Ordnance Survey

STREET ATLAS
North Hampshire

Contents

III	Key to map symbols
IV	Key to map pages
VI	Administrative and post code boundaries
1	Street maps
209	Town map of Portsmouth
210	Town map of Southampton
211	Index of hospitals, railway stations, schools, shopping centres, street names and universities

PHILIP'S

First edition published 1991
Second edition published 1994
First colour edition published 1998
Reprinted in 1998,1999 by

Ordnance Survey® and George Philip Ltd, a division of
Romsey Road   Octopus Publishing Group Ltd
Maybush   2-4 Heron Quays
Southampton   London
SO16 4GU   E14 4JP

ISBN 0-540-07471-3 (hardback)
ISBN 0-540-07472-1 (spiral)

To the best of the Publishers' knowledge, the information in this atlas was
correct at the time of going to press. No responsibility can be accepted
for any errors or their consequences.

The representation in this atlas of a road, track or path is no evidence
of the existence of a right of way.

**The mapping between pages 1 and 210 (inclusive) in this atlas is
derived from Ordnance Survey® OSCAR® and Land-Line® data,
and Landranger® mapping.**

Ordnance Survey, OSCAR, Land-Line and Landranger are registered trade
marks of Ordnance Survey, the national mapping agency of Great Britain.

Printed and bound in Spain by Cayfosa

Digital Data

The exceptionally high-quality mapping
found in this book is available as digital
data in TIFF format, which is easily
convertible to other bit-mapped (raster)
image formats.

The index is also available in digital form
as a standard database table. It contains
all the details found in the printed index
together with the National Grid reference
for the map square in which each entry
is named and feature codes for places
of interest in eight categories such as
education and health.

For further information and to discuss
your requirements, please contact the
Ordnance Survey Solutions Centre on
01703 792929.

Motorway (with junction number)

Primary route (dual carriageway and single)

A road (dual carriageway and single)

B road (dual carriageway and single)

Minor road (dual carriageway and single)

Other minor road

Road under construction

Pedestrianised area

Railway

Tramway, miniature railway

Rural track, private road or narrow road in urban area

Gate or obstruction to traffic (restrictions may not apply at all times or to all vehicles)

Path, bridleway, byway open to all traffic, road used as a public path

The representation in this atlas of a road, track or path is no evidence of the existence of a right of way

Adjoining page indicators

British Rail station

Underground station

Docklands Light Railway station

Private railway station

Bus, coach station

Ambulance station

Coastguard station

Fire station

Police station

Accident and Emergency entrance to hospital

Hospital

Church, place of worship

Information centre (open all year)

Parking

Post Office

Important buildings, schools, colleges, universities and hospitals

Prim Sch

County and unitary authority boundaries

River Medway Water name

Stream

River or canal (minor and major)

Water

Tidal water

Woods

Houses

Non-Roman antiquity

Roman antiquity

Acad	Academy	Mon	Monument
Cemy	Cemetery	Mus	Museum
C Ctr	Civic Centre	Obsy	Observatory
CH	Club House	Pal	Royal Palace
Coll	College	PH	Public House
Ent	Enterprise	Recn Gd	Recreation Ground
Ex H	Exhibition Hall	Resr	Reservoir
Ind Est	Industrial Estate	Ret Pk	Retail Park
Inst	Institute	Sch	School
Ct	Law Court	Sh Ctr	Shopping Centre
L Ctr	Leisure Centre	Sta	Station
LC	Level Crossing	TH	Town Hall/House
Liby	Library	Trad Est	Trading Estate
Mkt	Market	Univ	University
Meml	Memorial	YH	Youth Hostel

■ The dark grey border on the inside edge of some pages indicates that the mapping does not continue onto the adjacent page

■ The small numbers around the edges of the maps identify the 1 kilometre National Grid lines

The scale of the maps is 5.52 cm to 1 km (3½ inches to 1 mile)

0   ¼   ½   ¾   1 mile

0   250m   500m   750m   1 kilometre

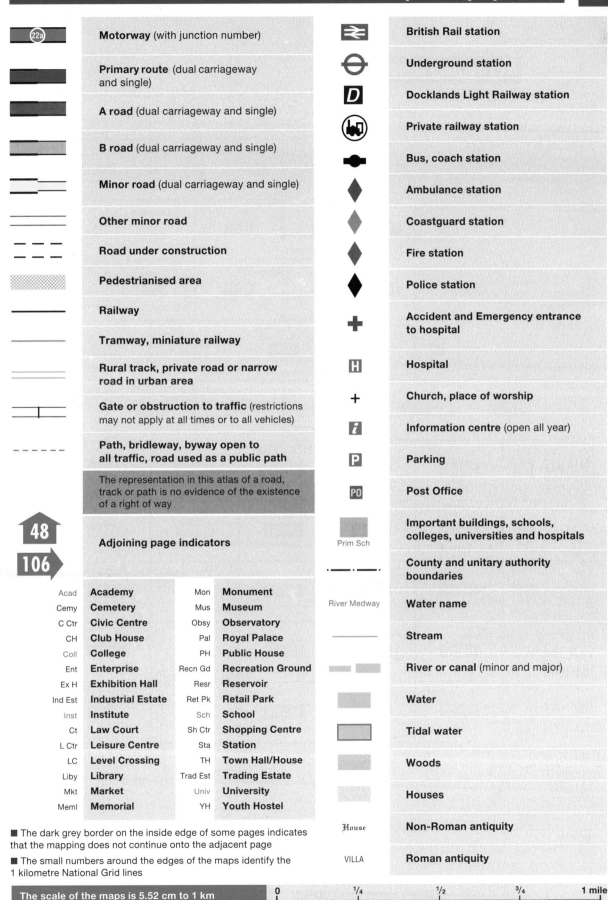

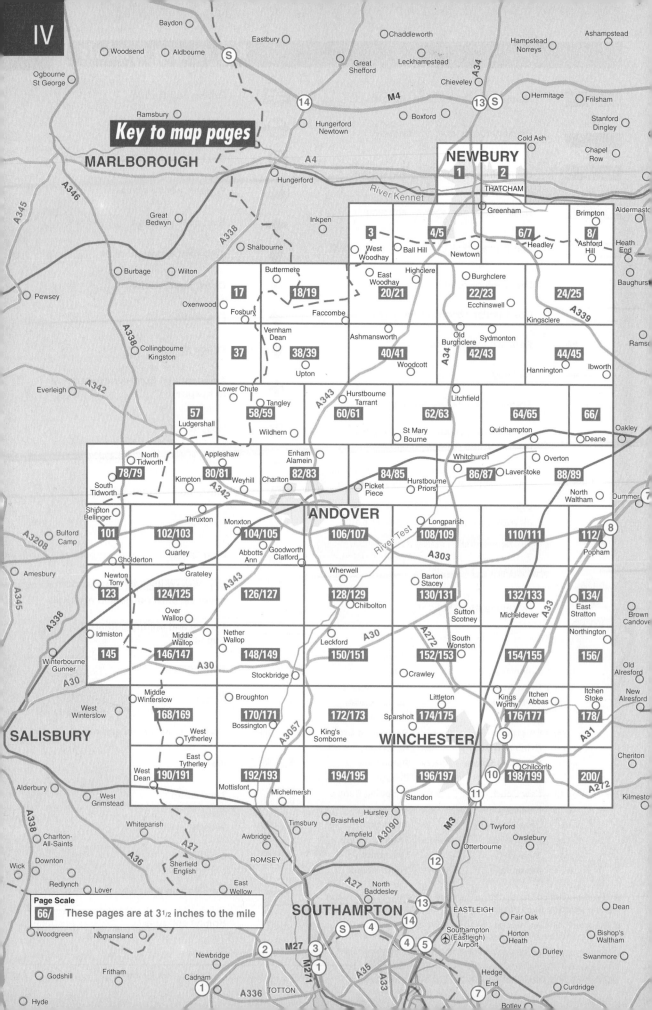

IV

Key to map pages

MARLBOROUGH

NEWBURY 1 2

THATCHAM

ANDOVER

WINCHESTER

SALISBURY

SOUTHAMPTON

Page Scale
66/ These pages are at 3½ inches to the mile

3 | 4/5 | 6/7 | 8/
17 | 18/19 | 20/21 | 22/23 | 24/25
37 | 38/39 | 40/41 | 42/43 | 44/45
57 | 58/59 | 60/61 | 62/63 | 64/65 | 66/
78/79 | 80/81 | 82/83 | 84/85 | 86/87 | 88/89
101 | 102/103 | 104/105 | 106/107 | 108/109 | 110/111 | 112/
123 | 124/125 | 126/127 | 128/129 | 130/131 | 132/133 | 134/
145 | 146/147 | 148/149 | 150/151 | 152/153 | 154/155 | 156/
168/169 | 170/171 | 172/173 | 174/175 | 176/177 | 178/
190/191 | 192/193 | 194/195 | 196/197 | 198/199 | 200/

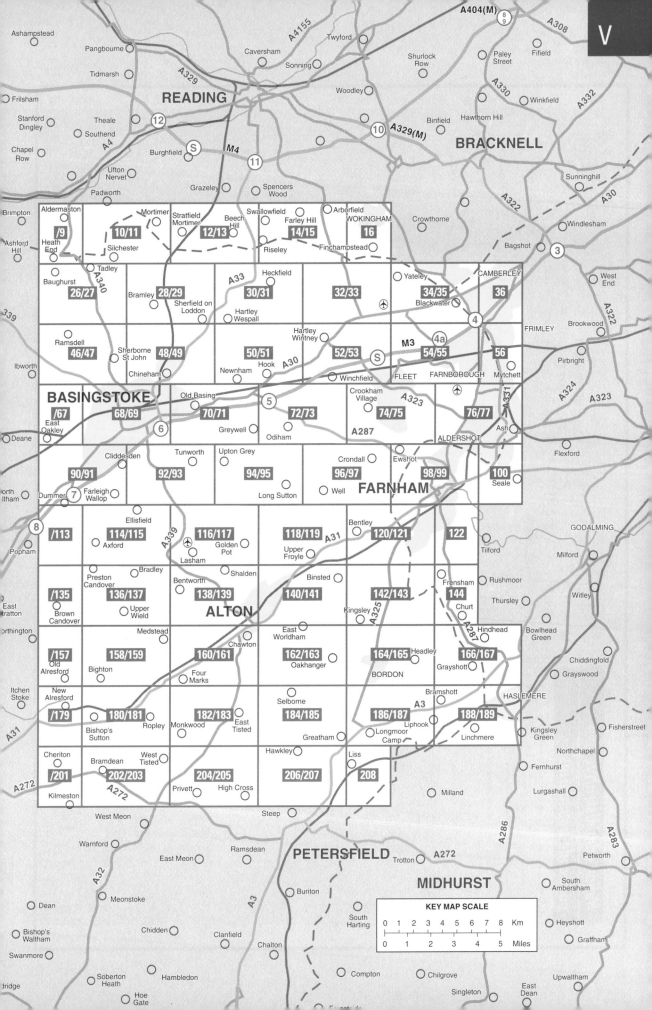

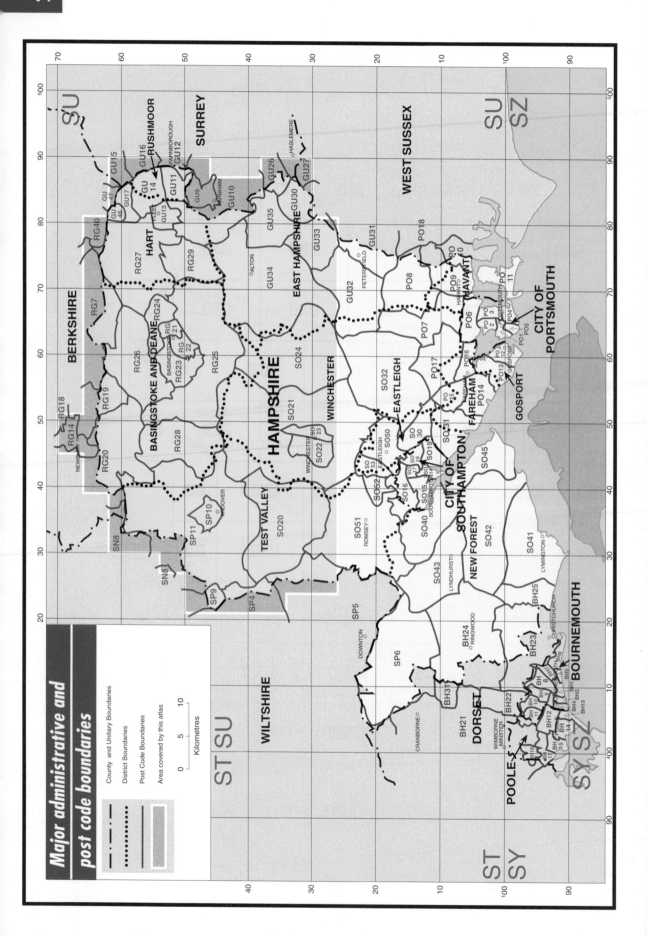

Major administrative and post code boundaries

County and Unitary Boundaries
District Boundaries
Post Code Boundaries
Area covered by this atlas

Kilometres

0   5   10
0   5   10

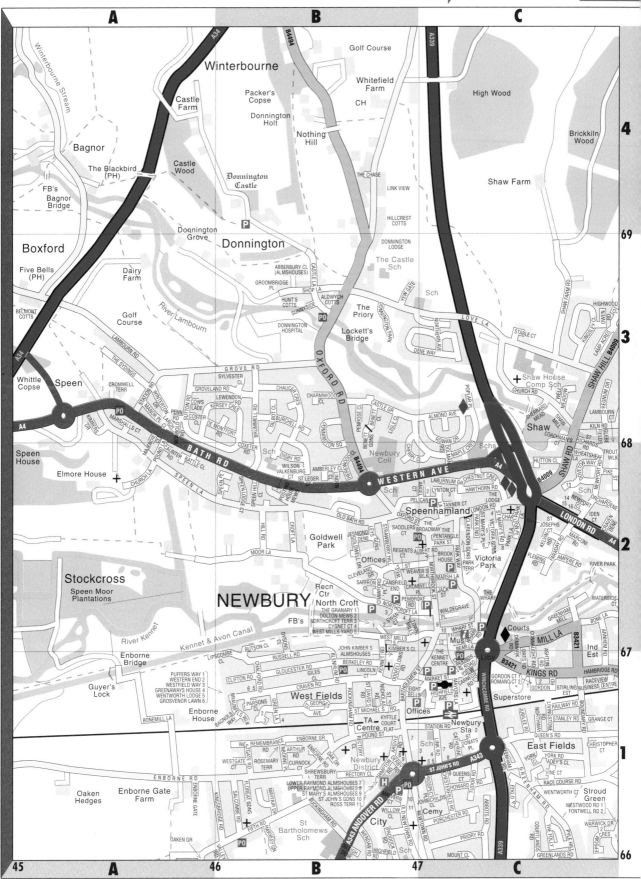

C1
1 THOMAS MERRIMAN CT
2 ASHRIDGE CT
3 FAIR CLOSE HOUSE
4 LINK HOUSE
5 MADEIRA PL
6 KENNET PL
7 SHEFFORD LODGE
8 ILCHESTER CT
9 HILARY HOUSE

C2
1 CORPORATION COTTS
2 WESTBOURNE TERR
3 SPEENHAMLAND CT
4 ST MARY'S CT
5 BEECH CT
6 ASH CT
7 CHESTNUT CT
8 CONISTON CT
9 BRIDGE ST

10 MANSION HOUSE ST
11 MARKET PL
12 THE ARCADE
13 LESLIE SOUTHERN CT
14 NORTH VIEW GDNS
15 KENNET PL
16 SOUTH VIEW GDNS

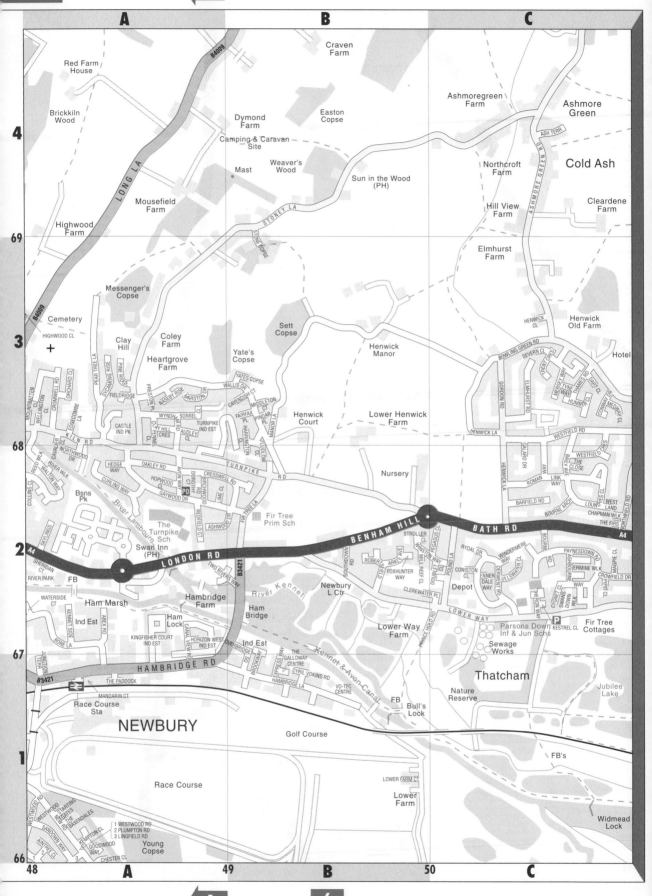

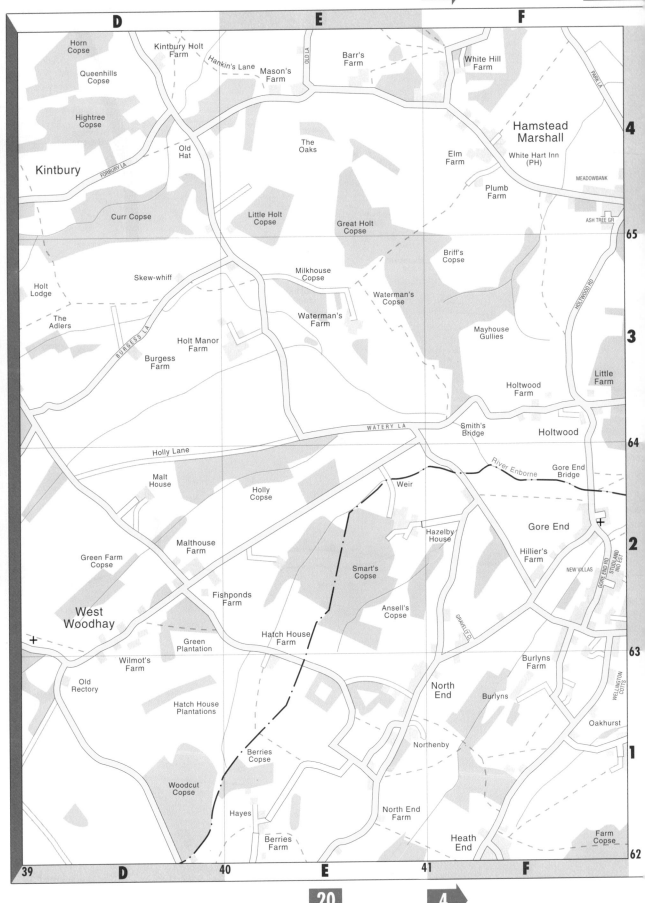

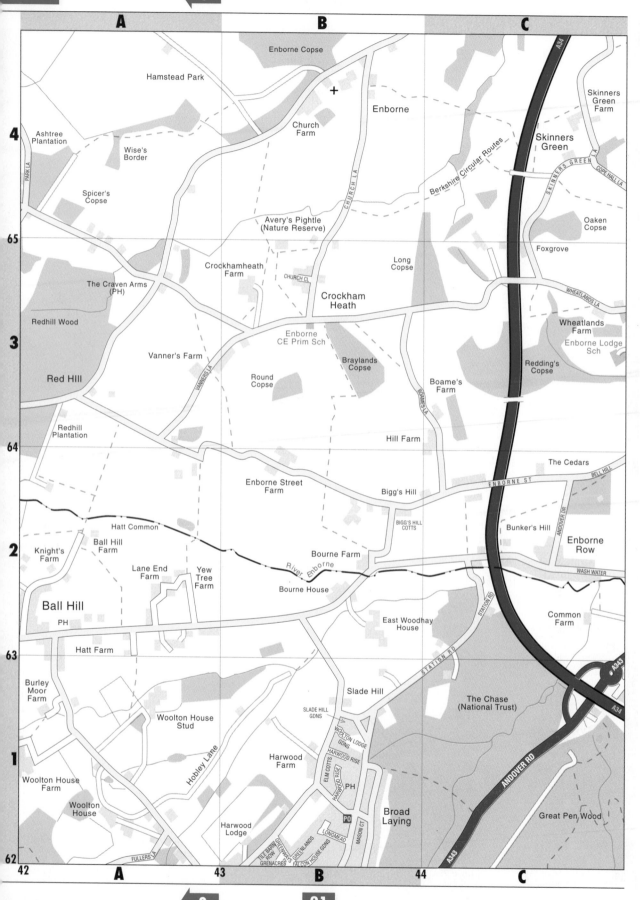

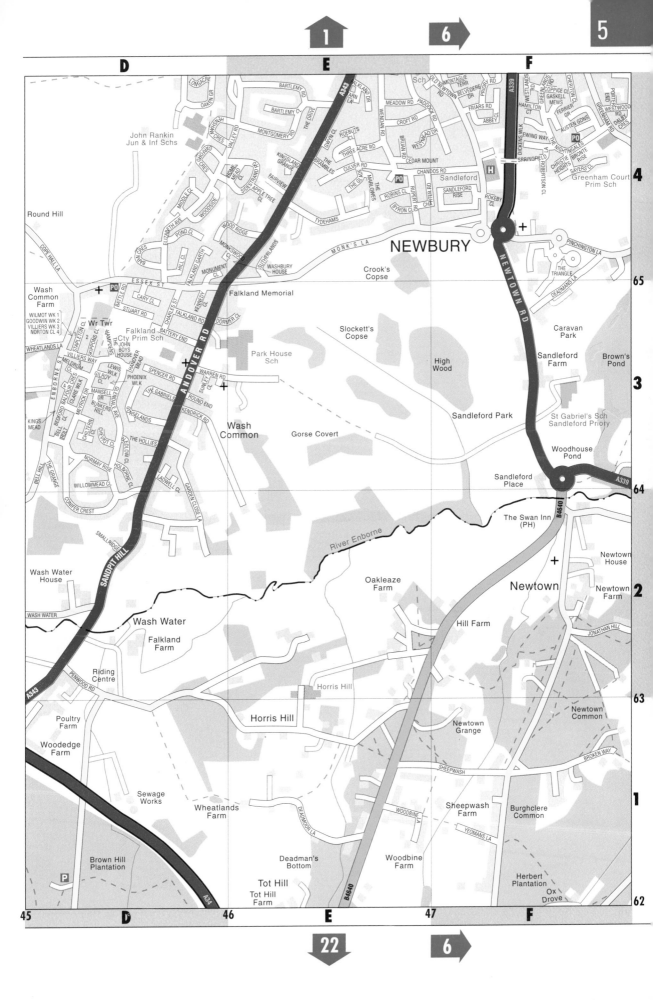

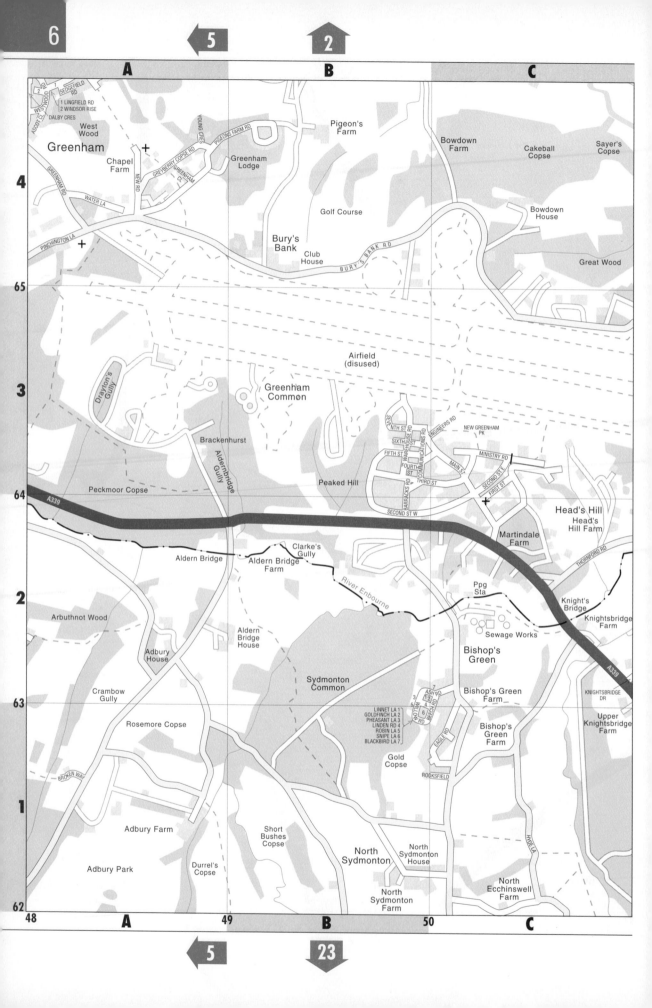

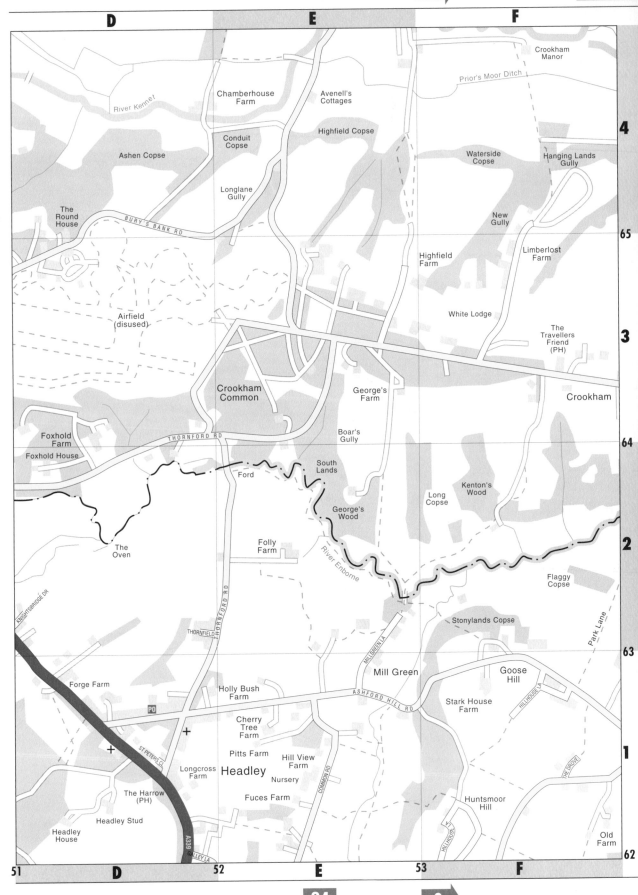

D **E** **F**

Crookham
Manor

Prior's Moor Ditch

Chamberhouse
Farm

Avenell's
Cottages

4

River Kennet

Highfield Copse

Conduit
Copse

Ashen Copse

Waterside
Copse

Hanging Lands
Gully

Longlane
Gully

New
Gully

The
Round
House

BURY'S BANK RD

65

Limberlost
Farm

Highfield
Farm

White Lodge

Airfield
(disused)

The
Travellers
Friend
(PH)

3

Crookham
Common

George's
Farm

Crookham

Foxhold
Farm

THORNFORD RD

Boar's
Gully

64

Foxhold House

Ford

South
Lands

Kenton's
Wood

Long
Copse

The
Oven

Folly
Farm

George's
Wood

River Enborne

2

Flaggy
Copse

KNIGHTSBRIDGE DR

THORNFORD RD

THORNFIELD RD

Stonylands Copse

MILLGREEN LA

Park Lane

63

Forge Farm

Mill Green

Goose
Hill

Holly Bush
Farm

ASHFORD HILL RD

Stark House
Farm

HILLHOUSE LA

PO

Cherry
Tree
Farm

+

+

Pitts Farm

Hill View
Farm

COMMON RD

THE DROVE

1

Longcross
Farm

Headley

Nursery

ST PETERS CL

Fuces Farm

Huntsmoor
Hill

The Harrow
(PH)

HILLHOUSE

Headley Stud

Old
Farm

Headley
House

A339

GALLEY LA

62

51 **D** **52** **E** **53** **F**

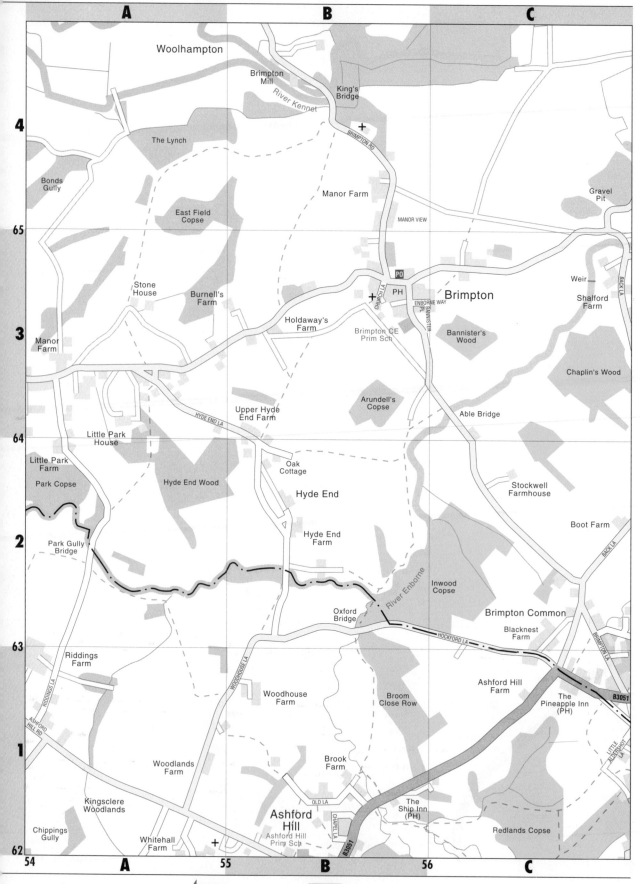

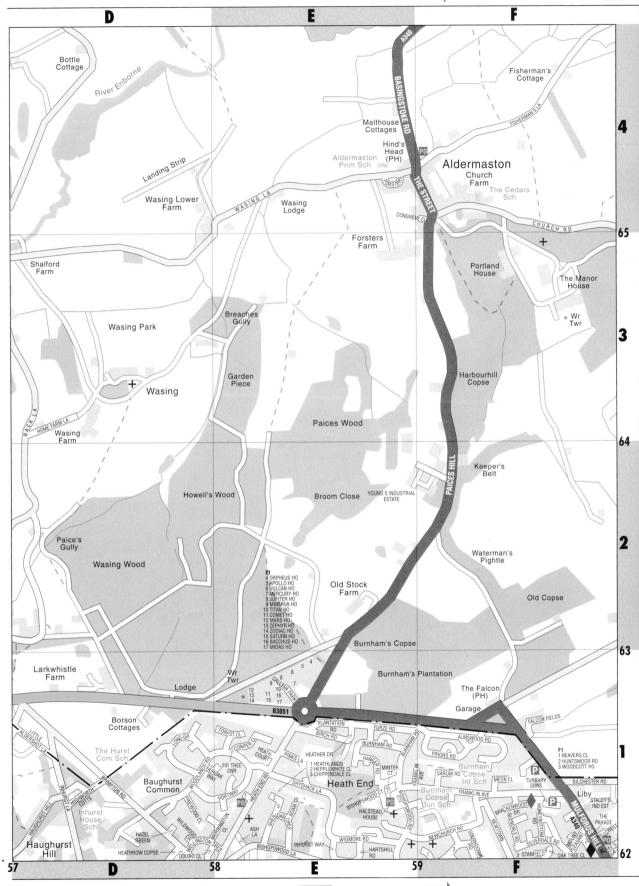

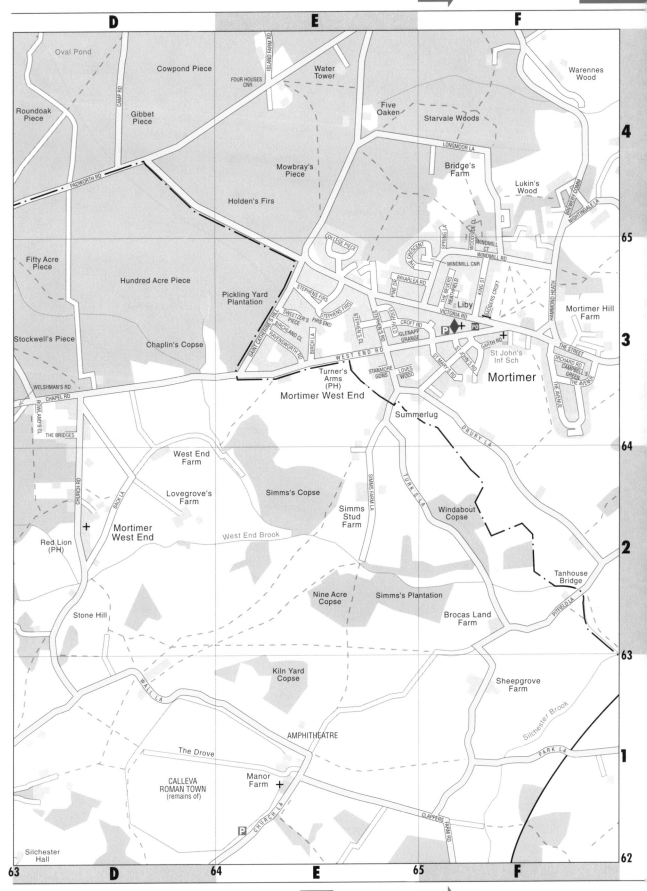

D
E
F

Oval Pond

Cowpond Piece

FOUR HOUSES CNR

ISLAND FARM RD

Water Tower

Warennes Wood

Roundoak Piece

CAMP RD

Gibbet Piece

Five Oaken

Starvale Woods

4

Mowbray's Piece

LONGMOOR LA

Bridge's Farm

Lukin's Wood

NIGHTINGALE LA

BREWERY COMM

PADWORTH RD

Holden's Firs

COLLEGE PIECE

SPRING LA

THE CRESCENT

WOODSIDE CL

WINDMILL CT

WINDMILL RD

65

Fifty Acre Piece

Hundred Acre Piece

Pickling Yard Plantation

STEPHENS FIRS

SWEETZER'S PIECE

STEPHENS FIRS END

PINE DR

BRIARLEA RD

WINDMILL CNR

THE REVERS

HEATHFIELD

KING ST

BADGERS CROFT

HAMMOND HEATH

Liby

Mortimer Hill Farm

Stockwell's Piece

Chaplin's Copse

SAINT CATHERINE'S HILL

BIRCHLAND CL

RAVENSWORTH RD

BIRCH LA

STEPHENS CL

STEPHENS'S RD

LEIGH FIELD

CROFT RD

GLENAPP GRANGE

VICTORIA RD

P

PO

ST MARY'S RD

ST JOHN'S RD

GARTH RD

St John's Inf Sch

THE STREET

ORCHARD RD

CAMPBELL'S GREEN

THE AVENUE

3

WELSHMAN'S RD

CHAPEL RD

ROWLAND'S CL

THE BRIDGES

WEST END RD

Turner's Arms (PH)

STANMORE GDNS

LOVES WOOD

Mortimer West End

Summerlug

DRURY LA

Mortimer

64

West End Farm

CHURCH RD

BACK LA

Lovegrove's Farm

Simms's Copse

SIMMS FARM LA

Simms Stud Farm

TURK'S LA

Windabout Copse

Red Lion (PH)

Mortimer West End

West End Brook

Tanhouse Bridge

2

Stone Hill

Nine Acre Copse

Simms's Plantation

Brocas Land Farm

PITFIELD LA

63

Kiln Yard Copse

Sheepgrove Farm

WALL LA

Silchester Brook

AMPHITHEATRE

The Drove

PARK LA

1

CALLEVA ROMAN TOWN (remains of)

Manor Farm

CHURCH LA

CLAPPERS FARM RD

Silchester Hall

63

D

64

E

65

F

62

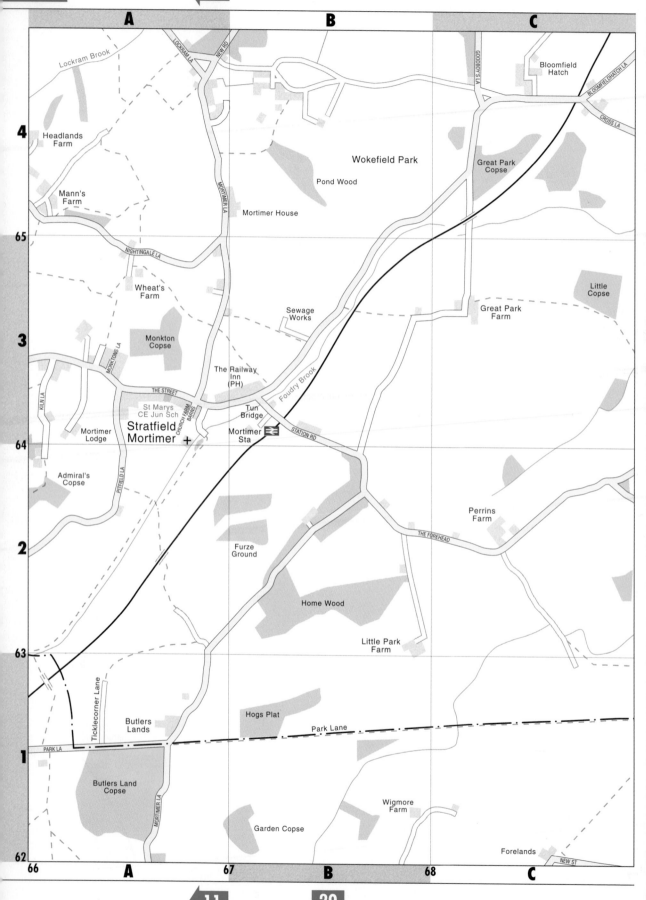

A   B   C

Lockram Brook

LOCKRAM LA

NEW RD

GOODBOY'S LA

Bloomfield
Hatch

BLOOMFIELDHATCH LA

CROSS LA

4

Headlands
Farm

Wokefield Park

Great Park
Copse

Mann's
Farm

MORTIMER LA

Pond Wood

Mortimer House

65

NIGHTINGALE LA

Little
Copse

Wheat's
Farm

Sewage
Works

Great Park
Farm

3

MONKTONS LA

Monkton
Copse

The Railway
Inn
(PH)

Foudry Brook

KILN LA

THE STREET

St Marys
CE Jun Sch

CHURCH FARM BARNS

Tun
Bridge

**Stratfield
Mortimer** +

Mortimer
Sta

STATION RD

64

Mortimer
Lodge

PITFIELD LA

Admiral's
Copse

Perrins
Farm

THE FOREHEAD

2

Furze
Ground

Home Wood

Little Park
Farm

63

Ticklecorner Lane

Butlers
Lands

Hogs Plat

Park Lane

1

PARK LA

Butlers Land
Copse

MORTIMER LA

Wigmore
Farm

Garden Copse

Forelands

NEW ST

62

66   A   67   B   68   C

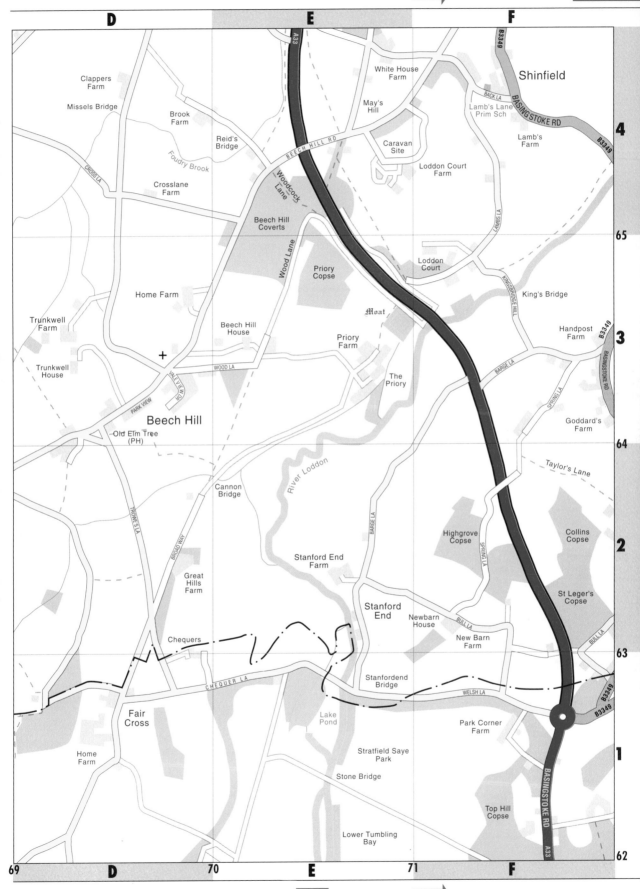

D **E** **F**

Clappers Farm

Missels Bridge

Brook Farm

Reid's Bridge

Foudry Brook

CROSS LA

Crosslane Farm

A33

BEECH HILL RD

Woodcock Lane

Beech Hill Coverts

Wood Lane

Priory Copse

White House Farm

May's Hill

Caravan Site

Loddon Court Farm

B3349

Shinfield

BACK LA

Lamb's Lane Prim Sch

BASINGSTOKE RD

Lamb's Farm

4

65

Loddon Court

LAMB'S LA

KINGSBRIDGE HILL

King's Bridge

Home Farm

Trunkwell Farm

Trunkwell House

Beech Hill House

WOOD LA

Priory Farm

Moat

The Priory

BARGE LA

SPRING LA

Handpost Farm

B3349

BASINGSTOKE RD

Goddard's Farm

3

64

PARK VIEW

VALLEY VIEW RD

Beech Hill

Old Elm Tree (PH)

River Loddon

Cannon Bridge

Taylor's Lane

TROWE'S LA

BROAD WAY

Great Hills Farm

Stanford End Farm

BARGE LA

Highgrove Copse

SPRING LA

Collins Copse

St Leger's Copse

2

Home Farm

Fair Cross

Chequers

CHEQUER LA

Stanford End

Stanfordend Bridge

Newbarn House

BULL LA

New Barn Farm

WELSH LA

BULL LA

B3349

63

Lake Pond

Stratfield Saye Park

Stone Bridge

Lower Tumbling Bay

Park Corner Farm

Top Hill Copse

BASINGSTOKE RD

A33

1

62

13

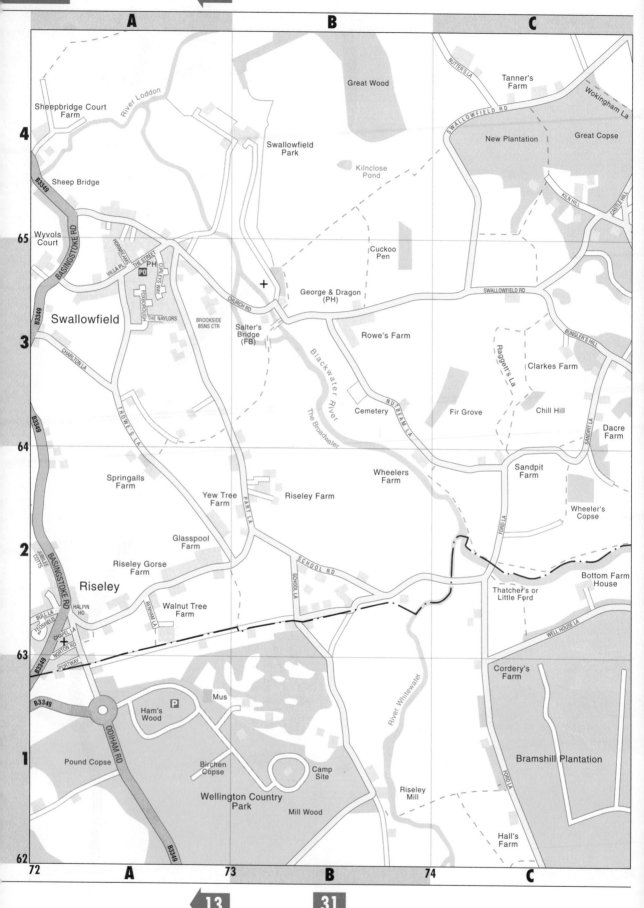

13
31

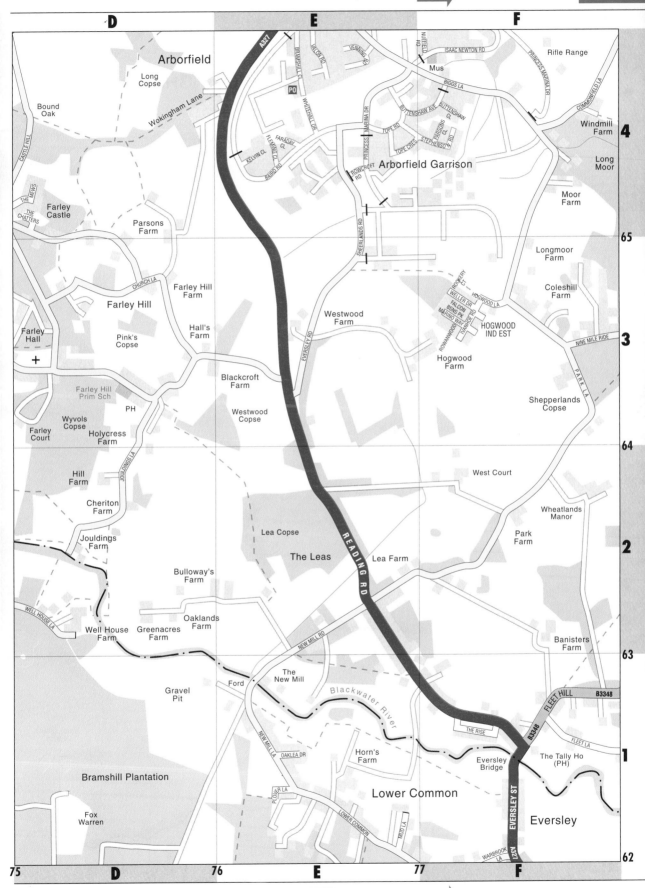

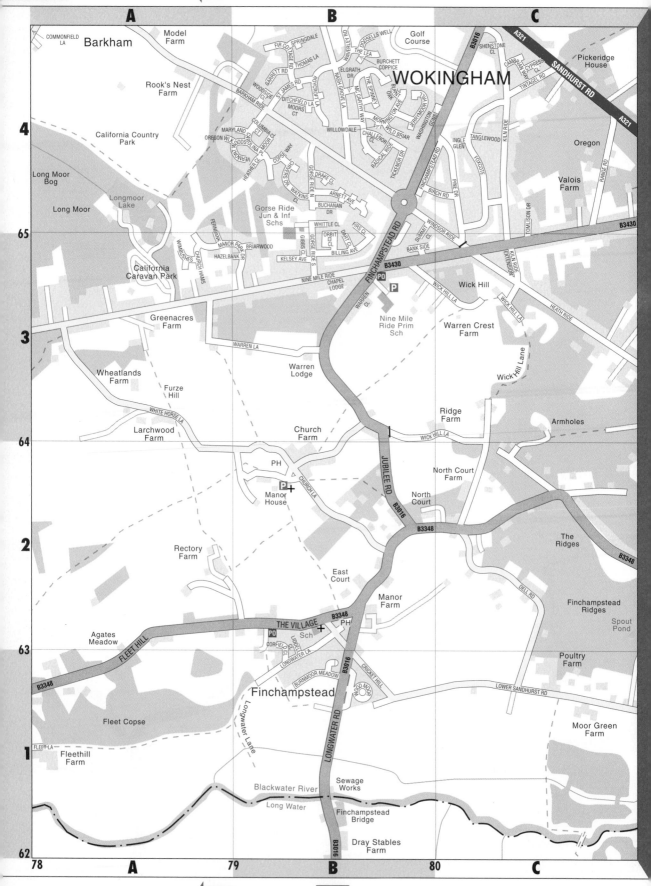

Barkham
COMMONFIELD LA

Model Farm

Rook's Nest Farm

California Country Park

Long Moor Bog

Long Moor

Longmoor Lake

California Caravan Park

WOKINGHAM

Golf Course

FIR COTTAGE RD
SPRINGDALE
THOMAS LA
GARRETT RD
WOODSIDE CL
ST JAMES RD
DITCHFIELD LA
MOORS CT
COLUMBIA CT
MARYLAND
OREGON WLK
VERMONT CL
COSY NOLA PL
HEATHER CL
MOOR CL
FERNBANK
WIMBLESHES
CHURCH HAMS
MANOR PARK DR
HAZELBANK
BRIARWOOD
GIBBS CL
KELSEY AVE
NINE MILE RIDE
CHAPEL LODGE

SHENSTONE CL
CAM & IAN MAN
CYPRESS CL
TINTAGEL CL

SANDHURST RD

Pickeridge House

Oregon

Valois Farm

DRSSELLS WELL
THE LEA
BURCHETT COPPICE
ELGRATH DR
MCCARTHY WAY
WILLOWDALE
NASH GROVE LA
CHALLENOR CL
RADICAL RIDE
TICKENOR DR
MORNING
WILD BRIAR
JERRYMOOR
WASHINGTON
FINCHAMPSTEAD RD
BIRCH RD
PINE DR
INGLE GLEN
TANGLEWOOD
KILN RIDE
FOXCOTE

TOMLISON DR
HEATH RIDE

B3016

A321

B3430

Gorse Ride Jun & Inf Schs

WHITTLE CL
ORBIT CL
DART CL
FIRS CL
BILLING AVE
ARNETT AVE
DRAKE CL
GORSE RIDE N
GORSE RIDE S
BUCHANAN DR
CORSE WAY
WATKINS DR

B3430

P

Nine Mile Ride Prim Sch

WARREN CL

WINDSOR RIDE
SUMMIT CL
BANK SIDE

WICK HILL LA

Wick Hill

Warren Crest Farm

KILN RIDE EXTENSION

Greenacres Farm

WARREN LA

Warren Lodge

Wheatlands Farm

Furze Hill

WHITE HORSE LA

Larchwood Farm

Church Farm

Ridge Farm

Armholes

Wick Hill Lane

WICK HILL LA

PH

Manor House

P

Rectory Farm

JUBILEE RD

North Court Farm

North Court

B3016

B3348

The Ridges

B3348

East Court

Manor Farm

DELL RD

Finchampstead Ridges

Spout Pond

Agates Meadow

FLEET HILL

THE VILLAGE
PO
CORFIELD CL
LIDDELL
LONGWATER LA

B3348
Sch
PH

B3016

CRICKET HILL

Poultry Farm

LOWER SANDHURST RD

Moor Green Farm

B3348

Fleet Copse

BURNMOOR MEADOW

Finchampstead

LONGWATER RD

Longwater Lane

FLEET LA
Fleethill Farm

Blackwater River

Long Water

Sewage Works

Finchampstead Bridge

Dray Stables Farm

B3016

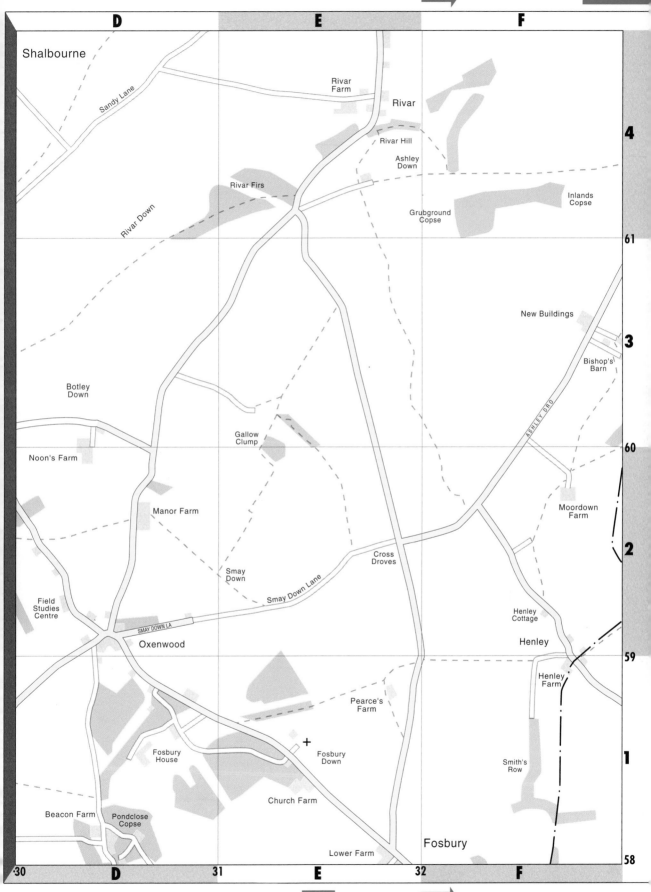

Shalbourne

Sandy Lane

Rivar Farm

Rivar

Rivar Hill

Ashley Down

Rivar Firs

Rivar Down

Grubground Copse

Inlands Copse

New Buildings

Bishop's Barn

Botley Down

Gallow Clump

ASHLEY DRO.

Noon's Farm

Manor Farm

Moordown Farm

Smay Down

Cross Droves

Smay Down Lane

Field Studies Centre

Henley Cottage

SMAY DOWN LA

Henley

Oxenwood

Henley Farm

Pearce's Farm

Fosbury House

Fosbury Down

Smith's Row

Church Farm

Beacon Farm

Pondclose Copse

Fosbury

Lower Farm

30   D   31   E   32   F   58

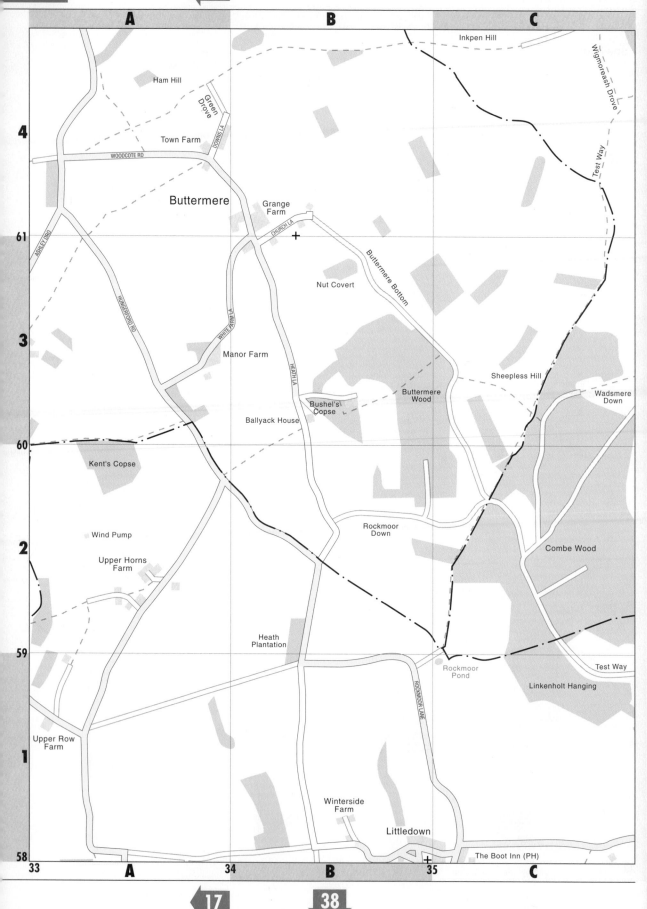

A   B   C

Inkpen Hill

Ham Hill

Green Drove

DENNIS LA

Town Farm

WOODCOTE RD

Wigmoreash Drove

Test Way

4

Buttermere

Grange Farm

CHURCH LA

ASHLEY DRO

61

Nut Covert

Buttermere Bottom

HUNGERFORD RD

WHITE PARISH LA

3

Manor Farm

HEATH LA

Sheepless Hill

Buttermere Wood

Wadsmere Down

Bushel's Copse

Ballyack House

Kent's Copse

60

Wind Pump

Rockmoor Down

Combe Wood

2

Upper Horns Farm

Heath Plantation

59

Rockmoor Pond

Test Way

Linkenholt Hanging

ROCKMOOR LANE

Upper Row Farm

1

Winterside Farm

Littledown

The Boot Inn (PH)

58

A
B
C

4

Park Copse

Copse Farm

Rectory Farm

Barn Croft

FULLERS LA

Malverleys

East Woodhay

St Martin's CE Prim Sch

Lodge

PH

Church Farm

VICTORIA COTTS

East End

61

East End Farm

Stargrove

Rabbit Pit Farm

3

Lower Eastwick Copse

Upper Eastwick Copse

Wayfarer's Wlk

Brick Kiln Farm

Jones' Farm

60

Dean Hill

Pilot Hill

2

Apsley Farm

The Oaks

West Down Copse

Kydd's Copse

Buckhanger Copse

59

Kilmore

Wayfarer's Wlk

1

The Clump

Roe Wood

Hitchen

The Keeper's Bungalow

58

Faccombe Manor

Curzon Street Farm

Robins Croft Copse

Privet Copse

39

A

40

B

41

C

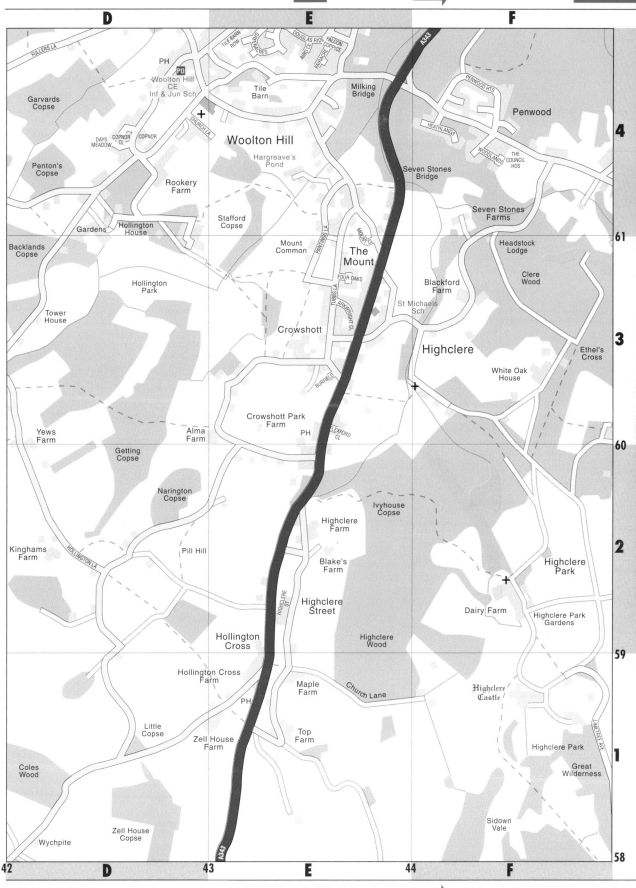

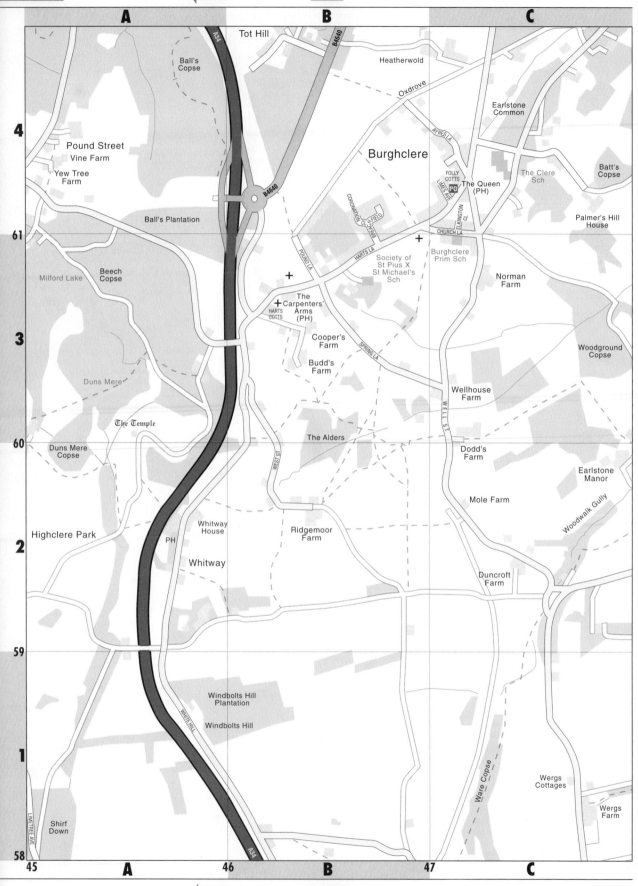

A B C

4

61

3

60

2

59

1

58

45 A 46 B 47 C

Tot Hill

Heatherwold

Oxdrove

Earlstone Common

Burghclere

The Clere Sch

Batt's Copse

Pound Street

Vine Farm

Yew Tree Farm

FOLLY COTTS

The Queen (PH)

Palmer's Hill House

Ball's Copse

Ball's Plantation

Milford Lake

Beech Copse

Society of St Pius X St Michael's Sch

Burghclere Prim Sch

Norman Farm

The Carpenters' Arms (PH)

HARTS COTTS

Cooper's Farm

Woodground Copse

Duns Mere

Budd's Farm

Wellhouse Farm

The Temple

Duns Mere Copse

The Alders

Dodd's Farm

Earlstone Manor

Highclere Park

PH

Whitway House

Ridgemoor Farm

Mole Farm

Woodwalk Gully

Whitway

Duncroft Farm

Windbolts Hill Plantation

Windbolts Hill

Ware Copse

Wergs Cottages

Shirf Down

Wergs Farm

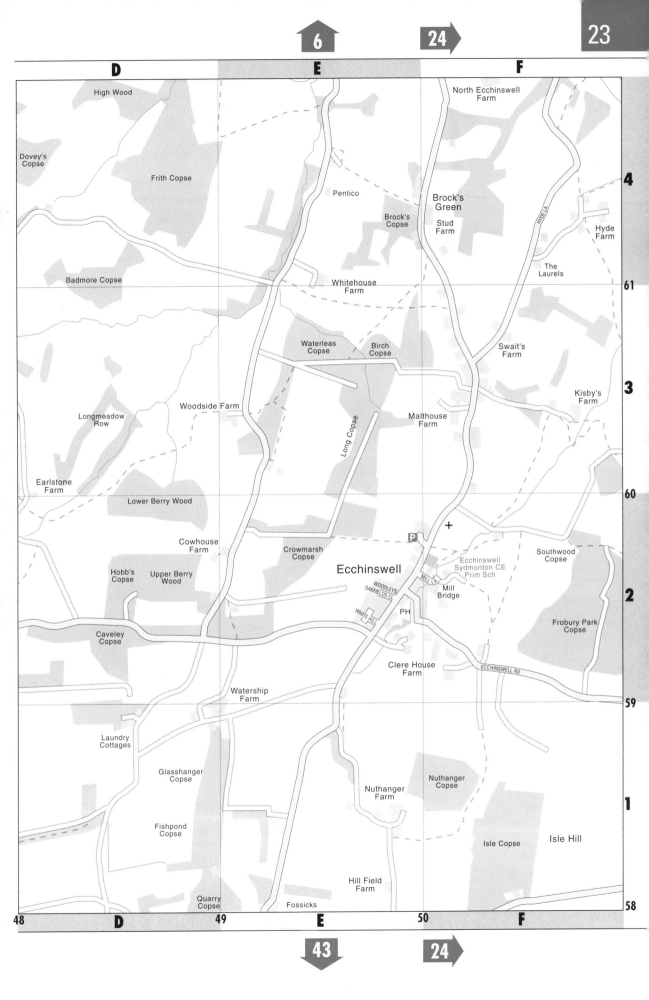

D
E
F

4

61

3

60

2

59

1

58

High Wood

Dovey's
Copse

Frith Copse

Pentico

Brock's
Green

North Ecchinswell
Farm

HYDE LA

Brock's
Copse

Stud
Farm

Hyde
Farm

Badmore Copse

Whitehouse
Farm

The
Laurels

Waterleas
Copse

Birch
Copse

Swait's
Farm

Woodside Farm

Long Copse

Malthouse
Farm

Kisby's
Farm

Longmeadow
Row

Earlstone
Farm

Lower Berry Wood

P

Ecchinswell
Sydmonton CE
Prim Sch

Southwood
Copse

Cowhouse
Farm

Crowmarsh
Copse

Ecchinswell

MILL LA

Mill
Bridge

Hobb's
Copse

Upper Berry
Wood

WOODLEYS
OAKFIELDS CL

WHITE HILL

PH

Frobury Park
Copse

Caveley
Copse

Clere House
Farm

ECCHINSWELL RD

Watership
Farm

Laundry
Cottages

Glasshanger
Copse

Nuthanger
Farm

Nuthanger
Copse

Fishpond
Copse

Isle Copse

Isle Hill

Quarry
Copse

Fossicks

Hill Field
Farm

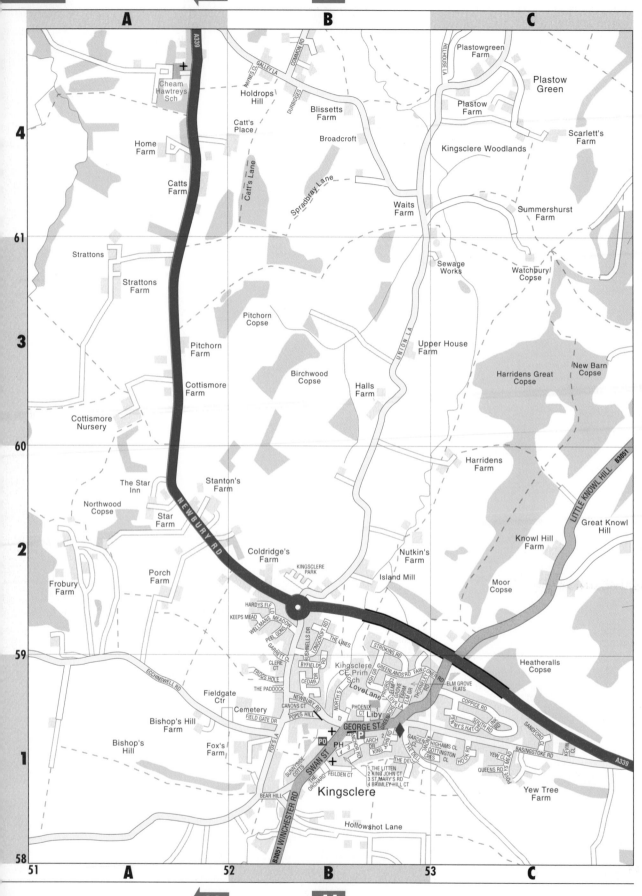

A B C

4

61

3

60

2

59

1

58

Cheam Hawtreys Sch
Home Farm
Catts Farm
Holdrops Hill
Catt's Place
Catt's Lane
Blissetts Farm
Broadcroft
Spradbray Lane
Plastowgreen Farm
Plastow Green
Plastow Farm
Scarlett's Farm
Kingsclere Woodlands
HILLHOUSE LA
GALLEY LA
COMMON RD
DURRIDGES
PAYNS CL
Waits Farm
Summershurst Farm
Strattons
Strattons Farm
Pitchorn Copse
Sewage Works
Watchbury Copse
UNION LA
Pitchorn Farm
Upper House Farm
Cottismore Farm
Birchwood Copse
Halls Farm
Harridens Great Copse
New Barn Copse
Cottismore Nursery
Harridens Farm
The Star Inn
Stanton's Farm
B3051
LITTLE KNOWL HILL
Great Knowl Hill
Northwood Copse
Star Farm
NEWBURY RD
Coldridge's Farm
Nutkin's Farm
Knowl Hill Farm
Frobury Farm
Porch Farm
KINGSCLERE PARK
Island Mill
Moor Copse
HARDYS FLE
KEEPS MEAD
WELLMANS MEADOW
PEEL GDNS
GARRETT CL
CLERE CT
BUSHNELLS DR
BYFIELDS
LONGCROFT RD
THE LINES
STROKINS RD
Heatheralls Copse
ECCHINSWELL RD
Fieldgate Ctr
THE PADDOCK
NEWBURY RD
CEDAR
FROGS HOLE
CANONS CT
POPES HILL
Cemetery
FIELD GATE DR
Kingsclere CE Prim Sch
GREENLANDS RD
ASH GR
PRIORS CL
ELM GR
GREENACRE
FAIRCLOSE RD
ELM GROVE FLATS
ELM GR
Love Lane
PHOENIX CT
Liby
Bishop's Hill Farm
FOX'S LA
GEORGE ST
Fox's Farm
Bishop's Hill
PO
PH
SWAN ST
SUNNYSIDE COTTS
ORCHARD
BEAR HILL
FEILDEN CT
Kingsclere
NORTH ST
SWAN ST
WINCHESTER RD
B3051
LARCH DR
JOHN RD
KING
THE DELL
THORNLEY
COPPICE RD
SOUTH RD
GARDENS CL
HIGHAMS CL
COTTINGTON CL
HOOK RD
PNY'S HAT
CRES
QUEENS RD
YEW CL
PNYS MEAD
SANDFORD
BASINGSTOKE RD
KEVIN
A339
Yew Tree Farm
Hollowshot Lane
1 THE LITTEN
2 KING JOHN CT
3 ST MARY'S RD
4 BRIMLEY HILL CT

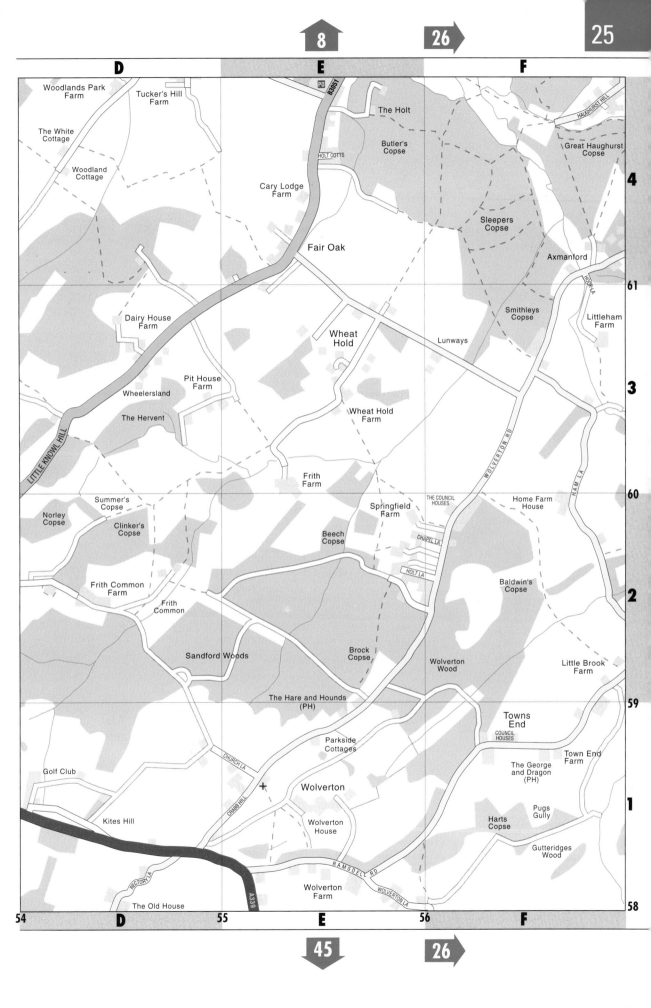

D E F

Woodlands Park Farm
Tucker's Hill Farm
The Holt
HAUGHURST HILL

The White Cottage
Butler's Copse
Great Haughurst Copse

Woodland Cottage
HOLT COTTS
4

Cary Lodge Farm
Sleepers Copse

Fair Oak
Axmanford

HOOK LA
61

Dairy House Farm
Wheat Hold
Lunways
Smithleys Copse
Littleham Farm

Pit House Farm
3

Wheelersland
Wheat Hold Farm

The Hervent

WOLVERTON RD
HAM LA

Summer's Copse
Frith Farm
THE COUNCIL HOUSES
Home Farm House
60

Norley Copse
Springfield Farm

Clinker's Copse
Beech Copse
CHAPEL LA

Frith Common Farm
HOLT LA
Baldwin's Copse
2

Frith Common
Brock Copse

Sandford Woods
Wolverton Wood
Little Brook Farm

The Hare and Hounds (PH)
59

Towns End
COUNCIL HOUSES

CHURCH LA
Parkside Cottages
Town End Farm

Golf Club
The George and Dragon (PH)

Wolverton
Harts Copse
Pugs Gully
1

Kites Hill
CRABB HILL
Wolverton House
Gutteridges Wood

RECTORY LA
A339
RAMSDELL RD
WOLVERTON LA

The Old House
Wolverton Farm
58

54 D 55 E 56 F

LITTLE KNOWL HILL

B3051

PO

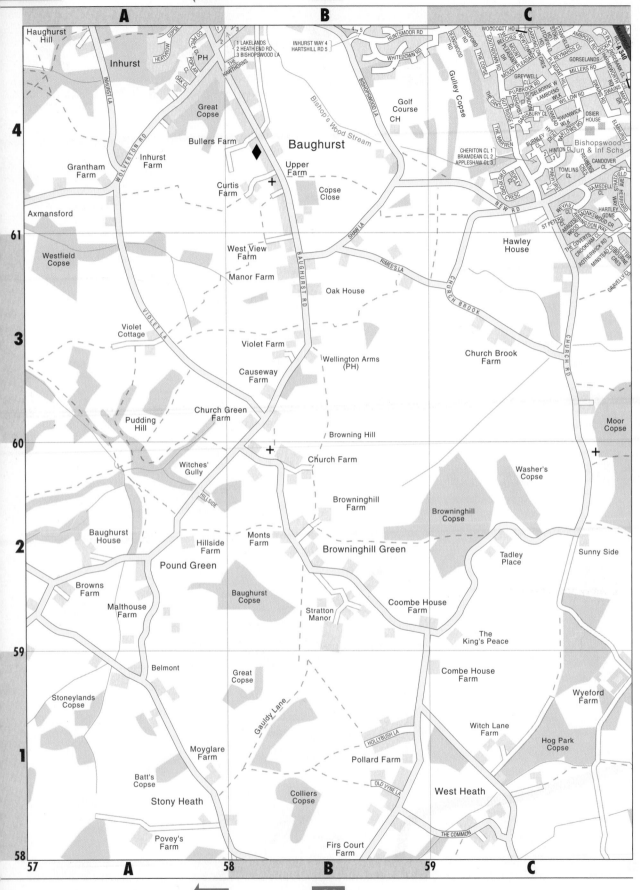

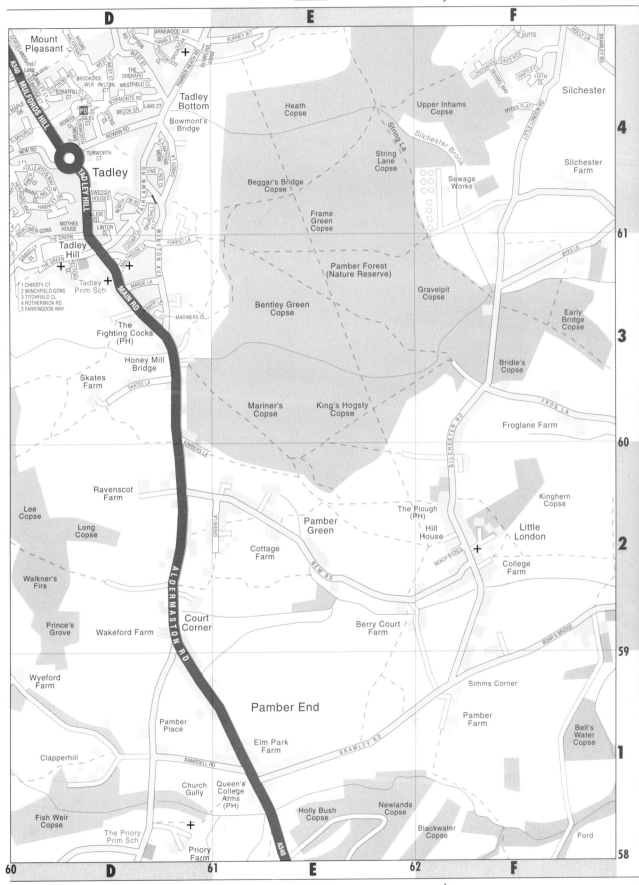

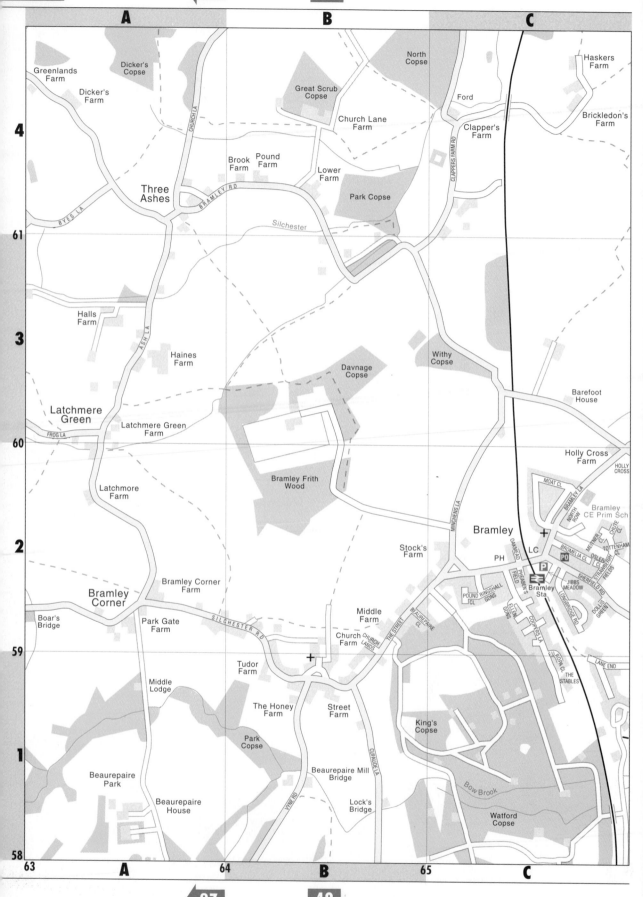

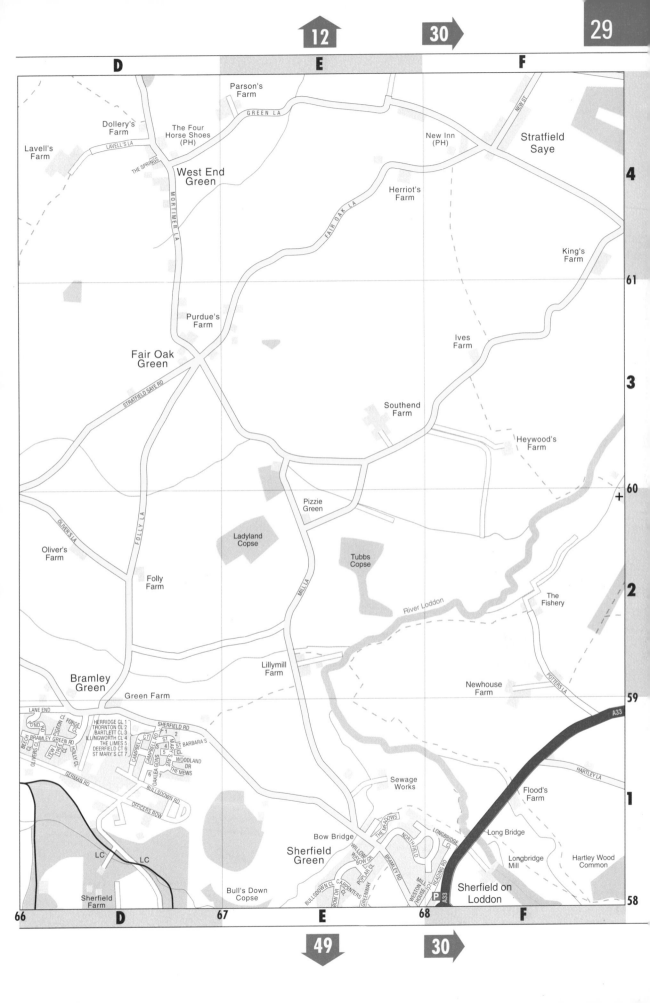

D
E
F

Parson's Farm

GREEN LA

NEW ST

Dollery's Farm

LAVELL'S LA

The Four Horse Shoes (PH)

New Inn (PH)

Stratfield Saye

Lavell's Farm

THE SPRINGS

West End Green

MORTIMER LA

Herriot's Farm

FAIR OAK LA

King's Farm

4

61

Purdue's Farm

Fair Oak Green

Ives Farm

STRATFIELD SAYE RD

Southend Farm

3

Heywood's Farm

OLIVER'S LA

FOLLY LA

Pizzie Green

60

+

Oliver's Farm

Ladyland Copse

Tubbs Copse

The Fishery

2

Folly Farm

MILL LA

River Loddon

POTTERS LA

Lillymill Farm

Newhouse Farm

59

Bramley Green

Green Farm

A33

LANE END

HERRIDGE CL 1
THORNTON CL 2
BARTLETT CL 3
ILLINGWORTH CL 4
THE LIMES 5
DEERFIELD CT 6
ST MARY'S CT 7

SHERFIELD RD

HARTLEY LA

BEECH CL
PIGEON CL
FORGE CL
UND.
NEW TREE CL
BRAMLEY GREEN RD
OLIVERS CL
HOLLY CL
CAMPBELL CT
CAMPBELL RD
ST MARY'S AVE
ST MARY CL
ST BARBARA'S
WOODLAND DR
OAKLEA GDNS
THE MEWS

Flood's Farm

1

GERMAN RD

BULLSDOWN RD

Sewage Works

Long Bridge

OFFICERS ROW

WILLOW CL
THE MEADOWS
BOW GR
NORTHFIELD
LONGBRIDGE CL

Longbridge Mill

Hartley Wood Common

LC

LC

Bow Bridge

Sherfield Green

BRAMLEY RD
MILL HOUSE CL
READING RD

P

Sherfield on Loddon

A33

Sherfield Farm

Bull's Down Copse

BULLSDOWN CL
BOW DR
CARPENTERS CL
GREENWAY
POPLAR CL
WESTON CL

58

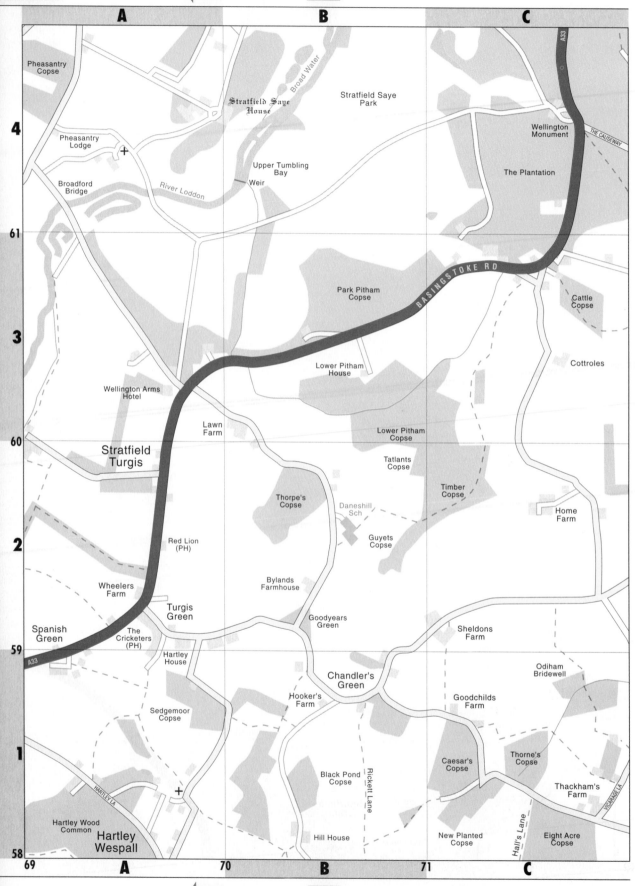

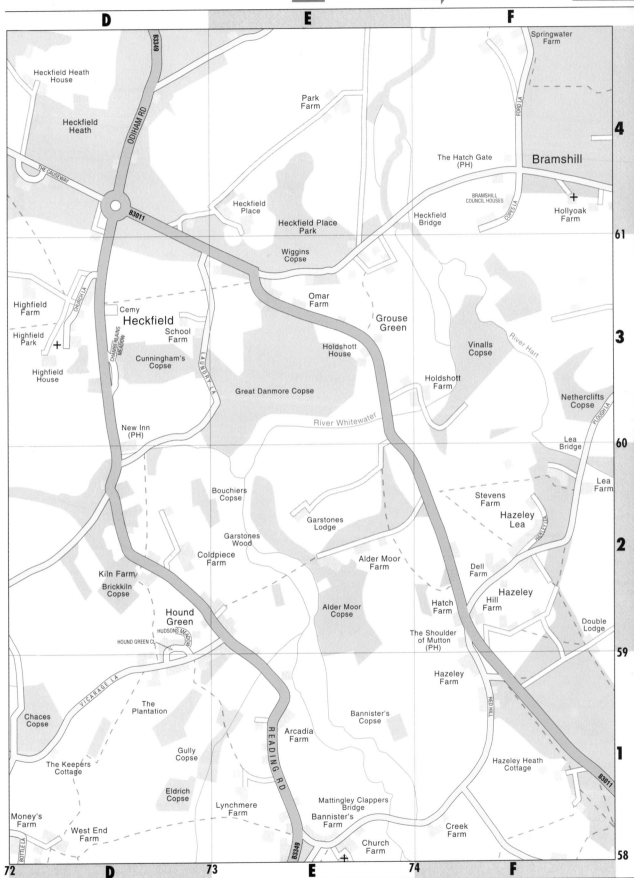

A B C

4

61

3

60

2

59

1

58

75 A 76 B 77 C

Bramshill
Plantation

St Neot's
Sch

WARBROOK LA

Warbrook
(Con Ctr)

A327

B3272
EVERSLEY RD

Warren
Farm

ST NEOT'S RD

Yalden's
Farm

Church
Farm

A327

Refuse
Tip

PLOUGH LA

Moor Place
Farm

Heath
Warren

Cudbury Clump

The Welsh Drive

Peatmoor
Copse

Warren Heath

Three Castles Path

Sir Richard's Drive

Bramshill Park

Bramshill House
(Police Coll)

Deer Park   Long
Water

High Bridge

Birch
Bottom

Sand &
Gravel Pit

River Hart

Chalwin's
Copse

Hazeley
Heath

Crabtree Copse

Crabtree
Lodge

Hulford's Copse

B3011

Purdies Farm

Warren Hill
Farm

Warren Hill Plantation

A30

Hatts
Cottage

Hazeley
Heath

SPRINGWELL LA

HULFORDS LA

STAR HILL

Star
Hill

B3011

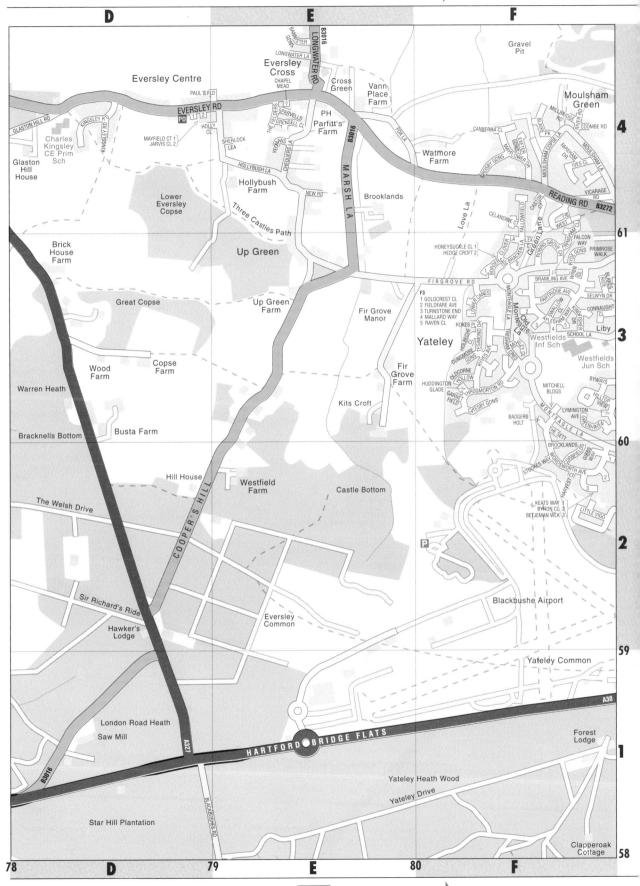

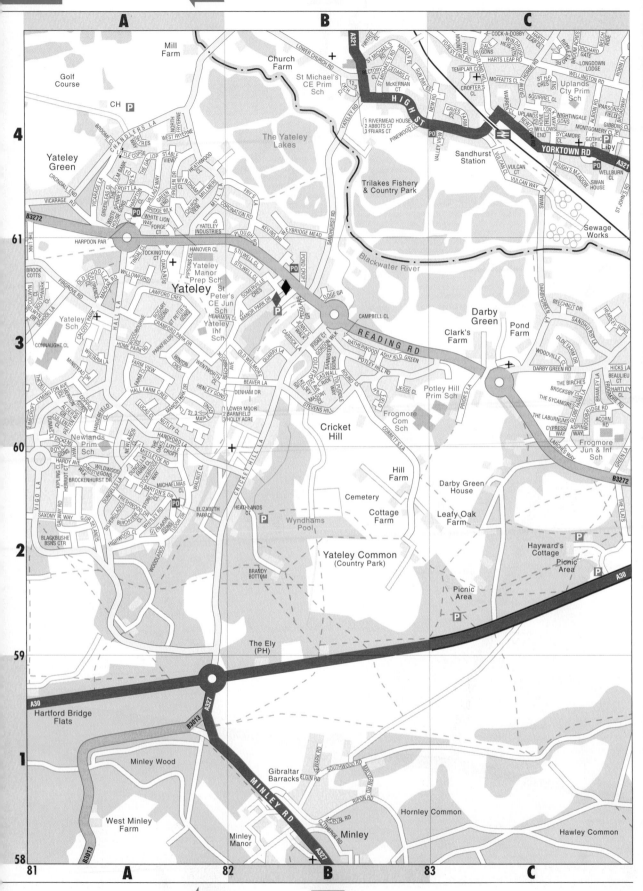

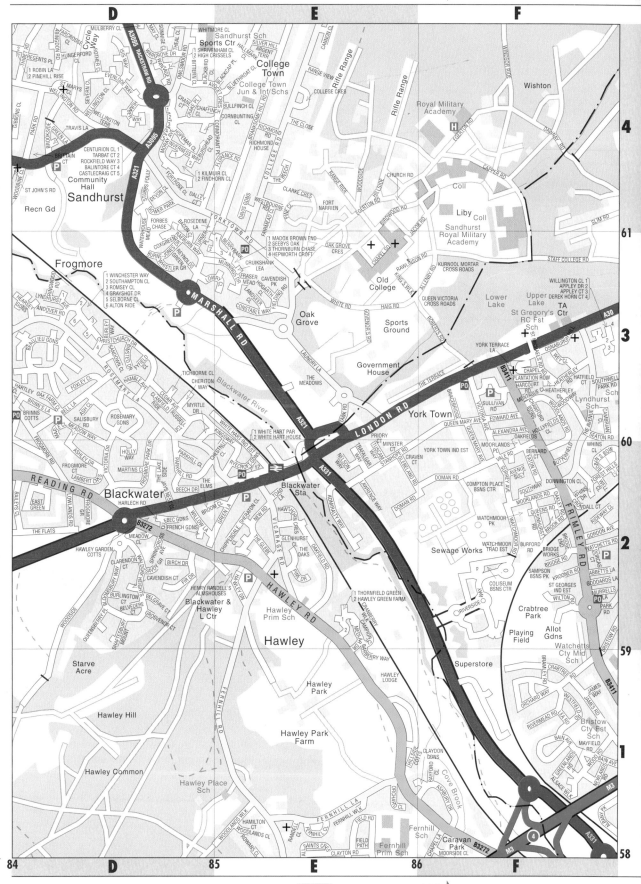

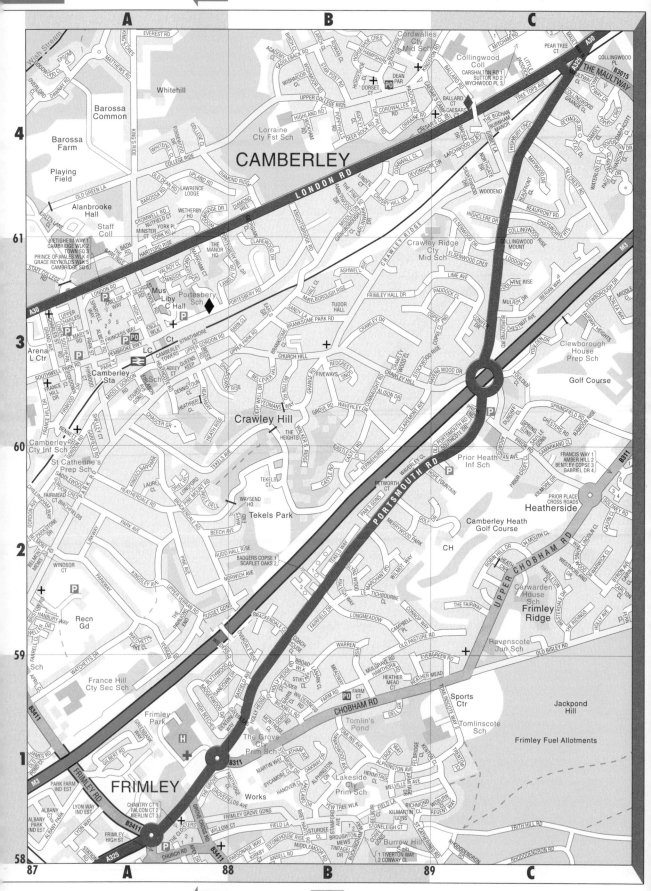

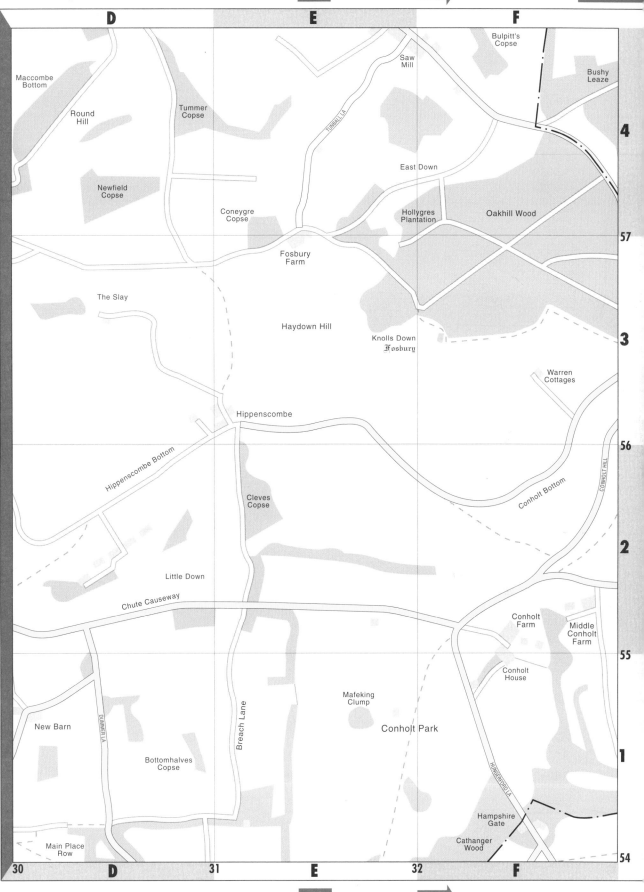

Maccombe Bottom

Round Hill

Tummer Copse

Bulpitt's Copse

Bushy Leaze

Saw Mill

East Down

Newfield Copse

Coneygre Copse

Hollygres Plantation

Oakhill Wood

Fosbury Farm

TURNBALL LA

The Slay

Haydown Hill

Knolls Down

Fosbury

Warren Cottages

Hippenscombe

Hippenscombe Bottom

Cleves Copse

Conholt Bottom

CONHOLT HILL

Little Down

Chute Causeway

Conholt Farm

Middle Conholt Farm

Conholt House

New Barn

DUMMER LA

Bottomhalves Copse

Breach Lane

Mafeking Clump

Conholt Park

HUNGERFORD LA

Hampshire Gate

Main Place Row

Cathanger Wood

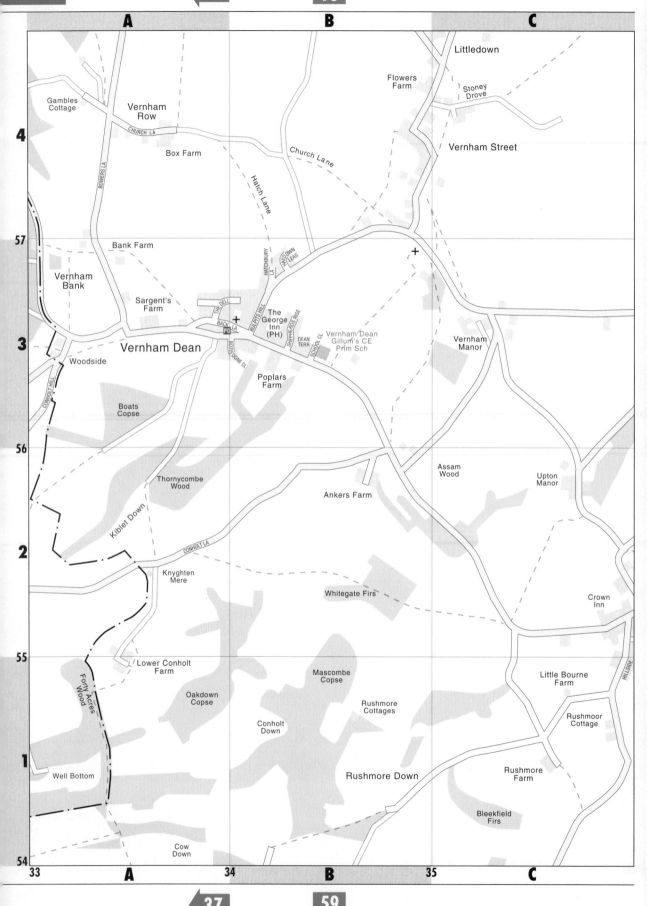

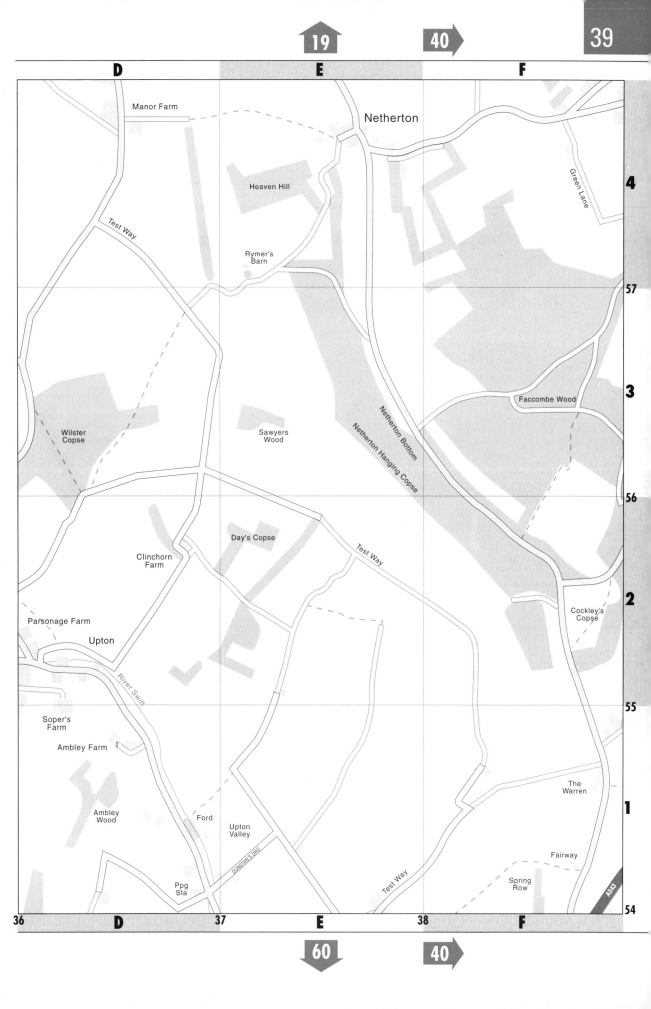

A B C

PH

Privet Copse

Robins
Croft
Copse

Manor
Farm

The Isle

Woodhay
Poor

The Plough
(PH)

BARN CLOSE LA

CROSS LA

4

Ashmansworth

Bartlett's
Down

HIGHFIELD

PO

London Lane

Steeles
Farm

Spencefield
Copse

57

Codley
Copse

Hipple La

Hall Lane

Alexander
Farm

Kimmer Farm

Church
Farm

+

3

Lower
Manor
Farm

The
Bushes

A343

56

Faccombe Wood

Sidley
Wood

Ten
Acre
Brow

2

Sidley
Bottom

Doyley
Manor

Lye
Copses

55

DOILEY HILL

Lye
Farm

Doyley Manor
Farm

P

Esseborne
Manor
(Hotel)

Splatts
Copse

Long
Copse

1

Doiley Hill
Farm

Doiley
Wood

Sladen
Green
Farm

DOILEY BOTTOM

A343

Lower
Doiley
Farm

Sladen
Green

54

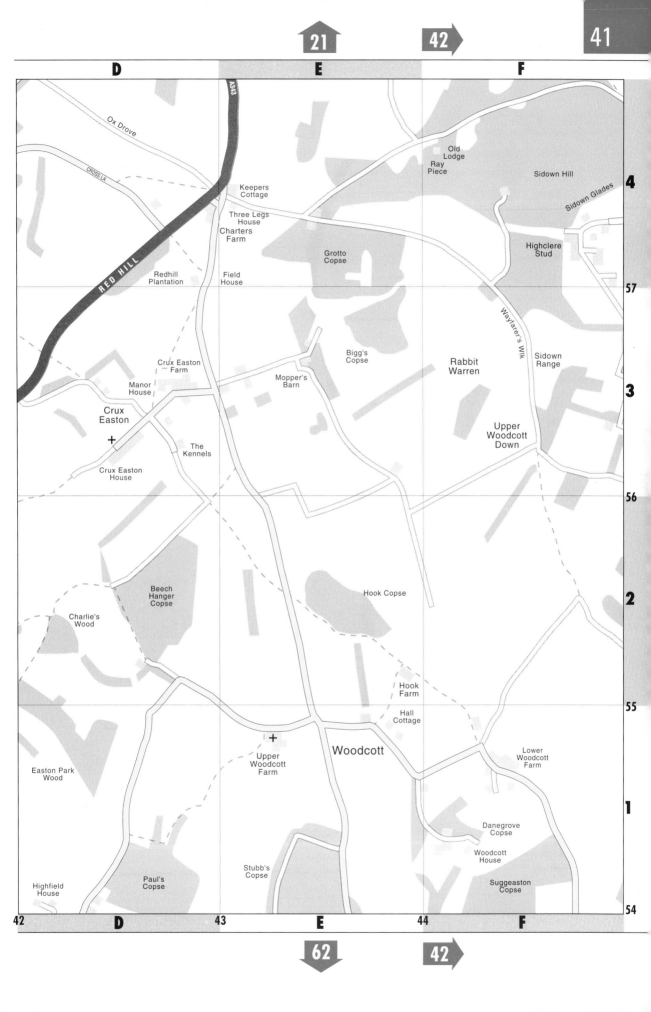

D
E
F

Ox Drove

CROSS LA

A343

RED HILL

Keepers
Cottage

Three Legs
House

Charters
Farm

Redhill
Plantation

Field
House

Old
Lodge

Ray
Piece

Sidown Hill

Sidown Glades

Highclere
Stud

Grotto
Copse

4

57

Crux Easton
Farm

Manor
House

Crux
Easton

Crux Easton
House

The
Kennels

Mopper's
Barn

Bigg's
Copse

Wayfarer's Wlk

Rabbit
Warren

Sidown
Range

3

Upper
Woodcott
Down

56

Charlie's
Wood

Beech
Hanger
Copse

Hook Copse

2

Hook
Farm

Hall
Cottage

55

Easton Park
Wood

Upper
Woodcott
Farm

Woodcott

Lower
Woodcott
Farm

1

Danegrove
Copse

Woodcott
House

Highfield
House

Paul's
Copse

Stubb's
Copse

Suggeaston
Copse

54

A   B   C

4

Lanecombe
Copse

Ivory
Farm

A34

Manor
Farm

WEIR
COTTS

BEACON PASS

P

Old Burghclere

Hall

THE LIME KILN
COTTS

Grave

57

Beacon Hill

Black
Valley

3

Wayfarer's Walk

Down Farm

56

Chapman's Dell

Hare Warren
Down

Lower Woodcott
Down

Thorndown
Plantation

Great Litchfield
Down

2

Seven
Barrows

55

Shell's
Copse

1

Bixley
Copse

Old Orchard
Copse

A34

JUBILEE CL

Little Down

Down Farm

54

45   A   46   B   47   C

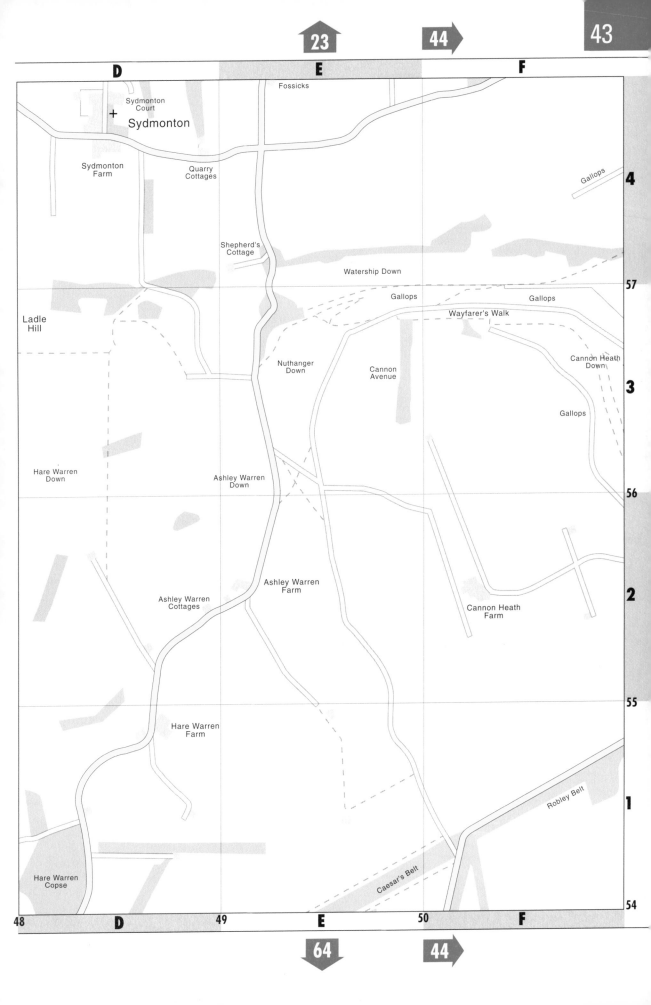

D
E
F

4

Fossicks

Sydmonton
Court
+
Sydmonton

Sydmonton
Farm

Quarry
Cottages

Gallops

Shepherd's
Cottage

Watership Down

57

Gallops

Gallops

Ladle
Hill

Wayfarer's Walk

Cannon Heath
Down

Nuthanger
Down

Cannon
Avenue

3

Gallops

Hare Warren
Down

Ashley Warren
Down

56

Ashley Warren
Farm

Cannon Heath
Farm

2

Ashley Warren
Cottages

Hare Warren
Farm

55

Robley Belt

1

Hare Warren
Copse

Caesar's Belt

54

48
D
49
E
50
F

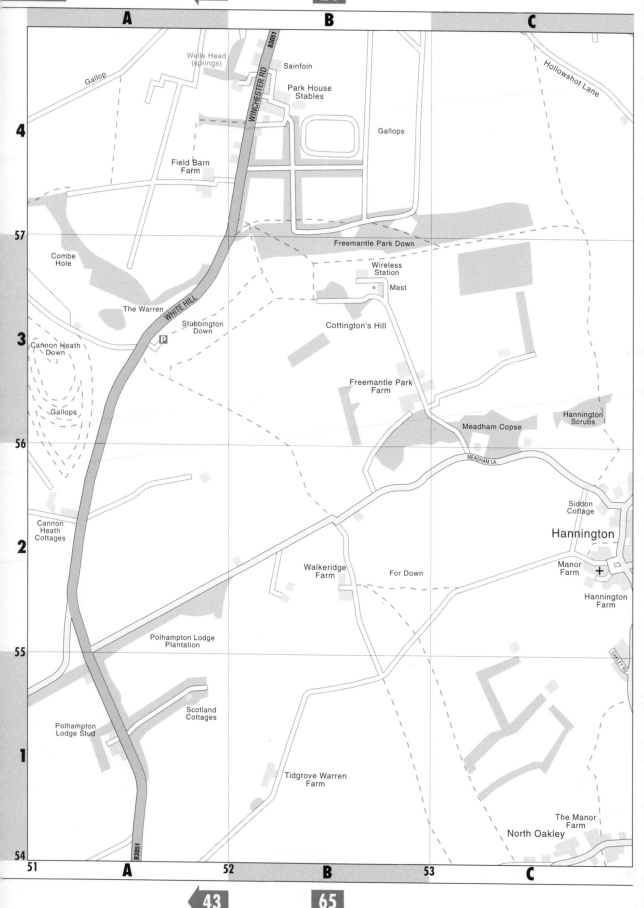

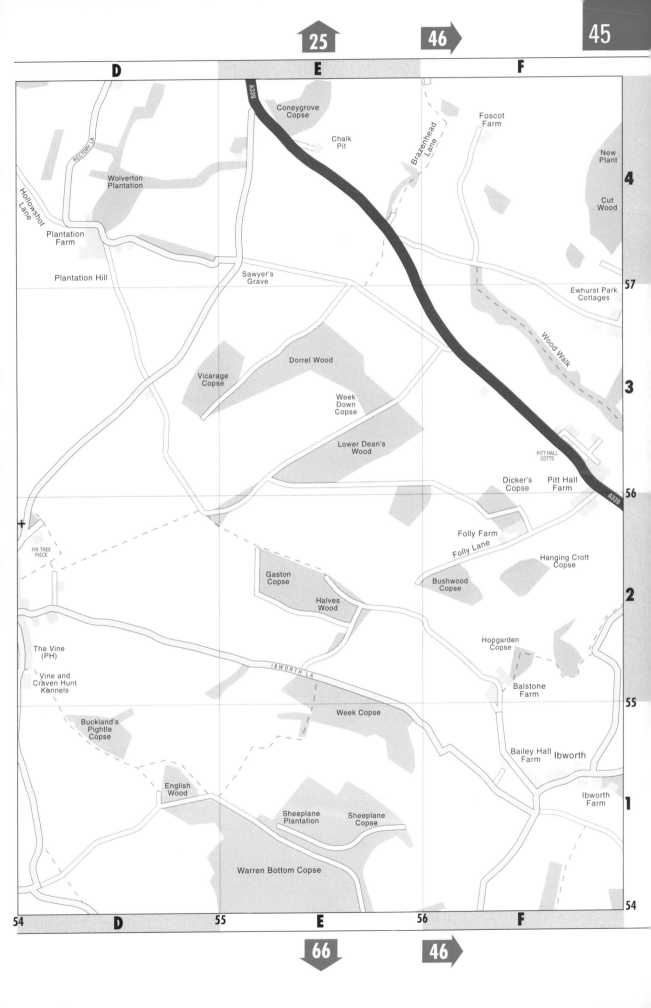

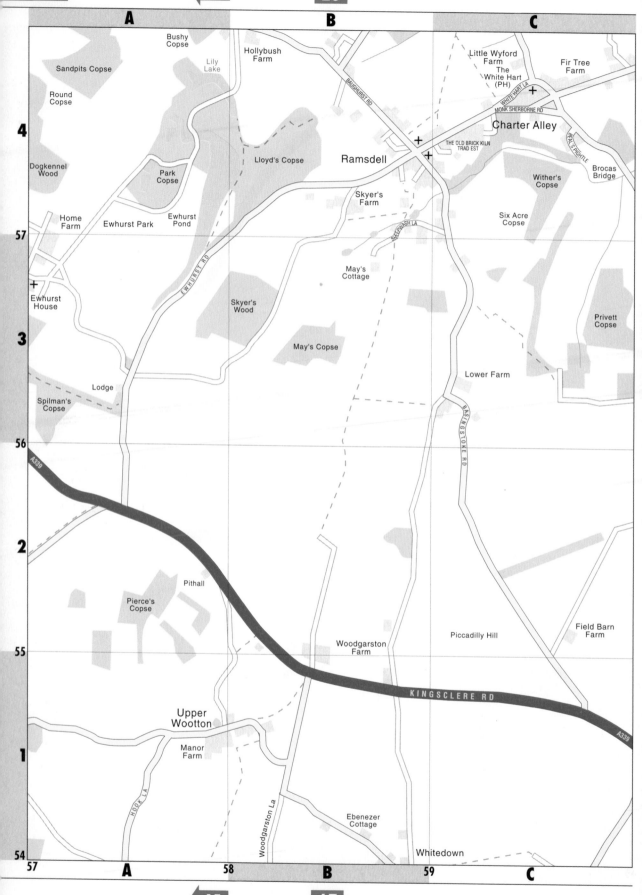

A **B** **C**

Sandpits Copse

Bushy Copse

Lily Lake

Hollybush Farm

Little Wyford Farm
The White Hart (PH)

Fir Tree Farm

Round Copse

WHITE HART LA

MONK SHERBORNE RD

Charter Alley

4

BAUGHURST RD

Dogkennel Wood

Park Copse

Lloyd's Copse

Ramsdell

THE OLD BRICK KILN TRAD EST

Wither's Copse

PEAL'S PIGHTLE

Brocas Bridge

Home Farm

Ewhurst Park

Ewhurst Pond

Skyer's Farm

Six Acre Copse

57

EWHURST RD

SHEEPWASH LA

Ewhurst House

Skyer's Wood

May's Cottage

Privett Copse

3

May's Copse

Lower Farm

Lodge

Spilman's Copse

BASINGSTOKE RD

56

A339

2

Pithall

Pierce's Copse

Woodgarston Farm

Piccadilly Hill

Field Barn Farm

55

KINGSCLERE RD

A339

Upper Wootton

1

Manor Farm

HOOK LA

Woodgarston La

Ebenezer Cottage

54

Whitedown

57 **A** 58 **B** 59 **C**

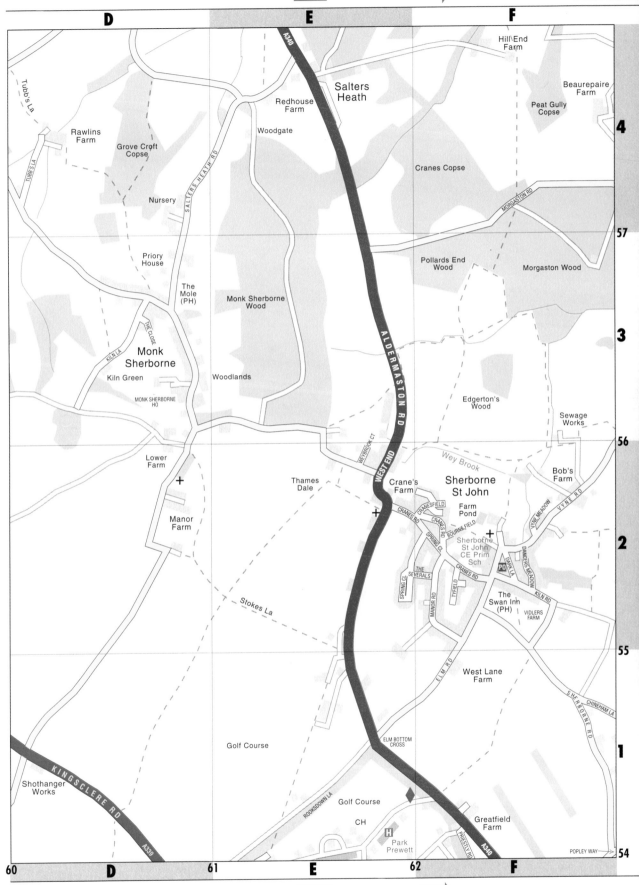

D
E
F

Tubb's La

Rawlins Farm

Grove Croft Copse

Nursery

Priory House

The Mole (PH)

Monk Sherborne

Kiln Green

MONK SHERBORNE HO

Woodlands

KILN LA

THE CLOSE

SALTERS HEATH RD

Redhouse Farm

Woodgate

Salters Heath

Monk Sherborne Wood

A340

Hill\End Farm

Beaurepaire Farm

Peat Gully Copse

Cranes Copse

MORGASTON RD

Pollards End Wood

Morgaston Wood

ALDERMASTON RD

Edgerton's Wood

Sewage Works

4

57

3

Lower Farm

Manor Farm

Thames Dale

Stokes La

Crane's Farm

CRANES RD

WEYBROOK CT

WEST END

Sherborne St John

Wey Brook

Farm Pond

CRANESFIELD

BOURNE FIELD

Sherborne St John CE Prim Sch

SPRING CL

SPRING CL

THE SEVERALS

MANOR RD

TYFIELD

CRANES RD

DARK LA

PO

The Swan Inn (PH)

VIDLERS FARM

DANGERS MEADOW

KILN RD

VYNE MEADOW

VYNE RD

Bob's Farm

56

2

55

KINGSCLERE RD

A339

Shothanger Works

Golf Course

ROOKSDOWN LA

Golf Course

CH

H

Park Prewett

West Lane Farm

ELM RD

ELM BOTTOM CROSS

Greatfield Farm

SHERBORNE RD

CHINEHAM LA

PRIESTLY RD

A340

POPLEY WAY

1

54

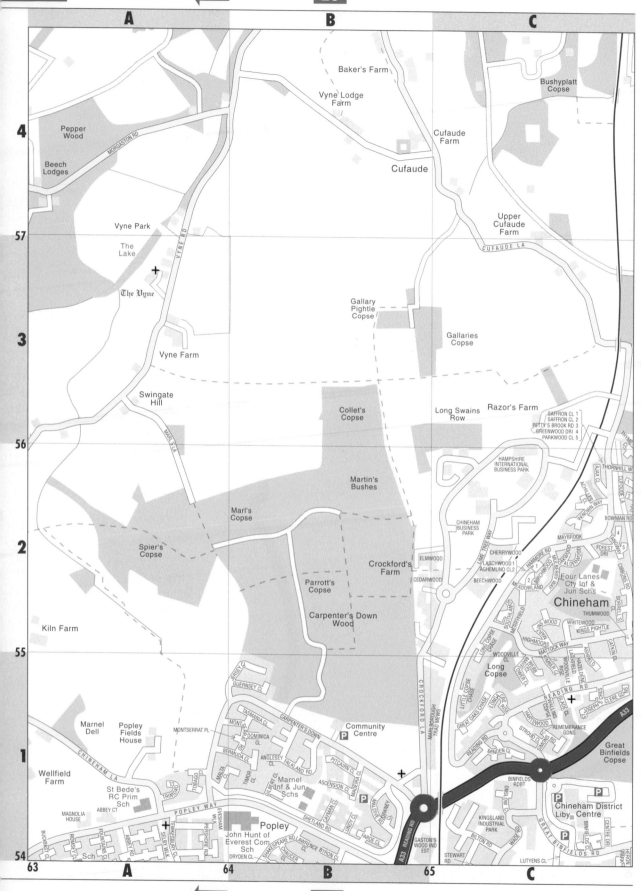

4

Pepper Wood

Beech Lodges

Baker's Farm

Vyne Lodge Farm

Bushyplatt Copse

Cufaude Farm

Cufaude

Morgaston Rd

57

Vyne Park

The Lake

Vyne Rd

The Vyne

Upper Cufaude Farm

CUFAUDE LA

Gallary Pightle Copse

Gallaries Copse

3

Vyne Farm

Swingate Hill

Collet's Copse

Long Swains Row

Razor's Farm

SAFFRON CL 1
SAFFRON CL 2
PETTY'S BROOK RD 3
GREENWOOD DRI 4
PARKWOOD CL 5

MARL'S LA

56

Martin's Bushes

HAMPSHIRE INTERNATIONAL BUSINESS PARK

THYME CL

THORNHILL W

CUFAUDE LA

Marl's Copse

CHINEHAM BUSINESS PARK

RENOWN WAY

ACHILLES CL

AJAX CL

BOWMAN RD

2

Spier's Copse

Parrott's Copse

Crockford's Farm

ELMWOOD

CEDARWOOD

CHERRYWOOD

LARCHWOOD 1
AGHEMUND CL 2

BEECHWOOD

LIME TREE WAY

HANMORE RD

MEADOWLAND

MAYBROOK

Four Lanes Cty Inf & Jun Schs

Chineham

THUMWOOD

FOREST DRI

Carpenter's Down Wood

Kiln Farm

WOODVILLE CL

WHITEWOOD

KINGS PIGHTLE

HIGHMOORS

MATTOCK WAY

55

Long Copse

Marnel Dell

Popley Fields House

JERSEY CL

GUERNSEY CL

TASMANIA CL

CARPENTER'S DOWN

Community Centre

MONTSERRAT PL

CHINEHAM LA

Wellfield Farm

Marnel Inf & Jun Schs

Popley

CROCKFORD LA

MARLBOROUGH TRAD MEWS

READING RD

A33

Great Binfields Copse

1

St Bede's RC Prim Sch

ABBEY CT

POPLEY WAY

John Hunt of Everest Com Sch

BINFIELDS RDBT

Chineham District Liby Centre

Kingsland Industrial Park

MAGNOLIA HOUSE

GASTON'S WOOD IND EST

Great Binfields Copse

54

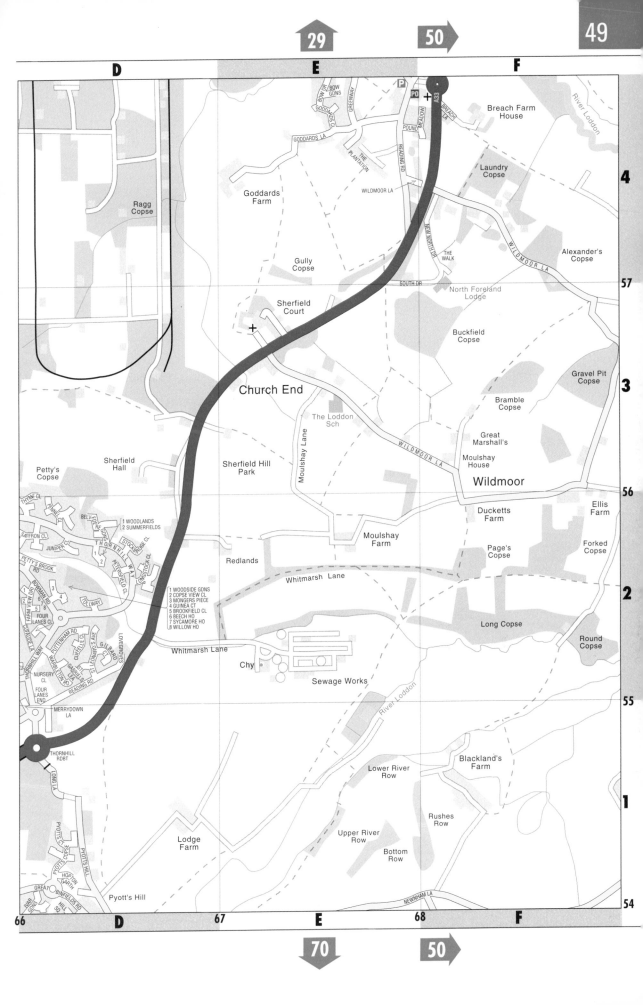

D
E
F

BOW DR
BOW GDNS
GODDARDS CL
GREENWAY
GODDARDS LA
THE PLANTATION
POUND MEADOW
READING RD
WILDMOOR LA
P
PO
A33
BREACH LA

Breach Farm House

Laundry Copse

Ragg Copse

Goddards Farm

Gully Copse

NEW NORTH DR
THE WALK
SOUTH DR

WILDMOOR LA

Alexander's Copse

North Foreland Lodge

4

57

Sherfield Court

Buckfield Copse

Gravel Pit Copse

Church End

Bramble Copse

3

The Loddon Sch

Moulshay Lane

WILDMOOR LA

Great Marshall's
Moulshay House

Wildmoor

Petty's Copse

Sherfield Hall

Sherfield Hill Park

THYME CL
FENNEL
SAFFRON CL
JUNIPER
BELVEDERE CL
RE GUINE CL
STOCKERS
THORNTHILL WY
TOSTOCK CL
1 WOODLANDS
2 SUMMERFIELDS
PETERSFIELD CL
PETTY'S BROOK RD
BOWMAN RD
FINCH VIEW DR
BIRCH WY
TOLLWAY
FOUR LANES CL
CITRADELA WY
PUTTENHAM RD
WARBLETON RD
ST LEONARDS AVE
CUFFELL CL
GILBARD
LOVEGROVES
GARDNER WY
BARGROVE
NURSERY CL
FOUR LANES END
READING RD
MERRYDOWN LA
THORNHILL RDBT
LONG LA

1 WOODSIDE GDNS
2 COPSE VIEW CL
3 MONGERS PIECE
4 GUINEA CT
5 BROOKFIELD CL
6 BEECH HO
7 SYCAMORE HO
8 WILLOW HO

Redlands

Whitmarsh Lane

Whitmarsh Lane

Chy

Sewage Works

Moulshay Farm

Ducketts Farm

Page's Copse

Ellis Farm

Forked Copse

Long Copse

Round Copse

River Loddon

River Loddon

56

2

55

Lodge Farm

Lower River Row

Upper River Row

Bottom Row

Blackland's Farm

Rushes Row

NEWNHAM LA

1

54

PYOTTS COPSE
PYOTTS HILL
HOPTON GARTH
GREAT BINFIELDS RD
HILL SQ
AMBER GDNS
Pyott's Hill

Topford Cottage

Webb's Hill

Kilnclose Copse

Hall's Lane

Peter's Copse

Webb's Copse

Lower Home Copse

Cooper's Farm

4

ROTHERWICK LA

Poplars Farm

Upper Høme Copse

Allen Moor

Hays Farm

Allenmoor Lane

Mill Farm

The Fox (PH)

Lyde Green Farm

Lance Levy Farm

MILL LA

FROG LA

Lyde Green

Black Wood

57

Wedman's Farm

WEDMAN'S PL

Soperslip Copse

River Loddon

Lyde River

Winnells Copse

LAMPARDS CL

WEDMAN'S LA

Rooks Farm

Rotherwick

COWFOLD LA

HOOK RD

3

Tim's Copse

Whitewater CE Prim Sch

THE STREET

The Coach and Horses (PH)

Summerstead Farm

The Old Rectory

Wildmoor Farm

56

The Old House

GREEN LA

Sewage Works

Runten's Farm

Club House

2

Golf Course

Cedar Clump

North Runten's Copse

Tylney Park

Tylney House

Home Farm

55

Tynley Hall

Shirlen's Copse

College Copse

Beehive Farm

Outdoor Education Centre

RIDGE LA

Hill Copse

Compfield Copse

College Copse

GOOSE GREEN

GREAT SHELDON COPP

PAINTERS PIGHTLE

1

Hale Farm

SHAW PIGHTLE

SCURES RD

GARDEN CL

TRUST CL

SHELDON CL

FERRELL FIELD

Deanlands Farm

TYLNEY LA

Newnham

BROWN CROFT

HAYFIELD

STABLE CL

CARLETON CL

NEWNHAM LA

Newnham Green Farm

PH

BOWLING GREEN DR

HOP GARDEN RD

Lyde Mill

Webb's Copse

Owen's Farm

BLUEHAVEN WLK

54

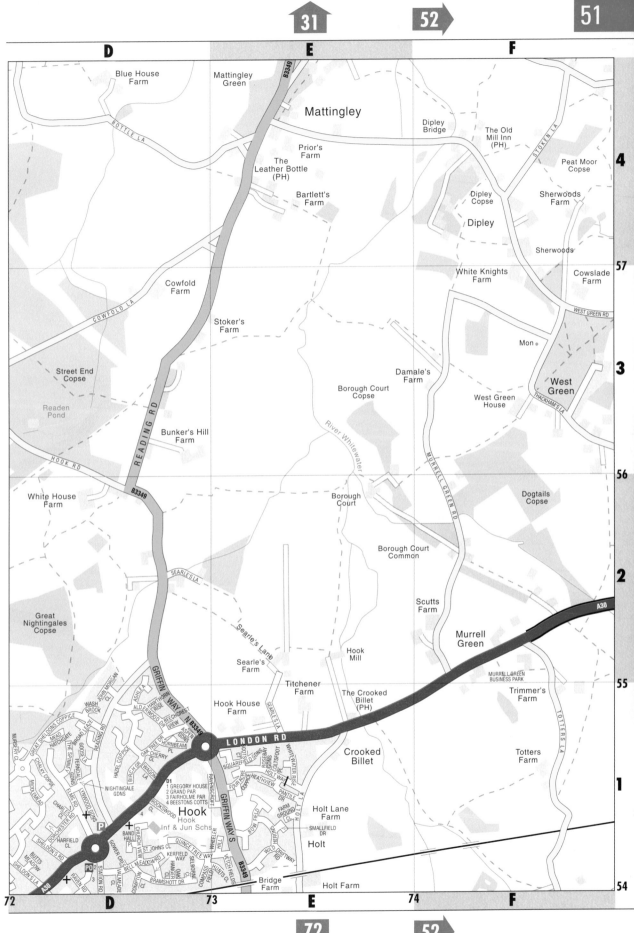

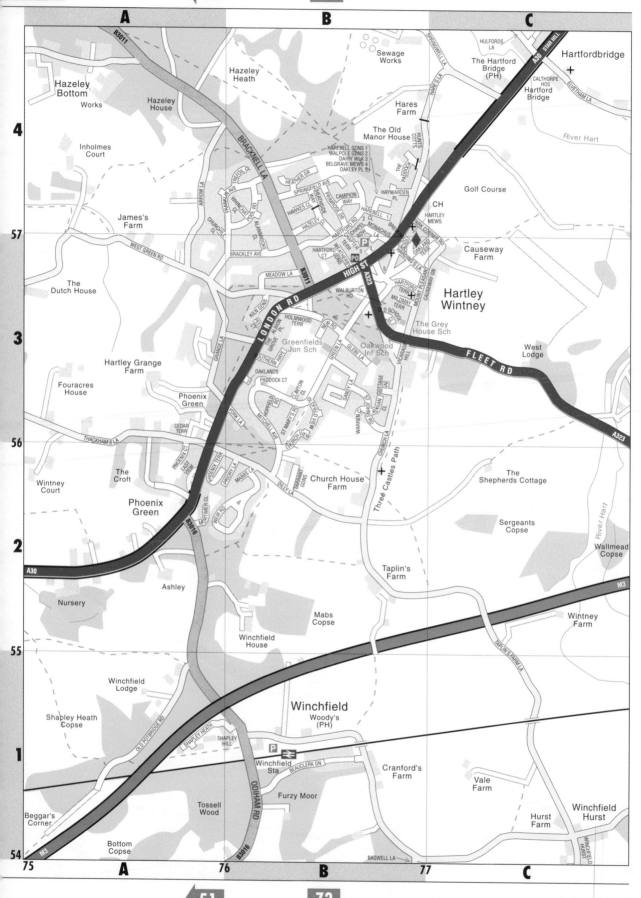

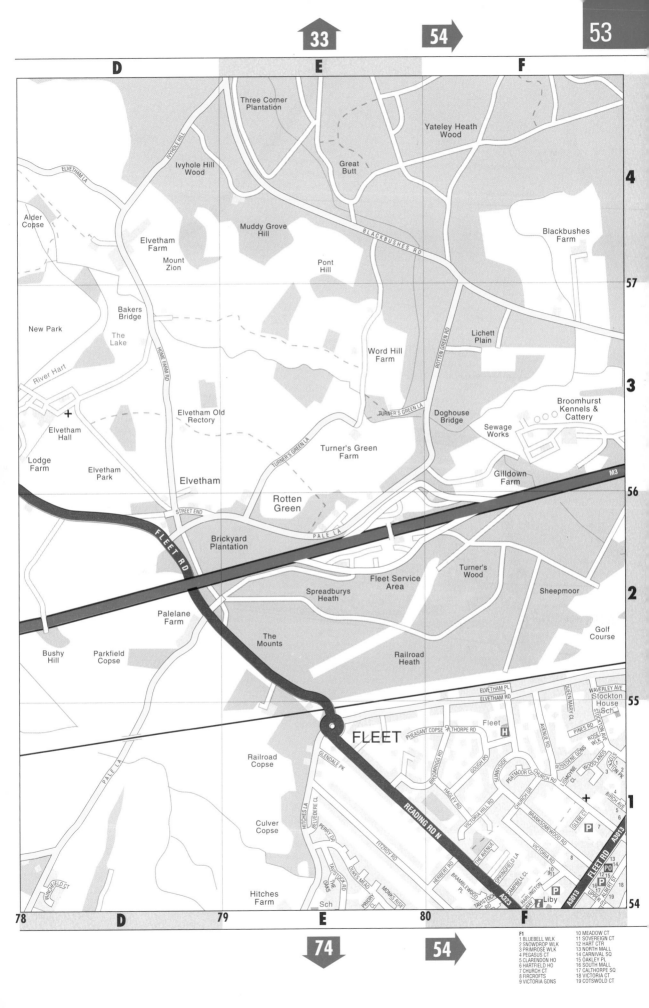

D E F

4

57

3

56

2

55

1

54

Three Corner Plantation

Yateley Heath Wood

ELVETHAM LA

Ivyhole Hill Wood

IVYHOLE HILL

Great Butt

BLACKBUSHES RD

Blackbushes Farm

Alder Copse

Muddy Grove Hill

Elvetham Farm

Mount Zion

Pont Hill

Bakers Bridge

New Park

The Lake

HOME FARM RD

Word Hill Farm

Lichett Plain

ROTTEN GREEN RD

River Hart

Elvetham Old Rectory

Elvetham Hall

TURNER'S GREEN LA

Doghouse Bridge

Broomhurst Kennels & Cattery

Sewage Works

Lodge Farm

Elvetham Park

Elvetham

Turner's Green Farm

TURNER'S GREEN LA

Gilldown Farm

M3

Rotten Green

FLEET RD

STREET END

Brickyard Plantation

PALE LA

Fleet Service Area

Turner's Wood

Sheepmoor

Palelane Farm

Spreadburys Heath

The Mounts

Railroad Heath

Golf Course

Bushy Hill

Parkfield Copse

PALE LA

ELVETHAM PL
ELVETHAM RD

WAVERLEY AVE
Stockton House Sch

QUEEN MARY CL

PINES RD

Fleet H

ROSE WLK

ROSEBERIE GDNS

WOODLANDS

STOCKTON AVE

FLEET

PHEASANT COPSE

CALTHORPE RD

AVENUE RD

LISMOYNE CL

BIRCH AVE

Railroad Copse

GLENDALE PK

BROOMRIGG RD

GOUGH RD

SUNNYSIDE

PEATMOOR CL

CHURCH RD

CHURCH GR

BRANSOMEWOOD RD

GLEBE CT

HITCHES LA

BELVEDERE CL

VICTORIA HILL RD

HAGLEY RD

READING RD N

P

P

A3013

FLEET RD

Culver Copse

PERRY DR

FITZROY RD

DIKES MEAD

THE OAKS

MOWS RISE

PRIORY CL

Sch

HERBERT RD

BRAMBLEWOOD PL

THE AVENUE

SPRINGFIELD LA

CAMPBELL CL

A323

HARLINGTON WAY

Liby

VICTORIA RD

TAVISTOCK RD

P

PO

P

UPPER ALBERT ST

WINCHFIELD CT

Hitches Farm

78 D 79 E 80 F

F1
1 BLUEBELL WLK
2 SNOWDROP WLK
3 PRIMROSE WLK
4 PEGASUS CT
5 CLARENDON HO
6 HARTFIELD HO
7 CHURCH CT
8 FIRCROFTS
9 VICTORIA GDNS
10 MEADOW CT
11 SOVEREIGN CT
12 HART CTR
13 NORTH MALL
14 CARNIVAL SQ
15 OAKLEY PL
16 SOUTH MALL
17 CALTHORPE SQ
18 VICTORIA CT
19 COTSWOLD CT

A B C

4

Minley Farm

Minley Wood

Minley Warren

Home Farm

Lower Minley Cottages

Hawley Common

Hawley Lake

MINLEY RD

A327

57

Crown and Cushion (PH)

LINKLATER'S COTTS

BLACKBUSHES RD

Mallards Copse

M3

4a

3

Tobridge Copse

Brook House

Bramshot Copse

Ancels Copse

A327

M3

BARLEY WAY HARVEST CRES

1 RYELAND CL
2 COLBRED CNR
3 FALLOWFIELD

ANCELLS CT

THE GATES

ANCELLS RD

The Bungalow

BRAMSHOT LA

56

CH B3013

Great Bramshot Farm

KERRY SHETLAND WAY

THRESHERS

FALKNER HOUSE

Little Bramshot Farm

Ash Copse

FENNEL

MARJORAM CL

LYNDSEY CL

HYTHARD DR

A327

B3014

FLEET RD B3014

DEXTER WAY GUERNSEY DR JERSEY

SUSSEX GDNS

GALLOWAY CL

SANKEY LA

2

Golf Course

CYGNET CT 1
WATERSIDE MEWS 2

OLD COVE RD

LAKESIDE CT

HANOVER RD

FOREST DEAN

SHIRE AVE

FOXWOOD WOODGATE

COVE RD

A3013

B3014

SUMMIT AVE

A327

OLD WOOD CHASE

KNOLL CT

Fleet Sta

MINLEY RD

P

WATERFRONT BUSINESS PARK

Fleet Pond
(Nature Reserve)

KENNELS LA

P

55

ELVETHAM RD WENSLEY

COACH HOUSE GDNS

HILLCREST CRANBROOK

THE MOUNT

STATION IND EST

DARSET AVE

BRAMSHOT DR

WELLINGTON AVE

CHESTNUT GR

Gelvert Stream

KNOLL CL

SEYMOUR CT

PINEWOOD HILL

AVONDALE RD

Fugelmere Wlk

KENILWORTH RD

FUGELMERE WLK

FUGELMERE CRES

MONKSIDE GDNS

WOODSIDE GDNS

KENWITH AVE

1

WAVERLEY RD

STOCKTON AVE WEST

MINSTER CL

B3010

Wks

CHURCH

OLD SCHOOL CL

CLARENCE RD

BEARWOOD

THE LAURELS

ABBOTS BURNSIDE

KENT RD

SOUTHBY DR

KENILWORTH RD

BROOK GDNS

WESTOVER RD

LOCKSTOCK WAY

WOOD LA

HONISTER GDNS

HONISTER RD

LLIANS WAY

CYPRESS RD

PONDTAIL RD

LYNDALE DR

Test & Evaluation Establishment

Pyestock

Sewage Works

KINGS RD

B3010

FLEET

Oakley Park

GEORGE RD

KEATS GDNS

ALBANY RD

ALSANN RD

ADAMS CL COOMBE

CAMBRAY RD HOWARD RD

GUILFORD RD

HERRIES RD

CEDAR DR

ROWAN CL

ELMS RD

ALTON RD

JORDANS WLK

FRINGHAM RD

FARNHAM RD

Pondtail

Playing Field

54

81 A 82 B 83 C

A1
1 PINEWOOD CT
2 KINGS PAR
3 GAINSBOROUGH CT
4 ST PHILIPS CT
5 CLARENCE CT
6 GEORGINA CT
7 WINDSOR CT
8 KINGSWOOD CT
9 WESTFIELD CT
10 ST JOHN'S CT
11 CLARE CT

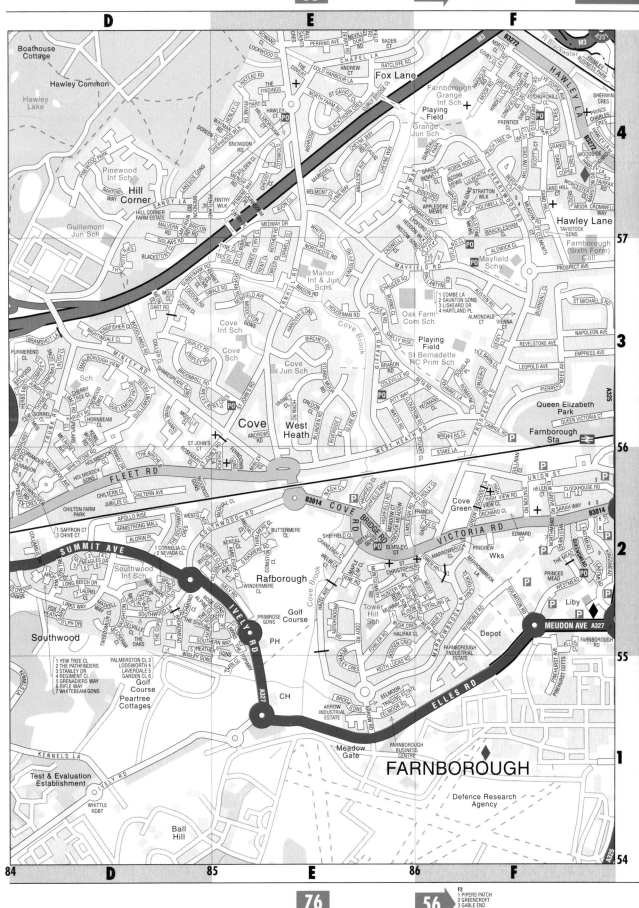

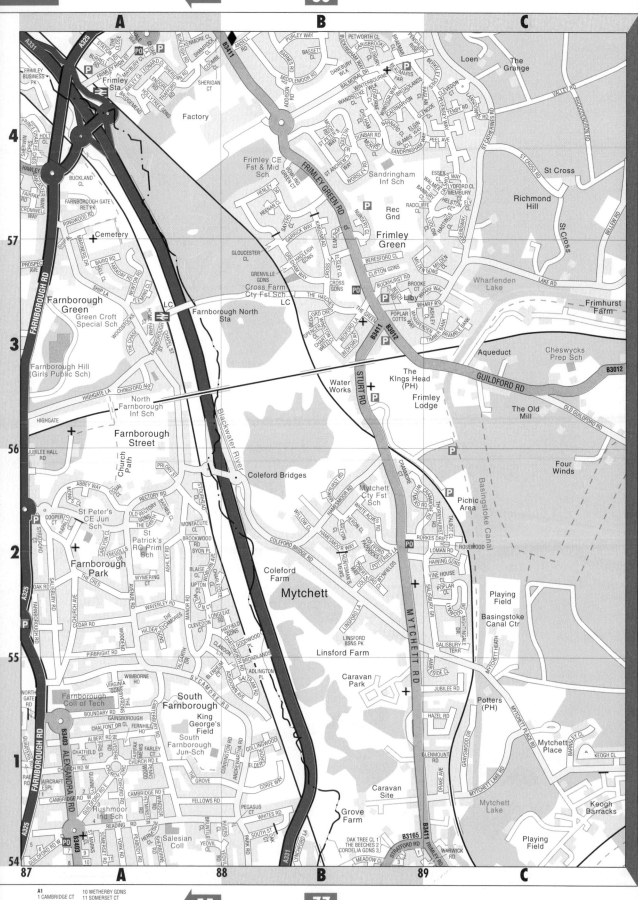

A1
1 CAMBRIDGE CT
2 BARTON CT
3 DENBY CT
4 REDE CT
5 NEELEM CT
6 KASHMIR CT
7 BULLER CT
8 WYKEHAM HO
9 ALEXANDRA CT
10 WETHERBY GDNS
11 SOMERSET CT

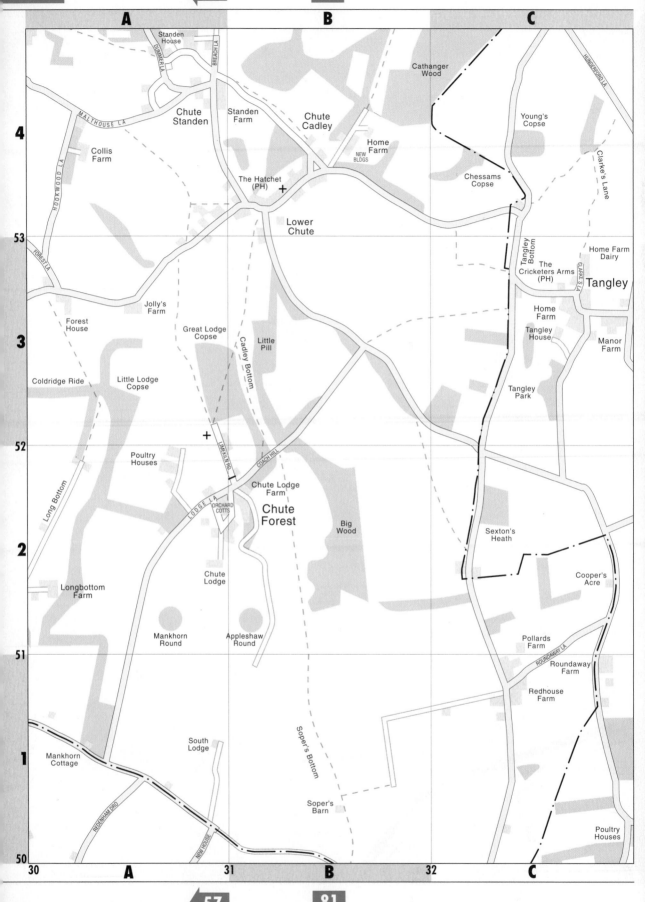

Standen
House

Chute
Standen

Standen Farm

Chute
Cadley

Cathanger
Wood

Young's
Copse

Clarke's Lane

Collis
Farm

Home
Farm

NEW
BLDGS

Chessams
Copse

MALTHOUSE LA

DUMMER LA

BREACH LA

HOOKWOOD LA

The Hatchet
(PH)

Lower
Chute

Home Farm
Dairy

Tangley
Bottom

The
Cricketers Arms
(PH)

CLARKE'S LA

Tangley

FOREST LA

Jolly's
Farm

Home
Farm

Forest
House

Great Lodge
Copse

Little
Pill

Tangley
House

Manor
Farm

Coldridge Ride

Little Lodge
Copse

Cadley Bottom

Tangley
Park

Poultry
Houses

Chute Lodge
Farm

Sexton's
Heath

LIMEKILN RD

COACH HILL

Long Bottom

LODGE LA

ORCHARD
COTTS

Chute
Forest

Big
Wood

Cooper's
Acre

Longbottom
Farm

Chute
Lodge

Pollards
Farm

Mankhorn
Round

Appleshaw
Round

Roundaway
Farm

ROUNDAWAY LA

Redhouse
Farm

South
Lodge

Soper's Bottom

Mankhorn
Cottage

REDENHAM DRO

NEW HOUSE

Soper's
Barn

Poultry
Houses

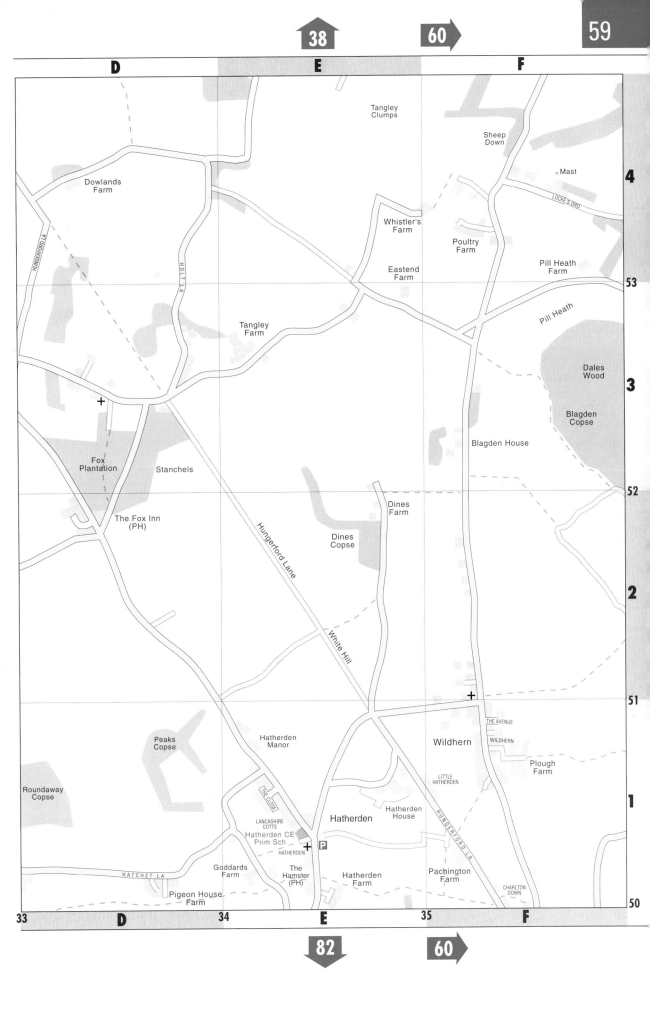

D E F

Tangley Clumps

Sheep Down

• Mast

4

LOCKE'S DRO

Dowlands Farm

Whistler's Farm

Poultry Farm

Pill Heath Farm

HOLT LA

HUNGERFORD LA

Eastend Farm

Pill Heath

53

Tangley Farm

Dales Wood

3

Blagden Copse

+

Blagden House

Fox Plantation

Stanchels

Dines Farm

52

The Fox Inn (PH)

Dines Copse

Hungerford Lane

2

White Hill

+

51

THE AVENUE

Peaks Copse

Hatherden Manor

Wildhern

WILDHERN

Plough Farm

Roundaway Copse

LITTLE HATHERDEN

HUNGERFORD LA

1

THE CLOSE

LANCASHIRE COTTS

Hatherden CE Prim Sch

+

HATHERDEN

P

Hatherden House

Hatherden

HATCHET LA

Goddards Farm

The Hamster (PH)

Hatherden Farm

Pachington Farm

CHARLTON DOWN

Pigeon House Farm

50

A   B   C

4

Ibthorpe

Upper Ibthorpe
Farm

HORSESHOE LA

Ibthorpe Manor
Farm

Prosperous
Farm

A343

Locke's
Barn

LOCKE'S DRO

Yewtree
Farm

Adams
Farm

Test Way

DOLOMANS LA

DINES CL

Hurstbourne
Tarrant

THE RANK

The
Dene

KNIGHTS LA

THE CRESCENT

DEAN RISE

53

Windmill Hill
Down

WINDMILL LA

Dolomans La

The George
and Dragon
(PH)

PO

B3048

CHURCH ST

Parsonage Farm

Windmills Farm

DOCTORS DRO

River Swift

STOKE RD

B3048

Windmills

Windmill
Hill

Hurstbourne
Tarrant
CE Prim Sch

Lower
Farm

3

Blagden
Copse

Hurstbourne
Common

Hurstbourne
Hill

Bourne Rivulet

52

Doles
Copse

Test Way

Doles Wood

2

Doles
Farm

Doles
House

Bourne
Park

Frenches
Farm

Rag
Wood

51

Lee's
Wood

Frenche's
Lodge

1

GREEN DRO

Rag
Copse

Straits
Copse

NEWBURY RD

MAC OLLUM RD

Great
Stubbage

Long
Copse

Ridges
Copse

A343

50

36   A   37   B   38   C

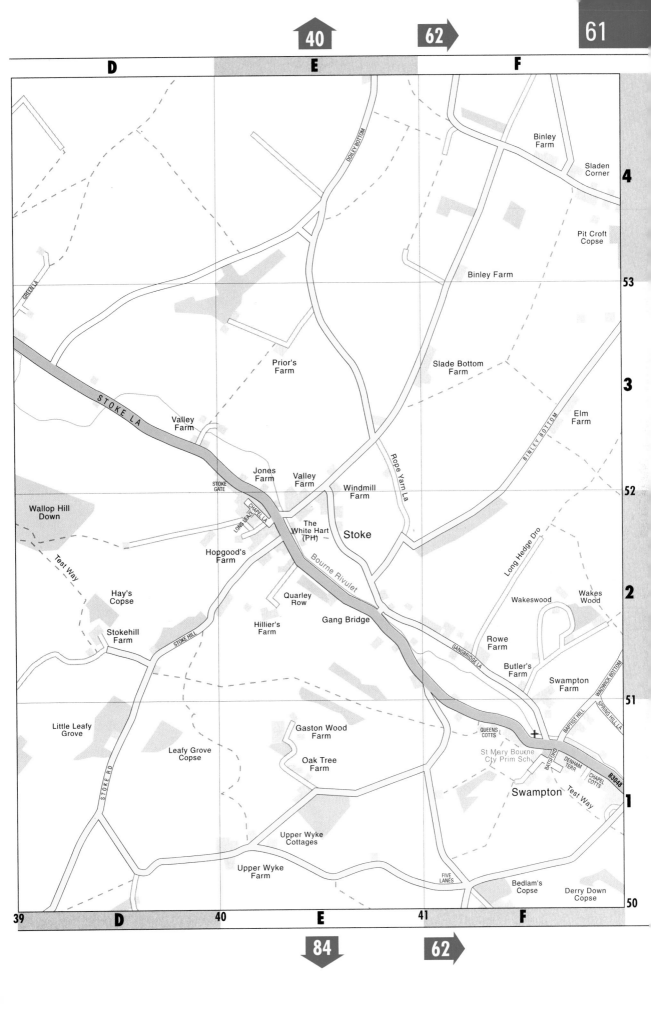

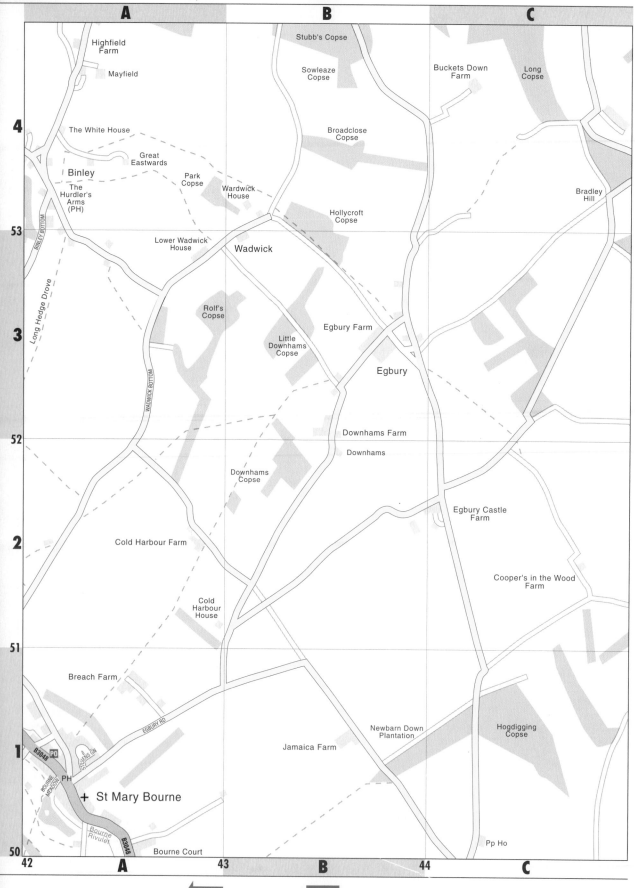

A   B   C

Highfield Farm

Mayfield

Stubb's Copse

Sowleaze Copse

Buckets Down Farm

Long Copse

4

The White House

Broadclose Copse

Great Eastwards

Binley

Park Copse

Wardwick House

Bradley Hill

The Hurdler's Arms (PH)

Hollycroft Copse

53

Lower Wadwick House

Wadwick

Binley Bottom

Long Hedge Drove

Rolf's Copse

Egbury Farm

3

Little Downhams Copse

Egbury

Wadwick Bottom

Downhams Farm

52

Downhams

Downhams Copse

Egbury Castle Farm

2

Cold Harbour Farm

Cooper's in the Wood Farm

Cold Harbour House

51

Breach Farm

Egbury Rd

Stevens Gn

Newbarn Down Plantation

Hogdigging Copse

1

B3048

PO

PH

Bourne Meadow

Jamaica Farm

+ St Mary Bourne

Bourne Rivulet

B3048

Bourne Court

Pp Ho

50

42   A   43   B   44   C

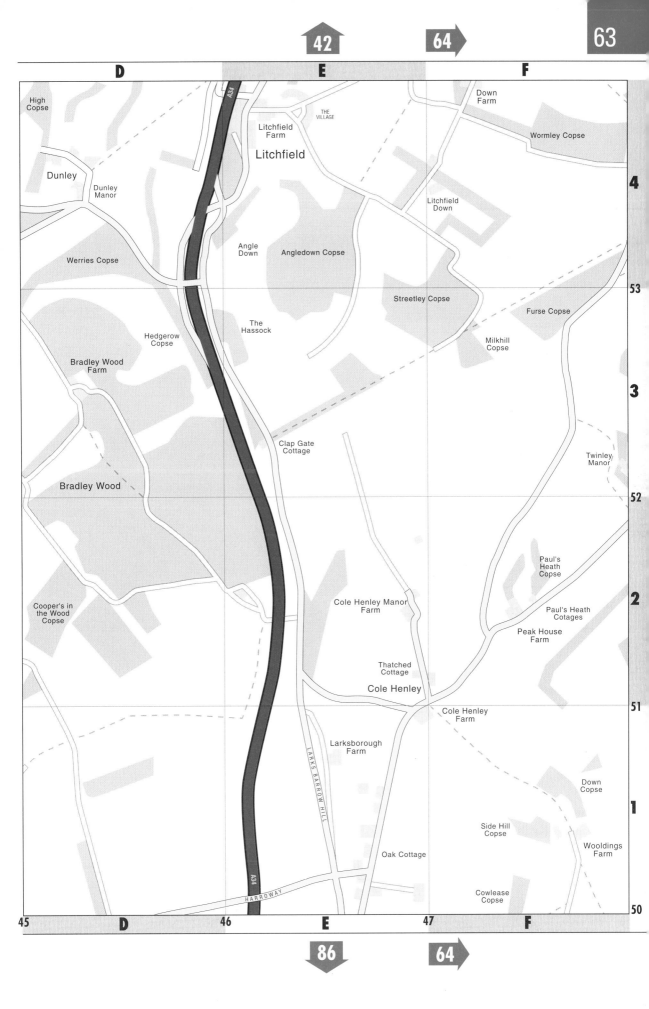

D   E   F

High
Copse

A34

Down
Farm

Litchfield
Farm

THE
VILLAGE

Wormley Copse

Litchfield

Dunley

Dunley
Manor

4

Litchfield
Down

Werries Copse

Angle
Down

Angledown Copse

53

Streetley Copse

Furse Copse

The
Hassock

Hedgerow
Copse

Milkhill
Copse

Bradley Wood
Farm

3

Twinley
Manor

Clap Gate
Cottage

Bradley Wood

52

Paul's
Heath
Copse

Cooper's in
the Wood
Copse

Cole Henley Manor
Farm

2

Paul's Heath
Cotages

Peak House
Farm

Thatched
Cottage

Cole Henley

Cole Henley
Farm

51

LARKS BARROW HILL

Larksborough
Farm

Down
Copse

1

Side Hill
Copse

Wooldings
Farm

Oak Cottage

A34

Cowlease
Copse

HARROWAY

50

45   D   46   E   47   F

A   B   C

4

Owls
Lodge

Caesar's Belt

Palmer's
Bushes

Robley Belt

Ridgeway
Copse

53

Keeper's Cottage

Old Farmhouse

Ridgeway
Farm

Willesley Warren
Cottages

Willesley Warren
Farm

Dunn's
Wood

3

Paul's
Wood.

Twinley
Manor

52

Little Twinley's
Copse

The
Peak

Whitnal

2

New
Barn

La
Bresse

51

WATCH LA

COURT DRO

1

The
Orchards

The
Cottage

Harroway Belt

Lordsfield
Plantation

Ash Bed
Plantation

Northfield
Plantation

Northington Belt

Sewage
Works

50

48   A   49   B   50   C

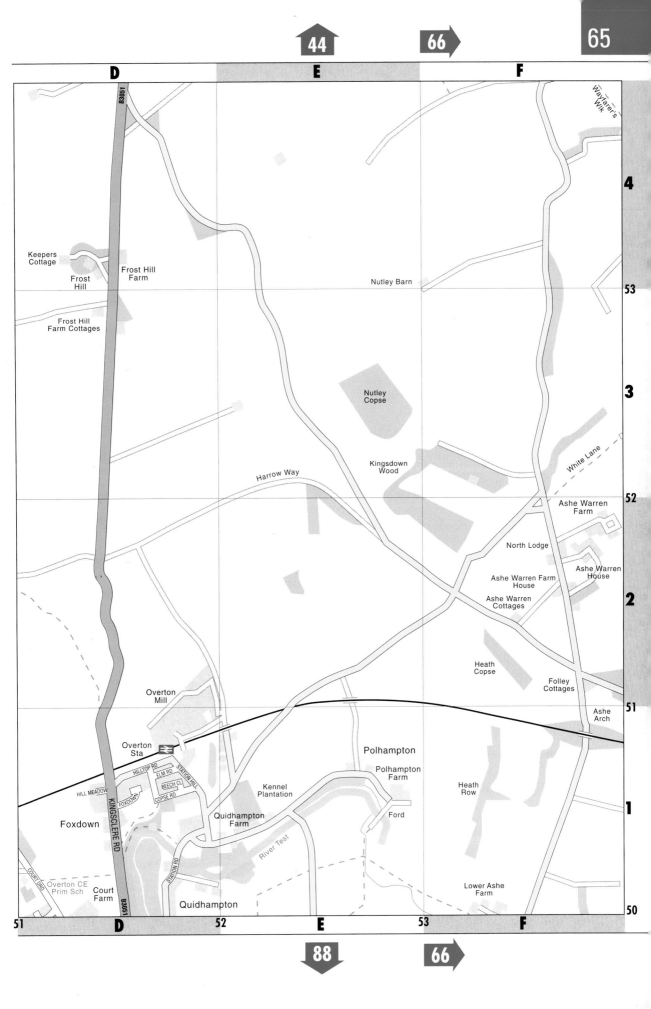

Wayfarer's Wlk

D
E
F

4

Keepers
Cottage
Frost Hill
Farm
Nutley Barn
53
Frost
Hill
Frost Hill
Farm Cottages

Nutley
Copse
3

Kingsdown
Wood
White Lane

Harrow Way
Ashe Warren
Farm
52
North Lodge
Ashe Warren
House
Ashe Warren Farm
House
2
Ashe Warren
Cottages

Heath
Copse
Folley
Cottages

Overton
Mill
Ashe
Arch
51

Overton
Sta

Polhampton

HILLTOP RD
STATION HILL
Polhampton
Farm

ELM RD
BEECH CL
HILL MEADOW
FOXDOWN
COPSE RD
Kennel
Plantation
Heath
Row

KINGSCLERE RD
Quidhampton
Farm
Ford
1

Foxdown
STATION RD
River Test

COURT DRO
Overton CE
Prim Sch
Court
Farm
B3051
Quidhampton
Lower Ashe
Farm
50

51
D
52
E
53
F

A   B   C

Warren Bottom Copse

Freemantle Farm

Freemantle Farm Cottages

Sunny View

The Gables

4

Hay Wood

Wayfarer's Walk

Lynwood

Pamelia

Lockley Copse

HOOK LA

53

Frith Wood

Rosemont

WHITE LA

Shear Down Farm

White Lane

Patchbourne Wood

SUMMER DOWN LA

Malshanger House

3

Great Deane Wood

Summer Down Copse

Malshanger Park

Wayfarer's Walk

Home Farm

Home Farm Cottages

52

Stubb's Copse

Little Deane Wood

Blandy's Farm

MALSHANGER LA

Sourley Row

SUMMERDOWN COTTS

Summer Down Farm

2

IVY DOWN LA

Deane Down Farm

Deane Down

HARROW WAY

Sewage Works

Motel

B3400

51

Clarken Green

STATION RD

Wayfarer's Walk

The Spinney

Park Farm

1

Deane House Cottages

Church Oakley

RECTORY RD

ANDOVER RD

Deane House

DEANES COTTS

Deane

Manor Farm

Oakley Park

B3400

Deane Park

50

54   A   55   B   56   C

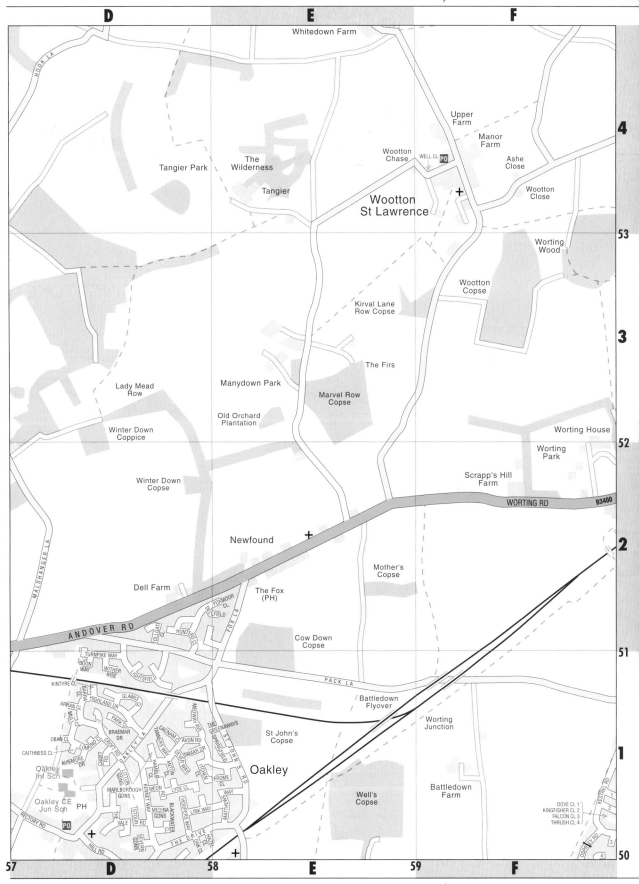

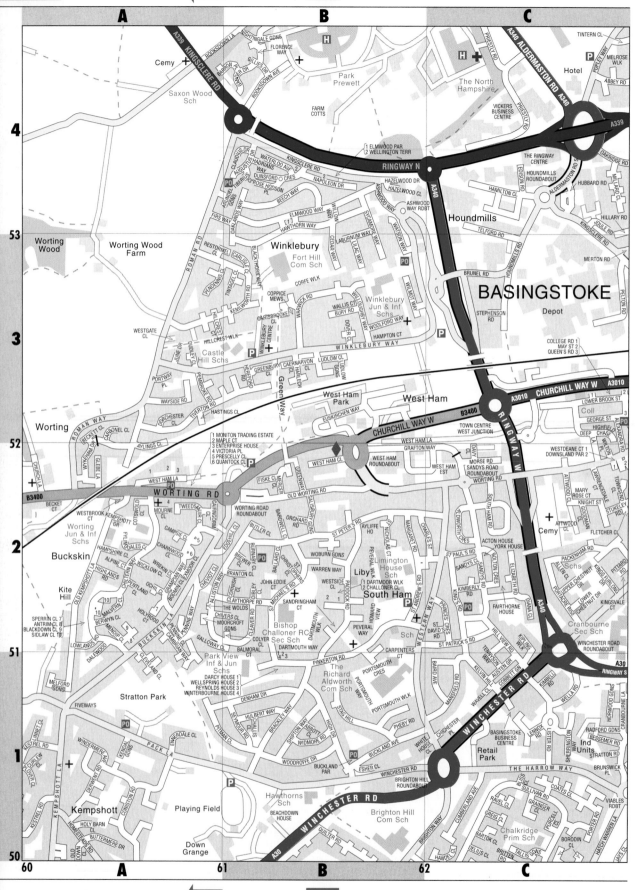

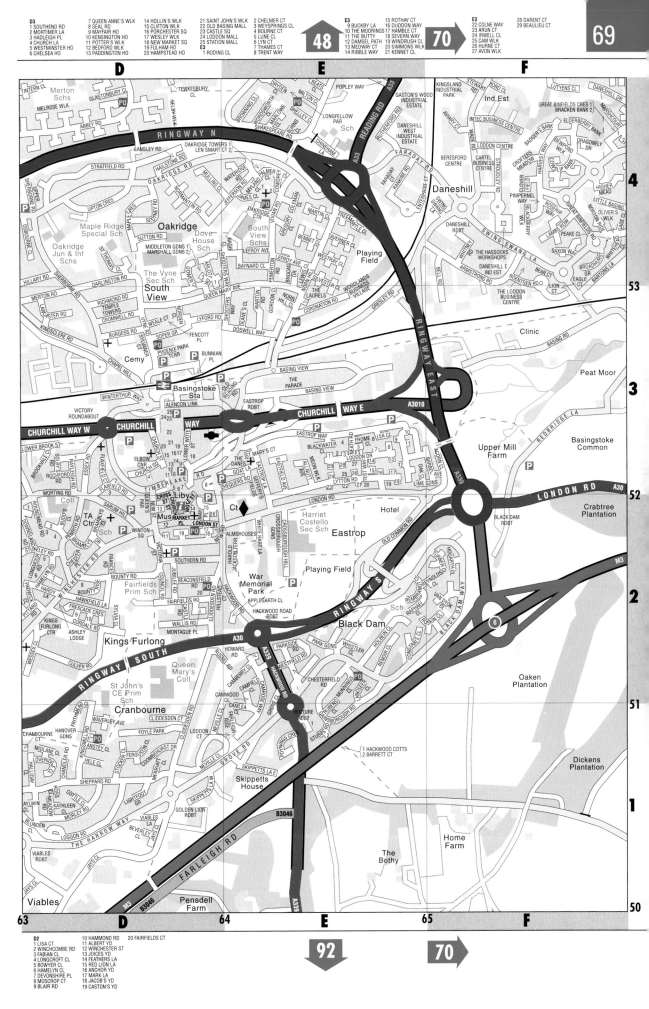

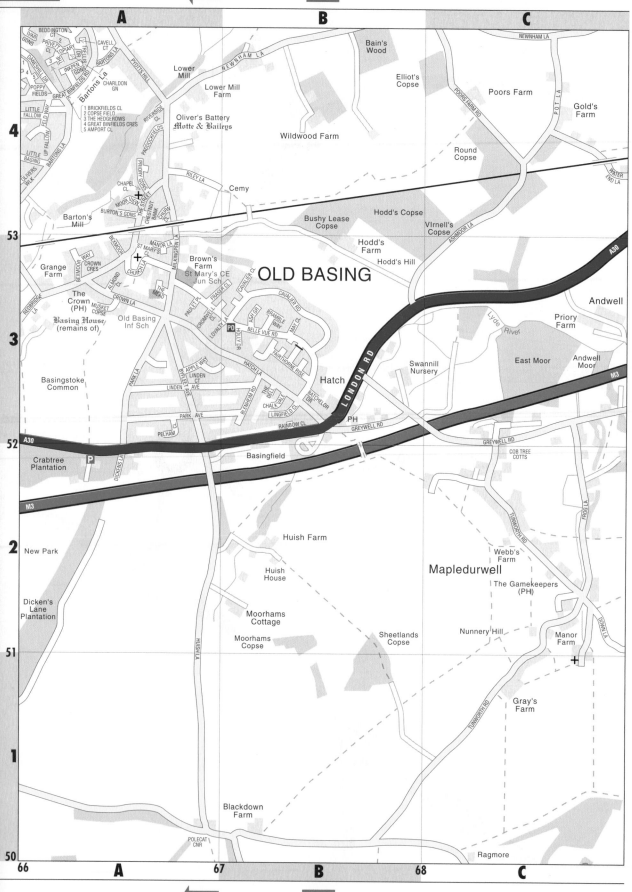

OLD BASING

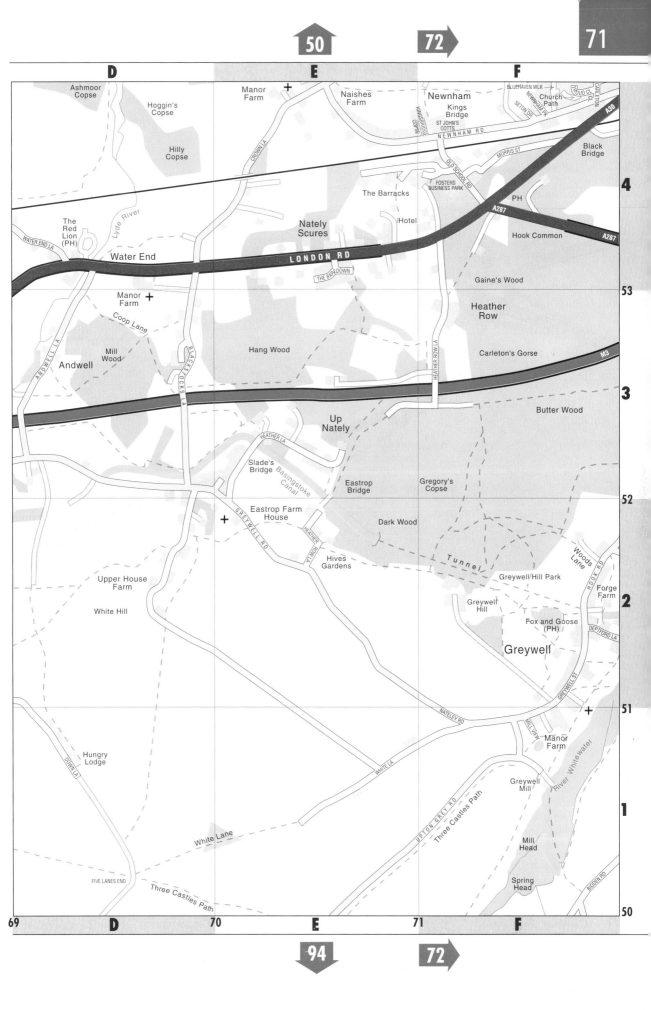

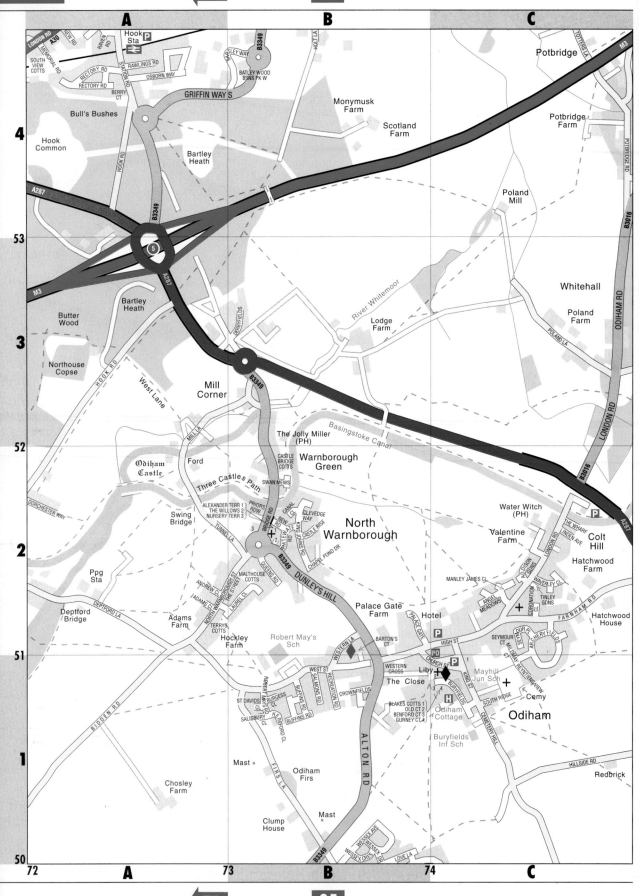

London Rd A30 New Rd Raven Rd Hook Sta P Rawlings Rd Batley Way B3349 Holt La Potbridge M3 Potters La

Memorial Rd Station Rd Osborn Way Batley Wood Bsns Pk W Potbridge Farm

Rectory Rd Berry Ct Griffin Way S Monymusk Farm Scotland Farm B3016 Potbridge Rd

Bull's Bushes Bartley Heath Poland Mill

Hook Common Poland Farm Odiham Rd Whitehall

A287 B3349 River Whitemoor Poland La

M3 Bartley Heath Lodge Farm London Rd

Butter Wood Hook Rd West Lane Mill Corner B3349 Basingstoke Canal B3016

Northouse Copse Mill La The Jolly Miller (PH) Water Witch (PH) P The Wharf Inden Ave Colt Hill

Odiham Castle Ford Castle Bridge Cotts Warnborough Green Valentine Farm London Rd Hatchwood Farm

Dorchester Way Three Castles Path Swan Mews Ad Dixon Gdns Waverley Cl

Swing Bridge Tunnel La Alexander Terr 1 The Willows 2 Nursery Terr 3 Priors Row New Rd Whitewater Rd King Johns Rd Castle Rise Clevedge Way North Warnborough Manley James Cl Tinley Gdns Coronation Cl Hatchwood House

Ppg Sta Chapel Pond Dr Angel Meadows Farnham Rd

Deptford Bridge Deptford La Adams Farm North Warnborough St Malthouse Cotts Laurel Cl Queens Rd Dunley's Hill Palace Gate Farm Hotel Palace Gate High St Seymour Ct Mildmay Reyntiens View Archery Fields

Bidden Rd Andrew Cl Adams Cl The Street Terrys Cotts Hockley Farm Robert May's Sch Western La Barton's Ct P Church St King St PO P Mayhill Jun Sch South Ridge Cemy Odiham

Robert May's Cl Burgess West St Salmons Rd Recreation Rd Crownfields Western Cross Liby The Close Buryfields Blakes Cotts 1 Old Ct 2 Benford Ct 3 Gurney Ct 4 H Odiham Cottage Buryfields Inf Sch Cemetery Hill Hillside Rd Redbrick

St Davids Cl Salisbury Cl H Hereford Cl Buffins Rd Buffins Rd

Mast Firs La Odiham Firs Alton Rd

Chosley Farm Clump House Mast Wess La Wessex Cres Love La B3349

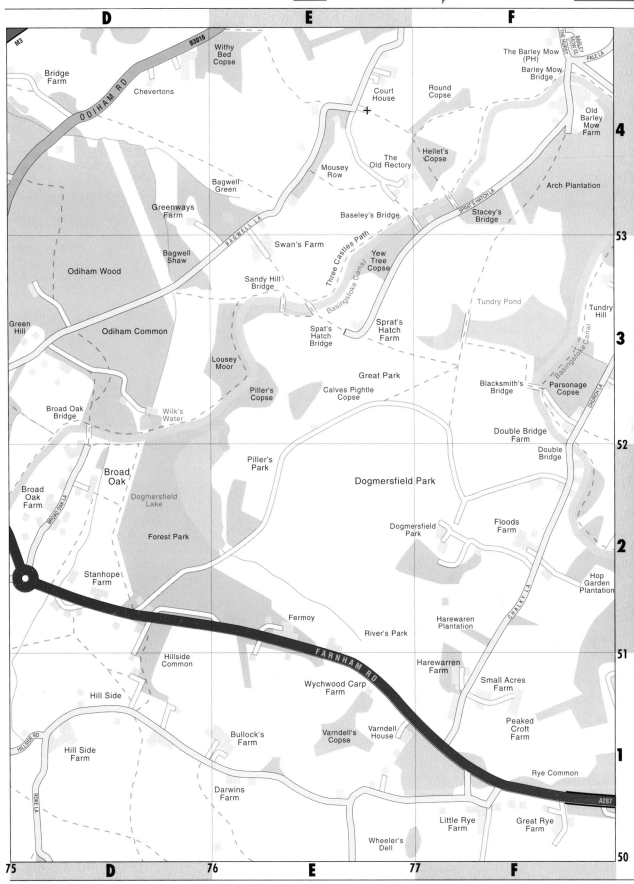

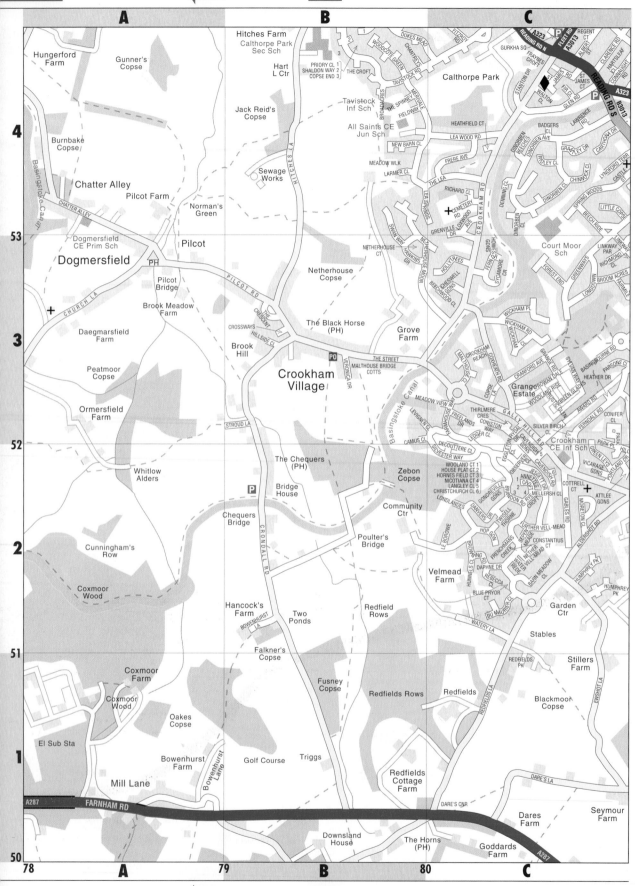

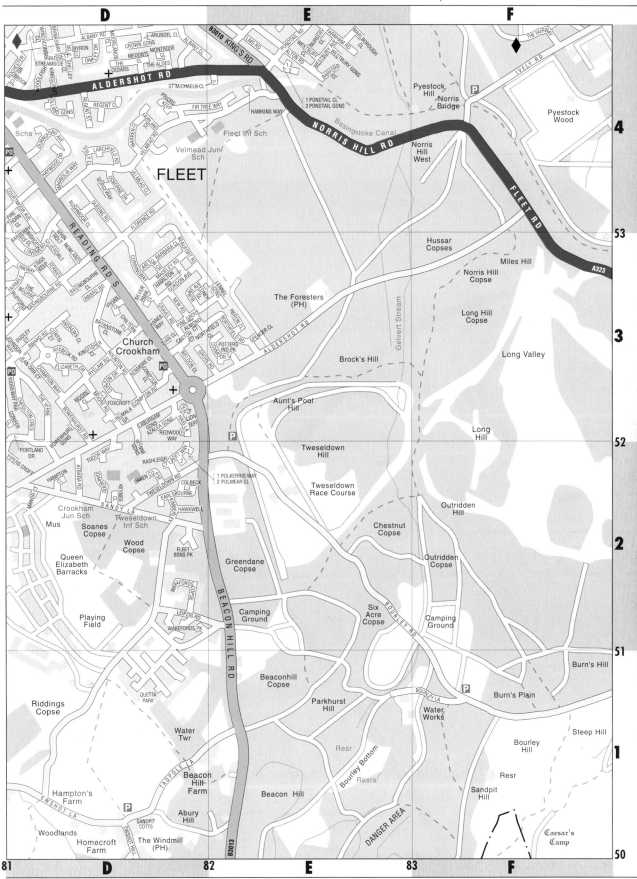

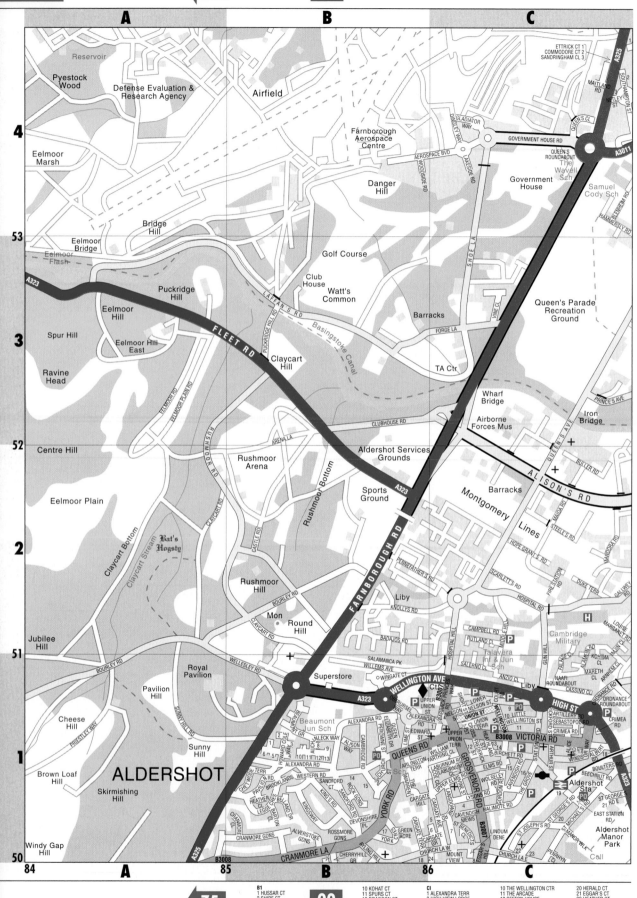

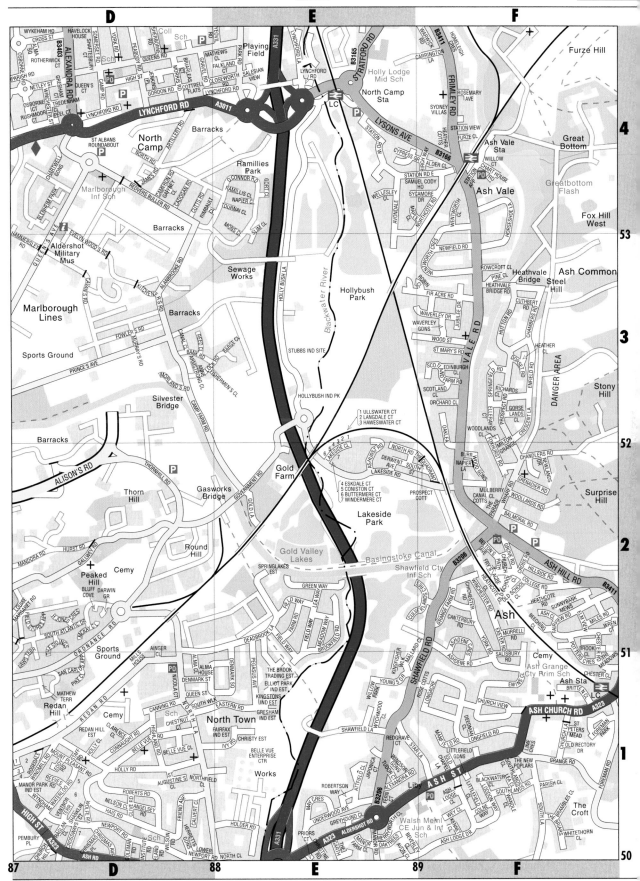

D1
1 REDAN GDNS
2 AMBER CT
3 POUND RD
4 WINDMILL CT
5 SUNNY VIEW CL
6 BEMBRIDGE CT
7 RYDE CT

C3
1 MELKSHAM HO
2 SAVERNAKE HO
3 CALNE HO
4 PEWSEY HO
5 WESTBURY HO
6 PETERSFIELD HO

7 ANDOVER HO
8 SOUTHAMPTON HO
9 WINCHESTER HO
10 PORTSMOUTH HO
C4
1 COLLINS CT
2 VOCKINS CL

3 AUCHINLECK HO
4 CUNNINGHAM HO
5 MONTGOMERY HO
6 ALEXANDER HO
7 CHESTNUT AVE
8 ROWAN CT
9 SWINDON HO

10 DEVIZES HO
11 WARMINSTER HO
12 SALISBURY HO
13 TROWBRIDGE HO
14 WILSON HO
15 PRINCES CT

D3
1 URCHFONT HO
2 MALMESBURY HO
3 AMESBURY HO
D4
1 JUNIPER CT
2 FOREST CT

3 WILLOW MEWS
4 ROSEWOOD CT
5 MAPLE TERR
6 PINETREE HO

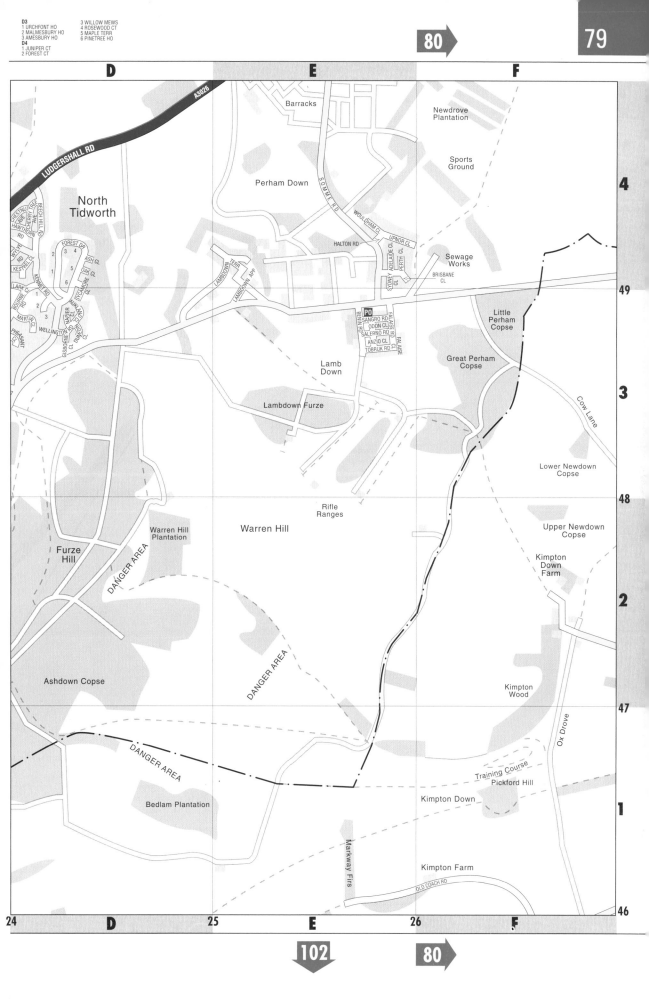

D **E** **F**

LUDGERSHALL RD
A3026

North
Tidworth

CHESTNUT AVE
CHERRY TREE RD
BEECH HILL RD
HAWTHORN RD
WYLYE RD
KESTREL CL
LARK CL
KENNY RD
FOREST DR
ASH CL
OAK CL
SYCAMORE CL
BOURNE RD
MARTIN CL
PHEASANT CL
WELLINGTON CL
GISBORNE CL
NAPIER CL
DUNDAS CL
DURNFORD CL
AVON LAKE
CL

Barracks

Perham Down

S O M M E   R D
WOULDHAM CL
HALTON RD
UPNOR CL
ADELAIDE CL
PERTH CL
SYDNEY CL
BRISBANE CL

Newdrove
Plantation

Sports
Ground

4

Sewage
Works

49

LAMBDOWN TERR
LAMBDOWN APP

PO
SANGRO RD
ODON CL
BENIN RD
SALERNO RD
ANZIO CL
TOBRUK RD
FALAISE RD
FALAISE RD
FALAISE

Lamb
Down

Little
Perham
Copse

Great Perham
Copse

Cow Lane

Lambdown Furze

3

Lower Newdown
Copse

Rifle
Ranges

48

Warren Hill

Upper Newdown
Copse

Warren Hill
Plantation

DANGER AREA

Furze
Hill

Kimpton
Down
Farm

2

Ashdown Copse

DANGER AREA

Kimpton
Wood

47

Ox Drove

DANGER AREA

Training Course

Pickford Hill

Bedlam Plantation

Kimpton Down

1

Markway Firs

Kimpton Farm

OLD COACH RD

46

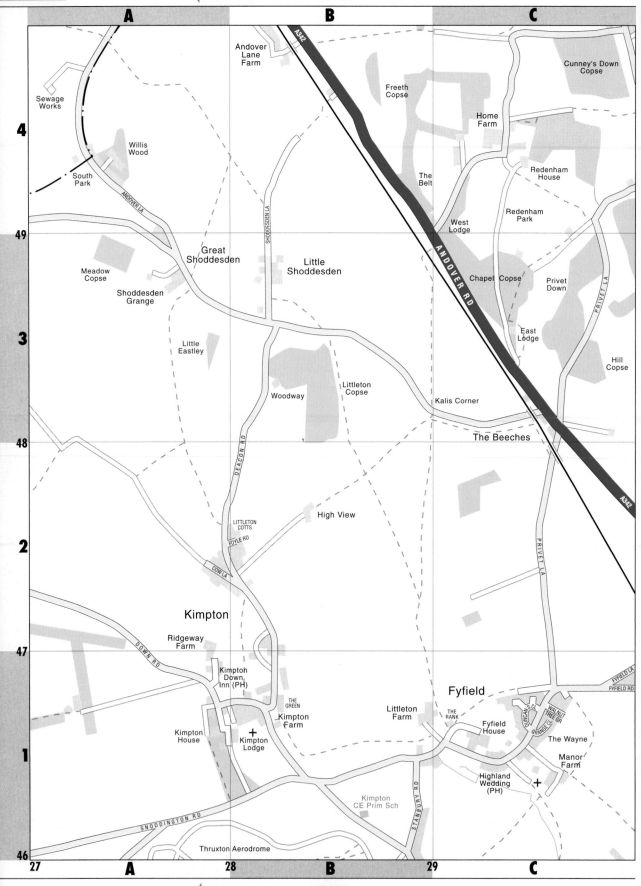

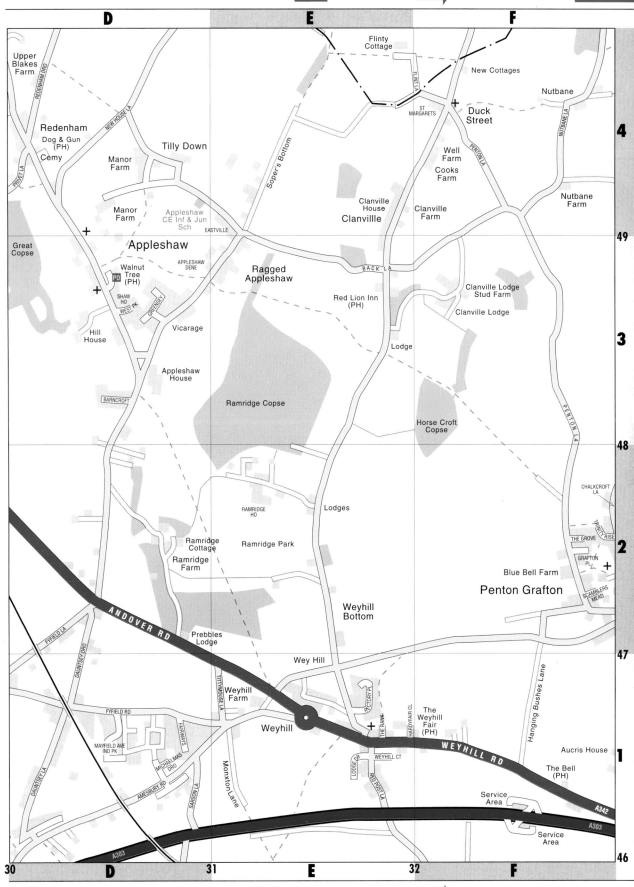

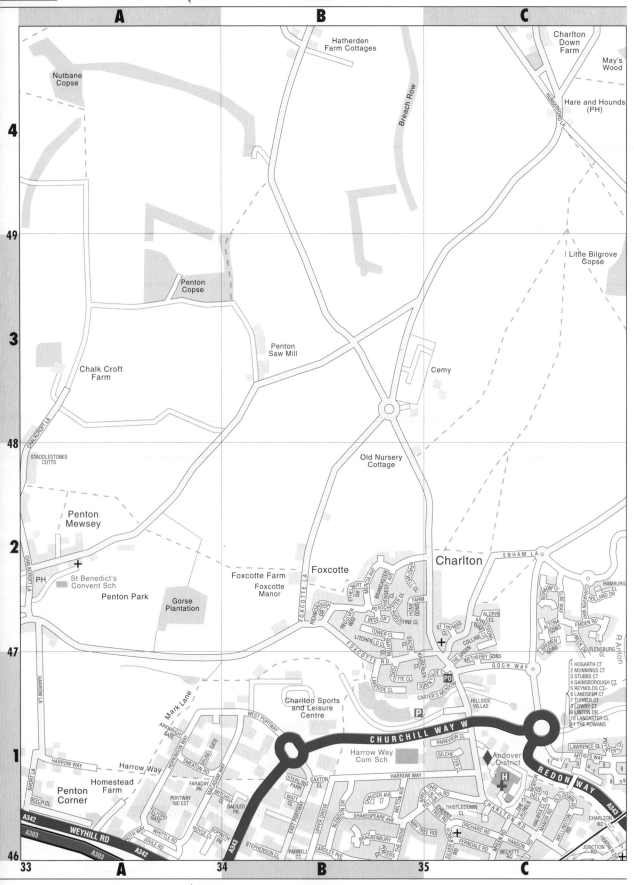

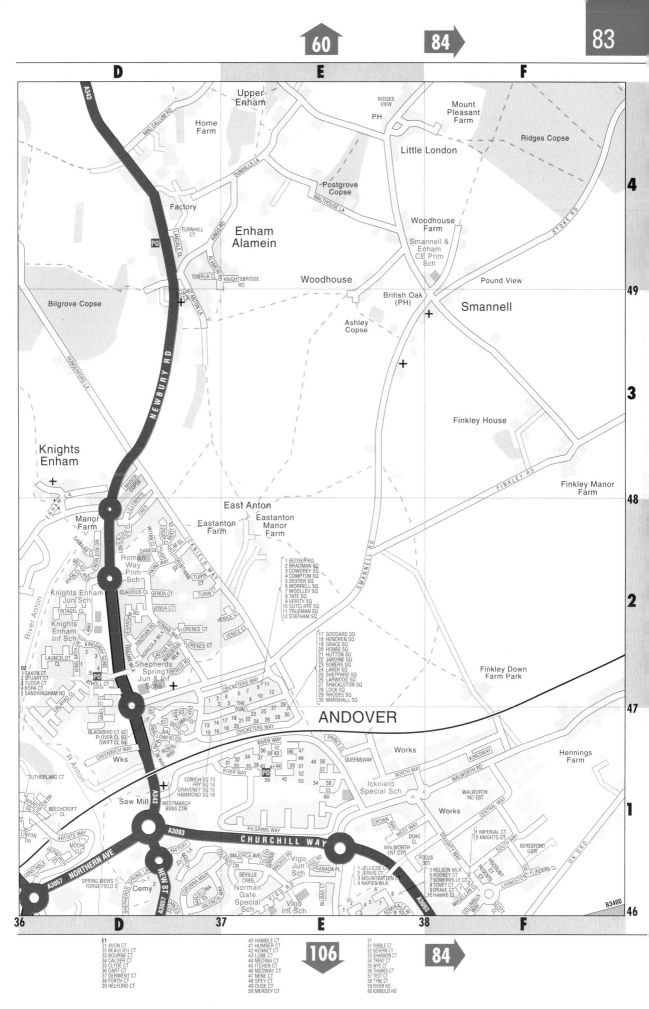

D E F

4

49

3

48

2

47

1

46

Upper Enham
Home Farm
Factory
TURNHILL CT
Enham Alamein
MAC CALLUM RD
KINGS RD
DUNHILLS LA
MALTHOUSE LA
Postgrove Copse
RIDGES VIEW
PH
Little London
Mount Pleasant Farm
Ridges Copse
Woodhouse Farm
Smannell & Enham CE Prim Sch
Pound View
TOBRUK CL
KNIGHTSBRIDGE RD
Woodhouse
British Oak (PH)
Smannell
Bilgrove Copse
Ashley Copse
Finkley House
STOKE RD
Knights Enham
NEWBURY RD
HUNGERFORD LA
ENHAM LA
FINKLEY RD
Finkley Manor Farm
Manor Farm
East Anton
Eastanton Farm
Eastanton Manor Farm
SMANNELL RD

1 BEDSER SQ
2 BRADMAN SQ
3 COWDREY SQ
4 COMPTON SQ
5 DEXTER SQ
6 WORRELL SQ
7 WOOLLEY SQ
8 TATE SQ
9 VERITY SQ
10 SUTCLIFFE SQ
11 TRUEMAN SQ
12 STATHAM SQ

17 GODDARD SQ
18 HENDREN SQ
19 GRACE SQ
20 HOBBS SQ
21 HUTTON SQ
22 JARDINE SQ
23 SOBERS SQ
24 LAKER SQ
25 SHEPPARD SQ
26 LARWOOD SQ
27 SHACKLETON SQ
28 LOCK SQ
29 RHODES SQ
30 MARSHALL SQ

Roman Way Prim Sch
Knights Enham Jun Sch
Knights Enham Inf Sch
River Anton
ICKNIELD WAY
TURIN CT
GENOA CT
GENOA CT
CLAUDIUS CL
VENICE CT
VENICE CT
FLORENCE CT
FLORENCE CT
ROMAN WAY
HADRIAN RD
AGRICOLA WLK
CAESAR RD
TRAJAN WLK
VESPASIAN RD
TIBERIUS RD
Shepherds Spring Jun & Inf Schs
Finkley Down Farm Park

ANDOVER

Hennings Farm
Works
Queensway
KINGSWAY
NORTH WAY
WALWORTH RD
CENTRAL WAY
Icknield Special Sch
Walworth Ind Est
Works
CROWN WAY
WEST WAY
DUKE CL
Walworth Ent Ctr
SOUTH WAY
DOUGHTY WAY
1 IMPERIAL CT
2 KNIGHTS CT
Beresford Gate
FLINDERS CL
OX DRO

CRICKETERS WAY
THE OVAL
River Way
RIVER WAY
PRINCE CL
EDRICH SQ 13
FRY SQ 14
GRAVENEY SQ 15
HAMMOND SQ 16
WESTMARCH BSNS CTR
Saw Mill
A343
A3093
PILGRIMS WAY
CHURCHILL WAY
B3400

Sutherland Ct
R Anton
Beechcroft Cl
NORTHERN AVE
A3057
NEW ST
A3093
Spring Mews 1
Forge Field 2
Cemy
Norman Gate Special Sch
MAJORCA AVE
SEVILLE CRES
Vigo Jun Sch
GRANADA PL
Vigo Inf Sch
1 JELLICOE CT
2 RODNEY CT
3 MOUNTBATTEN CT
4 NAPIER WLK
5 NELSON WLK
6 RODNEY CT
7 SOMERVILLE CT
8 TOVEY CT
9 DRAKE CT
10 HAWKE CL
ADMIRALS W
MAGELLAN CL
COLUMBUS WAY
Focus 303

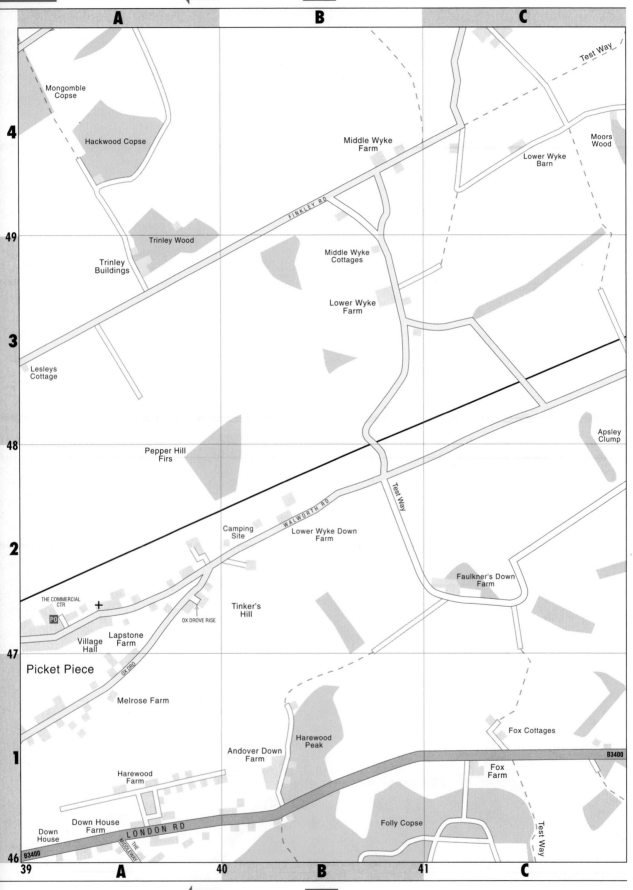

A **B** **C**

4

Mongomble Copse

Hackwood Copse

Middle Wyke Farm

Lower Wyke Barn

Moors Wood

Test Way

49

Trinley Wood

FINKLEY RD

Middle Wyke Cottages

Trinley Buildings

Lower Wyke Farm

3

Lesleys Cottage

Apsley Clump

48

Pepper Hill Firs

Test Way

WALWORTH RD

Camping Site

Lower Wyke Down Farm

2

THE COMMERCIAL CTR

PO

Tinker's Hill

Faulkner's Down Farm

OX DROVE RISE

Village Hall

Lapstone Farm

47

Picket Piece

OX DRO

Melrose Farm

Fox Cottages

1

Andover Down Farm

Harewood Peak

Fox Farm

B3400

Harewood Farm

Down House Farm

Folly Copse

Down House

LONDON RD

THE MIDDLEWAY

Test Way

46

B3400

39   **A**   40   **B**   41   **C**

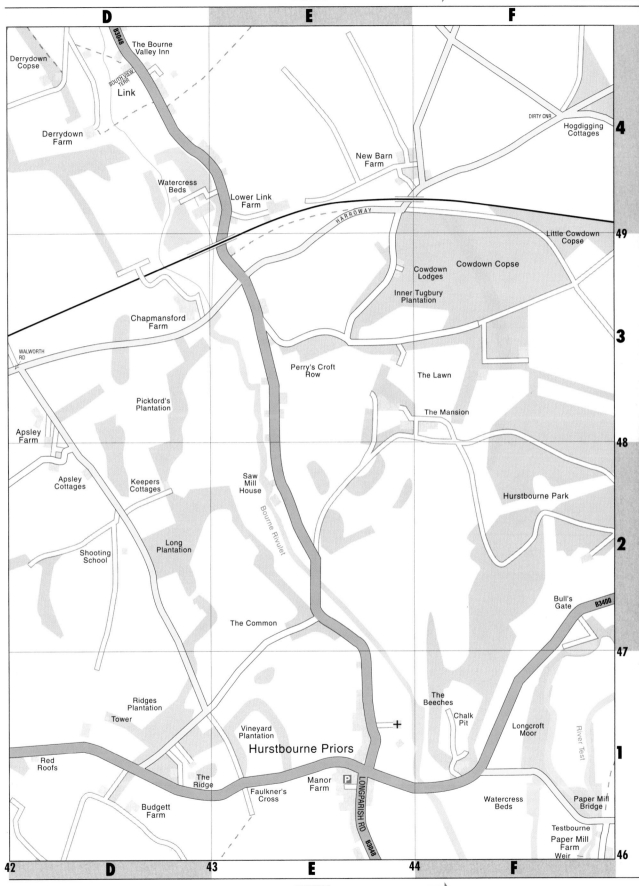

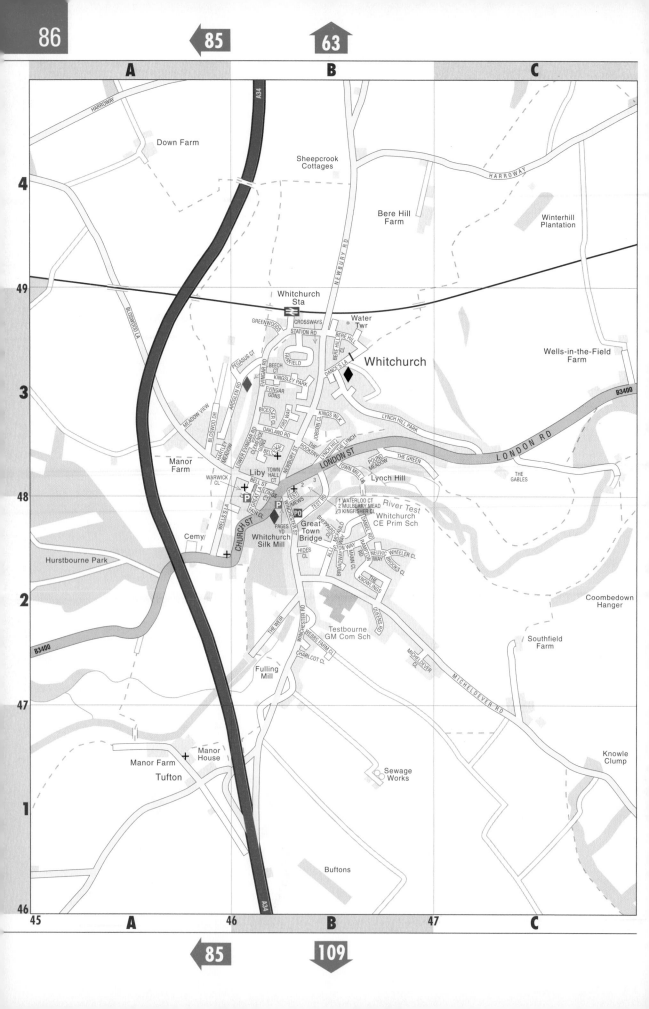

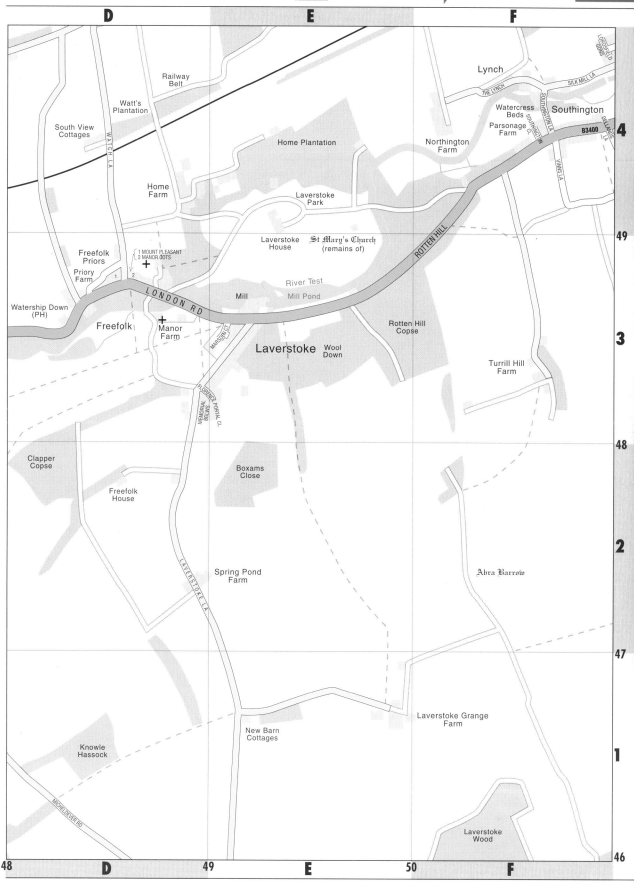

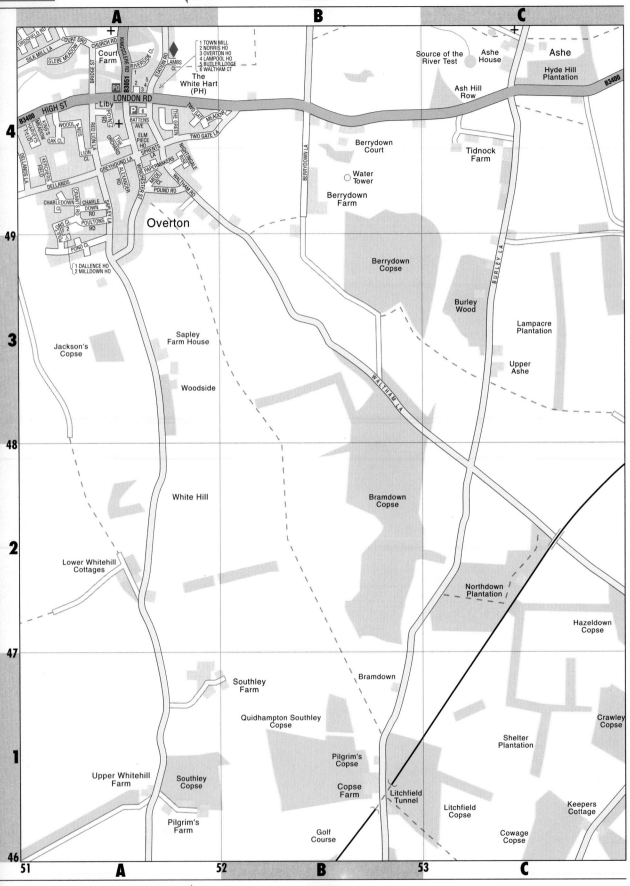

A B C

Court Farm

1 TOWN MILL
2 NORRIS HO
3 OVERTON HO
4 LAMPOOL HO
5 BUTLER LODGE
6 WALTHAM CT

The White Hart (PH)

ORDSFIELD RD
SILK MILL LA
COURT DRO
GLEBE MEADOW
CHURCH RD
BRIDGE ST
KINGSCLERE RD
RIVERSIDE CL
STATION RD
LAMBS CL

Source of the River Test

Ashe House

Ashe

Hyde Hill Plantation

B3400

Ash Hill Row

LONDON RD

Liby

HIGH ST

B3400

KING'S MEADOW
HARVEST FIELD
WOODLANDS
OAK CL
RED LION LA
LION CL
PRYNT'Z RD
THE ORCHARD
BATTENS AVE
ELM PIECE HO
SPRENTS
TWO GATE MEADOW
TWO GATE LA
THE GREEN

4

Berrydown Court

Tidnock Farm

BERRYDOWN LA

Water Tower

KERCHERS FIELD
DELLANDS LA
DELLANDS
CHARLEDOWN CL
CRANTS RD
CHARLE DOWN RD
POULTONS RD
GREYHOUND LA
ALEXANDER RD
WINCHESTER ST
SAPLEY LA
PAPERMAKERS
NIGHTINGALE RISE
MIERE
WALTHAM RD
POUND RD

Overton

Berrydown Farm

49

ONS CL
POND
POND CL

1 DALLENCE HO
2 MILLDOWN HO

Berrydown Copse

BURLEY LA

Burley Wood

Lampacre Plantation

3

Jackson's Copse

Sapley Farm House

Upper Ashe

Woodside

WALTHAM LA

48

White Hill

Bramdown Copse

2

Lower Whitehill Cottages

Northdown Plantation

Hazeldown Copse

47

Southley Farm

Bramdown

Quidhampton Southley Copse

Crawley Copse

1

Pilgrim's Copse

Shelter Plantation

Upper Whitehill Farm

Southley Copse

Copse Farm

Litchfield Tunnel

Litchfield Copse

Keepers Cottage

Pilgrim's Farm

Golf Course

Cowage Copse

46

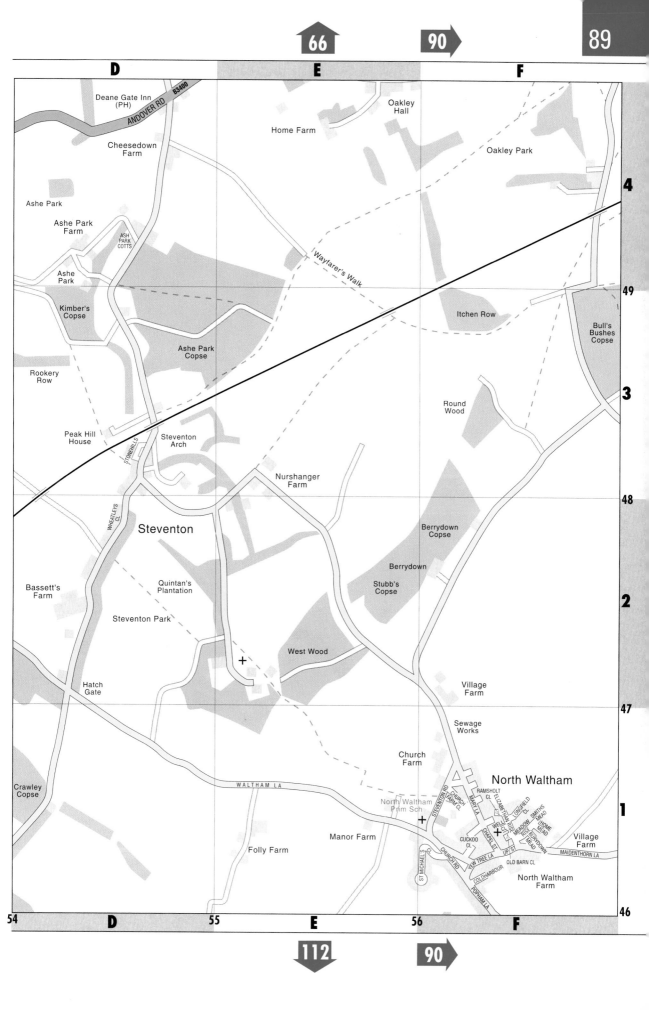

D   **E**   **F**

Deane Gate Inn (PH)
ANDOVER RD   B3400
Home Farm
Oakley Hall
Cheesedown Farm
Oakley Park

4

Ashe Park
ASH PARK COTTS
Ashe Park Farm
Wayfarer's Walk

Ashe Park
49
Kimber's Copse
Itchen Row
Bull's Bushes Copse

Ashe Park Copse
Rookery Row
Round Wood
3

Peak Hill House
Steventon Arch
STONEHILLS
Nurshanger Farm

48
WHEATLEY'S CL
Steventon
Berrydown Copse

Bassett's Farm
Quintan's Plantation
Berrydown
Stubb's Copse
2

Steventon Park
West Wood
+
Village Farm

Hatch Gate
47

Crawley Copse
Sewage Works

Church Farm
North Waltham

WALTHAM LA
North Waltham Prim Sch
STEVENTON RD
CHURCH FARM CL
MARY LA
RAMSHOLT CL
ELIZABETHAN RISE
LONGFIELD CL
MEADOW RISE
SMITHS FIELD
HOME MEAD
BURYTOWN READ

1
Manor Farm
Folly Farm
+
CUCKOO CL
CHAPEL ST
WELL LA
UP ST
Village Farm
MAIDENTHORN LA

ST MICHAELS CL
CHURCH RD
YEW TREE LA
COLDHARBOUR
OLD BARN CL
North Waltham Farm
POPHAM LA

46

54   **D**   **55**   **E**   **56**   **F**

A B C

4

THE DRIVE
KINGS ORCH
WESTBROOK CL
BARN LA
UPPER FARM RD
CEDAR TREE CT
EAST TREE CT
BEECH TREE CL
APPLETREE CL
NEW TREE CL
HILL RD
St John's PIECE
GOODRIS FIRS
St John's Rd

Breach Farm

Breach Cottages

Jeffery's Copse

WATER RIDGES
SUNNY MEAD
SAXON CL
PETERSFIELD
FAIRVIEW MEADOW
Sewage Works

Pardown

OSPREY CL
THRUSH CL
LARK CL
STARLING CL
MOTIVALS
EAGLE CL
WOODPECKER CL
PHEASANT CL
HERON WAY
MAGPIE CL
BLACKBIRD CL
SEAGULL CORMORANT
GANNET CL
JACKDAW CL
FINZEY DRO
PETREL CL
CROFT
SANDPIPER WAY
BITTERN CL
BRAMBLING CL
AURLET CL
TERN
LARK CRES
FULMAR CL
GREENFINCH
MALLARD CRES
GRACEMERE CRES
WOODMERE CROFT
RAINHAM CL
GREBE

Small's Copse

49

Pardown Copse

Bull's Bushes Copse

Bull's Bushes Farm

3

Little Stubbs Copse

South Wood

WINCHESTER RD

A30

BEGGARWOOD LA

CH

Great Stubbs Copse

48

Wayfarer's Walk

Dean Heath Copse

Southwood Farm

Golf Course

Kempshott Park

2

Ganderdown Copse

The Copse (Caravan Site)

Peak Copse

The Cedars

M3

Oakdown Farm

47

7

Wayfarer's Walk

CH

Golf Course

Rowley Copse

1

The Sun Inn (PH)

CHAPEL CL
DOWN ST
GLEBE CL
PORTERS CL
PO
POST OFFICE
LA

Dummer

FARLEIGH LA
Clump Farm

MAIDENTHORN LA

Mast

Tel Ex

The Queen (PH)

QUEENSFIELD

Dummer Clump

Nutley Lane

46

A30

M3

Cemy

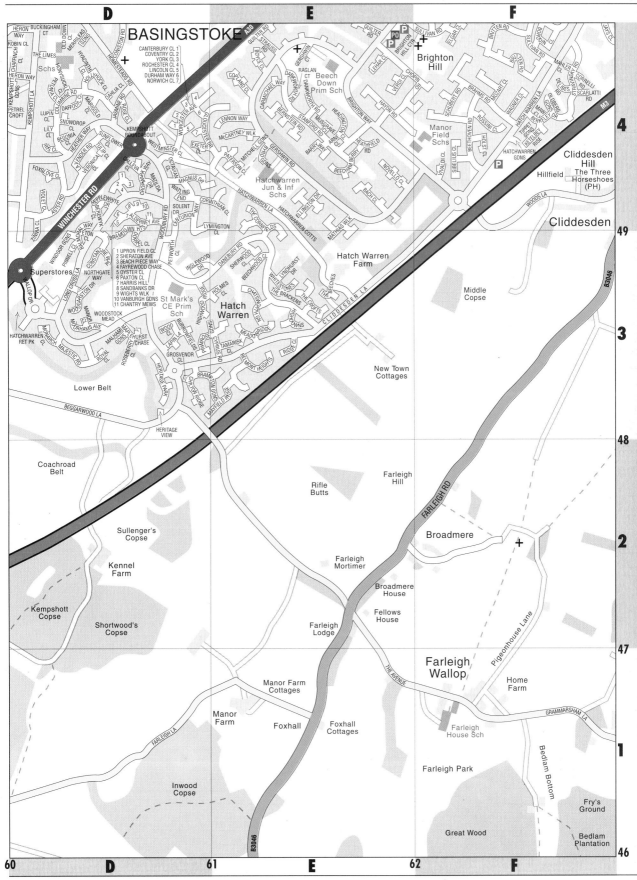

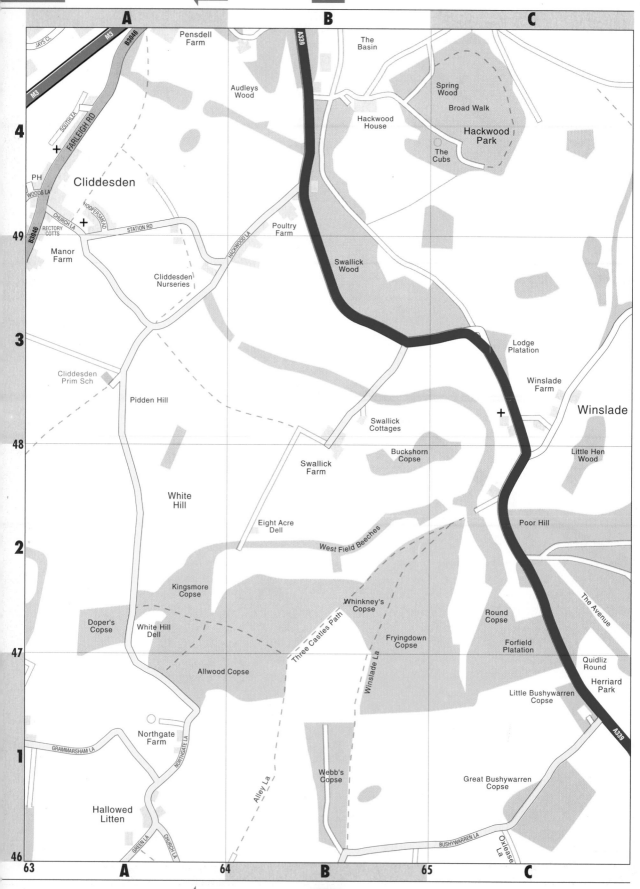

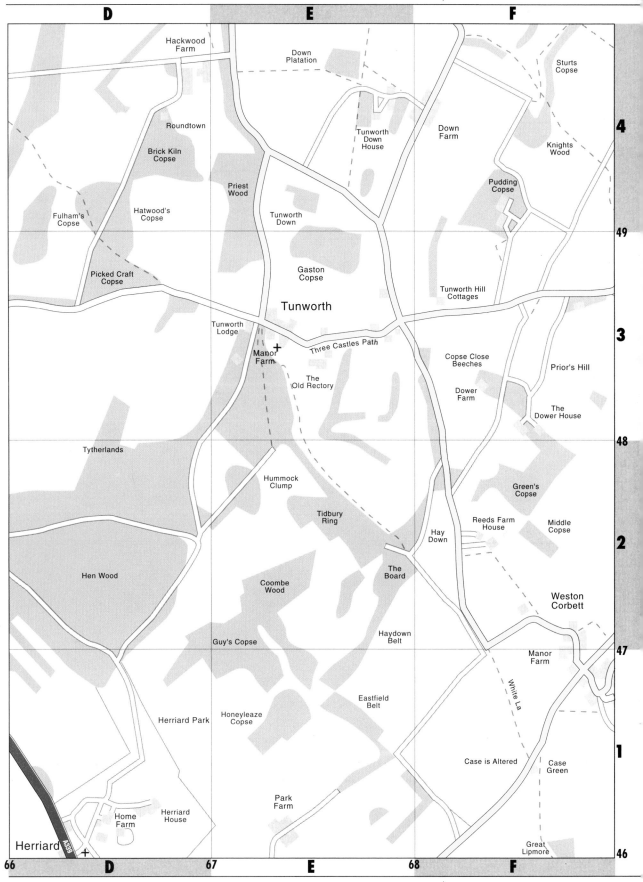

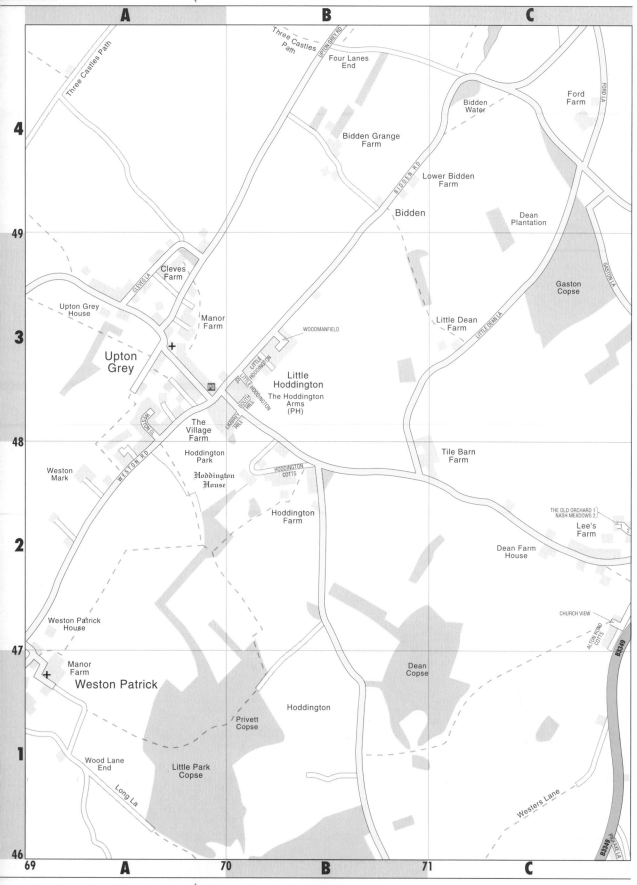

Three Castles Path

Three Castles Path

UPTON GREY RD

Four Lanes End

FORD LA

B3349

Bidden Water

Ford Farm

4

Bidden Grange Farm

BIDDEN RD

Lower Bidden Farm

Dean Plantation

Bidden

49

GASTON LA

Cleves Farm

Gaston Copse

CLEVES LA

Upton Grey House

Manor Farm

WOODMANFIELD

Little Dean Farm

LITTLE DEAN LA

3

Upton Grey

+

LITTLE HODDINGTON

Little Hoddington

PO

LITTLE HODDINGTON

The Hoddington Arms (PH)

SOUTH HILL

WESTON CL

The Village Farm

LIMBREY HILL

48

Tile Barn Farm

Weston Mark

WESTON RD

Hoddington Park

HODDINGTON COTTS

Hoddington House

THE OLD ORCHARD 1

NASH MEADOWS 2

Hoddington Farm

Lee's Farm

2

Dean Farm House

Weston Patrick House

CHURCH VIEW

ALTON ROAD COTTS

B3349

47

Manor Farm

+

Dean Copse

Weston Patrick

Hoddington

Privett Copse

Wood Lane End

Westers Lane

1

Little Park Copse

Long La

PACKLANE LA

B3349

46

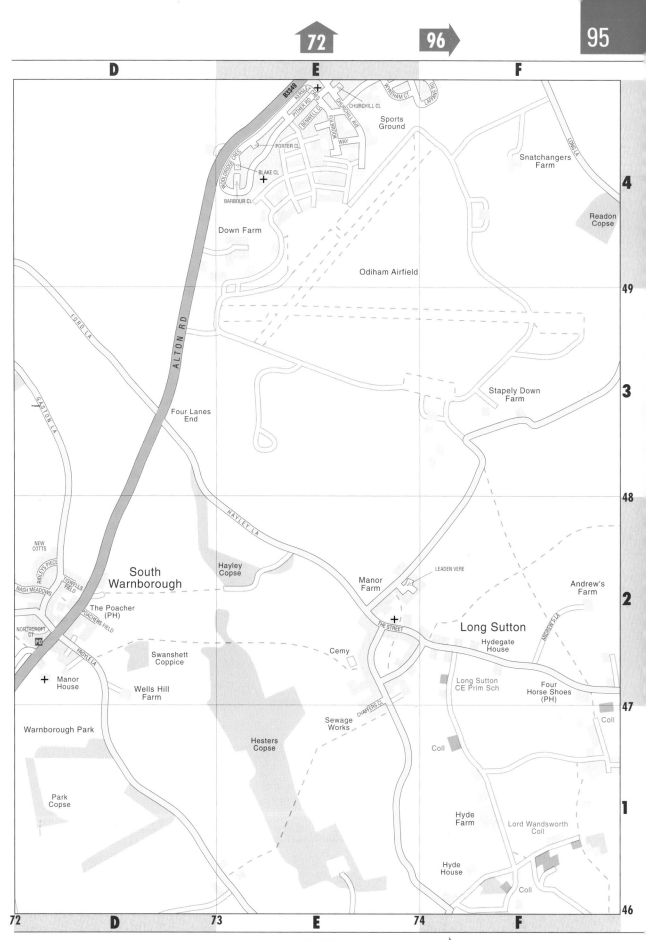

95
73

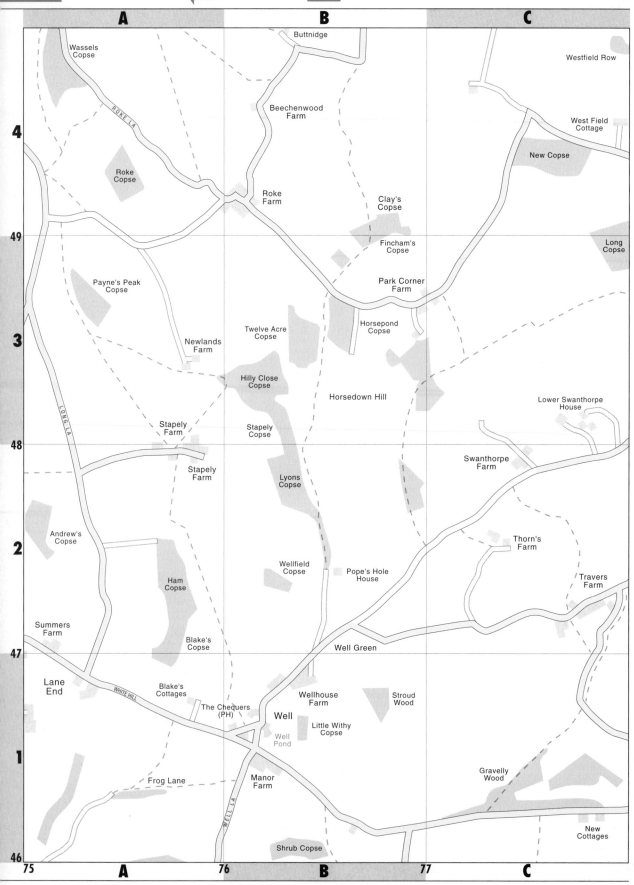

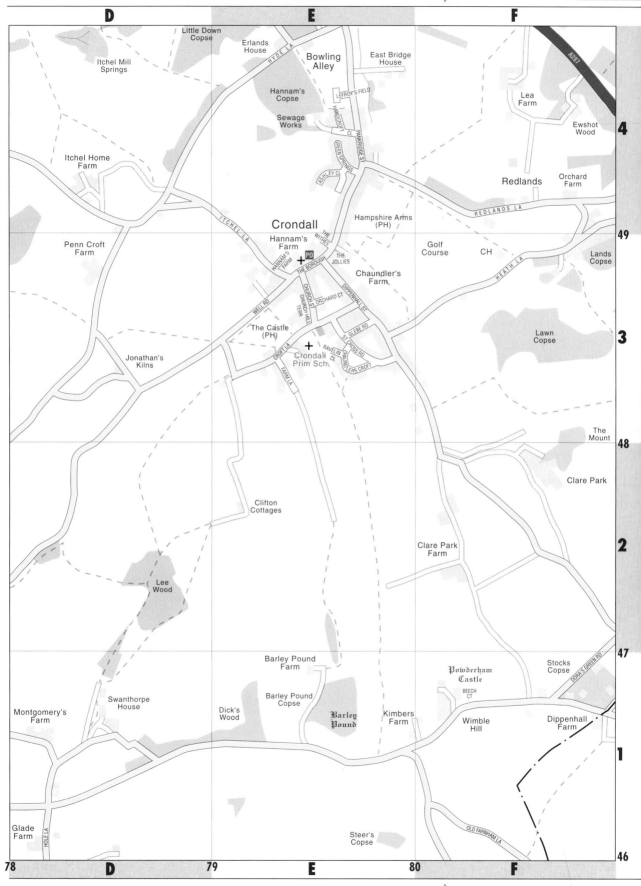

Little Down Copse
Erlands House
Bowling Alley
East Bridge House
Itchel Mill Springs
Hannam's Copse
Sewage Works
HYDE LA
LEFROY'S FIELD
HANDCROFT CL
PAINBRIDGE ST
GREEN SPRINGS
ASHLEY CL
Lea Farm
Ewshot Wood
A287
Itchel Home Farm
Redlands
Orchard Farm
ITCHEL LA
Crondall
Hampshire Arms (PH)
REDLANDS LA
HEATH LA
Penn Croft Farm
Hannam's Farm
HANNAM'S FARM
THE WITHES
PO
THE BOROUGH
THE JOLLIES
Chaundler's Farm
Golf Course
CH
Lands Copse
49
Well Rd
WELL RD
CHURCH RD
CHURCH HILL
TERR
ORCHARD CT
DIPPENHALL ST
GLEBE RD
ST CROSS RD
CHAUNDLERS CROFT
The Castle (PH)
Crondall Prim Sch
RAVELIN CL
CROFT LA
FARM LA
Jonathan's Kilns
Lawn Copse
3
The Mount
48
Clare Park
Clifton Cottages
Clare Park Farm
2
Lee Wood
47
Barley Pound Farm
Powderham Castle
Stocks Copse
DORA'S GREEN RD
Swanthorpe House
Barley Pound Copse
Dick's Wood
Barley Pound
Kimbers Farm
BEECH CT
Wimble Hill
Dippenhall Farm
Montgomery's Farm
1
Glade Farm
HOLE LA
Steer's Copse
OLD FARNHAM LA
46

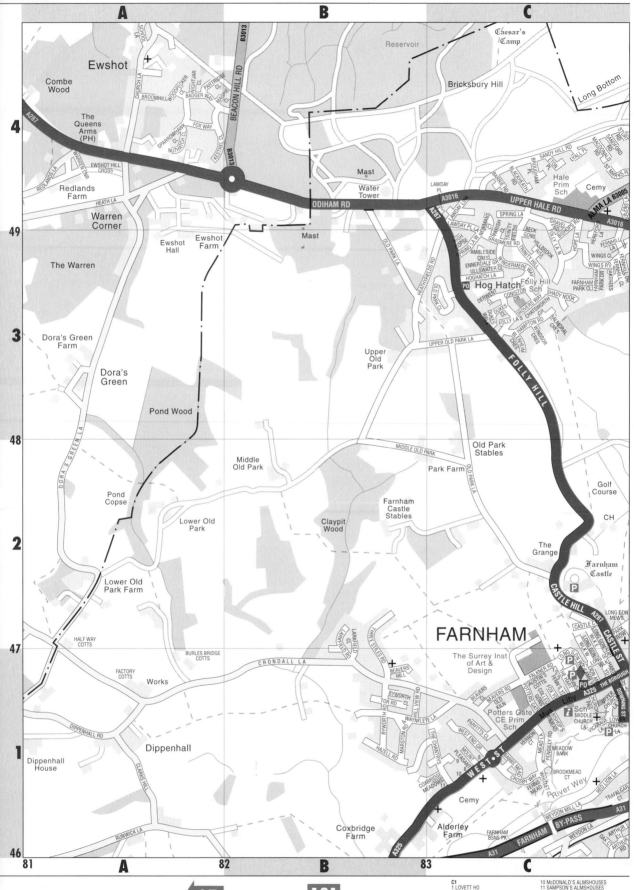

C1
1 LOVETT HO
2 WESTMEAD
3 COBBETTS MEWS
4 LION AND LAMB WAY
5 TIMBER CL
6 CRAVEN HO
7 ARUNDELL PL
8 TRIMMER'S ALMSHOUSES
9 CHANTRYS CT
10 McDONALD'S ALMSHOUSES
11 SAMPSON'S ALMSHOUSES

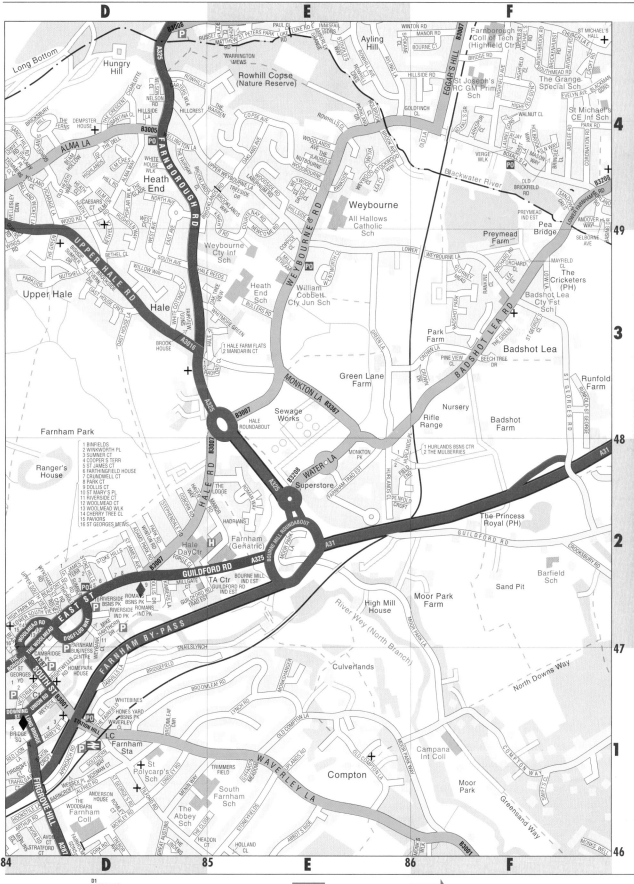

D1
1 BORELLI YD
2 BORELLI MEWS
3 PROVIDENCE PL
4 ABBEY CT
5 ST ANDREW S CT

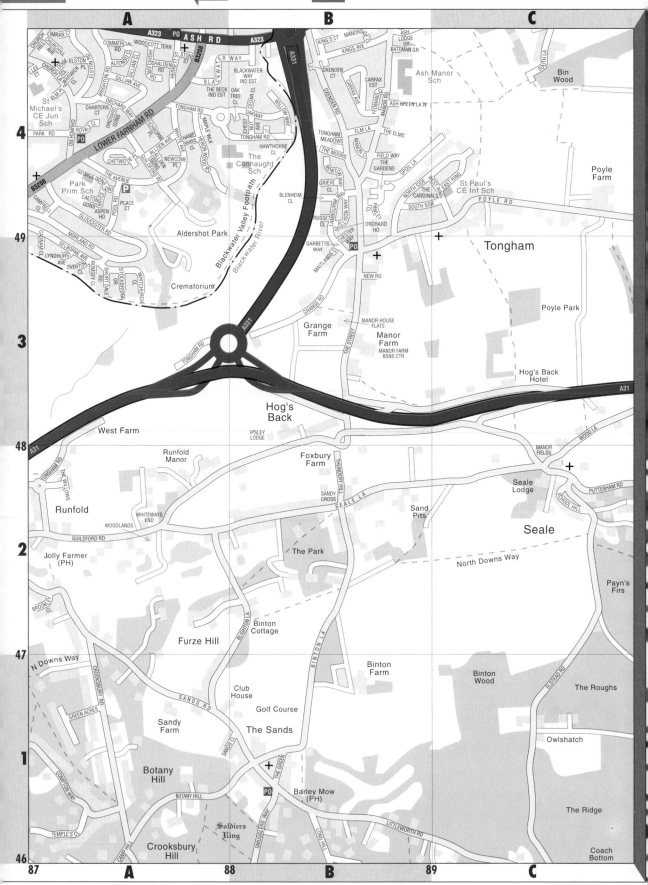

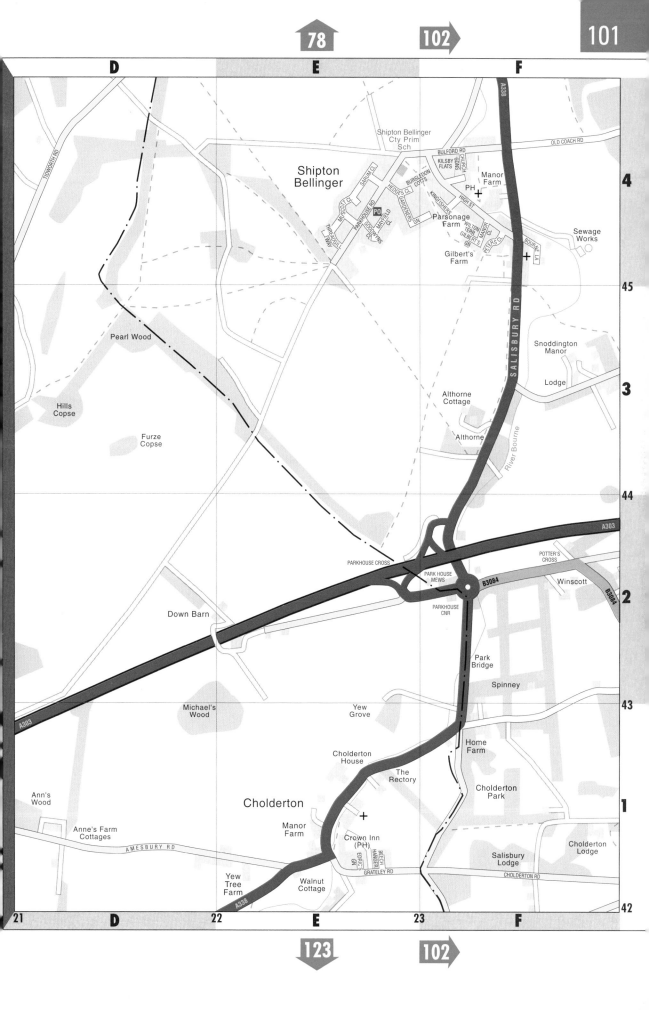

D
E
F

4

Shipton Bellinger Cty Prim Sch

Shipton Bellinger

BULFORD RD
KILSBY FLATS
CHURCH
Manor Farm
PH

BURSLEDON COTTS
SARUM CL
HEDGES CL
GARDENERS GN
GOODWINS CL
MAYFIELD CL
PARKHOUSE RD
MCSCOT CL
PO
THREADGILL WAY
KINGFISHERS
HIGH ST
Parsonage Farm
WILTON TERR
GILBERT'S GN
MANOR CL
PETERS CL
BOURNE LA

Gilbert's Farm

Sewage Works

45

SALISBURY RD

Pearl Wood

Snoddington Manor

Lodge

Hills Copse

Furze Copse

Althorne Cottage

3

Althorne

River Bourne

44

A303

A338

OLD COACH RD

PARKHOUSE CROSS

PARK HOUSE MEWS

POTTER'S CROSS

Winscott

B3084

B3084

2

PARKHOUSE CNR

Down Barn

Park Bridge

Spinney

A303

Michael's Wood

Yew Grove

43

Home Farm

Cholderton House

The Rectory

Cholderton Park

Ann's Wood

Cholderton

Anne's Farm Cottages

AMESBURY RD

Manor Farm

Crown Inn (PH)

EDRICS GN

BEECH HANGER

GRATELEY RD

Salisbury Lodge

Cholderton Lodge

1

CHOLDERTON RD

Yew Tree Farm

Walnut Cottage

A338

42

21
D
22
E
23
F

A   B   C

Shipton
Plantation

OLD COACH RD

OLD COACH RD

SNODDINGTON RD

Shipton
Wood

4

Snoddington Down
Farm

45

Racedown
Farm

RACEDOWN
COTTS

3

Snoddington
Hill

A303

Thruxton
Down House

44

A303

Thimble
Hall

Middlecot
House

Thruxton
Farm

Thruxton
Hill

2

B3084

Hugh's
Settlement

Fairhaven

Cholderton
Hill

CHOLDERTON RD

43

Victoria
Copse

Horseshoe
Meadow
Farm

Curlews

Windy Dido

Cholderton Park

Coronation
Belt

1

Lodge

Quarley
Hill

GRATELEY DRO

42

B3084

24   A   25   B   26   C

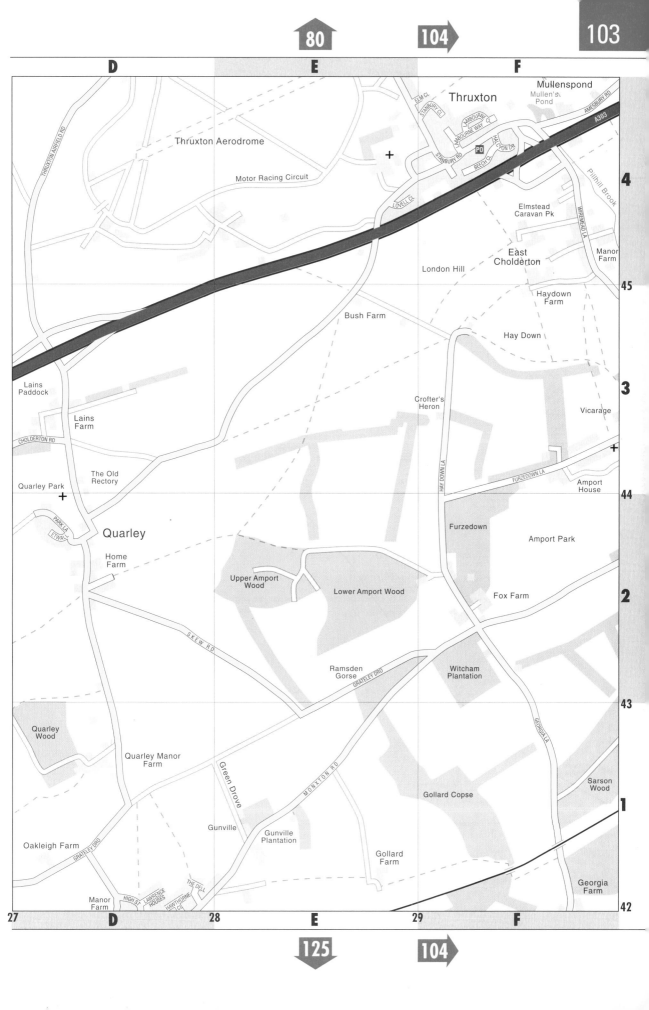

Mullenspond

Thruxton

Mullen's Pond

AMESBURY RD

A303

THRUXTON AIRFIELD RD

Thruxton Aerodrome

ELM CL

STANBURY CL

LAMBOURNE CL

LAMBOURNE WAY

PO

STANBURY RD

HALCYON DR

BEECH CL

Motor Racing Circuit

LOVELL CL

Elmstead Caravan Pk

WIREMEAD LA

PILLHILL BROOK

Manor Farm

East Cholderton

4

London Hill

Haydown Farm

45

Bush Farm

Hay Down

3

Lains Paddock

Crofter's Heron

Vicarage

Lains Farm

CHOLDERTON RD

HAY DOWN LA

FURZEDOWN LA

Amport House

The Old Rectory

44

Quarley Park

PARK LA

Furzedown

Amport Park

ELM WAY

Quarley

Home Farm

Upper Amport Wood

Lower Amport Wood

Fox Farm

2

SKEW RD

Ramsden Gorse

GRATELEY DRO

Witcham Plantation

43

Quarley Wood

Quarley Manor Farm

GREEN DROVE

MONXTON RD

Gollard Copse

GEORGIA LA

Sarson Wood

1

Oakleigh Farm

GRATELEY DRO

Gunville

Gunville Plantation

Gollard Farm

Georgia Farm

Manor Farm

HIGH ST

LAWRENCE HOUSES

HAWTHORNE CL

THE DELL

42

A   B   C

A303

4

The Hawk Conservancy

Works

Andover Airfield

Monxton Lane

RED POST LA

MONXTON RD

45

Hunt's Lane

Piper's Hill

SUNNYBANK

ANDOVER RD

WIREMEAD LA

SARSON CL

Manor Farm

Upper Mill Farm

CHAPEL CL

MOUNT PLEASANT

Amport

THE EIGHTS

Amport Inn (PH)

The Black Swan (PH)

Pillhill Brook

3

Watercress Beds

Sarson

FURZEDOWN LA

Sarson Farm

GREEN LA

ABBOTTS ANN RD

CHALKPIT LA

Watercress Beds

CATTLE LA

AMPORT FIRS

Amport CE Prim Sch

SHEPPARD ALMSHOUSES

Monxton

KEEPER'S HILL

The Triangle

Two Rivers Farm

44

HILLSIDE

DUCK ST

Manor Farm

BROAD RD

Hook Lane

Abbott's Ann Parochial Prim Sch

PO

MANOR CL

2

WARREN DR

DUNKIRT LA

BILBERY

Sarsons Wood

Great Wood

The Drove

43

Keeper's Cottage

Dunkirt Lane

1

Woodlands Prospect Farm

Eastover Farm

Sarson Furze Down

Dunkirt Barn

Eastover Farm Cottages

The Groves

SALISBURY RD

A343

The Morrells

Eastover Copse

42

30   31   32

A   B   C

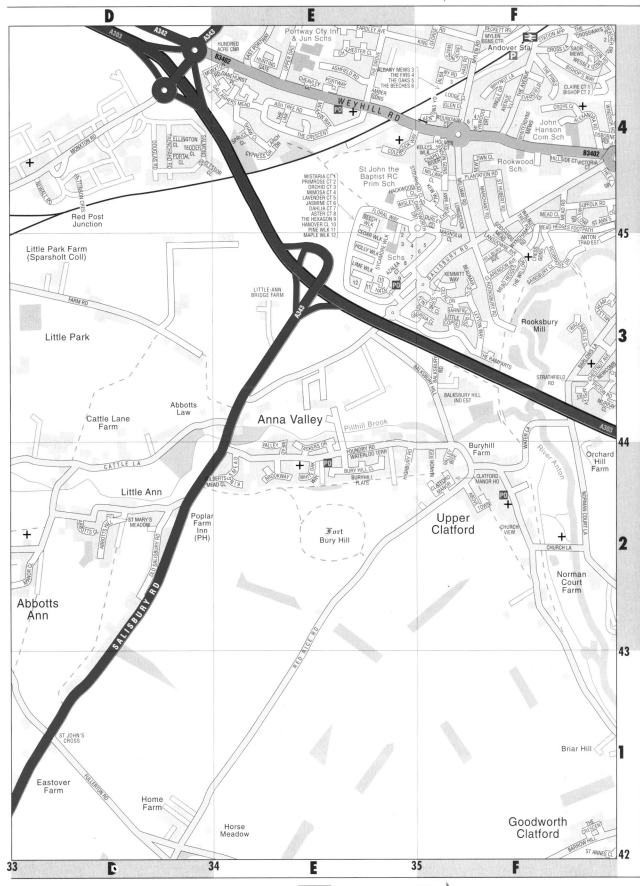

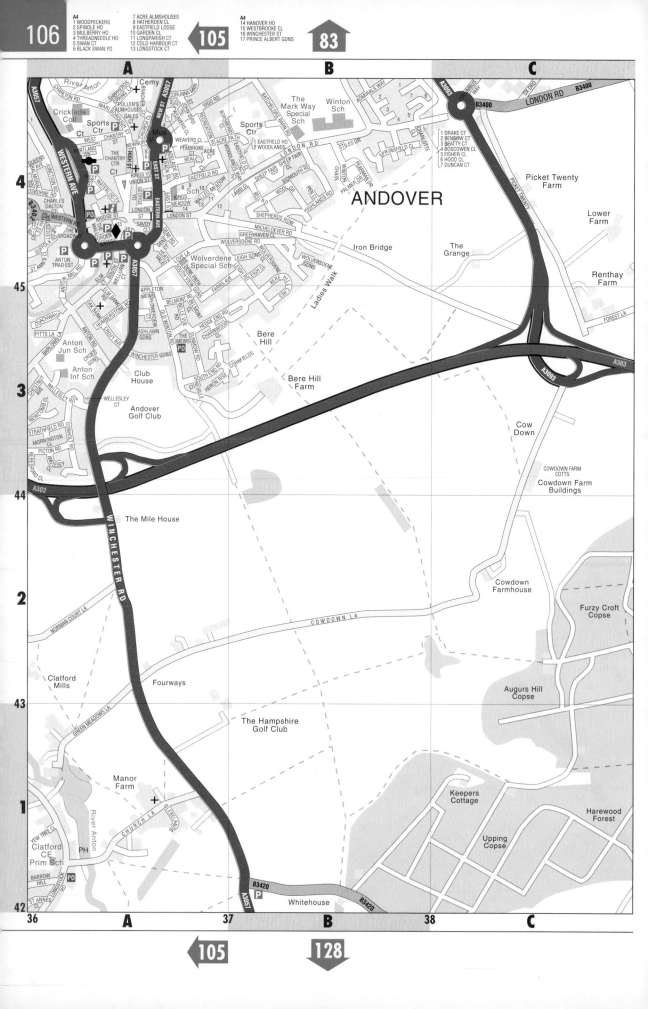

106

A4
1 WOODPECKERS
2 SPINDLE HO
3 MULBERRY HO
4 THREADNEEDLE HO
5 SWAN CT
6 BLACK SWAN YD

7 ACRE ALMSHOUSES
8 HATHERDEN CL
9 EASTFIELD LODGE
10 GARDEN CL
11 LONGPARISH CT
12 COLD HARBOUR CT
13 LONGSTOCK CT

105

A4
14 HANOVER HO
15 WESTBROOKE CL
16 WINCHESTER ST
17 PRINCE ALBERT GDNS

83

ANDOVER

1 DRAKE CT
2 BENBOW CT
3 BEATTY CT
4 BOSCOWEN CL
5 FISHER CL
6 HOOD CL
7 DUNCAN CT

D
E
F

Andover Down

Dane End Copse

Houndshott Copse

Test Way

Whiteditch Copse

Pond Copse

4

Round Bush Copse

Harewood Forest

Burnt Copse

Deadman's Plack Copse

Green's Copse

Pound Copse

45

Gravelly Bank Copse

Deadmans Plack Monument

THE MIDDLEWAY

FOREST LA

Old Pound Earthwork

Ridgeway Copse

Cowdown Copse

3

Ball's Cottages

OLD MICHELDEVER RD

44

Cole's Copse

Burnt Lodge Copse

Cowdown Copse

Forton

B3048

Harewood Forest

Snows Copse

2

Forton Farm House

Hartway Copse

Beechen Copse

HAREWOOD FOREST IND EST

B3048

Ladies House Copse

43

A303

Test Way

Pachington Farm

Gavelacre

LONGPARISH RD

Park Brow Copse

Park Farm

Patchington Copse

River Test

1

Hassock Copse

Stoneyard Copse

B3048

42

A B C

4

Three Halve Copse

Bourne Rivulet

Tracy's Dell

Watercress Beds

Paul's Dell

Wood Walk Plantation

East Aston

45

Mill House

B3048 LONGPARISH RD

DRURY CL

NORTH ACRE

Longparish House

Cricketers Inn

Watercress Beds

Larkwhistle Farm

3

Longparish

River Test

Vale Farm

Big Firs

Lower Mill

Lower Farm

GLADSTONE TERR

THE MIDDLEWAY

Middleton Park

The Plough Inn

Middleton

MILL LA

SOUTHSIDE RD

THE WITHIES

44

Middleton House

Longparish Cty Prim Sch

B3048

Southside Farm

2

Drayton

MONXER WILLIAMS RD

THE AVENUE

Drayton Camp

Lodge Farm

43

A303

Drayton Down

1

Bransbury Manor Farm

Motel

Bransbury

River Dever

Sewage Works

A303

Playing Field

Weir

Bransbury Hill

42

42 A 43 B 44 C

D E F

4

45

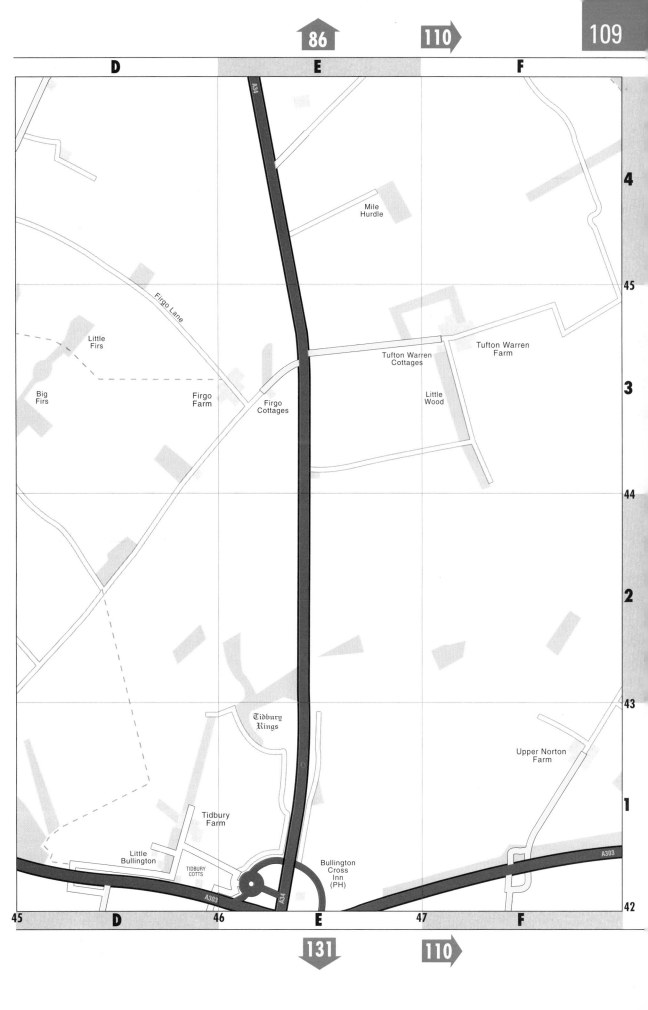

Mile
Hurdle

Firgo Lane

Little
Firs

Tufton Warren
Cottages

Tufton Warren
Farm

Big
Firs

Firgo
Farm

Firgo
Cottages

Little
Wood

3

44

2

43

Tidbury
Rings

Upper Norton
Farm

1

Tidbury
Farm

Little
Bullington

TIDBURY
COTTS

Bullington
Cross
Inn
(PH)

A303

42

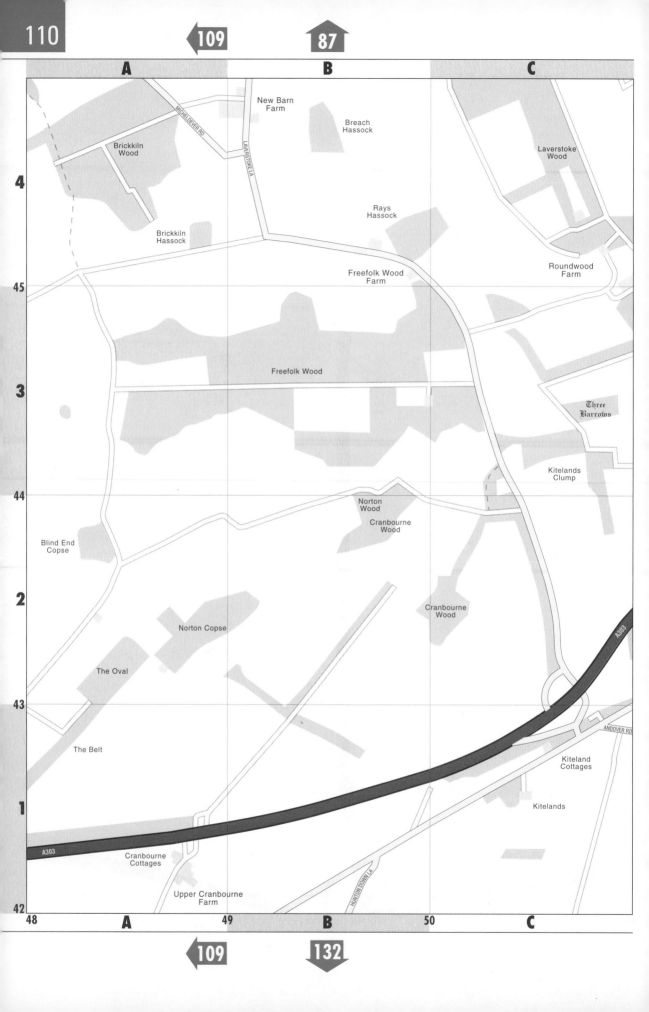

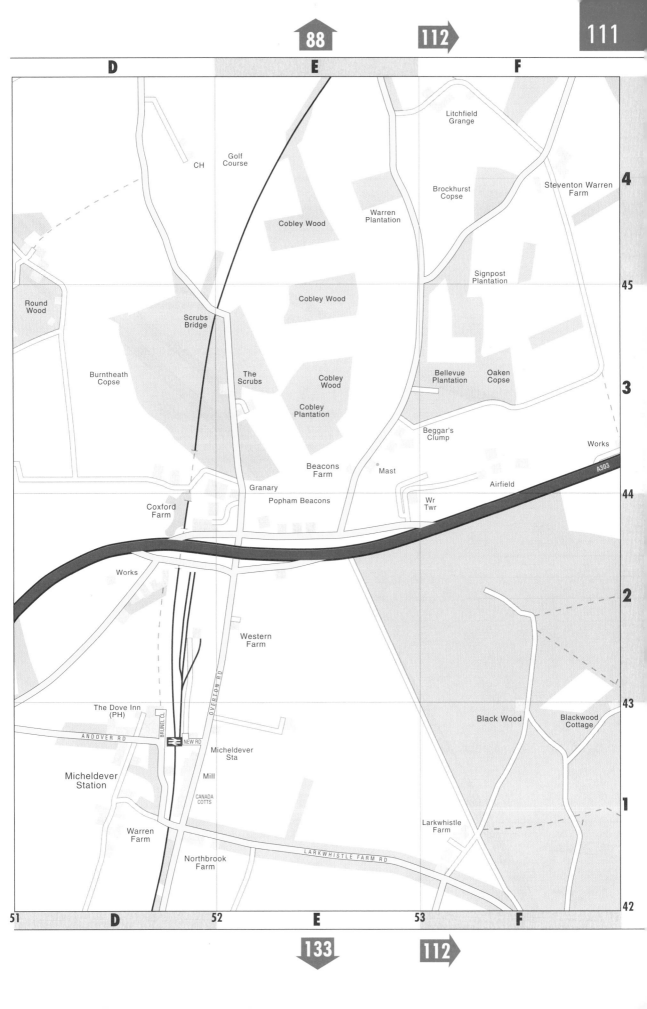

D
E
F

Litchfield Grange

CH
Golf Course

4

Brockhurst Copse

Steventon Warren Farm

Cobley Wood

Warren Plantation

45

Round Wood

Scrubs Bridge

Cobley Wood

Signpost Plantation

Burntheath Copse

The Scrubs

Cobley Wood

Bellevue Plantation

Oaken Copse

3

Cobley Plantation

Beggar's Clump

Works

Beacons Farm

Mast

A303

Granary

Airfield

44

Coxford Farm

Popham Beacons

Wr Twr

Works

2

Western Farm

The Dove Inn (PH)

OVERTON RD

43

Black Wood

Blackwood Cottage

ANDOVER RD

BRUNEL CL.

NEW RD

Micheldever Sta

Micheldever Station

Mill

CANADA COTTS

1

Larkwhistle Farm

Warren Farm

Northbrook Farm

LARKWHISTLE FARM RD

42

A **B** **C**

4

45

3

44

2

43

1

42

54 **A** 55 **B** 56 **C**

Ashen Grove Copse

The Fox (PH)

POPHAM LA

Wheatsheaf Hotel

A30

A303

Misholt Copse

Waltham Trinleys

8

Hellier's Copse

Bramley Wood

M3

Cocksford Firs East

Cocksford Down

A303

West Farm

Popham Court Farm

Popham

Popham Court Farm

Bittley Copse

Black Wood

The Old Vicarage

Vicarage Farm

College Wood

BRADLEY COTTS

Bradley Farm

Manor Farm

Woodmancott

London Lodge

Rownest Wood

THE CALVERT CTR

Innersdown Farm

A33

M3

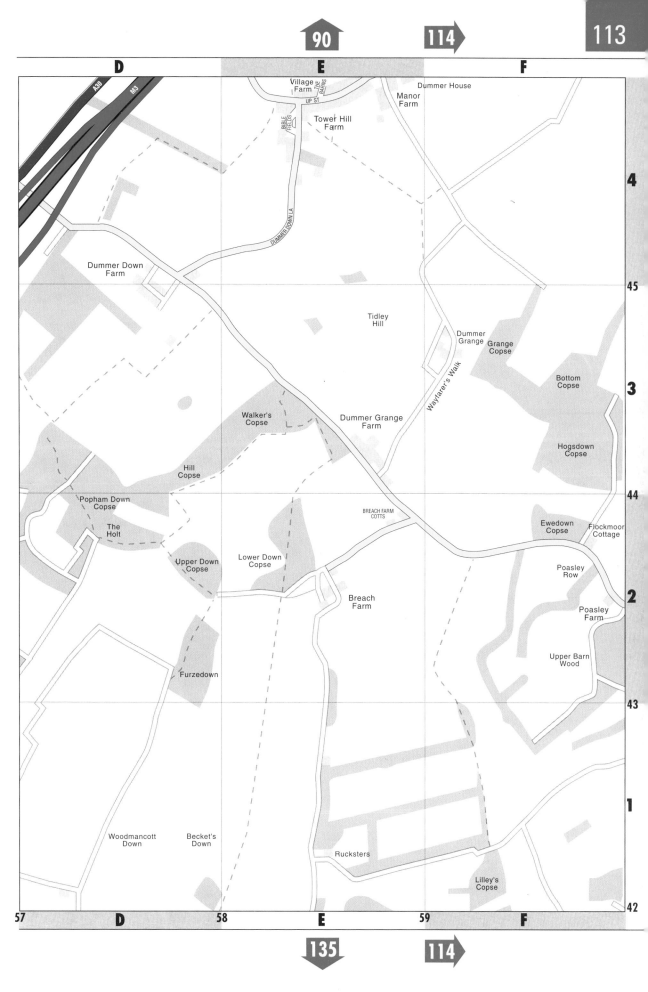

A30
M3

D
E
F

4

Village
Farm
THE BARNS
UP ST
Dummer House

Manor
Farm

Tower Hill
Farm

BIBLE FIELDS

DUMMER DOWN LA

Dummer Down
Farm

45

Tidley
Hill

Dummer
Grange
Grange
Copse

Bottom
Copse

3

Wayfarer's Walk

Walker's
Copse

Dummer Grange
Farm

Hogsdown
Copse

Hill
Copse

44

Popham Down
Copse

BREACH FARM
COTTS

Ewedown
Copse

Flockmoor
Cottage

The
Holt

Upper Down
Copse

Lower Down
Copse

Poasley
Row

2

Breach
Farm

Poasley
Farm

Upper Barn
Wood

Furzedown

43

1

Woodmancott
Down

Becket's
Down

Rucksters

Lilley's
Copse

42

57
D
58
E
59
F

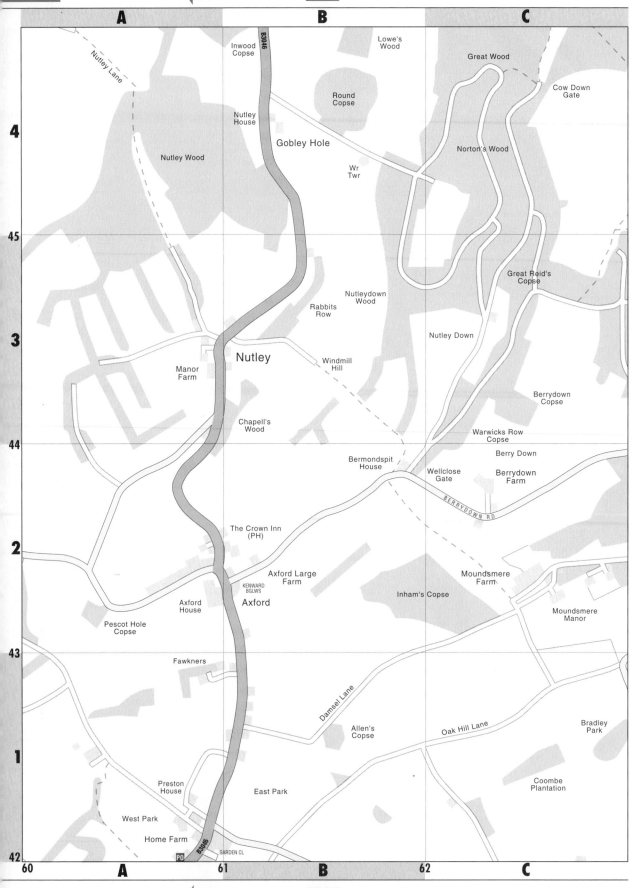

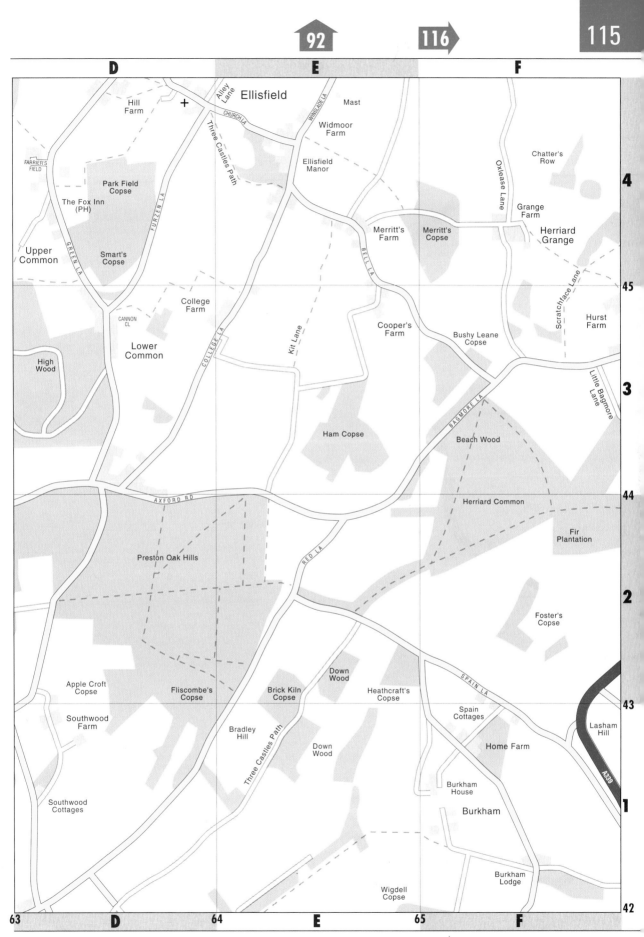

Ellisfield

Hill Farm

FARRIER'S FIELD

Park Field Copse

The Fox Inn (PH)

Upper Common

Smart's Copse

Mast

Widmoor Farm

Ellisfield Manor

Merritt's Farm

Merritt's Copse

Oxlease Lane

Chatter's Row

Grange Farm

Herriard Grange

Scratchface Lane

4

45

College Farm

CANNON CL

Lower Common

High Wood

Kit Lane

Cooper's Farm

Bushy Leane Copse

Hurst Farm

Little Bagmore Lane

3

Ham Copse

Beach Wood

BAGMORE LA

AXFORD RD

Herriard Common

44

Preston Oak Hills

RED LA

Fir Plantation

2

Foster's Copse

Apple Croft Copse

Fliscombe's Copse

Brick Kiln Copse

Down Wood

Heathcraft's Copse

SPAIN LA

Spain Cottages

Lasham Hill

43

Southwood Farm

Bradley Hill

Three Castles Path

Down Wood

Home Farm

A339

Southwood Cottages

Burkham House

Burkham

1

Burkham Lodge

Wigdell Copse

42

GREEN LA

FURZEN LA

COLLEGE LA

Alley Lane

CHURCH LA

Three Castles Path

WINSLADE LA

BELL LA

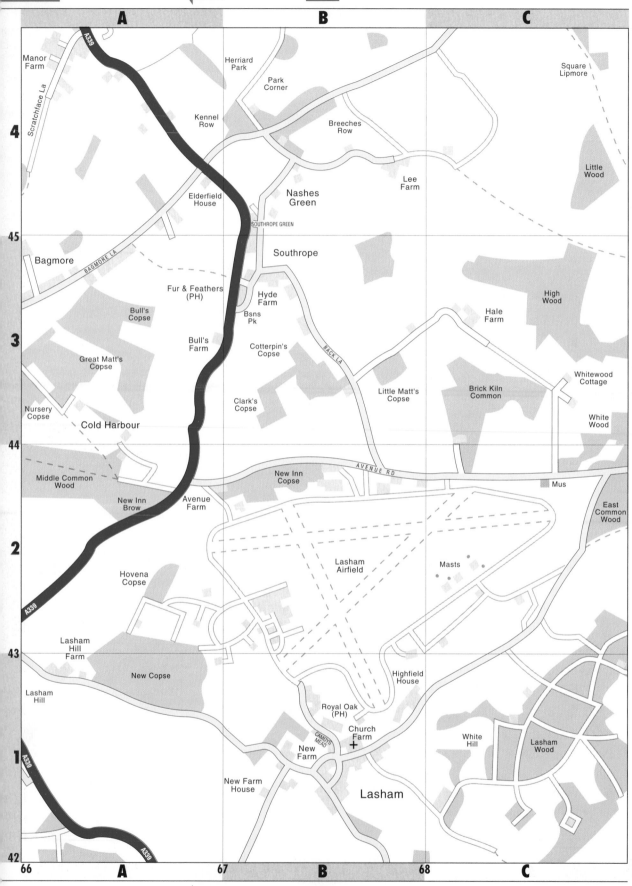

A
B
C

4

Manor Farm

Scratchface La

A339

Herriard Park

Park Corner

Kennel Row

Breeches Row

Square Lipmore

Little Wood

Nashes Green

Elderfield House

Lee Farm

SOUTHROPE GREEN

45

Bagmore

BAGMORE LA

Southrope

Fur & Feathers (PH)

Hyde Farm

Bsns Pk

High Wood

Bull's Copse

Hale Farm

3

Great Matt's Copse

Bull's Farm

Cotterpin's Copse

BACK LA

Little Matt's Copse

Brick Kiln Common

Whitewood Cottage

Nursery Copse

Clark's Copse

White Wood

Cold Harbour

44

Middle Common Wood

New Inn Copse

AVENUE RD

Mus

East Common Wood

New Inn Brow

Avenue Farm

A339

2

Hovena Copse

Lasham Airfield

Masts

Lasham Hill Farm

43

New Copse

Highfield House

Lasham Hill

Royal Oak (PH)

CAMOYS MEAD

Church Farm

White Hill

Lasham Wood

A339

1

New Farm

New Farm House

Lasham

A339

42

66
A
67
B
68
C

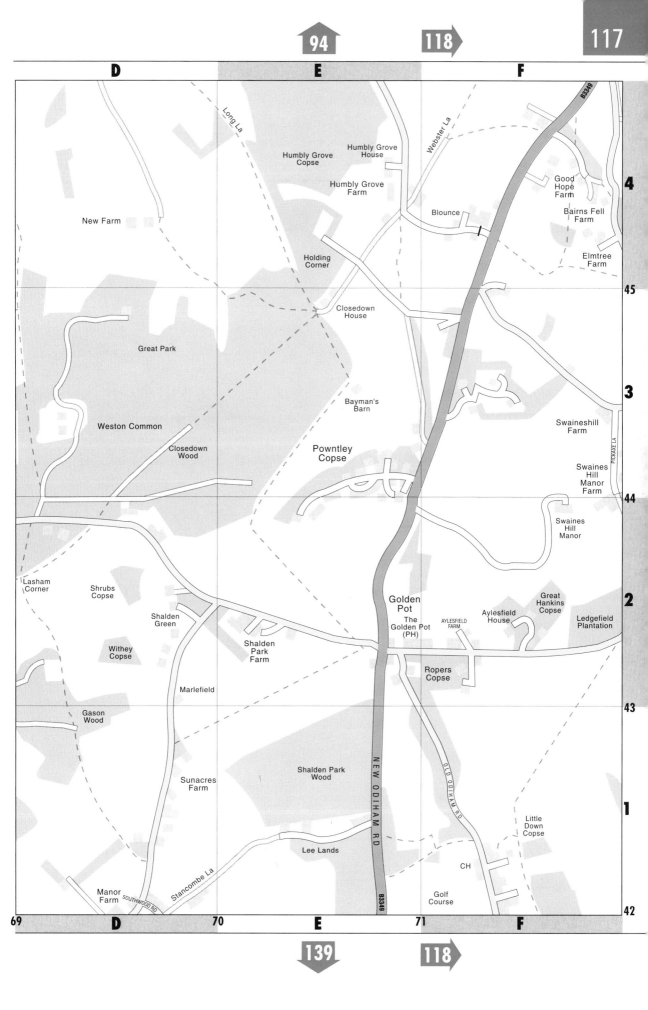

D
E
F

Long La

Humbly Grove
Copse

Humbly Grove
House

Webster La

B3349

Good
Hope
Farm

4

New Farm

Humbly Grove
Farm

Blounce

Bairns Fell
Farm

Elmtree
Farm

Holding
Corner

45

Closedown
House

Great Park

3

Bayman's
Barn

Swaineshill
Farm

Weston Common

Closedown
Wood

Powntley
Copse

PICKAXE LA

Swaines
Hill
Manor
Farm

44

Swaines
Hill
Manor

Lasham
Corner

Shrubs
Copse

Golden
Pot

Great
Hankins
Copse

2

Shalden
Green

The
Golden Pot
(PH)

AYLESFIELD
FARM

Aylesfield
House

Ledgefield
Plantation

Withey
Copse

Shalden
Park
Farm

Ropers
Copse

Marlefield

43

Gason
Wood

NEW ODIHAM RD

Shalden Park
Wood

OLD ODIHAM RD

Little
Down
Copse

1

Sunacres
Farm

CH

Manor
Farm

SOUTHWOOD RD

Stancombe La

Lee Lands

Golf
Course

42

69
D
70
E
71
F

B3349

A B C

4

New Farm

Vinney
Copse

Sheephouse
Copse

Pickaxe
Copse

White House
Farm

Highnam
Copse

Sutton
Common

45

PICKAXE LA

West
View

Great
Wood

Gaston
Copse

3

Broadlands
Copse

Little
Wood

SONCROFT LA

Yarnhams
Farm

Hawkins
Wood

44

Beech Hangers Lane

Mast

Liddenfield
Copse

Stowell
Copse

Dicket's
Plantation

Fielders
Copse

Yarnhams
Cottages

Stowell
Cottage

2

Ham Wood

Shrub Croft
Copse

Masts

43

Spollycombe
Copse

Peakham
Copse

Holybourne
Down

BROCKHAM HILL LA

Brockham Hill
Farm Cottages

Brockham Hill
Barn

New Lane

1

Round
Wood

Howard's Lane

42

72 A 73 B 74 C

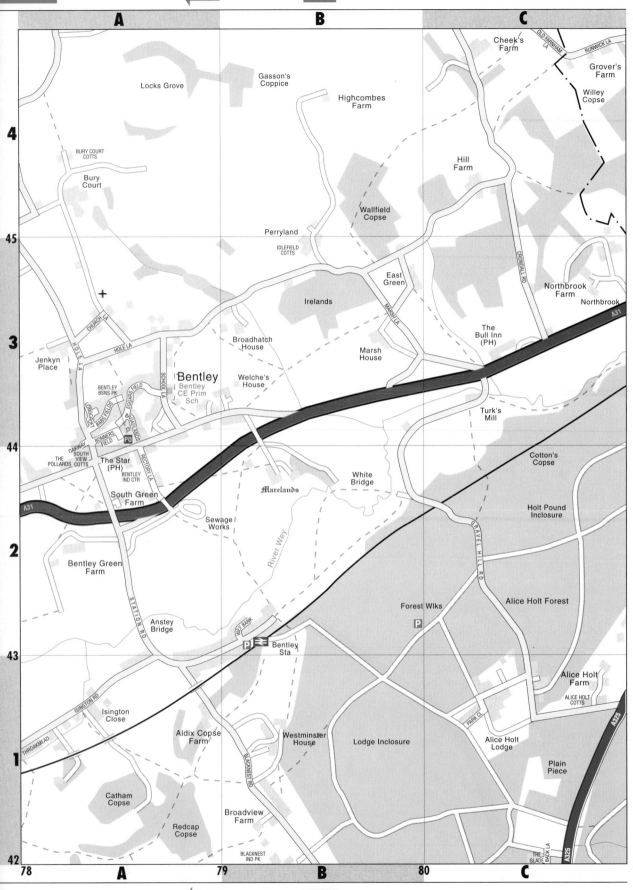

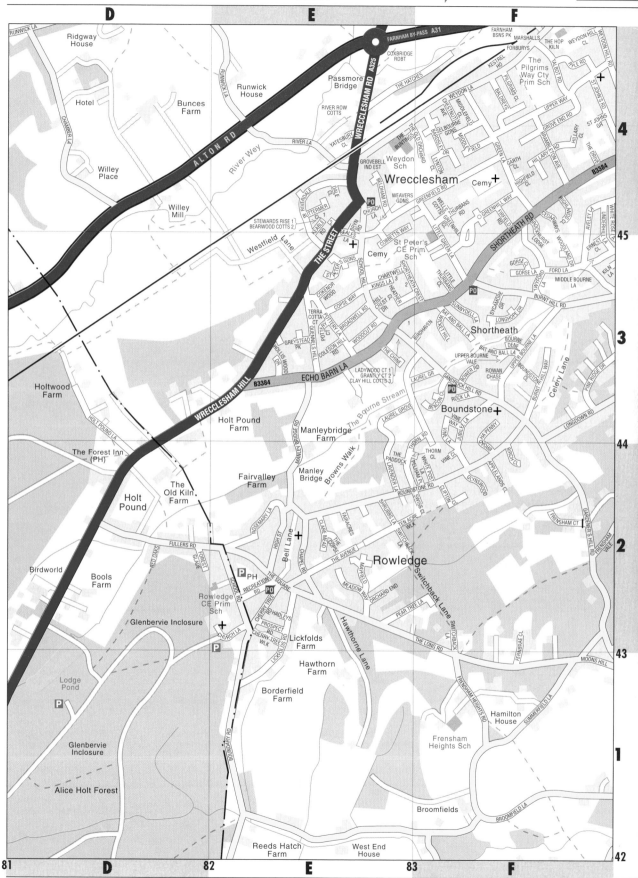

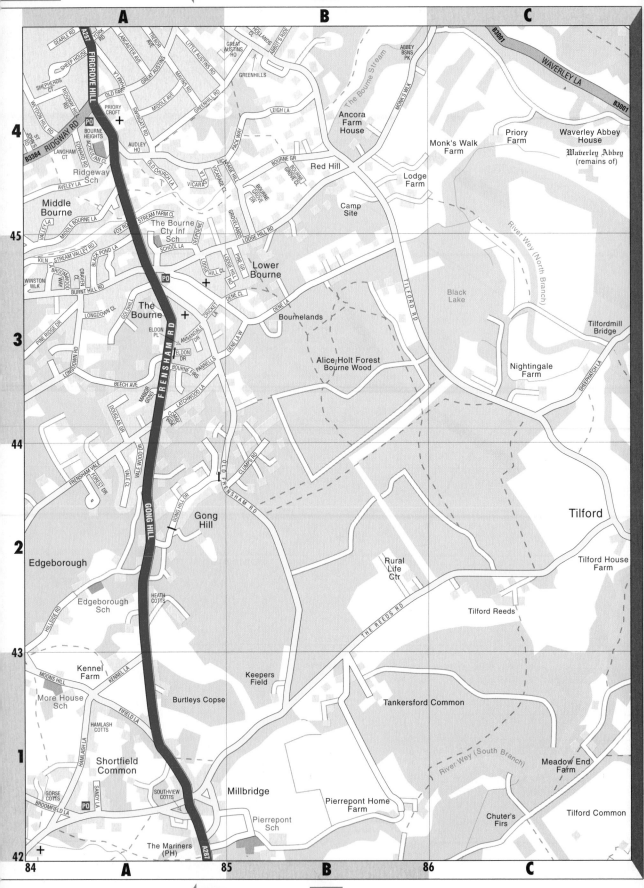

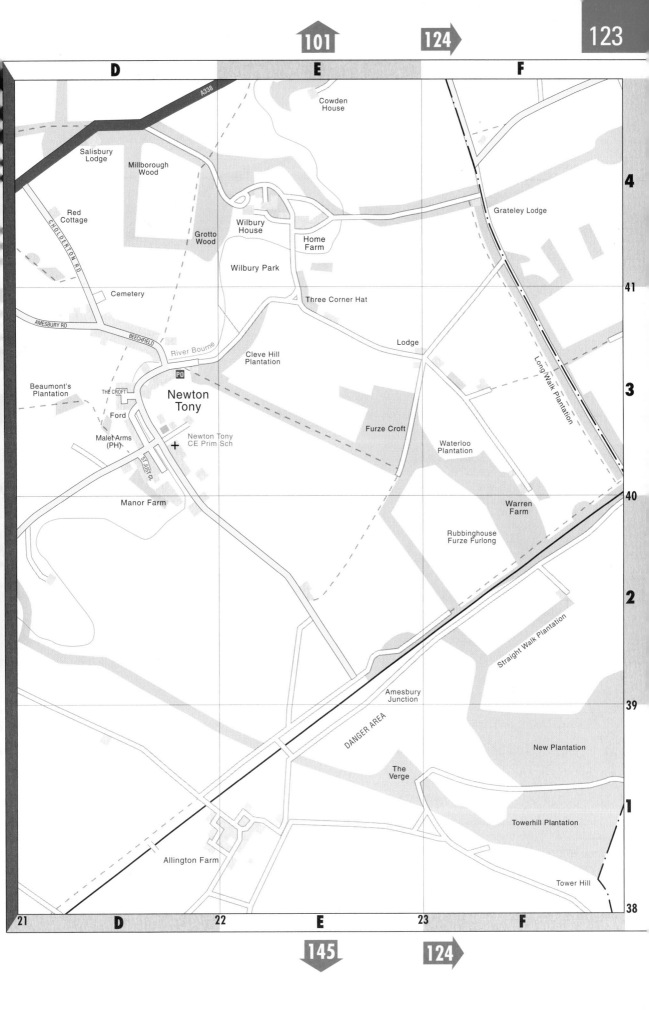

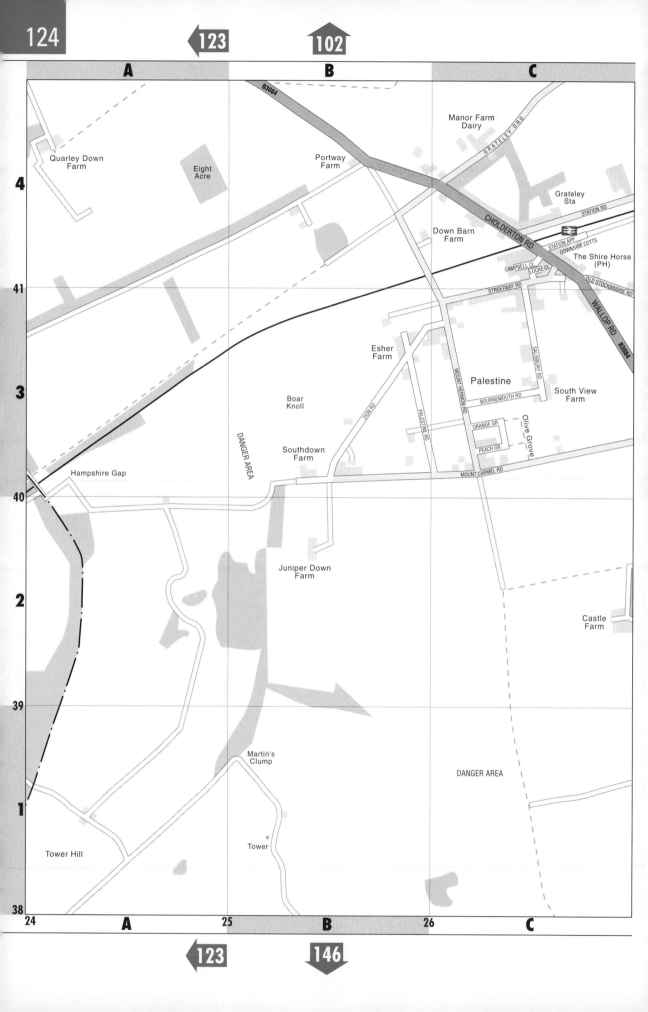

A   B   C

4

Quarley Down Farm

Eight Acre

Portway Farm

B3084

Manor Farm Dairy

GRATELEY DRO.

Grateley Sta

STATION RD

CHOLDERTON RD

Down Barn Farm

STATION APP

DOWNSIDE COTTS

The Shire Horse (PH)

41

CAMPBELL CL

LOCKE CL

STREETWAY RD

OLD STOCKBRIDGE RD

WALLOP RD

B3084

Esher Farm

SALISBURY RD

Palestine

3

Boar Knoll

ZION RD

MOUNT HERMON RD

BOURNEMOUTH RD

South View Farm

DANGER AREA

Southdown Farm

PALESTINE RD

ORANGE GR

PEACH GR

OLIVE GROVE

MOUNT CARMEL RD

Hampshire Gap

40

Juniper Down Farm

2

Castle Farm

39

Martin's Clump

DANGER AREA

1

Tower Hill

Tower

38

24   A   25   B   26   C

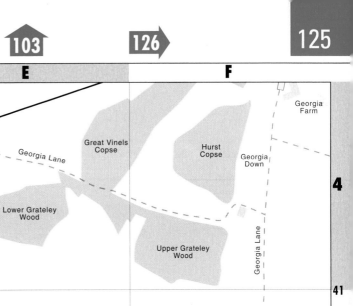
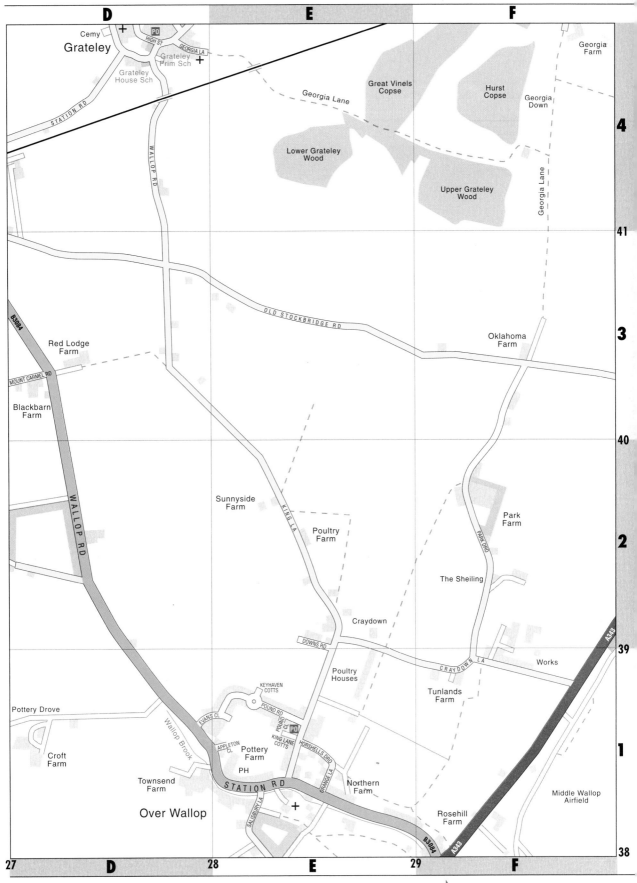

D

Cemy
Grateley
PO
High St
GEORGIA LA
Grateley Prim Sch
Grateley House Sch

STATION RD

WALLOP RD

E

Georgia Lane

Great Vinels Copse

Lower Grateley Wood

Upper Grateley Wood

F

Georgia Farm

Hurst Copse

Georgia Down

Georgia Lane

4

41

B3084

Red Lodge Farm

MOUNT CARMEL RD

Blackbarn Farm

OLD STOCKBRIDGE RD

Oklahoma Farm

3

40

WALLOP RD

Sunnyside Farm

KING LA

Poultry Farm

Park Farm

The Sheiling

2

Craydown

DOWNS RD

CRAYDOWN LA

Works

39

Pottery Drove

Croft Farm

Wallop Brook

EVANS CL

APPLETON CL

KEYHAVEN COTTS

POUND RD

POUND CL

PO

King Lane Cotts

Poultry Houses

Tunlands Farm

PARK DRO

Pottery Farm

PH

Townsend Farm

SALISBURY LA

HORSHELLS DRO

ORANGE LA

Northern Farm

Rosehill Farm

Middle Wallop Airfield

1

Over Wallop

STATION RD

B3083

A343

38

27

D

28

E

29

F

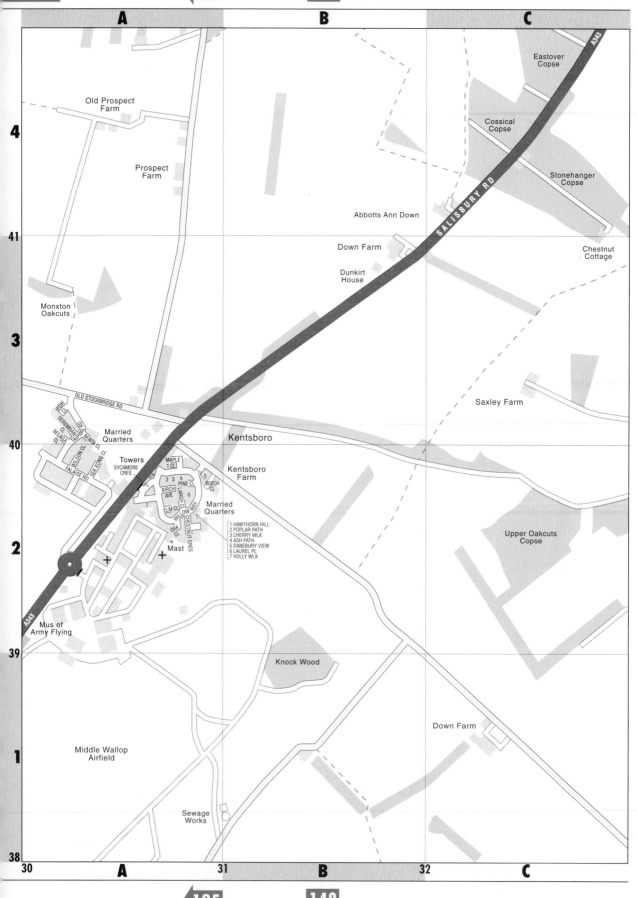

A
B
C

4

Old Prospect Farm

Prospect Farm

Eastover Copse

Cossical Copse

Stonehanger Copse

Abbotts Ann Down

41

Down Farm

Chestnut Cottage

Dunkirt House

Monxton Oakcuts

SALISBURY RD

A343

3

Saxley Farm

OLD STOCKBRIDGE RD

Married Quarters

Kentsboro

40

Towers
SYCAMORE CRES

MAPLE
1 CL

Kentsboro Farm

2 3 4
PINE CL

5
BEECH CL

BIRCH AVE

6

ELM CL

LARCH CL

WILLOW WAY

CHESTNUT CRES

Married Quarters

1 HAWTHORN HILL
2 POPLAR PATH
3 CHERRY WLK
4 ASH PATH
5 DANEBURY VIEW
6 LAUREL PL
7 HOLLY WLK

OAK CL

Upper Oakcuts Copse

2

Mast

Mus of Army Flying

A343

39

Knock Wood

Down Farm

1

Middle Wallop Airfield

Sewage Works

38

30
A
31
B
32
C

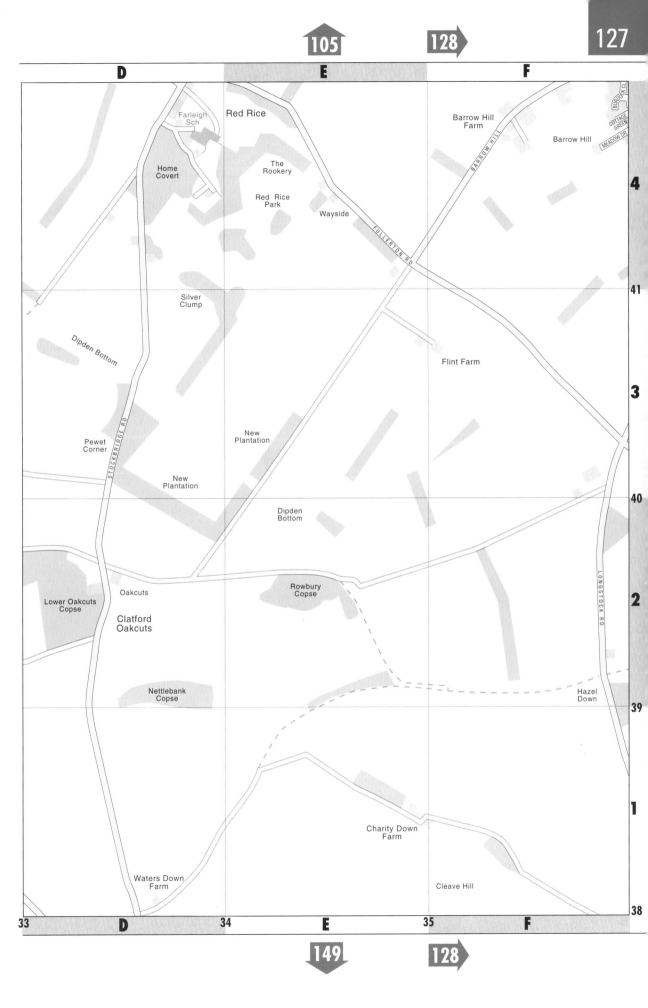

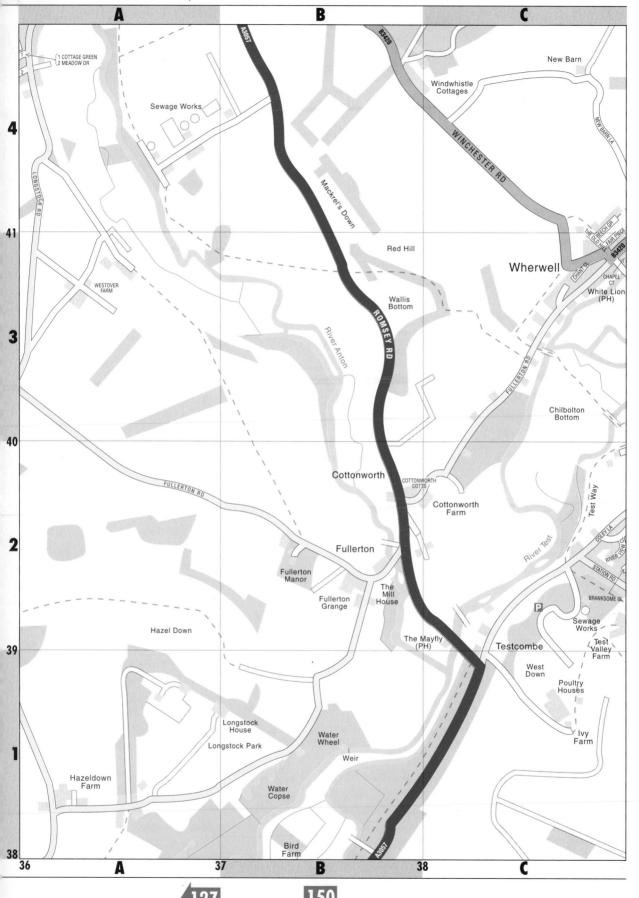

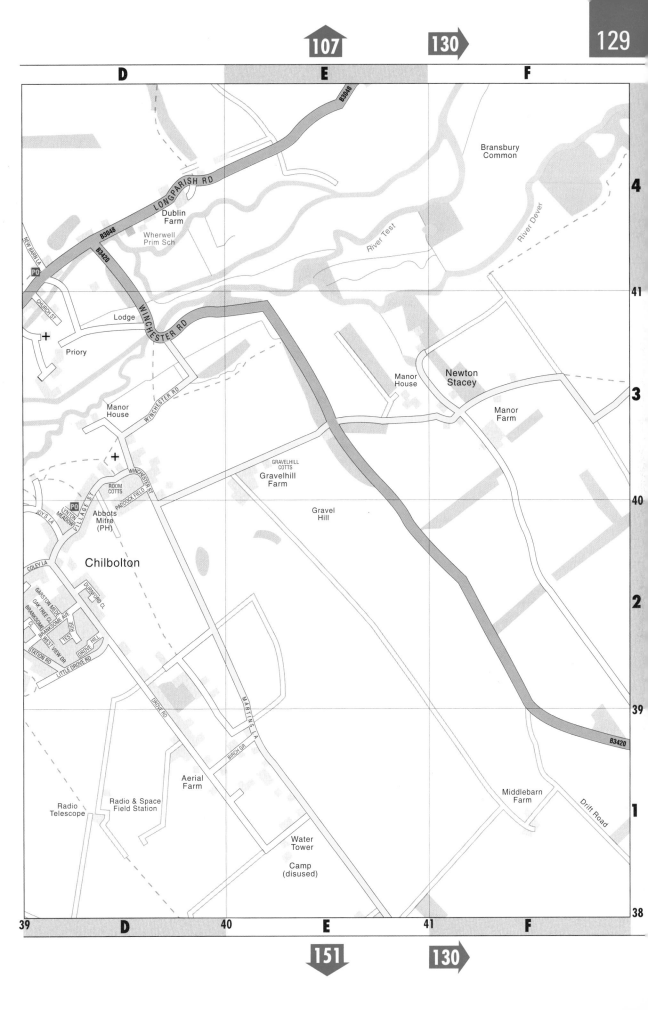

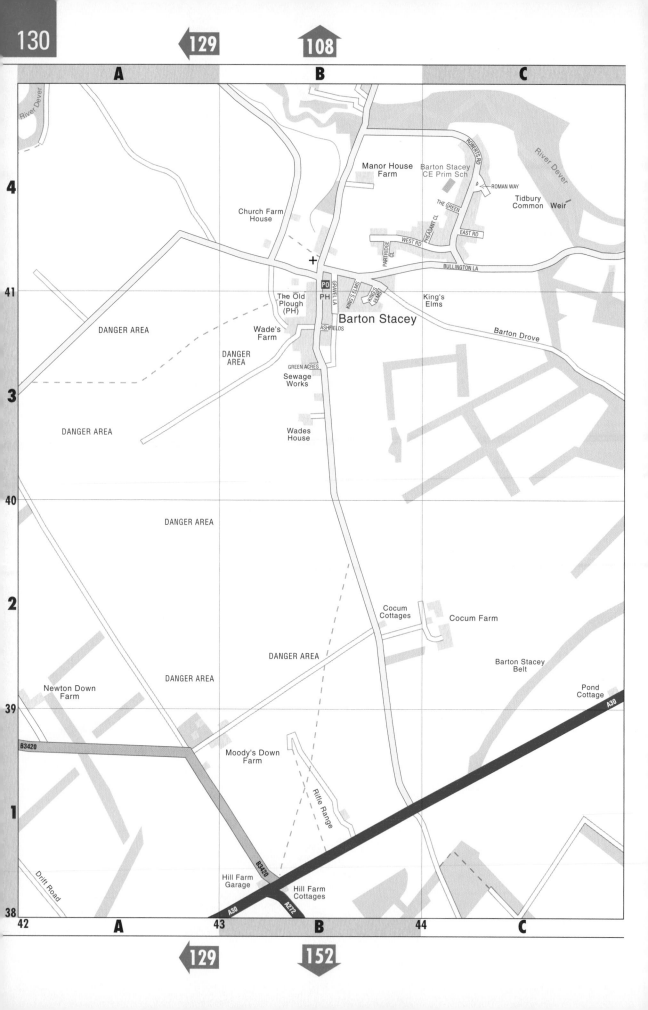

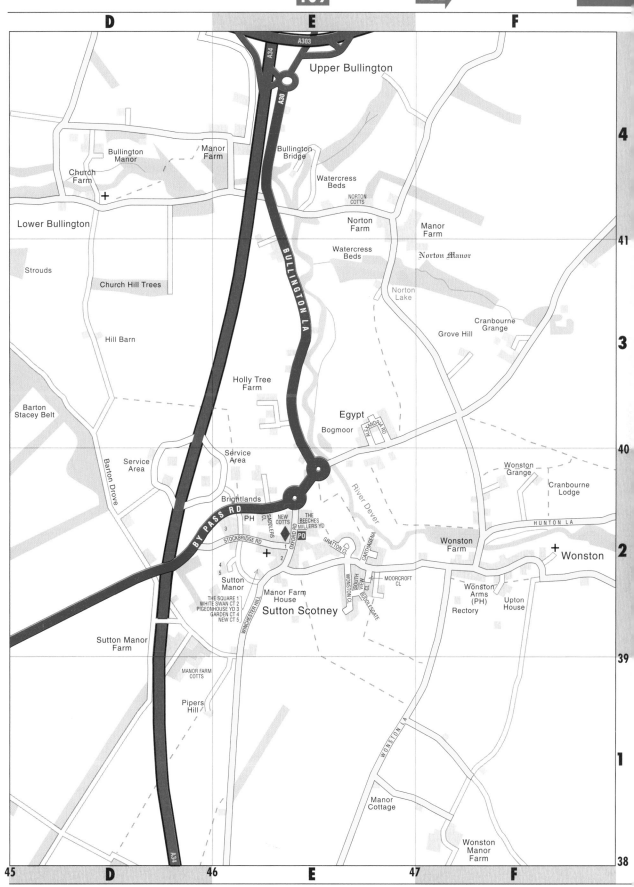

Upper Bullington

A303

A30

A34

4

Manor
Farm

Bullington
Manor

Bullington
Bridge

Church
Farm

Watercress
Beds

NORTON
COTTS

Lower Bullington

Norton
Farm

Manor
Farm

41

Strouds

BULLINGTON LA

Watercress
Beds

Norton Manor

Church Hill Trees

Norton
Lake

Cranbourne
Grange

Hill Barn

Grove Hill

3

Holly Tree
Farm

Egypt

Bogmoor

ALEXANDRA RD

Barton
Stacey Belt

Service
Area

Service
Area

River Dever

40

Wonston
Grange

Cranbourne
Lodge

Barton Drove

Brightlands

BY PASS RD

PH

NEW
COTTS

SADDLERS
CL

THE
BEECHES
MILLERS YD

HUNTON LA

PO

OXFORD RD

GRATTON CL

Wonston
Farm

Wonston ✠ Wonston

STOCKBRIDGE RD

SOUTH
VIEW

CARTHAGENA

2

3

1

MOORCROFT
CL

4

2

WONSTON CL

BIDDLESGATE

5

Sutton
Manor

Wonston
Arms
(PH)

Upton
House

Manor Farm
House

WINCHESTER HILL

Rectory

THE SQUARE 1
WHITE SWAN CT 2
PIGEONHOUSE YD 3
GARDEN CT 4
NEW CT 5

Sutton Scotney

39

Sutton Manor
Farm

MANOR FARM
COTTS

Pipers
Hill

WONSTON LA

1

Manor
Cottage

A34

Wonston
Manor
Farm

38

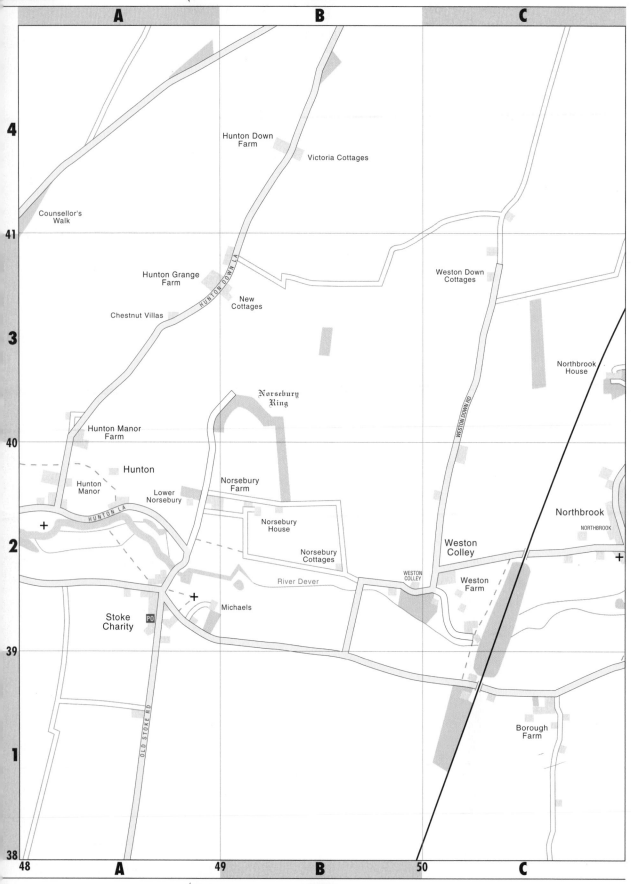

A   B   C

4

Hunton Down
Farm

Victoria Cottages

Counsellor's
Walk

41

Hunton Grange
Farm

HUNTON DOWN LA

New
Cottages

Weston Down
Cottages

Chestnut Villas

WESTON DOWN RD

3

Northbrook
House

Norsebury
Ring

Hunton Manor
Farm

40

Hunton

Hunton
Manor

Norsebury
Farm

Northbrook

NORTHBROOK

Lower
Norsebury

Norsebury
House

Weston
Colley

HUNTON LA

2

Norsebury
Cottages

WESTON
COLLEY

Weston
Farm

River Dever

Michaels

Stoke
Charity

PO

39

OLD STOKE RD

Borough
Farm

1

48   A   49   B   50   C

38

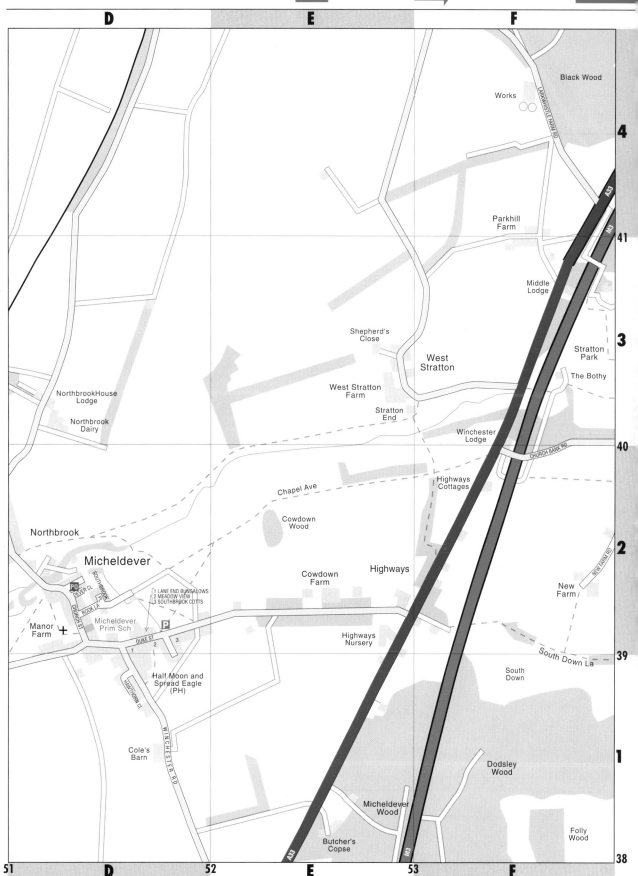

D E F

Black Wood

Works

LARKWHISTLE FARM RD

A33

M3

Parkhill Farm

4

41

Middle Lodge

Shepherd's Close

West Stratton

3

Stratton Park

West Stratton Farm

The Bothy

NorthbrookHouse Lodge

Stratton End

Northbrook Dairy

Winchester Lodge

40

Chapel Ave

Highways Cottages

CHURCH BANK RD

Cowdown Wood

Northbrook

Cowdown Farm

Highways

2

New Farm

NEW FARM RD

Micheldever

SOUTHBROOK PL

PO
DEVER CL

1 LANE END BUNGALOWS
2 MEADOW VIEW
3 SOUTHBROOK COTTS

ROOK LA

South Down La

39

Manor Farm

Micheldever Prim Sch

CHURCH ST

P

DUKE ST

2

3

1

South Down

Highways Nursery

Half Moon and Spread Eagle (PH)

HAWTHORN CL

1

Dodsley Wood

Cole's Barn

WINCHESTER RD

Micheldever Wood

A33

M3

Butcher's Copse

Folly Wood

38

51 D 52 E 53 F

A   B   C

Biddles wood

Black Wood

Embley Wood

A33

M3

Stratton Park

Lone Farm

41

Whiteway Farm

The Cowleys

Stratton House

Norn's Copse

Well House Copse

Candover Copse

3

Cross

East Stratton Farm

40

East Stratton

EAST STRATTON

Hazely Copse

Foxhill

New Farm Rd

The Plough Inn

STRATTON CL

BARING CL

Thorny Down Wood

Burnt House Copse

2

CHURCH BANK RD

Black Hut Copse

COPSE LA

STRATTON LA

Duke's Copse

NORTHINGTON CORNER

39

South Down Lane

Totford Copse

South Down

Burcot Farm

Dodsley Wood

1

Wayfarer's Walk

38

54   A   55   B   56   C

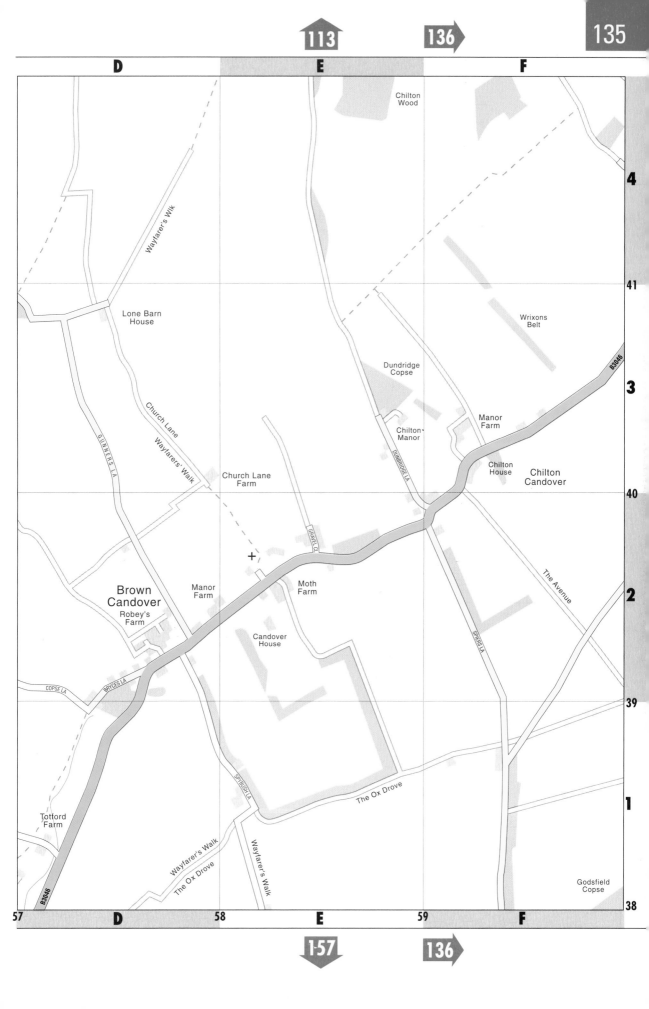

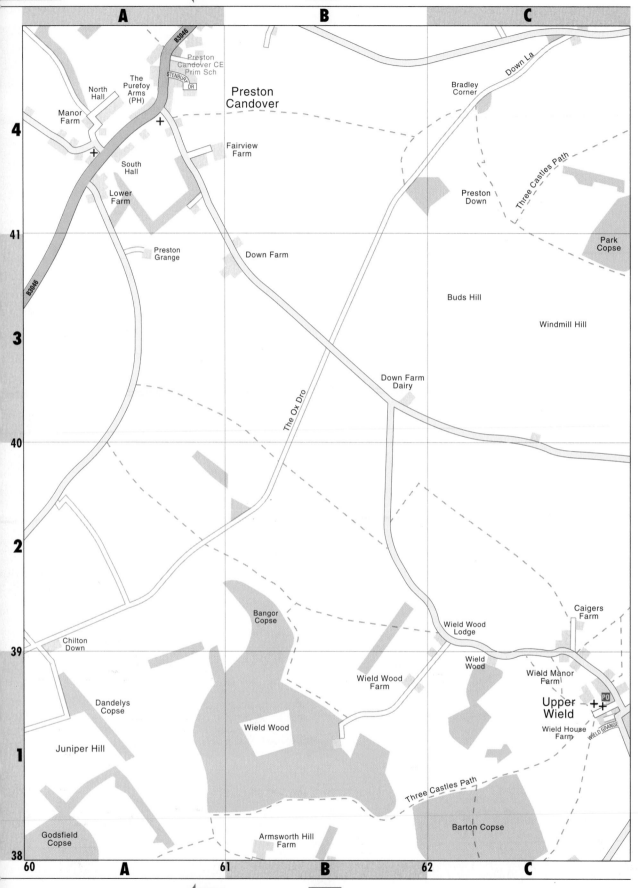

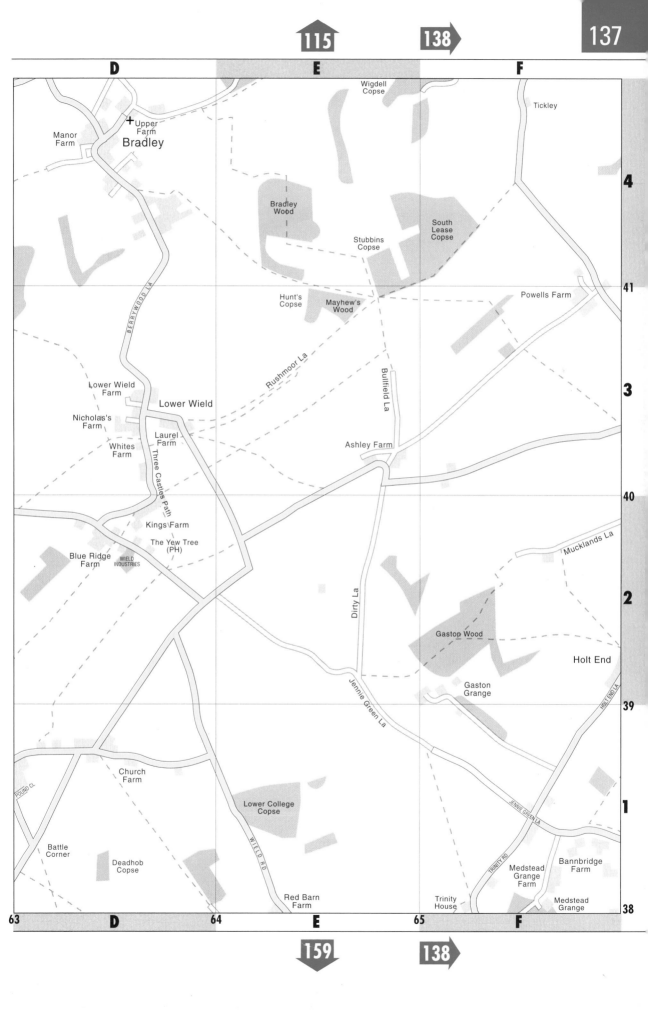

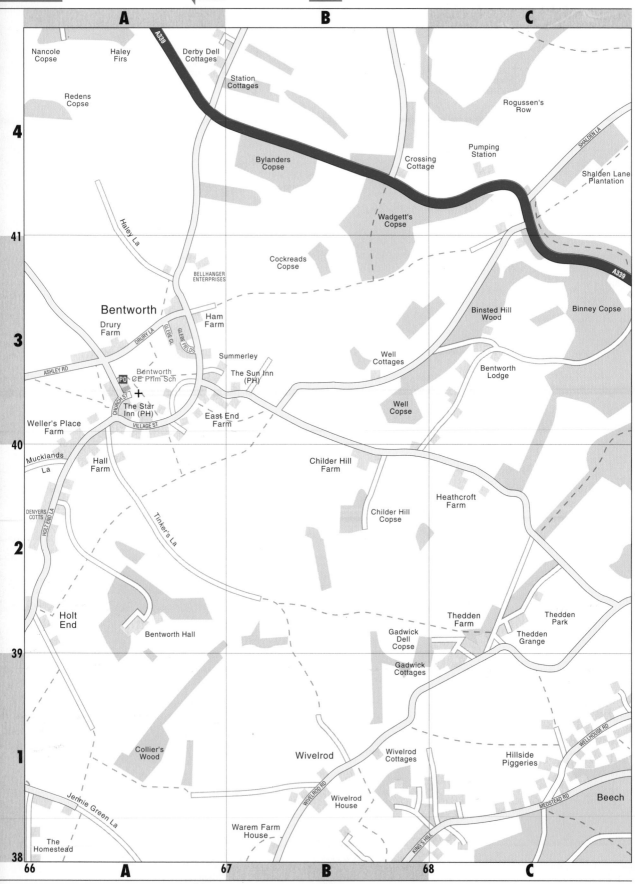

A339
Nancole Copse
Haley Firs
Derby Dell Cottages
Station Cottages
Rogussen's Row
SHALDEN LA
Redens Copse
4
Pumping Station
Shalden Lane Plantation
Bylanders Copse
Crossing Cottage
Haley La
Wadgett's Copse
A339
41
BELLHANGER ENTERPRISES
Cockreads Copse
Binney Copse
Bentworth
Ham Farm
Binsted Hill Wood
Drury Farm
GLEBE CL
GLEBE FIELDS
3
Summerley
Well Cottages
Bentworth Lodge
DRURY LA
ASHLEY RD
Bentworth CE Prim Sch
The Sun Inn (PH)
PO
CHURCH ST
The Star Inn (PH)
East End Farm
Well Copse
Weller's Place Farm
VILLAGE ST
40
Mucklands La
Hall Farm
Childer Hill Farm
Heathcroft Farm
DENYERS COTTS
HOLT END LA
Tinker's La
Childer Hill Copse
2
Thedden Park
Holt End
Thedden Farm
Thedden Grange
Bentworth Hall
Gadwick Dell Copse
39
Gadwick Cottages
Collier's Wood
Wivelrod
Wivelrod Cottages
Hillside Piggeries
1
WELLHOUSE RD
Jennie Green La
WIVELROD RD
Wivelrod House
MEDSTEAD RD
Beech
Warem Farm House
KING'S HILL
The Homestead
38
66   A   67   B   68   C

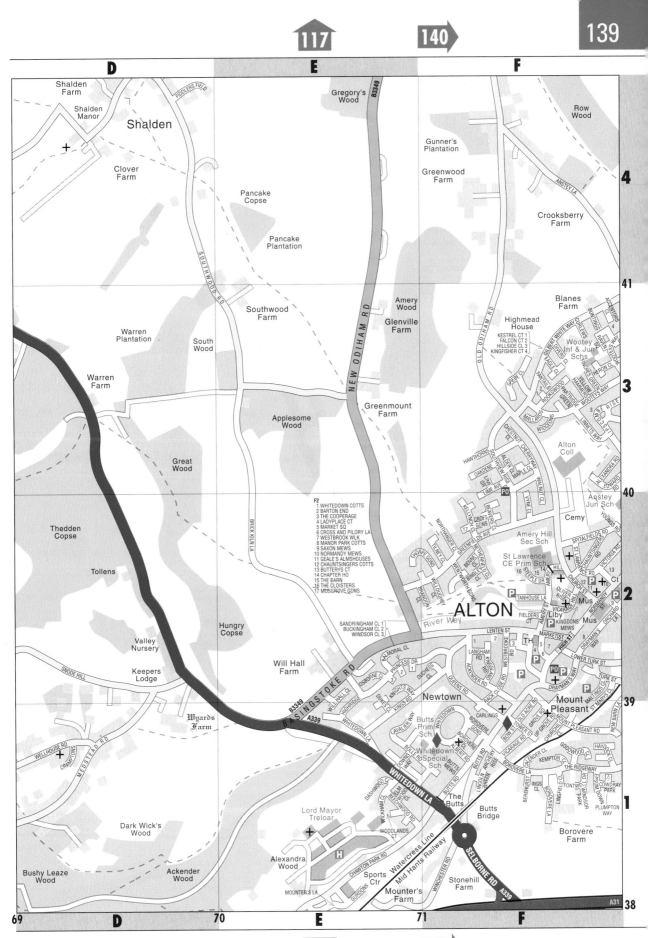

D   E   F

Shalden
Farm
Shalden
Manor
FIDDLERS FIELD
Shalden
Clover
Farm
Pancake
Copse
Pancake
Plantation
SOUTHWOOD RD
Southwood
Farm
Warren
Plantation
South
Wood
Warren
Farm
Great
Wood
Applesome
Wood

Gregory's
Wood
B3349
Gunner's
Plantation
Greenwood
Farm
Row
Wood
ANSTEY LA
Crooksberry
Farm

4

41

NEW ODIHAM RD
Amery
Wood
Glenville
Farm
Greenmount
Farm
OLD ODIHAM RD

Blanes
Farm
Highmead
House
KESTREL CT 1
FALCON CT 2
HILLSIDE CL 3
KINGFISHER CT 4
GILBERT WHITE WAY
CURLEWS
BUNTINGS
DIVERS
EAGLE CL
Wootey
Inf & Jun
Schs
ACKENDERS
BARN
ACRES GREENWAY
HERON CL
ACHES
WOOTEYS WAY
LINNETS WAY
ALEXANDRA RD
EDWARD RD

3

Thedden
Copse
Tollens

BRICK KILN LA
Hungry
Copse

HAWTHORNS
SOUTHVIEW RISE
OAKDENE
LIME AVE
ALDER RISE
CHESTNUT CL
CHERRY WAY
MAPLE CL
WALNUT CL
WYNE CL
Alton
Coll
PO
Anstey
Jun Sch
Cemy
YOUNGS RD

40

F2
1 WHITEDOWN COTTS
2 BARTON END
3 THE COOPERAGE
4 LADYPLACE CT
5 MARKET SQ
6 CROSS AND PILORY LA
7 WESTBROOK WLK
8 MANOR PARK COTTS
9 SAXON MEWS
10 NORMANDY MEWS
11 GEALE'S ALMSHOUSES
12 CHAUNTSINGERS COTTS
13 BUTTERYS CT
14 CHAPTER HO
15 THE BARN
16 THE CLOISTERS
17 MUSGROVE GDNS

Amery Hill
Sec Sch
St Lawrence
CE Prim Sch
SPITALFIELDS RD
VICTORIA RD
ST LAWRENCE RD
CHURCH ST
Ct
P
P
Mus
NORMANDY
ORCHARD LA

2

SANDRINGHAM CL 1
BUCKINGHAM CL 2
WINDSOR CL 3
River Wey
ALTON
THORPE GDNS
NORTHANGER CT
GREENFIELDS AVE
KELLYNCH RD
WILLOUGHBY
BRANDON CL
WENTWORTH GDNS
BINGLEY CL
NETHERFIELD CT
BEINE
FIELDERS
CT
LENTEN ST
Liby
KINGDONS
MEWS
VICARAGE
AMERY ST
STEELE DR
AMERY HILL
OLIVER
RISE
MARKET ST
HIGH ST
Mus

P
TANHOUSE LA
BALMORAL CL
PRINCESS DR
DUCHESS
LANGHAM
RD
WESTBROOK RD
TH
P
PO
P
DRAYMAN'S WAY
LOWER TURK ST
TURK ST
MALTINGS
P

Valley
Nursery
Keepers
Lodge
SNODE HILL
Will Hall
Farm

BASINGSTOKE RD
B3349
A339
WILL HALL CL
HIGHRIDGE
JOSBORNE CL
KNIGHTS WAY
KINGS WAY
DUNCAN
QUEENS RD
ACKENDER RD
RACK CLOSE RD
Newtown
CARLINGS
GROVE RD
TOWER ST
UP GROVE RD
CHURCHILL
Mount
Pleasant
MOUNT PLEASANT RD
ST MARY'S CL
NEW BARN LA
HAYOCK

39

Wyards
Farm
WELLHOUSE RD
CRAMPTONS
MEDSTEAD RD
Butts
Prim
Sch
CAVALIER WAY
WHITEDOWN LA
Whitedown
Special
Sch
BUTTS RD
WHITEDOWN
ALBERT RD
BOROVERE CL
OLD ACRE RD
BUTTS
MEWS
BOROVERE
GDNS
BOW'S RD
LINCOLN
ARCHERY
RISE
BUTTS RD
VICARAGE RD
CALENDER CL
BEREHURST
INGS CL
BOROVERE LA
KEMPTON
LINGFIELD
OLD ODIHAM RD
FONTWELL RD
WINDSOR
THE RIDGEWAY
GOODWOOD
COWDRAY
PARK
EPSOM DOWNS
PLUMPTON
WAY

1

Dark Wick's
Wood
Bushy Leaze
Wood
Ackender
Wood

WICKHAM CL
DASHWOOD
BELHAM
BEECHWOOD RD
WOODLANDS
CT
Lord Mayor
Treloar
H
Alexandra
Wood
CHAWTON PARK RD
MOUNTER'S LA
GURDONS
Sports
Ctr
Mounter's
Farm
Watercress Line
Mid Hants Railway
WINCHESTER RD
The
Butts
Butts
Bridge
Stonehill
Farm
SELBORNE RD
A339
Borovere
Farm
A31

38

69   D   70   E   71   F

139
118

A   **B**   **C**

4

Row
Wood

Cadnam
Farm

1 GILMOUR GDNS
2 GOODWYNS GREEN

41

Holybourne

Howard's La

BROCKHAM HILL LA

Manor
Farm

Howards
Farm

Howard's La

CHURCH LA

Bonham's
Farm

Cuckoo's
Corner

Haw
Bridge

Hawbridge
Farm

WISTERIA
MEWS

PO

PH

LONDON RD

A31

BONHAMS

BOURNE PL

GREENS

RACEMAKERS CL

VINDOMIS

SMITHY

LOWER NEATHAM MILL LA

INHAMS RD

Lord Mayor
Treloar Coll
of F Ed

Andrews
Endowed CE
Prim Sch

New
PADDOCK

MALTHOUSE MEWS

MONFORD DR

Our Lady of
Providence
Convent Sch

Eggar's
Sec Sch

Upper
Neatham Mill
Farm

Neatham

River Wey

Manor
Farm

BAKERS RD

TOCKS

MANOR RD

LINK RD

WOOTEYS
WAY

JENNIFER WAY

SWALLOW
CL

ROBIN

DOVE
CL

MARTINS
CL

ANSTEY LA

PLOVERS
WAY

WREN
CL

WILLIAM
WAY

KING
GR

ALLEN CL

HAROLD
RD

DOWDEN
GDNS

POUND
RD

GEALE'S

SPERS

CRES

EDWARD RD

LANSDOWNE RD

GEALE'S

CHALKCRAFTS

PARK CLOSE RD

EGGAR'S
CL

ANSTEY MILL LA

ANSTEY RD

GASKEL CL

COMPLINS

UPPER NEATHAM MILL LA

THORNTON
END

Anstey

Lynch
Hill

B3004

NEWMAN LA

Copt
Hill

Golden Chair
Hill

Stirvill's
Copse

3

P

41... 40

Sch

EASTBROOKE

NURSERY RD

VICTORIA RD

ADAMS WAY

KERRIDGE
INDUSTRIAL ESTATE

THE
GARTH

LITTLEFIELD

GROVE PARK
INDUSTRIAL
ESTATE

MILL LA

RIVERWEY
INDUSTRIAL
ESTATE

Sewage
Works

Golden Chair
Farm

40

Sch

VICTORIA
ST

NORMANDY ST

KORE MEWS

BRAMLEY

Mid Hants Rly
Watercress Line

Alton
Sta.

PAPER

DICKER ST

SPITALHATCH

CAKER STREAM RD

MILL LANE
INDUSTRIAL ESTATE

THE
KILNS

Spitalhatch

ALTON
BUSINESS
CENTRE

OMNI
BUSINESS
CENTRE

OMEGA
PARK

Neatham Down

Monk Wood

2

KINGSMEAD

ASHDELL RD

GOODYERS

WATESIDE

WILSOM
CL

WILSOM RD

Wilsom

1 FERNDOWN CT
2 ASHLEY CT
3 ROSETREE COTTS
4 ORCHARD TERR
5 RIVER VIEW COTTS
6 ORCHARD HO
7 BLENHEIM CL
8 KINGSMEAD COTTS
9 MANOR PARK COTTS
10 SHERWOOD TERR

Hangers Way

STATIONS

SPICERS RD

CURTIS RD

MORELAND
CL

GAUVAIN CL

VAUGHANS

CROWLEY DR

HUNTSMEAD

WINDMILL HILL

THE RIDGEWAY

SALSBURY CL

WINCANTON
CL

WINDMILL LA

1 SANDOWN CL
2 ASCOT CL

Water La

CH

Little Caker
Bridge

Meadow
Wixes

Wixes

CAKER'S LA

Golf
Course

Cox's
Copse

Clay's
Farm

CLAY'S LA

Shelley's
Barn

SHELLEY'S LA

WYCK LA

Old House
Farm

Kiln
House

A31

Park Farm

PH

BLANKET ST

B3004

39

1

38

72   A   73   B   74   C

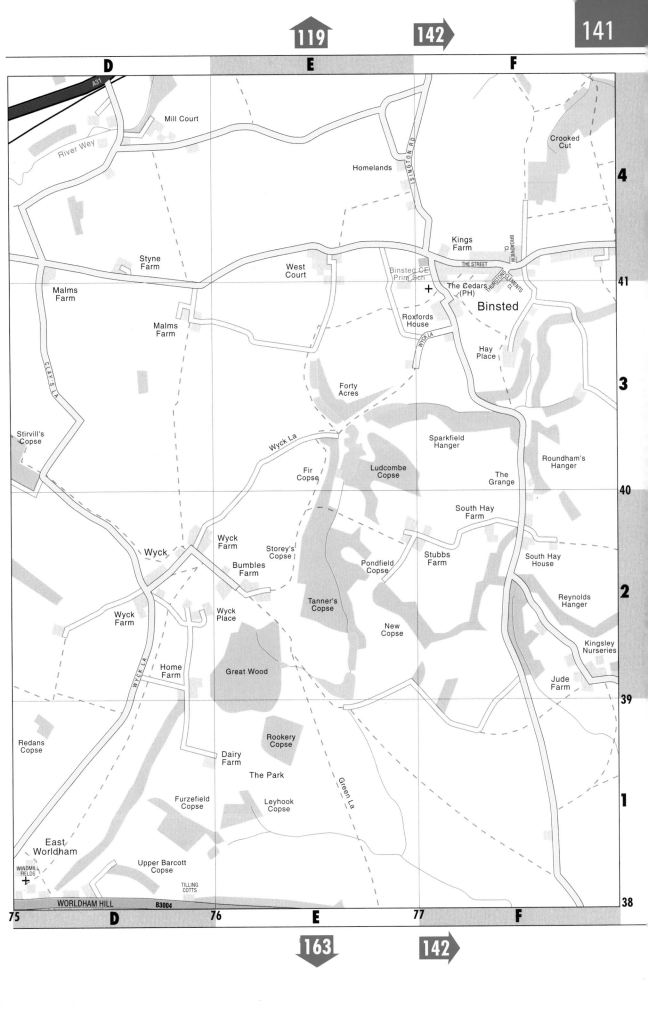

D E F

4

Mill Court

River Wey

A31

Homelands

ISINGTON RD

Crooked Cut

Kings Farm

BROADVIEW CL

THURSTONE CLEMENTS CL

THE STREET

Styne Farm

West Court

Binsted CE Prim Sch

The Cedars (PH)

Binsted

41

Malms Farm

Malms Farm

Roxfords House

WYCK LA

Hay Place

CLAY'S LA

Forty Acres

3

Stirvill's Copse

Wyck La

Sparkfield Hanger

Roundham's Hanger

Fir Copse

Ludcombe Copse

The Grange

40

Wyck

Wyck Farm

Storey's Copse

South Hay Farm

Bumbles Farm

Wyck Place

Pondfield Copse

Stubbs Farm

South Hay House

Reynolds Hanger

2

Wyck Farm

Tanner's Copse

New Copse

Kingsley Nurseries

WYCK LA

Home Farm

Great Wood

Jude Farm

39

Redans Copse

Dairy Farm

Rookery Copse

Green La

1

The Park

Furzefield Copse

Leyhook Copse

East Worldham

WINDMILL FIELDS

Upper Barcott Copse

TILLING COTTS

WORLDHAM HILL

B3004

38

75 D 76 E 77 F

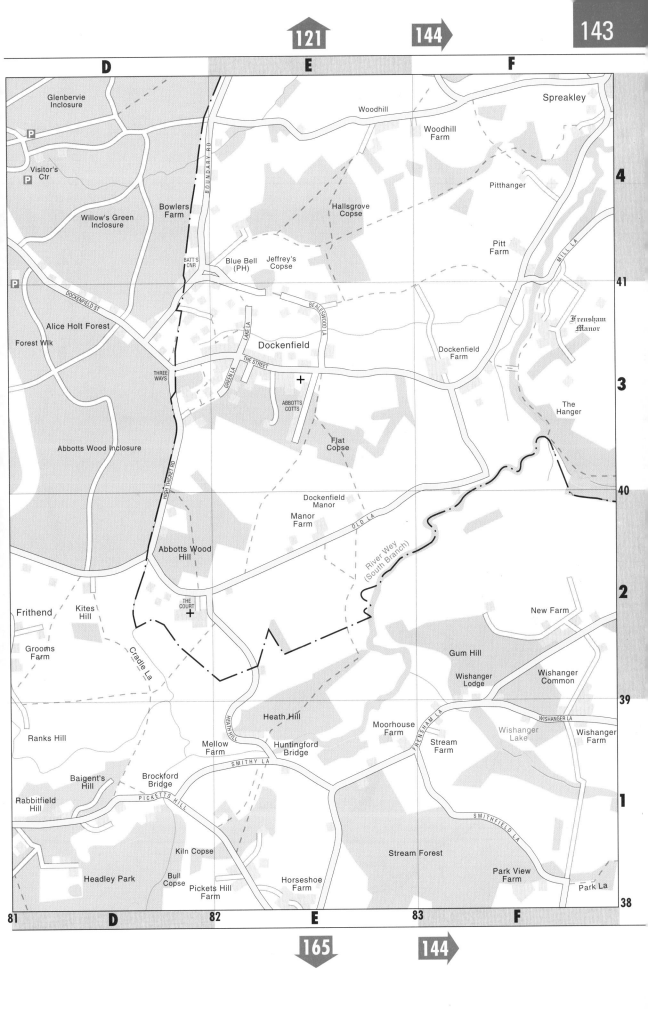

D
E
F

Glenbervie Inclosure

P

Visitor's Ctr
P

Spreakley

Woodhill

Woodhill Farm

4

Pitthanger

Bowlers Farm

Willow's Green Inclosure

P

BATT'S CNR

Blue Bell (PH)

Jeffrey's Copse

Hallsgrove Copse

Pitt Farm

MILL LA

41

BOUNDARY RD

Alice Holt Forest

Forest Wlk

DOCKENFIELD ST

LAKE LA

BEALESWOOD LA

Dockenfield

Frensham Manor

THE STREET

Dockenfield Farm

THREE WAYS

GREEN LA

Abbotts Wood Inclosure

ABBOTTS COTTS

Flat Copse

The Hanger

3

HIGH THICKET RD

Dockenfield Manor

Manor Farm

OLD LA

40

Abbotts Wood Hill

River Wey (South Branch)

New Farm

2

Frithend

Kites Hill

THE COURT

Gum Hill

Grooms Farm

Cradle La

Wishanger Lodge

Wishanger Common

39

Ranks Hill

HEATHHILL

Heath Hill

Moorhouse Farm

FRENSHAM LA

WISHANGER LA

Wishanger Lake

Wishanger Farm

Mellow Farm

Huntingford Bridge

Stream Farm

Baigent's Hill

Brockford Bridge

SMITHY LA

1

Rabbitfield Hill

PICKETTS HILL

SMITHFIELD LA

Kiln Copse

Bull Copse

Pickets Hill Farm

Horseshoe Farm

Stream Forest

Park View Farm

Park La

Headley Park

81
D
82
E
83
F
38

◀ **143**
122 ▲

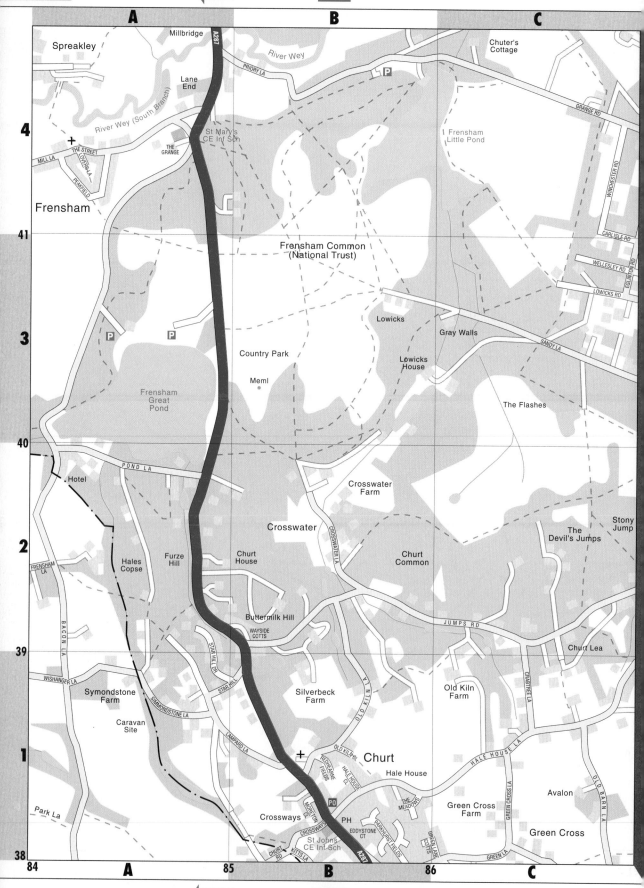

A **B** **C**

Spreakley

Millbridge

River Wey

Chuter's
Cottage

Lane
End

PRIORY LA

GRANGE RD

4

River Wey (South Branch)

St Mary's
CE Inf Sch

Frensham
Little Pond

MILL LA

THE STREET

OVEN LA

THE
GRANGE

WINCHESTER RD

Frensham

PEACHFIELD

41

CARLISLE RD

Frensham Common
(National Trust)

WELLESLEY RD

EGLINTON RD

LOWICKS RD

3

P

P

Lowicks

Gray Walls

SANDY LA

Country Park

Lowicks
House

Meml

The Flashes

Frensham
Great
Pond

40

Hotel

POND LA

Crosswater
Farm

Stony
Jump

Crosswater

The
Devil's Jumps

FRENSHAM LA

2

Hales
Copse

Furze
Hill

Churt
House

CROSSWATER LA

Churt
Common

BACON LA

Churt Lea

39

WISHANGER LA

Buttermilk Hill

JUMPS RD

CRABTREE LA

WAYSIDE
COTTS

Symondstone
Farm

SIMMONDSTONE LA

Silverbeck
Farm

OLD KILN LA

Old Kiln
Farm

STAR HILL DR

STAR HILL

Caravan
Site

LAMPARD LA

1

Churt

GREEN CROSS LA

OLD BARN LA

Old Kiln

Hale House

HALE HOUSE LA

Avalon

Park La

REDTHORNE FIELDS

HALE HOUSE CL

THE
MEADOWS

Green Cross
Farm

Green Cross

Crossways

MORETON

PO

PH

EDDYSTONE
CT

FAIRCHURST FIELDS

GREEN LANE COTTS

CHURT RD

CROSSWAYS

St Johns
CE Inf Sch

KITTS LA

A287

GREEN LA

38

84 **A** 85 **B** 86 **C**

◀ **143**
166 ▼

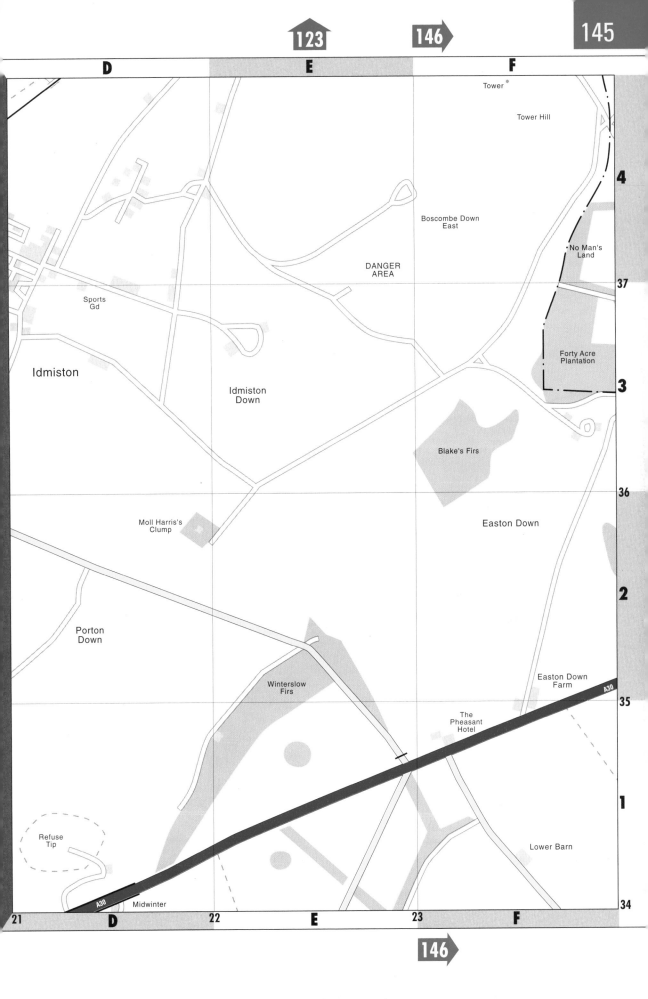

Tower
Tower Hill

D E F

4

Boscombe Down
East

No Man's
Land

DANGER
AREA

37

Forty Acre
Plantation

Sports
Gd

3

Idmiston

Idmiston
Down

Blake's Firs

36

Moll Harris's
Clump

Easton Down

Porton
Down

2

Winterslow
Firs

Easton Down
Farm

A30

35

The
Pheasant
Hotel

1

Refuse
Tip

Lower Barn

A30
Midwinter

34

21 D 22 E 23 F

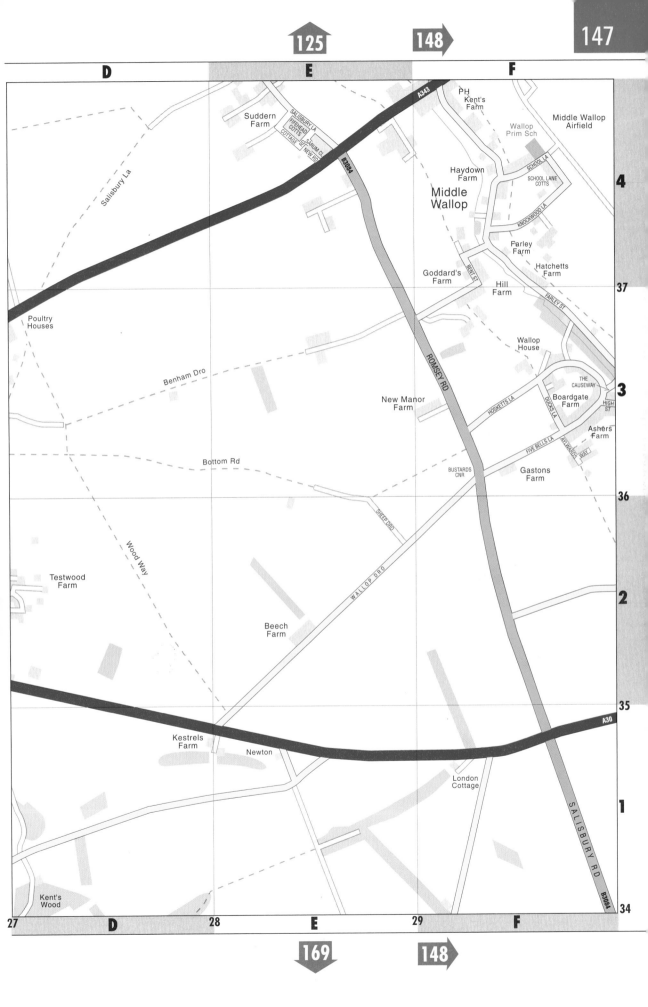

147
126

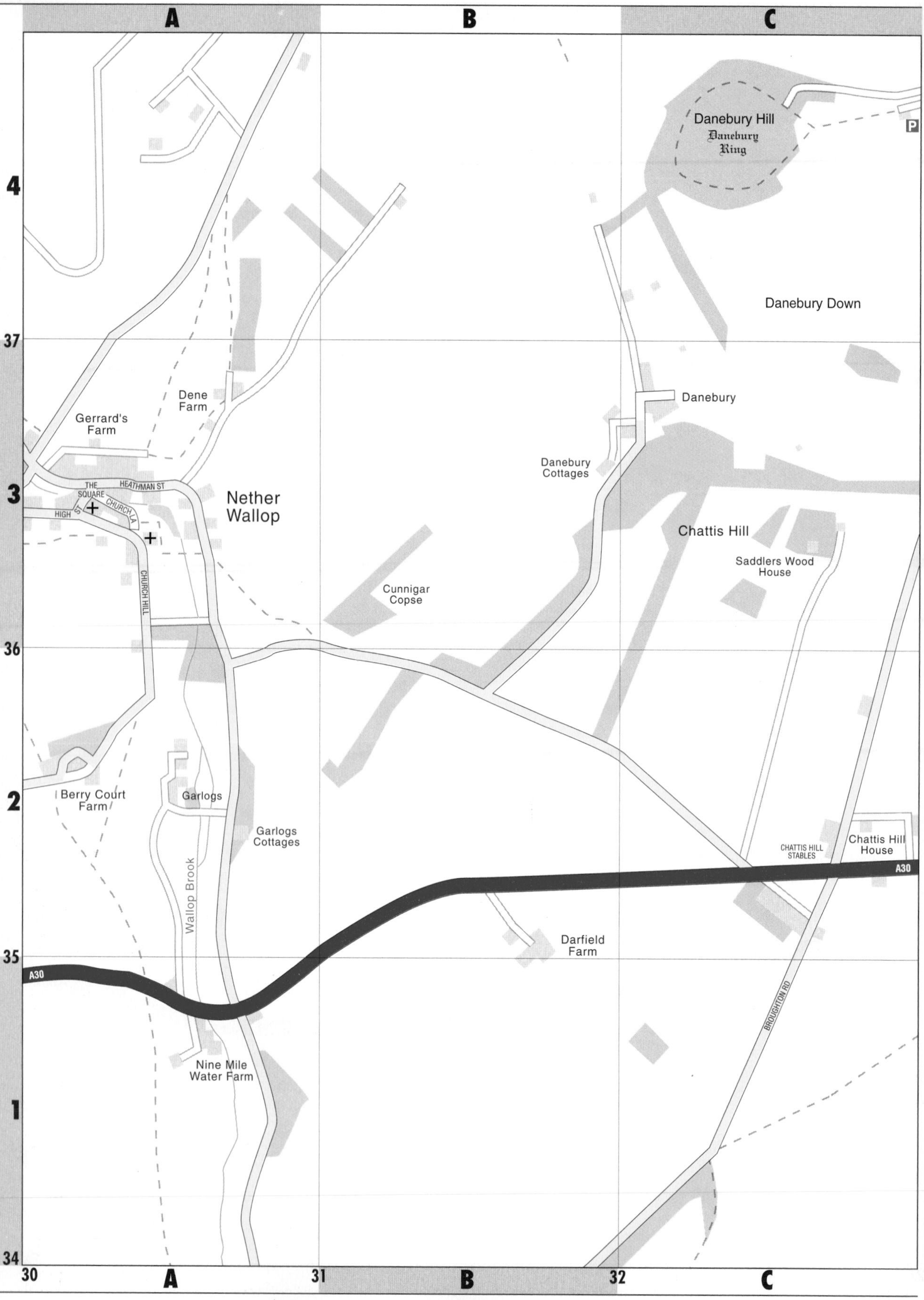

A **B** **C**

4

Danebury Hill
Danebury Ring

P

Danebury Down

37

Dene
Farm

Danebury

Gerrard's
Farm

Danebury
Cottages

THE
SQUARE   HEATHMAN ST

3   HIGH   CHURCH LA

ST
Nether
Wallop

Chattis Hill

Saddlers Wood
House

CHURCH HILL

Cunnigar
Copse

36

2

Berry Court
Farm   Garlogs

Garlogs
Cottages

CHATTIS HILL
STABLES

Chattis Hill
House

A30

Wallop Brook

Darfield
Farm

35

A30

Nine Mile
Water Farm

BROUGHTON RD

1

34

30   31   32

A **B** **C**

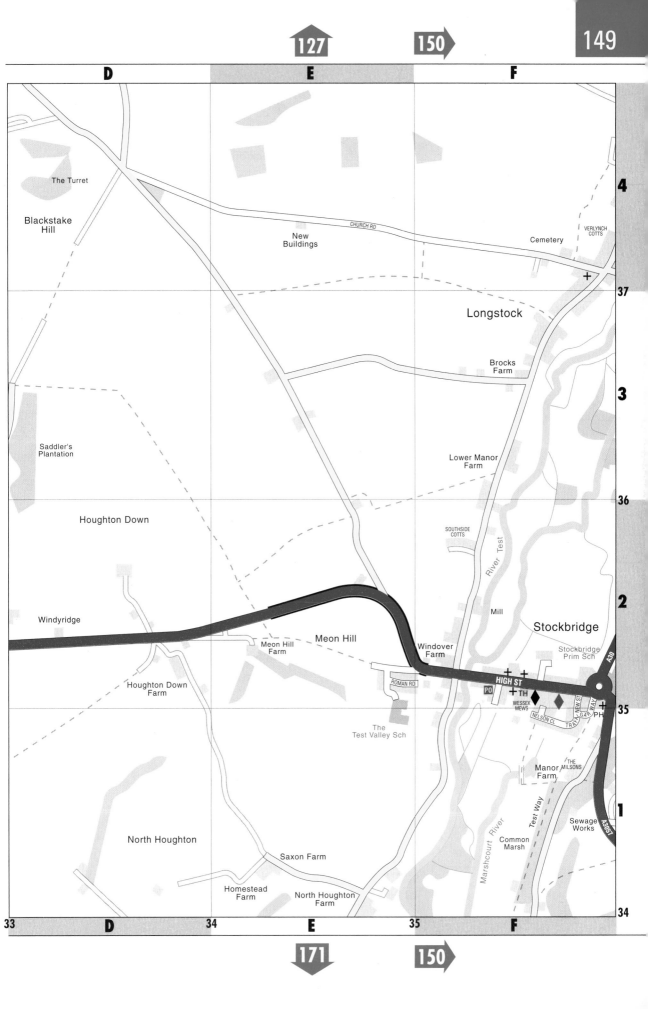

A B C

4

37

CH

3

36

2

35

1

34

36 A 37 B 38 C

Little Common

Abbotts
Manor
Farm

Leckford

PO
LECKFORD

Leckford Abbas

Leckford
Dairy

Leckford
Plantation

River Test

Great
Common

Charity Farm
House

Aqueduct

Baker's
Farm

Lone Barn

LECKFORD LA

Riches
Plantation

Atners
Hill

Atners
Towers

Test Way

Golf Course

Chilcombe
Copse

Leckford
Camp

A3057

London Hill
Farm

Wynrush

LONDON RD

A30

A3057

Fair View
Farm

Little Dean
Farm

LITTLE
DEAN
CT

LITTLE
DEAN
HOUSE

OLD LONDON RD

A30

Sch

WINTON HILL

Cemetery

B3049

Woolbury Ring

Sandydown
Farm

Stockbridge Down

Home
Farm

PERRY LA

P

P

The
Plantation

Lamberts

P

Ridge's Grove

B3049

A3057

SOMBORNE PARK RD

Teg
Down

Windovers

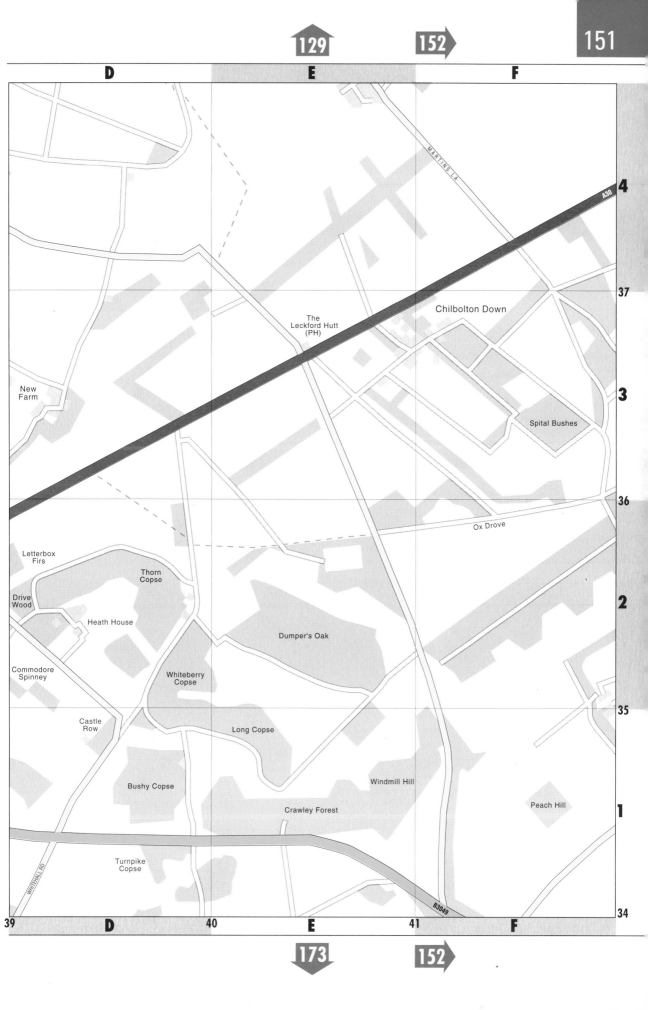

129
152

D   E   F

MARTINS LA

A30

4

Chilbolton Down

37

The
Leckford Hutt
(PH)

3

Spital Bushes

New
Farm

36

Ox Drove

Letterbox
Firs

Thorn
Copse

Drive
Wood

2

Heath House

Dumper's Oak

Commodore
Spinney

Whiteberry
Copse

35

Castle
Row

Long Copse

Bushy Copse

Windmill Hill

Peach Hill

1

Crawley Forest

WHITEHALL RD

Turnpike
Copse

B3049

34

39   D   40   E   41   F

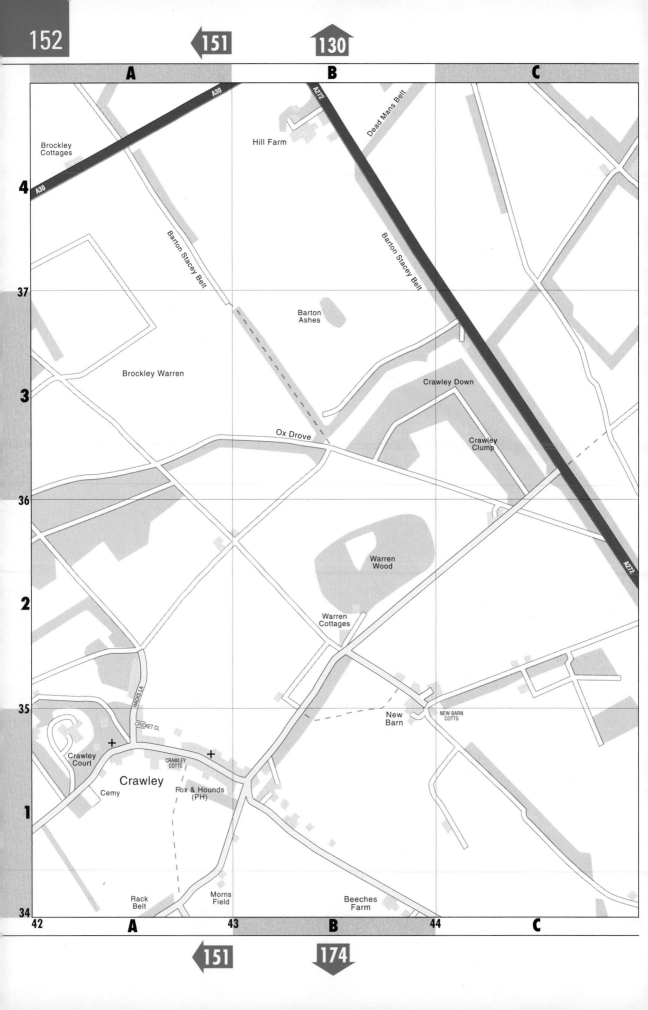

A   **B**   **C**

A30

A272

Brockley
Cottages

Hill Farm

Dead Mans Belt

4

A30

Barton Stacey Belt

Barton Stacey Belt

37

Barton
Ashes

Brockley Warren

Crawley Down

3

Ox Drove

Crawley
Clump

36

A272

Warren
Wood

2

Warren
Cottages

35

New
Barn

NEW BARN
COTTS

HACKS LA

CRICKET CL

Crawley
Court

CRAWLEY
COTTS

Crawley

Cemy

Fox & Hounds
(PH)

1

Rack
Belt

Morns
Field

Beeches
Farm

34

42   **A**   43   **B**   44   **C**

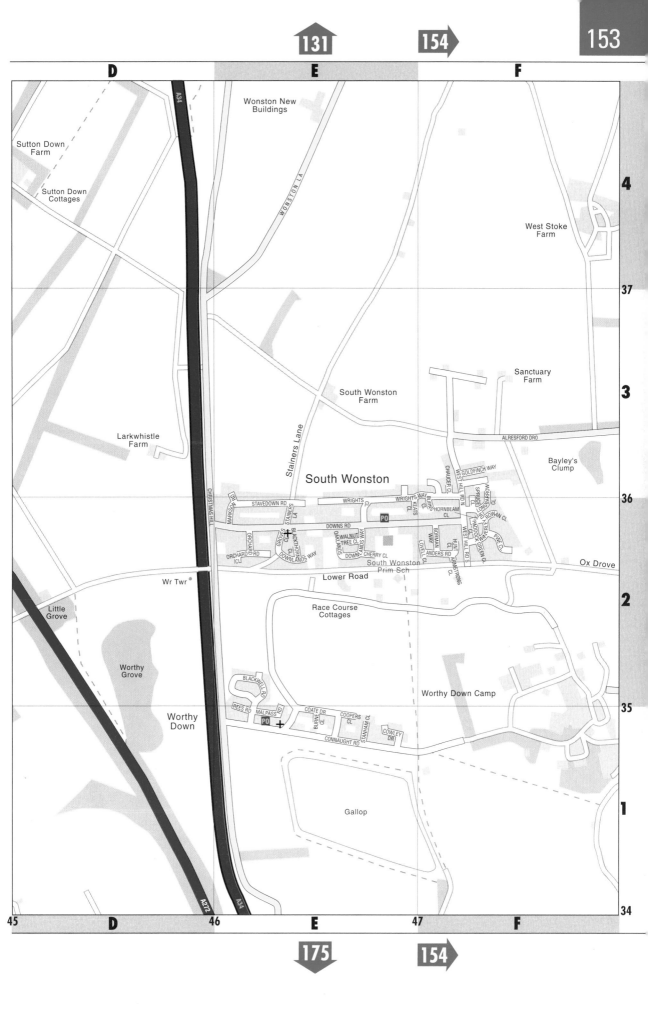

D E F

4

37

3

Wonston New Buildings

Sutton Down Farm

Sutton Down Cottages

West Stoke Farm

South Wonston Farm

Sanctuary Farm

Larkwhistle Farm

Stainers Lane

ALRESFORD DRO

Bayley's Clump

South Wonston

36

CHAUCER CL

GOLDFINCH WAY

WEST HILL RD N

MARKSON CL

STAVEDOWN RD

WRIGHTS CL

WRIGHTS WAY

BURNS CL

HORNBEAM CL

SPRUCE CL

LONGBARROW

ROWAN CL

KEATS CL

PO

DOWNS RD

WALNUT TREE CL

OAKLANDS

DOWN STONY WAY

PADDOCK

PINE CL

WAVERLEY

GREEN CL

ORCHARD CL

GROVE

STAINERS LA

BLACKTHORN CL

DOWNLANDS WAY

BORHAM WAY

LOVELL CL

LANDERS RD

HUNT

ARMSTRONG CL

ORCHARD RD

CHERRY CL

South Wonston Prim Sch

Ox Drove

Wr Twr

Lower Road

2

Little Grove

Race Course Cottages

Worthy Grove

Worthy Down Camp

35

Worthy Down

BLACKWELL RD

REES RD

MALPASS RD

PO

COATE DR

BURNE CL

COOPERS CL

STANHAM CL

COWLEY DR

CONNAUGHT RD

1

Gallop

A272

A34

34

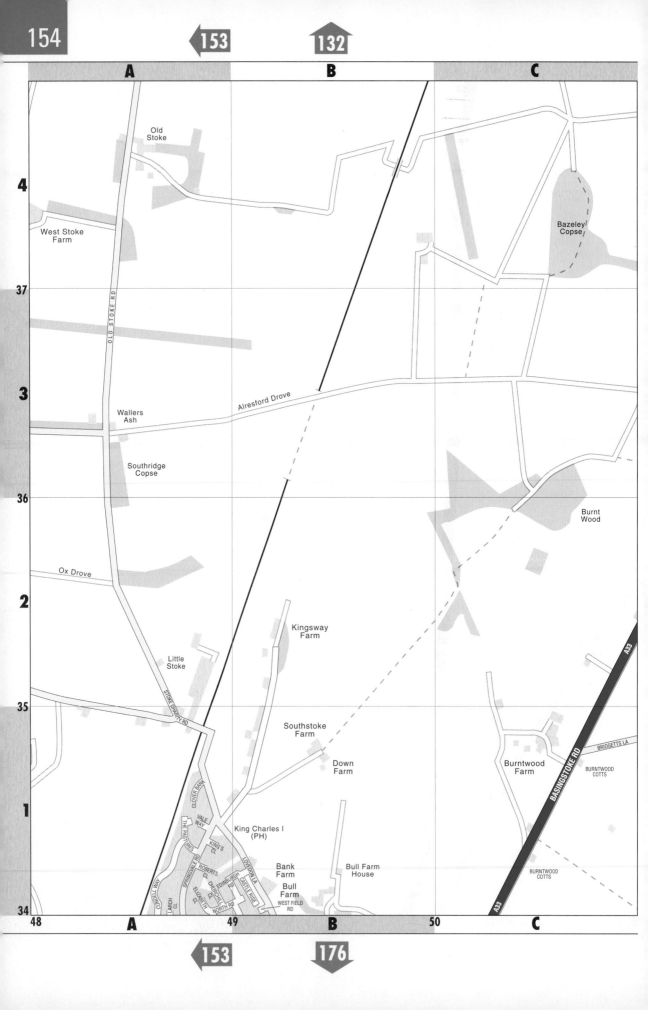

153
132

A　　　　B　　　　C

4

Old Stoke

West Stoke Farm

Bazeley Copse

37

OLD STOKE RD

3

Alresford Drove

Wallers Ash

Southridge Copse

Burnt Wood

36

Ox Drove

2

Kingsway Farm

Little Stoke

STOKE CHARITY RD

35

Southstoke Farm

Down Farm

Burntwood Farm

BRIDGETTS LA

BURNTWOOD COTTS

A33

BASINGSTOKE RD

CLOVER BANK

1

VALE WAY

KING'S CL

King Charles I (PH)

LOVEDON LA

THE PASTURES

SPRINGVALE RD

ROBERTS CL

EDINBURGH RD

CHURCHILL CL

CASTLE RISE

Bank Farm

Bull Farm House

Bull Farm

BURNTWOOD COTTS

CUNDELL WAY

LARCH CL

ELIZABETH CL

NORTH RD

WEST FIELD RD

34

48　　　　A　　　　49　　　　B　　　　50　　　　C

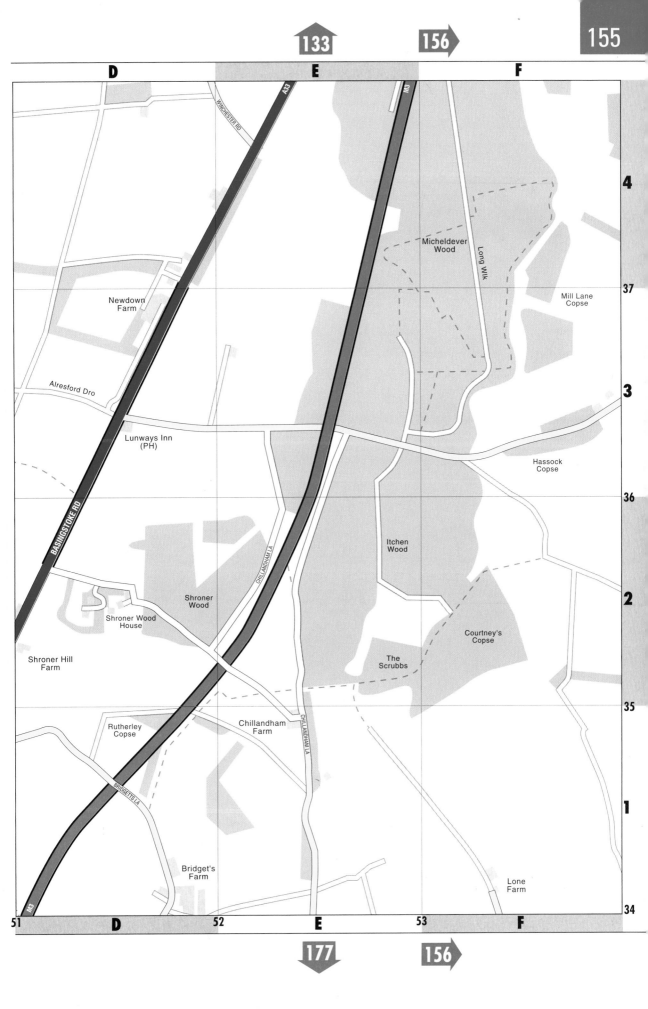

D E F

4

37

3

36

2

35

1

34

WINCHESTER RD

A33

M3

Micheldever Wood

Long Wlk

Mill Lane Copse

Newdown Farm

Alresford Dro

Hassock Copse

Lunways Inn (PH)

BASINGSTOKE RD

CHILLANDHAM LA

Itchen Wood

Shroner Wood

Shroner Wood House

Courtney's Copse

Shroner Hill Farm

The Scrubbs

Rutherley Copse

Chillandham Farm

CHILLANDHAM LA

BRIDGETS LA

M3

Bridget's Farm

Lone Farm

155
134

A　　　**B**　　　**C**

Lawn
Copse

Northington
Down

Kites
Hill

Northington

4

Northington Down
Farm

Lawn
Cottage

Swarraton

Northfield
Plantation

37

B3046

Piggery

Newhouse
Farm

The Grange
Farm

Newhouse

New
Lodge

3

Swarraton
Lodge

The Grange
Park

B3046

The Grange

East
Lodge

36

The Grange
Lake

2

Lynch
Row

35

Abbotstone
Farm

Wayfarers Wlk

NORTHINGTON RD

Abbotstone

1

New
Cottages

Three Castles Path

Itchen Stoke
Down

Watercress
Beds

Wayfarers Wlk

Itchen Down
Farm

34

54　　　　55　　　　56

A　　　**B**　　　**C**

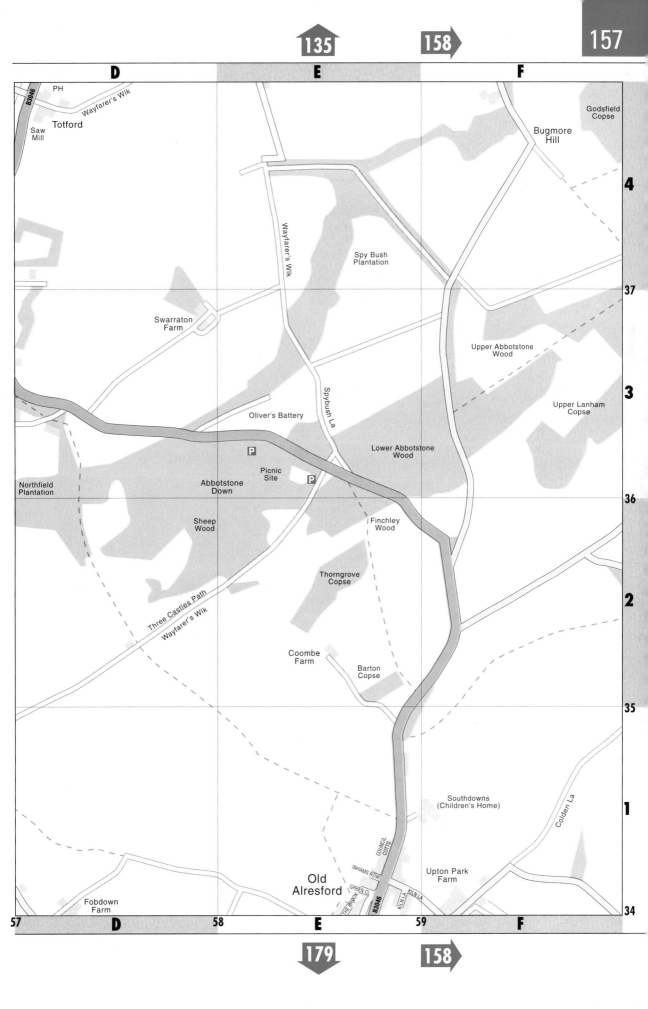

PH

B3046

Wayfarer's Wlk

Saw
Mill

Totford

Godsfield
Copse

Bugmore
Hill

4

Wayfarer's Wlk

Spy Bush
Plantation

37

Swarraton
Farm

Upper Abbotstone
Wood

Spybush La

3

Oliver's Battery

Upper Lanham
Copse

P

Lower Abbotstone
Wood

Picnic
Site

P

Northfield
Plantation

Abbotstone
Down

36

Sheep
Wood

Finchley
Wood

Thorngrove
Copse

Three Castles Path

2

Wayfarer's Wlk

Coombe
Farm

Barton
Copse

35

Southdowns
(Children's Home)

Colden La

1

COUNCIL
COTTS

INHAMS ROW

Old
Alresford

Upton Park
Farm

Fobdown
Farm

THE BROOK

GREEN CL

B3046

KILN LA

KILN LA

34

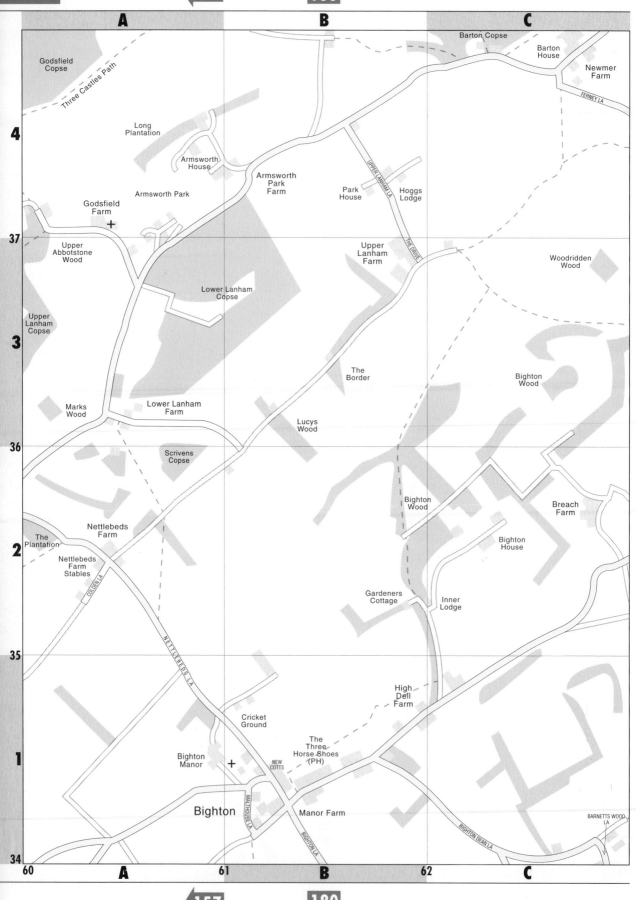

A   B   C

Godsfield
Copse

Three Castles Path

Long
Plantation

Armsworth
House

Armsworth Park

Godsfield
Farm

Upper
Abbotstone
Wood

Upper
Lanham
Copse

Marks
Wood

Lower Lanham
Farm

Scrivens
Copse

Nettlebeds
Farm

The
Plantation

Nettlebeds
Farm
Stables

Bighton
Manor

Bighton

Barton Copse

Barton
House

Newmer
Farm

FERNEY LA

Armsworth
Park
Farm

Park
House

Hoggs
Lodge

UPPER LANHAM LA

Upper
Lanham
Farm

THE DRIVE

Woodridden
Wood

Lower Lanham
Copse

The Border

Bighton
Wood

Lucys
Wood

Bighton
Wood

Breach
Farm

Bighton
House

GOLDEN LA

NETTLEBEDS LA

Gardeners
Cottage

Inner
Lodge

High
Dell
Farm

Cricket
Ground

NEW
COTTS

The
Three
Horse Shoes
(PH)

MALTHOUSE LA

BIGHTON LA

Manor Farm

BIGHTON DEAN LA

BARNETTS WOOD
LA

4

37

3

36

2

35

1

34

60   A   61   B   62   C

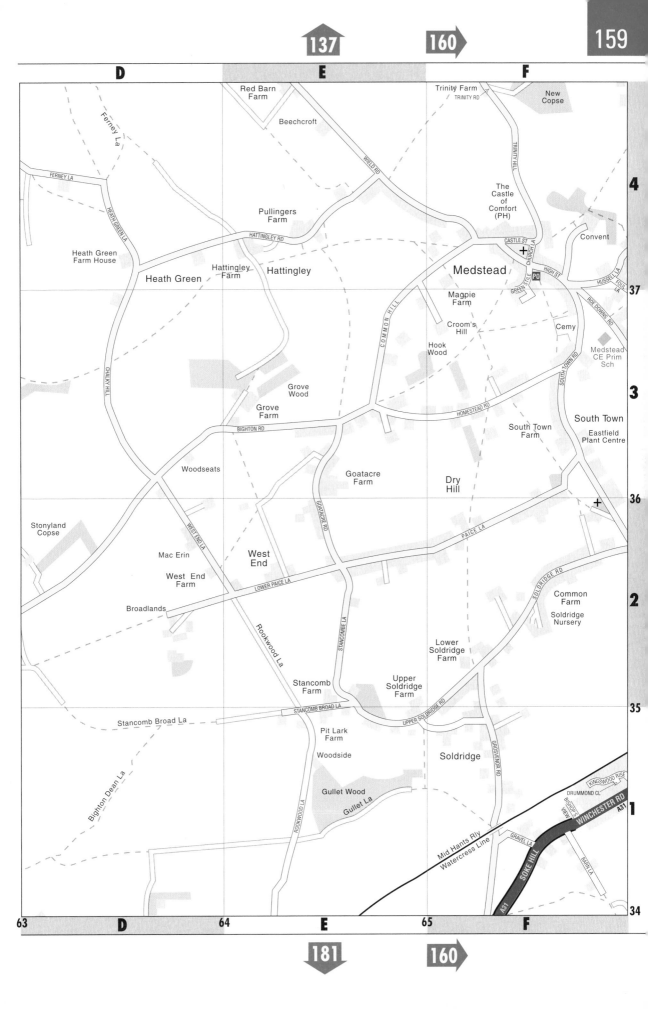

D   E   F

Red Barn Farm

Beechcroft

Trinity Farm

TRINITY RD

New Copse

Ferney La

FERNEY LA

WIELD RD

TRINITY HILL

4

HEATH GREEN LA

HATTINGLEY RD

The Castle of Comfort (PH)

Convent

Heath Green Farm House

Pullingers Farm

CASTLE ST

CHURCH LA

HIGH ST

HUSSELL LA

FOLL LA

Heath Green

Hattingley Farm

Hattingley

Medstead

GREEN STILE

PO

37

CHALKY HILL

COMMON HILL

Magpie Farm

Croom's Hill

Hook Wood

Cemy

ROE DOWNS RD

Medstead CE Prim Sch

Grove Wood

3

Grove Farm

BIGHTON RD

HOMESTEAD RD

South Town

South Town Farm

SOUTH TOWN RD

South Town

Eastfield Plant Centre

Woodseats

Goatacre Farm

Dry Hill

36

Stonyland Copse

WEST END LA

GOATACRE RD

PAICE LA

Mac Erin

West End

SOLDRIDGE RD

Common Farm

West End Farm

LOWER PAICE LA

Soldridge Nursery

2

Broadlands

ROOKWOOD LA

STANCOMBE LA

Lower Soldridge Farm

Stancomb Farm

Upper Soldridge Farm

STANCOMB BROAD LA

UPPER SOLDRIDGE RD

35

Stancomb Broad La

GROSVENOR RD

Bighton Dean La

Pit Lark Farm

Woodside

Soldridge

KINGSWOOD RISE

DRUMMOND CL

ROOKWOOD LA

Gullet Wood

Gullet La

BISHOP'S VIEW

WINCHESTER RD

A31

1

Mid Hants Rly Watercress Line

GRAVEL LA

SOKE HILL

BARN LA

A31

34

63   D   64   E   65   F

159
138

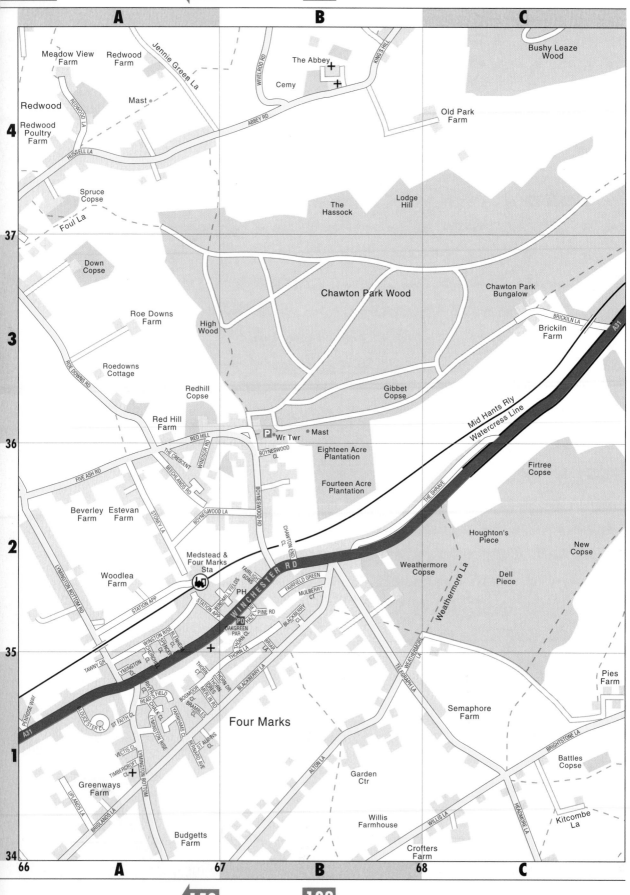

Meadow View Farm
Redwood Farm
Jennie Green La
The Abbey
Cemy
Bushy Leaze Wood

Redwood
Mast
Old Park Farm

Redwood Poultry Farm
REDWOOD LA
ABBEY RD
HUSSELL LA
WIVELROD RD
KING'S HILL

Spruce Copse
The Hassock
Lodge Hill

Foul La
Chawton Park Bungalow

Down Copse
Chawton Park Wood
BRICKILN LA
Brickiln Farm
A31

Roe Downs Farm
High Wood

Roedowns Cottage
Gibbet Copse

ROE DOWNS RD
Redhill Copse
Mid Hants Rly
Watercress Line

Red Hill Farm
RED HILL
WINDSOR RD
P
Wr Twr
Mast
Firtree Copse

THE CRESCENT
BOYNESWOOD CL
Eighteen Acre Plantation

FIVE ASH RD
BEECHLANDS RD
BOYNESWOOD RD
Fourteen Acre Plantation
THE SHRAVE
Houghton's Piece
New Copse

Beverley Farm
Estevan Farm
STONEY LA
BOYNES-WOOD LA
CHAWTON END CL

Woodlea Farm
Medstead & Four Marks Sta
WINCHESTER RD
Weathermore Copse
Weathermore La
Dell Piece

LYMINGTON BOTTOM RD
PH
FAIRLIGHT GDNS
WINDMILL FIELDS
FAIRFIELD GREEN
MULBERRY CT

STATION APP
STATION APP
PO
PINE RD
BLACKBERRY CL
Pies Farm

WINSTON RISE
OAKGREEN PAR
THORN LA
BRIAR
BLACKBERRY LA
TELEGRAPH LA
WEATHERMORE

TAWNY GR
LYMINGTON CL
CHURCH CL
SPENCER CL
THORN CL
THORN DR

PENROSE WAY
GLOUCESTER CL
ST FAITH CL
READ'S FIELD
CHALK CL
BOGMOOR CL
MERLIN RD
BRAMBLES CL
Semaphore Farm
BRIGHTSTONE LA
Battles Copse

A31
VECTIS CL
TIMBERCROFT CL
LYMINGTON RISE
LYMINGTON BOTTOM
WARNHAMS CL
ST ALBINS CL
BERNARD AVE
Four Marks
ALTON LA
HEADMORE LA
Kitcombe La

Greenways Farm
UPLANDS LA
BRISLANDS LA
Garden Ctr

Budgetts Farm
Willis Farmhouse
WILLIS LA
Crofters Farm

159
182

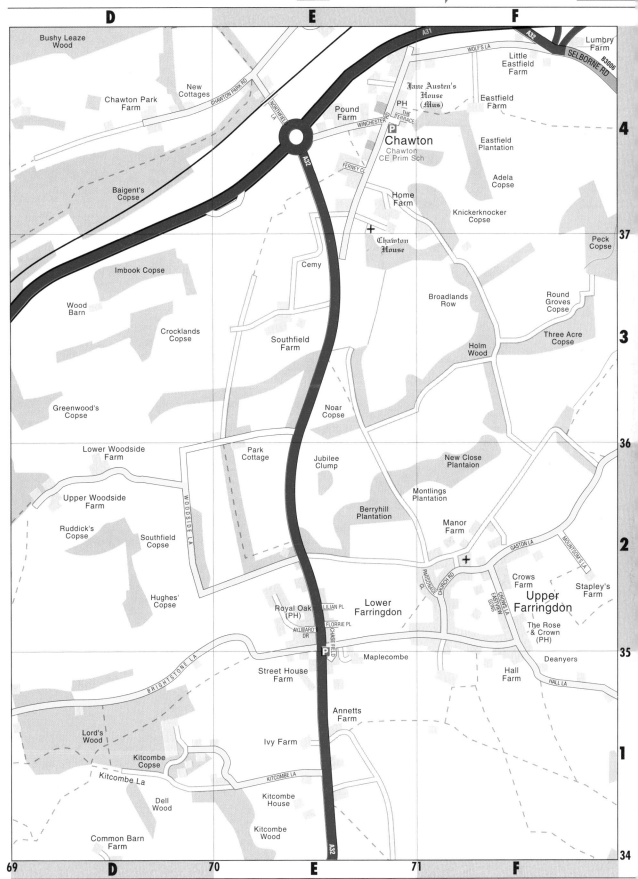

D
E
F

Bushy Leaze Wood

A31

A32

WOLF'S LA

Little Eastfield Farm

Lumbry Farm

SELBORNE RD

B3006

New Cottages

CHAWTON PARK RD

Chawton Park Farm

NORTHFIELD LA

Pound Farm

PH

THE TERRACE

Jane Austen's House (Mus)

Eastfield Farm

4

WINCHESTER RD

P

Chawton

Eastfield Plantation

Baigent's Copse

A32

Chawton CE Prim Sch

FERNEY CL

Home Farm

Adela Copse

Knickerknocker Copse

Imbook Copse

Cemy

Chawton House

37

Peck Copse

Wood Barn

Broadlands Row

Round Groves Copse

Crocklands Copse

Southfield Farm

Holm Wood

Three Acre Copse

3

Greenwood's Copse

Noar Copse

Lower Woodside Farm

Park Cottage

Jubilee Clump

New Close Plantaion

36

Upper Woodside Farm

WOODSIDE LA

Montlings Plantation

Ruddick's Copse

Southfield Copse

Berryhill Plantation

Manor Farm

GASTON LA

MOUNTSOM'S LA

2

Hughes' Copse

PARSONAGE CL

CHURCH RD

Crows Farm

Stapley's Farm

Upper Farringdon

Royal Oak (PH)

LILIAN PL

Lower Farringdon

CROWS LA

EASTVIEW GDNS

AYLWARD'S DR

FLORRIE PL

CHASE FIELD

The Rose & Crown (PH)

P

Maplecombe

35

BRIGHTSTONE LA

Street House Farm

Hall Farm

Deanyers

HALL LA

Lord's Wood

Annetts Farm

Kitcombe Copse

Ivy Farm

1

Kitcombe La

KITCOMBE LA

Dell Wood

Kitcombe House

Common Barn Farm

Kitcombe Wood

A32

34

69
D
70
E
71
F

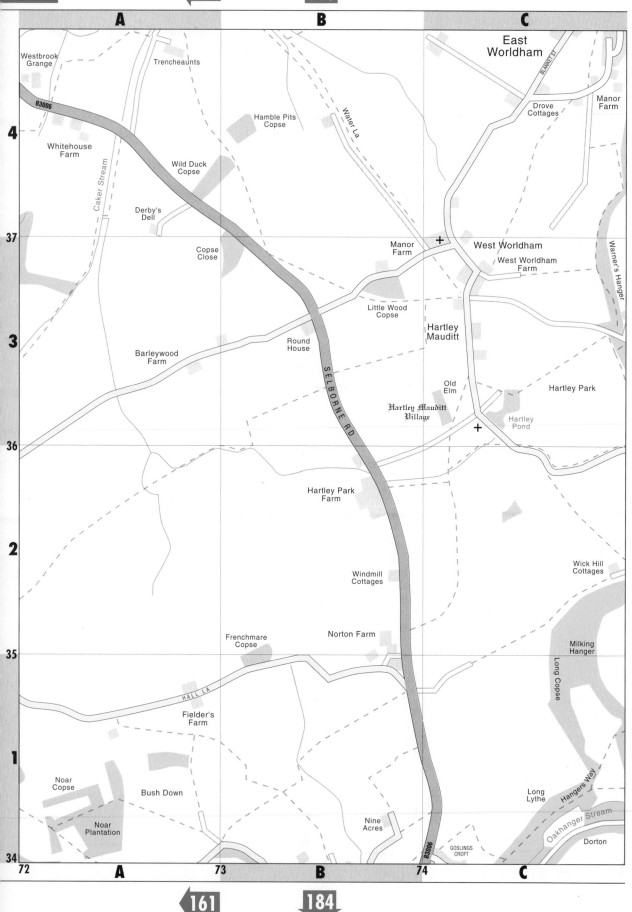

A

B

C

East
Worldham

Westbrook
Grange

Trencheaunts

BLANKET ST

Drove
Cottages

Manor
Farm

B3006

Hamble Pits
Copse

Water La

4

Whitehouse
Farm

Wild Duck
Copse

Caker Stream

Derby's
Dell

Manor
Farm

+

West Worldham

West Worldham
Farm

Warner's Hanger

37

Copse
Close

Little Wood
Copse

Hartley
Mauditt

Barleywood
Farm

Round
House

SELBORNE RD

Old
Elm

Hartley Park

3

Hartley Mauditt
Village

+

Hartley
Pond

36

Hartley Park
Farm

Wick Hill
Cottages

2

Windmill
Cottages

Milking
Hanger

Frenchmare
Copse

Norton Farm

Long Copse

35

HALL LA

Fielder's
Farm

Hangers Way

1

Noar
Copse

Bush Down

Long
Lythe

Oakhanger Stream

Noar
Plantation

Nine
Acres

B3006

GOSLINGS
CROFT

Dorton

34

72

A

73

B

74

C

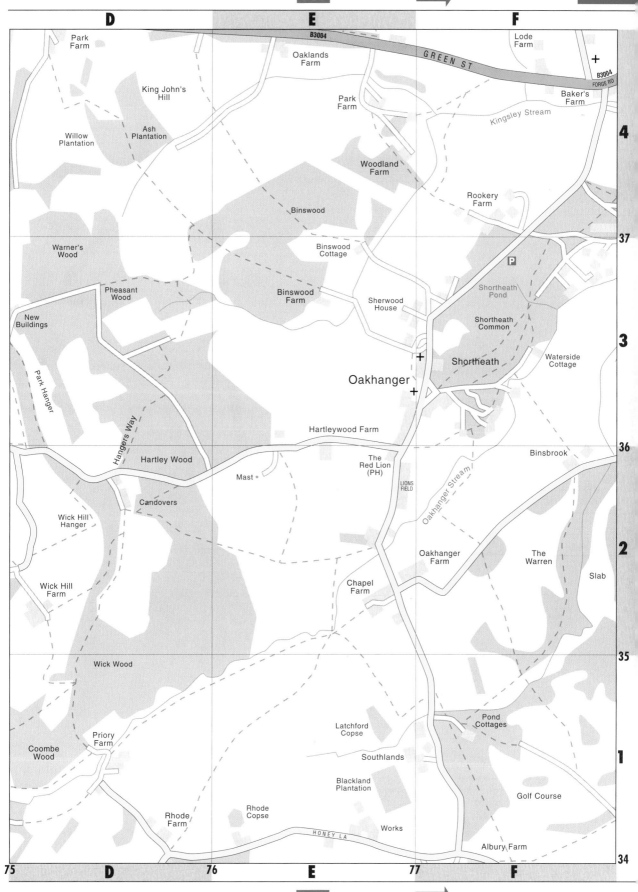

B3004

Park
Farm

Oaklands
Farm

GREEN ST

Lode
Farm

B3004
FORGE RD

King John's
Hill

Park
Farm

Baker's
Farm

Kingsley Stream

4

Willow
Plantation

Ash
Plantation

Woodland
Farm

Rookery
Farm

Warner's
Wood

Binswood

Binswood
Cottage

37

P

Shortheath
Pond

Pheasant
Wood

Binswood
Farm

Sherwood
House

Shortheath
Common

New
Buildings

Waterside
Cottage

Park Hanger

3

Oakhanger

Shortheath

Hangers Way

Hartleywood Farm

Hartley Wood

Mast

The
Red Lion
(PH)

Binsbrook

36

LIONS
FIELD

Oakhanger Stream

Candovers

Wick Hill
Hanger

Oakhanger
Farm

The
Warren

2

Wick Hill
Farm

Chapel
Farm

Slab

Wick Wood

35

Coombe
Wood

Priory
Farm

Latchford
Copse

Pond
Cottages

Southlands

1

Rhode
Farm

Rhode
Copse

Blackland
Plantation

Golf Course

HONEY LA

Works

Albury Farm

34

163
142

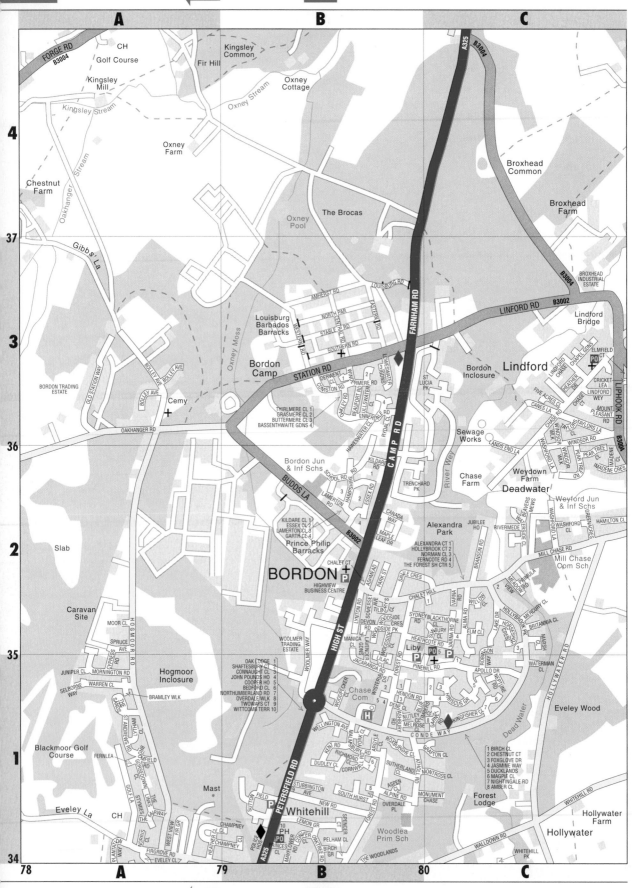

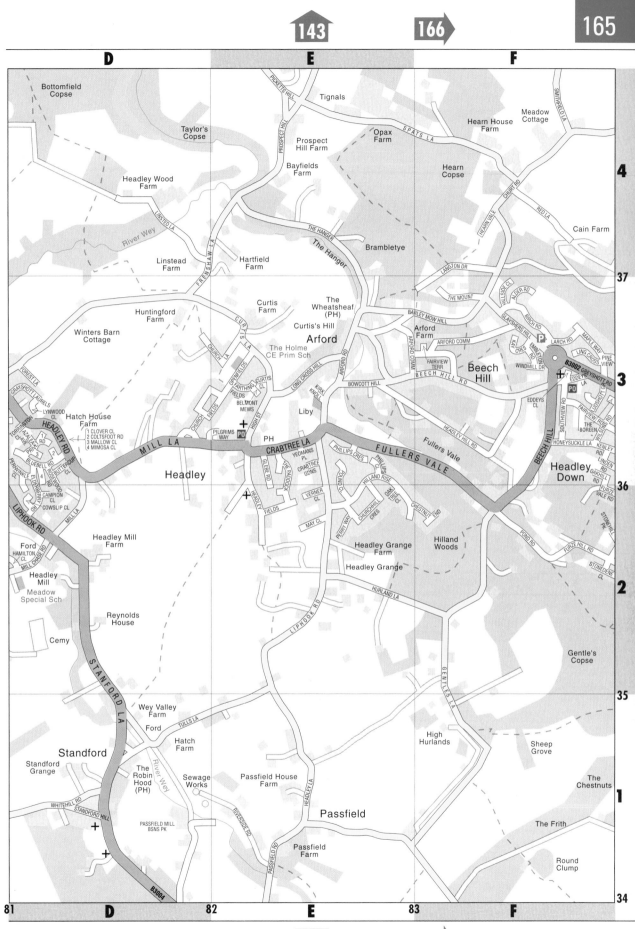

4

37

3

36

2

35

1

34

Bottomfield Copse

Taylor's Copse

Headley Wood Farm

Prospect Hill

Tignals

Prospect Hill Farm

Bayfields Farm

Opax Farm

SPATS LA

PICKETTS HILL LA

Hearn House Farm

Meadow Cottage

SMITHFIELD LA

Hearn

Hearn Copse

Cain Farm

CHURT RD

RED LA

River Wey

LINSTED LA

Linstead Farm

Hartfield Farm

FRENSHAW LA

THE HANGER

The Hanger

Brambletye

LANGTON DR

THE MOUNT

HEARN VALE

Winters Barn Cottage

Huntingford Farm

Curtis Farm

The Wheatsheaf (PH)

Curtis's Hill

Arford

CURTIS LA

CHURCH LA

BARLEY MOW HILL

Arford Farm

ARFORD COMM

Beech Hill

HILLSIDE CL

ALDER RD

BIRCH RD

GLAYSHERS HILL

KAY CRES

B3002 GREYSHOTT RD

PINE VIEW

LING CROSS HILL

MAPLE WAY

KEMLEY CL

The Holme CE Prim Sch

OPENFIELDS

DARTHING FIELDS

CURTIS CL

LONG CROSS HILL

ARFORD RD

ARFORD COMM

FAIRVIEW TERR

BEECH HILL RD

WINDMILL DR

LARCH RD

PO

EMBLETON RD

BEECH HILL

FAIRVIEW ROAD

EDDEYS CL

THE BOREEN

HONEYSUCKLE LA

KENLEY RD

LINDEN RD

FORREST LA

GRAYSHOTT LAURELS

Hatch House Farm

BELMONT MEWS

HIGHFILD

Liby

KIRK KNOLL

BOWCOTT HILL

Fullers Vale

HEADLEY HILL RD

Headley Down

FURZE VALE RD

LYNWOOD CL

TORRINGTON CL

AZALEA CL

PRIMROSE CL

BLUEBELL RD

PERIWINKLE CL

ROSEWOOD CL

BUTTERCUP CL

CAMPION CL

COWSLIP CL

1 CLOVER CL
2 COLTSFOOT RD
3 MALLOW CL
4 MIMOSA CL

HEADLEY RD

MILL LA

PILGRIMS WAY

PO

PH

Headley

CHURCH FIELDS

GLEBE RD

CRABTREE LA

THE PADDOCK

YEOMANS PL

CRABTREE GDNS

FULLERS VALE

PHILLIPS CRES

PHILLIPS CL

POND CL

HILLAND RISE

EDDEDYS CL

SOUTHVIEW RD

STONEHILL

FURZE HILL RD

STONEDENE CL

LIPHOOK RD

Ford

HAMILTON CL

Headley Mill

Meadow Special Sch

MILL CHASE RD

MILL LA

Headley Mill Farm

Reynolds House

VERNER CL

HEADLEY FIELDS

MAY CL

PERRY WAY

CHURCHILL CRES

OAK TREE CL

CHESTNUT END

Headley Grange Farm

Headley Grange

Hilland Woods

POND RD

Gentle's Copse

Cemy

STANFORD LA

LIPHOOK RD

HURLAND LA

GENTLE'S LA

Wey Valley Farm

Ford

TULLS LA

Hatch Farm

River Wey

Passfield House Farm

HEADLEY LA

High Hurlands

Sheep Grove

The Chestnuts

Standford

Standford Grange

The Robin Hood (PH)

Sewage Works

PASSFIELD MILL BSNS PK

WHITEHILL RD

STANDFORD HILL

B3004

RIVERSIDE RD

PASSFIELD RD

Passfield

Passfield Farm

The Frith

Round Clump

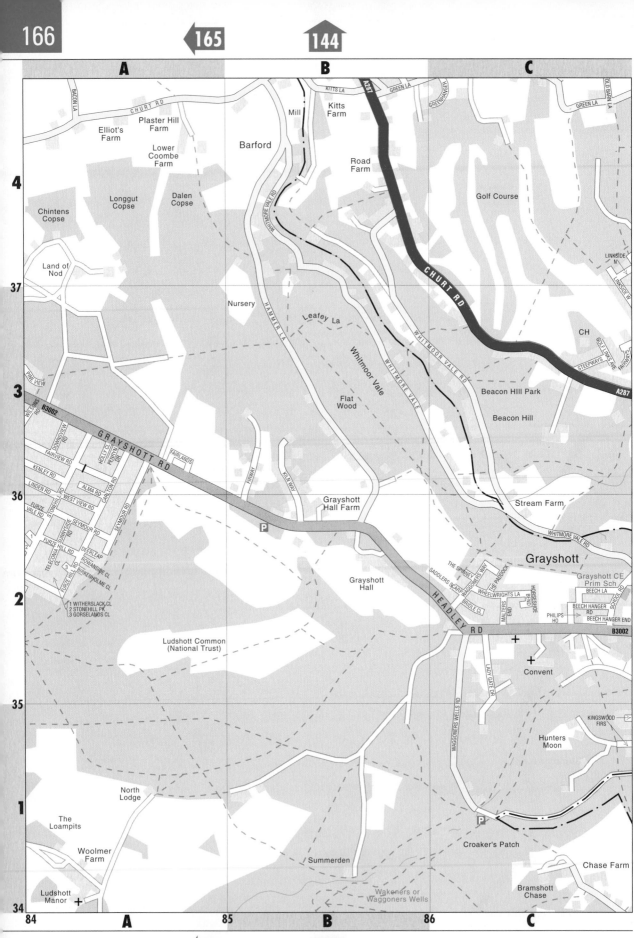

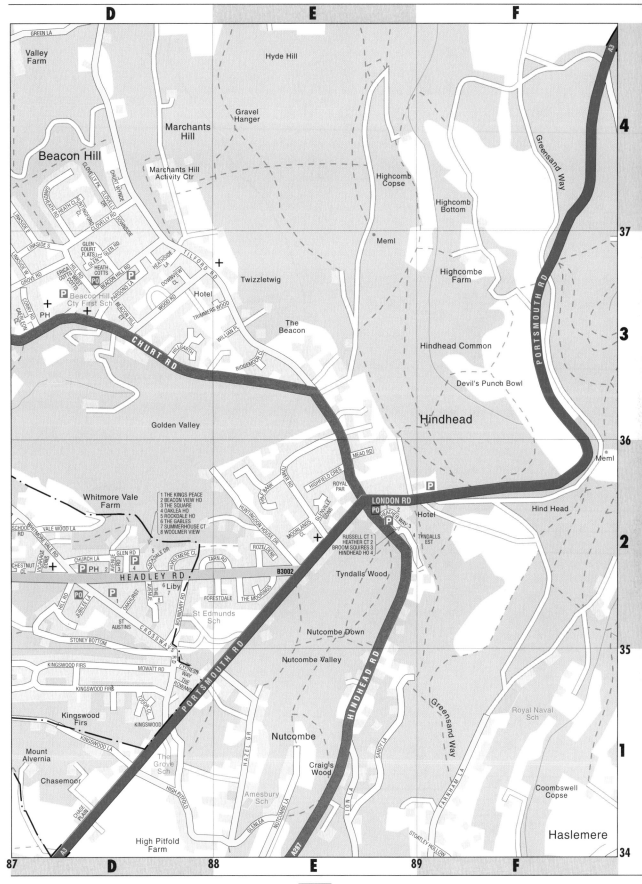

D E F

4

Valley Farm

Hyde Hill

Marchants Hill

Gravel Hanger

Beacon Hill

Greensand Way

Marchants Hill Activity Ctr

Highcomb Copse

Highcomb Bottom

37

GLEN COURT FLATS

Highcombe Farm

PORTSMOUTH RD

Meml

Twizzletwig

Hotel

3

The Beacon

Hindhead Common

CHURT RD

Golden Valley

Devil's Punch Bowl

Hindhead

36

Meml

Whitmore Vale Farm

1 THE KINGS PEACE
2 BEACON VIEW HO
3 THE SQUARE
4 OAKLEA HO
5 ROCKDALE HO
6 THE GABLES
7 SUMMERHOUSE CT
8 WOOLMER VIEW

MEAD RD

Hind Head

LONDON RD

Hotel

2

Royal Par

RUSSELL CT 1
HEATHER CT 2
BROOM SQUIRES 3
HINDHEAD HO 4

TYNDALLS EST

HEADLEY RD

B3002

Tyndalls Wood

Liby

St Edmunds Sch

FORESTDALE

THE MOORINGS

Nutcombe Down

35

PORTSMOUTH RD

Nutcombe Valley

Greensand Way

Royal Naval Sch

Kingswood Firs

HINDHEAD RD

Kingswood

Nutcombe

1

Mount Alvernia

The Grove Sch

Chasemoor

Craigs Wood

Coombswell Copse

Amesbury Sch

High Pitfold Farm

A287

Haslemere

34

87 D 88 E 89 F

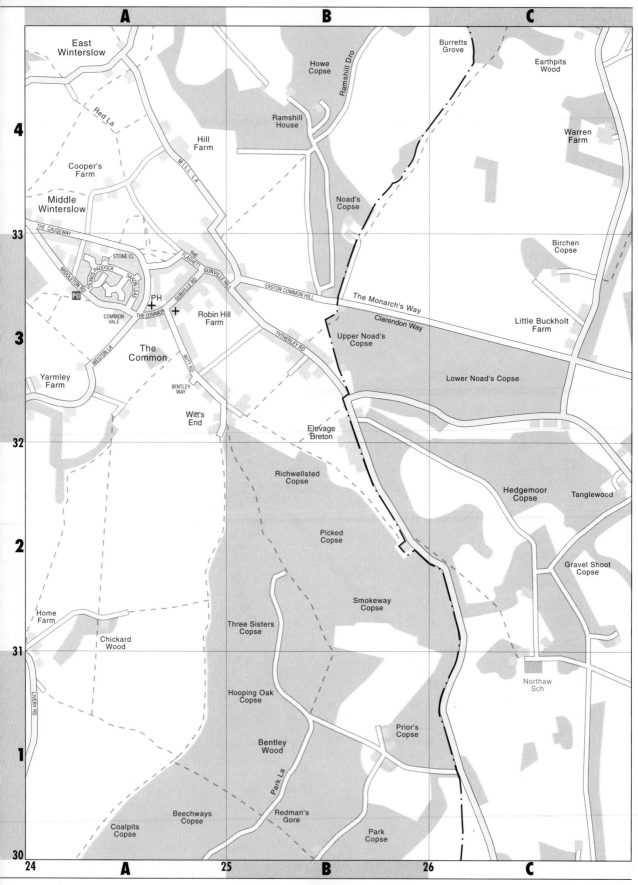

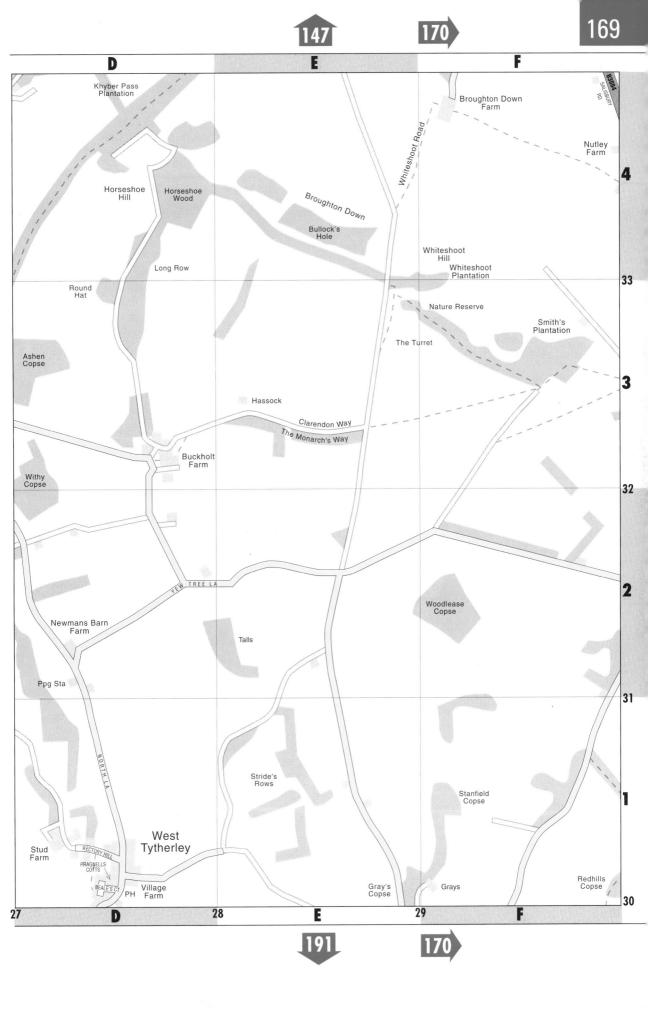

A **B** **C**

Waterloo
Farm

Works

B3084

Nutley
Farm

Manor
Farm

The Buildings

Eveley
Wood

4

SALISBURY RD

Broughton
Prim Sch

VENISON TERR
DIXONS LA

Broughton Drove

Steven's Drove

Cemy

HIGH ST

HINWOOD CL

PAYNES LA

PAYNES CL

Broughton

CHAPEL CT

CHAPEL LA

OLD FORGE GDNS

RECTORY LA

33

WHITESHOOT

PLOUGH

GUNS

GREENACRE

Broughton
House

PO

PH

QUEENWOOD RD

QUEENWOOD RISE

The Monarch's Way

Church
Farm

RUCKHOLT RD

BEECHCROFT COTTS

COOLERS FARM

ROOKERY LA

Clarendon Way

3

ROMSEY RD

The
Manse

Coolers
Farm

Wallop Brook

Hyde
Farm

SOUTH RD

Ford

Hayter's
Farm

Hayter's
Copse

Clarendon Way

Balls
Plantation

32

Broughton
Hill

THE HOLLOW

Roake
Farm

HORSEBRIDGE RD

Avenue
Cottages

Honeycomb

2

Little
Wood

BEECH TREE WLK

Fir Hill

31

Hildon
House

Queenwood
Farm

Queenwood Avenue

Acorn
Ground

Heywood
Farm

1

Dumore
Copse

Straits Copse

Crown
Farm

Copse
Corner

Redhills
Copse

B3084

30

30 **A** **31** **B** **32** **C**

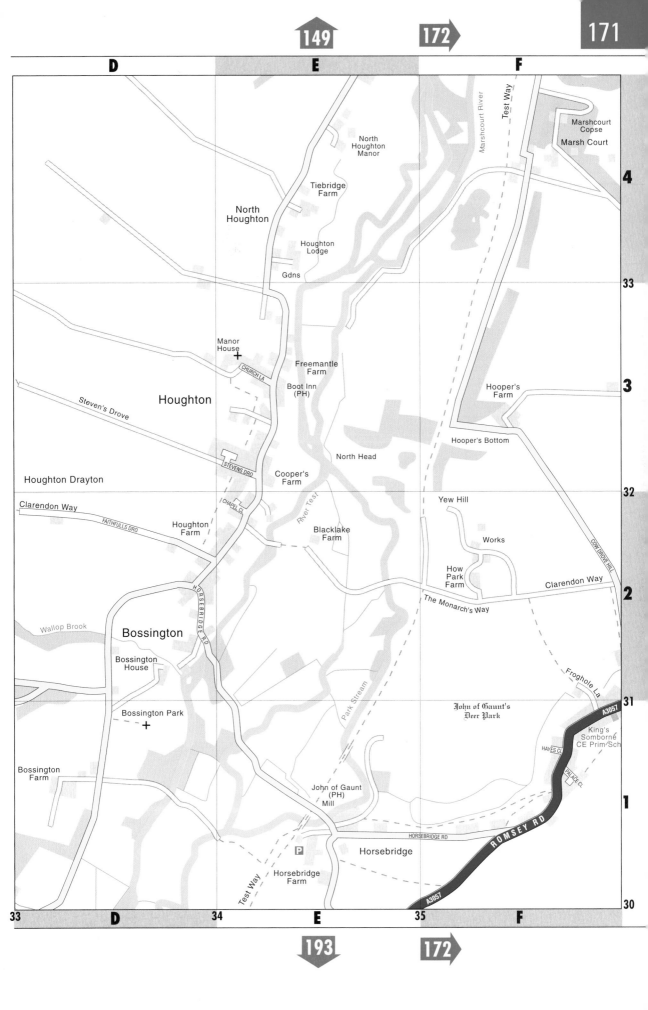

D E F

4

33

3

32

2

31

1

30

Marshcourt River
Test Way
Marshcourt Copse
Marsh Court

North Houghton Manor

Tiebridge Farm

North Houghton

Houghton Lodge
Gdns

Hooper's Farm

Manor House
CHURCH LA
Freemantle Farm
Boot Inn (PH)

Houghton

Steven's Drove

Hooper's Bottom

North Head

STEVENS DRO

Houghton Drayton

Cooper's Farm

Yew Hill

Clarendon Way
FAITHFULLS DRO

CHAPEL CL

Houghton Farm

Blacklake Farm

River Test

Works

How Park Farm

COW DROVE HILL

Clarendon Way

Wallop Brook

Bossington

HORSEBRIDGE RD

The Monarch's Way

Bossington House

Park Stream

Frognole La

Bossington Park

John of Gaunt's Deer Park

A3057

King's Somborné CE Prim Sch

HAYES CL

Bossington Farm

John of Gaunt (PH) Mill

PALACE CL

P

HORSEBRIDGE RD

Horsebridge

ROMSEY RD

Test Way

Horsebridge Farm

A3057

171
150

A B C

4

A3057

Marshcourt Farm

North Park Farm

Windovers

Whitehall

North Park Wood

Winter Down Copse

SOMBORNE PARK RD

WHITEHALL RD

33

Little Somborne House

Little Somborne

Park Farm

3

New Lease Farm

CHALK HILL

32

CHALK VALE

Chalkvale Cottage

COW DROVE HILL
Cemy

New Farm

Ashley Manor Farm

Ashley

2

STOCKBRIDGE RD
A3057

Recn Gd

NEW LA

Manor Farm

RIVERSIDE CL

WINCHESTER RD

MUSS LA

NUTCHERS DRO

Ashley Glebe Farm

ROMSEY RD

OLD VICARAGE LA

31

THE CROSS

PO

Ashley Manor

Old Palace Farm

CHURCH RD

King's Somborne

Allot Gdns

Brickkiln Drove

THE GORRINGS

SCOTT CL

ELDON CL

SOPWITH CL

1

HUMBERS VIEW

Ashley New Buildings

Clarendon Way

ELDON RD

FURZEDOWN RD

30

36 A 37 B 38 C

171
194

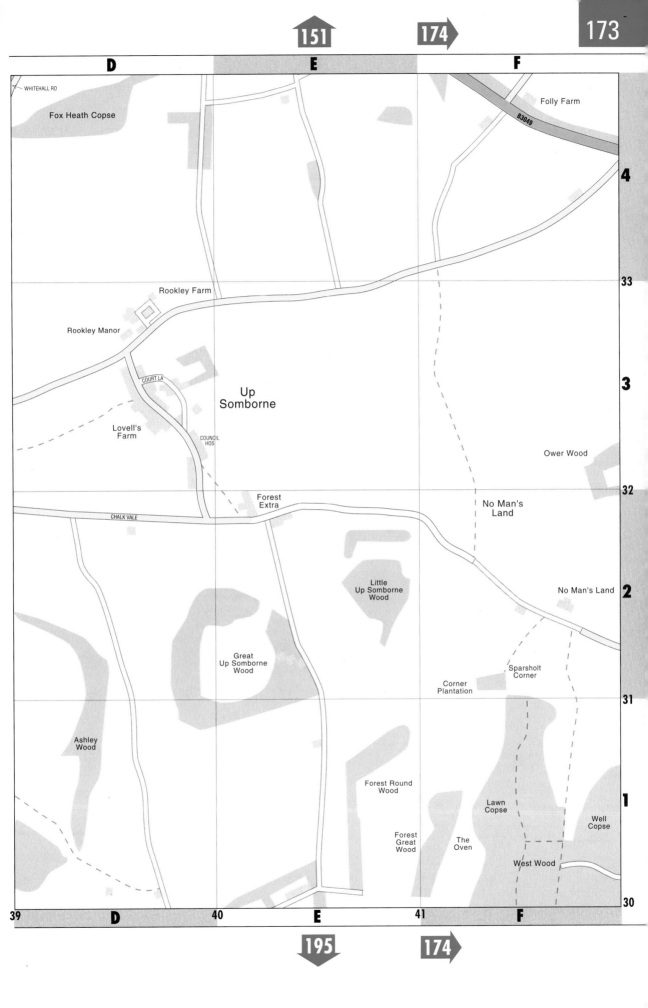

151
174

D **E** **F**

WHITEHALL RD

Fox Heath Copse

Folly Farm

B3049

4

33

Rookley Farm

Rookley Manor

COURT LA

Up
Somborne

3

Lovell's
Farm

COUNCIL
HOS

Ower Wood

Forest
Extra

No Man's
Land

32

CHALK VALE

No Man's Land

2

Little
Up Somborne
Wood

Great
Up Somborne
Wood

Sparsholt
Corner

Corner
Plantation

31

Ashley
Wood

Forest Round
Wood

Lawn
Copse

Well
Copse

1

Forest
Great
Wood

The
Oven

West Wood

30

39 **D** 40 **E** 41 **F**

A B C

173

152

Rack Belt

B3049
PH
RACK & MANGER
COTTS

Kirton
Farm

Littleton
House

Long
Park

4

STOCKBRIDGE RD

Ball Down
Service Station

Cradle
Copse

Long
Wood

33

Ball Down
Farm

Northwood Park
Farm

3

Bushmoor
Copse

Northwood
Park

Westley

WESTLEY LA

B3049

32

Sparsholt Coll
Hampshire

HILLSIDE
COTTS

WESTLEY
COTTS

Privet
Copse

Lainston
House
Hotel

Lainston
Farm

St Peter's
Church

2

Moor Court
Farm

MOOR COURT LA

LOCK'S LA

CHURCH LA

HOME LA

LAMBOURNE CL

The Plough Inn
(PH)

WATLEY LA

Dean

Dean
Farm

Newbarn
Farm

Sparsholt CE
Prim Sch

PO

Sparsholt

WOODMAN LA

WOODMAN CL

BOSTOCK CL

Church
Farm

DEAN LA

31

SHEDDON
PL

Well Copse

Ham Green

1

Burrow Road

Stockers Down

Lanham
Plantation

Heath's
Copse

West Wood

Rabbit
Warren

30

42 43 44

A B C

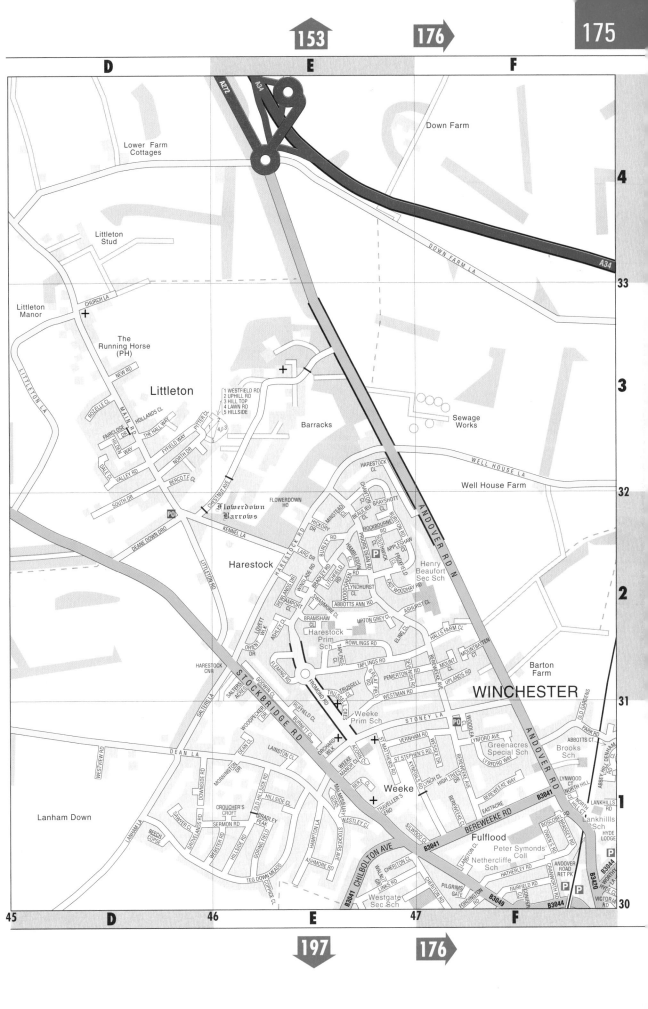

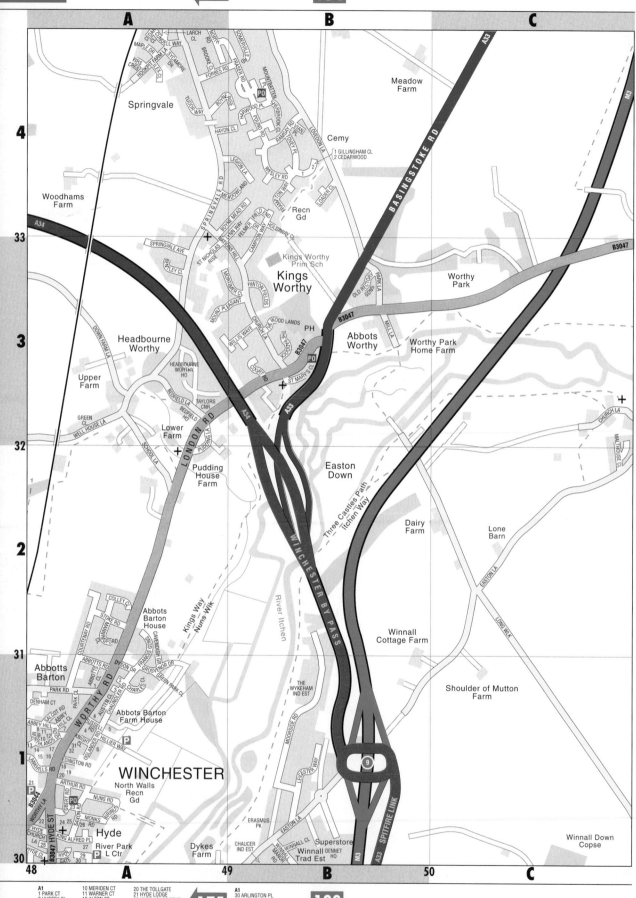

A1
1 PARK CT
2 HUSSEY CL
3 CORAM CL
4 CONEY GN
5 SIMONDS CT
6 COLBOURNE CT
7 COVENTRY CT
8 KENILWORTH CT
9 STRATFORD CT
10 MERIDEN CT
11 WARNER CT
12 ALTON CT
13 WARWICK CL
14 WARWICK CT
15 TWYFORD CT
16 FARINGDON CT
17 REGENT CT
18 WOODLANDS CT
19 DONNINGTON CT
20 THE TOLLGATE
21 HYDE LODGE
22 HYDE HOUSE GDNS
23 DANES RD
24 HYDE CHURCH PATH
25 BARTHOLOMEW CL
26 ST BEDE'S CT
27 ALSWITHA TERR
28 ROSEWARNE CT
29 KING ALFRED TERR

A1
30 ARLINGTON PL
31 DALZELL
32 YORK HO

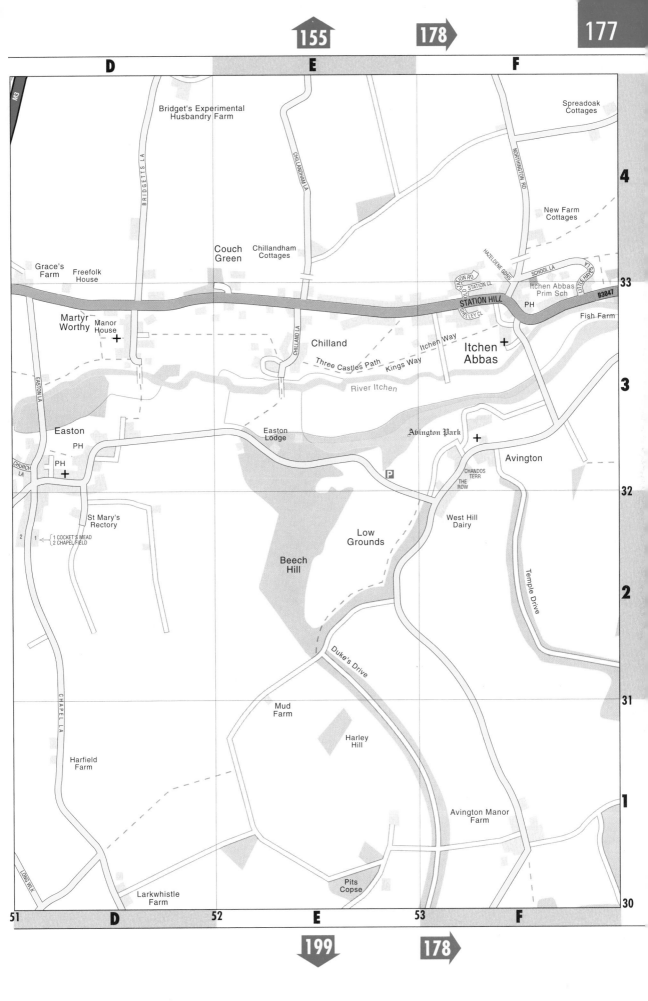

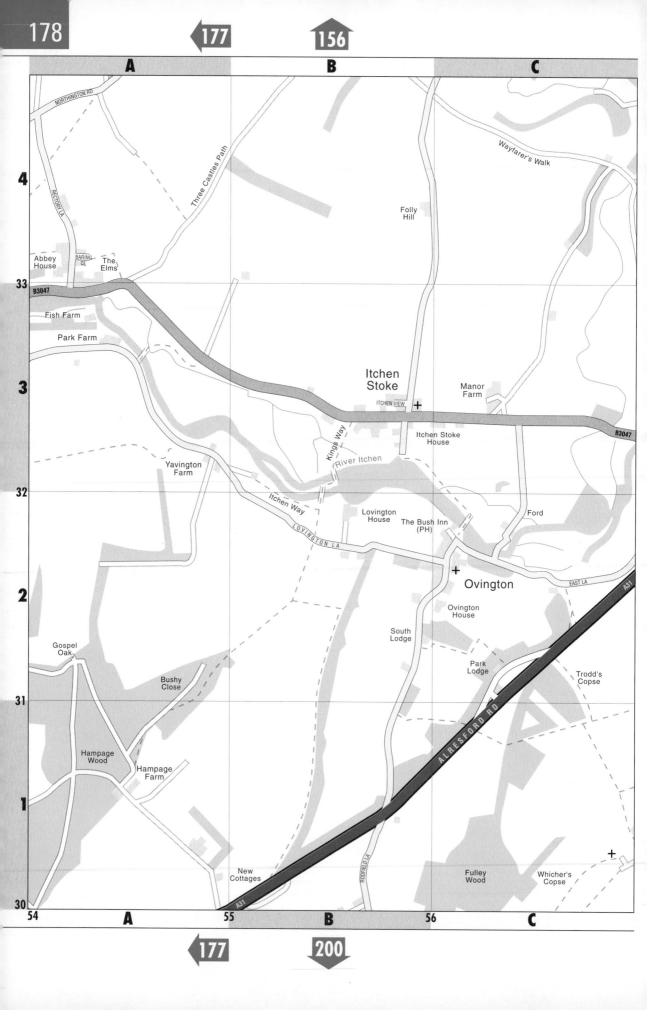

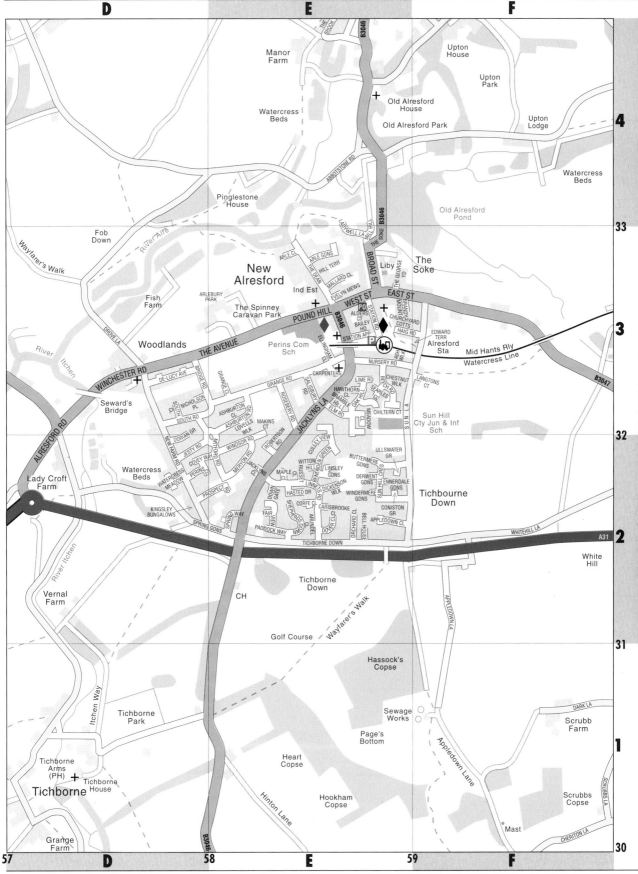

D E F

4

33

3

32

2

31

1

30

Manor Farm

Watercress Beds

Old Alresford House

Old Alresford Park

Upton House

Upton Park

Upton Lodge

Watercress Beds

Pinglestone House

Old Alresford Pond

Fob Down

River Arle

New Alresford

Arle Cl
Arle Gdns
Hill Terr
The Dean
Hill Rd
Mallard Cl
Evelyn Mews

Liby

The George Yd

The Soke

BROAD ST

Fish Farm

ARLEBURY PARK

The Spinney Caravan Park

Ind Est

WEST ST
EAST ST

PO

ALDERS CT
BAILEY HO
STATION APP

CHURCHYARD COTTS
HAIG RD

MOUNT PL
BRANDON
ASH GROVE

Edward Terr

Woodlands

POUND HILL

B3046

EL INGHAM

Alresford Sta

Mid Hants Rly
Watercress Line

B3047

DROVE LA

THE AVENUE

Perins Com Sch

STATION RD

WINCHESTER RD

DE-LUCY AVE

BRIDGE RD

GRANGE CL

Grange Rd

SALISBURY RD

ROSEBERY RD

CARPENTERS

JACKLYNS LA

NURSERY RD

LIME RD

HAWTHORN CL

CHESTNUT WLK

BEECH RD

ASH RD

Langtons CT

River Itchen

Seward's Bridge

NICHOLSON PL

SOUTH CL

ASHBURTON CL

ASHBURTON CT

MAKINS WLK

BRAMBLE CL

HILL CL

ELM RD

MEADOW

CHILTERN CT

SEARLES

SUN LA

Sun Hill Cty Jun & Inf Sch

ALRESFORD RD

SOUTH RD

NEW FARM RD

DORIAN GR

JESTY RD

WINDSOR RD

MERYON RD

COVEY WAY

PERINS

ROBERTSON RD

JACKLYNS CL

CULLEY VIEW

WITTON HILL

MAPLE CL

BENED... GREEN

RUSSET CL

LINSLEY GDNS

DICKENSON WLK

DERWENT GDNS

ULLSWATER GR

BUTTERMERE GDNS

ENNERDALE GDNS

WINDERMERE GDNS

Tichbourne Down

Watercress Beds

WATERCRESS MEADOW

PROSPECT RD

DOWN GATE

SHEPHERDS DOWN

HASTED DR

LINNES CL

CORFE CL

CARISBROOKE CL

ARUNDEL CL

ORCHARD CL

CONISTON GR

APPLEDOWN CL

BELL HOUSE

Tichbourne Down

Lady Croft Farm

Kingsley Bungalows

SPRING GDNS

SPRING WAY

FAIR VIEW DR

PADDOCK WAY

DOCK CL

TICHBORNE DOWN

WHITEHILL LA

A31

White Hill

Vernal Farm

River Itchen

CH

Tichborne Down

Golf Course

Wayfarer's Walk

Hassock's Copse

Sewage Works

Scrubb Farm

DARK LA

Tichborne Park

Page's Bottom

APPLEDOWN LANE

SCRUBBS LA

Itchen Way

Heart Copse

Tichborne Arms (PH)

Tichborne House

Tichborne

Hinton Lane

Hookham Copse

Mast

Scrubbs Copse

CHERITON LA

Grange Farm

B3046

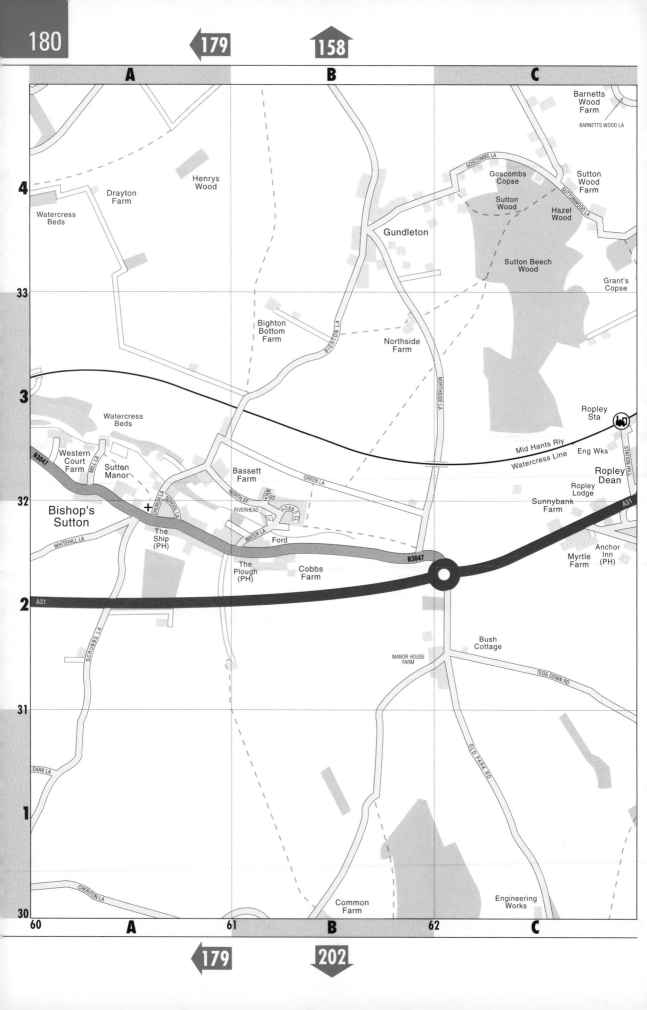

A   **B**   **C**

Barnetts
Wood
Farm

BARNETTS WOOD LA

GOSCOMBS LA

Goscombs
Copse

Sutton
Wood
Farm

4

Drayton
Farm

Henrys
Wood

Sutton
Wood

Hazel
Wood

SUTTONWOOD LA

Watercress
Beds

Gundleton

Sutton Beech
Wood

Grant's
Copse

33

Bighton
Bottom
Farm

Northside
Farm

BIGHTON LA

NORTHSIDE LA

Ropley
Sta

3

Watercress
Beds

Mid Hants Rly

Watercress Line

Eng Wks

Ropley
Dean

STATION HILL

B3047

Western
Court
Farm

MILL LA

Sutton
Manor

Bassett
Farm

GREEN LA

Ropley
Lodge

Sunnybank
Farm

A31

32

Bishop's
Sutton

CHURCH LA

SCHOOL LA

NORTH ST

HOME CL

RIVERHEAD

HOBBS CL

The
Ship
(PH)

WATER LA

Ford

Cobbs
Farm

B3047

Myrtle
Farm

Anchor
Inn
(PH)

WHITEHILL LA

The
Plough
(PH)

Bush
Cottage

2

A31

MANOR HOUSE
FARM

TEGG DOWN RD

SCRUBBS LA

31

OLD PARK RD

DARK LA

1

CHERITON LA

Common
Farm

Engineering
Works

30

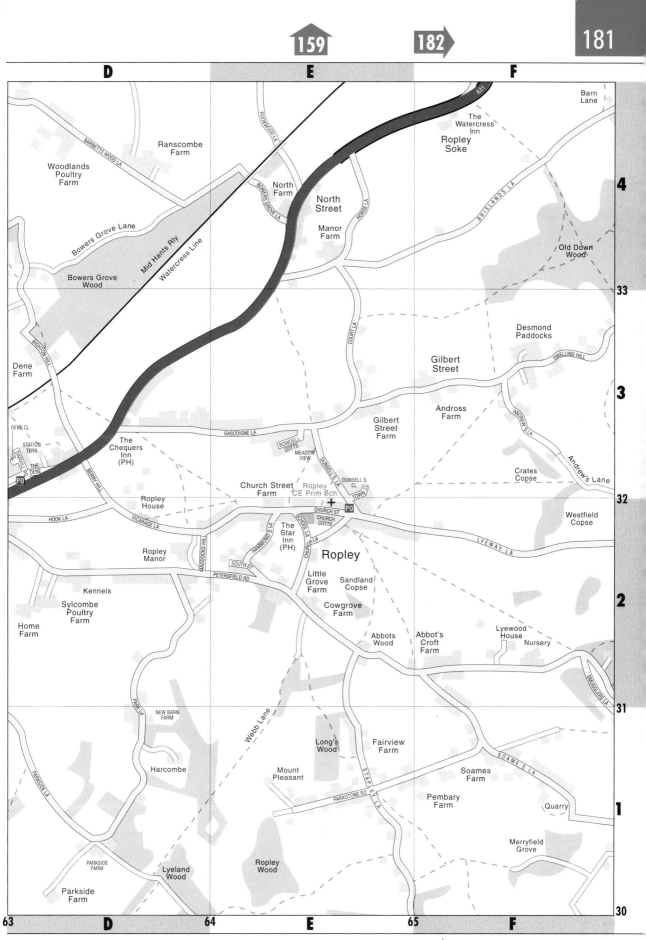

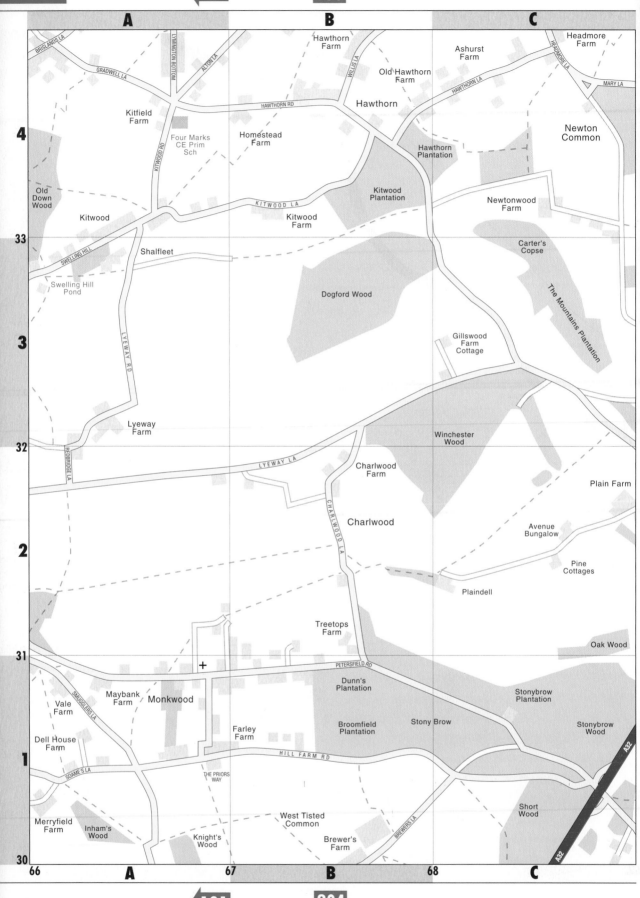

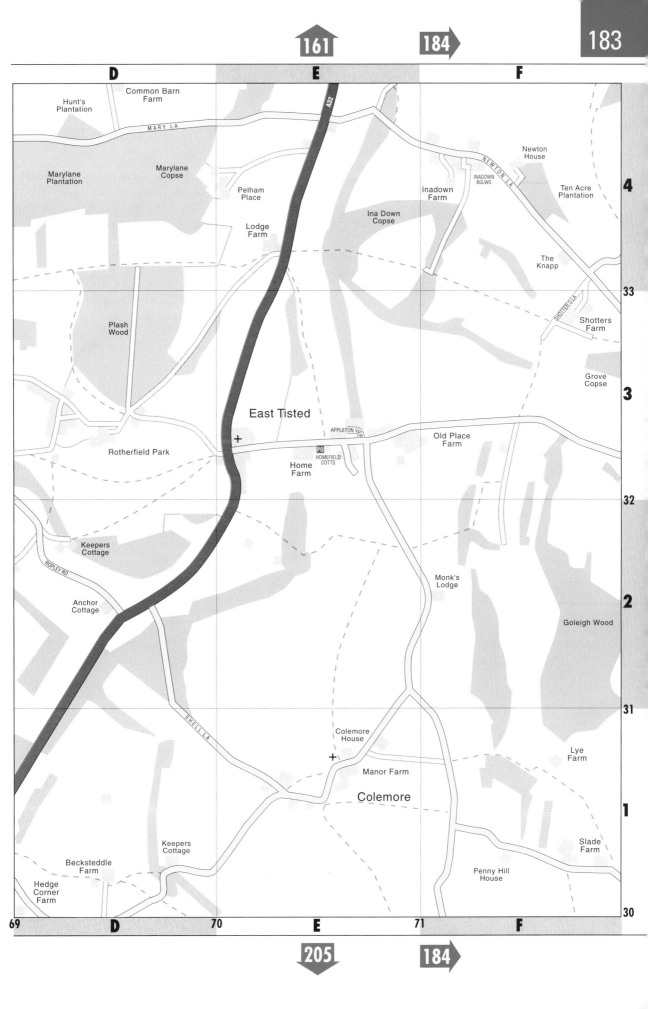

D
E
F

Hunt's Plantation

Common Barn Farm

MARY LA

A32

Marylane Plantation

Marylane Copse

Pelham Place

Newton House

NEWTON LA

Inadown Farm

INADOWN BGLWS

Ten Acre Plantation

4

Lodge Farm

Ina Down Copse

The Knapp

33

Plash Wood

SHOTTER'S LA

Shotters Farm

Grove Copse

3

East Tisted

APPLETON VIEW

Old Place Farm

Rotherfield Park

PO
HOMEFIELD COTTS

Home Farm

32

Keepers Cottage

ROPLEY RD

Monk's Lodge

Anchor Cottage

2

Goleigh Wood

31

SHELL LA

Colemore House

Lye Farm

Manor Farm

Colemore

1

Keepers Cottage

Slade Farm

Becksteddle Farm

Hedge Corner Farm

Penny Hill House

30

69
D
70
E
71
F

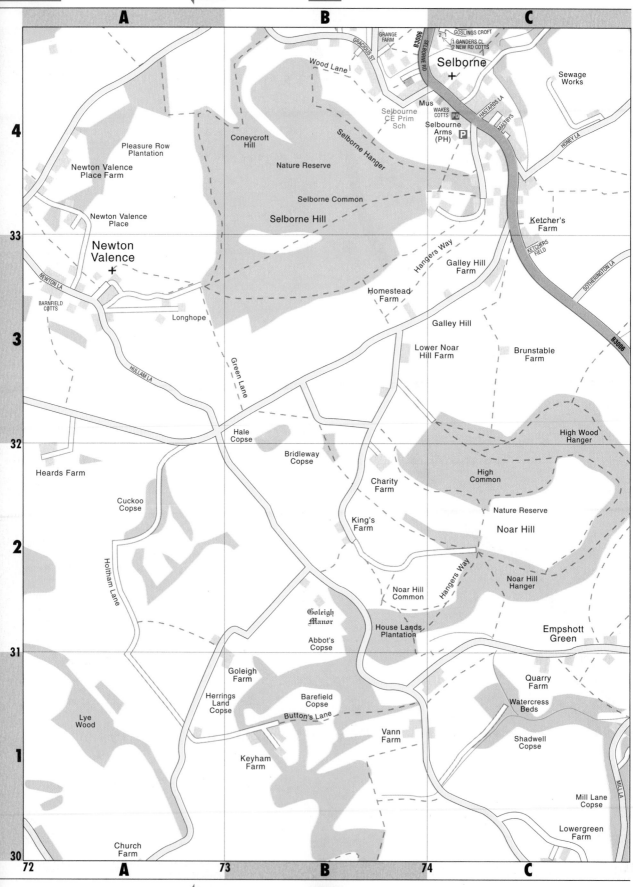

183 162

A B C

4

Pleasure Row
Plantation

Newton Valence
Place Farm

Coneycroft
Hill

Wood Lane

GRACIOUS ST

GRANGE
FARM

GOSLINGS CROFT
1 GANDERS CL
2 NEW RD COTTS

Selborne

Sewage
Works

Selbourne
CE Prim
Sch

Mus

WAKES
COTTS

Selbourne
Arms
(PH)

P

PO

HASTARDS LA

MALTBYS

HONEY LA

Nature Reserve

Selborne Hanger

Newton Valence
Place

Selborne Common

Selborne Hill

Ketcher's
Farm

33

**Newton
Valence**

Hangers Way

Galley Hill
Farm

KETCHERS
FIELD

KETCHERS
FIELD

SOTHERINGTON LA

NEWTON LA

Homestead
Farm

BARNFIELD
COTTS

Longhope

Galley Hill

B3006

3

HULLAM LA

Green Lane

Lower Noar
Hill Farm

Brunstable
Farm

32

Heards Farm

Hale
Copse

Bridleway
Copse

Charity
Farm

High Wood
Hanger

High
Common

Cuckoo
Copse

King's
Farm

Nature Reserve

Noar Hill

2

Holtham Lane

Noar Hill
Common

Hangers Way

Noar Hill
Hanger

Goleigh
Manor

House Lands
Plantation

Empshott
Green

Abbot's
Copse

31

Goleigh
Farm

Quarry
Farm

Herrings
Land
Copse

Barefield
Copse

Watercress
Beds

Lye
Wood

Button's Lane

Vann
Farm

Shadwell
Copse

1

Keyham
Farm

MILL LA

Mill Lane
Copse

Lowergreen
Farm

30

Church
Farm

183 206

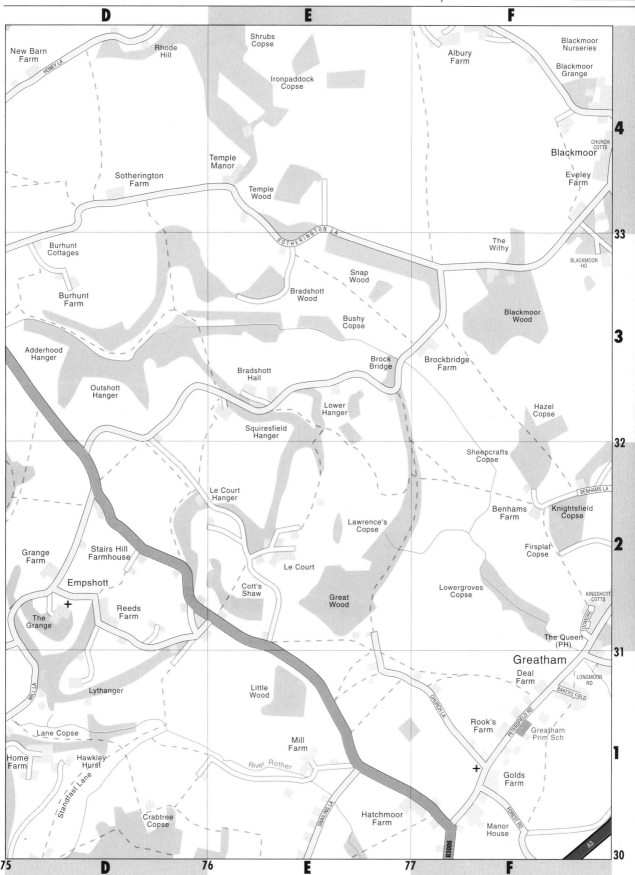

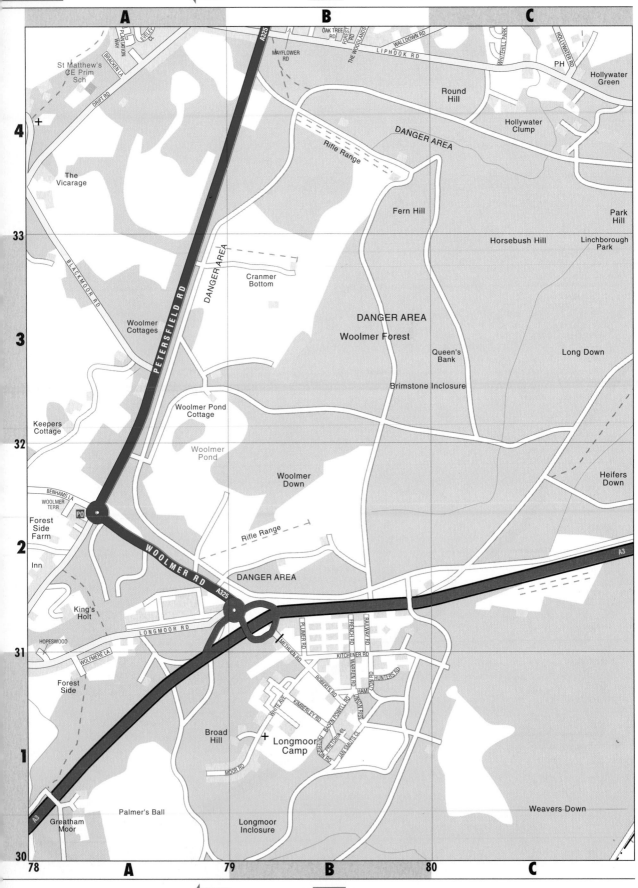

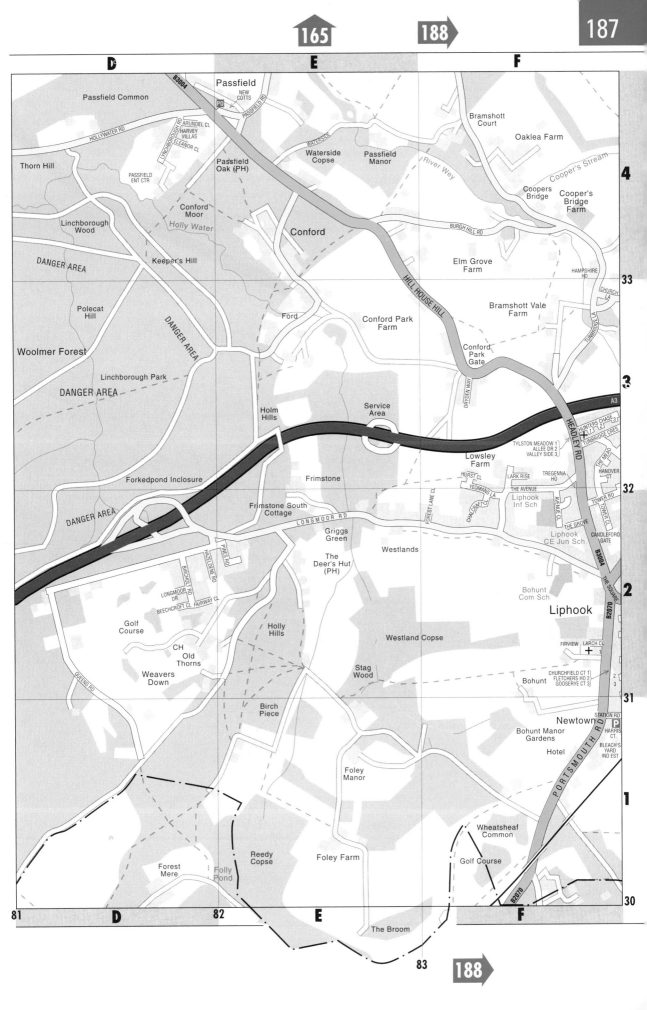

D   E   F

Passfield Common
Thorn Hill
HOLLYWATER RD
ARUNDEL CL
HARVEY VILLAS
ELEANOR CL
LYNCHBOROUGH RD
B3004
Passfield
PO
NEW COTTS
PASSFIELD RD
Passfield Oak (PH)
Conford Moor
Holly Water
Linchborough Wood
Keeper's Hill
PASSFIELD ENT CTR
WATERSIDE
Waterside Copse
Passfield Manor
River Wey
Bramshott Court
Oaklea Farm
Cooper's Stream
4

DANGER AREA
Conford
Ford
BURGH HILL RD
Coopers Bridge
Cooper's Bridge Farm

Polecat Hill
Woolmer Forest
DANGER AREA
DANGER AREA
Linchborough Park
Conford Park Farm
HILL HOUSE HILL
Elm Grove Farm
Bramshott Vale Farm
HAMPSHIRE HO
CHURCH LA
TUNBRIDGE LA
33

Holm Hills
Service Area
Conford Park Gate
DRYDEN WAY
A3
HEADLEY RD
HUNTERS CHASE
TUNBRIDGE CRES
3

DANGER AREA
Forkedpond Inclosure
Frimstone
Frimstone South Cottage
LONGMOOR RD
Griggs Green
Lowsley Farm
TYLSTON MEADOW 1
ALLEE DR 2
VALLEY SIDE 3
HURST CL
YEOMANS LA
THE AVENUE
CHALCRAFT CL
FOREST LANE CL
LARK RISE
TREGENNA HO
Liphook Inf Sch
AVENUE CL
THE GROVE
Liphook CE Jun Sch
THE MEAD
HANOVER CT
TOWER RD
TOWER CL
CANDLEFORD GATE
32

PINES RD
HAZELDENE RD
BIRCHOLT RD
LONGMOOR DR
BEECHCROFT CL
FAIRWAY CL
The Deer's Hut (PH)
Westlands
Westland Copse
Bohunt Com Sch
Liphook
B2070
B3004
THE SQUARE
2

Golf Course
Weavers Down
CH
Old Thorns
Holly Hills
Stag Wood
FIRVIEW
LARCH CL
Bohunt
CHURCHFIELD CT 1
FLETCHERS HO 2
GOOSERYE CT 3

QUEENS RD
Birch Piece
Newtown
STATION RD
HARRIS CT
BLEACH'S YARD IND EST
PORTSMOUTH RD
31

Foley Manor
Bohunt Manor Gardens
Hotel
1

Forest Mere
Folly Pond
Reedy Copse
Foley Farm
Wheatsheaf Common
Golf Course
B2070
30

81   D   82   E   F
The Broom
83

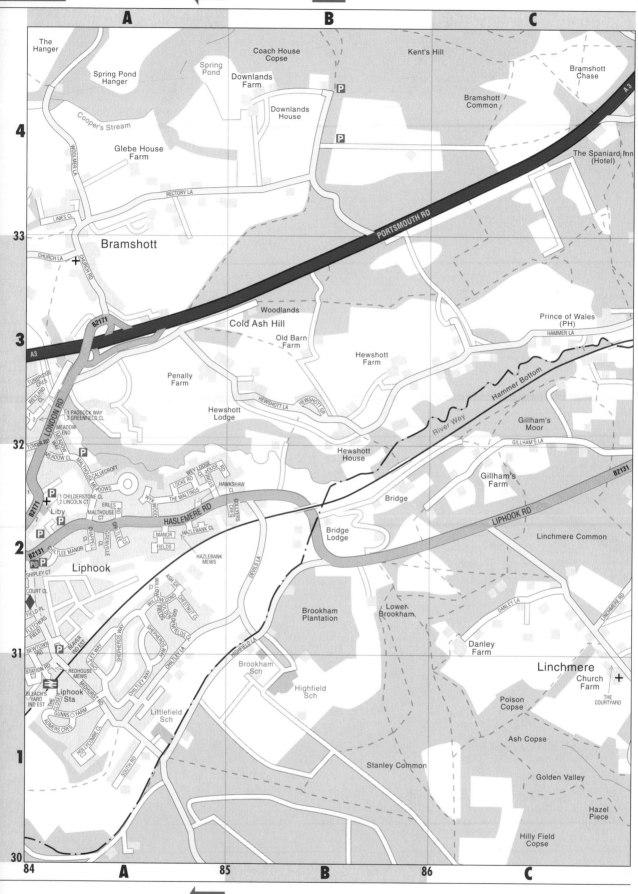

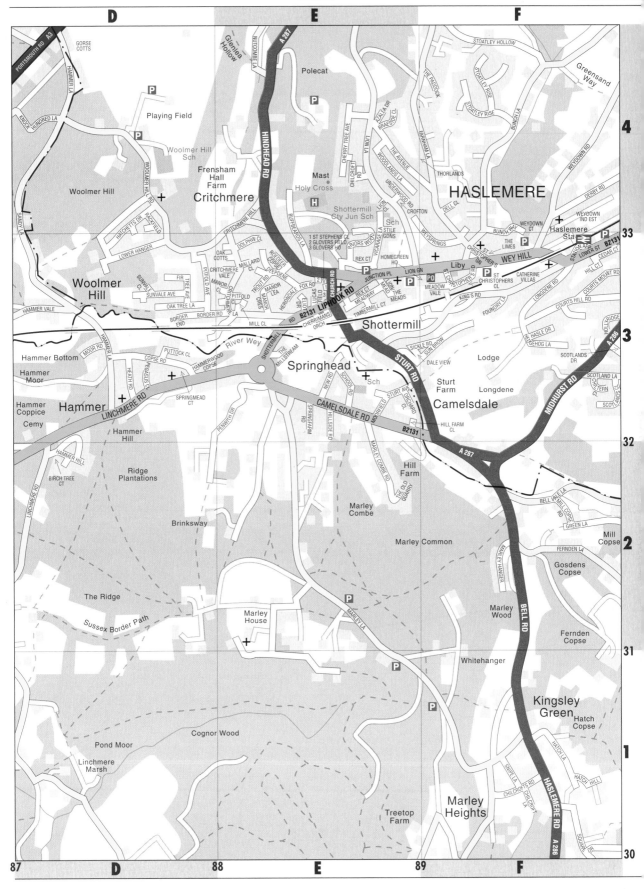

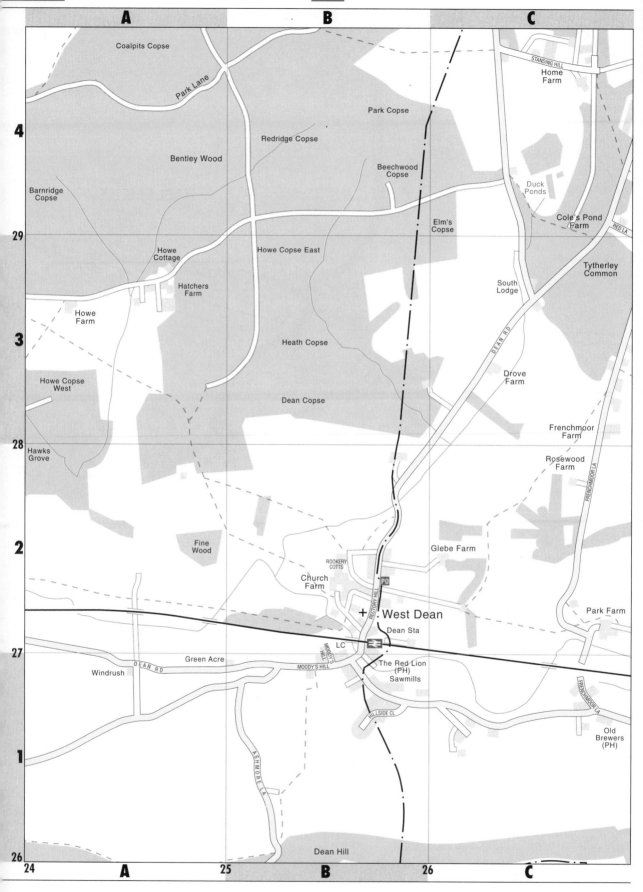

Coalpits Copse

Park Lane

Park Copse

4

Redridge Copse

Bentley Wood

Beechwood Copse

Barnridge Copse

Elm's Copse

Home Farm

STANDING HILL

Duck Ponds

Cole's Pond Farm

RED LA

29

Howe Copse East

Tytherley Common

Howe Cottage

South Lodge

Hatchers Farm

DEAN RD

Howe Farm

Drove Farm

3

Heath Copse

Howe Copse West

Frenchmoor Farm

Dean Copse

Rosewood Farm

FRENCHMOOR LA

28

Hawks Grove

Fine Wood

2

Glebe Farm

ROOKERY COTTS

Church Farm

PO

Park Farm

RECTORY HILL

+ West Dean

Dean Sta

LC

27

Green Acre

MOODY'S HILL

The Red Lion (PH)

DEAN RD

Windrush

MOODY'S HILL

Sawmills

FRENCHMOOR LA

HILLSIDE CL

Old Brewers (PH)

1

ASHMORE LA

26

Dean Hill

24   **A**   25   **B**   26   **C**

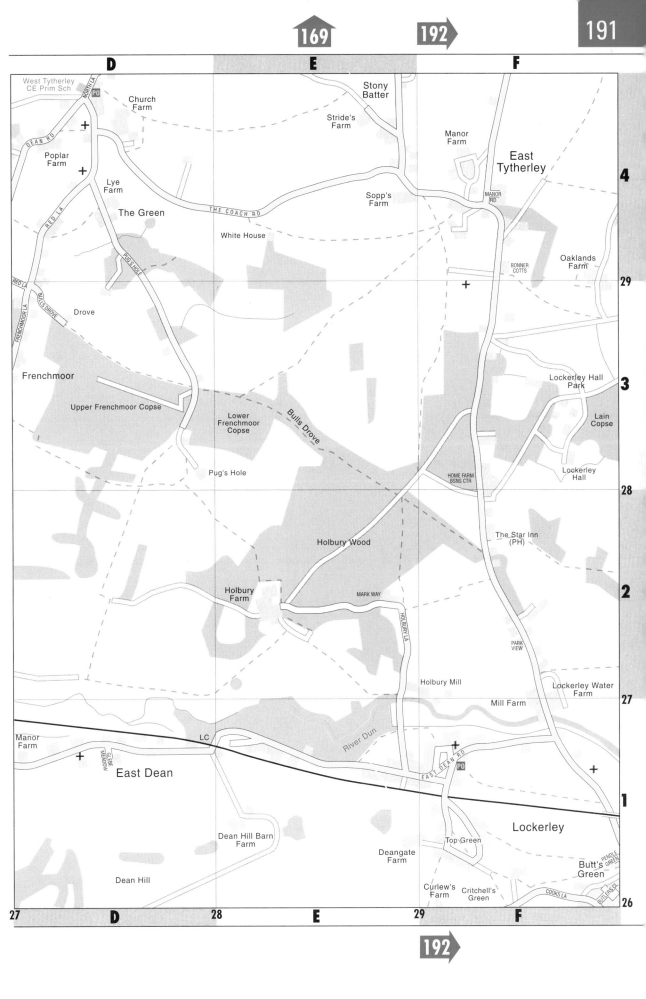

D
E
F

West Tytherley CE Prim Sch
PO
Church Farm
Stony Batter
Stride's Farm
Manor Farm
East Tytherley
4
DEAN RD
Poplar Farm
Lye Farm
The Green
Sopp's Farm
MANOR RD
RED LA
THE COACH RD
White House
BONNER COTTS
Oaklands Farm
29
PUG'S HOLE
FRENCHMOOR LA
RED LA
BULLS DROVE
Drove
Lockerley Hall Park
Frenchmoor
Upper Frenchmoor Copse
Lower Frenchmoor Copse
Bulls Drove
Lain Copse
3
Pug's Hole
HOME FARM BSNS CTR
Lockerley Hall
28
Holbury Wood
The Star Inn (PH)
Holbury Farm
MARK WAY
2
HOLBURY LA
PARK VIEW
Holbury Mill
Lockerley Water Farm
27
Mill Farm
Manor Farm
LC
River Dun
EAST DEAN RD
PO
GLEBE MEADOW
East Dean
1
Lockerley
Dean Hill Barn Farm
Top Green
Deangate Farm
Butt's Green
PENDLE GREEN
Dean Hill
Curlew's Farm
Critchell's Green
COOKS LA
BUTLERS CL
26

27
D
28
E
29
F
26

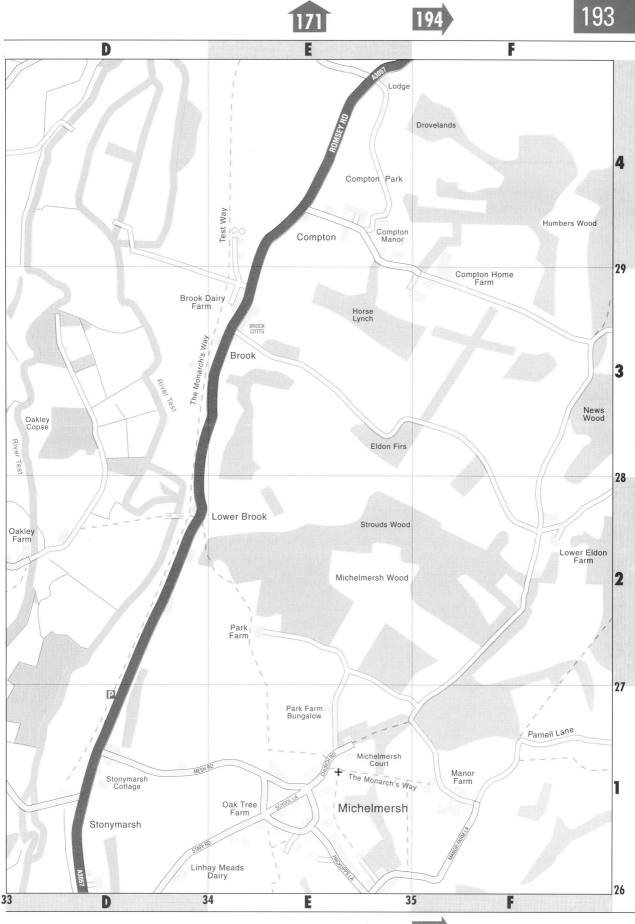

A3057

ROMSEY RD

Lodge

Drovelands

Compton Park

Humbers Wood

Test Way

Compton

Compton Manor

Compton Home Farm

Brook Dairy Farm

BROOK COTTS

The Monarch's Way

Brook

Horse Lynch

News Wood

River Test

Oakley Copse

Eldon Firs

River Test

Lower Brook

Oakley Farm

Strouds Wood

Lower Eldon Farm

Michelmersh Wood

Park Farm

Park Farm Bungalow

Parnell Lane

Stonymarsh Cottage

MESH RD

CHURCH RD

Michelmersh Court

The Monarch's Way

Manor Farm

Oak Tree Farm

SCHOOL LA

Michelmersh

Stonymarsh

A3057

STAFF RD

Linhay Meads Dairy

HACKUPS LA

MANOR FARM LA

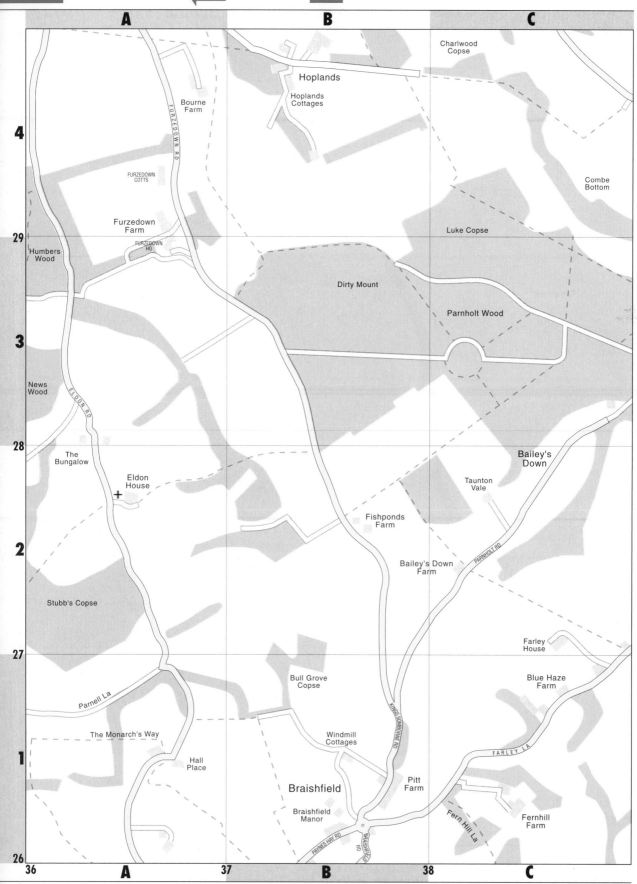

Charlwood
Copse

Hoplands

Hoplands
Cottages

Bourne
Farm

FURZEDOWN RD

4

Combe
Bottom

FURZEDOWN
COTTS

Furzedown
Farm

Luke Copse

29

FURZEDOWN
HO

Humbers
Wood

Dirty Mount

Parnholt Wood

3

ELDON RD

News
Wood

28

Bailey's
Down

The
Bungalow

Eldon
House

Taunton
Vale

Fishponds
Farm

PARNHOLT RD

2

Bailey's Down
Farm

Stubb's Copse

Farley
House

27

Bull Grove
Copse

Blue Haze
Farm

Parnell La

KINGS SOMBORNE RD

The Monarch's Way

Windmill
Cottages

FARLEY LA

1

Hall
Place

Braishfield

Pitt
Farm

Fern Hill La

Fernhill
Farm

Braishfield
Manor

PAYNES HAY RD

BRAISHFIELD

26

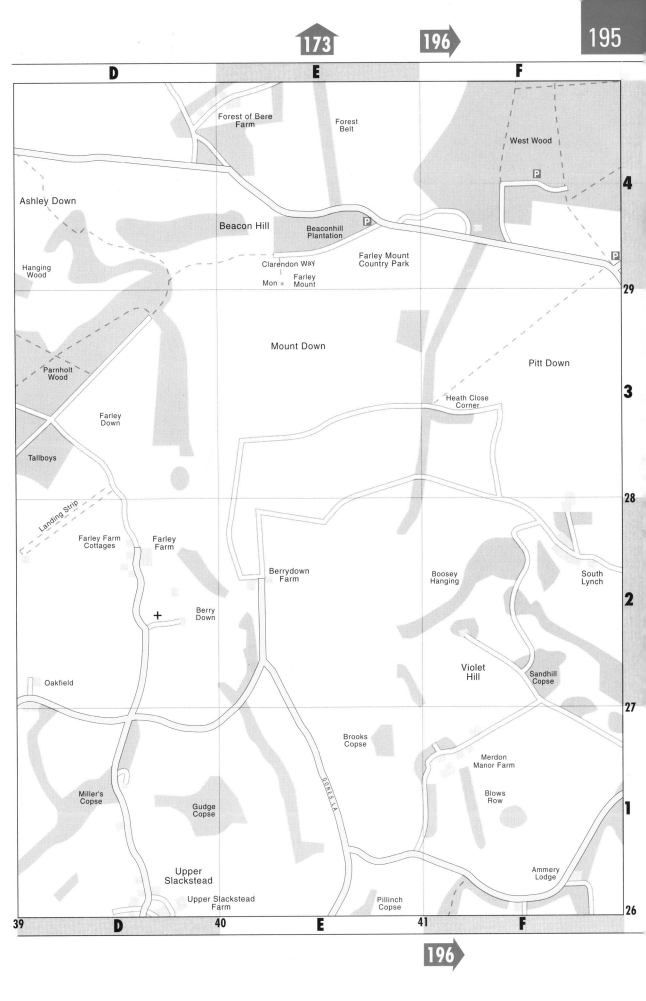

D   E   F

Forest of Bere
Farm

Forest
Belt

West Wood

P

4

Ashley Down

Beacon Hill

Beaconhill
Plantation

P

Farley Mount
Country Park

P

29

Hanging
Wood

Clarendon Way

Mon •

Farley
Mount

Mount Down

Pitt Down

Parnholt
Wood

Heath Close
Corner

3

Farley
Down

Tallboys

28

Landing Strip

Farley Farm
Cottages

Farley
Farm

Berrydown
Farm

Boosey
Hanging

South
Lynch

2

+

Berry
Down

Oakfield

Violet
Hill

Sandhill
Copse

27

Miller's
Copse

Brooks
Copse

Merdon
Manor Farm

Gudge
Copse

DORES LA

Blows
Row

1

Ammery
Lodge

Upper
Slackstead

Upper Slackstead
Farm

Pillinch
Copse

26

195
174

A   **B**   **C**

4

West Wood

Burrow Copse

Ashmore Hill Copse

Crab Wood

Crabwood Farm House

Mast

P

Clarendon Way

Crabwood House

SARUM RD

29

Pittdown Plantation

3

Pitt Down

Little Pittdown Plantation

Enmill House

Enmill Barn

Enmill LA

Vale Farm

Enmill Farm

Pitt View

28

Pages Copse

Grovelands Copse

FARLEY MOUNT RD

SPARSHOLT RD

Stopham's Copse

White House

A3090

Yew Tree

Pitt Copse

MILLERS LA

2

Larkfarm Plantation

27

Southlynch Plantation

Standon Farm

Standon

Juniper Bank

Nan Trodd's Hill

Down Farm

Butcher's Plantation

1

Merdon Castle

A3090

PORT LA

26

42   **A**   43   **B**   44   **C**

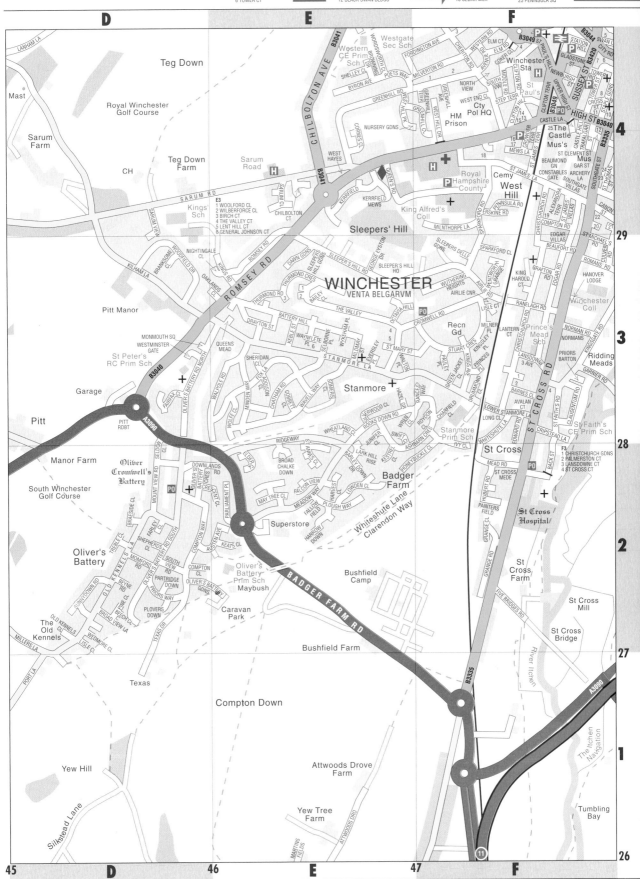

F4	F4	F4	
1 RONALD BOWKER CT	7 KINGSDALE CT	13 CLIFTON LODGE NO 1	19 FAIRLAWN HO
2 FULFLOOD CT	8 BILBERRY CT	14 CLIFTON LODGE NO 2	20 ST MICHAEL'S GDNS
3 FORDINGTON RD	9 FABERS YD	15 ARBOUR CT	21 CULVERWELL GDNS
4 SPICER CT	10 CHARLECOTE MEWS	16 MACKLIN HO	22 MALT HO
5 CAPITAL HO	11 ST PAULS PL	17 HIGHFIELD TERR	23 LIONS HALL
6 TOWER CT	12 BLACK SWAN BLDGS	18 CEDAR WLK	24 ST THOMAS' PAS
			25 PENINSULA SQ

175 **198** **197**

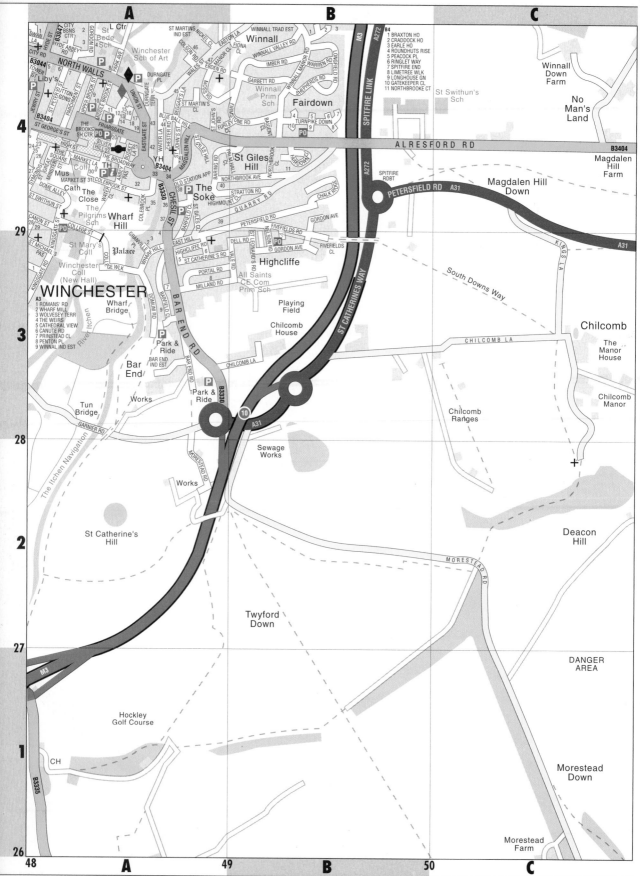

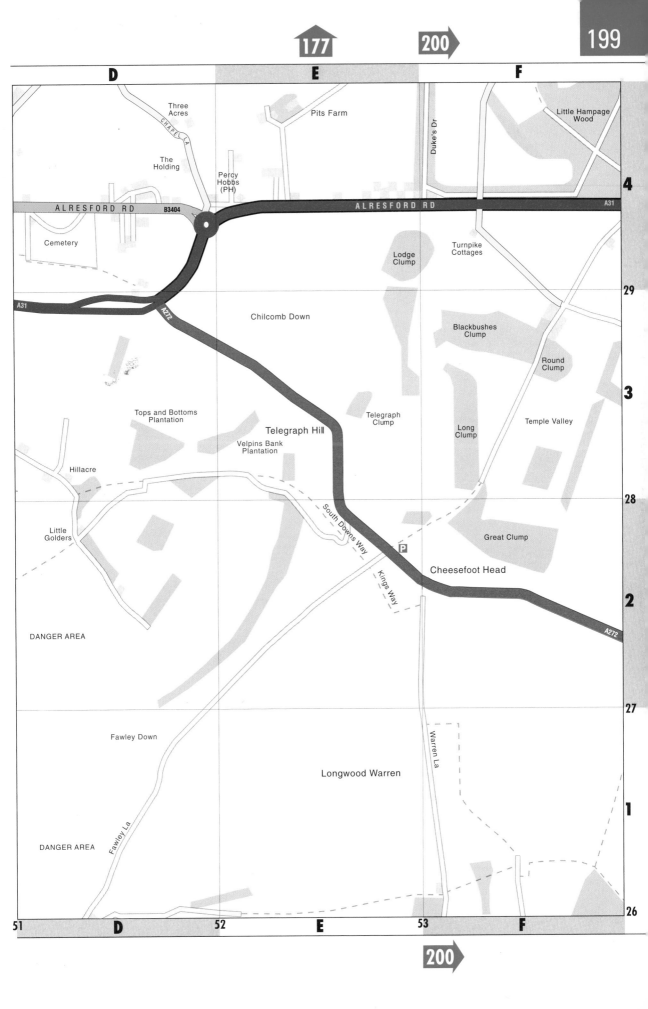

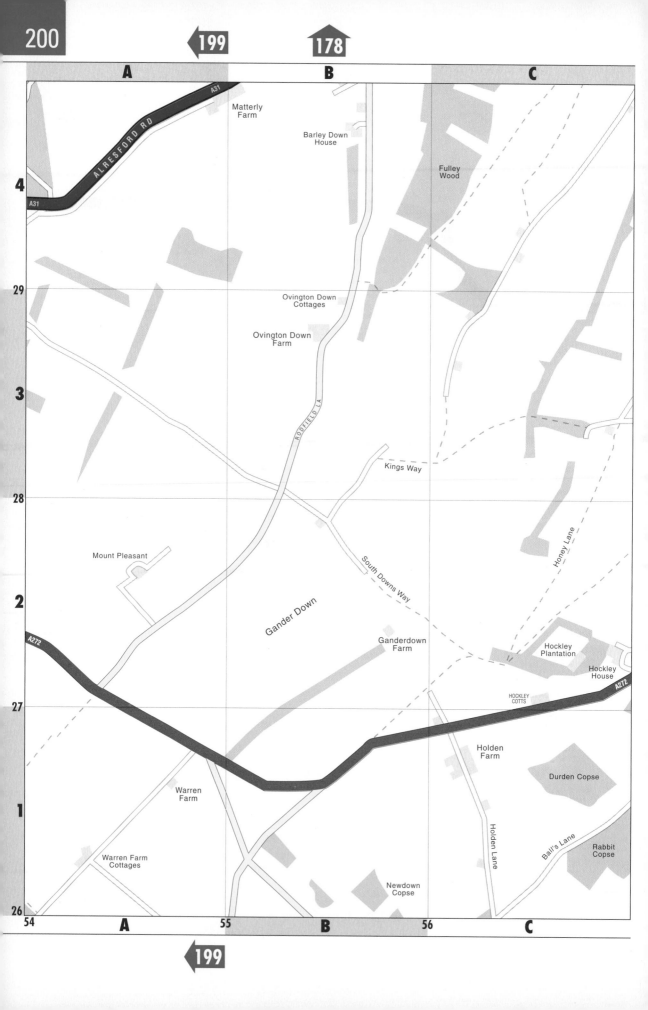

A   B   C

ALRESFORD RD
A31
A31

Matterly Farm

Barley Down House

Fulley Wood

4

29

Ovington Down Cottages

Ovington Down Farm

RODFIELD LA

3

Kings Way

28

Honey Lane

Mount Pleasant

South Downs Way

2

Gander Down

Ganderdown Farm

Hockley Plantation

Hockley House

A272

A272

HOCKLEY COTTS

27

Holden Farm

Durden Copse

Warren Farm

1

Holden Lane

Ball's Lane

Rabbit Copse

Warren Farm Cottages

Newdown Copse

26

54   A   55   B   56   C

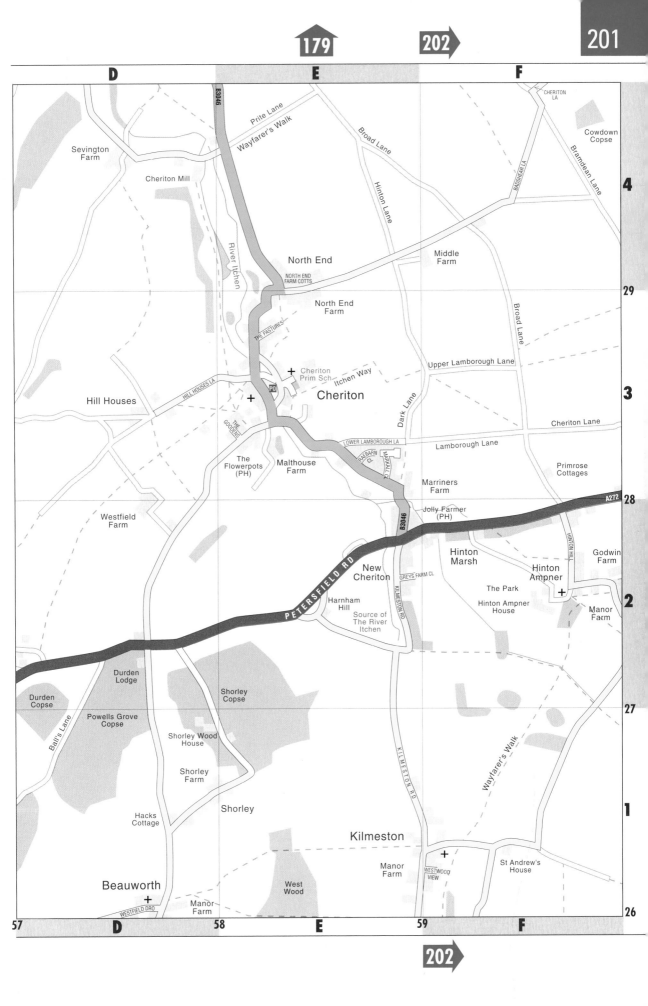

A **B** **C**

CHERITON LA

Common Farm

Old Park Wood

Tenant Woods

OLD PARK RD

Bullbeck Copse

4

Cheriton Wood

Breach Plain Cottages

Wood Farm Cottages

29

Marriners Farm

Wood Farm

WOOD LA

Alresford Lane

Kelsey Farm

3

Cheriton Lane

Kalamunnda Farm

Woodlane Farm

New Cottages

West End Farm

Lacey's Farm

WOODLANE CL

28

A272

Bramdean

CHURCH LA

WOODCOTE COTTS

Woodcote Manor House

Bramdean Manor

Manor Farm

Bramdean Farm

TITHELANDS LA

Hinton Ampner

The Malthouse

2

Manor Farm

Godwin's Plantation

Humpty's Down

A272

27

New Pond Cottages

Joan's Acre

1

Broom Wood

Brockwood Park

Joan's Acre Wood

Brockwood Park Farm

DELL COTTS

BROCKWOOD BOTTOM

26

60 **A** **61** **B** **62** **C**

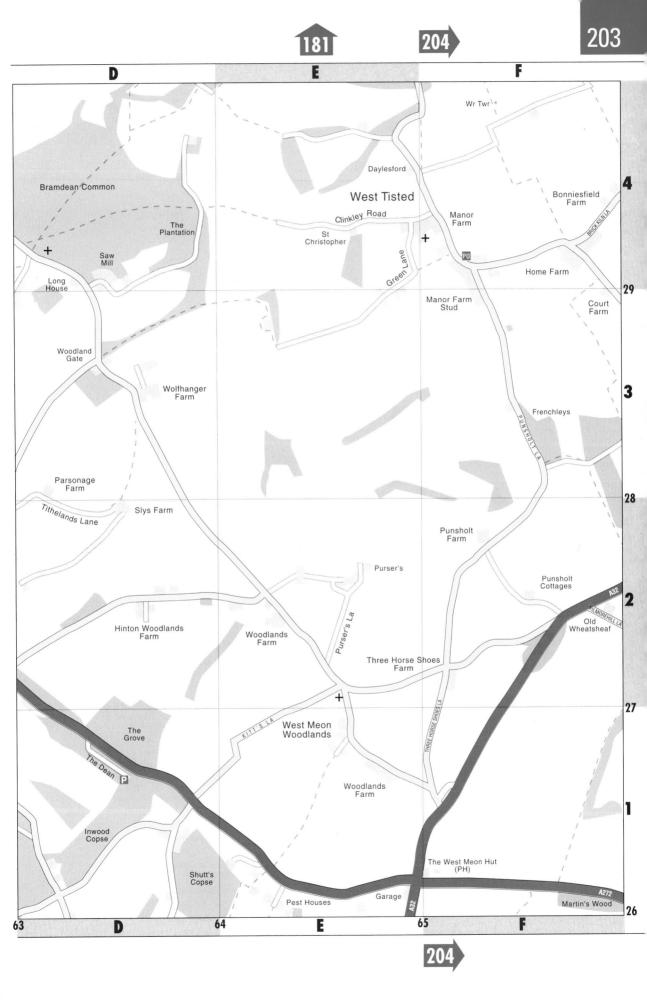

D
E
F

Wr Twr

Daylesford

Bramdean Common

West Tisted

Bonniesfield Farm

4

The Plantation

Clinkley Road

Manor Farm

BRICK KILN LA

Saw Mill

St Christopher

+

Green Lane

PO

Home Farm

29

Long House

Manor Farm Stud

Court Farm

Woodland Gate

PUNSHOLT LA

Wolfhanger Farm

Frenchleys

3

Parsonage Farm

28

Tithelands Lane

Slys Farm

Punsholt Farm

Purser's

Punsholt Cottages

A32

2

Hinton Woodlands Farm

Purser's La

Old Wheatsheaf

FILMOREHILL LA

Woodlands Farm

Three Horse Shoes Farm

+

27

KITT'S LA

West Meon Woodlands

THREE HORSE SHOES LA

The Grove

The Dean

P

Woodlands Farm

1

Inwood Copse

Shutt's Copse

The West Meon Hut (PH)

A32

Pest Houses

Garage

A272

Martin's Wood

26

63
D
64
E
65
F

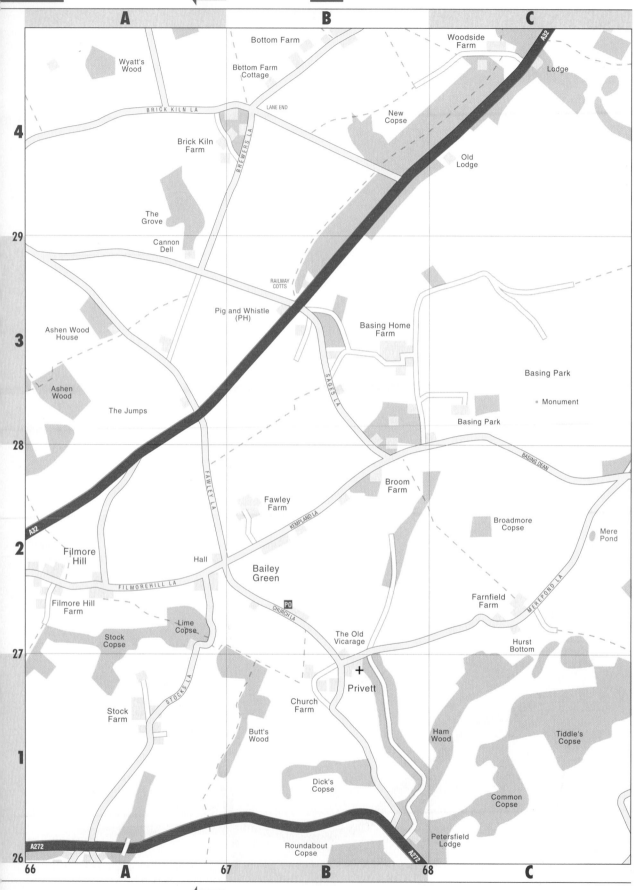

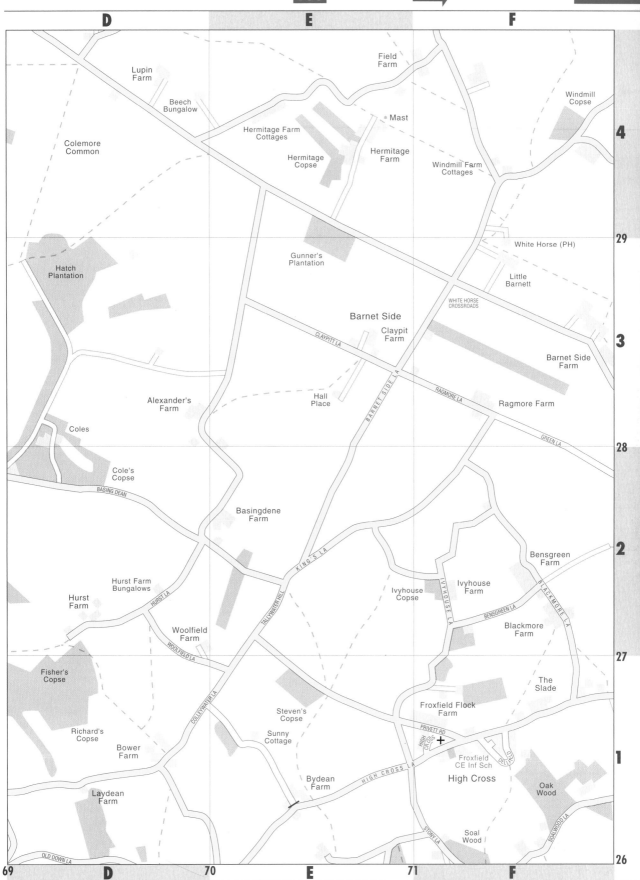

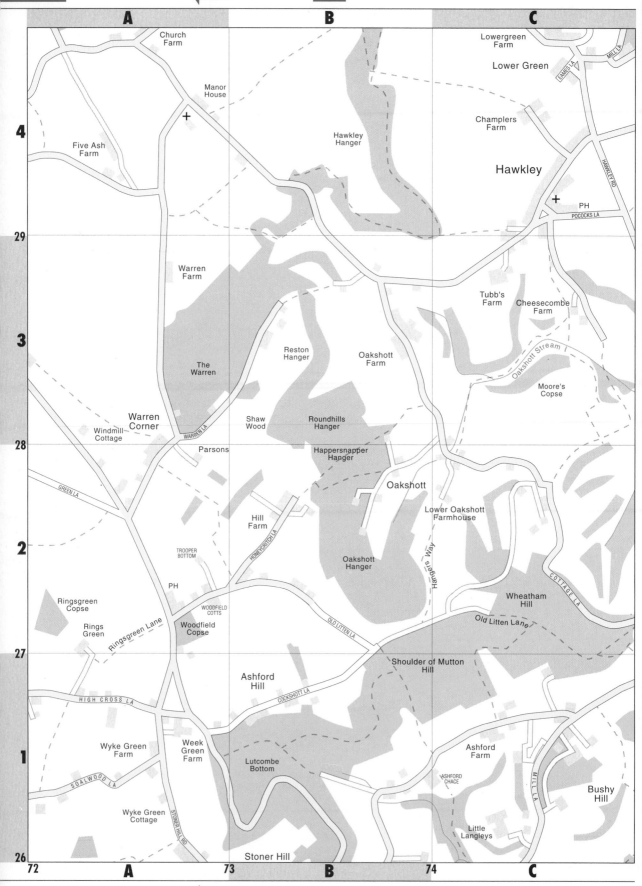

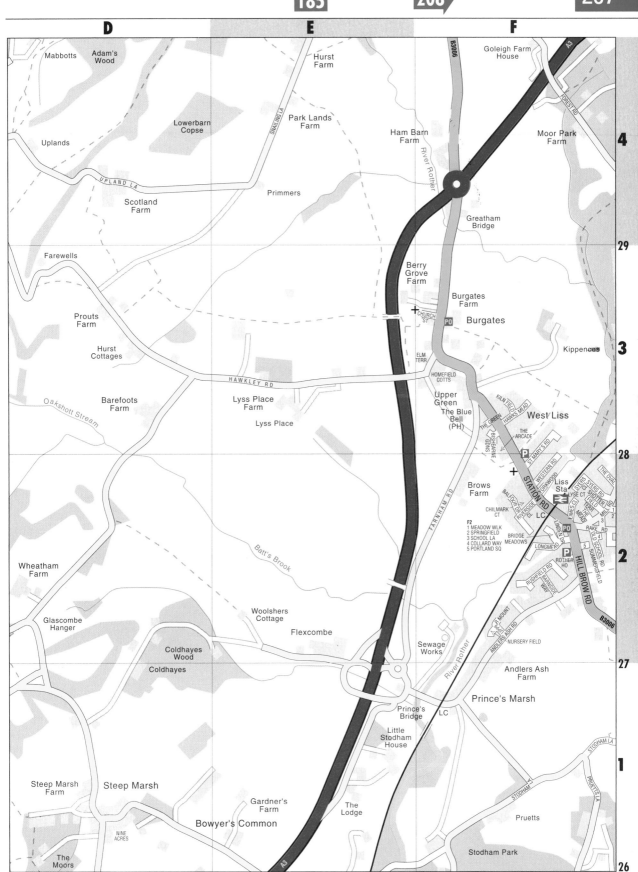

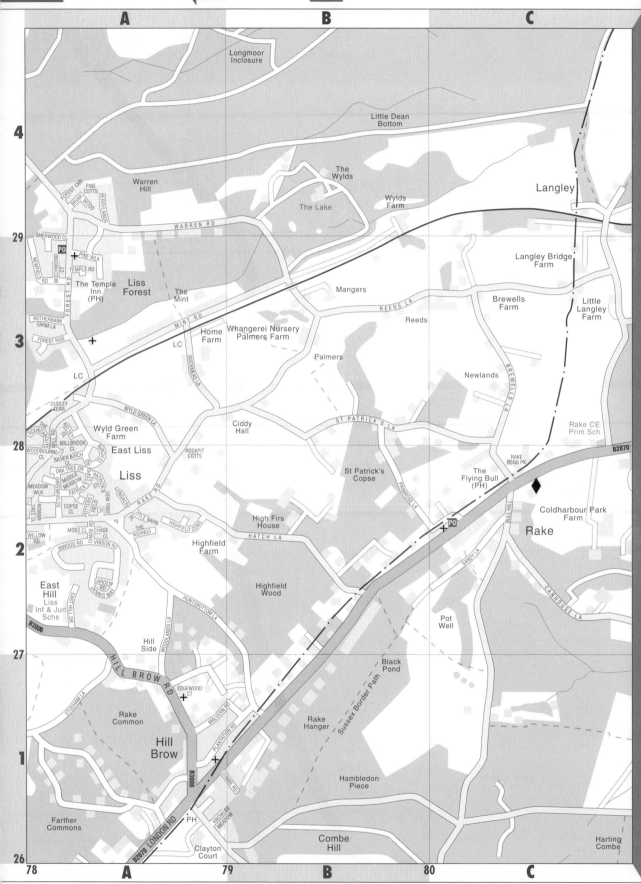

Longmoor Inclosure

Little Dean Bottom

4

Warren Hill

The Wylds

Langley

The Lake

Wylds Farm

FOREST CNR
PINE COTTS
BRIAR WOOD
BERRYLANDS
WARREN RD

29

Langley Bridge Farm

SHERWOOD CL

PO

PINE WLK

TEMPLE RD

Mangers

REEDS LA

Reeds

Brewells Farm

Little Langley Farm

NEWFIELD RD
BEECHWOOD CT

The Temple Inn (PH)

Liss Forest

The Mint

MINT RD

Home Farm

Whangerei Nursery
Palmers Farm

ROTHERBANK FARM LA

FOREST RD

FOREST RISE

LC

DUCKMEAD LA

Palmers

Newlands

BREWELLS LA

Rake CE Prim Sch

LC

DUDLEY TERR

WYLD GREEN LA

St PATRICK'S LA

B2070

Wyld Green Farm

Ciddy Hall

28

KELSEY CL

MILLBROOK CL

East Liss

ROCKPIT COTTS

RAKE BSNS PK

WOODBOURNE CL
SILVER BIRCH CL

Liss

St Patrick's Copse

The Flying Bull (PH)

Coldharbour Park Farm

OAK TREE DR
GREENFIELDS CL

MEADOW WLK

St PATRICK'S RD

MIDDLE MEADOW

RAKE RD

YEW TREE CL

PRIMROSE LA

PO

Rake

ROWAN TREE CL

COPSE CL
POTTERS

Little Barn

HIGHFIELD GDNS

High Firs House

BULL HILL

WILLOW RD

MOSS CL
CHASE CL

THE RIDINGS

HATCH LA

2

INWOOD RD
VINSON RD

Highfield Farm

Highfield Wood

SANDY LA

East Hill
Liss Inf & Jun Schs

CARDEW RD
DENNIS WAY

CANHOUSE LA

B3006

EAST HILL DR

HUNTSBOTTOM LA

WOODLANDS LA

Pot Well

27

STODHAM LA

Hill Side

Black Pond

Rake Common

EDGEWOOD CT

MALVERN RD

Rake Hanger

Sussex Border Path

HILL BROW RD

1

Hill Brow

B3006

PLANTATION RD

COMBE RD

Hambledon Piece

Farther Commons

PH

B2070 LONDON RD

KNOWLES MEADOW

Clayton Court

Combe Hill

Harting Combe

26

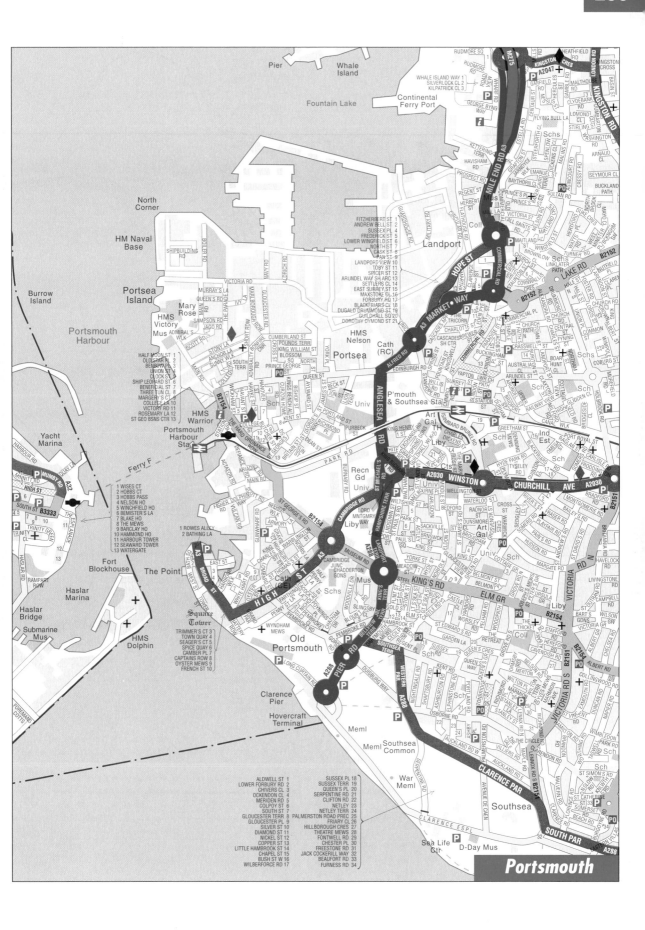

Portsmouth

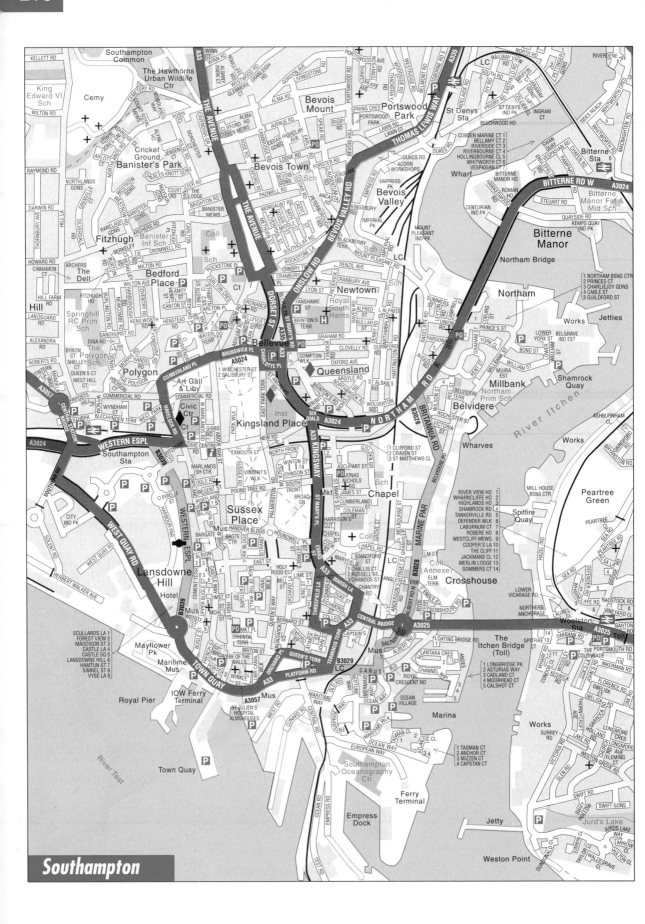

Street names are listed alphabetically and show the locality, the Postcode District, the page number and
a reference to the square in which the name falls on the map page

Victoria Gdns 9 Fleet GU13........ 53 F1

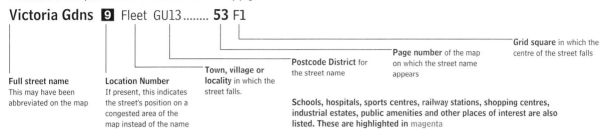

Full street name
This may have been
abbreviated on the map

Location Number
If present, this indicates
the street's position on a
congested area of the
map instead of the name

**Town, village or
locality** in which the
street falls.

Postcode District for
the street name

Page number of the map
on which the street name
appears

Grid square in which the
centre of the street falls

Schools, hospitals, sports centres, railway stations, shopping centres,
industrial estates, public amenities and other places of interest are also
listed. These are highlighted in magenta

Abbreviations used in the index

App	Approach	Cl	Close	Ent	Enterprise	La	Lane	Rdbt	Roundabout
Arc	Arcade	Comm	Common	Espl	Esplanade	N	North	S	South
Ave	Avenue	Cnr	Corner	Est	Estate	Orch	Orchard	Sq	Square
Bvd	Boulevard	Cotts	Cottages	Gdns	Gardens	Par	Parade	Strs	Stairs
Bldgs	Buildings	Ct	Court	Gn	Green	Pk	Park	Stps	Steps
Bsns Pk	Business Park	Ctyd	Courtyard	Gr	Grove	Pas	Passage	St	Street, Saint
Bsns Ctr	Business Centre	Cres	Crescent	Hts	Heights	Pl	Place	Terr	Terrace
Bglws	Bungalows	Dr	Drive	Ho	House	Prec	Precinct	Trad Est	Trading Estate
Cswy	Causeway	Dro	Drove	Ind Est	Industrial Estate	Prom	Promenade	Wlk	Walk
Ctr	Centre	E	East	Intc	Interchange	Ret Pk	Retail Park	W	West
Cir	Circus	Emb	Embankment	Junc	Junction	Rd	Road	Yd	Yard

Town and village index

Abbotts Ann 105 D2	Cliddesden 91 F4	Headley, Nr Greenham . 7 E1	Mortimer 11 F3	South Warnborough ... 95 D2
Aldermaston 9 F4	Cold Ash 2 C4	Heckfield 31 D3	Mottisfont .... 192 Cl	South Wonston 153 E3
Aldershot 76 A1	Colemore .... 183 El	Herriard .... 93 Dl	Mytchett 56 B2	Sparsholt 174 B2
Alton 139 F2	Combe 19 E4	High Cross 205 F1	Nether Wallop 148 A3	St Mary Bourne .... 62 Al
Amport 104 A3	Crawley .... 152 Al	Highclere 21 F3	New Alresford 179 E3	Standon 196 A1
Andover 106 B4	Crondall 97 E4	Hill Brow .... 208 Al	Newbury 1 B2	Steep Marsh 207 D1
Appleshaw 81 D3	Crookham Village 74 B3	Hindhead 167 F3	Newnham .... 50 Bl	Steventon 89 D2
Arborfield 15 D4	Deane .... 66 Al	Hook .... 51 Dl	Newton Tony 123 D3	Stockbridge 149 F2
Ash 77 F2	Dogmersfield 74 A3	Houghton 171 D3	Newton Valence 184 A3	Stoke 61 E2
Ashford Hill .... 8 Bl	Dummer .... 90 Bl	Hurstbourne Priors ..... 85 El	Newtown 5 F2	Stratfield Mortimer 12 A3
Ashley 172 C2	East Dean .... 191 Dl	Hurstbourne Tarrant .. 60 C4	North Tidworth 79 D4	Stratfield Saye 29 F4
Ashmansworth 40 C4	East Stratton 134 A2	Ibworth 45 F1	North Waltham .... 89 Fl	Stratfield Turgis 30 A2
Axford 114 B2	East Tisted 183 E3	Idmiston 145 D3	North Warnborough ... 72 B2	Sutton Scotney 131 E2
Ball Hill 4 A2	East Tytherley 191 F4	Itchen Abbas 177 F3	Northington 156 C4	Swallowfield 14 A3
Barton Stacey 130 B3	East Woodhay 20 B4	Itchen Stoke 178 B3	Oakhanger 163 E3	Sydmonton 43 D4
Basingstoke 68 C3	East Wordham 162 C4	Kilmeston .... 201 El	Oakley .... 67 El	Tadley 27 D4
Baughurst 26 B4	Ecchinswell 23 E2	Kimpton 80 A2	Odiham .... 72 Cl	Tangley 58 C3
Beacon Hill 167 D4	Ellisfield 115 E4	King's Somborne 172 A1	Old Alresford .... 157 El	Thatcham .... 2 Cl
Beech Hill 13 D3	Enborne 4 B4	Kings Worthy 176 B3	Old Basing 70 B3	Thruxton 103 F4
Bentley 120 A3	Enham Alamein 83 E4	Kingsclere .... 24 Bl	Old Burghclere 42 B4	Tichborne .... 179 Dl
Bentworth 138 A3	Eversley .... 15 Fl	Kingsley .... 142 Al	Over Wallop .... 125 Dl	Tilford 122 C2
Bighton .... 158 Bl	Ewshot 98 A4	Kintbury 3 D4	Overton 88 A4	Tongham 100 C3
Binsted 141 F3	Farleigh Wallop .... 91 Fl	Knights Enham 83 D3	Ovington 178 C2	Upper Bullington 131 E4
Bishop's Green 6 C2	Farley Castle 15 D4	Lasham .... 116 Bl	Oxenwood 17 D2	Upper Chute 57 F4
Bishop's Sutton 180 A2	Farley Hill 15 D3	Laverstoke 87 E3	Padworth 10 C4	Upper Clatford 105 F2
Blackwater 35 D2	Farnborough .... 55 Fl	Leckford 150 B4	Pamber End .... 27 El	Upper Farringdon 161 F2
Bordon 164 B2	Farnham 98 C2	Linchmere .... 188 Cl	Pamber Heath 10 B1	Upper Froyle .... 119 Dl
Bossington 171 D2	Finchampstead .... 16 Bl	Lindford 165 C3	Penton Grafton 81 F2	Upper Wield .... 136 Cl
Bradley 137 D4	Fleet .... 54 Al	Liphook 188 A2	Picket Piece .... 84 Al	Upton Grey 94 A3
Braishfield 194 B1	Fosbury 17 F1	Liss 208 A2	Popham 112 C2	Vernham Dean 38 A3
Bramdean 202 B2	Four Marks .... 160 Bl	Litchfield 63 E4	Preston Candover 136 B4	West Dean 190 B2
Bramley 28 C2	Frensham 144 A4	Little Somborne 172 C3	Privett 204 B1	West Tisted 203 E4
Bramshill 31 F4	Froxfield 205 F1	Littleton 175 D3	Quarley 103 D2	West Tytherley .... 169 Dl
Bramshott 188 A3	Fyfield .... 80 Cl	Lockerley .... 191 Fl	Quidhampton 65 D1	West Woodhay 3 D2
Brimpton 8 C3	Golden Pot 117 E2	Long Sutton 95 F2	Rake 208 C2	Weyhill 81 E1
Broughton 170 B4	Goodworth Clatford . 105 Fl	Longmoor Camp 186 B1	Ramsdell 46 B4	Wherwell 128 C3
Brown Candover 135 D2	Grateley 125 D4	Longparish 108 B3	Riseley 14 A2	Whitchurch 86 B3
Burghclere 22 B4	Grayshott 166 C2	Longstock 149 F3	Ropley 181 E2	Wildhern 59 F1
Buttermere 18 A4	Greatham .... 185 Fl	Lower Froyle 119 E3	Rotherwick 50 C3	Winchester 197 E3
Camberley 36 B4	Greenham 6 A4	Ludgershall .... 57 Dl	Sandhurst 35 D4	Winchfield .... 52 Bl
Charlton 82 C2	Greywell 71 F2	Maplederwell 70 C2	Seale 100 C2	Winterbourne 1 B4
Charter Alley 46 C4	Hamstead Marshall 3 F4	Mattingley 51 E4	Selborne 184 C4	Wokingham 16 B4
Chawton 161 E4	Hannington 44 C2	Medstead 159 F4	Shalden 139 D4	Wonston 131 F2
Cheriton 201 E3	Hartley Wespall .... 30 Al	Micheldever 133 D2	Sherborne St John 47 F2	Woodcott 41 E1
Chilbolton 129 D2	Hartley Wintney 52 C3	Michelmersh .... 193 El	Sherfield on Loddon ... 29 Fl	Woolton Hill 21 E4
Chilcomb 198 C3	Haslemere 189 F4	Middle Wallop 147 F4	Shinfield 13 F4	Wooton St Lawrence .. 67 E4
Chineham 48 C2	Hatherden 59 E1	Middle Winterslow ... 168 A4	Shipton Bellinger 101 E4	Yateley 34 A3
Cholderton .... 101 El	Hawkley 206 C4	Monk Sherborne 47 D3	Silchester .... 10 Cl	
Churt .... 144 Bl	Hawley 35 E2	Monkwood 182 A1	Smannell 83 F3	
Chute Forest 58 B2	Headley 165 D3	Monxton 104 B3	South Tidworth 78 C2	

Abbatt Cl SP11 .... 57 D1
Abberbury Cl (Almshouses)
   RG14 .... 1 B3
Abbetts La GU47 .... 35 F2
Abbey Bsns Pk GU9 ...... 122 B4
Abbey Cl RG14 .... 5 F4
Abbey Ct Basingstoke RG24 .... 48 A1
   Camberley GU15 .... 36 A3
   4 Farnham GU9 .... 99 D1
Abbey Hill Cl SO23 .... 176 A1
Abbey Hill Rd SO23 ...... 175 F1
Abbey Pas SO23 .... 198 A4
Abbey Rd Alton GU34 .... 160 B4
   Basingstoke RG22 .... 69 D4
   Medstead GU34 .... 160 B4
Abbey Sch The GU9 .... 99 D1
Abbey St GU15 .... 99 D1
Abbey Way GU14 .... 56 A2
Abbot's Ride GU9 .... 99 E1
Abbots Cl Fleet GU13 ...... 54 A1
   North Tidworth SP9 ...... 78 C4
Abbots Ct GU46 .... 34 B4
Abbots Rd Newbury RG14 .... 1 C1
   North Tidworth SP9 ...... 78 C4
Abbotstone Rd SO24 ...... 179 E4
Abbotswood Cl RG26 ...... 26 C4
Abbott Cl RG23 .... 68 B1
Abbott's Ann Parochial
   Prim Sch SP11 .... 104 C2
Abbott's Ann Rd
   Abbotts Ann SP11 .... 104 B3
   Monxton SP11 .... 104 B3
Abbotts Ann SP11 .... 105 D2
Abbotts Ann Rd SO22 .... 175 E2
Abbotts Cl Abbotts Ann SP11 .... 105 D2
   Winchester SO23 .... 176 A1
Abbotts Cotts SO34 .... 143 E3
Abbotts Ct SO22 .... 175 F1
Abbotts Hill SP11 .... 105 D2
Abbotts Rd SO23 .... 176 A1
Abex Rd RG14 .... 2 A2
Abingdon Rd GU17 .... 35 D3
Above Town SP11 .... 105 F2
Academy Cl GU17, GU47 .... 36 B4
Accentors Cl GU9 .... 139 F3
Achelian Cl GU9 .... 122 A4
Achilles Cl RG24 .... 48 C2
Ackender Rd GU34 .... 139 F2
Acorn Cl RG23 .... 69 F3
Acorn Mews GU14 .... 55 F4
Acorn Rd RG27 .... 34 C3
Acre Almshouses 7 SP10 .... 106 A4
Acre Ct SP10 .... 106 A4
Acre Path SP10 .... 106 A4
Acton Ho RG22 .... 68 C2
Adam Cl RG7 .... 9 E1
Adampur Rd SP9 .... 78 B2
Adams Cl RG29 .... 72 A2
Adams Dr GU13 .... 54 B1
Adams Ho GU34 .... 140 A2
Adams Park Rd GU9 ...... 99 D2
Adams Way GU34 .... 140 A2
Addison Cl SP10 .... 197 E3
Addison Gdns RG29 ...... 72 C2
Addison Rd GU14 .... 56 B4
Adelaide Cl SP9 .... 79 E4
Adelaide Rd SP10 .... 106 A4
Adlington Pl GU14 .... 56 B1
Admers Cres GU30 .... 188 A1
Admirals Way SP10 .... 83 E1
Admiralty Way GU47 ...... 35 E2
Adrian Cl RG27 .... 52 B3
Aerospace Bvd GU11 ...... 76 C4
Aghemund Cl RG24 .... 48 C2
Agra Rd SP9 .... 78 B2
Agricola Wlk SP10 .... 83 D2
Ainger Cl GU12 .... 77 D2
Aintree Cl RG14 .... 2 A1
Airborne Forces Mus GU13 .... 76 C3
Aircraft Espl GU14 .... 56 A1
Aird Cl RG20 .... 21 E4
Airlie Cnr SO22 .... 197 F3
Airlie Rd SO22 .... 197 F3
Ajax Cl RG24 .... 48 C2
Alamein Rd Aldershot GU11 .... 76 C1
   Enham Alamein SP11 .... 83 D4
Alanbrooke Cl RG27 ...... 52 B3
Alanbrooke Rd GU11, GU12 .... 77 D3
Albany Cl GU13 .... 75 D4
Albany Ct Camberley GU15 .... 36 A1
   Fleet GU13 .... 54 A1
Albany Mews SP10 .... 105 F4
Albany Pk Ind Est GU15 .... 36 A1
Albany Pk GU15 .... 36 A1
Albany Pk Ind Est GU47 .... 35 F1
Albany Rd Andover SP11 .... 105 F4
   Fleet GU13 .... 75 D4
Albert Rd Aldershot GU14 .... 76 C1
   Alton GU34 .... 139 F1
   Camberley GU13 .... 36 A3
   Farnborough GU16 ...... 56 A1
   Newbury RG14 .... 1 C2
Albert St GU13 .... 54 A1
Albert Yd 11 RG21 .... 69 D2
Albion Pl RG27 .... 52 B3
Albion Rd GU46 .... 34 C4
Alder Cl Alton GU34 ...... 139 F3
   Ash GU12 .... 77 F4
Alder Gr GU46 .... 34 A3
Alder Rd GU35 .... 165 F3
Aldermaston Prim Sch RG26 .... 9 E4
Aldermaston Rd
   Basingstoke RG23 .... 68 C4
   Pamber End RG26 .... 27 D2
   Sherborne St John RG26 .... 47 E3

Aldermaston Rd S RG22 .... 68 C4
Alderney Ave RG22 .... 91 D4
Alders Ct SO24 .... 179 E3
Aldershot Military Mus GU12 .... 77 D3
Aldershot Rd Ash GU12 .... 77 E1
   Fleet GU13 .... 75 D4
   Fleet, Church Crookham GU13 .... 75 E3
   Aldershot Sta GU11 ...... 76 C1
Alderwood RG24 .... 48 C2
Alderwood Dr RG27 .... 51 D1
Aldrin Cl SP11 .... 82 C2
Aldrin Pl GU14 .... 55 D2
Aldwick Cl GU14 .... 55 F3
Aldworth Cres RG22 ...... 68 C2
Aldwych Cotts RG14 ...... 1 B3
Alencon Link RG24 .... 69 D3
Alexander Ho 5 SP9 ...... 78 C4
Alexander Rd RG25 .... 88 A4
Alexander Terr RG29 ...... 72 B2
Alexandra Ave GU15 ...... 35 F3
Alexandra Ct Bordon GU35 .... 164 C2
   9 Farnborough GU14 .... 56 A1
Alexandra Rd Aldershot GU11 .... 76 B1
   Alton GU34 .... 139 F3
   Andover SP11 .... 105 F4
   Ash GU11 .... 77 E1
   Basingstoke RG21, RG24 .... 68 C3
   Farnborough GU14 ...... 56 A1
Alexandra Terr
   1 Aldershot GU11 ...... 76 C1
   Winchester SO23 .... 197 F4
Alexandria Rd SO21 ...... 131 E3
Alfonso Cl GU9 .... 100 A4
Alfred Rd GU9 .... 99 D1
Alfred St GU11 .... 76 C1
Alice Holt Cotts GU10 .... 120 C1
Alice Rd GU11, GU12 ...... 76 C1
Alison Cl GU14 .... 55 E2
Alison Dr GU15 .... 36 B3
Alison Way GU11 .... 76 B1
Alison's Rd GU11 .... 76 C2
Alexandra Terr
   1 Aldershot GU11 ...... 76 C1
All Hallows Catholic Sch
   GU9 .... 99 E4
All Saints CE Com Prim Sch
   SO23 .... 198 A3
All Saints CE Jun Sch GU13 .... 74 B4
All Saints Cres GU15, GU16 .... 35 E1
Allden Ave GU9 .... 100 A4
Allden Gdns GU12 .... 100 A4
Allee Dr GU30 .... 187 F3
Allen Cl Alton GU34 ...... 140 A3
   Basingstoke RG21 .... 68 C2
Allenby Rd GU17 .... 35 F3
Alliston Way
   Basingstoke RG22 .... 68 A2
   Whitchurch RG28 .... 86 B2
Allnutt Ave RG21 .... 69 E3
Alma Cl GU11 .... 77 D1
Alma La GU9 .... 99 D4
Alma Rd Bordon GU35 .... 164 C2
   Headley GU35 .... 166 A3
Alma Sq GU12 .... 77 D4
Alma Way GU9 .... 99 D4
Almond Ave RG14 .... 1 C3
Almond Cl
   2 Farnborough GU14 .... 55 F4
   Old Basing RG24 .... 70 A3
Almond Ct GU13 .... 75 D3
Almondale Ct GU14 ...... 55 F3
Almshouses RG21 .... 69 D2
Almswood Rd RG26 ...... 9 F1
Aloes The GU13 .... 75 D4
Alphington Ave GU15, GU16 .... 36 B1
Alphington Gn GU15 ...... 36 B1
Alpine Cl GU14 .... 55 D2
Alpine Ct RG21 .... 68 A2
Alresford Dro
   Chilcomb SO21, SO23 .... 199 E4
   Ovington SO24 .... 178 C1
   Tichborne SO24 .... 178 C1
   Winchester SO21, SO23 .... 198 B4
   Alresford Sta SO24 ...... 179 E3
Alsace Wlk GU15 .... 35 F1
Alswitha Terr 27 SO23 .... 176 A1
Alton Bsns Ctr GU34 .... 140 A2
Alton Coll GU34 .... 139 F3
Alton Ct 12 SO23 .... 176 A1
Alton Inf Sch GU34 ...... 140 A2
Alton La GU34 .... 160 B1
Alton Rd Farnham GU10 .... 121 D4
   Fleet GU13 .... 75 E4
   Odiham RG29 .... 95 D3
   South Warnborough RG25 .... 95 D3
Alton Ride GU35 .... 35 D4
Alton Road Cotts RG25 .... 94 C2
Alton Sta GU34 .... 140 A2
Altona Gdns SP10 .... 82 C2
Alverstoke Gdns GU11 .... 76 B1
Amber Cl GU35 .... 164 C1
Amber Ct 2 GU12 .... 77 D1
Amber Gdns SP10 .... 105 E4
Amber Hill GU15 .... 36 C2
Amberley Cl RG14 .... 1 B2
Amberley Grange GU9 .... 99 E4
Amberwood Dr GU16 .... 36 B4
Ambleside Ct
   Farnborough GU14 ...... 55 E2
   Mytchett GU14 .... 56 C1
Ambleside Cres GU10 .... 98 C3
Ambrose Rd RG26 .... 26 C4
Amery Hill GU34 .... 139 F2
Amery Hill Sec Sch GU34 .... 139 F2
Amery St GU34 .... 139 F2
Amesbury Ho 3 SP9 ...... 79 D3
Amesbury Rd Cholderton SP4 .... 101 D1
   Newton Tony SP4 .... 123 D3
   Penton Grafton SP11 ...... 81 D1

Amesbury Sch GU26 ...... 167 E1
Amherst Rd GU35 .... 164 B3
Ampere Rd RG14 .... 1 C2
Amport CE Prim Sch SP11 .... 104 A3
Amport Cl Old Basing RG24 .... 70 A4
   Winchester SO22 .... 175 E2
Amport Firs SP11 .... 104 A3
Amport Ho 7 SP9 .... 78 C3
Amport La SP11 .... 80 A4
Amport Rd Appleshaw SP11 .... 80 C3
   Blackwater GU17 .... 35 D3
   Deane RG25 .... 66 B1
   Fyfield SP11 .... 80 C3
   Kimpton SP11 .... 80 C3
   Ludgershall SP11 .... 80 C3
   Micheldever SO21 .... 111 D1
   Monxton SP11 .... 104 B3
   Newbury RG14, RG20 .... 5 D3
   Oakley RG25 .... 66 B1
   Penton Grafton SP11 .... 80 C3
   Winchester SO21, SO22, SO23 .... 175 F1
Andover Rd N SO22 ...... 175 F2
Andover Road Ret Pk SO23 .... 175 F1
Andover Sta SP10 .... 105 F4
Andover Way GU11 .... 99 F4
Andrew Cl RG29 .... 72 A2
Andrew Ct GU14 .... 55 E4
Andrew's La
   Long Sutton RG29 .... 95 F2
   Ropley SO24 .... 181 F3
Andrewartha Rd GU14 .... 56 B1
Andrews Cl GU13 .... 75 D3
Andrews Endowed CE
   Prim Sch GU34 .... 140 B3
Andrews Rd GU14 .... 55 E3
Andwell La
   Mapledurwell RG24 ...... 71 D3
   Newnham RG27 .... 71 D3
Angel Ct RG14 .... 1 C2
Angel Meadows RG29 .... 72 C2
Anglesey Rd GU12 .... 77 D1
Anglesey Ave GU14 ...... 55 E4
Anglesey Cl Andover SP10 .... 106 A3
   Basingstoke RG24 .... 48 B1
Angora Way GU13 .... 54 A2
Annandale Dr GU10 ...... 122 A3
Anne Armstrong Cl GU14 .... 77 D3
Annes Way GU13 .... 75 D3
Annettes Croft RG27 ...... 74 C2
Ansell Rd GU16 .... 36 B1
Anstey Cl RG21 .... 69 D1
Anstey Jun Sch GU34 .... 139 F2
Anstey La Alton GU34 .... 139 F4
   Shalden GU34 .... 139 F4
Anstey Mill Cl GU34 ...... 140 A3
Anstey Mill La GU34 ...... 140 A3
Anstey Rd GU34 .... 140 A3
Anton Cl RG23 .... 67 D1
Anton La SP11 .... 83 D3
Anton Mill Rd SP10 ...... 106 A4
Anton Rd SP10 .... 106 A3
Anton Schs SP10 .... 106 A4
Anton Trad Est SP10 ...... 106 A4
Antrim Cl RG21 .... 68 A2
Anzio Cl Aldershot GU11 .... 76 C1
   North Tidworth SP9 ...... 79 E3
Apex Dr GU15 .... 36 A1
Apollo Dr GU35 .... 164 C1
Apollo Ho 5 RG26 .... 9 E1
Apollo Rise GU14 .... 55 D2
Apple Tree Cl RG14 ...... 5 E4
Apple Tree Gr SP10 ...... 82 B1
Apple Way RG24 .... 70 A3
Appledore Mews GU14 .... 55 F4
Appledown Cl SO24 ...... 179 E2
Appledown La SO24 ...... 179 F2
Applegarth Cl RG21 ...... 69 E2
Applelands Cl GU10 ...... 121 F2
Appleshaw CE Schs SP11 .... 81 D4
Appleshaw Cl Tadley RG26 .... 26 C4
   Winchester SO22 .... 175 E2
Appleshaw Dene SP11 .... 81 D3
Appleton Cl SO20 .... 125 E1
Appleton Mews SP10 .... 106 A3
Appleton View SO34 ...... 183 E3
Appley Ct GU15 .... 35 F3
Appley Dr GU17 .... 35 F3
Approach Rd GU9 .... 99 D1
April Cl GU15 .... 36 A1
Apsley Cl SP10 .... 105 F3
Arbour Ct 18 SO22 ...... 197 F4
Arcade The
   11 Aldershot GU11 ...... 76 C1
   Liss GU33 .... 207 F3
   12 Newbury RG14 .... 1 C2
Archery Fields RG29 ...... 72 C2
Archery La SO22 .... 197 F4
Archery Rise GU34 .... 139 F1
Arcot Rd SP9 .... 78 C2
Ardglen Rd RG28 .... 86 B3
Ardrossan Ave GU16 ...... 36 C3
Arena L Ctr GU16 .... 36 A3
Arena La GU11 .... 76 B3
Arford Comm GU35 ...... 165 E3
Arford Rd GU35 .... 165 E3
Argent Terr GU17 .... 35 E4

Argente Cl GU13 .... 54 A2
Argyle Cl GU35 .... 164 B1
Argyle Rd GU14 .... 1 B1
Arkle Ave RG19 .... 2 B2
Arkwright Cl RG20 .... 21 E3
Arkwright Gate SP10 ...... 82 A1
Arle Cl SO24 .... 179 E3
Arle Gdns SO24 .... 179 E3
Arlebury Pk SO24 .... 179 E3
Arlington Pl 2 RG21 .... 198 A4
Arlington Terr GU11 ...... 76 B1
Arlott Dr RG21 .... 69 D4
Armitage Dr RG21 .... 36 B1
Armstrong Cl SO21 ...... 153 F2
Armstrong Mall GU11 .... 55 D2
Armstrong Rd RG21 ...... 69 F4
Armstrong Rise SP10 .... 82 C2
Arne Cl RG22 .... 91 E4
Arnett Ave RG40 .... 16 B4
Arnewood Ave RG26 ...... 10 A1
Arnham Cl GU11 .... 76 C1
Arnhem Rd RG14 .... 1 C2
Arran Cl RG23 .... 67 D1
Arrow Ind Est GU14 ...... 55 E1
Arrow La RG27 .... 52 A4
Arrow Rd GU14 .... 55 E1
Arthur Cl GU9 .... 98 C1
Arthur Rd Farnham GU11 .... 99 D1
   Newbury RG14 .... 1 B1
   Winchester SO23 .... 176 A1
Arthur St GU11 .... 76 C1
Artillery Rd Aldershot GU11 .... 76 C1
   Farnborough GU12 ...... 77 D4
Artists Way SP10 .... 83 D1
Arun Ct 23 RG21 .... 69 E3
Arundel Cl Fleet GU13 .... 75 D4
   Liphook GU30 .... 187 D4
   New Alresford SO24 ...... 179 E2
Arundel Gdns RG22 ...... 68 B4
Arundell Pl 7 GU9 .... 98 C1
Ascension Cl RG24 .... 48 B1
Ascot Cl Alton GU34 ...... 140 A1
   Newbury RG14 .... 6 A4
Ash Church Rd GU12 .... 77 F1
Ash Cl Ash GU12 .... 77 F2
   Blackwater GU17 .... 35 D3
   North Tidworth SP9 ...... 79 D4
Ash Ct 6 RG14 .... 1 C2
Ash Gr Kingsclere RG20 .... 24 B1
   Liphook GU30 .... 188 A2
   Old Basing RG24 .... 70 B3
Ash Grange Cty
   Prim Sch GU12 .... 77 F1
Ash Green La W GU12 .... 100 B4
Ash Hill Rd GU12 .... 77 F2
Ash La Baughurst RG26 .... 9 E1
   Latchmere Green RG26 .... 28 A3
Ash Lodge Cl GU12 ...... 77 F1
Ash Lodge Dr GU12 ...... 77 F1
Ash Manor Sch GU12 .... 100 B4
Ash Park Cotts RG25 .... 89 D4
Ash Path SO20 .... 126 A2
Ash Rd Aldershot GU12 .... 100 A4
   Bishop's Green RG14 .... 6 C2
Ash St GU12 .... 77 F1
Ash Sta GU12 .... 77 F1
Ash Terr RG18 .... 2 C4
Ash Tree Cl GU14 .... 55 D2
Ash Tree Gr RG20 .... 3 F4
Ash Tree Rd SP10 .... 105 E4
Ash Vale Sta GU12 .... 77 F4
Ash Wlk SO24 .... 179 E3
Ashbarn Cres SO22 ...... 197 E3
Ashbourne Way RG19 .... 2 C2
Ashburton Cl GU12 ...... 179 E3
Ashburton Rd SO24 ...... 179 E3
Ashbury Dr GU15 .... 35 F1
Ashbury Rd GU35 .... 164 B1
Ashdell Rd GU34 .... 140 A2
Ashdene Cres GU12 ...... 77 F2
Ashdene Rd GU12 .... 77 F1
Ashdown Ave GU14 ...... 56 B1
Ashdown Terr SP9 .... 78 C3
Ashfield RG24 .... 48 C2
Ashfield Gn GU17 .... 34 B3
Ashfield Rd SP10 .... 105 E4
Ashfields SO20 .... 130 B3
Ashford Chace GU32 .... 206 C1
Ashford Hill Prim Sch RG19 .... 8 B1
Ashford Hill Rd RG14 .... 7 E1
Ashlawn Gdns SP10 ...... 106 A3
Ashlea RG27 .... 51 D1
Ashley Cl Camberley GU16 .... 56 C3
   Crondall GU10 .... 97 E4
   Winchester SO22 .... 175 E2
Ashley Ct GU34 .... 140 A2
Ashley Dr GU47 .... 35 D2
Ashley Dro Buttermere RG40 .... 17 F3
   Oxenwood RG40 .... 17 F3
Ashley Lodge RG21 ...... 69 D2
Ashley Rd Bentworth GU34 .... 138 A3
   Farnborough GU14 ...... 56 A2
Ashmead GU35 .... 164 B2
Ashmoor La RG24 .... 70 C3
Ashmore Green Rd RG18 .... 2 C4
Ashmore La SP5 .... 190 B1
Ashmore Rd SO21 .... 175 C1
Ashridge GU14 .... 55 E4
Ashridge Ct 2 RG14 ...... 1 C1
Ashton Rd GU14 .... 1 C1
Ashurst Cl Tadley RG26 .... 26 C4
   Winchester SO22 .... 175 E2
Ashurst Rd GU12 .... 77 E2
Ashwell Ave GU15 .... 36 B3
Ashwood Dr RG14 .... 2 A2
Ashwood Way RG22 ...... 68 B4
Ashwood Way Rdbt RG22 .... 68 B4
Aspen Cl GU35 .... 164 B1

Aspen Gdns RG27 .... 51 D1
Aspen Ho GU12 .... 100 A4
Aspin Way GU47 .... 34 C3
Aster Ct SP10 .... 105 E3
Aster Rd RG22 .... 91 D4
Atbara Rd GU13 .... 75 D2
Atholl Ct SP10 .... 83 D2
Atholl Rd GU35 .... 164 B1
Attenborough Cl GU13 .... 54 A2
Attfield Cl GU12 .... 77 E1
Attlee Gdns RG27 .... 74 C2
Attwood Cl RG23 .... 68 C2
Attwoods Dro SO21 ...... 197 E1
Auchinleck Ho 3 SP9 .... 78 C4
Auchinleck Way GU11 .... 76 B1
Audley Cl RG14 .... 2 A3
Audley Ho GU9 .... 122 A4
Augustine Cl SP10 .... 82 B2
Augustus Dr RG23 .... 68 B4
Augustus Wlk SP10 ...... 83 D2
Aukland Cl SP9 .... 79 D3
Auklet Ct RG25 .... 90 C4
Austen Ave SO22 .... 197 E2
Austen Cl SO23 .... 176 A1
Austen Gdns RG14 .... 5 F4
Austen Gr RG22 .... 68 C1
Austen Rd GU14 .... 55 F3
Austin's Cotts GU9 .... 98 C1
Avalan Ct SO22 .... 197 F3
Aveley La GU10 .... 122 A4
Avenue Cl Andover SP10 .... 105 F4
   Liphook GU30 .... 187 F2
Avenue Rd Farnborough GU14 .... 56 A2
   Fleet GU13 .... 53 F1
   Grayshott GU26 .... 167 D2
   Lasham GU34 .... 116 B2
Avenue Sucy GU17 .... 35 F2
Avenue The Aldershot GU12 .... 100 A4
   Andover SP10 .... 105 F4
   Barton Stacey SP11 ...... 108 B2
   Camberley GU15 .... 35 F3
   Farleigh Wallop RG22 .... 91 E1
   Farnham GU10 .... 121 E2
   Fleet GU13 .... 53 F1
   Grayshott GU26 .... 167 D2
   Haslemere GU27 .... 189 E4
   Hatherden SP11 .... 59 F1
   Liphook GU30 .... 187 F2
   Mortimer RG7 .... 11 F3
   New Alresford SO24 ...... 179 E3
   South Tidworth SP9 ...... 78 C2
Avery Ct 17 GU11 .... 76 C1
Aviary Ct RG24 .... 69 F4
Aviemore Rd RG26 ...... 67 D1
Avocet Cres GU17 .... 35 E4
Avon Cl Ash GU12 .... 77 E1
   Farnborough GU14 ...... 55 E4
Avon Ct 31 Andover SP11 .... 83 E1
   Farnham GU9 .... 99 D1
Avon Rd Farnham GU9 .... 99 D1
   Oakley RG23 .... 67 D1
   South Tidworth SP9 ...... 78 C3
Avon Way RG14 .... 2 A2
Avon Wlk 27 RG21 .... 69 E3
Avondale Cl GU12 .... 77 E4
Avondale Rd Aldershot GU9 .... 99 F4
   Fleet GU13 .... 54 A1
Award Rd GU13 .... 74 C3
Axford La RG25 .... 115 D2
Ayjay Cl GU9 .... 99 F4
Aylesfield Farm GU34 .... 117 F2
Aylesham Way GU46 ...... 33 F3
Ayliffe Ho RG21 .... 68 B2
Ayling Cl GU11 .... 99 E4
Ayling Hill GU11 .... 76 B1
Ayling La GU11 .... 99 E4
Aylings Cl RG23 .... 68 A2
Aylward's Dr GU34 .... 161 E2
Aylwards Way SO20 ...... 147 F3
Aylwin Cl RG21 .... 69 D1
Ayres La RG20 .... 22 C4
Ayrshire Gdns GU13 ...... 54 A2
Azalea Ave GU35 .... 165 D3
Azalea Ct SP10 .... 105 E3
Azalea Dr GU27 .... 189 E4
Azalea Gdns GU13 .... 75 D3
Azalea Way GU15 .... 36 C3

Babbs Mead GU9 .... 98 C1
Babs Fields GU10 .... 120 A3
Bacchus Ho 16 RG26 .... 9 E1
Bach Cl RG22 .... 91 E4
Back La Appleshaw SP11 .... 81 E3
   Binsted GU34 .... 142 C4
   Brimpton RG26 .... 9 D3
   Mottisfont SO51 .... 192 C3
   Shinfield RG7 .... 13 F4
   Silchester RG7 .... 11 D2
   Southrope RG25 .... 116 B3
   Vernham Dean SP11 ...... 38 B3
Back St SO23 .... 197 F2
Bacon Cl GU15 .... 35 D3
Bacon La GU10 .... 144 A2
Badajos Rd GU11 .... 76 B2
Baden Powell Rd GU33 .... 186 B1
Bader Ct GU14 .... 55 E4
Badger Farm Rd SO22 .... 197 E2
Badger Way GU9 .... 98 A4
Badger's Bank RG24 ...... 69 F4
Badgers Cl GU13 .... 74 C4
Badgers Copse GU16 .... 36 B2
Badgers Croft RG7 .... 11 F3
Badgers Holt GU46 ...... 33 F3
Badgerwood Dr GU15 .... 36 A1
Badshear La SO24 .... 201 F4
Badshot Lea Cty Fst Sch GU9 .... 99 F3
Badshot Lea Rd GU11 .... 99 F3
Badshot Pk GU9 .... 99 F3

Bagmore La Bradley RG25 ...... 115 F3
Herriard RG25 ...... 115 F3
Bagnols Way RG14 ...... 1 B1
Bagwell La Odiham RG29 ...... 73 E3
Winchfield RG29 ...... 73 E3
Baigent Cl SO23 ...... 198 B4
Bailey Cl Camberley GU16 ...... 56 A4
Winchester SO22 ...... 197 E3
Bailey Ho SO24 ...... 179 E3
Baileys Cl GU15 ...... 35 D2
Bain Av GU47 ...... 35 F1
Baird Av RG22 ...... 68 C1
Baird Rd Arborfield RG2 ...... 15 E4
Farnborough GU14 ...... 56 A3
Bakehouse Mews 9 GU11 ...... 76 C1
Bakers Field GU33 ...... 185 F1
Baldreys GU10 ...... 121 F4
Balfour Cres RG14 ...... 5 D3
Balfour Dr GU33 ...... 207 F2
Balintore Ct GU47 ...... 35 D4
Balksbury Hill 105 E3
Balksbury Hill Ind Est SP11 ...... 105 F3
Balksbury Rd SP11 ...... 105 F3
Balksbury Schs SP10 ...... 105 E3
Ball and Wicket La GU9 ...... 99 D4
Ballantyne Rd GU14 ...... 55 F3
Ballard Cl RG22 ...... 68 B2
Ballard Ct GU15 ...... 36 C4
Ballard Rd GU15 ...... 36 C4
Balmoral Cl GU34 ...... 139 E2
Balmoral Cres GU9 ...... 98 C3
Balmoral Ct RG22 ...... 68 B2
Balmoral Dr GU14 ...... 56 B4
Balmoral Rd Andover SP10 ...... 106 A4
Ash GU12 ...... 77 F2
Balmoral Way RG25 ...... 91 D4
Bamber La GU34 ...... 119 D2
Banbury Cl GU16 ...... 56 C4
Band Hall Pl RG27 ...... 51 D1
Bank Rd GU14 ...... 77 D3
Bank Side RG40 ...... 16 B3
Bankside GU9 ...... 99 E4
Bannister Gdns
Eversley GU46 ...... 33 E4
Yateley GU46 ...... 34 B3
Bannister Pl RG19 ...... 8 B3
Baptist Hill SP11 ...... 61 F1
Bar End Ind Est SO23 ...... 198 A3
Bar End Rd SO23 ...... 198 A3
Barbara Cl SO13 ...... 75 D3
Barbel Ave RG17 ...... 69 F3
Barberry Cl GU13 ...... 75 D3
Barberry Way GU17 ...... 35 E1
Barbour Cl RG29 ...... 95 E4
Barcelona Cl SP10 ...... 83 D1
Bardsley Dr GU10 ...... 121 F4
Bardwell Cl RG22 ...... 68 B2
Baredown The RG27 ...... 71 E4
Barfield Cl SO23 ...... 198 A3
Barfield Rd RG18 ...... 2 C2
Barfield Sch GU9 ...... 99 F2
Barford Cl GU13 ...... 75 E4
Barge Cl GU12 ...... 77 E3
Barge La RG7 ...... 13 E2
Baring Cl East Stratton SO21 ...... 134 A2
Itchen Abbas SO21 ...... 178 A4
Baring Rd SO23 ...... 198 A4
Barkham Ride RG40 ...... 16 B4
Barley Down Dr SO22 ...... 197 E2
Barley Mow Ct RG27 ...... 73 F4
Barley Mow Hill GU35 ...... 165 E3
Barley Way GU15 ...... 54 A3
Barlows SP10 ...... 105 F3
Barlows Rd RG26 ...... 26 C4
Barn Cl GU16 ...... 36 B3
Barn Close La RG20 ...... 40 C4
Barn Cres RG14 ...... 5 D4
Barn La Four Marks GU34 ...... 159 F1
Oakley RG22 ...... 90 A4
Barn Meadow Cl GU13 ...... 74 C2
Barn The 15 GU12 ...... 139 F2
Barnard Cl GU14 ...... 56 B4
Barncroft Appleshaw SP11 ...... 81 D3
Farnham GU9 ...... 99 D1
Barnes Cl Farnborough GU16 ...... 56 A2
Winchester SO23 ...... 197 F3
Barnes Rd GU16 ...... 56 B4
Barnet Side La GU32 ...... 205 E3
Barnetts Wood La SO24 ...... 181 D4
Barnfield GU46 ...... 34 A3
Barnfield Cl GU34 ...... 119 D2
Barnfield Cotts GU34 ...... 184 A3
Barnfield Rise SP10 ...... 105 F3
Barns The RG25 ...... 113 E4
Barnside Way GU33 ...... 207 F2
Barnsley Cl GU16 ...... 56 C1
Baroda Rd SP9 ...... 78 B2
Barossa Rd GU15 ...... 36 A4
Barra Cl RG23 ...... 67 D1
Barrack Rd GU11 ...... 76 C1
Barracks Rd RG14 ...... 6 B3
Barrett Ct RG21 ...... 69 E1
Barrie Rd GU10 ...... 98 C4
Barron Pl RG22 ...... 68 B4
Barrow Hill SO20 ...... 127 F4
Barry Way RG22 ...... 91 E4
Bartholomew St RG14 ...... 1 B1
Bartholomew Cl 25 SO23 ...... 176 A1
Bartlemy Cl RG14 ...... 5 E4
Bartlemy Rd RG14 ...... 5 E4
Bartlett Cl RG26 ...... 29 D1
Bartley Way RG29 ...... 72 B4
Bartok Cl RG22 ...... 68 C1
Barton Cl Aldershot GU11 ...... 76 B1
Charlton SP10 ...... 82 B2
Barton Ct 2 GU14 ...... 56 A1
Barton End 2 GU34 ...... 139 F2

Barton Stacey CE Prim Sch
SO21 ...... 130 C4
Barton's Ct RG29 ...... 72 B2
Bartons La RG24 ...... 70 A4
Bartons Way GU14 ...... 55 D4
Basing Dean GU34 ...... 204 C2
Basing Dr GU11 ...... 99 F4
Basing Ho RG24 ...... 70 A3
Basing Rd RG24 ...... 69 E3
Basing View RG21 ...... 69 E3
Basingbourne Cl GU13 ...... 75 D3
Basingbourne Rd GU13 ...... 75 D3
Basingstoke Bsns Ctr RG22 ...... 68 C1
Basingstoke Canal Ctr GU16 ...... 56 C2
Basingstoke Coll Of Tech
Basingstoke 68 C3
Basingstoke 69 D2
Basingstoke Rd
Aldermaston RG26 ...... 9 E4
Alton RG34 ...... 139 E2
Kings Worthy SO23 ...... 176 B4
Kingsclere RG20 ...... 24 C1
Monk Sherborne RG26 ...... 46 C3
Ramsdell RG26 ...... 46 C3
Swallowfield RG7 ...... 14 A3
Basingstoke Sta RG24 ...... 69 D3
Bassenthwaite Gdns GU35 ...... 164 B3
Bassett Cl GU12 ...... 56 B4
Bat and Ball La GU9 ...... 121 F3
Batchelor Dr RG24 ...... 70 B3
Batchelors Barn Rd SP10 ...... 106 B4
Bateman Gr GU34 ...... 100 B3
Bath Rd Camberley GU15 ...... 36 A3
Newbury RG14 ...... 1 A2
Thatcham RG18, RG19 ...... 2 C2
Batley Wood
Bsns Pk W RG29 ...... 72 B4
Batsford SP11 ...... 61 F1
Batt's Cnr GU35 ...... 143 D4
Battens Ave RG25 ...... 88 A4
Battery End RG14 ...... 5 D3
Battery Hill SO22 ...... 197 E3
Battle Cl RG14 ...... 1 A2
Battle Rd RG14 ...... 5 D3
Baughurst Rd
Baughurst RG26 ...... 26 B3
Ramsdell RG26 ...... 46 B4
Baverstocks GU34 ...... 140 A3
Bawlings The GU15 ...... 36 A3
Baxendales The RG14 ...... 2 A1
Bayfield Ave GU15 ...... 36 B1
Bayford Cl GU15 ...... 35 F1
Baynard Cl RG21 ...... 69 E4
Baywood Cl GU14 ...... 55 D3
Bazaar Rd SP9 ...... 78 B3
Beach Piece Way RG22 ...... 91 D4
Beach's Cres RG26 ...... 27 F2
Beachdown Ho RG22 ...... 68 B1
Beacon Cl GU47 ...... 121 F3
Beacon Hill Ct GU26 ...... 167 D3
Beacon Hill Cty First Sch
GU26 ...... 167 D3
Beacon Hill Rd
Beacon Hill GU26 ...... 167 D3
Crondall GU13 ...... 75 E2
Fleet GU13 ...... 75 E2
Beacon Pass GU34 ...... 42 A4
Beacon View Ho GU26 ...... 167 D2
Beaconsfield Rd RG21 ...... 69 D2
Beal's Pightle RG26 ...... 46 C4
Beale's Ct SP10 ...... 106 A4
Beale's Ct SP5 ...... 169 D1
Beales La GU10 ...... 121 E4
Bealeswood La GU35 ...... 143 E3
Beam Hollow GU9 ...... 99 D4
Bear Ct RG24 ...... 69 F4
Bear Hill RG20 ...... 24 B1
Bear La Farnham GU11 ...... 99 D2
Newbury RG14 ...... 1 C2
Bearwood Cotts GU10 ...... 121 E4
Bearwood Gdns GU13 ...... 54 A1
Beatty Ct SP10 ...... 106 B4
Beauclerk Gn RG27 ...... 52 B1
Beaufort Rd Bordon GU35 ...... 164 B3
Farnham GU9 ...... 99 D2
Fleet GU13 ...... 75 D3
Winchester SO23 ...... 197 F3
Beaufront Cl GU15 ...... 36 C4
Beaufront Rd GU15 ...... 36 C4
Beaulieu Cl SO22 ...... 175 E2
Beaulieu Ct
32 Andover SP10 ...... 83 D1
28 Basingstoke RG21 ...... 69 E3
Blackwater GU17 ...... 34 C3
Beaulieu Gdns GU47 ...... 35 D3
Beaumaris Cl SP10 ...... 105 F3
Beaumaris Par GU16 ...... 56 B4
Beaumont Gn SO22 ...... 197 E4
Beaumont Gr GU11 ...... 76 B1
Beaumont Jun Sch GU11 ...... 76 B1
Beaurepaire Cl RG26 ...... 46 C4
Beaver Ind Est GU30 ...... 188 A2
Beaver La GU46 ...... 34 B3
Beavers Cl Alton GU34 ...... 139 F2
1 Tadley RG26 ...... 9 F1
Beavers Hill GU9 ...... 98 B1
Beavers Mews GU35 ...... 164 C2
Beavers Rd GU9 ...... 98 C1
Beck Gdns GU9 ...... 98 C3
Beck Ind Est The GU12 ...... 100 A4
Becket Ct RG22 ...... 68 A2
Beckett Cl RG23 ...... 68 A3
Beckett Rd SP10 ...... 105 F4
Beckford Ho SO23 ...... 176 A3
Bedfield La SO23 ...... 176 A3

Bedford Ave GU16 ...... 56 B3
Bedford Cl Bordon GU35 ...... 164 B1
Newbury RG14 ...... 5 D3
Bedford Cres GU16 ...... 56 B3
Bedford La GU16 ...... 56 B3
Bedford Wlk 12 RG21 ...... 69 D3
Bedser Sq SP10 ...... 83 D2
Beech Ave Camberley GU16 ...... 56 A2
Farnham GU10 ...... 122 A3
Beech Cl Bramley RG26 ...... 29 D1
Middle Wallop SO20 ...... 126 A2
Overton RG25 ...... 65 D1
Penton Grafton SP11 ...... 82 A1
Thruxton SP11 ...... 103 F4
Winchester SO22 ...... 197 D2
Beech Copse SO22 ...... 175 D1
Beech Ct Crondall GU10 ...... 97 F1
5 Newbury RG14 ...... 1 C2
Beech Down Prim Sch RG22 ...... 91 E4
Beech Dr GU17 ...... 35 D2
Beech Gr GU17 ...... 128 C4
Beech Hanger SP4 ...... 101 E1
Beech Hanger End RG26 ...... 166 C2
Beech Hanger Rd GU26 ...... 166 C2
Beech Hill GU35 ...... 165 F3
Beech Hill Rd Headley GU35 ...... 165 E3
North Tidworth SP9 ...... 79 D4
Shinfield RG7 ...... 13 E4
Beech Ho RG24 ...... 49 D2
Beech Rd Bishop's Green RG14 ...... 6 C1
Camberley GU15 ...... 56 B3
Farnborough GU14 ...... 55 F4
New Alresford SO24 ...... 179 E3
Beech Ride Fleet GU13 ...... 74 C4
Sandhurst GU47 ...... 34 C4
Beech The GU17 ...... 35 E4
Beech Tree Cl RG22 ...... 90 A4
Beech Tree Dr GU9 ...... 99 F3
Beech Tree Wlk
Broughton SO20 ...... 170 B2
East Tytherley SO20 ...... 170 B2
Beech Way GU23 ...... 68 B4
Beech Wlk SP10 ...... 105 E4
Beecham Berry RG22 ...... 91 E4
Beechbrook Ave GU46 ...... 34 B3
Beechcrest View RG27 ...... 51 D1
Beechcroft Cl Andover SP10 ...... 83 D1
Liphook GU30 ...... 187 D2
Beechcroft Cotts SO20 ...... 170 A3
Beeches The Andover SP10 ...... 105 F4
Ash GU12 ...... 56 B1
Basingstoke RG22 ...... 91 E3
Tadley RG26 ...... 26 C4
Wonston SO21 ...... 131 E2
Beechfield SP4 ...... 123 D3
Beeching Cl GU12 ...... 77 F2
Beechnut Dr GU46 ...... 34 C3
Beechnut Rd GU11 ...... 76 C1
Beechwood RG24 ...... 48 C2
Beechwood Cl
Basingstoke RG22 ...... 91 E3
Fleet GU13 ...... 74 C3
Beechwood Ct GU33 ...... 208 A3
Beechwood Rd GU34 ...... 139 E1
Beestons Cotts RG27 ...... 51 D1
Beethoven Rd RG22 ...... 91 E4
Beeton's Ave GU11 ...... 77 F2
Beggar's La SO23 ...... 198 A4
Beggarwood La RG22 ...... 91 D3
Begonia Cl RG22 ...... 91 D4
Belaga Cl SO20 ...... 126 A4
Beldham Rd GU10 ...... 121 E4
Belgrave Ct GU17 ...... 35 D2
Belgrave Mews RG27 ...... 52 B3
Bell Cl GU15 ...... 56 A3
Bell Hill Enborne RG20 ...... 4 C2
Newbury RG14 ...... 4 C2
Bell Ho SO24 ...... 179 E2
Bell Holt RG14 ...... 5 D3
Bell La Blackwater GU17 ...... 35 D3
Ellisfield RG25 ...... 115 E4
Bell Meadow Rd RG27 ...... 51 D1
Bell Rd Andover SP10 ...... 106 B4
Basingstoke RG24 ...... 69 F4
Linchmere GU27 ...... 189 F2
Bell St Ludgershall SP11 ...... 57 D1
Whitchurch RG28 ...... 86 B3
Bell Vale La GU27 ...... 189 F2
Belland Dr GU11 ...... 76 B1
Belle Vue Cl GU11 ...... 77 D1
Belle Vue Ent Ctr GU12 ...... 77 E1
Belle Vue Inf Sch GU12 ...... 77 D1
Belle Vue Rd Aldershot GU12 ...... 77 D1
Andover SP10 ...... 106 A3
Old Basing RG24 ...... 70 B3
Bellever Hill GU15 ...... 36 B3
Bellevue RG28 ...... 86 B3
Bellew Rd GU16 ...... 56 C3
Bellhanger Ents GU34 ...... 138 A3
Belmont Cl Andover SP10 ...... 106 A3
Farnborough GU14 ...... 55 E4
Belmont Cotts RG14 ...... 1 A3
Belmont Hts RG22 ...... 91 E3
Belmont Mews
Camberley GU15 ...... 36 A2
Headley GU35 ...... 165 E3
Belmont Rd Andover SP10 ...... 106 A3
Camberley GU15 ...... 36 A2
Belstone Mews GU14 ...... 55 F4
Belton Rd GU15 ...... 36 B3
Belvedere Cl GU13 ...... 53 E1
Belvedere Ct GU17 ...... 35 D2
Belvedere Dr RG14 ...... 5 F4
Belvedere Gdns RG24 ...... 49 D2
Belvedere Rd GU14 ...... 56 A1

Belvoir Cl GU15 ...... 36 B1
Bembridge Ct 6 GU12 ...... 77 D1
Benbow Ct SP10 ...... 106 B4
Benenden Gn SO24 ...... 179 E2
Benett Gdns GU14 ...... 1 B3
Benford Ct RG29 ...... 72 C1
Benger's La SO51 ...... 192 B1
Benham Hill Newbury RG14 ...... 2 B2
Thatcham RG18 ...... 2 B2
Benham La RG7 ...... 14 A2
Benhams La GU33 ...... 186 A3
Benin Rd SP9 ...... 79 E3
Bennet Cl Alton GU34 ...... 139 F2
Basingstoke RG21 ...... 69 E4
Bennett Cl GU15 ...... 36 A3
Bensgreen La GU32 ...... 205 F2
Bent St GU15 ...... 147 F4
Benta Cl SO20 ...... 126 A3
Bentley Bsns Pk GU10 ...... 120 A3
Bentley CE Prim Sch GU10 ...... 120 A3
Bentley Cl SO23 ...... 176 A3
Bentley Copse GU15 ...... 36 C2
Bentley Ind Ctr GU10 ...... 120 A2
Bentley Ind Est GU10 ...... 120 A2
Bentley Sta GU10 ...... 120 B2
Bentley Way SP5 ...... 168 A3
Bentworth CE
Prim Sch GU34 ...... 138 A3
Benwell Cl RG29 ...... 95 E4
Bercote Cl SO22 ...... 175 D3
Bere Cl SO22 ...... 175 E1
Bere Hill RG28 ...... 86 B3
Bere Hill Cl RG28 ...... 86 B3
Bere Hill Cres SP10 ...... 106 B4
Berehurst GU34 ...... 139 F1
Beresford Cl Andover SP10 ...... 106 A3
Camberley GU14 ...... 56 B3
Beresford Ctr RG24 ...... 69 F4
Beresford Gate SP10 ...... 83 F1
Bereweeke Ave SO22 ...... 175 F1
Bereweeke Cl SO22 ...... 175 F1
Bereweeke Rd SO22 ...... 175 F1
Bereweeke Way SO22 ...... 175 F1
Berewyk Cl RG22 ...... 91 D4
Berkeley Cl SO23 ...... 54 A1
Berkeley Cres GU16 ...... 56 C4
Berkeley Dr RG22 ...... 91 F4
Berkeley Rd RG14 ...... 1 B1
Berkshire Rd GU16 ...... 36 B4
Bermuda Cl RG24 ...... 48 B1
Bernard Ave GU34 ...... 160 A1
Bernard Ct GU17 ...... 35 F2
Bernstein Rd RG22 ...... 91 E4
Berry Ct RG20 ...... 72 A4
Berry Hill SO24 ...... 181 D3
Berrybank GU17 ...... 35 E3
Berrydown La Axford RG25 ...... 114 C2
Overton RG25 ...... 88 B4
Berrylands GU33 ...... 208 A4
Berrywood La
Bradley RG25 ...... 137 D3
Upper Wield RG25 ...... 137 D3
Berwyn Cl RG23 ...... 68 A2
Bessemer Rd RG23 ...... 68 C1
Beta Rd GU14 ...... 55 F3
Bethel Cl GU33 ...... 99 D3
Bethel La GU9 ...... 99 D3
Betjeman Wlk GU46 ...... 33 F2
Beveren Cl GU13 ...... 54 A2
Beverley Cl Ash GU12 ...... 77 E1
Basingstoke RG24 ...... 69 D1
Beverley Cres GU14 ...... 55 E1
Bevers The RG7 ...... 11 F3
Bexmoor RG24 ...... 70 A3
Bexmoor Way RG24 ...... 70 A3
Beyne Rd SO22 ...... 197 D2
Bible Fields RG25 ...... 113 E4
Bicester Ct RG28 ...... 86 B3
Bicknell Rd GU16 ...... 36 B1
Bidden Rd Odiham RG29 ...... 94 B4
Upton Grey RG25 ...... 94 B4
Biddesden La SP11 ...... 57 D1
Bideford Ct GU14 ...... 55 F4
Bietigheim Wlk GU15 ...... 36 A3
Bigg's Hill Cotts RG20 ...... 4 B2
Biggs La RG40 ...... 15 F4
Bighton Dean La SO24 ...... 158 C1
Bighton Hill SO24 ...... 181 D3
Bighton La
Bighton SO24 ...... 180 B3
Bishop's Sutton SO24 ...... 180 B3
Bighton Rd SO24 ...... 159 E3
Bilbao Ct SP10 ...... 83 E1
Bilberry Cl 8 SO22 ...... 197 F4
Billing Ave RG40 ...... 16 B3
Bilton Rd RG24 ...... 48 C1
Binfields GU9 ...... 99 D2
Binfields Cl RG24 ...... 48 C1
Binfields Rdbt RG24 ...... 48 C1
Bingley Cl GU34 ...... 139 F2
Binley Bottom SP11 ...... 61 F3
Binley Ct RG26 ...... 27 D4
Binsted CE Prim Sch GU34 ...... 141 F4
Binsted Dr GU17 ...... 35 D3
Binton La GU12 ...... 100 B2
Birch Ave Fleet GU13 ...... 53 F1
Middle Wallop SO20 ...... 126 A2
Birch Cl Bordon GU35 ...... 164 C1
Camberley GU15 ...... 36 B4
Farnham GU10 ...... 121 F2
Liss GU33 ...... 208 A2
Birch Ct 3 SO22 ...... 197 E3
Birch Dr GU17 ...... 35 D2
Birch Gr Bordon GU35 ...... 164 B1
Chilbolton SO20 ...... 129 E1
Hook RG27 ...... 51 D1
Birch Ho 4 GU14 ...... 55 F4
Birch La RG7 ...... 11 E3

Birch Rd Headley GU35 ...... 165 F3
Tadley RG26 ...... 9 E1
Wokingham RG40 ...... 16 C4
Birch Tree Ct GU27 ...... 189 D2
Birch Way GU12 ...... 77 F4
Birches The Blackwater GU47 ...... 34 C4
Farnborough GU14 ...... 55 D2
Birchett Rd Aldershot GU11 ...... 76 C1
Farnborough GU14 ...... 55 E3
Birchfields GU16 ...... 36 A2
Birchland Cl RG7 ...... 11 E3
Bircholt Rd GU30 ...... 187 D2
Birchview GU46 ...... 34 A2
Birchwood RG24 ...... 48 C2
Birchwood Rd RG14 ...... 2 A2
Birdhaven GU9 ...... 121 F3
Birdwood Rd GU47 ...... 35 E4
Birdworld GU10 ...... 121 D2
Birinus Rd SO23 ...... 176 A1
Birkenholme Cl GU35 ...... 166 A2
Bishearne Gdns GU33 ...... 207 F3
Bishop Challoner RC Sec Sch
RG22 ...... 68 B2
Bishop Ct SP10 ...... 105 F4
Bishop Sumner Dr GU9 ...... 99 D3
Bishop's Mead GU9 ...... 98 C1
Bishop's View GU34 ...... 159 F1
Bishop's Way SP10 ...... 105 F4
Bishops Cl Fleet GU13 ...... 75 D3
South Tidworth SP9 ...... 78 C2
Bishops Gn GU9 ...... 98 C3
Bishopswood Ct RG7 ...... 9 E1
Bishopswood La RG26 ...... 26 B4
Bishopswood Rd RG26 ...... 9 E1
Bishopswood Schs RG26 ...... 26 C4
Bittern Cl Basingstoke RG22 ...... 90 C4
Sandhurst GU17 ...... 35 D4
Black Dam Rdbt RG24 ...... 69 F2
Black Dam Way RG24 ...... 69 F2
Black Pond La GU9 ...... 122 A3
Black Swan Bldgs 12 SO22 ...... 197 F4
Black Swan Yd 6 SP10 ...... 106 A4
Blackberry Cl SO24 ...... 160 B2
Blackberry La GU33 ...... 160 B1
Blackberry Wlk RG22 ...... 69 F4
Blackbird Cl Basingstoke RG23 ...... 90 C4
Sandhurst GU47 ...... 35 D4
Blackbird Ct SP10 ...... 83 D1
Blackbird La RG20 ...... 6 C2
Blackbushe Bsns Ctr GU17 ...... 34 A2
Blackbushes Rd RG27 ...... 53 E4
Blackcap Pl GU15 ...... 35 E4
Blackdown Cl RG22 ...... 68 A2
Blackheath Rd GU9 ...... 98 C4
Blackman Gdns GU11 ...... 99 F4
Blackmoor Golf Course
GU35 ...... 164 A1
Blackmoor Ho GU33 ...... 185 F3
Blackmoor La GU34 ...... 186 A3
Blackmore La GU32 ...... 205 F2
Blacknest Golf Course
GU34 ...... 142 B3
Blacknest Ind Pk GU34 ...... 142 B4
Blacknest Rd GU34 ...... 120 B1
Blackstocks La
Mapledurwell RG24 ...... 71 D3
Newnham RG27 ...... 71 D3
Blackstone Cl GU14 ...... 55 D3
Blackthorn Cl SO21 ...... 153 E2
Blackthorn Cres GU14 ...... 55 E4
Blackthorn Way RG21 ...... 68 B3
Blackthorne Cl GU35 ...... 164 C2
Blackwater Cl Ash GU12 ...... 77 F1
Basingstoke RG21 ...... 69 E3
Oakley RG23 ...... 67 D1
Blackwater & Hawley L Ctr
GU47 ...... 35 E2
Blackwater Sta GU47 ...... 35 E2
Blackwater Way GU12 ...... 100 A4
Blackwater Way Ind Est
GU10 ...... 100 B4
Blackwell Rd SO21 ...... 153 E2
Blair Rd 9 RG21 ...... 69 D2
Blaire Pk GU46 ...... 33 F4
Blaise Cl GU14 ...... 56 A2
Blake Cl RG29 ...... 95 E4
Blake's La RG27 ...... 10 A1
Blake's Ride GU46 ...... 33 F3
Blakes Cotts RG29 ...... 72 C1
Blanket St GU34 ...... 162 C4
Bleach's Yard Ind Est GU30 ...... 188 A1
Bledlow GU14 ...... 5 D3
Blendon Dr SP10 ...... 82 B1
Blenheim Cl Alton GU34 ...... 140 A2
Four Marks GU34 ...... 160 A2
Tongham GU12 ...... 100 B4
Blenheim Cres GU9 ...... 98 C4
Blenheim Lodge GU16 ...... 56 A1
Blenheim Pk GU12 ...... 77 D4
Blenheim Rd
Farnborough GU12 ...... 76 C4
Newbury RG14 ...... 1 B1
Old Basing RG24 ...... 70 B3
Blighton La GU10 ...... 100 B2
Bliss Cl GU12 ...... 68 C1
Block Cotts RG7 ...... 10 C3
Bloomfieldhatch La RG7 ...... 12 C2
Bloomsbury Way GU47 ...... 35 D2
Bloswood Dr RG28 ...... 86 A3
Bloswood La RG28 ...... 86 A3
Blue Ball Hill SO23 ...... 198 A4
Blue Pryor Ct GU14 ...... 55 D3
Blue Timbers Cl GU35 ...... 164 B1
Bluebell Rd GU35 ...... 165 D3
Bluebell Wlk 1 GU13 ...... 53 F1

Bluehaven Wlk RG27 .... 50 C1
Blues Hayes Cl SP10 .... 106 A4
Bluethroat Cl GU15 .... 35 E4
Bluff Cove GU11 .... 77 D2
Blunden Cl RG24 .... 69 D1
Blunden Rd GU14 .... 55 E3
Blythwood Dr GU15 .... 36 A1
Boames La RG20 .... 4 B3
Boar's Bridge RG26 .... 27 F2
Bodmin Cl RG22 .... 68 A3
Bogmoor Cl GU34 .... 160 A1
Bohunt Com Sch GU30 ...... 187 F2
Bohunt Manor Gdns GU30 ... 187 F1
Bolle Rd GU14 .... 139 E1
Bolley Ave GU35 .... 164 A3
Bolton Cres RG22 .... 68 C2
Bond Cl RG21, RG23 .... 69 F4
Bone La RG14 .... 2 A2
Bonemill La GU11 .... 1 A1
Bonhams Cl GU34 .... 140 C4
Bonner Cotts SP5 .... 191 F4
Bonners Field GU10 .... 120 A3
Boon Way RG23 .... 67 D1
Border Gates SP10 .... 106 A4
Border End GU27 .... 189 D3
Border Rd GU27 .... 189 D3
Borderside GU46 .... 33 F3
Bordon Cl RG26 .... 26 C4
Bordon Schs GU35 .... 164 B2
Bordon Trad Est GU35 .... 164 A3
Boreen The GU35 .... 165 F3
Borelli Mews **2** GU9 .... 99 D1
Borelli Yd **1** GU11 .... 99 D1
Borkum Cl SP10 .... 82 C2
Borman Way SO21 .... 153 F2
Borodin Cl RG22 .... 91 F4
Borough The Crondall GU10 ... 97 E3
   Farnham GU9 .... 98 C1
Borovere Cl GU34 .... 139 F1
Borovere Gdns GU34 .... 139 F1
Borovere La GU34 .... 139 F1
Boscobel Rd SO21 .... 175 F1
Boscowen Cl SP10 .... 106 A4
Bostock Cl SO21 .... 174 B2
Botany Hill Farnham GU10 ... 100 A1
   Seale GU10 .... 100 A1
Botisdone Cl SP11 .... 38 B3
Bottle La RG27 .... 51 D4
Boulters Rd GU11 .... 76 C1
Boundary Rd Binsted GU10 ... 121 C1
   Farnborough GU16 .... 56 A1
   Frensham GU10 .... 121 E1
   Grayshott GU26 .... 167 D2
   Newbury RG14 .... 1 C1
Boundstone Cl GU10 .... 121 F3
Boundstone Rd GU10 .... 121 F2
Bounty Rd RG21 .... 69 D2
Bounty Rise RG21 .... 69 D2
Bourley Rd Aldershot GU13 ... 75 E2
   Crondall GU13 .... 75 E2
   Fleet GU13 .... 75 E2
Bourne Arch RG18 .... 2 C2
Bourne Ct
   Aldershot GU9 .... 99 F4
   33 Andover SP10 .... 83 E1
   4 Basingstoke RG24 .... 69 E3
Bourne Cty Inf Sch The
   GU10 .... 122 A3
Bourne Dene GU10 .... 121 F3
Bourne Field RG26 .... 47 F2
Bourne Firs GU10 .... 122 A3
Bourne Gr GU10 .... 122 B4
Bourne Grove Cl GU10 .... 122 B4
Bourne Grove Dr GU10 .... 122 B4
Bourne Hts GU10 .... 122 A4
Bourne La SP9 .... 101 D4
Bourne Meadow SP11 .... 62 A1
Bourne Mill Ind Est GU9 .... 99 C2
Bourne Pl GU10 .... 140 C4
Bourne Rd
   North Tidworth SP9 .... 78 C3
   Thatcham RG19 .... 2 C2
Bourne The GU13 .... 75 D3
Bourne View SP9 .... 78 C4
Bournemouth Rd SP11 .... 124 C3
Bow Dr RG26 .... 29 E1
Bow Field RG27 .... 51 E1
Bow Gdns RG24 .... 49 E4
Bow Gr RG26 .... 29 E1
Bow St GU34 .... 139 F1
Bowcott Hill GU35 .... 165 E3
Bowenhurst Gdns GU13 .... 75 D3
Bowenhurst La GU13 .... 74 B2
Bowenhurst Rd GU13 .... 75 D3
Bower Rd GU10 .... 121 F3
Bowers Grove La SO24 .... 181 E4
Bowers La SP11 .... 38 A4
Bowling Green Ct GU14 .... 56 B4
Bowling Green Dr RG24 .... 50 C1
Bowling Green Rd RG18 .... 2 C3
Bowman Rd GU14 .... 49 D2
Bowmonts Rd RG26 .... 27 D4
Bowyer Cl **5** RG22 .... 69 D2
Boxall's Gr GU11 .... 99 F4
Boxall's La GU9 .... 99 F4
Boyce Cl RG22 .... 91 E4
Boyne Mead Rd SO23 .... 176 B4
Boyne Rise SO23 .... 176 A4
Boyneswood Cl GU34 .... 160 B2
Boyneswood La GU34 .... 160 A2
Boyneswood Rd GU34 .... 160 B2
Brabon Rd GU14 .... 55 E3
Bracebridge GU15 .... 35 F3
Bracher Cl SP10 .... 106 A4
Bracken Bank RG21 .... 69 F4

Bracken La Bordon GU46 ...... 186 A4
   Yateley GU46 .... 33 F3
Brackenbury SP10 .... 82 B1
Brackendale Cl GU15 .... 36 B2
Brackendale Rd GU15 .... 36 A2
Brackens The GU22 .... 91 E3
Brackenwood Dr RG26 .... 9 F1
Bracklesham Cl GU14 .... 55 F4
Brackley Ave RG27 .... 52 B3
Brackley Way RG22 .... 68 B1
Bracknell La RG27 .... 52 B4
Bradley Cotts SO21 .... 112 A1
Bradley Peak SO22 .... 175 E1
Bradley Rd SO22 .... 175 E2
Bradman Sq SP10 .... 83 D2
Bradwell Pl SP10 .... 82 B2
Braemar Cl GU14 .... 56 B4
Braemar Dr RG23 .... 67 D1
Braeside Cl
   Haslemere GU27 .... 189 E4
   Winchester SO22 .... 197 D2
Brahms Rd RG22 .... 91 F4
Braishfield Rd SO51 .... 194 B1
Bramble Bank GU14 .... 56 C3
Bramble Hill SO24 .... 179 E3
Bramble Way RG24 .... 70 B3
Brambles Cl Ash GU12 .... 77 F1
   Four Marks GU34 .... 160 A1
Brambles The RG14 .... 5 E4
Brambleton Ave GU10 .... 121 F4
Bramblewood Pl GU13 .... 53 F1
Brambling Cl RG22 .... 90 C4
Bramblys Cl RG21 .... 69 D2
Bramblys Dr RG21 .... 69 D2
Bramdean Cl RG26 .... 26 C4
Bramdown Hts RG22 .... 91 D4
Bramley CE Prim Sch RG26 ... 28 C2
Bramley Cl GU34 .... 140 A2
Bramley Green Rd RG26 .... 29 D1
Bramley La Blackwater GU17 ... 34 C3
   Bramley RG26 .... 28 C2
Bramley Rd Camberley GU17 ... 35 F1
   Pamber End RG26 .... 27 E1
   Sherfield on Loddon RG27 .... 29 E1
   Three Ashes RG26 .... 28 A4
Bramley Sta RG26 .... 28 C2
Bramley Wlk GU35 .... 164 A1
Bramling Ave GU46 .... 33 F3
Brampton Gdns RG22 .... 91 E3
Bramshaw Ct SO22 .... 175 E2
Bramshill Cl RG2 .... 15 E4
Bramshill Council Hos RG27 ... 31 F4
Bramshill Ho (Police Coll)
   RG27 .... 32 A2
Bramshot Dr GU13 .... 54 A1
Bramshot La GU13 .... 54 C3
Bramshott Dr RG27 .... 51 D1
Brancaster Ave SP10 .... 82 B2
Brandon Cl GU34 .... 139 F2
Brandon Rd GU13 .... 74 C2
Brandy Bottom GU46 .... 34 B2
Brandy Mount SO24 .... 179 E3
Branksome Ave SO20 .... 129 D2
Branksome Cl
   Camberley GU16 .... 36 B3
   Chilbolton SO20 .... 129 D2
   Winchester SO22 .... 197 D3
Branksome Hill Rd GU47 .... 35 E4
Branksome Park Rd GU15 .... 36 B3
Branksomewood Rd GU13 .... 53 F1
Branson Rd GU35 .... 164 C2
Branton Cl RG22 .... 68 B2
Brassey Rd GU22 .... 175 F1
Braunfels Wlk RG14 .... 1 B1
Braxton Ho **1** SO23 .... 198 B4
Breach Farm Cotts RG25 .... 113 E2
Breach La
   Sherfield on Loddon RG24 ..... 49 F4
   Upper Chute SP11 .... 58 A4
Breachfield RG20 .... 22 B4
Brecon Rd GU14 .... 55 D4
Bremen Gdns SP10 .... 82 C2
Brendon Rd GU14 .... 55 D4
Bret Harte Rd GU15 .... 36 B1
Brew House La RG27 .... 52 B3
Brewells La GU33 .... 208 C2
Brewer Cl RG22 .... 68 B2
Brewers Cl GU14 .... 55 F3
Brewers La SO24 .... 204 B4
Brewery Comm RG7 .... 11 F4
Briar La GU34 .... 160 B2
Briar Way RG26 .... 27 D4
Briar Wood GU33 .... 208 A4
Briarlea Rd RG7 .... 11 E3
Briarleas Ct GU13 .... 77 D4
Briars Cl GU14 .... 55 D2
Briars The GU11 .... 77 F1
Briarwood Rd GU34 .... 16 B3
Brick Kiln La Alton GU34 ...... 139 E2
   West Tisted SO24 .... 204 A4
Brickfields Cl RG24 .... 70 A4
Brickiln La GU34 .... 160 C3
Bricksbury Hill GU11 .... 99 D4
Bridge Cl RG26 .... 27 D4
Bridge Meadows GU33 .... 207 F2
Bridge Rd Aldershot GU11 ...... 99 F4
   Camberley GU15 .... 35 F2
   Farnborough GU14 .... 55 E2
   New Alresford SO24 .... 179 D3
   North Warnborough RG29 ..... 72 B2
Bridge Sq GU9 .... 99 D1
Bridge St Andover SP10 .... 106 A4
   9 Newbury RG14 .... 1 C2
   Overton RG25 .... 88 A4
   34 Winchester SO23 .... 198 A4
Bridge Wlk GU46 .... 34 A4
Bridge Works GU15 .... 35 F2
Bridgefield GU9 .... 99 D1

Bridgemead GU16 .... 56 A4
Bridges The RG7 .... 11 D3
Bridgetts La SO21 .... 155 D1
Bridle Cl GU26 .... 166 C2
Bridle Ct **7** GU14 .... 76 B1
Brighton Hill Com Sch RG22 ... 68 B1
Brighton Hill Ctr RG22 .... 91 E4
Brighton Hill Rdbt RG22 .... 68 B1
Brighton Rd GU10 .... 100 A4
Brighton Way RG22 .... 91 E4
Brightstone La GU34 .... 161 D1
Brightwells Rd GU9 .... 99 D1
Brimley Hill Ct RG20 .... 24 B1
Brimpton CE Prim Sch RG19 ... 8 B3
Brimpton La RG19 .... 8 C2
Brimpton Rd Baughurst RG26 ... 9 D1
   Brimpton RG7 .... 8 B4
Brindle Cl GU9 .... 99 F4
Brinkway GU13 .... 75 D4
Brinn's La GU47 .... 35 D3
Brinns Cotts GU15 .... 35 D3
Brisbane Cl SP9 .... 79 E4
Brislands La SO24 .... 181 F4
Bristow Cres GU15 .... 36 A2
Bristow Cty Fst Sch GU47 ...... 35 E1
Bristow Rd GU17 .... 35 F2
Britannia Cl GU35 .... 164 C2
Brittain Cl GU17 .... 35 D4
Britten Cl GU12 .... 77 F1
Britten Rd RG22 .... 91 F4
Broad Chalke Down SO22 ..... 197 E2
Broad Ha'penny GU10 .... 121 F3
Broad Leaze RG7 .... 11 D1
Broad Oak La RG29 .... 73 D2
Broad Rd SP11 .... 104 B2
Broad St SO24 .... 179 E3
Broad View La SO22 .... 197 D2
Broad Way RG7 .... 13 D2
Broad Wlk GU15 .... 36 B1
Broadacres GU13 .... 74 B4
Broadhalfpenny La RG7 .... 10 A1
Broadhurst GU14 .... 55 D2
Broadhurst Gr RG24 .... 69 F4
Broadlands Camberley GU16 ... 56 B4
   Farnborough GU14 .... 56 B1
Broadlands Cl GU34 .... 120 A3
Broadmead GU14 .... 55 D2
Broadoak RG26 .... 27 D4
Broadview Cl GU34 .... 141 F4
Broadway GU28 .... 86 B2
Broadway The
   Andover SP10 .... 106 A4
   Newbury RG14 .... 1 C1
   Sandhurst GU17 .... 34 C4
   Winchester SO23 .... 198 A4
Broadwell Rd GU9 .... 121 E3
Brocas Dr RG21 .... 69 E4
Brockenhurst Dr GU46 .... 34 A3
Brockenhurst Rd GU14 .... 99 F4
Brockham Hill La GU34 .... 118 A1
Brockhurst Lodge GU10 .... 121 F4
Brocklands GU46 .... 33 F2
Brocksby Cl GU46 .... 34 C3
Brockwood Bottom SO24 ...... 202 C1
Broken Way Burghclere RG14 ... 6 A1
   Newtown RG14 .... 6 A1
Bromelia Cl RG26 .... 28 C2
Bronte Rise RG14 .... 5 F4
Brook Ave GU11 .... 99 E4
Brook Cl Ash GU12 .... 77 F2
   Fleet GU13 .... 75 D4
Brook Cotts
   King's Somborne SO51 .... 193 E3
   Yateley SO17, GU47 .... 34 A3
Brook Gdns GU14 .... 55 E1
Brook Gn RG26 .... 27 D4
Brook Ho Farnham GU11 .... 99 D3
   Newbury RG14 .... 1 C2
Brook Rd GU15 .... 35 F2
Brook The SO24 .... 179 E4
Brook Trad Est The GU12 .... 77 E1
Brooke Cl SO23 .... 176 A4
Brooke Ct GU16 .... 56 B3
Brookfield Rd GU12 .... 77 E2
Brookham Sch GU30 .... 188 B1
Brookhouse Rd GU14 .... 55 E2
Brooklands GU11 .... 76 B1
Brooklands Cl GU9 .... 99 D4
Brooklands Rd GU9 .... 99 E4
Brooklands Way GU9 .... 99 E4
Brookley Cl GU10 .... 100 A2
Brookly Gdns GU13 .... 54 A1
Brookmead Ct GU9 .... 98 C1
Brooks Cl RG28 .... 86 B2
Brooks Sch SO22 .... 175 F1
Brookside Farnham GU9 .... 99 D3
   Sandhurst GU15 .... 35 D4
Brookside Bsns Ctr RG7 .... 14 A3
Brookside Wlk RG26 .... 27 D4
Brookvale Cl RG21 .... 69 D3
Brookway Newbury RG14 .... 2 B1
   Upper Clatford SP10 .... 105 E2
Brookwood Rd GU16 .... 56 A2
Broom Acres Fleet GU13 .... 74 C3
   Sandhurst GU46 .... 34 C4
Broom Cl GU47 .... 35 E2
Broom Squires GU26 .... 167 E2
Broome Cl GU46 .... 34 A4
Broomfield La GU34 .... 121 F1
Broomfield Rd GU35 .... 164 A1
Broomhill GU10, GU9 .... 98 A4
Broomhill Rd GU14 .... 55 D3
Broomleaf Cnr GU9 .... 99 D1
Broomleaf Rd GU9 .... 99 D1
Broomrigg Rd GU13 .... 53 F1
Broomwood Way GU10 .... 122 A3
Brougham Pl GU9 .... 98 C4
Broughton Mews GU16 .... 36 B1

Broughton Rd SO20 .... 148 C1
Brown Croft RG24 .... 50 C1
Browning Rd RG24 .... 69 E4
Browning Dr SO22 .... 197 E4
Brownsover Rd GU14 .... 55 D2
Broxhead Ind Est GU35 .... 164 C3
Bruan Rd GU14 .... 5 E4
Brummell Rd RG14 .... 1 B3
Brunel Cl SO21 .... 111 D1
Brunel Gate SP10 .... 82 A1
Brunel Rd RG22 .... 68 C3
Brunswick Pl RG22 .... 68 C1
Bruntile Cl GU14 .... 56 A1
Bryanstone Cl GU13 .... 75 D3
Bryce Gdns GU12 .... 100 A4
Bryces La SO21 .... 135 D2
Bryn Rd GU10 .... 121 E4
Buchan The GU15 .... 36 C4
Buchanan Dr RG40 .... 16 B4
Buckby La **9** RG21 .... 69 E3
Buckfast Cl RG24 .... 48 A1
Buckholt Rd SO20 .... 170 A3
Buckhurst Rd GU16 .... 56 B3
Buckingham Cl GU34 .... 139 E2
Buckingham Ct RG22 .... 91 D4
Buckingham Rd RG14 .... 1 B1
Buckland Ave RG22 .... 68 B1
Buckland Cl GU14 .... 56 A4
Buckland Par GU21 .... 68 A2
Buckskin La RG21 .... 68 A2
Budd's Cl RG21 .... 69 D2
Buddlesgate SO21 .... 131 E2
Budds La GU35 .... 164 B2
Buffbeards La GU27 .... 189 E4
Buffins Rd RG29 .... 72 B1
Bulbery SP11 .... 104 C2
Bulford Rd
   Shipton Bellinger SP9 .... 101 F4
   South Tidworth SP9 .... 78 B2
Bull Hill GU33 .... 208 C2
Bull La RG7 .... 13 F2
Buller Ct **7** GU14 .... 56 A1
Buller Rd GU11 .... 76 C2
Bulls Rd GU9 .... 99 E3
Bullfinch Cl GU15 .... 35 E4
Bullington La
   Barton Stacey SO21 .... 130 C4
   Upper Bullington SO21 .... 131 D3
   Wonston SO21 .... 131 D3
Bulls Drove SP5 .... 191 D3
Bullsdown Ct RG27 .... 29 E1
Bullsdown Rd RG26 .... 29 D1
Bulpits Hill SP11 .... 38 B3
Bunch La GU27 .... 189 E4
Bunch Way GU27 .... 189 E4
Bungler's Hill RG7 .... 14 C3
Bunnian Pl RG24 .... 69 D3
Buntings GU34 .... 139 F3
Buntings The GU9 .... 121 E4
Burchell Rd RG14 .... 1 B3
Burchett Coppice RG40 .... 16 B4
Burdock Cl SO20 .... 127 F4
Burfield RG20 .... 21 E3
Burford Rd GU47 .... 35 F2
Burgess Cl RG29 .... 72 B1
Burgess La RG20 .... 3 D2
Burgess Rd RG21 .... 69 D3
Burgh Hill Rd GU30 .... 187 D3
Burghclere Prim Sch RG20 .... 22 C3
Burghead Cl GU15 .... 35 D4
Burgoyne Rd GU16 .... 36 C3
Buriton Rd SO22 .... 175 E2
Burleigh Rd GU14 .... 56 A4
Burles Bridge Cotts GU9 .... 98 A1
Burley La RG25 .... 88 C3
Burley Rd RG22 .... 175 E2
Burley Way GU47 .... 35 D3
Burlington Ct
   6 Aldershot GU11 .... 76 C1
   Blackwater GU15 .... 35 D2
Burnaby Rd RG22 .... 68 B2
Burne Cl SO21 .... 153 E1
Burnett Cl SO22 .... 175 E1
Burney Bit RG26 .... 27 E4
Burnham Copse Schs RG26 ..... 9 F1
Burnham Manor GU16 .... 36 C4
Burnham Rd GU9 .... 9 E1
Burnley Cl RG26 .... 26 C4
Burnmoor Meadow RG40 .... 16 B1
Burns Ave GU13 .... 75 D3
Burns Cl Basingstoke RG21 ..... 69 E4
   Farnborough GU14 .... 55 E3
   South Wonston SO21 .... 153 F2
Burnsall Cl GU14 .... 55 F3
Burnside GU11 .... 54 A1
Burnt Hill Rd GU10 .... 121 F3
Burnt Hill Way GU10 .... 121 F3
Burnt Oak RG40 .... 16 B4
Burntwood Cotts SO21 .... 154 C1
Burrell Rd GU14 .... 56 A4
Burrow Hill Sch GU15 .... 36 B1
Burrowfields RG22 .... 91 D3
Burrwood Gdns GU12 .... 77 F2
Bursledon Cotts SP9 .... 101 F4
Burton's Gdns RG24 .... 70 A4
Bury Court Cotts GU34 .... 120 A4
Bury Hill GU17 SP10 .... 105 E2
Bury Rd RG22 .... 68 B3
Bury's Bank Rd
   Greenham RG19 .... 6 B4
   Thatcham RG19 .... 6 B4
Burydown Mead RG25 .... 89 F1
Buryfields RG29 .... 72 C1
Buryhill Inf Sch RG29 .... 72 C1
Buryhill Flats SP10 .... 105 E2
Bushells Dr RG20 .... 24 B2
Bushywarren La RG22 .... 92 C1

Busk Cres GU14 .... 55 E2
Bustards Cnr SO20 .... 147 F3
Butler Ct RG22 .... 68 B2
Butler Lodge RG25 .... 88 A4
Butlers Cl SO51 .... 191 F1
Butson Cl RG41 .... 1 B2
Buttenshaw Ave RG7 .... 15 E4
Buttenshaw Cl RG40 .... 15 F4
Buttercup Cl GU35 .... 165 D3
Butterfield GU47 .... 35 F2
Buttermer Cl GU10 .... 121 E4
Buttermere Cl
   Bordon GU35 .... 164 B3
   Farnborough GU14 .... 55 E2
Buttermere Ct GU12 .... 77 E2
Buttermere Dr RG22 .... 68 A1
Buttermere Gdns SO24 .... 179 E2
Butterys Ct **13** GU34 .... 139 F2
Butts Hill SP11 .... 57 F4
Butts Meadow RG27 .... 51 D1
Butts Prim Sch GU34 .... 139 F1
Butts Rd GU34 .... 139 F1
Butts The RG26 .... 27 F4
Butty The **11** RG21 .... 69 E3
By Pass Rd SO21 .... 131 D2
Byes La Silchester RG26 .... 27 D3
   Three Ashes RG26 .... 28 A4
Byfields Rd RG20 .... 24 B1
Byfleet Ave RG24 .... 70 A3
Byfrons The GU16 .... 56 A1
Byrd Gdns RG22 .... 91 E4
Byron Ave Camberley GU15 .... 36 C2
   Winchester SO22 .... 197 E4
Byron Cl Basingstoke RG24 .... 48 B1
   Fleet GU13 .... 75 D4
   Newbury RG14 .... 5 E4
   Yateley GU46 .... 33 F2
Byways GU46 .... 33 F3
Byworth Cl GU9 .... 98 B1
Byworth Rd GU9 .... 98 B1

Cabrol Rd GU14 .... 55 F3
Cabul Rd SP9 .... 78 B2
Cadet Way GU13 .... 75 D2
Cadnam Cl Aldershot GU10 ... 100 A3
   Oakley RG23 .... 67 D1
Cadogan Rd GU12 .... 77 D4
Caerleon Cl GU16 .... 167 D3
Caerleon Dr SP10 .... 83 D2
Caernarvon GU16 .... 56 B4
Caernarvon Cl RG23 .... 68 B3
Caesar Ct **13** GU11 .... 76 B1
Caesar Rd SP10 .... 83 D2
Caesar's Camp Rd GU15 .... 36 C4
Caesar's Cl GU15 .... 36 C4
Caesars Ct Camberley GU15 ... 36 C4
   Farnham GU9 .... 99 D4
Cairn Cl GU15 .... 36 C2
Cairngorm Cl RG22 .... 68 A2
Cairngorm Pl GU14 .... 55 E4
Caithness Cl RG23 .... 67 D1
Caker Stream Rd GU34 .... 140 A2
Caker's La Alton GU34 .... 140 B1
   East Worldham GU34 .... 140 B1
Calard Dr RG18 .... 2 C2
Calard Rd RG18 .... 2 C3
Calcott Pk GU46 .... 34 A3
Calder Ct **34** SP10 .... 83 E1
Calender Cl GU34 .... 139 F1
California Ctry Pk RG40 .... 16 A4
Calleva Cl RG22 .... 91 D4
Calleva Pk RG26 .... 9 E1
Calne Ho **3** SP9 .... 78 C3
Calshot Way GU16 .... 56 C4
Calthorpe Hos RG27 .... 52 C4
Calthorpe Park Sec Sch
   GU13 .... 74 B4
Calthorpe Rd GU13 .... 53 F1
Calthorpe Sq **17** GU13 .... 53 F1
Calton Gdns GU11 .... 100 A4
Calvecroft GU30 .... 188 A2
Calvert Cl GU12 .... 77 D1
Calvert Ctr The SO21 .... 112 B1
Calvin Cl GU15 .... 36 C2
Cam Wlk **25** RG21 .... 69 E3
Cambell Rd SP11 .... 108 B1
Camberley Cty Inf Sch 36 A3
Camberley Heath Golf Course
   GU15 .... 36 C2
Camberley Sta GU15 .... 36 A3
Camberley Towers GU15 .... 36 A3
Camberry Cl RG24 .... 69 E2
Cambrian Cl GU17 .... 35 F3
Cambrian Rd GU14 .... 55 D4
Cambrian Way
   Basingstoke RG22 .... 68 A2
   Wokingham RG40 .... 16 C4
Cambridge Ct **1** GU14 .... 56 A1
Cambridge Military Hospl
   GU11 .... 76 C2
Cambridge Pl GU9 .... 99 D1
Cambridge Rd GU11 .... 76 B1
Cambridge Rd E GU16 .... 56 A1
Cambridge Rd W GU16 .... 56 A1
Cambridge Sq GU15 .... 36 A3
Cambridge Wlk GU15 .... 54 B1
Camelot SP10 .... 83 D1
Camelsdale Cty Prim Sch
   GU27 .... 189 E3
Camelsdale Rd GU27 .... 189 E3
Cameron Cl GU12 .... 77 D4
Camfield Cl RG22 .... 69 E2
Camlea Cl RG21 .... 69 E1
Camoys Mead GU34 .... 116 B1
Camp Farm Rd GU11 .... 77 D3
Camp Hill GU11 .... 100 A1

Camp Rd Bordon GU35 .... 164 B2
Farnborough GU12 .... 77 D4
Padworth RG7 .... 11 D4
Campana Int Coll GU9 .... 99 F1
Campbell Cl
 Aldershot GU11 .... 100 A4
 Fleet GU13 .... 53 F1
 Yateley GU47 .... 34 B3
Campbell Ct RG26 .... 29 D1
Campbell Pl GU16 .... 36 B2
Campbell Rd Aldershot GU11 ...... 76 C2
 Bramley RG27 .... 29 D1
Campbell St SP11 .... 124 C4
Campbell's Gn RG7 .... 11 F3
Campion Cl Hawley GU17 .... 35 E2
 Lindford GU35 .... 165 D2
Campion Way
 Hartley Wintney RG27 .... 52 B4
 Kings Worthy SO23 .... 176 B4
Campsie Cl RG23 .... 68 A2
Camrose Way RG21 .... 69 E2
Camus Cl GU13 .... 74 B3
Camwood Cl RG21 .... 69 E2
Canada Cotts SO21 .... 111 D1
Canada Way GU35 .... 164 B2
Canal Cl Farnborough GU11 .... 77 D3
 North Warnborough RG29 .... 72 B2
Canal Cotts GU11 .... 77 F2
Canal View Rd RG14 .... 2 A2
Candleford Gate GU30 .... 187 F2
Candover Ct RG26 .... 26 C4
Canes La GU35 .... 164 C3
Canhouse La GU33 .... 208 C2
Canning Rd GU14 .... 77 D1
Cannon Cl Ellisfield RG25 .... 115 D3
 Sandhurst GU15 .... 35 E4
Canon St SO23 .... 197 F4
Canons Ct SP9 .... 78 C2
Canons Ct RG20 .... 24 B1
Cansfield End RG14 .... 1 B2
Canterbury Cl RG22 .... 91 D4
Canterbury Rd Ash GU12 .... 77 F2
 Farnborough GU14 .... 56 A1
Canute Rd GU14 .... 198 A3
Capital Ho SO22 .... 197 F4
Capper Rd GU15 .... 35 F4
Carbonel Ct RG22 .... 68 A3
Cardew Rd GU33 .... 208 A2
Cardinals The GU10 .... 100 B4
Carfax Ave GU11 .... 100 A4
Carfax Est GU10 .... 100 B4
Cargate Ave GU11 .... 76 C1
Cargate Gr GU11 .... 76 C1
Cargate Hill GU11 .... 76 B1
Cargate Terr GU11 .... 76 B1
Carisbrooke GU14 .... 56 B4
Carisbrooke Cl
 Basingstoke RG22 .... 68 B3
 New Alresford SO24 .... 179 E2
Carleton Cl RG27 .... 50 C1
Carlinwark Dr GU15 .... 36 B4
Carlisle Cl RG22 .... 68 B3
Carlisle Rd GU10 .... 144 C4
Carlton Cl GU15 .... 36 C2
Carlton Cres GU13 .... 75 D3
Carlton Rd GU35 .... 166 A3
Carlyon Cl
 Farnborough GU14 .... 56 A2
 Mytchett GU14 .... 56 B2
Carmarthen Cl GU14 .... 55 F4
Carmichael Way RG22 .... 91 D4
Carnegie Rd RG14 .... 1 C1
Carnival Sq [14] GU13 .... 53 F1
Carolina Pl RG40 .... 16 B4
Carpenter Rd SP11 .... 108 B1
Carpenter's Down RG24 .... 48 B1
Carpenters SO24 .... 179 E3
Carpenters Cl Alton GU34 .... 140 B3
 Sherfield on Loddon RG27 ...... 29 E1
Carpenters Ct RG23 .... 68 B2
Carrick La GU46 .... 34 B3
Carrington Cres RG26 .... 26 C4
Carrington La GU12 .... 77 F4
Carshalton Rd GU16 .... 36 C4
Cartel Bsns Ctr RG21 .... 69 F4
Carter's Meadow SP10 .... 82 C1
Carters Wlk GU9 .... 99 D4
Carthagena SO21 .... 131 E2
Carthona Dr GU13 .... 74 C4
Carwarden House Sch GU15 .... 36 C2
Cary Cl RG14 .... 5 D3
Cassino Cl GU11 .... 76 C1
Castle Ave GU14 .... 197 F4
Castle Bridge Cotts RG29 .... 72 B2
Castle Cl GU15 .... 36 B2
Castle Ct GU9 .... 98 C2
Castle Gr RG14 .... 1 B3
Castle Hill Farley Castle RG2 ... 15 D4
 Farnham GU9 .... 98 C2
 Winchester SO22 .... 197 F4
Castle Hill Schs RG23 .... 68 B3
Castle Ind Pk RG14 .... 2 A3
Castle La RG14 .... 1 B3
Castle Rd Aldershot GU11 .... 76 B2
 Basingstoke RG21 .... 69 D2
 Camberley GU15 .... 36 B2
Castle Rise
 Kings Worthy SO23 .... 154 B1
 North Warnborough RG29 .... 72 B2
Castle Sch The RG14 .... 1 B3
Castle Sq [23] RG21 .... 69 D3
Castle St Farnham GU9 .... 98 C2
 Fleet GU13 .... 74 C4
 Medstead GU34 .... 159 F4
Castlecraig Ct GU15 .... 35 D4
Caston's Yd [19] RG21 .... 69 D2
Castor Ct Fleet GU13 .... 75 D3
 Yateley GU46 .... 33 F4

Caswall Ride GU46 .... 34 B3
Caswell Cl GU14 .... 55 E3
Catesby Gdns GU15 .... 33 F3
Cathedral View [5] SO23 .... 198 A3
Catherine Ct [14] GU11 .... 76 B1
Catherine Rd RG14 .... 1 C1
Catherine Villas GU27 .... 189 F3
Catkin Cl RG24 .... 48 C2
Cattle La SP11 .... 104 C3
Caunter Rd RG14 .... 1 A2
Causeway Gn RG27 .... 52 B3
Causeway The
 Heckfield RG27 .... 31 D4
 Middle Winterslow SP5 .... 168 A4
 Nether Wallop SO20 .... 147 F3
Cavalier Cl Newbury RG14 .... 2 A3
 Old Basing RG24 .... 70 B3
Cavalier Way GU34 .... 139 E1
Cavalry Ct [4] GU11 .... 76 B1
Cavan's Rd GU12 .... 77 D3
Cavell Ct RG24 .... 70 A4
Cavendish Ct
 Blackwater GU47 .... 35 D2
 Newbury RG14 .... 2 B3
Cavendish Gdns GU13 .... 74 C2
Cavendish Gr SO23 .... 176 A2
Cavendish Mews GU11 .... 76 C1
Cavendish Pk GU15 .... 35 E3
Cavendish Rd Aldershot GU11 ..... 76 C1
 Fleet GU13 .... 74 C2
Caves Farm Cl GU46 .... 34 C4
Caxton Cl SP10 .... 82 B1
Cayman Cl RG24 .... 48 B1
Cedar Ave GU47 .... 35 D3
Cedar Cl
 Aldershot GU10 .... 100 B4
 Kings Worthy SO23 .... 176 A4
 Tadley RG26 .... 27 D3
Cedar Ct GU27 .... 189 F3
Cedar Dr Fleet GU13 .... 54 B1
 Kingsclere RG20 .... 24 B1
Cedar La GU16 .... 56 A4
Cedar Rd GU14 .... 56 A2
Cedar Terr RG27 .... 52 A3
Cedar Tree Cl RG22 .... 90 A4
Cedar Way RG22 .... 68 B3
Cedar Wlk Andover SP10 .... 105 E4
 [18] Winchester SO22 .... 197 F4
Cedars Cl GU46 .... 34 B4
Cedars Sch The RG26 .... 9 F4
Cedars The GU13 .... 75 D4
Cedarways GU10 .... 121 F4
 Kings Worthy SO23 .... 176 B4
Celandine Ct GU46 .... 33 F4
Celtic Dr SP11 .... 105 F3
Cemetery Hill RG29 .... 72 C1
Cemetery Rd GU13 .... 74 C4
Central Rd GU35 .... 164 B3
Central Way SP10 .... 83 F1
Centre Dr RG24 .... 48 C1
Centurion Cl GU17 .... 35 D4
Centurion Way RG22 .... 91 D4
Chaffers Ct RG29 .... 95 E2
Chaffinch Cl
 Basingstoke RG22 .... 91 D4
 Sandhurst GU15 .... 35 D4
Chalcraft Cl GU30 .... 187 F2
Chalcrafts GU34 .... 140 A3
Chalet Cl GU35 .... 164 B2
Chalet Hill GU35 .... 164 B2
Chalfont Dr GU16 .... 56 A1
Chalford Rd GU14 .... 1 B1
Chalk Cl GU34 .... 160 A1
Chalk Hill GU30 .... 172 C3
Chalk Vale Ashley SO20 .... 172 C2
 King's Somborne SO20 .... 172 C2
 Old Basing RG24 .... 70 B3
Chalkcroft La SP11 .... 81 F2
Chalkpit La SP11 .... 104 B3
Chalkridge Prim Sch RG22 .... 68 C1
Chalky Copse RG27 .... 51 D1
Chalky Hill GU34 .... 159 D3
Chalky La RG27 .... 73 F2
Challenor Cl RG40 .... 16 B4
Challis Cl RG22 .... 68 B1
Challis St SP11 .... 57 D1
Challoner Cl RG23 .... 68 B2
Chamberlain Rd GU14 .... 121 D4
Chamberlains Meadow
 RG27 .... 31 D3
Chambers Rd GU12 .... 77 F3
Chamomile Gdns GU14 .... 55 D3
Champion Way GU13 .... 75 D3
Champney Cl GU35 .... 164 A1
Chandler Rd RG21 .... 69 D1
Chandlers La GU46 .... 34 A4
Chandlers Rd GU12 .... 77 F2
Chandos Rd GU14 .... 5 E4
Chandos Terr SO21 .... 177 F3
Chant Cl SP11 .... 128 C3
Chantreys GU13 .... 74 B4
Chantry Ct GU16 .... 36 A1
Chantry Ctr The SP10 .... 106 A4
Chantry Mews RG22 .... 91 D4
Chantry St SP10 .... 106 A4
Chantrys The GU9 .... 98 C1
Chapel Cl Amport SP11 .... 104 A3
 Dummer RG22 .... 90 B1
 Old Basing RG24 .... 70 A4
Chapel Cotts SP11 .... 61 F1
Chapel Ct
 Broughton SO20 .... 170 A4
 Wherwell SP11 .... 128 C3
Chapel Field SO21 .... 177 D2
Chapel Gdns GU35 .... 164 D3
Chapel Hill RG21 .... 69 D3

Chapel La
 Aldermaston RG26 .... 10 B3
 Ashford Hill RG7 .... 8 B1
 Baughurst RG26 .... 25 F2
 Broughton SO20 .... 170 A4
 Enham Alamein SP10 .... 83 D3
 Farnborough GU14 .... 55 E4
 Itchen Abbas SO21 .... 177 D2
 Riseley RG7 .... 14 A2
 Stoke SP11 .... 61 E2
Chapel Lodge RG26 .... 16 B3
Chapel Mead GU46 .... 33 E4
Chapel Pond Dr RG29 .... 72 B2
Chapel Rd Camberley GU17 .... 35 F3
 Farnham GU9 .... 121 E2
 Silchester RG7 .... 11 D3
Chapel River Cl SP10 .... 105 F4
Chapel Row RG27 .... 52 B4
Chapel Sq GU47 .... 35 E3
Chapel St Farnborough GU16 ...... 56 A3
 North Waltham RG25 .... 89 F1
Chapman Wlk RG18 .... 2 C2
Chappell Cl GU30 .... 188 A2
Chapter Ho [14] GU34 .... 139 F2
Chapter Terr RG27 .... 52 B3
Charfield Ct SO22 .... 197 F3
Charlcot Cl RG28 .... 86 B2
Charldon Gn RG24 .... 70 A4
Charlecote Cl GU14 .... 56 A2
Charlecote Mews [10] SO22 ...... 197 F4
Charledown Cl RG25 .... 88 A4
Charledown Rd RG25 .... 88 A4
Charles Cl Hook RG27 .... 51 D1
 Winchester SO23 .... 176 A1
Charles Dalton Ct SP10 .... 106 A4
Charles Kingsley CE Prim Sch
 RG27 .... 33 D4
Charles St Basingstoke RG22 ..... 68 C2
 Newbury RG14 .... 5 D3
Charlotte Cl Andover SP10 .... 106 B4
 Farnham GU9 .... 99 D4
Charlton Down SP11 .... 59 F1
Charlton La RG7 .... 14 A3
Charlton Pl RG14 .... 1 C2
Charlton Rd SP10 .... 82 C1
Charlton Sports and L Ctr
 SP10 .... 82 B1
Charlwood La
 East Tisted SO24 .... 182 B2
 Ropley SO24 .... 182 B2
Charmwood Cl RG14 .... 1 B3
Charnwood Cl
 Andover SP10 .... 106 A3
 Basingstoke RG22 .... 68 A2
Chart House Rd GU11 .... 77 F4
Charter Rd RG14 .... 5 E4
Charters Ct GU12 .... 100 A4
Chartwell Camberley GU14 .... 56 B3
 Farnham GU10 .... 121 E3
Chartwell Gdns GU12 .... 77 D4
Chase Cl GU35 .... 208 A2
Chase Com Hospl GU35 .... 164 B1
Chase Ct GU35 .... 164 C3
Chase Field GU34 .... 161 E2
Chase Plain GU26 .... 167 D1
Chase Rd Lindford GU35 .... 164 C3
 Liss GU33 .... 208 A2
Chase The
 Farnborough GU14 .... 56 A3
 Newbury RG14 .... 1 B4
Chasewater Ct [7] GU11 .... 76 C1
Chatfield Cl GU14 .... 56 A1
Chatham Rd SO22 .... 197 E3
Chatsworth Dr SP10 .... 105 E4
Chatsworth Gn RG22 .... 91 E3
Chatsworth Gr GU9 .... 98 C3
Chatsworth Hts GU15 .... 36 C4
Chatsworth Rd RG16 .... 56 B2
Chatter Alley GU13 .... 74 A4
Chatters The RG2 .... 15 D4
Chattis Hill Stables SO20 ...... 148 C2
Chaucer Av SP10 .... 82 B1
Chaucer Cl Basingstoke RG24 ..... 48 B1
 South Wonston SO21 .... 153 F3
Chaucer Cres RG14 .... 1 B3
Chaucer Gr GU15 .... 36 A3
Chaucer Ind Est SO23 .... 176 B1
Chaucer Rd GU14 .... 55 E3
Chaundler Rd SO23 .... 176 A1
Chaundlers Croft GU10 .... 97 E3
Chauntsingers Cotts [12]
 GU34 .... 139 F2
Chauntsingers Rd GU34 .... 139 F2
Chawton CE Prim Sch
 GU34 .... 161 E4
Chawton Cl SO22 .... 175 E2
Chawton End Cl GU34 .... 160 B2
Chawton Park Rd GU34 .... 139 E1
Cheam Hawtreys Sch RG20 .... 24 A4
Cheap St RG14 .... 1 C1
Cheavley Cl SP10 .... 105 E4
Chelmer Ct [2] RG21 .... 69 E3
Chelsea Ho [6] RG21 .... 69 D3
Chequer La RG7 .... 13 E1
Chequers La GU46 .... 33 E4
Chequers Rd RG21 .... 69 E3
Cherberry Cl GU13 .... 54 A2
Cheriton Cl
 Tadley RG26 .... 26 C4
 Winchester SO22 .... 175 E1
Cheriton La SO24 .... 180 A1
Cheriton Prim Sch SO24 .... 201 E3
Cheriton Rd SO22 .... 197 F4
Cheriton Way GU47 .... 35 D3
Cherrimans Orch GU27 .... 189 E3
Cherry Cl Hook RG27 .... 51 D1
 Newbury RG14 .... 1 B2
 South Wonston SO21 .... 153 E2

Cherry Tree Ave
 Haslemere GU27 .... 189 E4
 North Tidworth SP9 .... 79 D4
Cherry Tree Cl
 Farnborough GU14 .... 55 D3
 Farnham GU9 .... 99 D2
Cherry Tree Rd Andover SP10 ..... 82 C1
 Farnham GU10 .... 121 E2
Cherry Tree Wlk GU9 .... 121 E2
Cherry Wlk SO20 .... 126 A2
Cherryhill Gr GU11 .... 76 B1
Cherryway GU14 .... 139 F3
Cherrywood Rd GU14 .... 55 F4
Chesil St SO23 .... 198 A4
Chesil Terr [37] SO23 .... 198 A4
Chesilton Cres GU13 .... 75 D3
Chester Cl Ash GU12 .... 77 F1
 Newbury RG14 .... 2 A1
Chester Pl RG21 .... 69 D2
Chester Rd Ash GU12 .... 77 F1
 Winchester SO22 .... 198 A4
Chester Way GU12 .... 100 B4
Chesterfield Rd RG21 .... 69 E2
Chesters GU16 .... 36 C3
Chestnut Ave
 Aldershot GU12 .... 100 B4
 Andover SP10 .... 105 F3
 Camberley GU15 .... 36 C3
 Farnham GU10 .... 121 F4
 Littleton SO22 .... 175 D2
 North Tidworth SP9 .... 79 D4
Chestnut Bank RG24 .... 70 A4
Chestnut Cl Alton GU34 .... 139 F3
 Blackwater GU15 .... 35 E2
 Fleet GU13 .... 54 B2
 Grayshott GU26 .... 167 D2
 Liphook GU30 .... 188 A2
Chestnut Cres
 Middle Wallop SO20 .... 126 A2
 Newbury RG14 .... 1 C2
Chestnut Ct Aldershot GU11 ...... 77 D1
 Bordon GU35 .... 164 C1
 [7] Newbury RG14 .... 1 C2
Chestnut End GU35 .... 165 F2
Chestnut Gr GU13 .... 54 A1
Chestnut Rd GU14 .... 55 F3
Chestnut Wlk SO24 .... 179 E3
Cheswell Gdns GU13 .... 74 C3
Cheswycks Prep Sch GU14 .... 56 C3
Chetwode Pl GU10 .... 100 A4
Chetwode Terr GU11 .... 76 B1
Cheviot Cl Basingstoke RG22 ..... 68 A2
 Farnborough GU14 .... 55 E4
 Fleet GU13 .... 54 A2
 Newbury RG14 .... 5 D3
Cheyne Way GU14 .... 55 E4
Chichester Cl SP10 .... 105 E4
Chichester Pl RG22 .... 68 C1
Chichester Rd GU12 .... 77 F2
Chilbolton Ave SO22 .... 197 E4
Chilcombe Hts [39] SO23 .... 198 A4
Chilcombe La
 Chilcomb SO23 .... 198 C3
 Winchester SO23 .... 198 B3
Chilcroft La GU27 .... 189 F1
Chilcroft Rd GU27 .... 189 F1
Chilcrofts Rd GU27 .... 189 F1
Childerstone Cl GU30 .... 188 A2
Chilham Cl GU14 .... 56 B4
Chilland La SO21 .... 177 E3
Chillandham La SO21 .... 155 E1
Chillingham Way GU15 .... 36 A2
Chilmark Ct GU33 .... 207 F2
Chiltern Ave GU15 .... 55 D2
Chiltern Cl
 Farnborough GU14 .... 55 D2
 Haslemere GU27 .... 189 F3
 Newbury RG14 .... 5 D3
Chiltern Ct SO24 .... 179 E3
Chiltern Way RG22 .... 68 A2
Chiltlee Cl GU30 .... 188 A2
Chiltlee Manor GU30 .... 188 A2
Chiltley La GU30 .... 188 A1
Chiltley Way GU30 .... 188 A1
Chilton Farm Pk GU14 .... 55 D2
Chilton Ridge RG22 .... 91 D3
Chine The GU10 .... 121 E3
Chineham Bsns Pk RG24 .... 48 C2
Chineham District Ctr RG24 ..... 48 C1
Chineham La
 Basingstoke RG21 .... 69 E4
 Basingstoke, Popley RG24 ...... 48 A1
 Sherborne St John RG24 .... 48 A1
Chineham Park Cty Prim Sch
 RG24 .... 69 E4
Chingford Ave GU14 .... 56 A3
Chinnock Cl GU13 .... 74 C4
Chippendale Cl
 Baughurst RG26 .... 9 E1
 Blackwater GU17 .... 35 E2
Chive Ct GU14 .... 55 D2
Chivers Cl RG22 .... 68 B2
Chivers Dr RG40 .... 16 B4
Chobham Rd GU15 .... 36 B1
Cholderton Rd
 Cholderton SP4 .... 102 B2
 Grateley SP11 .... 124 C4
 Newton Tony SP4 .... 123 D4
 Quarley SP4 .... 102 B2
Chopin Rd RG22 .... 91 E4
Chrismas Ave GU12 .... 77 D1
Chrismas Pl GU12 .... 77 D1
Christchurch CE Prim Sch RG27 ... 74 C2
Christchurch Dr GU17 .... 35 D3
Christchurch Gdns [1] SO23 ..... 197 F4
Christchurch Rd SO23 .... 197 F3
Christie Hts RG14 .... 5 E4

Christie Wlk GU47 .... 34 A2
Christine Cl GU12 .... 77 E1
Christopher Ct RG14 .... 1 C1
Christy Ct RG26 .... 27 D4
Christy Est GU12 .... 77 E1
Chudleigh Ct [5] GU14 .... 55 F2
Church Ave GU14 .... 56 A2
Church Bank Rd SO21 .... 133 F3
Church Brook RG26 .... 26 C3
Church Circ GU16 .... 56 A1
Church Cl Andover SP10 .... 106 A4
 Enborne RG20 .... 4 B3
Church Cotts
 Ropley SO24 .... 181 E2
 Selborne GU33 .... 185 F4
Church Ct [7] GU11 .... 53 F1
Church Farm Barns RG7 .... 12 A3
Church Farm Cl RG25 .... 89 F1
Church Fields GU35 .... 165 D3
Church Gdns SP9 .... 101 F4
Church Gr GU13 .... 53 F1
Church Hams RG40 .... 16 A3
Church Hill
 Aldershot GU12 .... 100 A4
 Camberley GU15 .... 36 B3
 Nether Wallop SO20 .... 148 A3
Church Hill Terr GU10 .... 97 E3
Church La
 Alton GU34 .... 140 B4
 Ash GU12 .... 77 F1
 [4] Basingstoke RG21 .... 69 D3
 Basingstoke, Worting RG22 ..... 68 A2
 Baughurst RG26 .... 25 E1
 Bentley GU10 .... 120 A3
 Binsted GU9 .... 121 E2
 Bishop's Sutton SO24 .... 180 A2
 Bramdean SO24 .... 202 B2
 Bramshott GU30 .... 188 A3
 Brimpton RG7 .... 8 B3
 Burghclere RG20 .... 22 C4
 Buttermere SN8 .... 18 B4
 Cliddesden RG22 .... 92 A4
 Combe RG17 .... 19 E3
 Dogmersfield GU13 .... 74 A3
 Ellisfield RG25 .... 115 E4
 Enborne RG20 .... 4 B4
 Ewshot GU9 .... 98 A4
 Farley Hill RG2 .... 15 D3
 Farnborough GU14 .... 55 E2
 Farnham GU10 .... 121 E4
 Finchampstead RG40 .... 16 B2
 Froxfield GU30 .... 204 B2
 Goodworth Clatford SP10 .... 106 A1
 Grayshott GU26 .... 167 D2
 Greatham GU33 .... 185 F1
 Hartley Wintney RG27 .... 52 B3
 Headley GU35 .... 165 E3
 Heckfield RG27 .... 31 D3
 Houghton SO20 .... 171 E3
 Itchen Abbas SO21 .... 176 C3
 Kings Worthy SO23 .... 176 B3
 Littleton SO22 .... 175 D3
 Medstead GU34 .... 159 F4
 Mottisfont SO51 .... 192 C1
 Nether Wallop SO20 .... 148 A3
 Newbury RG14 .... 1 A2
 Old Basing RG24 .... 70 A3
 Ropley SO24 .... 181 E2
 Silchester RG7 .... 11 E1
 South Tidworth SP9 .... 78 C2
 Sparsholt SO21 .... 174 B2
 Upper Clatford SP10 .... 105 F2
 Vernham Dean SP11 .... 38 A4
 Woolton Mill RG20 .... 21 D4
Church La E GU9 .... 99 F4
Church La W GU11 .... 76 C1
Church Lands RG26 .... 28 B2
Church Pas GU9 .... 98 C1
Church Path GU12 .... 77 F2
Church Rd
 Aldermaston RG26 .... 9 F4
 Aldershot GU12 .... 100 A4
 Bramshott GU30 .... 188 A3
 Camberley GU15 .... 36 A1
 Fleet GU13 .... 53 F1
 Haslemere GU27 .... 189 E3
 King's Somborne SO20 .... 172 A1
 Longstock SO20 .... 149 E4
 Michelmersh SO51 .... 193 E1
 Newbury RG14 .... 1 C3
 North Waltham RG25 .... 89 F1
 Overton RG25 .... 88 A4
 Pamber Heath RG26 .... 10 B1
 Sandhurst GU15 .... 35 E4
 Silchester RG7 .... 11 D2
 Swallowfield RG7 .... 14 B3
 Tadley RG26 .... 26 C3
 Upper Farringdon GU34 .... 161 F2
Church Rd E GU14 .... 56 A1
Church Rd W GU14 .... 56 A1
Church Sq RG24 .... 69 D3
Church St
 Aldershot GU11 .... 76 B1
 Alton GU34 .... 139 F2
 Basingstoke RG21 .... 69 D2
 Basingstoke RG23, RG24, RG25 .. 69 D3
 Bentworth GU34 .... 138 A3
 Crondall GU10 .... 97 E3
 Hurstbourne Tarrant SP11 ...... 60 C4
 Liss GU33 .... 207 F3
 Michelmersh SO21 .... 133 D2
 North Warnborough RG29 .... 72 B2
 Ropley SO24 .... 181 E2
 Wherwell SP11 .... 129 D3
 Whitchurch RG28 .... 86 B2

Church View
Ash GU12 .... 77 F1
Hartley Wintney RG27 .... 52 B3
Hook RG27 .... 51 D1
South Warnborough RG25 ...... 94 C2
Upper Clatford SP10 .... 105 F2
Yateley GU47 .... 34 A4
Churchdale 23 GU11 .... 76 C1
Churchfield Ct GU30 .... 187 F2
Churchfields GU35 .... 142 A1
Churchill Ave
Aldershot GU12 .... 100 A4
Odiham RG29 .... 95 E4
Churchill Cl
Alton GU34 .... 139 F1
Farnborough GU14 .... 55 F4
Four Marks GU34 .... 160 A1
Hartley Wintney RG27 .... 52 A4
North Tidworth SP9 .... 78 B4
Odiham RG29 .... 95 E4
Tadley RG26 .... 27 D4
Churchill Cres
Farnborough GU14 .... 55 F4
Headley GU35 .... 165 E2
Churchill Way Andover SP10 .. 83 E1
Basingstoke RG21 .... 69 D3
Churchill Way E RG21, RG25 .. 69 E3
Churchill Way W
Andover SP10 .... 82 B1
Basingstoke RG22 .... 68 C3
Churchyard Cotts SO24 ...... 179 E3
Churn Cl RG24 .... 70 A4
Churt RG10 Beacon Hill GU26 . 166 C4
Churt GU10 .... 166 C4
Headley GU35 .... 166 C4
Churt Wynde GU26 .... 167 D4
Chute Cl RG26 .... 28 C2
Cibbons Rd RG24 .... 48 C2
City Bsns Ctr SO23 .... 198 A4
City Rd SO23 .... 197 F4
Claire Ct SP10 .... 105 F4
Clandon Ct GU14 .... 56 B2
Clanfield Ride GU17 .... 35 D3
Clappers Farm Rd RG7 .... 11 F1
Clapps Gate Rd RG26 .... 10 B1
Clare Ct 11 GU13 .... 54 A1
Clare Mead GU10 .... 121 E2
Clare Wlk RG14 .... 5 D3
Claremont Ave GU16 .... 36 B3
Clarence Cl GU12 .... 77 D1
Clarence Ct 5 GU13 .... 54 A1
Clarence Dr GU15 .... 36 C4
Clarence Rd GU13 .... 54 A1
Clarendon Ave SP10 .... 105 F3
Clarendon Ct GU17 .... 35 D2
Clarendon Cty Schs SP9 ..... 78 C3
Clarendon Gdns RG14 .... 1 C2
Clarendon Ho 5 GU13 .... 53 F1
Clarendon Terr SP9 .... 78 B2
Clarewood Dr GU16 .... 36 B3
Clarke Cres GU47 .... 35 E4
Clarke's La SP11 .... 58 C3
Clarks Hill GU9 .... 98 A1
Clatford CE Prim Sch
SP11 .... 106 A1
Clatford Manor SP10 .... 105 F2
Clatford Manor Ho SP10 .... 105 F2
Claudius Cl SP10 .... 83 D2
Claudius Dr RG22 .... 68 B4
Clausentum Rd SO23 .... 197 F3
Clay Hill Cotts GU10 ...... 121 E3
Clay Hill Cres RG14 .... 2 A3
Clay's La Binsted GU34 ..... 141 D3
East Worldham GU34 .... 140 C1
Claycart Rd Aldershot GU11 .. 76 A2
Aldershot GU11 .... 76 B2
Claydon Gdns GU17 .... 35 F1
Claypit La GU32 .... 205 E3
Claythorpe Rd
RG23, RG24, RG25 .... 68 B2
Clayton Cl RG27 .... 52 B3
Clayton Rd GU17 .... 35 E1
Cleaver Rd RG21 .... 68 B2
Clem's Way SO51 .... 192 A1
Clemence Gdns RG28 .... 86 B3
Clements Cl GU34 .... 141 F4
Clere Ct RG20 .... 24 B1
Clere Gdns RG24 .... 48 C1
Clere Sch The RG20 .... 22 C4
Clerewater Pl RG19 .... 2 C2
Clevedge Way RG29 .... 72 B2
Clevedon Ct Camberley GU14 . 56 C4
Farnborough GU14 .... 56 A2
Cleveland Cl RG23 .... 68 A1
Cleveland Gr RG14 .... 1 B2
Cleves La RG25 .... 94 A3
Clewborough Dr GU15 .... 36 C3
Clewborough House Prep Sch
GU15 .... 36 C3
Cliddesden Ct RG21, RG25 ... 69 D1
Cliddesden La RG21 .... 91 E3
Cliddesden Prim Sch RG25 ... 92 A3
Cliddesden Rd RG21 .... 69 D1
Clifton Cl GU10 .... 121 E2
Clifton Gdns GU14 .... 56 B3
Clifton Hill SO22 .... 197 F4
Clifton Lodge No 1 13 SO22 . 197 F4
Clifton Lodge No 2 14 SO22 . 197 F4
Clifton Rd Newbury RG14 ..... 1 B1
Winchester SO22 .... 197 F4
Clifton Terr SO22 .... 197 F4
Clifton Wlk 15 RG21 .... 69 D3
Clitheroe Rd GU46 .... 34 B1
Clive Rd GU12 .... 77 D1
Clockhouse Rd GU14 .... 55 F2

Cloisters The
16 Alton GU34 .... 139 F2
Camberley GU15 .... 36 A1
Close The
Camberley GU16 .... 56 A4
Farnham GU9 .... 99 D1
Hatherden SP11 .... 59 E1
Liphook GU30 .... 188 A1
Monk Sherborne RG26 .... 47 D3
Sandhurst GU15 .... 35 E4
Thatcham RG18 .... 2 C2
Closeworth Rd GU12 .... 77 E4
Clouston Rd GU14 .... 55 E3
Clovelly Dr GU26 .... 167 D4
Clovelly Pk GU26 .... 167 D4
Clovelly Rd GU26 .... 167 D4
Clover Bank SO23 .... 154 A1
Clover Cl GU35 .... 165 D3
Clover Field RG21 .... 69 F4
Clover La GU46 .... 33 F3
Club La SP9 .... 78 C2
Clubhouse Rd GU11 .... 76 B3
Clumps Rd GU10 .... 122 B2
Clyde Ct 35 SP11 .... 83 E1
Coach Hill SP11 .... 58 B2
Coach House Cl GU15 .... 36 B2
Coach House Gdns GU13 ...... 54 A2
Coach Rd The
East Tytherley SP5 .... 191 F4
West Tytherley SP5 .... 191 F4
Coachman's Ct RG14 .... 1 C3
Coachways SP11 .... 106 A3
Coate Dr SO21 .... 153 E1
Coates Cl RG22 .... 68 C1
Cob Tree Cotts RG24 .... 70 C2
Cobbett Cl SO22 .... 197 E3
Cobbett Gn RG22 .... 68 C1
Cobbett's La GU46 .... 34 B3
Cobbetts Mews 3 GU9 .... 98 C1
Cobbetts Way GU9 .... 121 E3
Cock-a-Dobby GU46 .... 34 C4
Cocket's Mead SO21 .... 177 D2
Cockshott La GU32 .... 206 B1
Cody Rd GU14 .... 55 E2
Coe Cl GU11 .... 76 C1
Cokenor Wood GU10 .... 121 E3
Coker Cl SO22 .... 197 F4
Colbeck GU13 .... 75 D2
Colbourne Ct 6 SO23 ...... 176 A1
Colbred Cnr GU13 .... 54 A1
Cold Harbour Ct 12 SP10 ... 106 A4
Cold Harbour La GU14 .... 55 E4
Colden La SO24 .... 158 A2
Coldharbour RG25 .... 89 F1
Coldrey Cotts GU14 .... 119 E2
Coleford PI SO23 .... 198 A4
Coleford Bridge Rd
Farnborough GU14 .... 56 B2
Mytchett GU16 .... 56 B2
Coleford Cl GU16 .... 56 B2
Coleford Paddocks GU14 ..... 56 B2
Coleman Cl RG21 .... 69 E4
Coleman Rd GU12 .... 77 D1
Colenzo Dr SP10 .... 83 E1
Coleridge Ave GU46 .... 34 B3
Coleson Hill Rd GU9 .... 121 E3
Coleville Rd GU14 .... 55 E3
Coley La SP11 .... 128 C2
Coliseum Bsns Ctr GU17 ..... 35 F2
Collard Way 4 GU33 .... 207 F2
College Cl GU15 .... 36 A4
College Cres GU14 .... 35 E4
College Gdns GU9 .... 98 C1
College La RG25 .... 115 D3
College Piece RG7 .... 11 E3
College Rd Ash GU12 .... 77 F2
Basingstoke RG22 .... 68 C3
Sandhurst GU47 .... 35 E4
College Ride GU16 .... 36 A4
College St SO23 .... 198 A4
College Town Schs GU47 ..... 35 E4
College Wlk SO23 .... 198 A3
Colley Cl SO23 .... 176 A2
Colleywater La GU34 .... 205 D2
Collier Cl GU14 .... 55 D3
Collingwood Coll GU16 ...... 36 C4
Collingwood Grange Cl GU16 . 36 C4
Collingwood Mount GU15 ..... 36 C3
Collingwood Pl GU15 .... 36 C4
Collingwood Rise GU15 ...... 36 C4
Collins Cl SP10 .... 82 C2
Collins Ct 11 SP9 .... 78 C4
Collyers Cres GU30 .... 188 B2
Colne Way Ash GU14 .... 77 F1
22 Basingstoke RG21 .... 69 E3
Colson Cl 46 SO23 .... 198 A4
Colson Rd SO23 .... 198 A4
Coltsfoot Pl RG27 .... 51 E1
Coltsfoot Rd GU35 .... 165 D3
Columbia Ct RG40 .... 16 B4
Columbine Rd RG22 .... 91 D4
Columbus Dr GU14 .... 55 D2
Columbus Way SP10 .... 83 F1
Colwyn Cl GU46 .... 34 A3
Colyer Cl RG22 .... 68 B2
Combe La GU14 .... 55 F3
Combe Rd GU33 .... 208 A1
Combe Rise GU10 .... 122 A3
Comet Ho 11 RG26 .... 9 E1
Comfrey Cl GU14 .... 55 D3
Commercial Ctr The SP11 .... 84 A2
Commercial Rd GU11 .... 100 A4
Commodore Ct GU11 .... 76 C4
Common Hill GU34 .... 159 E3
Common Rd RG19 .... 7 E1

Common The
Middle Winterslow SP5 ...... 168 A3
Ramsdell RG26 .... 26 C1
Common Vale SP5 .... 168 A3
Commonfield La RG40 .... 15 F4
Communications Rd RG14 ...... 6 B3
Compass Field RG27 .... 51 D1
Complins GU34 .... 140 B3
Compton Cl Fleet GU13 ...... 75 D3
Hook RG27, RG29 .... 51 D1
Winchester SO22 .... 197 D2
Compton Place Bsns Ctr
GU47 .... 35 F2
Compton Rd Fleet GU13 ...... 75 D3
Winchester SO23 .... 197 F4
Compton Sq SP10 .... 83 E2
Compton Way
Farnham GU11 .... 99 F1
Winchester SO22 .... 197 D2
Conde Way GU35 .... 164 B1
Coney Gn 4 SO23 .... 176 A1
Congreve Cl RG7 .... 9 F4
Conholt Hill SP11 .... 37 F2
Conholt Rd SP10 .... 106 A3
Conifer Cl Baughurst RG26 ... 9 E1
Bordon GU35 .... 164 B1
Fleet GU13 .... 74 C3
Winchester SO22 .... 175 F1
Conifer Crest RG14 .... 5 D2
Conifer Dr GU15 .... 36 C3
Coniston Cl
Farnborough GU14 .... 55 E2
Thatcham RG19 .... 2 C2
Coniston Ct Ash GU12 .... 77 E2
8 Newbury RG14 .... 1 C2
Coniston Dr GU9 .... 98 C3
Coniston Gr SO24 .... 179 E2
Coniston Rd
Basingstoke RG22 .... 68 A1
Bordon GU35 .... 164 B3
Coniston Way GU13 .... 74 C3
Connaught Cl Bordon GU35 .. 164 B1
Yateley GU46 .... 34 A3
Connaught Rd
Aldershot GU11 .... 77 D1
Camberley GU15 .... 36 B3
Fleet GU13 .... 54 A1
Kings Worthy SO21 .... 153 E1
Newbury RG14 .... 1 C1
Connaught Sch The GU12 .... 100 B4
Connop Way GU15 .... 36 B2
Conservatory The 38 SO23 . 198 A4
Constable Cl RG24 .... 69 E2
Constable Ct SP10 .... 83 D1
Constable Way SP10 .... 35 E3
Constables Gate SO22 ...... 197 F4
Constantine Way RG22 .... 91 D3
Constantius Ct RG27 .... 74 C2
Conway Cl GU15 .... 36 B1
Conway Dr
Farnborough GU14 .... 55 D2
Thatcham RG18 .... 2 C3
Cooks SO51 .... 191 F1
Coolarne Rise GU15 .... 36 C3
Coolers Farm SO20 .... 170 B3
Coombe Cl GU16 .... 56 A4
Coombe Dr GU13 .... 54 B1
Coombe Rd GU46 .... 33 F4
Coombehurst Dr RG21 .... 69 D1
Cooper Ct GU16 .... 56 A2
Cooper Ho GU35 .... 164 B1
Cooper's Hill GU46 .... 33 D2
Cooper's Terr GU9 .... 99 D2
Cooperage The 3 GU34 ..... 139 F2
Coopers Cl SO51 .... 153 E1
Coopers La RG26 .... 28 C2
Cope Hall La RG14 .... 5 D4
Copes La RG27 .... 31 F4
Copland Cl RG22 .... 91 E4
Copnor Cl RG20 .... 21 D4
Copnor Rd RG20 .... 21 D4
Coppice Cl
Baughurst RG26 .... 26 A4
Farnham GU10 .... 99 E3
Newbury RG14 .... 5 F4
Winchester SO22 .... 175 E1
Coppice Gdns GU46 .... 34 A3
Coppice Mews RG21 .... 68 B3
Coppice Rd RG20 .... 24 C1
Copse Ave GU9 .... 99 E4
Copse Cl Camberley GU16 .... 36 C3
Liss GU33 .... 208 A2
Copse End Camberley GU16 ... 36 B3
Fleet GU13 .... 74 B4
Copse Field RG24 .... 70 A4
Copse La
Brown Candover SO21 .... 134 C2
Fleet GU13 .... 74 C3
Copse Rd Linchmere GU27 ... 189 D3
Overton RG25 .... 65 D1
Copse The Farnborough GU14 . 55 D2
Farnham GU10 .... 121 E2
Tadley RG26 .... 26 C4
Copse View Cl RG24 .... 49 D2
Copse Way Farnham GU10 .... 121 E3
Wokingham RG40 .... 16 B4
Coram Cl 3 SO23 .... 176 A1
Cordale Rd RG21 .... 69 D2
Cordelia Gdns GU14 .... 56 B1
Cordwalles Cty Mid Sch
GU15 .... 36 B4
Cordwalles Rd GU15 .... 36 B4
Corfe Cl SO24 .... 179 E2
Corfe Gdns GU15 .... 36 B1
Corfe Way GU14 .... 56 B1
Corfe Wlk RG22 .... 68 B3
Corfield Cl RG40 .... 16 B2
Coriander Cl GU14 .... 55 D2

Corinthian Cl
Basingstoke RG22 .... 91 D4
Knights Enham RG21 .... 83 D2
Cormorant Cl RG23 .... 90 C4
Cormorant Pl GU15 .... 35 E4
Cornbunting Cl GU15 .... 35 D4
Cornelia Cl GU12 .... 55 D2
Cornfields Andover SP10 ... 106 B3
Yateley GU46 .... 33 F2
Cornfields The RG22 .... 91 E4
Cornish Cl RG22 .... 68 B2
Cornwall Cl GU15 .... 36 B4
Cornwall Rd GU35 .... 164 B1
Coronation Cl
Burghclere RG20 .... 22 B4
Odiham RG29 .... 72 C2
Coronation Rd Aldershot GU9 . 99 F4
Basingstoke RG21 .... 69 E3
Ludgershall SP11 .... 57 D1
North Tidworth SP9 .... 78 C4
Yateley GU46 .... 34 B4
Corporation Cotts 1 RG14 ... 1 C1
Correlli Rd RG22 .... 91 E4
Corringway GU13 .... 75 D3
Corry Rd GU26 .... 167 D3
Corunna Main SP10 .... 83 D1
Cossack La 11 SO23 .... 198 A4
Cossack Lane Ho 13 SO23 ... 198 A4
Coster Cl RG14 .... 1 A1
Cotswold Cl
Basingstoke RG23 .... 68 A2
Farnborough GU14 .... 55 E4
Cotswold Ct 19 GU13 .... 53 F1
Cottage Gdns GU14 .... 55 E2
Cottage Gn
Goodworth Clatford SP11 ... 128 A4
Hartley Wintney RG27 .... 52 B3
Cottage La GU32 .... 206 C2
Cottage Rd SO20 .... 147 E4
Cottington Cl RG20 .... 24 B1
Cottle Cl RG21 .... 69 D1
Cottonworth Cotts SP11 .... 128 B2
Cottrell Ct GU14 .... 77 D4
Cottrell Flats GU12 .... 77 D4
Council Cotts SO24 .... 157 E1
Council Hos Baughurst RG26 . 25 F1
Little Somborne SO24 ...... 173 D3
Council Hos The
Baughurst RG26 .... 25 F2
Highclere RG20 .... 21 F4
Council Rd RG21 .... 69 D2
Court Cl GU30 .... 188 A2
Court Dro RG25 .... 64 C1
Court Gdns GU15 .... 36 A3
Court La
Little Somborne SO24 ...... 173 D3
Ropley SO24 .... 181 E3
Court Moor Sch GU13 .... 74 C4
Court Rd Aldershot GU11 .... 76 C1
Kings Worthy SO23 .... 176 B3
Court The SO23 .... 143 D2
Courtenay Rd Farnham GU9 ... 99 E4
Winchester SO23 .... 176 A2
Courtlands Rd RG14 .... 1 C1
Courtmoor Ave GU13 .... 75 D4
Courts Hill Rd GU27 .... 189 F3
Courts Mount Rd GU27 ...... 189 F3
Courtyard The GU30 .... 188 C1
Cove Inf Sch GU14 .... 55 E3
Cove Jun Sch GU14 .... 55 E3
Cove Rd Farnborough GU14 ... 55 E2
Fleet GU13 .... 54 B2
Cove Sch GU14 .... 55 E3
Coventry Cl RG22 .... 91 D4
Coventry Ct 7 SO23 .... 176 A1
Covert The GU14 .... 55 E4
Coverts The RG26 .... 26 C3
Covey Cl GU14 .... 55 F4
Covey Way SO24 .... 179 D2
Cow Drove Hill SO20 .... 172 A2
Cow La SP11 .... 80 A2
Cowdown Farm Cotts
SP10 .... 106 C3
Cowdown La SP10 .... 106 B2
Cowdray Pk GU34 .... 139 F1
Cowdrey Cl RG21 .... 69 E4
Cowdrey Sq SP10 .... 83 D2
Cowfold La RG27 .... 51 D3
Cowley Dr SO21 .... 153 E1
Cowslade RG14 .... 1 A3
Cowslip Bank RG21 .... 69 F4
Cowslip Cl GU35 .... 165 D2
Coxbridge Meadows GU9 ..... 98 C1
Coxbridge Rdbt GU10 .... 121 E4
Coxeter Rd RG14 .... 1 B2
Coxheath Rd GU13 .... 74 C3
Coxmoor Cl GU13 .... 75 D3
Crabb Hill RG26 .... 25 E1
Crabtree Gdns GU35 .... 165 E3
Crabtree La Churt GU10 .... 144 C1
Headley GU35 .... 165 E3
Crabtree Rd GU47 .... 35 F1
Craddock Ho 2 SO23 ...... 198 B4
Crake Pl GU47 .... 35 D4
Cramptons SO24 .... 139 D1
Cranberry Wlk GU47 .... 35 E2
Cranborne Ct RG21 .... 69 D1
Cranbourne La GU15 .... 68 C1
Cranbourne Sec Sch RG21 ... 68 C2
Cranbrook Ct GU13 .... 54 A2
Crane Cl GU15 .... 35 D4
Cranes Rd RG26 .... 47 F2
Cranesfield RG26 .... 47 F2
Cranford Ave GU13 .... 74 C4
Cranford Dr GU34 .... 140 B3
Cranford Park Dr GU46 ...... 34 A3
Cranleigh Ct GU14 .... 55 E2
Cranmore Cl GU11 .... 76 B1

Cranmore Ct GU16 .... 56 B2
Cranmore Gdns GU14 .... 76 B1
Cranmore La GU11 .... 76 B1
Cranmore Rd GU16 .... 56 C2
Cranworth Rd SO22 .... 175 F1
Craven Cl GU10 .... 122 A3
Craven Ct GU47 .... 35 E2
Craven Dene RG14 .... 1 C2
Craven Ho 6 GU9 .... 98 C1
Craven Rd RG14 .... 1 B1
Crawford Gdns GU17 .... 35 F3
Crawford Pl RG14 .... 1 B2
Crawlboys La SP11 .... 57 D2
Crawlboys Rd SP11 .... 57 D2
Crawley Cotts SO21 .... 152 A1
Crawley Dr GU16 .... 36 B3
Crawley Hill GU15 .... 36 B3
Crawley Ridge GU15 .... 36 B3
Crawley Ridge Cty Mid Sch
GU15 .... 36 B4
Crawley Wood Cl GU15 .... 36 B3
Crawts Rd RG25 .... 88 A4
Craydown La SO20 .... 125 F1
Credon Cl GU14 .... 55 E3
Crerar Cl GU14 .... 55 D2
Crescent Cl SO22 .... 197 D2
Crescent La GU12 .... 77 F3
Crescent The
Andover SP10 .... 105 E4
Crookham Village GU13 ...... 74 B3
Farnborough GU14 .... 56 A2
Farnham GU11 .... 99 D4
Four Marks GU34 .... 160 A2
Goodworth Clatford SP10 ... 105 F1
Hurstbourne Tarrant SP11 ... 60 C4
Mortimer RG7 .... 11 E3
Cress Gdns SP10, SP11 ..... 105 F3
Cresswell Rd RG14 .... 2 A2
Cricket Cl SO21 .... 152 A1
Cricket Hill RG40 .... 16 B1
Cricket Hill La GU17, GU46 . 34 B2
Cricket La GU10 .... 122 A3
Cricket Lea GU35 .... 164 C3
Cricketers Way SP10 .... 83 E1
Cricklade Coll SO24 .... 106 A4
Crimea Rd GU11 .... 76 C1
Cripley Rd GU14 .... 55 D3
Cripstead La SO23 .... 197 F3
Critchmere Hill GU27 ...... 189 E4
Critchmere La GU27 .... 189 E3
Critchmere Vale GU27 ...... 189 E3
Crockford La RG24 .... 48 B1
Croft Ave SP11 .... 106 A3
Croft Gdns Alton GU34 ..... 139 F2
Andover SP10 .... 106 A3
Croft La Crondall GU10 ..... 97 E3
Newbury RG14 .... 1 B2
Yateley GU46 .... 34 A4
Croft Rd Aldershot GU9 ..... 99 F4
Mortimer RG7 .... 11 E3
Newbury RG14 .... 5 E4
Oakley RG23 .... 67 D1
Croft The Fleet GU13 .... 74 B4
Newbury Tony SP4 .... 123 D3
Crofter's Cl GU46 .... 34 C4
Crofters Meadow RG21 ...... 69 F4
Crofton GU27 .... 189 E4
Crofts The RG22 .... 91 E3
Cromwell Cl RG24 .... 70 A3
Cromwell Pl RG14 .... 1 C2
Cromwell Rd
Basingstoke RG24 .... 69 D3
Camberley GU15 .... 36 A4
Newbury RG14 .... 2 A3
Winchester SO22 .... 197 F3
Cromwell Terr RG14 .... 1 A3
Cromwell Way GU14 .... 56 A4
Crondall Ct GU47 .... 35 F2
Crondall End GU46 .... 34 A4
Crondall La GU9 .... 98 B1
Crondall Prim Sch GU10 ..... 97 E3
Crondall Rd Bentley GU10 .. 120 C3
Crondall GU13 .... 74 B2
Crookham Village GU13 ...... 74 B2
Crookham CE Inf Sch GU13 ... 74 C2
Crookham Cl RG26 .... 26 C3
Crookham Jun Sch GU13 ..... 75 D2
Crookham Rd GU13 .... 74 C4
Crookham Reach GU10 .... 74 C2
Crooksbury Rd GU12 .... 100 A2
Cropmark Way RG22 .... 91 D4
Crosby Gdns GU46 .... 33 F4
Crosby Hill Dr GU15 .... 36 B4
Crosby Way GU9 .... 98 C1
Cross Farm Cty Fst Sch
GU16 .... 56 B3
Cross Gdns GU14 .... 56 B3
Cross Keys Pas 22 SO23 .... 198 A4
Cross La Andover SP11 ..... 105 F4
Ashmansworth RG20 .... 41 D4
Beech Hill RG7 .... 13 D4
Camberley GU15 .... 56 B3
Cross & Pillory La 6 GU34 . 139 F2
Cross Rd RG12 .... 77 F2
Cross St Aldershot GU11 .... 76 C1
Basingstoke RG21 .... 69 D3
Farnborough GU14 .... 77 D4
Winchester SO23 .... 197 F4
Cross The SO20 .... 172 A1
Crossborough Gdns RG21 ..... 69 E2
Crossborough Hill RG21 ..... 69 E2
Crosswater La GU14 .... 144 B2
Crossways The SP10 ..... 105 F4
Churt GU10 .... 144 B1
Crookham Village GU13 ...... 74 B3
Whitchurch RG28 .... 86 B3
Croucher's Croft SO22 .... 175 E1

Crowder Terr SO22 .... 197 F4
Crowfield Dr RG19 .... 2 C2
Crowley Dr GU34 .... 140 A2
Crown Cres RG24 .... 70 A3
Crown Dr GU9 .... 99 F3
Crown Gdns GU13 .... 75 D4
Crown La Farnham GU11 .... 99 F3
  Newnham RG27 .... 71 E4
  Old Basing RG24 .... 70 A3
Crown Way SP10 .... 83 E1
Crows La GU34 .... 161 F2
Crowthorne Rd GU46 .... 34 C4
Croyde Cl GU14 .... 55 F3
Croye SP10 .... 105 F4
Cruikshank Lea GU15 .... 35 E3
Crundwell Ct GU9 .... 99 D2
Cuckoo Cl GU13 .... 89 F1
Cufaude La RG24 .... 48 C4
Cuffelle Cl RG24 .... 49 D2
Cufoude La RG24 .... 48 C2
Cullen GU47 .... 34 A3
Cullens Mews 4 GU11 .... 76 C1
Culley View SO24 .... 179 E2
Culver Mews 29 SO23 .... 198 A4
Culver Rd Basingstoke RG21 .... 69 D2
  Newbury RG14 .... 5 E4
  28 Winchester SO23 .... 198 A4
Culverlands Cres GU12 .... 77 F2
Culverwell Gdns 21 SO23 .... 197 F4
Cumberland Ave RG22 .... 68 C1
Cundell Way SO23 .... 154 A1
Cundellway SO23 .... 176 A4
Cunningham Ho 4 SP9 .... 78 C4
Cunnington Rd GU14 .... 56 B1
Curlew Cl RG21 .... 68 A1
Curlews GU34 .... 139 F3
Curleys Way RG7 .... 14 A3
Curling Way GU14 .... 2 A2
Curly Bridge Cl GU14 .... 55 E4
Curnock Ct RG14 .... 1 B1
Curtis Cl GU35 .... 165 E3
Curtis Ct GU13 .... 75 D3
Curtis La GU35 .... 165 E3
Curtis Rd GU34 .... 140 A2
Curzon Dr GU13 .... 75 D3
Cusden Dr SP10 .... 83 E1
Cuthbert Rd GU14 .... 77 F3
Cutts Rd GU12 .... 77 D4
Cuxhaven Way SP10 .... 82 C2
Cygnet Cl RG19 .... 2 C2
Cygnet Ct Fleet GU13 .... 54 A2
  Newbury RG14 .... 1 B2
Cygnets GU13 .... 54 A2
Cypress Cl RG40 .... 16 C4
Cypress Dr GU13 .... 54 B1
Cypress Gr Andover SP10 .... 105 E4
  Ash GU12 .... 77 E4
Cypress Rd GU35 .... 164 A1
Cypress Way
  Blackwater GU17 .... 34 C3
  Grayshott GU26 .... 167 D1
Cyprus Rd RG22 .... 91 E3
Cyril Vokins Rd RG14 .... 2 B1

Dacre Cl SP10 .... 82 B2
Daffodil Cl RG22 .... 91 D4
Dahlia Cl RG22 .... 91 D4
Dahlia Ct SP10 .... 105 E3
Dairy Wlk RG27 .... 52 B3
Dalby Cres RG14 .... 6 A4
Dale Cl Farnham GU10 .... 121 E4
  Littleton SO22 .... 175 D3
Dale Gdns GU17, GU47 .... 34 C4
Dale View GU27 .... 189 F3
Dalewood RG22 .... 68 A2
Dallence Ho RG25 .... 88 A4
Dalley Ct GU15 .... 35 D4
Dalzell 31 SO23 .... 176 A1
Damsel Path 12 RG21 .... 69 E3
Dance's La RG28 .... 86 B3
Dancers Meadow RG26 .... 47 F2
Dances Cl SP10 .... 83 D1
Danebury Rd RG22 .... 91 E3
Danebury Ring SO20 .... 148 C4
Danebury View SO20 .... 126 A2
Danebury Wlk GU16 .... 56 B4
Danegeld Cl SP10 .... 83 D2
Danehurst Pl SP10 .... 105 E4
Danemark Ct 4 SO23 .... 198 A4
Danes 22 SO23 .... 176 A1
Danes The RG21 .... 69 E3
Daneshill Dr RG24 .... 70 A4
Daneshill East Ind Est RG21 .... 69 F4
Daneshill Rdbt RG21 .... 69 F4
Daneshill Sch RG27 .... 30 B2
Daneshill West Ind Est RG21 .... 69 E4
Daniel Rd RG28 .... 86 B2
Dankworth Rd RG22 .... 91 E4
Danley La GU27 .... 188 C2
Danvers Dr GU13 .... 74 C2
Daphne Dr GU13 .... 74 C2
Darby Green La GU46 .... 34 C3
Darby Green Rd GU17 .... 34 C3
Darcy Ho RG22 .... 68 B1
Dare's Cnr GU13 .... 74 C1
Dare's La GU13 .... 74 C1
Darent Ct 23 RG21 .... 69 E3
Dark La
  Bishop's Sutton SO24 .... 179 F1
  Sherborne St John RG26 .... 47 F2
Darlington Rd RG21 .... 69 D4
Darracott Cl GU15 .... 36 C4
Darset Ave GU13 .... 54 A1
Dart Cl Thatcham RG18 .... 2 C3
  Wokingham RG40 .... 16 B3
Dart Ct 36 SP10 .... 83 E1
Dart Rd GU14 .... 55 D3
Dartmoor Wlk RG22 .... 68 B2

Dartmouth Way RG22 .... 68 B2
Dartmouth Wlk RG22 .... 68 B2
Darvill Rd SO24 .... 181 D3
Darvills La GU9 .... 99 D1
Darwin Gr GU12 .... 77 D2
Dashwood Cl GU34 .... 139 E1
Dasna RG SP9 .... 78 B3
Daunch Cl SP9 .... 78 B4
Dauntsey Dro SP11 .... 81 D2
Dauntsey La SP11 .... 81 D1
Davis Gdns GU15 .... 35 E4
Davy Cl RG22 .... 68 C2
Dawn Gdns SO22 .... 197 E3
Dawnay Rd Camberley GU47 .... 35 F4
  Sandhurst GU15 .... 35 F4
Days Meadow RG20 .... 21 D4
De Lunn Bldgs 5 SO23 .... 198 A4
De Montfort Rd RG14 .... 1 B3
De-lucy Ave SO24 .... 179 D3
Deadbrook La GU11 .... 77 E2
Deadmans La RG19 .... 5 F3
Deadmoor La RG14 .... 5 E2
Dean Cl SO22 .... 175 E1
Dean La Sparsholt SO22 .... 175 D1
  Winchester SO22 .... 175 D1
Dean Par GU15 .... 36 B4
Dean Rd West Dean SP5 .... 190 A1
  West Tytherley SP5 .... 190 C3
Dean Rise SP11 .... 60 C4
Dean Sta SP5 .... 190 B2
Dean Terr SP11 .... 38 B3
Dean The SO24 .... 179 E3
Deane Down Dro SO22 .... 175 D2
Deane's Cl RG21 .... 69 E3
Deanes Cotts RG25 .... 66 A1
Deans Cl SP10 .... 78 C2
Deanswood Rd RG26 .... 26 C4
Decouttere Cl GU13 .... 74 C2
Deedman Cl GU12 .... 77 F1
Deep La RG22 .... 68 C3
Deep Well Dr GU15 .... 36 B3
Deepdene Farnham GU10 .... 122 A4
  Haslemere GU27 .... 189 E3
Deer Rock Rd GU15 .... 36 B4
Deerfield Ct RG26 .... 29 D1
Deerleap GU35 .... 166 A2
Delibes Rd RG22 .... 91 F4
Delius Cl RG22 .... 68 C1
Dell Cl GU27 .... 189 F4
Dell Cotts SO24 .... 202 C1
Dell Gr GU15 .... 36 B1
Dell Rd Andover SP10 .... 82 C1
  Finchampstead RG40 .... 16 C2
  Winchester SO23 .... 198 B3
Dell The Farnham GU9 .... 99 D4
  Grateley SP11 .... 103 E1
  Kingsclere RG20 .... 24 B1
  Old Basing RG24 .... 70 B3
  Vernham Dean SP11 .... 38 A3
  Yateley GU47 .... 34 A3
Dellands RG25 .... 88 A4
Dellands La RG25 .... 88 A4
Dellfield Froxfield GU32 .... 205 F1
  Oakley RG23 .... 67 E2
Delville GU14 .... 55 D2
Dempster Ho GU9 .... 99 D4
Denby Ct 3 GU16 .... 56 A1
Dene Cl Bordon GU35 .... 164 B1
  Farnham GU10 .... 122 B3
  Ropley SO24 .... 181 D3
Dene Ct SP10 .... 106 A4
Dene La GU10 .... 122 B3
Dene La W GU10 .... 122 B3
Dene Path SP10 .... 106 A4
Dene Rd Andover SP10 .... 106 A4
  Farnborough GU14 .... 55 E2
Dene The SO24 .... 181 D3
Dene Way RG14 .... 1 C3
Denham Cl SO23 .... 175 F1
Denham Dr Basingstoke RG22 .... 68 B1
  Yateley GU17 .... 34 A3
Denham Terr SP11 .... 61 F1
Denman Cl GU13 .... 54 B1
Denmark Rd RG14 .... 1 C2
Denmark Sq GU11 .... 77 E1
Denmark St GU12 .... 77 D1
Denmead RG26 .... 26 C4
Dennet Ho SO23 .... 176 B1
Denning Cl GU10 .... 74 C4
Dennis Way GU33 .... 208 A2
Dennistoun Cl GU15 .... 36 A3
Denton Way GU15 .... 36 A1
Denyers Cotts GU34 .... 138 A2
Deptford La Greywell RG29 .... 72 A2
  Odiham RG29 .... 72 A2
Derby Rd Haslemere GU27 .... 189 F4
  Newbury RG14 .... 1 B1
Derbyfields RG29 .... 72 B3
Derek Horn Ct GU47 .... 35 F3
Derry Rd GU14 .... 55 E4
Derwent Ave GU12 .... 77 E2
Derwent Cl Bordon GU35 .... 164 B3
  Farnborough GU14 .... 55 E2
  Farnham GU10, GU9 .... 98 C3
Derwent Ct 37 SP10 .... 83 E1
Derwent Gdns SO24 .... 179 E2
Derwent Rd
  Basingstoke RG21 .... 68 A1
  Thatcham RG19 .... 2 C2
Devenish Rd SO22 .... 175 E2
Dever Cl SO21 .... 133 D2
Dever Way RG14 .... 67 D1
Devils La GU30 .... 188 B2
Devizes Ho 10 SP9 .... 78 C4
Devon Cl Fleet GU13 .... 54 A2
  Sandhurst GU15 .... 35 D4
Devon Rd GU35 .... 164 B2

Devonshire Dr GU16 .... 36 B4
Devonshire Pl
  Aldershot GU11 .... 76 B1
  7 Basingstoke RG21 .... 69 D2
Dewpond Wlk RG21 .... 69 F4
Dexter Sq SP10 .... 83 E2
Dexter Way GU13 .... 54 A2
Diamond Hill GU15 .... 36 B4
Diamond Ridge GU16 .... 36 A4
Diana Cl GU12 .... 68 C2
Dibley Cl RG22 .... 68 B2
Dickens La GU34 .... 70 A2
Dickens Way GU17 .... 34 A3
Dickens Wlk RG14 .... 5 F4
Dickenson Wlk SO24 .... 179 E2
Dicker's La GU34 .... 140 A2
Digby Rd RG14 .... 1 B2
Dilly La RG27 .... 52 B2
Dine Cl GU14 .... 60 C4
Dingley Way GU11 .... 76 C4
Dinorben Ave GU13 .... 74 C4
Dinorben Beeches GU13 .... 74 C4
Dinorben Cl GU13 .... 74 C4
Dippenhall Rd GU9 .... 98 A1
Dippenhall St GU10 .... 97 E3
Dirty Cnr RG14 .... 85 F4
Ditchfield La RG40 .... 16 B4
Divers Cl GU34 .... 139 F3
Dixons La SO20 .... 170 A4
Dockenfield St GU35 .... 143 D3
Doctors Dro SP11 .... 60 B4
Dogflud Way GU9 .... 99 D2
Dodsells Well RG40 .... 16 B4
Dogmersfield CE Prim Sch RG27 .... 74 A4
Doiley Bottom SP11 .... 40 B1
Doiley Hill SP11 .... 40 B2
Dollis Cl GU9 .... 99 D2
Dollis Dr GU9 .... 99 D2
Dollis Gr RG26 .... 28 C2
Dolman Rd GU14 .... 1 C2
Dolomans La SP11 .... 60 C4
Dolphin Cl RG27 .... 189 E3
Dolton Mews RG14 .... 1 B2
Doman Rd GU15 .... 35 F2
Dome Al SO23 .... 198 A4
Dominica Cl RG22 .... 48 B1
Domum Rd SO23 .... 198 A3
Donnington Castle RG14 .... 1 B4
Donnington Cl GU15 .... 35 F2
Donnington Ct 19 SO23 .... 176 A1
Donnington Hospital RG14 .... 1 B3
Donnington Lodge RG14 .... 1 B3
Donnington Pk RG14 .... 1 B3
Donnington Sq RG14 .... 1 B3
Dora's Green La GU9 .... 98 A2
Dorcas Cl GU47 .... 35 F2
Dorchester Cl RG22 .... 68 A3
Dorchester Rd RG27 .... 51 D1
Dorchester Way RG29 .... 72 A2
Doreen Cl GU14 .... 55 E4
Dorian Gr SO24 .... 179 D2
Dormer Cl RG14 .... 5 D3
Dorney Ct RG14 .... 2 A2
Dorrel Cl RG22 .... 91 D3
Dorset Cl GU15 .... 36 B4
Dorset Rd GU12 .... 77 F3
Doswell Way RG21 .... 69 E3
Douai Cl GU14 .... 56 A2
Doublet Cl RG19 .... 2 C2
Doughty Way SP10 .... 83 F1
Douglas Gr GU10 .... 122 A1
Douglas Pl GU14 .... 55 F3
Douglas Rd SP10 .... 105 D4
Douglas Ride RG20 .... 21 E4
Douro RG7 .... 9 D1
Dove Cl Andover SP10 .... 83 D1
  Basingstoke RG22 .... 67 F1
Dove Cl GU34 .... 140 A2
Dove House Special Sch RG21 .... 69 E4
Dover Cl Basingstoke RG22 .... 68 B3
  New Alresford SO24 .... 179 E2
Doveton Way RG14 .... 1 C2
Dowden Gr GU34 .... 140 A3
Down Farm La SO23 .... 175 F4
Down Gate SO24 .... 179 E2
Down La RG25 .... 71 E1
Down Rd SP11 .... 80 A2
Down St RG25 .... 90 B1
Downing St GU9 .... 98 C1
Downlands Rd SO22 .... 197 D2
Downlands Way SO21 .... 153 E2
Downs La SN8 .... 18 A4
Downs Rd SO21 .... 153 E2
Downs Way GU34 .... 139 E1
Downside GU26 .... 167 D4
Downside Cotts SP11 .... 124 C4
Downside Rd SO22 .... 175 D1
Downsland Par RG22 .... 68 C2
Downsland Rd RG24 .... 69 D2
Downsview Rd GU35 .... 166 A3
Downview Cl GU26 .... 167 D3
Doyle Gdns GU46 .... 34 A2
Dragonfly Dr RG21 .... 69 F4
Dragoon Ct 12 GU11 .... 76 B1
Drake Ave GU16 .... 56 C1
Drake Cl RG40 .... 16 B4
Drake Ct SP10 .... 83 E1
Drayman's Way GU34 .... 139 F2
Drayton St SP11 .... 197 E3
Drift Rd Bordon GU35 .... 186 A4
  Selborne GU35 .... 186 A4
Driftway Rd RG27 .... 51 E1
Drive The Farnham GU10 .... 121 F4
  Newbury RG14 .... 5 F4
  Oakley RG23 .... 67 D1
  Old Alresford SO24 .... 158 B3

Drove Hill SO20 .... 129 D2
Drove La SO24 .... 179 D3
Drove Rd SP11 .... 129 D2
Drove The RG14 .... 7 F1
Drovers End GU13 .... 54 B2
Drovers Way GU10 .... 98 C3
Droxford Cres RG26 .... 26 C4
Drummond Cl
  Four Marks GU34 .... 159 F1
  Winchester SO22 .... 197 F3
Drury Cl SP11 .... 108 A2
Drury La Bentworth GU34 .... 138 A3
  Mortimer RG7 .... 11 F3
Dryden Cl RG24 .... 48 B1
Dryden Rd GU14 .... 55 E3
Dryden Way GU30 .... 187 F3
Du Maurier Cl GU13 .... 74 C2
Duchess Cl GU34 .... 139 F2
Duck St GU11 .... 104 C2
Ducklands GU35 .... 164 C1
Duckmead La GU33 .... 208 A3
Ducks La SO22 .... 147 F3
Duddon Way 16 RG21 .... 69 E3
Dudley Cl Basingstoke RG23 .... 68 A3
  Bordon GU35 .... 164 B1
Dudley Cl GU13 .... 75 D3
Dudley Terr GU33 .... 208 A3
Duke Cl SP10 .... 83 E1
Duke St SO21 .... 133 D2
Duke Terr GU11 .... 76 C2
Dukes Cl Alton GU34 .... 139 E1
  Farnham GU9 .... 98 C3
Dukes Mead GU13 .... 53 E1
Dukes Ride RG26 .... 27 F4
Dukes Wlk GU12 .... 98 C3
Dumas Cl GU34 .... 34 A3
Dummer Down La RG25 .... 113 E4
Dummer La SP11 .... 37 D1
Dunbar Rd GU16 .... 56 B4
Dunbridge La
  Brown Candover SO24 .... 135 E3
  Mottisfont SO51 .... 192 B1
Dunbridge Sta SO51 .... 192 B1
Duncan Cl SP10 .... 106 B4
Duncan's Cl SP11 .... 80 C1
Dundaff Cl GU15 .... 36 C3
Dunedin Gr RG23 .... 79 D3
Dungells Farm Cl GU46 .... 34 A2
Dungells La GU46 .... 34 A2
Dunhills La
  Enham Alamein SP10 .... 83 D1
  Smannell RG24 .... 83 E4
Dunkirt La SP11 .... 104 C2
Dunley's Hill RG29 .... 72 B2
Dunmow Hill GU13 .... 54 A1
Dunmow Rd SP10 .... 106 A3
Dunsell's Cl GU34 .... 181 E3
Dunsell's La SO24 .... 181 E3
Dunsford Cres RG23 .... 68 B4
Dunsmore Gdns GU46 .... 33 F3
Dunstall Pk GU14 .... 55 F4
Dunstan's Dro SP11 .... 39 E1
Durbidges RG19 .... 24 B4
Durham Way RG21 .... 91 D4
Durnford Rd SO20 .... 129 D2
Durngate Pl SO23 .... 198 A4
Durngate Terr SO23 .... 198 A4
Durnsford Ave GU13 .... 75 D4
Dyson Dr SO23 .... 176 A1
Dysons Cl RG14 .... 1 B2

Eagle Cl Alton GU34 .... 139 F3
  Basingstoke RG22 .... 90 C4
Eagle Ct RG21 .... 69 F3
Eagle Rd RG19 .... 6 C1
Eames La GU33 .... 206 C4
Eardley Ave SP10 .... 82 B1
Earle Ho 8 SO23 .... 198 A4
Earls Gr GU15 .... 36 B3
Earlsbourne GU13 .... 75 D2
Earlsdown 40 SO23 .... 198 A4
East Acre GU9 .... 99 D3
East Dean Rd SO51 .... 191 F1
East Hill Dr GU33 .... 208 A2
East La SO24 .... 178 C2
East Portway SP10 .... 82 B1
East Ring GU10 .... 100 C4
East St Andover SP10 .... 106 A4
  Farnham GU9 .... 99 D2
  New Alresford SO24 .... 179 E3
East Station Rd GU12 .... 76 C1
East Stratton SO21 .... 134 A2
East Tree RG25 .... 90 A4
East View RG27 .... 52 A2
East Woodhay Rd SO22 .... 175 E2
Eastacre SO22 .... 175 F1
Eastbrooke Rd GU34 .... 140 A2
Eastern Ave SP10 .... 106 A4
Eastern Rd Aldershot GU12 .... 77 E1
  Bordon GU35 .... 164 B3
Eastfield Ave GU14 .... 69 E3
Eastfield Cl 9 SP10 .... 106 A4
Eastfield Ho SP10 .... 106 B4
Eastfield Lodge SP10 .... 106 A4
Eastfield Rd SP10 .... 106 A4
Eastgate St SO23 .... 198 A4
Eastlyn Rd RG26 .... 10 B1
Eastmead GU14 .... 55 F2
Easton Common Hill SP5 .... 168 B3
Easton La SO21 .... 177 D3
Easton Lane Bsns Pk 47 SO23 .... 198 A4
Eastrop La RG21 .... 69 E3
Eastrop Rdbt RG24 .... 69 E3
Eastrop Way RG21 .... 69 E3

Eastville SP11 .... 81 E4
Eaton Rd GU15 .... 35 F2
Ebble Cl SP9 .... 78 C4
Ebden Rd SO23 .... 198 A4
Ecchinswell Rd
  Ecchinswell RG20 .... 24 A1
  Kingsclere RG20 .... 24 A1
Ecchinswell & Sydmonton CE Prim Sch RG20 .... 23 F2
Echo Barn La GU10 .... 121 F3
Eddeys Cl GU35 .... 165 F3
Eddeys La GU35 .... 165 F3
Eddy Rd GU12 .... 77 D1
Eddystone Ct GU10 .... 144 B1
Edgar Cl SP10 .... 83 D2
Edgar Rd SO23 .... 197 F4
Edgar Villas SO23 .... 197 F3
Edgeborough Sch GU10 .... 122 A2
Edgecombe La RG14 .... 2 A3
Edgehill RG21 .... 68 B2
Edgewood Ct GU33 .... 208 A1
Edinburgh Cl Ash GU12 .... 77 F3
  Kings Worthy SO23 .... 154 A1
Edington Rd SO23 .... 176 A1
Edison Rd RG23 .... 68 C4
Edney Cl GU13 .... 75 D3
Edric's Gn SP4 .... 101 E1
Edrich Sq SP11 .... 83 D1
Edward Ave GU15 .... 35 F3
Edward Ct GU14 .... 55 F2
Edward Rd Alton GU34 .... 140 A3
  Farnham GU10 .... 122 A4
  Winchester SO23 .... 197 F3
Edward St GU11 .... 76 C1
Edward Terr SO24 .... 179 F3
Eeklo Pl RG14 .... 1 C1
Eelmoor Plain Rd GU14 .... 76 A3
Eelmoor Rd Aldershot GU12 .... 76 A3
  Farnborough GU14 .... 55 E1
Eelmoor Trad Est GU14 .... 55 E1
Egbert Rd SO23 .... 176 A1
Egbury Rd SP11 .... 62 A1
Egerton Rd GU17 .... 35 E4
Eggar's Ct 21 GU11 .... 76 C1
Eggar's Hill GU9 .... 99 F4
Eggar's Sec Sch GU34 .... 140 A3
Eggars Cl GU34 .... 140 A2
Eggars Field GU10 .... 120 A3
Eggleton Cl GU15 .... 74 C2
Eglinton Rd GU10 .... 144 C3
Eight Bells RG14 .... 1 B1
Eights The SP11 .... 104 C3
Eland Rd GU14 .... 77 D1
Elane Ho SP11 .... 57 D1
Elbe Way SP10 .... 82 C2
Elbow Cnr RG21 .... 69 D3
Elder Cl SO22 .... 197 E2
Elderberry Bank RG24 .... 69 F4
Elderberry Rd GU35 .... 165 D3
Eldergrove GU14 .... 56 B1
Eldon Cl SO20 .... 172 A1
Eldon Dr GU10 .... 122 A3
Eldon Pl GU9 .... 122 A3
Eldon La Braishfield SO20 .... 194 A3
  King's Somborne SO20 .... 194 A3
Eleanor Cl GU30 .... 187 D4
Elgar Cl RG22 .... 91 F4
Elgin Rd GU46 .... 34 B1
Elgin Way SO16 .... 56 B4
Elgrath Dr RG40 .... 16 B4
Eling Cl SO22 .... 175 E2
Eliot Cl GU15 .... 36 C4
Eliot Dr GU27 .... 189 E3
Elizabeth Ave RG14 .... 5 D4
Elizabeth Cl SO23 .... 154 A1
Elizabeth Dr GU13 .... 75 D3
Elizabeth Par GU46 .... 34 A2
Elizabeth Rd RG23 .... 68 C2
Elizabethan Rise RG25 .... 89 F1
Elkington Cl RG22 .... 22 C4
Ellen Gdns RG26 .... 28 C2
Elleray Ct GU12 .... 77 F3
Elles Cl GU14 .... 55 F2
Elles La GU14 .... 55 F1
Ellingham Cl SO24 .... 179 E3
Ellington Cl SP10 .... 105 D4
Ellington Dr RG22 .... 91 E4
Elliot Park Ind Est GU12 .... 77 E1
Ellison Way GU12 .... 100 B4
Elm Bank GU46 .... 34 A4
Elm Bank Rd SP10 .... 106 A3
Elm Bottom Cross RG26 .... 47 E1
Elm Cl Bordon GU35 .... 164 C2
  Middle Wallop SO20 .... 126 A2
  Thruxton SP11 .... 103 E4
Elm Cotts RG14 .... 4 B1
Elm Cres GU9 .... 99 D4
Elm Ct Andover SP10 .... 106 A4
  Ludgershall SP11 .... 57 D1
  Winchester SO22 .... 197 F4
Elm Gr Farnham GU11 .... 99 D4
  Kingsclere RG20 .... 24 B1
Elm Grove Flats RG20 .... 24 B1
Elm Grove Pk RG20 .... 24 B1
Elm Grove Rd GU14 .... 55 F2
Elm La GU10 .... 100 B4
Elm Piece Ho RG25 .... 88 A4
Elm Pl SP10 .... 100 A4
Elm Rd Farnham GU9 .... 99 D4
  New Alresford SO24 .... 179 E3
  Overton RG25 .... 65 D1
  Sherborne St John RG26 .... 47 F1
  Winchester SO22 .... 197 F4
Elm Terr GU33 .... 207 F3
Elm View GU12 .... 77 F2

Elmay Ho SP11 .... 57 D1
Elmcroft Cl GU16 .... 56 B4
Elmfield Ct GU35 .... 164 C3
Elmhurst RG26 .... 27 D4
Elmhurst Ballet Sch GU15 .... 36 A3
Elmhurst Rd RG18 .... 2 C3
Elms Rd Aldershot GU11 .... 76 C1
Fleet GU13 .... 75 E4
Hook RG27 .... 51 D1
Elms The Andover SP11 .... 105 F4
Ash GU10 .... 100 B4
Blackwater GU15 .... 35 D2
Elmsleigh Rd GU14 .... 55 E2
Elmsley Ct GU14 .... 55 E2
Elmstead Caravan Pk SP11 .... 103 E4
Elmwood RG24 .... 48 C2
Elmwood Cl GU14 .... 139 E1
Elmwood Par RG22 .... 68 B4
Elmwood Way RG21 .... 68 B4
Elsenwood Cres GU15 .... 36 C3
Elsenwood Dr GU15 .... 36 C4
Elsley Cl GU14 .... 56 B3
Elstead Rd GU11 .... 100 C2
Elston Pl GU12 .... 100 A4
Elston Rd GU10 .... 100 A4
Elvetham Cl GU13 .... 54 A2
Elvetham La GU27 .... 53 D4
Elvetham Pl GU13 .... 53 F2
Elvetham Rd GU13 .... 53 F2
Ely Cl GU16 .... 56 C4
Embleton Rd GU35 .... 165 F3
Emden Rd SP10 .... 82 C2
Empress Ave GU14 .... 55 F3
Enborne CE Prim Sch RG20 .... 4 B3
Enborne Gr RG14 .... 1 B1
Enborne Lodge Sch RG14 .... 4 C3
Enborne Pl RG14 .... 1 B1
Enborne Rd RG14 .... 1 A1
Enborne St Enborne RG14 .... 4 C2
Newbury RG14 .... 4 C2
Enborne Way RG7 .... 8 B3
Enbourne Gate RG14 .... 1 A1
Enfield Rd GU12 .... 77 F3
Engineers Rd RG19 .... 6 C3
Enham SP11 .... 83 D2
Enmill La SO22 .... 196 C3
Ennerdale Cl GU14 .... 68 A1
Ennerdale Gdns SO24 .... 179 E2
Ennerdale Gr GU9 .... 98 C3
Ennerdale RG35 .... 164 B3
Ennerdale Way RG19 .... 2 C2
Enterprise Ct RG21 .... 69 E4
Enterprise Ho RG23 .... 68 A2
Epsom Cl GU15 .... 36 A4
Epsom Cres RG14 .... 1 C1
Epsom Down GU34 .... 139 F1
Erasmus Pk SO23 .... 176 B1
Erica Cotts GU26 .... 167 D3
Erleigh Dene RG14 .... 1 B1
Erles Rd GU30 .... 188 A2
Ermine Wlk RG19 .... 2 C2
Ernest Rd GU11 .... 121 F3
Erskine Cl RG26 .... 10 B1
Erskine Rd SO22 .... 197 F4
Esher Cl RG23 .... 68 B1
Eskdale Ct GU12 .... 77 E2
Essex Cl Bordon GU35 .... 164 B2
Camberley GU16 .... 56 C4
Essex Rd Basingstoke RG21 .... 69 D3
Bordon GU35 .... 164 B2
Essex St RG14 .... 5 D4
Ethelbert Ave SP10 .... 82 B2
Eton Cl RG22 .... 91 D3
Eton Pl GU9 .... 98 C4
Ettrick Ct GU14 .... 76 C4
Etwall SP11 .... 103 D2
Europa Cl RG26 .... 28 C2
Euskirchen Way RG22 .... 68 B3
Evans Cl SO20 .... 125 D1
Eveley Cl GU35 .... 164 A1
Evelyn Ave GU9 .... 99 F4
Evelyn Mews SO24 .... 179 E3
Evelyn Wood's Rd GU12 ...... 77 D3
Evenlode Way GU15 .... 35 D4
Everest Rd GU15 .... 36 A4
Evergreen Rd GU15 .... 36 B1
Eversfield Ct SP11 .... 105 F4
Eversley Pl SO22 .... 197 E3
Eversley Rd Arborfield RG40 .... 15 E4
Eversley GU46 .... 33 D4
Eversley St RG7 .... 15 F1
Evesham Wlk RG24 .... 48 A1
Evingar Gdns RG28 .... 86 B3
Evingar Rd RG28 .... 86 B3
Ewhurst Rd RG26 .... 46 A3
Ewins Cl GU12 .... 77 F1
Ewshot Hill GU13 .... 75 D1
Ewshot Hill Cross GU9 .... 98 A4
Ewshot La GU10 .... 74 B1
Exbury Way SP10 .... 105 F4
Exeter Cl RG22 .... 91 D4
Exeter Gdns GU46 .... 33 F4
Exeter Rd RG22 .... 77 F2
Exmoor Cl RG22 .... 68 A2
Express Way RG14 .... 2 B1

Fabers Yd SO22 .... 197 F4
Fabian Cl RG21 .... 69 D2
Factory Cotts GU9 .... 98 A1
Fair Cl RG28 .... 86 B2
Fair Close Ho RG14 .... 1 C1
Fair Oak La GU26 .... 29 E4
Fair Piece SP11 .... 128 C3
Fair View SO24 .... 179 E2
Fairacre RG20 .... 21 E4

Fairacres GU10 .... 121 E2
Fairclose Dr SO22 .... 175 D3
Faircrosse GU17 .... 35 D4
Fairdown Cl SO23 .... 198 B4
Fairfax Ind Est GU11 .... 77 E1
Fairfax Mews GU16 .... 56 A1
Fairfax Pl RG14 .... 2 B3
Fairfax Rd GU14 .... 56 A4
Fairfield RG28 .... 86 B3
Fairfield Dr GU15 .... 36 B2
Fairfield Gn GU34 .... 160 B2
Fairfield Rd SO21, SO22 ...... 175 F1
Fairfield The GU9 .... 99 D1
Fairfields Ct RG24 .... 69 D2
Fairfields Prim Sch RG21 .... 69 D2
Fairfields Rd RG21 .... 69 D2
Fairholm Gdns GU11 .... 99 D1
Fairholme Par RG27 .... 51 D1
Fairland Cl RG22 .... 75 D4
Fairlands GU35 .... 166 A3
Fairlawn Ho SO22 .... 197 F4
Fairlawn Rd RG26 .... 27 D4
Fairlight Gdns GU34 .... 160 B2
Fairmead Cl GU17 .... 35 E4
Fairmead Ct GU15 .... 36 A2
Fairmile GU13 .... 74 C3
Fairoak Way RG26 .... 9 D1
Fairthorne Ho RG22 .... 68 C2
Fairthorne Rise RG24 .... 70 B3
Fairview RG14 .... 5 E4
Fairview Gdns GU9 .... 99 D3
Fairview Meadow RG22 .... 90 A4
Fairview Rd Ash GU12 .... 77 F2
Headley GU35 .... 166 A3
Fairview Terr GU35 .... 165 F3
Fairway GU30 .... 187 D2
Fairway The Bordon GU35 .... 164 A1
Camberley GU16 .... 36 C2
Farnham GU9 .... 99 D4
Hawley GU13 .... 75 F4
Fairways Beacon Hill GU26 .. 166 C3
Thruxton SP11 .... 81 D1
Faithfulls Dro SO20 .... 171 D2
Falaise Ct Aldershot GU12 .... 76 C1
North Tidworth SP9 .... 79 E3
Falaise Rd
Middle Wallop SO20 .... 126 A2
North Tidworth SP9 .... 79 E3
Falcon Bsns Pk RG40 .... 15 F3
Falcon Cl Basingstoke RG23 .. 67 F1
North Tidworth SP9 .... 78 C4
Falcon Coppice RG20 .... 21 E4
Falcon Ct Alton GU34 .... 139 F3
Camberley GU16 .... 36 A1
Falcon Fields RG27 .... 9 F1
Falcon House Gdns RG20 .... 4 B1
Falcon Rd SP9 .... 78 C4
Falcon View SO22 .... 197 E2
Falcon Way GU46 .... 33 F3
Falkland Cl GU12 .... 77 E4
Falkland Cty Prim Sch RG14 .. 5 E3
Falkland Dr RG14 .... 5 E4
Falkland Garth RG14 .... 5 D4
Falkland Rd
Basingstoke RG24 .... 48 B1
Newbury RG14 .... 5 D3
Falkner Ho RG22 .... 54 B2
Falkner Rd GU9 .... 98 C1
Falkners Ct RG13 .... 54 B2
Fallow Field SO22 .... 197 E2
Fallowfield GU13 .... 54 B2
Falmouth Cl GU15 .... 36 C2
Fantails GU34 .... 139 F3
Faraday Cl RG40 .... 15 E4
Faraday Ct RG24 .... 69 E4
Faraday Pk SP10 .... 82 A1
Faraday Rd
Farnborough GU16 .... 56 A3
Newbury RG14 .... 1 C2
Farcrosse GU47 .... 35 D4
Fareham Dr GU46 .... 33 F4
Faringdon Ct SO23 .... 176 A1
Farleigh Hose Sch RG22 ..... 91 F1
Farleigh Wallop RG22 .... 91 D1
Farleigh Rd RG25 .... 92 A4
Farleigh Rise RG21 .... 69 E1
Farleigh Sch SP11 .... 127 D4
Farley Cl SO51 .... 194 C1
Farley Mount Ctry Pk SO21 .. 195 E4
Farley Mount Rd SO21 ...... 196 A2
Farley St SO20 .... 147 F3
Farm Cl GU46 .... 34 A3
Farm Cotts RG22 .... 68 B4
Farm Ct GU15 .... 36 B1
Farm Dr GU13 .... 54 A2
Farm Ground Cl RG27 ...... 51 E1
Farm La GU10 .... 97 E3
Farm Rd Abbotts Ann SP11 .. 105 D3
Aldershot GU12 .... 77 E2
Camberley GU16 .... 36 B1
Farm View GU46 .... 34 A3
Farm View Dr RG26 .... 49 D2
Farmhouse Way GU13 .... 74 C3
Farnborough Bsns Ctr GU14 .. 55 E1
Farnborough Coll of Tech
GU14 .... 56 A1
Farnborough Coll of Tech
(Highfield Ctr) GU9 ...... 99 F4
Farnborough Gate Ret Pk
GU14 .... 56 A4
Farnborough Grange Inf Sch
GU14 .... 55 F4
Farnborough Hill
(Girls Public Sch) GU14 .. 56 A3

Farnborough Ind Est GU14 .. 55 F2
Farnborough North Sta
GU14 .... 56 A3
Farnborough Rd
Aldershot GU11 .... 76 B2
Farnborough GU14 .... 76 B2
Farnborough (Sixth Form) Coll
GU14 .... 55 F3
Farnborough St GU14 .... 56 A3
Farnborough Sta GU14 ...... 55 F3
Farnham Bsns Ctr GU9 ...... 99 D3
Farnham Bsns Pk GU9 ...... 98 C1
Farnham By-Pass GU9 ...... 99 D1
Farnham Coll GU9 .... 99 D1
Farnham Hospl (Geriatric)
GU9 .... 99 E2
Farnham La SP11 .... 189 F4
Farnham Park Cl GU9 .... 98 C3
Farnham Park Dr GU9 ...... 98 C3
Farnham Rd Bordon GU35 .. 164 B3
Dogmersfield RG27 .... 73 E1
Fleet GU13 .... 75 E4
Liss GU33 .... 207 F2
Odiham RG29 .... 73 E1
Farnham Sta GU9 .... 99 D1
Farnham Trad Est GU9 ...... 99 E2
Faroe Cl RG24 .... 48 B1
Farrell Cl GU15 .... 36 A2
Farrier's Field GU35 .... 115 D4
Farringdon Way RG26 ...... 26 C4
Farrs Ave SP10 .... 106 A4
Farthing Fields GU35 .... 165 E3
Farthingfield Ho GU9 ...... 99 D2
Fawconer Rd RG20 .... 24 B1
Fawley La GU34 .... 204 A2
Fayrewood Chase RG22 ...... 91 D4
Feathers La GU21 .... 69 D2
Feilden Ct RG20 .... 24 B1
Felbridge Cl GU16 .... 36 B1
Feld Way RG24 .... 70 A4
Fellows Rd GU14 .... 56 A1
Felmer Dr SO23 .... 176 B4
Fencott Pl RG24 .... 69 D3
Fennel Cl Chineham RG24 .. 49 D2
Farnborough GU13 .... 54 C2
Newbury RG14 .... 2 A3
Ferbies GU33 .... 75 D3
Ferguson Cl RG21 .... 69 D1
Fern Cl GU16 .... 36 C2
Fern Ct GU12 .... 77 E1
Fern Dr GU13 .... 74 C3
Fernbank RG40 .... 16 A3
Fernbrae Cl GU10 .... 121 F2
Ferncote Rd GU35 .... 164 C2
Ferndale Gdns RG27 .... 51 D1
Ferndale Rd Andover SP10 .. 82 C1
Fleet GU13 .... 74 C3
Ferndown Ct GU34 .... 140 A2
Ferndown Gdns GU14 .... 55 E2
Ferney Cl GU13 .... 161 E4
Ferney La SO24 .... 159 D4
Fernhill Cl Farnborough GU14 .. 35 E1
Farnham GU9 .... 98 C3
Fernhill Dr GU9 .... 98 C3
Fernhill Ho GU14 .... 56 A1
Fernhill La Farnborough GU47 .. 35 E1
Farnham GU9 .... 98 C3
Fernhill Prim Sch GU47 .... 35 E1
Fernhill Rd GU14 .... 55 E3
Fernhill Sch GU14 .... 35 E1
Fernhill Wlk GU14 .... 35 E1
Ferniehurst GU15 .... 36 B2
Fernlea GU35 .... 164 A1
Ferns Mead GU9 .... 98 C1
Ferns The GU9 .... 99 D4
Ferrell Field RG27 .... 50 C1
Ferrier Gr RG14 .... 5 F4
Fiddlers Field GU34 .... 139 D4
Field End Farnham GU9 ...... 99 E2
Kings Worthy SO23 .... 176 B4
Field Gate Dr RG20 .... 24 B1
Field La GU16 .... 36 B1
Field Path GU14 .... 35 E1
Field Pl GU30 .... 188 A2
Field Rd GU14 .... 35 E1
Field Stores App GU11 ...... 77 D2
Field Way Aldershot GU12 .. 77 E2
Tongham GU12 .... 100 B4
Fielders Ct GU34 .... 139 F2
Fielders The GU46 .... 33 E4
Fieldfare Ave GU46 .... 33 F3
Fieldgate Ctr RG20 .... 24 B1
Fielding Rd GU17 .... 35 E3
Fieldridge RG14 .... 2 A3
Fieldway GU13 .... 74 B4
Fifehead Cotts SO20 .... 147 E4
Fifield La GU10 .... 122 A1
Fifth Rd GU14 .... 1 B1
Fifth St RG14 .... 6 B3
Filmorehill La GU34 .... 204 A2
Finch Cl RG26 .... 27 D4
Finchampstead CE Prim Sch
RG40 .... 16 B2
Finchampstead Rd
Wokingham RG40, RG41 .. 16 B3
Wokingham RG40 .... 16 B4
Finches Gn GU34 .... 139 F3
Findhorn Cl GU14 .... 35 D4
Findings The GU14 .... 55 E4
Fingle Dr SP10 .... 105 F4
Finkley Down Farm Pk SP10 .. 83 F2
Finkley Rd Smannell SP10 .. 84 B4
St Mary Bourne SP10 ...... 84 B4
Fintry Pl GU14 .... 55 E4
Fintry Wlk GU14 .... 55 E4
Fiona Cl SO23 .... 198 B4
Fir Acre Rd GU12 .... 77 F3
Fir Cottage Rd RG40 .... 16 B4

Fir Dr GU14 .... 35 D2
Fir Gr GU35 .... 164 A1
Fir Tree Alley GU11 .... 76 C3
Fir Tree Ave GU27 .... 189 D3
Fir Tree Cnr RG26 .... 9 E1
Fir Tree La RG14 .... 2 B2
Fir Tree Piece RG26 .... 45 D2
Fir Tree Prim Sch RG14 .... 2 B2
Fir Tree Way GU13 .... 75 D4
Fircrofts GU13 .... 53 F1
Fire Station Rd GU11 .... 76 C3
Fire Thorn Cl GU13 .... 75 D4
Firfield Rd GU10 .... 121 F4
Firglen Dr GU46 .... 34 A4
Firgrove Ct
Farnborough GU14 .... 55 F2
Farnham GU9 .... 99 D1
Firgrove Hill GU9 .... 99 D1
Firgrove Par GU14 .... 55 F2
Firgrove Rd Bordon GU35 .. 164 A1
Eversley GU46 .... 33 F3
Farnborough GU14 .... 55 F2
Yateley GU46 .... 33 F3
Firlands Ave GU16 .... 36 A3
Firs Cl Farnborough GU14 .. 56 A1
Wokingham RG40 .... 16 B4
Firs Cres SO23 .... 176 A4
Firs End RG7 .... 11 E3
Firs La RG29 .... 72 B1
Firs The Andover SP10 ...... 105 F4
Thatcham RG18 .... 2 C2
Firs Way Basingstoke RG22 .. 68 A4
Whitchurch RG28 .... 86 B3
First St RG14 .... 6 C3
Firth Cl RG26 .... 27 F4
Firtree Cl GU46 .... 34 B4
Firview GU30 .... 187 F2
Firway GU30 .... 166 B3
Firwood Ct GU15 .... 36 A3
Firwood Dr GU16 .... 36 A3
Fisher Cl SP10 .... 106 B4
Fisherman's La RG26 .... 9 F4
Fishermen's Cl GU11 .... 77 E3
Fiske Cl GU14 .... 68 B2
Fiske Ct GU14 .... 34 B3
Fitzroy Rd GU13 .... 53 E1
Five Acres Cl GU35 .... 164 C3
Five Ash Rd GU34 .... 160 A2
Five Bells La SO20 .... 147 F3
Five Bridges Rd SO22 ...... 197 F2
Five Lanes SP11 .... 61 F1
Five Lanes End RG27 ...... 71 D1
Fivefields Cl SO23 .... 198 B4
Fivefields Rd SO23 .... 198 B4
Fiveways Basingstoke RG22 .. 68 A4
Camberley GU15 .... 36 B3
Flashett The SP5 .... 168 A3
Flats The GU47 .... 35 D2
Flaxfield Ct RG21 .... 69 D3
Flaxfield Rd RG21 .... 69 D3
Fleet Bsns Pk GU13 .... 75 D2
Fleet Hill RG40 .... 16 A1
Fleet Hospl GU13 .... 53 F1
Fleet Inf Sch GU13 .... 75 E4
Fleet La RG40 .... 15 F1
Fleet Pond (Nature Reserve)
GU13 .... 54 B2
Fleet Rd Aldershot GU14 .... 76 B3
Farnborough GU13 .... 54 C2
Fleet GU13 .... 54 A1
Hartley Wintney RG27 .... 53 D2
Fleet Sta GU13 .... 54 A2
Fleming Cl Arborfield RG2 .. 15 E4
Farnborough GU14 .... 56 A3
Fleming Rd GU14 .... 1 C2
Flensburg Cl SP10 .... 82 C2
Fletcher Cl RG23 .... 68 C2
Fletchers Field GU30 .... 188 A2
Fletchers Ho RG30 .... 187 F2
Flexford Rd GU20 .... 21 E3
Flinders Cl SP10 .... 83 F1
Flint Cl SP10 .... 105 F3
Flint La Chute Forest SP11 .. 81 F4
Penton Grafton SP11 ...... 81 F4
Floral Way SP10 .... 105 E4
Floreat Gdns RG14 .... 1 B1
Florence Cl GU34 .... 34 A3
Florence Ct SP10 .... 83 D2
Florence Portal Cl RG28 .... 87 D3
Florence Rd Fleet GU13 .... 75 D4
Sandhurst GU47 .... 35 E4
Florence Way RG22 .... 68 B4
Florrie Pl GU34 .... 161 E2
Flowerdew Ct GU17 .... 35 D4
Flowerdown Ho SO22 ...... 175 E2
Focus 303 SP10 .... 83 E1
Folly Cotts RG20 .... 22 C4
Folly Hill GU9 .... 98 C3
Folly Hill Cty Inf Sch GU9 .. 98 C3
Folly La GU9 .... 29 D2
Folly La N GU9 .... 98 C3
Folly La S GU9 .... 98 C3
Folly The RG14 .... 1 C1
Fontwell Dr GU34 .... 139 F1
Fontwell Rd RG14 .... 1 C1
Forbes Chase GU17 .... 35 D4
Forbes Rd SO23 .... 176 A4
Forbury La RG20 .... 3 D4
Forburys GU10 .... 121 F4
Ford La Farnham GU9 ...... 121 F3
Odiham RG29 .... 95 D3
South Warnborough RG29 .. 94 C4
Swallowfield RG7 .... 14 C1
Fordington Ave SO22 .... 197 F4
Fordington Rd SO22 .... 175 F1
Forehead The RG7 .... 12 B2
Foreman Pk GU12 .... 77 F1
Foreman Rd GU12 .... 77 F1

Forest Cl RG26 .... 9 E1
Forest Cnr GU33 .... 208 A4
Forest Ct SP9 .... 79 D4
Forest Dean GU13 .... 54 B2
Forest Dr Chineham RG24 .. 48 C2
Farnham GU9 .... 122 A2
North Tidworth SP9 .... 79 D4
Forest End GU34 .... 74 C3
Forest End Rd GU47 .... 34 C4
Forest Glade GU10 .... 121 D2
Forest Hills GU17 .... 35 F2
Forest La Andover SP10 .... 106 C3
Lindford GU35 .... 165 D3
Tadley RG26 .... 27 D3
Upper Chute SP11 .... 57 F4
Forest Lane Cl GU30 .... 187 F2
Forest Rd Bordon GU35 .... 164 B1
Greatham GU33 .... 207 F4
Liss GU33 .... 208 A3
Forest Rise GU33 .... 208 A3
Forest Sh Ctr The GU35 .... 164 C2
Forestdale GU26 .... 167 E2
Forge Cl Bramley RG26 .... 29 D1
Farnham GU9 .... 99 D2
Forge Ct GU46 .... 34 A4
Forge Field SP10 .... 83 D1
Forge La GU11 .... 76 C3
Forge Rd Kingsley GU35 .... 142 C1
Kingsley GU35 .... 164 A4
Forsters RG26 .... 9 E4
Fort Hill Com Sch RG23 .... 68 B3
Fort Narrien GU47 .... 35 E4
Forth Cl GU14 .... 55 D3
Forth Ct SP10 .... 83 E1
Fortrose Cl GU47 .... 35 D4
Fossewood Dr GU15 .... 36 A4
Fosters Bsns Pk RG27 ...... 71 F4
Foul La GU34 .... 159 F4
Foundry La GU27 .... 189 F3
Foundry Rd SP10 .... 105 E2
Fountains Cl RG24 .... 48 A1
Four Acre Coppice RG27 .. 51 E1
Four Houses Cnr RG7 ...... 11 E4
Four Lanes Cl RG24 .... 49 D2
Four Lanes Cty Schs GU24 .. 48 C2
Four Lanes End RG24 ...... 49 D1
Four Marks CE Prim Sch
GU34 .... 182 A4
Four Oaks RG20 .... 21 E3
Four Ways GU15 .... 142 C4
Fourth St RG14 .... 6 B3
Fowler Rd GU14 .... 55 E2
Fowler's Rd GU11 .... 77 D3
Fox Dr GU46 .... 34 A4
Fox Heath GU14 .... 55 D2
Fox La Eversley GU46 .... 33 E4
Oakley RG22 .... 67 E2
Winchester SO22 .... 197 E3
Fox Rd Farnham GU10 ...... 122 A4
Haslemere GU27 .... 189 E3
Fox Way GU9 .... 98 A4
Fox Yd GU9 .... 98 C1
Fox's La RG20 .... 24 B1
Foxborough RG7 .... 14 A3
Foxcote RG40 .... 16 C4
Foxcote Cl SP10 .... 82 B1
Foxcote La SP10 .... 82 B2
Foxcote Rd SP10 .... 82 B2
Foxcroft GU13 .... 75 D3
Foxdown RG25 .... 65 D1
Foxdown Cl GU15 .... 36 A3
Foxglove Cl RG22 .... 91 D4
Foxglove Cl GU15 .... 164 C1
Foxhill Cres GU15 .... 36 C4
Foxhunter Way RG19 ...... 2 B2
Foxhurst Rd GU12 .... 77 F2
Foxley Cl GU15 .... 35 D3
Foxmoor Ct RG23 .... 67 E2
Foxwood GU13 .... 54 B2
Foye La GU13 .... 75 D3
Foyle Pk RG21 .... 69 D1
Foyle Rd SP11 .... 80 B2
Frampton Way SO23 .... 176 B4
France Hill Cty Sec Sch
GU15 .... 36 A1
France Hill Dr GU15 .... 36 A3
Frances Rd RG21 .... 69 D2
Francis Ct GU14 .... 55 E2
Francis Gdns SO23 .... 176 A2
Francis Way GU15 .... 36 C2
Franklin Ave
Hartley Wintney RG27 .... 52 B4
Tadley RG26 .... 9 F1
Fraser Cl RG24 .... 70 A3
Fraser Mead GU15 .... 35 E3
Fraser Rd SO23 .... 176 B4
Fraynes Croft GU13 .... 74 C4
Frederick St GU11 .... 76 C1
Freelands Dr GU13 .... 74 C3
Freemantle Cl RG21 .... 69 E4
French Gdns GU47 .... 35 D2
French Rd GU33 .... 186 B2
Frenchmans Creek GU13 .. 74 C2
Frenchmoor La
East Dean SP5 .... 190 C1
West Tytherley SP5 ...... 190 C2
Frensham Ave GU13 .... 54 B1
Frensham Cl GU46 .... 33 F3
Frensham Ct GU10 .... 121 F2
Frensham Heights Rd
GU10 .... 121 F1
Frensham Heights Sch
GU10 .... 121 F1
Frensham La Headley GU35 .. 165 D3
Lindford GU35 .... 165 D3
Frensham Rd GU10 .... 122 A3
Frensham Vale GU10 ...... 122 A2
Frescade Cres RG21 .... 69 D2

Freshwood Dr GU47 .... 34 A2
Friars Ct GU46 .... 34 B4
Friars Rd RG14 .... 5 F4
Friarsgate SO23 .... 198 A4
Friend Ave GU12 .... 77 D1
Friesian Cl GU13 .... 54 A2
Frimley Bsns Pk
  Camberley GU14 .... 56 A4
  Farnborough GU14 .... 55 F4
Frimley CE Fst & Mid Sch
  GU14 .... 56 B4
Frimley Green Rd GU14 .... 56 B4
Frimley Grove Gdns GU16 .... 36 B1
Frimley High St GU16 .... 56 A4
Frimley Park Hospl GU15 .... 36 A1
Frimley Rd Ash GU12 .... 77 F4
  Camberley GU17 .... 37 F2
Frimley Sta GU16 .... 56 A4
Frith End Rd GU35 .... 142 C3
Frith Hill Rd GU15 .... 36 C1
Frithmead Cl RG21 .... 69 D1
Frog La
  Latchmere Green RG26 .... 27 F3
  Mapledurwell RG25 .... 70 C2
  Rotherwick RG27 .... 50 B3
Frogmore Com Sch GU46 .... 34 B3
Frogmore Ct GU47 .... 35 D2
Frogmore Gr GU17 .... 35 D2
Frogmore Park Dr GU15, GU16 .. 35 D2
Frogmore Rd GU17 .... 35 D2
Frogmore Schs GU17 .... 34 C3
Frogs Hole RG20 .... 24 B1
Frome Cl Basingstoke RG21 .... 69 E3
  Oakley RG22 .... 67 E1
Fromond Rd SO22 .... 175 E2
Froud RG27 .... 71 F4
Froxfield CE Inf Sch GU32 .. 205 F1
Froxfield Cl SO22 .... 175 E2
Froyle La RG29 .... 95 D2
Fry Sq SP10 .... 83 D1
Fry's Acre GU12 .... 77 F2
Fry's La GU46 .... 34 B4
Fugelmere Rd GU13 .... 54 B1
Fugelmere Wlk GU13 .... 54 B1
Fulbrook Way RG29 .... 95 E4
Fulflood Ct [2] SO22 .... 197 F4
Fulham Ho [19] RG21 .... 69 D3
Fullers La RG20 .... 21 D4
Fullers Rd Binsted GU10 .... 121 D2
  Farnham GU10 .... 121 D2
Fullers Vale GU35 .... 165 E3
Fullerton Rd
  Goodworth Clatford SP11 .... 127 E4
  Upper Clatford SP11 .... 127 E4
  Wherwell SP11 .... 127 E4
Fullerton Way RG26 .... 27 D4
Fulmar Cl RG22 .... 90 C4
Furley Cl SO23 .... 198 A4
Further Vell-Mead GU13 .... 74 C2
Furze Cl GU12 .... 77 F4
Furze Hill Rd Headley GU35 .. 166 A2
  South Tidworth SP9 .... 78 C3
Furze Rd RG7 .... 9 E1
Furze Vale Rd GU35 .... 166 A2
Furzedown Cotts SO20 .... 194 A4
Furzedown Ho SO20 .... 194 A3
Furzedown La SP11 .... 103 F3
Furzedown Rd SO20 .... 194 A4
Furzen La RG25 .... 115 D4
Fuzzy Dro RG22 .... 90 C4
Fyfield Cl GU17 .... 35 D3
Fyfield La Appleshaw SP11 .... 81 D2
  Fyfield SP11 .... 81 D2
Fyfield Rd Fyfield SP11 .... 81 D1
  Thruxton SP11 .... 81 D1
Fylingdales Cl RG21 .... 68 A2

Gable End [3] GU14 .... 55 F2
Gables Cl GU14 .... 55 F2
Gables Rd GU13 .... 74 C2
Gables The Grayshott GU26 .. 167 D2
  Whitchurch RG28 .... 86 C3
Gabriel Dr GU15 .... 36 C2
Gabriels The RG14 .... 5 D3
Gaffney Cl GU11 .... 77 D4
Gage Cl RG21 .... 69 F4
Gainsborough Cl
  Camberley GU15 .... 36 B4
  Farnborough GU16 .... 56 A1
Gainsborough Ct
  Andover SP10 .... 82 C1
  [3] Fleet GU13 .... 54 A1
Gainsborough Rd
  RG21, RG23 .... 69 E1
Galahad Cl SP10 .... 83 D2
Gales Ct SP10 .... 106 A4
Galileo Pk SP10 .... 82 B1
Gallaghers Mead SP10 .... 105 E4
Galley La RG19 .... 24 B4
Gallop The GU46 .... 34 A4
Galloway Cl Basingstoke RG24 .. 68 B2
  Fleet GU13 .... 54 B2
Galloway Ctr The RG14 .... 2 B1
Gallwey Rd GU11 .... 77 D2
Gally Hill Rd GU13 .... 74 C2
Galway Rd GU14 .... 34 A2
Gander Dr RG22 .... 68 B4
Ganders Cl RG24 .... 184 C4
Gangbridge La SP11 .... 61 F2
Gannet Cl RG23 .... 90 C4
Gar St SO22 .... 197 F4
Garbett Rd SO23 .... 198 A4
Garbetts Way GU12 .... 100 B3
Garden Cl [10] Andover SP11 .. 106 A4
  Ellisfield RG25 .... 114 A1
  Farnborough GU14 .... 55 E2
  Hook RG27 .... 50 C1
  Kingsclere RG20 .... 24 B1

Garden Close La RG14 .... 5 D2
Garden La [15] SO23 .... 198 A4
Gardener's Hill Rd GU10 .... 121 F2
Gardeners Gn SP9 .... 101 E4
Gardens The GU10 .... 100 B4
Garfield Rd GU15 .... 36 A3
Garford Cres RG14 .... 5 D4
Garnet Field GU17, GU46 .... 33 F3
Garnet Rd GU35 .... 164 C1
Garnier Rd SO23 .... 198 A3
Garrett Cl RG20 .... 24 B1
Garrett Rd RG40 .... 16 A4
Garrick Way GU16 .... 56 B4
Garston Mede SO20 .... 129 D2
Garth Cl Bordon GU35 .... 164 B2
  Farnham GU10 .... 121 F4
Garth Rd RG7 .... 11 F3
Garth The Alton GU34 .... 140 A2
  Ash GU12 .... 77 E1
  Farnborough GU14 .... 56 A2
Gascoigne La SO24 .... 181 E3
Gaskell Cl GU34 .... 140 B3
Gason Hill Rd SP9 .... 78 C4
Gaston La
  South Warnborough RG29 .... 95 D3
  Upper Farringdon GU34 .... 161 F2
Gaston's Wood Ind Est
  RG21 .... 69 E4
Gatekeeper Cl [10] SO23 .... 198 B4
Gates The GU13 .... 54 B2
Gauvain Cl GU34 .... 140 A1
Gawaine Cl SP10 .... 83 D2
Gaywood Dr RG14 .... 2 A2
Geale's Almshouses [11] GU34 . 139 F2
Geale's Cres GU34 .... 140 A3
Geale's Ct GU34 .... 140 A3
Geffery's Fields RG24 .... 69 E3
General Johnson Ct [6]
  SO22 .... 197 E3
Genoa Ct SP10 .... 83 D2
Gentles La Bramshott GU30 .. 165 F2
  Headley GU35 .... 165 F2
George Eyston Dr SO22 .... 197 E3
George Gdns SP10 .... 100 A4
George Rd Fleet GU13 .... 54 A1
  North Tidworth SP9 .... 78 C4
George St Basingstoke RG22 .. 68 C3
  Kingsclere RG20 .... 24 B1
George Yd SP10 .... 106 A4
George Yd The SO24 .... 179 E3
Georgia Cl SP10 .... 105 F3
Georgia La Amport SP11 .... 103 F1
  Grateley SO20 .... 125 D4
Georgian Cl GU15 .... 36 B4
Georgina Ct [6] GU13 .... 54 A1
Georgina Gdns RG26 .... 27 D4
Gerald Sq GU14 .... 140 A3
Gershwin Ct RG22 .... 91 E4
Gershwin Rd RG22 .... 91 E4
Gibbet La GU15 .... 36 C4
Gibbons Cl GU17 .... 35 D4
Gibbs Cl RG40 .... 16 B3
Gibbs Way GU46 .... 33 F2
Gid La GU34 .... 119 D2
Giffard Dr GU14 .... 55 E3
Giffards Meadow GU9 .... 99 E1
Gilbard Ct RG24 .... 49 D2
Gilbert Cl RG24 .... 48 B1
Gilbert Rd GU15 .... 36 A1
Gilbert White Way GU34 .... 139 F3
Gilbert's Gn SP4 .... 101 F4
Gilberts Mead SP10 .... 105 E2
Giles Cl RG14 .... 1 B1
Giles Ct RG26 .... 27 D4
Giles Hill SO23 .... 198 A4
Giles Rd RG26 .... 27 D4
Gillham's La GU27 .... 188 C3
Gillian Ave GU10 .... 100 A4
Gillian Cl GU11 .... 100 A4
Gillies Dr RG22 .... 68 B4
Gillingham Cl SO23 .... 176 B4
Gilmour Gdns GU34 .... 140 A3
Gilroy Cl RG14 .... 5 D3
Gisborne Cl SP9 .... 79 D3
Glade Cl RG24 .... 48 C1
Glade The Binsted GU10 .... 120 C1
  Farnham GU9 .... 99 D4
  Newbury RG14 .... 5 E4
Gladiator Way GU11 .... 76 C4
Gladstone Terr SP11 .... 108 A3
Glamis Cl Camberley GU14 .... 56 A4
  Oakley RG23 .... 67 D1
Glaston Hill Rd GU46 .... 33 D4
Glastonbury Cl RG21 .... 69 D4
Glayshers Hill GU35 .... 165 F3
Glebe Cl Bentworth GU34 .... 138 A3
  Dummer RG25 .... 90 B1
  Tadley RG26 .... 27 D4
Glebe Ct GU13 .... 53 F1
Glebe Fields GU34 .... 138 A3
Glebe La Basingstoke RG24 .... 68 A2
  Hartley Wintney RG27 .... 52 B3
Glebe Meadow
  East Dean SP5 .... 191 D1
  Overton RG25 .... 88 A4
Glebe Rd Crondall GU10 .... 97 E3
  Farnborough GU14 .... 55 E3
  Headley GU35 .... 165 E3
Glebe The GU17 .... 35 E2
Glebefields RG14 .... 1 C3
Glebeland Rd GU17 .... 35 E2
Glebelands SP10 .... 106 A1
Glen Cl Andover SP10 .... 105 F4
  Beacon Hill GU26 .... 167 D3
Glen Court Flats GU26 .... 167 D3
Glen Rd Beacon Hill GU26 .... 167 D3
  Fleet GU13 .... 74 C4
  Grayshott GU26 .... 167 D2

Glen The RG26 .... 10 B1
Glenapp Grange RG7 .... 11 E3
Glenavon Gdns GU46 .... 34 A2
Glencoe Cl GU16 .... 56 C4
Glendale Ave RG14 .... 5 D3
Glendale Pk GU13 .... 53 E1
Glendale Rd RG26 .... 9 F1
Gleneagles Dr GU14 .... 55 D2
Glenhurst Cl GU47 .... 35 E2
Glenlea GU20 .... 167 E1
Glenlea Hollow GU27 .... 189 E4
Glenmount Rd GU16 .... 56 C1
Glenville Gdns GU26 .... 167 E2
Globe Farm La GU46 .... 34 C3
Glorney Mead GU9 .... 99 F3
Gloucester Cl
  Camberley GU16 .... 56 B3
  Four Marks GU34 .... 160 A1
Gloucester Dr RG22 .... 91 D4
Gloucester Rd
  Aldershot GU11 .... 100 A4
  Newbury RG14 .... 1 B1
Glovers Field GU27 .... 189 E3
Glovers Rd GU27 .... 189 E3
Glynswood Camberley GU15 .. 36 B2
  Farnham GU10 .... 121 F2
Goat La RG21 .... 69 E3
Goatacre Rd GU34 .... 159 E2
Goch Way SP10 .... 82 C1
Goddard Sq SP10 .... 83 E1
Goddards Cl RG24 .... 49 E4
Goddards Firs RG22 .... 90 B4
Goddards La Camberley GU17 .. 35 F2
  Sherfield on Loddon RG24 .... 49 E4
Goddards Mead SP11 .... 105 F4
Godden Cres GU14 .... 55 E2
Godson Ho [14] SO23 .... 198 A4
Godwin Cl SO22 .... 175 E1
Gold La GU11 .... 77 E2
Goldcrest Cl [1] GU46 .... 33 F3
Golden Fields GU30 .... 188 A2
Golden Lion Rdbt RG21 .... 69 D1
Goldenfields Cl GU30 .... 188 A2
Goldfinch Cl Alton GU34 .... 139 F1
  Camberley GU15 .... 36 A4
Goldfinch La GU34 .... 6 B2
Goldfinch Way SO21 .... 153 F3
Goldhill GU10, GU9 .... 122 A3
Goldney Rd GU15 .... 36 C2
Goldwell Dr RG14 .... 1 B2
Golf Dr GU15 .... 36 B2
Golf La GU35 .... 164 A1
Golf Links Ave GU26 .... 166 C3
Gondreville Gdns GU13 .... 74 C2
Gong Hill Farnham GU10 .... 122 A2
  Frensham GU10 .... 122 A2
Gong Hill Dr GU10 .... 122 A2
Goodboy's La RG7 .... 12 C4
Goodens The SO24 .... 201 E3
Goodman Cl RG22 .... 68 C2
Goodwin Wlk RG14 .... 5 D3
Goodwood Cl Alton GU34 .... 139 F1
  Camberley GU16 .... 56 A4
Goodwood Pl GU16 .... 56 B2
Goodwood Way RG14 .... 2 A1
Goodwyns Cl SP9 .... 101 E4
Goodwyns Gn GU34 .... 140 A3
Goodyers GU34 .... 140 A2
Goose Gn RG27 .... 50 C1
Goose La RG27 .... 51 D1
Gooserye Ct GU30 .... 187 F2
Gordon Ave Camberley GU15 .. 36 A3
  Fleet GU13 .... 75 D3
  Winchester SO23 .... 198 B3
Gordon Cl RG24 .... 69 E3
Gordon Cres GU15 .... 36 A2
Gordon Ct RG14 .... 1 C1
Gordon Rd Aldershot GU11 .... 76 C1
  Camberley GU15 .... 36 A3
  Farnborough GU11 .... 77 D4
  Newbury RG14 .... 1 C1
  Thatcham RG18 .... 2 C3
  Winchester SO23 .... 198 A4
Gordon Wlk GU17, GU46 .... 34 B3
Gore End Rd RG20 .... 3 F2
Goring Field SO22 .... 175 E1
Gorrings The SO20 .... 172 A1
Gorse Cl GU11 .... 121 F3
Gorse Cotts Frensham GU10 .. 122 A1
  Haslemere GU27 .... 189 D4
Gorse La GU10 .... 121 F3
Gorse Rd GU15 .... 36 B1
Gorse Ride N RG40 .... 16 B4
Gorse Ride S RG40 .... 16 B3
Gorse Ride Schs RG40 .... 16 B4
Gorsedown Cl GU35 .... 164 A1
Gorselands Farnham GU9 .... 99 D4
  Newbury RG14 .... 5 D3
  Tadley RG26 .... 26 C4
  Yateley GU46 .... 34 A2
Gorselands Cl Ash GU12 .... 77 F3
  Headley GU35 .... 166 A2
Gorseway GU13 .... 75 D4
Gort Cl GU12 .... 77 E4
Goscombs La SO24 .... 180 C4
Goslings Croft GU34 .... 184 C4
Gothic Ct GU17 .... 34 C4
Gough Rd GU13 .... 53 F1
Gough's Meadow GU17 .... 34 C4
Govenor's Rd GU15 .... 35 E3
Government House Rd
  GU11 .... 76 C4
Government Rd
  Aldershot GU14 .... 77 E2
  Farnborough GU14 .... 77 E2
Gower Cl RG21 .... 69 D4
Gower Cres RG27 .... 51 D1
Gower Pk GU17 .... 35 D4
Grace Bennett Cl GU14 .... 55 F4

Grace Reynolds Wlk GU15 .. 36 A3
Grace Sq SP10 .... 83 E1
Gracemere Cres RG25 .... 90 C4
Gracious Rd GU34 .... 184 B4
Gradwell La SO24 .... 182 A4
Grafton Cl GU35 .... 164 C1
Grafton Pl SP11 .... 81 F2
Grafton Rd SO23 .... 197 F3
Grafton Way RG24 .... 68 B2
Grainger Cl RG23 .... 68 C1
Grammarsham La RG25 .... 92 A1
Grampian Way RG21 .... 68 A2
Granada Pl SP10 .... 83 E1
Granary The RG14 .... 1 B2
Grand Ave GU15 .... 36 A3
Grand Par RG27 .... 51 D1
Grand Trunk Rd SP9 .... 78 B2
Grange Cl Fyfield SP11 .... 80 C1
  New Alresford SO24 .... 179 E3
  Winchester SO23 .... 197 F3
Grange Ct RG14 .... 1 C1
Grange Farm GU34 .... 184 B4
Grange Farm Rd GU11 .... 77 F2
Grange Jun Sch GU14 .... 55 F4
Grange La RG27 .... 52 A3
Grange Rd Ash GU11 .... 77 F1
  Camberley GU16 .... 36 B3
  Farnborough GU14 .... 55 F4
  Fleet GU13 .... 74 C3
  New Alresford SO24 .... 179 E3
  Tilford GU10 .... 144 C4
  Tongham GU12 .... 100 B3
  Winchester SO23 .... 197 F2
Grange Special Sch The
  GU11 .... 99 F4
Grange The Frensham GU10 .. 144 A4
  Newbury RG14 .... 5 D3
  Northington SO21 .... 156 C3
Grantley Dr GU13 .... 74 C4
Grantly Ct GU10 .... 121 E3
Granville Pl SO23 .... 198 A3
Grasmere Cl GU35 .... 164 B3
Grasmere Rd
  Farnborough GU14 .... 55 F2
  Farnham GU10 .... 98 C3
Graspan Rd SP11 .... 57 D1
Grateley Dro Amport SP11 .... 103 E2
  Grateley SP11 .... 103 D1
Grateley House Sch SO20 .... 125 D4
Grateley Prim Sch SP11 .... 125 D4
Grateley Rd SP4 .... 101 E3
Grateley Sta SP11 .... 124 C4
Grattons Cl SO21 .... 131 E3
Gravel Cl SO24 .... 135 E2
Gravel Hill Rd GU10 .... 120 C2
Gravel La Barton Stacey SO21 .. 130 B4
  Ropley SO24 .... 159 F1
Gravel Rd Farnborough GU11 .. 77 D4
  Farnham GU9 .... 98 C4
  Fleet GU13 .... 75 D3
Gravellhill Cotts SO20 .... 129 E3
Gravelly Cl Ball Hill RG20 .... 3 F2
  Tadley RG26 .... 27 D3
Graveney Sq SP10 .... 83 D1
Grayshot Dr GU15 .... 35 D3
Grayshott CE Prim Sch
  GU26 .... 166 C2
Grayshott Cl SO22 .... 175 E2
Grayshott Laurels GU35 .... 165 F3
Grayshott Rd GU35 .... 166 A3
Grayswood Dr GU16 .... 56 C1
Great Austins GU10 .... 122 A4
Great Austins Ho GU10 .... 122 B4
Great Binfields Cres RG24 .... 70 A4
Great Binfields Rd
  Chineham RG24 .... 49 D1
  Old Basing RG24 .... 70 A4
Great Field Rd SO22 .... 175 E2
Great La RG28 .... 86 B2
Great Minster St SO23 .... 198 A4
Great Oaks Chase RG24 .... 48 C1
Great Sheldons Coppice RG27 51 D1
Greatfield Cl GU14 .... 55 F4
Greatfield Rd GU14 .... 55 F4
Greatham Prim Sch GU33 .. 185 F1
Grebe Cl Alton GU34 .... 139 F3
  Basingstoke RG22 .... 90 C4
Green Acre RG14 .... 76 B1
Green Acres
  Barton Stacey SO21 .... 130 B3
  Farnham GU11 .... 100 A1
Green Cl Kings Worthy SO23 .. 176 A3
  Old Alresford SO24 .... 157 E1
  South Wonston SO21 .... 153 F2
Green Croft Special Sch 56 A3
Green Cotts La GU10 .... 144 B1
Green Dro SP11 .... 60 A1
Green End GU46 .... 34 A4
Green Glades GU13 .... 74 C3
Green Jacket Cl SO22 .... 197 F3
Green La
  Bishop's Sutton SO24 .... 180 B3
  Blackwater GU17 .... 34 C2
  Blackwater GU47 .... 35 E2
  Churt GU10 .... 144 C1
  Ellisfield RG25 .... 115 D4
  Farnham GU9 .... 99 D3
  Farnham, Wrecclesham GU10 .. 121 F4
  Frensham GU10 .... 143 C2
  Froxfield GU32 .... 205 D3
  Hartley Wintney RG27 .... 52 B3
  Monxton SP11 .... 104 B3
  Newbury RG14 .... 5 F4
  Pamber End RG26 .... 27 D2
  Rotherwick RG27 .... 50 C3
  Sandhurst GU17 .... 35 D4
  Stoke SP11 .... 61 D3
  West End Green RG26 .... 29 E4

Fre – Gro 219

Green Lane Cl GU15 .... 36 A4
Green Lane Cotts GU10 .... 144 C1
Green Leys GU13 .... 74 C2
Green Meadows La SP10 .... 106 A1
Green Park SO23 .... 176 A1
Green Springs GU10 .... 97 E4
Green St GU34 .... 163 F4
Green Stile GU34 .... 159 F4
Green The
  Barton Stacey SO21 .... 130 C4
  Camberley GU14 .... 56 B3
  Charlton SP10 .... 82 C1
  Farnham GU10, GU9 .... 99 F3
  Farnham, Upper Hale GU9 .... 99 D3
  Kimpton SP11 .... 80 B1
  Liss GU33 .... 207 F3
  Overton RG25 .... 88 A4
  Seale GU10 .... 100 B1
  Tadley RG26 .... 27 D3
  Whitchurch RG28 .... 86 B3
Green Way GU12 .... 77 E2
Green's School La GU14 .... 55 F2
Greenacre
  Broughton SO20 .... 170 A3
  Kingsclere RG20 .... 24 B1
Greenacres
  Bordon GU35 .... 164 C2
  Woolton Mill RG20 .... 21 E4
Greenacres Special Sch
  SO22 .... 175 F1
Greenaways Ho RG14 .... 1 B1
Greenaways The RG23 .... 67 E1
Greenbank Way GU15 .... 36 A1
Greenbirch Cl RG22 .... 90 C4
Greencroft [2] GU14 .... 55 F2
Greenfield Cl GU30 .... 188 A3
Greenfield Rd GU9 .... 121 F4
Greenfields GU33 .... 208 A2
Greenfields Ave GU34 .... 139 F2
Greenfields Jun Sch RG27 .... 52 B3
Greenham RG19 .... 6 A4
Greenham Court Prim Sch
  RG14 .... 5 F4
Greenham Mill RG14 .... 1 C2
Greenham Rd RG14 .... 5 F4
Greenhanger GU10 .... 166 C4
Greenhaven GU46 .... 33 F3
Greenhaven Cl SP10 .... 106 B4
Greenhill Cl
  Farnham GU10, GU9 .... 121 F4
  Winchester SO22 .... 197 F4
Greenhill Rd
  Farnham GU9 .... 122 A4
  Winchester SO22 .... 197 E4
Greenhill Terr SO22 .... 197 F4
Greenhill Way GU9 .... 121 F4
Greenhills GU9 .... 122 B4
Greenlands Rd
  Camberley GU17 .... 35 F1
  Kingsclere RG20 .... 24 B1
  Newbury RG14 .... 5 F4
Greenleas GU15 .... 36 B1
Greenleas Cl GU47 .... 34 A4
Greensey SP11 .... 81 D3
Greenway
  Basingstoke RG22 .... 68 B2
  Sherfield on Loddon RG24 .... 49 E4
Greenways GU13 .... 74 C3
Greenways Rd RG14 .... 4 B1
Greenwich Way SP10 .... 83 D1
Greenwood Dr RG24 .... 48 C2
Greenwoods RG28 .... 86 B3
Gregan Ct [15] GU11 .... 76 B1
Gregory Cl RG21 .... 69 E4
Gregory Ho RG27 .... 51 D1
Greig Cl RG21 .... 68 C1
Grenadier Rd GU12 .... 77 F2
Grenadiers Way GU14 .... 55 D2
Grensell Cl GU46 .... 33 E4
Grenville Cl GU30 .... 188 A2
Grenville Dr GU13 .... 74 C4
Grenville Gdns GU16 .... 56 B3
Gresham Cl GU14 .... 77 D4
Gresham Ind Est GU12 .... 77 E1
Gresham Way GU16 .... 56 B3
Gresley Rd RG21 .... 69 E4
Grey House Sch The RG27 .... 52 B3
Greyberry Copse Rd RG19 .... 6 A4
Greyfriars [19] SO23 .... 198 A4
Greyhound Cl GU12 .... 77 E1
Greyhound La RG25 .... 88 A4
Greys Ct [6] GU11 .... 76 B1
Greys Farm Cl SO24 .... 201 E2
Greystead Pk GU9 .... 121 E3
Greywell Cl RG26 .... 26 C4
Greywell St RG29 .... 71 F2
Grieve Cl GU10 .... 100 B4
Griffin Way N RG27 .... 51 D1
Griffin Way S RG27 .... 51 E1
Griffon Cl GU14 .... 55 D2
Groombridge Pl RG14 .... 1 B3
Grosvenor Cl RG22 .... 91 D3
Grosvenor Cl GU47 .... 35 D2
Grosvenor Dr SO23 .... 176 A1
Grosvenor Lawn RG14 .... 1 B1
Grosvenor Rd
  Aldershot GU11 .... 76 C1
  Medstead GU34 .... 159 F4
Grove Cl RG21 .... 69 E2
Grove Cross Rd GU15 .... 36 A1
Grove Cty Prim Sch The
  GU15 .... 36 B1
Grove End Rd GU9 .... 121 F4
Grove Park Ind Est GU34 .... 140 A2
Grove Pk GU34 .... 140 A2

Grove Rd Alton GU34 .... **139** F1
  Ash GU12 .... **77** F2
  Basingstoke RG21 .... **69** E1
  Beacon Hill GU26 .... **167** D3
  Camberley GU16 .... **36** B3
  Fleet GU13 .... **75** D3
  Newbury RG14 .... **1** B3
Grove Sch The GU26 .... **167** D1
Grove The Aldershot GU11 .... **76** C1
  Camberley GU16 .... **36** A1
  Farnborough GU16, GU17 .... **56** A1
  Hartley Wintney RG27 .... **52** B3
  Liphook GU30 .... **187** F2
  Penton Grafton SP11 .... **81** F2
Grovebell Ind Est GU10 .... **121** E4
Grovefields Ave GU16 .... **36** A1
Groveland Rd RG14 .... **1** B3
Grovelands GU9 .... **122** B4
Grovelands Rd SO22 .... **175** D1
Groves Cl SO21 .... **153** E2
Guernsey Cl RG24 .... **48** B1
Guernsey Dr GU13 .... **54** A2
Guildford Rd
  Aldershot GU12 .... **100** A4
  Camberley GU16 .... **56** C3
  Farnham GU10, GU9 .... **99** F2
  Fleet GU13 .... **54** B1
  Mytchett GU16 .... **56** C3
Guildford Rd E GU14 .... **56** A1
Guildford Rd Ind Est
  GU10, GU9 .... **99** E2
Guildford Rd Trad Est
  GU10, GU9 .... **99** D2
Guildford Rd W GU16 .... **56** A1
Guillemont Fields SO23 .... **55** D3
Guillemont Jun Sch GU14 .... **55** D4
Guinea Ct RG24 .... **49** D2
Gun Hill GU11 .... **76** C2
Gunners La SO51 .... **135** D3
Gunns Farm GU30 .... **188** A1
Gunville Hill SP5 .... **168** A3
Gunville Rd SP5 .... **168** A3
Gurdons GU34 .... **139** E1
Gurkha Mus The SO22 .... **197** F4
Gurkha Sq GU14 .... **74** C4
Gurney Ct RG29 .... **72** C1
Guttridge La RG26 .... **26** C4
Gwyn Cl RG14 .... **5** E4

H Jones Cres GU12 .... **77** D2
Hacks La SO21 .... **152** A2
Hackupps La SO51 .... **193** E1
Hackwood Cl SP10 .... **105** E4
Hackwood Cotts RG21 .... **69** E1
Hackwood La RG25 .... **92** B3
Hackwood Rd RG21 .... **69** E2
Hackwood Road Rdbt RG21 .... **69** D2
Hadleigh Gdns GU16 .... **56** B3
Hadleigh Pl RG21 .... **69** D3
Hadleys GU9 .... **121** E2
Hadrian Rd SP10 .... **83** D2
Hadrians GU9 .... **99** E2
Hadrians Way RG23 .... **68** B4
Hagley Rd GU13 .... **53** F1
Haig La GU13 .... **75** D3
Haig Rd Aldershot GU12 .... **77** D1
  Andover SP10 .... **105** F4
  New Alresford SO24 .... **179** E3
  Sandhurst GU17 .... **35** E3
Hailstone Rd RG21 .... **69** D4
Haining Gdns GU14 .... **56** C2
Halcyon Dr GU11 .... **103** F4
Hale Day Ctr GU9 .... **99** D2
Hale Farm Flats GU9 .... **99** E3
Hale House Cl GU10 .... **144** B1
Hale House La GU10 .... **144** C1
Hale Pl GU9 .... **99** E3
Hale Prim Sch GU9 .... **98** C4
Hale Rd GU9 .... **99** E2
Hale Reeds GU9 .... **99** E3
Hale Way GU14 .... **56** A4
Half Way Cotts GU9 .... **98** A2
Halifax Cl Andover SP10 .... **82** C1
  Farnborough GU14 .... **55** E2
Halimote Rd GU11 .... **76** C1
Hall Cl GU15 .... **36** B3
Hall Farm Cres GU46 .... **34** A3
Hall La Selborne GU34 .... **162** A1
  Upper Farringdon GU34 .... **162** A1
  Yateley GU46 .... **34** A3
Hall Rd GU34 .... **140** A3
Hall Way The SO22 .... **175** D3
Halliday Cl RG21 .... **69** D1
Hallmark Cl GU15 .... **35** E4
Halpin Ho RG7 .... **14** A2
Halstead Ho RG26 .... **9** E1
Halton SP9 .... **79** E4
Ham La RG25 .... **25** F3
Hamble Ave GU17 .... **35** D3
Hamble Cl RG23 .... **67** D1
Hamble Ct ⁴⁰ Andover SP10 .... **83** E1
  ⁷ Basingstoke RG21 .... **69** E3
Hamble Dr RG26 .... **27** D4
Hambledon Cl SO22 .... **175** E2
Hambleton Cl GU16 .... **36** C2
Hambridge La RG14 .... **2** B1
Hambridge Rd RG14 .... **2** A1
Hamburg Cl SP10 .... **82** C2
Hamelyn Cl ⁶ RG21 .... **69** D2
Hamelyn Rd RG21 .... **69** D2
Hamesmoor Rd GU16 .... **56** B2
Hamesmoor Way GU16 .... **56** B2
Hamilton Cl
  Basingstoke RG22 .... **68** C2
  Bordon GU35 .... **164** C2

Hamilton Ct
  Farnborough GU47 .... **35** E1
  Newbury RG14 .... **5** F4
Hamilton Rd Bordon GU13 .... **186** B1
  Fleet GU13 .... **75** D3
Hamlash Cotts GU10 .... **122** A1
Hamlash La GU10 .... **122** A1
Hammer Hill GU27 .... **189** D2
Hammer La
  Bramshott GU27 .... **188** C3
  Grayshott GU26 .... **166** B3
  Headley GU26 .... **166** B3
  Linchmere GU27 .... **189** D3
Hammer Vale GU27 .... **189** D4
Hammersly Rd GU11 .... **76** C4
Hammerwood Copse GU27 .... **189** D3
Hammond Heath RG7 .... **11** F3
Hammond Rd ¹⁰ RG21 .... **69** D2
Hammond Sq SP10 .... **83** D1
Hampdens The RG14 .... **5** D3
Hampshire Cl RG22 .... **68** A2
Hampshire Cross SP9 .... **78** C3
Hampshire Golf Club The
  SP10 .... **106** B1
Hampshire Ho GU30 .... **187** F4
Hampshire Int Bsns Pk
  RG24 .... **48** C2
Hampshire Rd Bordon GU35 .... **164** B2
  Camberley GU16 .... **36** B4
Hampstead Ho ²⁰ RG21 .... **69** D3
Hampton Cl GU13 .... **75** D2
Hampton Ct RG23 .... **68** B3
Hampton La SO22 .... **175** E1
Hampton Rd Farnham GU9 .... **98** C3
  Newbury RG14 .... **1** B1
Hanbury Way GU15 .... **36** A2
Handcroft Cl GU10 .... **97** E4
Handel Rd RG21 .... **68** C1
Handford La GU46 .... **34** A3
Hanger Rd RG26 .... **9** E1
Hanger The GU35 .... **165** E4
Hangerfield Cl GU46 .... **34** A3
Hanmore Rd RG24 .... **48** C2
Hannam's Farm GU10 .... **97** E3
Hanover Cl Andover SP10 .... **105** E3
  Camberley GU16 .... **36** B1
  Yateley GU17, GU46 .... **34** A4
Hanover Ct GU30 .... **187** F3
Hanover Dr GU13 .... **54** B2
Hanover Gdns
  Basingstoke RG21 .... **69** D1
  Farnborough GU14 .... **55** E3
Hanover Ho ¹⁴ SP10 .... **106** A4
Hanover Mead RG14 .... **5** D3
Hanson Cl GU15 .... **36** C4
Hanson Rd SP10 .... **82** C1
Harbour Rd GU14 .... **55** F4
Harcourt Rd GU47 .... **35** F3
Harding's La RG27 .... **52** B3
Hardy Ave GU46 .... **34** A2
Hardy La RG21 .... **69** D2
Hardyfair Cl SP11 .... **81** E1
Hardys Field RG20 .... **24** B2
Hare's La RG27 .... **52** C4
Harebell Cl RG27 .... **52** B4
Harebell Gdns RG27 .... **52** B4
Harestock Cl SO22 .... **175** E3
Harestock Cnr SO22 .... **175** E2
Harestock Prim Sch SO22 .... **175** E2
Harestock Rd SO22 .... **175** E2
Harewood Forest Ind Est
  SP10 .... **107** F2
Harfield Cl RG27 .... **51** D1
Harlech Cl RG22 .... **68** B3
Harlech Rd GU17 .... **35** D2
Harlington Way GU11 .... **53** F1
Harmsworth Rd RG26 .... **26** C4
Harold Gdns GU34 .... **140** A3
Harold Jackson Terr RG21 .... **69** F2
Harpdon Par GU46 .... **34** A4
Harpton Cl GU46 .... **34** A4
Harriet Costello Sec Sch
  RG21 .... **69** E2
Harrington Cl RG14 .... **2** B3
Harris Ct GU30 .... **187** F1
Harris Hill RG22 .... **91** D4
Harrow Down SO22 .... **197** D3
Harrow La SP10 .... **82** A1
Harrow Way Andover SP10 .... **82** B1
  Oakley RG23 .... **66** C2
  Penton Grafton SP10 .... **82** A1
Harrow Way Com Sch SP10 .... **82** B1
Harrow Way The RG22 .... **68** C1
Harroway RG28 .... **85** E4
Hart Cl GU14 .... **55** E4
Hart Ctr ¹² GU13 .... **53** F1
Hart L Ctr GU13 .... **74** B4
Hart The GU9 .... **98** C1
Hartfield Ho ⁶ GU13 .... **53** F1
Hartford Bridge Flats GU46 .... **33** E1
Hartford Ct RG27 .... **52** B3
Hartford Rd RG27 .... **52** B4
Hartford Rise GU15 .... **36** A3
Hartford Terr RG27 .... **52** B3
Hartland Pl GU14 .... **55** F3
Hartley Cl GU46 .... **34** C3
Hartley Gdns RG26 .... **26** C4
Hartley La RG26 .... **30** A1
Hartley Meadow RG28 .... **86** A3
Hartley Mews RG27 .... **52** B4
Hartleys RG26 .... **27** F4
Harts Cotts RG20 .... **22** B3
Harts Leap Cl GU17 .... **35** E3
Harts Leap Rd GU46 .... **34** C4
Harts Yd GU9 .... **98** C1
Hartshill Rd RG26 .... **9** E1

Hartsleaf Cl GU13 .... **74** C4
Hartswood RG24 .... **48** C1
Harvest Cl Winchester SO22 .... **197** E2
  Yateley RG14 .... **33** F2
Harvest Cres GU13 .... **54** A3
Harvest Gn RG14 .... **1** B1
Harvest Way RG21 .... **69** F4
Harvey Rd GU14 .... **55** D3
Harvey Villas GU30 .... **187** D4
Harveys Field RG25 .... **88** A4
Harwood Pl SO23 .... **176** A4
Harwood Rise RG14 .... **4** B1
Hasle Dr GU27 .... **189** F3
Haslemere Rd
  Linchmere GU27 .... **189** F1
  Liphook GU30 .... **188** A1
Haslemere Sta GU27 .... **189** F3
Hassocks Workshops The
  RG21 .... **69** F4
Hastards La GU34 .... **184** C4
Hasted Dr SO24 .... **179** E2
Hastings Cl Basingstoke RG22 .... **68** A3
  Camberley GU16 .... **56** C4
Hatch Hill GU27 .... **189** F1
Hatch La Linchmere GU27 .... **189** F1
  Liss GU33 .... **208** B2
  Old Basing RG24 .... **70** B3
Hatchbury La SP11 .... **38** B3
Hatches The Camberley GU16 .... **56** B3
  Farnham GU10 .... **121** E4
Hatchet La SP11 .... **59** D1
Hatchetts Dr GU27 .... **189** D4
Hatchwarren Cotts RG22 .... **91** E4
Hatchwarren Gdns RG22 .... **91** E4
Hatchwarren La RG22 .... **91** E3
Hatchwarren Ret Pk RG22 .... **91** D3
Hatchwarren Sch RG22 .... **91** E4
Hatfield Cl⁷ GU13 .... **75** D2
Hatfield Gdns GU16 .... **56** B2
Hatherden SP11 .... **59** E1
Hatherden CE Prim Sch
  SP11 .... **59** E1
Hatherden Cl ⁸ SP10 .... **106** A4
Hatherley Rd SO22 .... **175** F1
Hatherwood GU17 .... **34** B3
Hatt La SO51 .... **192** C1
Hattingley Rd GU34 .... **159** E4
Haughurst Hill RG26 .... **9** D1
Havelock Ho GU12 .... **77** D4
Haven Way GU9 .... **99** D2
Haweswater Cl GU35 .... **164** B3
Haweswater Ct GU11 .... **77** E3
Hawk Cl RG22 .... **90** C4
Hawk Conservancy The
  SP11 .... **104** A4
Hawke Cl SP10 .... **83** E1
Hawkes Cl RG27 .... **52** B4
Hawkfield La RG21 .... **69** D2
Hawkins Gr GU13 .... **74** B3
Hawkins Way GU13 .... **75** E4
Hawkley Dr RG26 .... **27** D4
Hawkley Rd Hawkley GU33 .... **207** E3
  Liss GU33 .... **207** E3
Hawks Mead GU33 .... **207** F3
Hawkshaw Cl GU30 .... **188** A2
Hawkswood Ave GU16 .... **36** B1
Hawkwell GU13 .... **75** D2
Hawley Cl GU14 .... **55** E4
Hawley Garden Cotts GU15 .... **35** D2
Hawley Gn GU17 .... **35** E2
Hawley Green Farm GU17 .... **35** E2
Hawley La GU14 .... **55** F4
Hawley Lodge GU17 .... **35** E1
Hawley Place Sch GU17 .... **35** E1
Hawley Prim Sch GU17 .... **35** E2
Hawley Rd Blackwater GU17 .... **35** E2
  Farnborough GU17 .... **35** F2
  Hawley GU17 .... **35** E2
Hawthorn Cl
  Micheldever SO21 .... **133** D1
  New Alresford SO24 .... **179** E3
Hawthorn Cres GU17 .... **35** E2
Hawthorn Hill SO20 .... **126** A2
Hawthorn La SO24 .... **182** C4
Hawthorn Rd
  Camberley GU15 .... **36** B1
  Four Marks SO24 .... **182** B4
  Newbury RG14 .... **1** C2
  North Tidworth SP9 .... **79** D4
Hawthorn Way RG23 .... **68** B4
Hawthorne Cl
  Aldershot GU10 .... **100** B4
  Grateley SP11 .... **103** E1
Hawthorns GU34 .... **139** F3
Hawthorns Sch RG22 .... **68** B1
Hawthorns The RG26 .... **26** B4
Hay Down La SP11 .... **103** F3
Haydn Cl SO23 .... **176** A4
Haydn Rd RG22 .... **91** E4
Haydock Cl GU34 .... **139** F1
Haydown Leas SP11 .... **38** B3
Hayes Cl SO20 .... **171** F1
Hayley La RG29 .... **95** E2
Haywarden Pl RG27 .... **52** B4
Haywood Dr GU13 .... **75** D4
Hazel Ave GU14 .... **55** E2
Hazel Cl Andover SP10 .... **105** E3
  Oakley RG23 .... **67** D1
Hazel Coppice RG27 .... **51** D1
Hazel Gn RG26 .... **9** D1
Hazel Gr Haslemere GU26 .... **167** E1
  Winchester SO22 .... **197** E3
Hazel Rd Four Marks GU34 .... **160** B2
  Mytchett GU16 .... **56** C1
Hazelbank RG40 .... **16** B3
Hazeldene RG24 .... **48** C1
Hazeldene Gdns SO21 .... **177** F4
Hazeldene Rd GU30 .... **187** D2

Hazeley Cl RG27 .... **52** B4
Hazeley Lea RG27 .... **31** F2
Hazell Rd GU9 .... **98** B1
Hazelwood Cl RG23 .... **68** B4
Hazelwood Dr RG23 .... **68** B4
Hazlebank Cl GU30 .... **188** A2
Hazlebank Mews GU30 .... **188** A2
Headbourne Worthy Ho
  SO23 .... **176** A3
Headington Cl RG22 .... **91** E4
Headley Fields GU35 .... **165** E4
Headley Hill Rd GU35 .... **165** F3
Headley La GU30 .... **165** E1
Headley Rd Grayshott GU26 .... **166** C2
  Lindford GU35 .... **165** D3
  Liphook GU30 .... **187** F3
Headmore La GU34 .... **160** C1
Headon Ct GU9 .... **99** D1
Hearmon Cl GU47 .... **34** B3
Hearn Vale GU35 .... **165** F4
Hearsey Gdns GU47 .... **34** C3
Heath Cl Beacon Hill GU26 .... **167** D4
  Farnham GU9 .... **99** D4
Heath Cnr GU15 .... **36** C2
Heath Cotts
  Beacon Hill GU26 .... **167** D3
  Frensham GU10 .... **122** A2
Heath Ct RG26 .... **9** E1
Heath End Rd Baughurst RG26 .... **9** E1
  Tadley RG26 .... **9** E1
Heath End Sch GU9 .... **99** E3
Heath Green La GU34 .... **159** D4
Heath Hill GU35 .... **143** E1
Heath La Buttermere SN8 .... **18** B3
  Crondall GU10 .... **97** F3
  Farnham GU9 .... **99** D4
Heath Rd Linchmere GU27 .... **189** D3
  Pamber Heath RG26 .... **10** B1
Heath Ride RG40 .... **16** C3
Heath Rise GU15 .... **36** A3
Heath Vale SP10 .... **106** A4
Heathcote Cl GU12 .... **77** F2
Heathcote Rd Ash GU12 .... **77** F2
  Bordon GU35 .... **164** C2
  Camberley GU16 .... **36** A3
Heather Cl Aldershot GU11 .... **76** B1
  Ash GU12 .... **77** F3
  Bordon GU35 .... **164** A1
  Farnham GU9 .... **121** E3
  Wokingham RG40 .... **16** B4
Heather Cotts GU12 .... **77** F4
Heather Ct
  ²² Aldershot GU11 .... **76** C1
  Hindhead GU26 .... **167** E2
Heather Dr Andover SP10 .... **105** F4
  Fleet GU13 .... **74** C3
  Lindford GU35 .... **164** C3
  Tadley RG26 .... **9** E1
Heather Gdns GU14 .... **55** E2
Heather Gr RG27 .... **52** B4
Heather La RG27 .... **71** E3
Heather Mead GU16 .... **36** B1
Heather Mead Ct GU15 .... **36** B1
Heather Row La
  Mapledurwell RG27 .... **71** F3
  Newnham RG27 .... **71** F3
Heather Way
  Basingstoke RG22 .... **91** D4
  Hindhead GU26 .... **167** E2
Heatherdale Rd GU15 .... **36** A2
Heatherley Cl GU17 .... **35** F3
Heatherley Rd GU17 .... **35** F3
Heatherly Cl GU15 .... **35** F3
Heatherside Schs GU13 .... **75** D4
Heathfield RG7 .... **11** F3
Heathfield Cl GU13 .... **74** C4
Heathfield Rd RG22 .... **91** E4
Heathland St GU13 .... **76** C1
Heathlands Baughurst RG26 .... **9** E1
  Highclere RG20 .... **21** F4
Heathlands Ct GU46 .... **34** B2
Heathman St SO20 .... **148** A3
Heathrow Copse RG26 .... **26** A4
Heathside La GU26 .... **167** D3
Heathside Way RG27 .... **52** B4
Heathvale Bridge Rd GU12 .... **77** F3
Heathview RG27 .... **51** E1
Heathway GU16 .... **36** A3
Heathway Cl GU16 .... **36** A3
Heathwood Cl GU14 .... **34** A4
Heathyfields Rd GU9 .... **98** C3
Heddon Wlk GU14 .... **55** F4
Hedge Croft GU46 .... **33** F3
Hedge End Rd SP10 .... **106** A3
Hedge Way RG14 .... **2** A2
Hedgehog La GU27 .... **189** F3
Hedgerows The RG24 .... **70** A4
Hedges Cl SP9 .... **101** E4
Heenan Cl GU16 .... **56** B4
Heights The GU15 .... **36** B3
Hele Cl RG24 .... **69** D1
Helen Ct GU14 .... **55** F2
Helford Ct ³⁰ SP10 .... **83** E1
Helston Cl GU14 .... **56** C4
Hendon Rd GU35 .... **164** B1
Hendren Sq SP10 .... **83** E1
Hengest Cl SP10 .... **82** B2
Henley Cl GU14 .... **55** E4
Henley Dr GU16 .... **56** B4
Henley Gdns GU17 .... **34** A3
Henry Beaufort Sec Sch
  SO22 .... **175** F2
Henry Randell's Almshouses
  GU15 .... **35** E2
Henshaw Cres RG14 .... **5** D4
Henwick Cl RG18 .... **2** C3
Henwick La RG18 .... **2** C1
Hepplewhite Cl RG26 .... **9** E1

Hepplewhite Dr RG22 .... **91** D4
Hepworth Cl SP10 .... **83** D1
Hepworth Croft GU15 .... **35** E3
Herald Ct ²⁰ GU11, GU12 .... **76** C1
Herbert Rd GU13 .... **53** F1
Herbs End GU14 .... **55** D3
Hereford Cl RG29 .... **72** B1
Hereford La GU9 .... **98** C4
Hereford Mead GU13 .... **54** A2
Hereford Rd RG23 .... **68** B3
Herewood Cl RG14 .... **1** B2
Heritage Pk RG22 .... **91** D3
Hermes Cl GU13 .... **54** B1
Hermitage Cl
  Camberley GU15 .... **36** B1
  Farnborough GU16 .... **56** A1
Heron Cl Alton GU34 .... **139** F3
  Fleet GU13 .... **75** E3
  Mytchett GU16 .... **56** B2
Heron Park RG24 .... **48** C1
Heron Rise SP10 .... **106** A3
Heron Way Basingstoke RG22 .... **90** C4
  Thatcham RG19 .... **2** C2
Heron Wood Rd GU12 .... **100** A4
Herondale GU27 .... **189** E3
Herrett St GU12 .... **100** A4
Herretts Gdns GU12 .... **77** D1
Herriard Way RG26 .... **27** D4
Herridge Cl RG26 .... **29** D1
Herriot Ct GU46 .... **34** A2
Hewshott Gr GU30 .... **188** B3
Hewshott La GU30 .... **188** B3
Hexagon The SP10 .... **105** E3
Hibiscus Gr GU35 .... **164** C1
Hickory Dr SO22 .... **175** E2
Hicks La GU46 .... **34** C3
Hides Cl RG28 .... **86** B2
High Beeches GU15 .... **36** A1
High Copse GU9 .... **98** C4
High Crissels GU17 .... **35** D4
High Cross GU32 .... **205** F1
High Cross La GU32 .... **205** E1
High Dr RG23 .... **68** B1
High Park Rd GU9 .... **99** D2
High Pitfold GU26 .... **167** D1
High St
  Aldershot GU11, GU12 .... **76** C1
  Alton GU34 .... **139** F2
  Andover SP10 .... **106** A4
  Bordon GU35 .... **164** B2
  Broughton SO20 .... **170** A4
  Camberley GU15 .... **36** A3
  Farnborough GU12 .... **77** D1
  Farnham GU9 .... **121** E2
  Grateley SO20 .... **125** D4
  Hartley Wintney RG27 .... **52** B3
  Headley GU35 .... **165** E3
  Medstead GU34 .... **159** F4
  Nether Wallop SO20 .... **148** A3
  Odiham RG29 .... **72** C2
  Overton RG25 .... **88** A4
  Sandhurst GU46 .... **34** B4
  Shipton Bellinger SP9 .... **101** F4
  Stockbridge SO20 .... **149** F2
  Winchester SO21, SO23 .... **197** F4
  ³³ Winchester SO21, SO23 .... **198** A4
High Thicket Rd GU35 .... **143** D3
High Trees Dr SO22 .... **175** F1
High View Cl GU14 .... **55** F2
High View Lodge ² GU11 .... **76** C1
High View Rd GU14 .... **55** F2
Highams Cl RG20 .... **24** B1
Highbury Cres GU16 .... **36** C4
Highbury Rd SP10 .... **105** E2
Highclere Castle RG20 .... **21** F1
Highclere Park Gdns RG20 .... **21** F2
Highclere Rd GU12 .... **100** A4
Highclere St RG20 .... **21** E2
Highcliffe Rd SO23 .... **198** A3
Highdown GU13 .... **54** A1
Highdowns RG22 .... **91** E3
Higher Mead RG24 .... **69** F4
Highfield RG20 .... **40** C4
Highfield Ave
  Aldershot GU10, GU9 .... **99** F4
  Newbury RG14 .... **1** C1
Highfield Chase RG21 .... **68** C3
Highfield Cl Aldershot GU9 .... **99** F4
  Farnborough GU14 .... **55** E2
  Farnham GU9 .... **121** F4
Highfield Cres GU26 .... **167** E2
Highfield Gdns GU33 .... **208** A2
Highfield La GU30 .... **188** B2
Highfield Path GU14 .... **55** E2
Highfield Rd
  Farnborough GU14 .... **55** E2
  Newbury RG14 .... **1** B1
Highfield Sch GU30 .... **188** B1
Highfield Terr ¹⁷ SO22 .... **197** F4
Highgate GU16 .... **56** A3
Highgate La GU14 .... **56** A3
Highland Dr Fleet GU13 .... **54** A2
  Oakley RG23 .... **67** D1
Highland Rd Aldershot GU14 .... **77** D1
  Camberley GU16 .... **36** B4
Highlands Cl GU10 .... **121** F4
Highlands Rd Andover SP10 .... **106** B4
  Basingstoke RG23 .... **68** A2
  Farnham GU11 .... **99** D4
Highmoors RG24 .... **48** C2
Highmount Cl SO23 .... **198** B4
Highridge GU34 .... **139** E2
Highrove GU14 .... **55** F4
Highview Bsns Ctr GU35 .... **164** B2
Highwood Cl Newbury RG14 .... **1** A1
  Yateley GU46 .... **34** A2
Highwood Ridge RG22 .... **91** D3
Highworth Cotts RG26 .... **9** D1

Hilary Ho 9 RG14 ... 1 C1
Hilden Way SO22 ... 175 D3
Hilder Gdns GU16 ... 56 A2
Hill Brow Rd
  Hill Brow GU33 ... 208 A1
  Liss GU33 ... 208 A1
Hill Cl RG14 ... 5 D4
Hill Corner Farm Est GU14 ... 55 D4
Hill Crest Dr GU9 ... 121 E3
Hill Ct GU27 ... 189 E3
Hill Farm Cl GU27 ... 189 E3
Hill Farm Rd SO24 ... 182 B1
Hill House Hill GU30 ... 187 F3
Hill Houses La SO24 ... 201 D3
Hill Meadow RG25 ... 65 D1
Hill Rd Barton Stacey SP11 ... 108 A1
  Beacon Hill GU26 ... 167 D3
  Farnham GU11 ... 99 D4
  Grayshott GU26 ... 167 D2
  Newbury RG14 ... 1 B2
  Oakley RG22 ... 90 A4
Hill Sq RG24 ... 49 D1
Hill Terr SO24 ... 179 E3
Hill Top SO22 ... 175 E3
Hill Top Ave SP9 ... 78 C4
Hill View Rd
  Basingstoke RG22 ... 68 C2
  Farnham GU9 ... 98 B1
Hilland Rise GU35 ... 165 E3
Hillary Cl GU9 ... 121 F4
Hillary Rd Basingstoke RG21 ... 69 D4
  Farnham GU9 ... 121 F4
Hillbrook Rise GU9 ... 98 C3
Hillbury Ave SP10 ... 105 F3
Hillcrest Farnham GU9 ... 99 D4
  Fleet GU13 ... 54 A2
  Tadley RG26 ... 9 F1
Hillcrest Cotts RG14 ... 1 B4
Hillcrest Ct RG21 ... 68 A3
Hillcrest Rd GU15 ... 36 C4
Hillcrest Wlk RG22 ... 68 A3
Hillfield GU17 ... 34 B3
Hillgarth GU26 ... 167 D3
Hillhouse La RG19, RG20 ... 7 F1
Hillier Way SO23 ... 176 A1
Hillsborough Ct GU14 ... 55 E4
Hillside Abbotts Ann SP11 ... 104 C2
  Baughurst RG26 ... 26 A2
  Littleton SO22 ... 175 E3
  Sandhurst GU15 ... 35 E4
  Upton SP11 ... 38 C1
Hillside Cl Alton GU34 ... 139 F3
  Crookham Village GU13 ... 74 B3
  Headley GU35 ... 165 F3
  West Dean SP5 ... 190 B1
  Winchester SO22 ... 175 E1
Hillside Cotts
  Farnborough GU47 ... 35 E1
  Sparsholt SO21 ... 174 A2
Hillside Cres GU16 ... 56 B4
Hillside Ct SP11 ... 105 F4
Hillside La GU9 ... 99 D4
Hillside Rd Aldershot GU9 ... 99 F4
  Ash GU12 ... 77 F2
  Farnham GU10 ... 122 A2
  Farnham, Weybourne GU9 ... 99 E4
  Linchmere GU27 ... 189 E3
  Odiham RG29 ... 72 B1
  Winchester SO22 ... 175 E1
Hillside Villas SP10 ... 82 C1
Hillstead Ct RG21 ... 69 D2
Hilltop Rd RG25 ... 65 D1
Hilltop View GU46 ... 33 F3
Hindell Cl GU14 ... 55 F4
Hindhead Ho GU26 ... 167 E2
Hindhead Rd GU27 ... 167 E1
Hinstock Cl GU14 ... 55 F2
Hinton Ampner Ho SO24 ... 201 F2
Hinton Cl RG26 ... 26 C4
Hinton Hill SO24 ... 201 F2
Hinwood Cl SO20 ... 170 A4
Hitches La
  Crookham Village GU13 ... 74 B4
  Fleet GU13 ... 74 B4
Hobbs Cl SO24 ... 180 A2
Hobbs Sq SP10 ... 83 E1
Hockford La RG7 ... 8 C2
Hockley Cotts SO24 ... 200 C2
Hockley Golf Course SO23 ... 198 A1
Hoddington Cotts RG25 ... 94 B2
Hogarth Cl Basingstoke RG24 ... 69 F2
  Sandhurst GU15 ... 35 E3
Hogarth Ct SP10 ... 82 C1
Hoghatch La GU9 ... 98 C3
Hogmoor Rd GU35 ... 164 A2
Hogwood Ind Est RG2 ... 15 F3
Hogwood La RG40 ... 15 F3
Holbeche Cl GU46 ... 33 F3
Holbein Cl RG21 ... 69 E2
Holborne Rd RG14 ... 5 D3
Holbrook Cl GU11, GU12 ... 99 E4
Holbrook Way GU10, GU9 ... 99 F4
Holbury La
  East Tytherley SO51 ... 191 E2
  Lockerley SO51 ... 191 E2
Holdaway Cl SO23 ... 176 B4
Holder Rd GU9 ... 77 E1
Hole La GU10 ... 120 A3
Holland Cl GU9 ... 99 E1
Holland Dr SP10 ... 82 C2
Holland Gdns GU13 ... 75 D4
Hollands Cl SO22 ... 175 D3
Hollies The RG14 ... 5 D3
Hollington La RG20 ... 21 D2
Hollis Wood Dr GU9 ... 121 E3
Hollow The SO20 ... 170 B3
Holly Acre GU47 ... 34 A3

Holly Ave GU15 ... 36 C2
Holly Bush La GU12 ... 77 E3
Holly Cl Aldershot GU12 ... 77 D1
  Bramley RG26 ... 29 D1
  Eversley GU46 ... 33 D4
  Farnborough GU14 ... 55 F2
  Headley GU35 ... 166 A3
Holly Cross RG26 ... 28 C2
Holly Dr RG24 ... 70 B3
Holly Gr RG26 ... 10 B1
Holly Hedge Cl GU15 ... 36 B1
Holly Hedge Rd GU15 ... 36 B1
Holly La RG26 ... 27 F4
Holly Lodge Mid Sch GU12 ... 77 E4
Holly Rd Aldershot GU12 ... 77 D1
  Farnborough GU14 ... 55 F2
Holly Way GU17 ... 35 D2
Holly Wlk Andover SP10 ... 105 E3
  Middle Wallop SO20 ... 126 A2
Hollybrook Cl GU35 ... 164 C2
Hollybrook Pk GU35 ... 164 C2
Hollybush Ind Pk GU12 ... 77 E3
Hollybush La Eversley GU46 ... 33 E4
  Ramsdell RG26 ... 26 B1
Hollycombe Cl GU30 ... 188 A1
Hollyfields Cl GU15 ... 35 F3
Hollyhock Cl RG22 ... 91 D4
Hollyridge GU27 ... 189 F3
Hollytree Gdns GU14 ... 56 A4
Hollytrees GU13 ... 74 C3
Hollywater Rd Bordon GU35 ... 164 C1
  Liphook GU30 ... 187 D4
Holmbrook Cl GU14 ... 55 D2
Holmbrook Gdns GU14 ... 55 D2
Holme CE Prim Sch The
  GU35 ... 165 E3
Holmes Cl RG22 ... 91 D4
Holmes Ct SP10 ... 105 F4
Holmwood Cotts GU34 ... 119 F2
Holmwood Terr RG27 ... 52 B3
Holst Cl RG22 ... 91 F4
Holt Cl GU14 ... 56 A4
Holt Cotts RG26 ... 25 E4
Holt End La GU34 ... 138 A2
Holt La Baughurst RG26 ... 25 E2
  Hook RG27 ... 51 E1
  Tangley SP11 ... 59 D4
Holt Pound La GU9 ... 121 D3
Holt Way RG27 ... 51 E1
Holtwood Rd RG20 ... 3 F3
Holy Barn Cl RG22 ... 68 A1
Holy Cross Hospl GU27 ... 189 E4
Holyrood Ct RG23 ... 68 A2
Holywell Cl GU14 ... 55 F4
Home Cl GU14 ... 180 B3
Home Farm Bsns Ctr SP5 ... 191 F3
Home Farm Cl GU16 ... 56 A3
Home Farm Gdns SP10 ... 82 B2
Home Farm La RG26 ... 9 D3
Home Farm Rd RG27 ... 53 D3
Home La SO21 ... 174 B2
Home Mead RG22 ... 89 F1
Home Mead Cl RG14 ... 5 E4
Home Park Rd GU14 ... 34 A3
Homefield Cotts
  East Tisted GU34 ... 183 E3
  Liss GU33 ... 207 F3
Homegreen Ho GU27 ... 189 F3
Homelea Cl GU14 ... 55 F4
Homeleigh Cres GU12 ... 77 F4
Homepark Ho GU11 ... 99 D1
Homerise Ho 1 SO23 ... 198 A4
Homestead Rd GU34 ... 159 F3
Homesteads Rd RG22 ... 91 D4
Hone Hill GU17 ... 34 C4
Hones Yard Bsns Pk GU9 ... 99 D1
Honey La GU34 ... 185 D4
Honeybottom Rd RG26 ... 9 F1
Honeycritch La GU32 ... 206 B2
Honeysuckle Cl
  Winchester SO22 ... 197 F2
  Yateley GU46 ... 33 F3
Honeysuckle La GU35 ... 165 F3
Honister Gdns GU13 ... 54 B1
Honysuckle Cl RG22 ... 91 D4
Hood Cl SP10, SP11 ... 106 B4
Hook La
  Baughurst RG26 ... 25 F4
  Oakley RG23 ... 67 D4
  Ropley RG26 ... 181 D2
  Wooton St Lawrence RG23 ... 67 D4
Hook Rd
  Greywell RG29 ... 72 A3
  Hook RG29 ... 72 A4
  Kingsclere RG20 ... 24 C1
  North Warnborough RG29 ... 72 A3
  Rotherwick RG27 ... 51 D3
Hook Schs RG27 ... 51 D1
Hook Sta RG27 ... 72 A4
Hookpit Farm La SO23 ... 176 A4
Hookstile La GU9 ... 99 D1
Hookwood La SP11 ... 58 A4
Hoopers Way RG23 ... 67 D1
Hoopersmead RG25 ... 92 A4
Hop Garden Rd RG27 ... 50 C1
Hop Gdn GU13 ... 74 C2
Hop Kiln The GU10 ... 121 F4
Hope Fountain GU16 ... 36 C2
Hope Grant's Rd GU12 ... 76 C2
Hope La GU9 ... 98 C3
Hopeman Rd GU47 ... 35 D2
Hopeswood GU33 ... 186 A1
Hopfield Rd RG27 ... 52 B3
Hopkinson Way SP10 ... 82 A1
Hopton Garth RG24 ... 49 D1
Hopwood Cl RG14 ... 2 A2
Horizon West Ind Est RG14 ... 2 A2
Horn Rd GU14 ... 55 D3

Hornbeam Cl
  Farnborough GU14 ... 55 D3
  South Wonston SO21 ... 153 F2
Hornbeam Pl RG27 ... 51 D1
Hornbeams RG7 ... 14 A3
Hornes Field Ct GU13 ... 74 C2
Horris Hill RG14 ... 5 E2
Horse La SO24 ... 181 E4
Horsebridge Rd
  Broughton SO20 ... 170 B2
  Houghton SO20 ... 171 D2
  King's Somborne SO20 ... 171 E1
Horseshoe Bend GU16 ... 166 C2
Horseshoe Cl GU16 ... 36 B4
Horseshoe Cres
  Bordon GU35 ... 164 C2
  Camberley GU16 ... 36 B4
Horseshoe La Ash GU12 ... 77 F4
  Hurstbourne Tarrant SP11 ... 60 B4
Horshells Dro SO20 ... 125 E1
Horwood Gdns RG23 ... 68 C1
Hosketts La GU30 ... 147 F3
Hospital Hill GU11, GU12 ... 76 C2
Hospital Rd GU11, GU12 ... 76 C2
Houghton Lodge Gdns
  SO20 ... 171 E4
Hound Green Cl RG27 ... 31 D2
Houndmills Rd RG22 ... 68 C3
Houndmills Rdbt RG22 ... 68 C4
House Plat Ct GU34 ... 74 C2
Houseman Rd GU14 ... 55 D3
Howard Cl GU13 ... 54 B1
Howard Cole Way GU11 ... 76 B1
Howard Dr GU13 ... 54 C2
Howard Rd Basingstoke RG21 ... 69 E2
  Newbury RG14 ... 1 C1
Howard View RG21 ... 68 B2
Howard's La GU34 ... 140 B4
Howes Gdns GU13 ... 74 C3
Hubbard Rd RG21 ... 68 C4
Huddington Glade GU46 ... 33 F3
Hudsons Meadow RG27 ... 50 C1
Huish La RG24 ... 70 A2
Hulbert Way RG22 ... 68 B1
Hullam La GU34 ... 184 A3
Humber Cl RG18 ... 2 C3
Humber Ct 41 SP10 ... 83 E1
Humber La SP9 ... 78 B2
Humber Way GU17 ... 35 D4
Humbers View SO20 ... 172 A1
Humberstone Rd SP10 ... 106 A3
Humphrey Pk GU13 ... 74 C2
Hundred Acre Cnr SP10 ... 105 D4
Hungerford Cl GU15 ... 35 D4
Hungerford La
  Hatherden SP10 ... 82 C4
  Knights Enham SP10 ... 82 C4
  Tangley SP11 ... 37 F1
  Upper Chute SP11 ... 37 F1
Hungerford Rd SN8 ... 18 A3
Hunnels Cl GU13 ... 74 C2
Hunt Cl SO21 ... 153 F2
Hunt's Cotts RG14 ... 1 B3
Hunter Rd GU14 ... 55 E2
Hunters Cl RG23 ... 67 E2
Hunters Rd GU33 ... 186 B1
Hunting Gate SP10 ... 105 E4
Huntingdon House Dr
  GU26 ... 167 E2
Huntingford Cl RG26 ... 167 D4
Hunton Down La
  Upper Bullington SO21 ... 132 B3
  Wonston SO21 ... 132 B3
Hunton La SO21 ... 132 A2
Hunts Cl RG27 ... 51 E1
Hunts Cotts RG27 ... 52 B4
Huntsbottom La
  Hill Brow GU33 ... 208 A2
  Liss GU33 ... 208 A2
Huntsman's Mews GU16 ... 56 B2
Huntsmead GU34 ... 140 A2
Huntsmoor Rd RG26 ... 26 B4
Hurland La GU35 ... 165 E2
Hurlands Bsns Ctr GU9 ... 99 E2
Hurlands Cl GU9 ... 99 E2
Hurlands Pl GU9 ... 99 E2
Hurne Ct 28 RG21 ... 69 E3
Hurst Cl GU30 ... 187 F3
Hurst Com Sch The RG26 ... 9 D1
Hurst La GU34 ... 205 D2
Hurst Rd Aldershot GU12 ... 77 D2
  Farnborough GU14 ... 55 F4
Hurst The RG27 ... 73 F4
Hurstbourne Tarrant
  CE Prim Sch SP11 ... 60 C3
Hurstmere Ct GU26 ... 167 D2
Hussar Ct 1 GU11 ... 76 B1
Hussell La GU34 ... 160 A4
Hussey Cl 2 SO23 ... 176 A1
Husseys La GU34 ... 119 E3
Hutton Cl RG14 ... 1 C2
Hutton Rd GU12 ... 77 F3
Hutton Sq SP10 ... 83 E1
Hyacinth Cl RG22 ... 91 D4
Hyde Abbey Rd SO23 ... 198 A4
Hyde Church La SO23 ... 176 A1
Hyde Church Path 24 SO23 ... 176 A1
Hyde Cl SO23 ... 175 F1
Hyde End Rd RG7 ... 8 A3
Hyde Gate SO23 ... 176 A1
Hyde House Gdns 22 SO23 ... 176 A1
Hyde La Crondall GU10 ... 97 E4
  Ecchinswell RG20 ... 23 F4
Hyde Lodge SO22 ... 175 F1
Hyde St SO23 ... 176 A1
Hydes Platt RG26 ... 27 F4
Hyson Cres SP11 ... 57 D1

Hythe Cl RG26 ... 26 C4
Iberian Way GU15 ... 36 C3
Ibworth La RG26 ... 45 E2
Ickneild Ho 80 SP10 ... 83 E1
Icknield Special Sch SP10 ... 83 E1
Icknield Way SP10 ... 83 D2
Iden Ct RG14 ... 1 C2
Idlefield Cotts GU10 ... 120 B3
Ilchester Ct 8 RG14 ... 1 C1
Ilex Cl Pamber Heath RG26 ... 10 B1
  Yateley GU46 ... 33 F3
Illingworth Cl RG26 ... 29 D1
Imadene Cl GU35 ... 164 C2
Imadene Cres GU35 ... 164 C2
Imber Rd SO23 ... 198 B4
Imjin Cl RG21 ... 76 C2
Imperial Ct SP10 ... 83 E1
Impstone Rd RG26 ... 10 B1
Imran Ct GU12 ... 100 A4
Inadown Bnglws GU34 ... 183 F4
Ingle Dell GU35 ... 36 A2
Ingle Glen RG40 ... 16 C4
Inglewood Dr RG22 ... 91 D3
Inhams Rd GU34 ... 140 B3
Inhams Row SO24 ... 157 E1
Inhams Way RG26 ... 27 F4
Inhurst House Sch RG26 ... 9 D1
Inhurst La RG26 ... 26 A4
Inhurst Way RG26 ... 9 E1
Inkpen Gdns RG24 ... 70 A4
Innisfail Gdns GU9 ... 99 E4
Institute Rd GU12 ... 77 D1
Instow Gdns GU14 ... 55 F4
Intec Bsns Ctr RG24 ... 69 F4
Inverness Way GU47 ... 35 D4
Invincible Rd GU14 ... 55 F2
Inwood Rd GU33 ... 208 A2
Ipoh Cl SO20 ... 126 A3
Ipsley Lodge GU12 ... 100 B3
Iris Ct RG22 ... 91 D4
Irvine Dr GU14 ... 55 E4
Irwell Cl 24 RG21 ... 69 E3
Isaac Newton Rd RG40 ... 15 F4
Isington La GU34 ... 119 F1
Isington Rd GU34 ... 119 F1
Isis Way GU47 ... 35 D4
Island Farm Rd RG7 ... 11 E4
Itchel La GU10 ... 97 E4
Itchen Abbas Prim Sch
  SO21 ... 177 F3
Itchen Cl RG23 ... 67 D1
Itchen Ct
  46 Andover SP10 ... 83 E1
  43 Winchester SO23 ... 198 A4
Itchen View SO24 ... 178 B3
Ivanhoe Rd RG40 ... 15 F3
Ivar Gdns RG24 ... 49 D1
Ively Rd GU14 ... 55 D1
Ives Cl GU46 ... 33 F4
Ivy Cl SO22 ... 197 F3
Ivy Down La RG23 ... 66 C2
Ivy La GU9 ... 98 C1
Ivy Rd GU14 ... 77 E1
Ivyhole Hill RG27 ... 53 D4
Ivyhouse La GU32 ... 205 F2
Jacaranda Rd GU35 ... 164 B1
Jack St RG14 ... 1 C2
Jackdaw Cl RG22 ... 90 C4
Jacklyns Cl SO24 ... 179 E2
Jacklyns La SO24 ... 179 E3
Jacob Rd GU47 ... 35 E4
Jacob's Yd 18 RG21 ... 69 D2
Jagdalik Rd SP9 ... 78 C2
James Cl RG21 ... 69 E4
James Rd Camberley GU47 ... 35 F1
  Farnborough GU12 ... 77 D4
James Way GU47 ... 35 F1
Jamrud Rd SP9 ... 78 B3
Jan Smuts Cl GU33 ... 186 B1
Jane Austen's Ho (Mus)
  GU34 ... 161 E4
Japonica Ct GU12 ... 77 E1
Jardine Sq SP10 ... 83 E1
Jarvis Cl GU46 ... 33 D4
Jasmine Ct SP10 ... 105 F3
Jasmine Rd RG22 ... 91 D4
Jasmine Way GU35 ... 164 C1
Jays Cl RG21 ... 69 D1
Jays Nest Cl GU17 ... 35 D2
Jean Orr Ct GU13 ... 75 D3
Jefferson Rd RG21 ... 69 E4
Jellicoe Ct SP10 ... 83 E1
Jenkins Pl GU12 ... 77 D4
Jenkyn Pl GU10 ... 120 A3
Jenner Way GU34 ... 140 A3
Jennie Green La SO24 ... 137 F1
Jenny's Wlk GU46 ... 34 B3
Jenson Gdns SP10 ... 105 F4
Jerrymoor Hill RG40 ... 16 B4
Jersey Cl
  Basingstoke RG24 ... 48 B1
  Fleet GU13 ... 54 A2
Jervis Ct SP10 ... 83 E1
Jesmond Dene RG14 ... 1 B2
Jesse Cl GU34 ... 34 B3
Jessett Dr GU13 ... 74 C2
Jesty Rd SO24 ... 179 D2
Jewry St SO23 ... 198 A4
Jibbs Meadow RG26 ... 28 C2
Jobson Cl RG28 ... 86 B3
John Boys Ho RG14 ... 5 D3
John Childs Cl RG14 ... 1 C1
John Cl GU9 ... 99 E4
John Eddie Ct RG22 ... 68 B2
John Hanson Com Sch
  SP10 ... 105 F4

John Hunt of Everest Com Sch
  RG24 ... 48 B1
John Kimber's Almshouses
  RG14 ... 1 B2
John Morgan Cl RG27 ... 51 D1
John Pounds Ho GU35 ... 164 B1
John Rankin Schs RG14 ... 5 D4
Johnson Way GU13 ... 75 D3
Joices Yd 13 RG21 ... 69 D2
Jollies The GU10 ... 97 E3
Jonathan Hill RG14 ... 5 F2
Jouldings La RG22 ... 15 D2
Joule Rd Andover SP10 ... 82 A1
  Basingstoke RG21 ... 68 C4
Joy's La SO20 ... 129 D2
Jubilee Cl Farnborough GU14 ... 55 D2
  Litchfield RG28 ... 42 B1
  Pamber Heath RG26 ... 10 B1
Jubilee Cotts RG7 ... 14 A2
Jubilee Ct GU12 ... 77 E3
Jubilee Hall Rd GU14 ... 56 A2
Jubilee Ho GU35 ... 164 C2
Jubilee La Farnham GU10 ... 121 F3
  Grayshott GU26 ... 167 D2
Jubilee Rd Aldershot GU11 ... 99 F4
  Basingstoke RG22 ... 69 D2
  Finchampstead RG40 ... 16 B2
  Mytchett GU16 ... 56 C1
  Newbury RG14 ... 1 C1
Jumps Rd GU10 ... 144 C2
Junction Pl GU27 ... 189 E3
Junction Rd SP10 ... 106 A4
Junction Terr RG14 ... 2 A1
June Dr RG22 ... 68 A3
Juniper Cl Bordon GU35 ... 164 A1
  Chineham RG24 ... 49 D2
  Winchester SO22 ... 197 E3
Juniper Ct 1 SP9 ... 79 D4
Juniper Gr GU14 ... 55 D3
Jupiter Ho 8 RG26 ... 9 E1
Karachi Cl SP9 ... 78 C4
Kashmir Ct 6 GU16 ... 56 A1
Kathleen Cl RG21 ... 69 D1
Kay Cres GU35 ... 165 F3
Keable Rd GU9 ... 121 E4
Keats Cl Basingstoke RG24 ... 69 E4
  South Wonston SO21 ... 153 F2
  Winchester SO21, SO22 ... 197 E2
Keats Gdns GU34 ... 54 A1
Keats Way GU46 ... 33 F2
Keble St SO22 ... 197 E3
Keeper's Hill SP11 ... 104 A3
Keepers La SO51 ... 192 B1
Keeps Mead RG20 ... 24 B2
Keith Lucas Rd GU14 ... 55 E1
Kellynch Cl GU34 ... 139 F2
Kellys Wlk SP10 ... 105 F4
Kelsey Ave RG40 ... 16 B3
Kelsey Cl GU33 ... 208 A3
Kelsey Gr GU47 ... 34 B3
Kelvin Dr GU14 ... 15 E4
Kelvin Hill RG22 ... 68 C1
Kelvin Rd RG14 ... 1 C2
Kemmitt Way SP10 ... 105 F3
Kempland La GU34 ... 204 B2
Kempshott Gdns RG22 ... 91 D4
Kempshott Gr RG21 ... 68 A2
Kempshott La RG22 ... 91 D4
Kempshott Schs RG22 ... 91 D4
Kempton Cl Alton GU34 ... 139 F1
  Newbury RG14 ... 2 A1
Kendal Cl GU14 ... 55 E2
Kendal Gdns RG23 ... 68 A1
Kendrick Rd GU14 ... 5 D3
Kenilworth Cres GU13 ... 54 B1
Kenilworth Ct 8 SO23 ... 176 A1
Kenilworth Rd
  Basingstoke RG22 ... 68 B3
  Farnborough GU14 ... 55 D3
  Fleet GU13 ... 54 A1
Kenley Rd GU33 ... 166 A3
Kenmore Cl Camberley GU14 ... 56 A4
  Fleet GU13 ... 75 D3
Kennedy Cl RG14 ... 5 D3
Kennel La Frensham GU10 ... 122 A1
  Littleton SO22 ... 175 E2
Kennels La GU14 ... 55 D1
Kennet Cl Ash GU12 ... 77 F1
  21 Basingstoke RG21 ... 69 E3
  Farnborough GU14 ... 55 E3
Kennet Ct
  42 Andover SP10 ... 83 E1
  6 Newbury RG14 ... 1 C1
Kennet Ctr The RG14 ... 1 C1
Kennet Pl 15 RG14 ... 1 C2
Kennet Rd Newbury RG14 ... 1 B1
  North Tidworth SP9 ... 79 D4
Kennet Side RG14 ... 2 A2
Kennet Way GU13 ... 67 D1
Kensington Ho 10 RG21 ... 69 D3
Kent Rd Bordon GU35 ... 164 B1
  Fleet GU13 ... 54 A1
Kenton Cl GU15 ... 36 B1
Kenward Bglws RG25 ... 114 B2
Kenwith Ave GU13 ... 54 B1
Kenyons Yd SP11 ... 105 F4
Keogh Cl GU16 ... 56 C1
Kerchers Field RG25 ... 88 A4
Kerfield Way RG27 ... 51 D1
Kerfield Mews SO22 ... 197 E4
Kerridge Ind Est GU34 ... 140 A2
Kerry Cl GU13 ... 54 A3
Kersey Cres RG14 ... 1 B3

Kersley Cres RG29 .... 95 E4
Kestrel Cl Ewshot GU9 .... 98 A4
North Tidworth SP9 .... 79 D4
Thatcham RG19 .... 2 C1
Winchester SO22 .... 197 E2
Kestrel Ct GU34 .... 139 F3
Kestrel Ho GU10 .... 121 E4
Kestrel Rd RG23 .... 67 F1
Ketchers Field GU34 .... 184 C3
Ketelbey Rise RG22 .... 91 F4
Kevin Cl RG20 .... 24 C1
Kevins Dr GU46 .... 34 B4
Kevins Gr GU13 .... 54 A1
Kew Wlk SP10 .... 105 F4
Keyhaven Cotts SO20 .... 125 E1
Keynes Cl GU13 .... 75 D2
Kildare Cl GU35 .... 164 B2
Kildare Rd GU35 .... 164 B2
Kilham La SO22 .... 197 D3
Kilmartin Gdns GU15 .... 36 B1
Kilmeston Rd Cheriton SO24 .... 201 E2
Kilmeston SO24 .... 201 E1
Kilmore Dr GU15 .... 36 C2
Kilmuir Cl GU15 .... 35 D4
Kiln Field GU33 .... 207 F3
Kiln Gdns RG27 .... 52 B3
Kiln Hill RG7 .... 14 C4
Kiln La Farnham GU10, GU9 .... 122 A3
Monk Sherborne RG26 .... 47 D3
Old Alresford SO24 .... 157 E1
Stratfield Mortimer RG7 .... 12 A3
Kiln Rd Newbury RG14 .... 2 A3
Sherborne St John RG26 .... 47 F2
Kiln Ride RG40 .... 16 C4
Kiln Ride Extension RG40 .... 16 C3
Kiln Way Aldershot GU11 .... 99 F4
Grayshott GU26 .... 166 B3
Kilns The GU34 .... 140 A2
Kilsby Flats SP9 .... 101 F4
Kimbell Rd RG22 .... 68 C1
Kimber Cl RG24 .... 48 C1
Kimber's Cl RG14 .... 1 B2
Kimberley GU13 .... 75 D2
Kimberley Cl SP10 .... 82 B1
Kimberley Rd GU33 .... 186 B1
Kimberly Rd RG22 .... 68 C2
Kimbers Dr RG14 .... 1 A3
Kimbers La Farnham GU11 .... 99 D2
Pamber End RG26 .... 27 D3
Kimpton CE Prim Sch SP11 .... 80 B1
King Alfred Pl SO23 .... 176 A1
King Alfred Terr 29 SO23 .... 176 A1
King Alfred's Coll SO22 .... 197 F4
King Arthur's Way SP10 .... 83 D2
King George Rd SP10 .... 105 F4
King Harold Ct SO22 .... 197 F3
King John Ct RG20 .... 24 B1
King John Rd RG20 .... 24 B1
King Johns Rd RG29 .... 72 B2
King La SO20 .... 125 E2
King Lane Cotts SO20 .... 125 E1
King's Somborne
CE Prim Sch SO20 .... 171 F1
King St Mortimer RG7 .... 11 F3
Odiham RG29 .... 72 C1
King's Cl SO23 .... 154 A1
King's Cres GU16 .... 36 A4
King's Ct GU12 .... 100 B4
King's Elms SO21 .... 130 B4
King's Hill GU34 .... 138 B1
King's La GU32 .... 205 E2
King's Meadow RG25 .... 88 A4
King's Rd Aldershot GU11 .... 76 B1
Basingstoke RG23 .... 68 C2
Haslemere GU27 .... 189 F3
King's Ride GU16 .... 36 A4
King's Wlk GU15 .... 35 E3
Kingfisher Cl
Basingstoke RG22 .... 67 F1
Bordon GU35 .... 164 C1
Farnborough GU14 .... 55 D3
Fleet GU13 .... 75 D3
Whitchurch RG28 .... 86 B3
Kingfisher Court Ind Est
RG14 .... 2 A2
Kingfisher Ct GU34 .... 139 F3
Kingfisher Dr GU46 .... 33 F3
Kingfisher Wlk GU12 .... 77 E1
Kingfishers SP9 .... 101 F4
Kings Ave Ash GU12 .... 100 B4
Winchester SO22 .... 197 F3
Kings Furlong Ctr RG24 .... 69 D2
Kings Furlong Dr RG22 .... 68 C2
Kings Furlong Schs RG22 .... 68 C2
Kings Head Yd 28 SO23 .... 198 A4
Kings Keep GU13 .... 75 D3
Kings La Chilcomb SO23 .... 198 C3
Farnham GU10 .... 121 E3
Kings Mead RG14 .... 5 D3
Kings Meadow SP10 .... 106 A4
Kings Orch RG20 .... 90 A4
Kings Par 2 GU13 .... 54 A1
Kings Peace The GU26 .... 167 D2
Kings Pightle GU13 .... 48 C2
Kings Rd
Alton GU34 .... 139 E2
Enham Alamein SP10 .... 83 D4
Fleet GU13 .... 54 A1
Newbury RG14 .... 1 C1
Silchester RG7 .... 10 C1
Kings Road W RG14 .... 1 C1
Kings Sch SO23 .... 197 D4
Kings Sch The RG21 .... 69 D2
Kings Somborne Rd SO51 .... 194 B1
Kings Wlk RG28 .... 86 B3

Kings Worthy Prim Sch
SO23 .... 176 B3
Kings Yd SP10 .... 106 A4
Kingsbridge Copse RG27 .... 71 F4
Kingsbridge Hill
Shinfield RG7 .... 13 F3
Swallowfield RG7 .... 13 F3
Kingsbridge Rd RG14 .... 1 B1
Kingsclear Pk GU15 .... 36 A2
Kingsclere CE Prim Sch
RG20 .... 24 B1
Kingsclere Pk RG20 .... 24 B2
Kingsclere Rd
Basingstoke RG21, RG23 .... 69 D3
Monk Sherborne RG26 .... 47 D1
Overton RG25 .... 65 D1
Upper Wootton RG26 .... 46 C1
Kingscroft GU13 .... 75 D4
Kingsdale Ct 7 SO22 .... 197 F4
Kingsgate Rd SO23 .... 197 F3
Kingsgate St SO23 .... 198 A3
Kingshott Cotts GU33 .... 185 F2
Kingsland Grange RG14 .... 5 E4
Kingsland Ind Pk RG21, RG24 .... 48 C1
Kingsland Rd RG14 .... 139 F2
Kingsley Ave GU15 .... 36 A2
Kingsley Bglws SO24 .... 179 D2
Kingsley Cl RG14 .... 1 C3
Kingsley Pk RG28 .... 86 B3
Kingsley Pl SO22 .... 197 F3
Kingsley Rd Eversley GU46 .... 33 D4
Farnborough GU14 .... 55 E3
Kingsmead Camberley GU14 .... 56 B4
Farnborough GU14 .... 55 F2
Upper Clatford SP10 .... 105 E2
Kingsmead Cotts GU34 .... 140 A2
Kingsmead Sh Ctr 9 GU14 .... 55 F2
Kingsmill Rd RG21 .... 69 D1
Kingston Rd GU15 .... 36 B4
Kingstons Ind Est GU12 .... 77 E1
Kingsvale Ct RG21 .... 68 C2
Kingsway Aldershot GU11 .... 76 B1
Andover SP10 .... 83 F1
Blackwater GU17 .... 35 E3
Kingsway Gdns SP10 .... 83 D2
Kingswood GU26 .... 167 D1
Kingswood Cl 8 GU33 .... 54 A1
Kingswood Firs GU26 .... 167 D1
Kingswood La GU26 .... 167 D1
Kingswood Rise GU34 .... 159 F1
Kintyre Ct RG23 .... 67 D1
Kipling Cl GU46 .... 34 A2
Kipling Wlk RG22 .... 68 C2
Kirk Knoll GU35 .... 165 E3
Kirkby Ct GU15 .... 36 B1
Kirkee Rd SP9 .... 78 C3
Kitchener Rd GU33 .... 186 B1
Kitchener's Rd GU12 .... 77 D3
Kitcombe La GU34 .... 161 E1
Kitt's La GU10 .... 203 E1
Kitts La GU10 .... 166 B4
Kitwood La SO24 .... 182 B4
Kitwood Rd SO24 .... 182 A4
Knapp La RG26 .... 27 D3
Knight Cl SO23 .... 176 A1
Knight St RG21 .... 68 C2
Knights Ct SP10 .... 83 F1
Knights Enham Schs SP11 .... 83 E4
Knights La RG20 .... 4 A2
Knights Rd GU11 .... 99 E4
Knights Way GU34 .... 139 E2
Knights Yd SP11 .... 60 C4
Knightsbridge Dr RG19 .... 6 C2
Knightsbridge Rd
Camberley GU15 .... 36 B4
Enham Alamein SP10 .... 83 E4
Knock Hundred La GU27 .... 189 D4
Knockwood La SO20 .... 147 F4
Knoll Cl GU13 .... 54 A1
Knoll Ct GU13 .... 54 A2
Knoll Rd Camberley GU15 .... 36 A3
Fleet GU13 .... 54 A1
Knoll Wlk GU15 .... 36 A3
Knollys Rd Aldershot GU11 .... 76 B2
Pamber Heath RG26 .... 10 B1
Knowle Cres RG20 .... 24 B1
Knowles Meadow GU33 .... 208 A1
Knowlings The RG28 .... 86 B2
Kohat Ct SP9 .... 78 B4
Kohat Ct 10 GU11 .... 76 B1
Kohat Rd SP9 .... 78 C3
Kohima Ct GU11 .... 76 C1
Krooner Rd GU47 .... 35 F2
Kurnool Mortar Cross Roads
GU15 .... 35 F3
Kyftle Court Flat RG14 .... 1 B1
Kynegils Rd SO22 .... 175 F1

Laburnam Gdns GU13 .... 75 D3
Laburnum Cl GU11 .... 76 C1
Laburnum Gr RG14 .... 1 C2
Laburnum Pas 3 GU11 .... 76 C1
Laburnum Rd
Aldershot GU11 .... 76 C1
Farnham GU9 .... 99 E4
Laburnum Way RG21 .... 68 B4
Laburnums The GU46 .... 34 C3
Ladwell Cl RG14 .... 5 D3
Lady Gate Dr GU26 .... 166 C2
Lady Godley Cl SP9 .... 78 C3
Ladyplace Ct 4 GU34 .... 139 F2
Ladywell La SO24 .... 179 E3
Ladywood Ave GU14 .... 55 D2
Ladywood Cl GU10 .... 121 E3
Laffan's Rd GU11 .... 76 B3
Laffans Rd RG29 .... 95 F4
Lahore Cl SP9 .... 78 C4

Lahore Rd SP9 .... 78 C3
Lake Ct RG26 .... 27 D4
Lake Dr GU35 .... 164 C2
Lake La GU13 .... 143 E3
Lake Rd GU16 .... 56 C3
Lake Side The GU17 .... 35 D2
Lakeland Dr GU15 .... 36 B1
Lakelands RG26 .... 26 A4
Laker Sq SP10 .... 83 E1
Lakeside Cl Ash GU12 .... 77 E2
Charlton SP10 .... 82 B1
Lakeside Ct GU13 .... 54 A2
Lakeside Cty Prim Sch
GU15 .... 36 B1
Lakeside Gdns GU14 .... 55 D4
Lakeside Rd Ash GU12 .... 77 E2
Farnborough GU11 .... 76 C4
Lama Ho GU12 .... 77 D1
Lamb Cl SP10 .... 106 B4
Lamb's Lane Prim Sch RG7 .... 13 F4
Lambdens W RG26 .... 26 C4
Lambdown App SP9 .... 79 E3
Lambdown Terr SP9 .... 79 E4
Lambert Cres GU15 .... 35 D2
Lambourn Ct RG14 .... 1 C3
Lambourn Rd RG14 .... 1 A3
Lambourne Cl
Sparsholt SO21 .... 174 A2
Thruxton SP11 .... 103 F4
Lambourne Way
Thruxton SP11 .... 103 F4
Tongham GU10 .... 100 B4
Lambs Cl RG25 .... 88 A4
Lambs La RG7 .... 13 F4
Lambs Row RG21, RG23 .... 69 F4
Lamerton Cl GU35 .... 164 B2
Lamerton Rd GU35 .... 164 B2
Lamp Acre RG14 .... 1 C3
Lampard La GU10 .... 144 A1
Lampards Cl RG27 .... 50 C3
Lampool Ho RG25 .... 88 A4
Lanark Cl GU16 .... 36 B1
Lancashire Cotts SP11 .... 59 E1
Lancaster Ave GU10 .... 122 A4
Lancaster Cl SP10 .... 82 C1
Lancaster Dr GU16 .... 36 A3
Lancaster Rd RG21 .... 69 D3
Lancaster Way GU14 .... 56 A4
Lancer Cl 5 GU11 .... 76 B1
Landale Cl SP11 .... 83 D4
Lands End La GU35 .... 164 C3
Landseer Cl
Basingstoke RG21 .... 69 E4
Sandhurst GU15 .... 35 E3
Landseer Ct SP10 .... 82 C1
West Tisted SO24 .... 204 B4
Lane End Bramley RG26 .... 29 D1
West Tisted SO24 .... 204 B4
Lane End Bglws SO21 .... 133 D2
Lane The RG26 .... 27 D4
Langdale Cl GU14 .... 55 E2
Langdale Ct GU12 .... 77 E3
Langham Cl GU10 .... 122 A4
Langham Rd GU34 .... 139 F2
Langley Cl GU13 .... 74 C2
Langley Dr GU15 .... 36 A3
Langton Cl SO22 .... 175 F1
Langton Dr GU35 .... 165 F4
Langtons Ct SO24 .... 179 D2
Lanham La Sparsholt SO22 .... 196 C4
Winchester SO22 .... 175 D1
Lankhills Sch SO22 .... 175 F1
Lankhills Rd SO23 .... 176 A1
Lansdowne Ave
Andover SP10 .... 105 E3
Winchester SO23 .... 197 F3
Lansdowne Ct 3 SO22 .... 197 F3
Lansdowne Rd
Aldershot GU11 .... 76 C1
Alton GU34 .... 140 A3
Camberley GU15 .... 36 C4
Lansley Rd RG24 .... 69 D4
Lantern Ct SO22 .... 197 F3
Lapin La RG22 .... 91 D3
Larch Cl Camberley GU16 .... 36 B4
Kings Worthy SO23 .... 154 A1
Liphook GU30 .... 187 F2
Middle Wallop SO20 .... 126 A2
Newbury RG14 .... 1 A3
Larch Dr Andover SP10 .... 105 E4
Kingsclere RG20 .... 24 B1
Larch Way GU14 .... 55 D2
Larches Way GU46 .... 34 C3
Larchfield Rd GU13 .... 75 D4
Larchwood GU24 .... 48 C2
Larchwood Glade GU15 .... 36 C4
Larg Dr SO22 .... 175 E2
Lark Cl
Andover SP11 .... 83 D1
Basingstoke RG22 .... 90 C4
North Tidworth SP9 .... 79 D3
Lark Hill Rise SO22 .... 197 E2
Lark Rise GU30 .... 187 F3
Larkfield RG24 .... 48 C1
Larkfield Cl GU9 .... 98 B1
Larkfield Rd GU9 .... 98 B1
Larks Barrow Hill RG28 .... 63 E1
Larkspur Cl GU9 .... 99 F4
Larkwhistle Farm Rd SO21 .... 111 E1
Larmer Cl GU13 .... 74 B4
Larwood Sq SP10 .... 83 E1
Lasham Airfield GU34 .... 116 B2
Latchmoor La GU9 .... 122 A4
Latham Ave GU15 .... 36 B1
Lauder Rd GU15 .... 36 B1
Launcelot Cl SP11 .... 83 D2
Laundry La Camberley GU17 .... 35 E2
Heckfield RG27 .... 31 D3
Sandhurst GU17 .... 35 E3

Laurel Cl Camberley GU15 .... 36 A2
Farnborough GU14 .... 55 D2
North Warnborough RG29 .... 72 B2
Laurel Gdns GU9 .... 99 F4
Laurel Grove GU10 .... 121 E3
Laurel Pl SO22 .... 126 A2
Laurels The Andover SP10 .... 82 C1
Basingstoke RG21 .... 69 E3
Farnham GU11 .... 99 E4
Fleet GU13 .... 54 A1
Lavell's La RG26 .... 29 D4
Lavender Ct SP10 .... 105 F3
Lavender Gdns GU35 .... 164 B2
Lavender La GU10 .... 121 E2
Lavender Rd RG22 .... 91 D4
Laverdale RG22 .... 55 D2
Laverstoke La RG28 .... 87 D2
Laverstoke Prim Sch RG28 .... 87 D3
Lawday Link GU9 .... 98 C4
Lawday Pl GU9 .... 98 C4
Lawday Pl La GU9 .... 98 C4
Lawford Cres GU46 .... 34 A3
Lawn Ho 17 SO23 .... 198 A4
Lawn Rd SO22 .... 175 E2
Lawn St 16 SO23 .... 198 A4
Lawns The GU14 .... 55 E2
Lawrence Cl Andover SP10 .... 82 C1
Basingstoke RG24 .... 48 B1
Lawrence Hos SP11 .... 103 D1
Lawrence Lodge GU16 .... 36 A4
Lawrence Rd GU13 .... 74 C4
Lawrence Way GU47 .... 35 C2
Lawrencedale Ct RG22 .... 68 C2
Laws Terr GU11 .... 77 D2
Lay Field RG27 .... 50 C1
Le Borowe GU13 .... 74 C2
Le Marchant Rd GU16 .... 36 B2
Lea Cl Ash GU12 .... 77 F1
Basingstoke RG21 .... 69 E3
Farnham GU11 .... 99 F3
Lea Ct GU9 .... 99 E4
Lea Rd GU15 .... 35 F1
Lea Springs GU13 .... 74 B4
Lea The Fleet GU13 .... 74 C4
Wokingham RG40 .... 16 A4
Lea Way GU12 .... 77 E2
Lea Wood Rd GU13 .... 74 C4
Leaden Vere RG29 .... 95 E2
Leckford Cl GU14 .... 55 F3
Leckford La Leckford SO20 .... 150 B4
Stockbridge SO20 .... 150 A3
Ledger Cl GU13 .... 74 C2
Lee Ct GU11 .... 100 A4
Lefroy Ave RG21 .... 69 E4
Lefroy's Field GU10 .... 97 E4
Legge Cres GU14 .... 76 B1
Legion La SO23 .... 176 B4
Lehar Ct RG22 .... 91 E4
Leicester Pl SP10 .... 106 A4
Leicester Way SO23 .... 176 B1
Leigh Cl SP10 .... 106 B4
Leigh Field RG7 .... 11 E3
Leigh Gdns SP10 .... 106 B4
Leigh La GU9 .... 122 B4
Leigh Rd SP10 .... 106 B4
Leipzig Rd GU13 .... 75 D2
Lemon Gr GU35 .... 164 B1
Len Smart Ct RG21 .... 69 E4
Lendore Rd GU16 .... 56 A4
Lennel Gdns GU13 .... 75 D3
Lennon Way RG22 .... 91 E4
Lennox Rd RG21 .... 68 C1
Lent Rise Ct 5 SO22 .... 197 E3
Lenten St GU34 .... 139 F2
Leonard Cl GU14 .... 56 A4
Leopold Ave GU14 .... 55 F3
Leslie Southern Ct 13 RG14 .... 1 C2
Lestock Way GU13 .... 54 B1
Levern Dr GU9 .... 99 D3
Levignen Cl GU13 .... 74 B3
Lewendon Rd RG14 .... 1 B3
Lewis Cl RG21 .... 69 E4
Lewis Wlk RG14 .... 5 D3
Ley Rd GU14 .... 55 D4
Leys Gdns RG14 .... 1 B2
Leyton Way SP10 .... 105 F3
Lickfolds Rd GU10 .... 121 E2
Liddell Cl RG40 .... 16 B2
Lightfoot Gr RG21 .... 69 D1
Lightsfield RG22 .... 67 D1
Lilac Cl GU35 .... 164 B1
Lilac Way RG23 .... 68 B3
Lilian Pl GU34 .... 161 E2
Lillywhite Cres SP10 .... 83 D2
Lily Cl RG22 .... 91 D4
Lime Ave Alton GU34 .... 139 F3
Camberley GU15 .... 36 C3
Lime Cl RG14 .... 2 A2
Lime Cres GU11 .... 77 F1
Lime Gdns RG21 .... 69 E3
Lime Gr GU34 .... 139 F3
Lime Kiln Cotts The GU34 .... 42 B4
Lime Rd SO24 .... 179 E3
Lime St GU11 .... 76 B1
Lime Tree Way RG24 .... 48 C2
Lime Wlk SP10 .... 105 F3
Limecroft GU17 .... 35 D2
Limekiln Rd SP11 .... 58 A2
Limes Ave RG20 .... 22 C4
Limes Cl Bramshott GU30 .... 188 A4
Liss SO23 .... 207 F2
Limes Rd GU11 .... 55 D3
Limes The Basingstoke RG22 .... 91 D4
Bramley RG26 .... 29 D1
Haslemere GU27 .... 189 F2
Limetree Ave RG20 .... 21 F1
Limetree Wlk 8 SO23 .... 198 B4

Limington House Sch RG22 .... 68 B2
Linchmere Rd GU27 .... 189 D3
Lincoln Cl Basingstoke RG22 .... 91 A4
Camberley GU15 .... 36 C2
Lincoln Ct Liphook GU30 .... 188 A2
Newbury RG14 .... 1 B1
Lincoln Gn GU34 .... 139 F1
Linden Ave Odiham RG29 .... 72 C2
Old Basing RG24 .... 70 A3
Linden Cl Ludgershall SP11 .... 57 D1
Newbury RG14 .... 1 B2
Linden Ct
Camberley GU15, GU16 .... 36 B4
Old Basing RG24 .... 70 A3
Linden Dr GU33 .... 207 F2
Linden Rd Bishop's Green RG20 .... 6 B2
Headley GU35 .... 166 A3
Lindens The GU9 .... 99 D1
Lindford Chase GU35 .... 164 C3
Lindford Rd GU35 .... 164 C3
Lindford Wey GU35 .... 164 C3
Lindum Cl 8 GU11 .... 76 C1
Lindum Dene GU11 .... 76 C1
Lines The RG20 .... 24 B2
Linford Rd GU35 .... 164 C3
Ling Cres GU35 .... 165 F3
Lingfield Cl Alton GU34 .... 139 F1
Old Basing RG24 .... 70 B3
Lingfield Rd GU14 .... 6 A4
Lingmala Gro GU13 .... 75 D3
Link Ho 4 RG14 .... 1 C1
Link Rd Alton GU34 .... 140 A3
Kingsclere RG20 .... 24 C1
Newbury RG14 .... 1 C1
Link The Andover SP10 .... 105 E4
Yateley GU17 .... 34 A4
Link View RG14 .... 1 B4
Link Way Oakley RG22 .... 67 D1
Thatcham RG18 .... 2 C2
Linklater's Cotts GU13 .... 54 C4
Links Cl SO22 .... 175 E1
Links The GU35 .... 164 A1
Links Way GU14 .... 55 D2
Linkside E GU26 .... 167 D4
Linkside N GU26 .... 166 C4
Linkside S GU26 .... 167 D3
Linkway Camberley GU15 .... 36 A2
Fleet GU13 .... 75 D3
Linkway Par GU13 .... 74 C3
Linnet Cl RG22 .... 68 A1
Linnet La RG19 .... 6 B2
Linnets Rd SO24 .... 179 E2
Linnets Way GU34 .... 139 F3
Linsford Bsns Pk GU16 .... 56 B2
Linsford La GU16 .... 56 B2
Linsley Gdns SO24 .... 179 E2
Linstead Rd GU14 .... 55 E4
Linsted La GU35 .... 165 D4
Linton Cl RG26 .... 27 D4
Linton Dr SP10 .... 83 D1
Lion and Lamb Way 4 GU9 .... 98 C1
Lion and Lamb Yd GU9 .... 98 C1
Lion Cl Haslemere GU27 .... 189 E4
Overton RG25 .... 88 A4
Lion Ct RG21 .... 69 F3
Lion Gn GU27 .... 189 E3
Lion La GU27 .... 189 E4
Lion Mead GU27 .... 189 E3
Lion Way GU13 .... 75 D3
Lions Field GU35 .... 163 E2
Lions Hall 22 SO22 .... 197 F4
Liphook CE Jun Sch GU30 .... 187 F2
Liphook Inf Sch GU30 .... 187 F2
Liphook Rd Bordon GU35 .... 186 B4
Bramshott GU30 .... 165 E2
Haslemere GU27 .... 189 E3
Headley GU35 .... 165 E2
Linchmere GU27 .... 188 C2
Lindford GU35 .... 164 C3
Liphook Sta GU30 .... 188 A1
Lipscombe Cl RG14 .... 1 B1
Lipscombe Rise GU34 .... 139 F3
Lisa Ct 1 RG21 .... 69 D2
Liskeard Dr GU14 .... 55 F3
Lisle Cl Newbury RG14 .... 1 B3
Winchester SO22 .... 197 D2
Lismoyne Cl GU13 .... 53 F1
Liss Schs GU33 .... 208 A1
Liss Sta GU33 .... 207 F2
Lister Rd GU13 .... 68 C1
Litchfield Cl SP10 .... 82 B2
Litchfield Ho RG26 .... 26 C4
Litchfield Rd SO22 .... 175 E2
Litten The RG20 .... 24 B1
Little Aldershot La RG7 .... 8 C1
Little Austins Rd GU10 .... 122 A4
Little Barn Pl GU34 .... 208 A4
Little Basing RG21 .... 69 F4
Little Copse Andover SP10 .... 105 F3
Fleet GU13 .... 74 C4
Yateley GU46 .... 34 A4
Little Copse Chase RG24 .... 48 C1
Little Croft GU46 .... 34 A3
Little Dean Ct SO20 .... 150 A2
Little Dean Ho SO20 .... 150 A2
Little Dean La
South Warnborough RG25 .... 94 C3
Upton Grey RG25 .... 94 C3
Little Drove Rd SO20 .... 129 D2
Little Fallow RG24 .... 70 A4
Little Green La GU10 .... 121 E3
Little Hatherden SP11 .... 59 F1
Little Hayes La SO21 .... 177 F4
Little Hoddington RG25 .... 94 B3
Little Hoddington Cl RG25 .... 94 B3
Little Knowl Hill RG20 .... 24 C2
Little London Rd RG26 .... 27 F4
Little Minster St 26 SO23 .... 198 A4

Little Paddock GU15 .... 36 C4
Little Thurbans Cl GU10 .... 121 F3
Little Vigo GU46 .... 33 F2
Little Wellington St GU11 .... 76 C1
Little-Ann Bridge Farm SP11 .... 105 E3
Littlefield Cl GU12 .... 77 F1
Littlefield Gdns GU12 .... 77 F1
Littlefield Rd GU34 .... 140 A2
Littlefield Sch GU34 .... 188 A1
Littleton Cotts SP11 .... 80 B2
Littleton La SO21 .... 175 D3
Littleton Rd SO22 .... 175 D2
Littleworth Rd GU10 .... 100 B1
Litton Gdns RG23 .... 67 D1
Livery Rd SP5 .... 168 A1
Livingstone Rd Andover SP10 .... 1 C1
  Newbury RG14 .... 1 C1
Lock Rd GU12 .... 77 D3
Lock Sq SP10 .... 83 E1
Lock's La SO21 .... 174 B2
Locke Cl SP11 .... 124 C4
Locke Rd GU30 .... 188 A1
Locke's Dro SP11 .... 60 A4
Lockerley Endowed CE Prim Sch SO51 .... 192 A1
Lockerley Rd SO51 .... 192 A1
Lockram La RG7 .... 12 A4
Lockwood Cl GU14 .... 55 E4
Loddon Cl GU15 .... 36 C3
Loddon Ct RG21 .... 69 E1
Loddon Ctr RG24 .... 69 F4
Loddon Dr RG21 .... 69 E3
Loddon Mall 20 RG21 .... 69 D3
Loddon Rd GU14 .... 55 D3
Loddon Sch The RG24 .... 49 E3
Loddon Way GU12 .... 77 F1
Lodge Cl SP10 .... 105 F4
Lodge Dr SP11 .... 81 E1
Lodge Gr GU46 .... 34 B3
Lodge Hill Cl GU9 .... 122 A3
Lodge Hill Rd GU9 .... 122 B3
Lodge La SP11 .... 58 A2
Lodge The Farnham GU9 .... 99 E2
  Newbury RG14 .... 1 C2
Lodsworth GU14 .... 55 D2
Loggon Rd RG21 .... 69 D1
Loman Rd GU16 .... 56 C2
Lomond Cl RG23 .... 67 D1
Londlandes GU13 .... 74 C2
London Rd Alton GU34 .... 140 B3
  Andover SP10 .... 106 B4
  Andover SP10 .... 106 C4
  Basingstoke RG21 .... 69 E2
  Blackwater GU15 .... 35 E3
  Camberley GU15 .... 36 A3
  Camberley GU15 .... 36 B4
  Hartley Wintney RG27 .... 52 B3
  Hill Brow GU33 .... 208 A1
  Hook RG27 .... 51 E1
  Kings Worthy SO23 .... 176 A3
  Laverstoke RG28 .... 87 D3
  Liphook GU30 .... 188 A3
  Newbury RG14 .... 2 A2
  Odiham RG29 .... 72 C2
  Odiham RG29 .... 72 C3
  Old Basing RG24 .... 70 B3
  Overton RG25 .... 88 A4
  Stockbridge SO20 .... 150 B2
  Whitchurch RG28 .... 86 C3
London St Andover SP10 .... 106 A4
  Basingstoke RG21 .... 69 D2
  Whitchurch RG28 .... 86 B3
Long Beech Dr GU14 .... 55 D2
Long Bridge GU9 .... 99 D1
Long Cl SO22 .... 197 F3
Long Copse Chase RG24 .... 48 C2
Long Cross Hill GU35 .... 165 D3
Long Cross La RG22 .... 91 D3
Long Gdn Mews GU9 .... 98 C1
Long Gdn Way GU9 .... 98 C1
Long Gdn Wlk GU9 .... 98 C1
Long Gdn Wlk E GU9 .... 98 C1
Long Gdn Wlk W GU9 .... 98 C1
Long Gr RG26 .... 9 D1
Long Hill GU11 .... 100 B1
Long La Chineham RG24 .... 49 D3
  Newbury RG14 .... 2 A4
  Odiham RG29 .... 96 A3
Long Leaze SP11 .... 61 E2
Long Rd The GU9 .... 121 F2
Long Sutton CE Prim Sch RG29 .... 95 F2
Long Wlk SO21 .... 176 C2
Longacre Ash GU12 .... 77 F1
  Liss GU33 .... 208 A2
  Newbury RG14 .... 5 D4
Longacre Rise RG24 .... 48 C3
Longbarrow Cl SO21 .... 153 F2
Longbridge Cl RG26 .... 29 F1
Longbridge Rd RG26 .... 28 C2
Longcroft GU10 .... 120 A3
Longcroft Cl 4 RG21, RG24, RG25 .... 69 D2
Longcroft Rd RG20 .... 24 B2
Longdene Rd GU27 .... 189 F3
Longdown GU13 .... 74 C3
Longdown Cl GU10 .... 122 A3
Longdown Lodge GU46 .... 34 C4
Longdown Rd GU10 .... 122 A3
Longfellow Par RG21, RG24, RG25 .... 69 E4
Longfield Cl Farnborough GU14 .... 55 F4
  North Waltham RG25 .... 89 F1
Longfield Rd Ash GU11 .... 77 F1
  Winchester SO23 .... 198 B4

Longford Cl GU15 .... 36 A2
Longhope Dr GU9 .... 121 F3
Longhouse Gn 9 SO23 .... 198 B4
Longleat Sq GU9 .... 56 A2
Longley Rd GU9 .... 99 D1
Longmead Fleet GU13 .... 75 D3
  Liss GU33 .... 207 F2
  Woolton Hill RG20 .... 4 B1
Longmeadow GU17 .... 36 B2
Longmoor Dr GU30 .... 187 D2
Longmoor La RG7 .... 11 F4
Longmoor Rd Basingstoke RG21 .... 69 D2
  Bordon GU33 .... 186 A2
  Greatham GU33 .... 186 A2
  Liphook GU30 .... 187 E2
Longparish CE Prim Sch SP11 .... 108 A2
Longparish Rd Hurstbourne Priors SP10 .... 85 E1
  Longparish SP11 .... 107 F1
  Wherwell SP11 .... 107 F1
Longs Ct RG28 .... 86 B3
Longstock Cl Andover SP10 .... 105 F4
  Chineham RG24 .... 49 D2
Longstock Ct 13 SP10 .... 106 A4
Longstock Rd Goodworth Clatford SP11 .... 128 A2
  Wherwell SP11 .... 128 A4
Longwater La Eversley GU46 .... 33 E4
  Finchampstead RG40 .... 16 B2
Longwater Rd Eversley RG40 .... 16 B1
  Finchampstead RG40 .... 16 B1
Lopcombe Corner SP4 .... 146 A2
Lord Mayor Treloar Coll of F Ed GU34 .... 140 A3
Lord Mayor Treloar Sch GU34 .... 119 D1
Lord Wandsworth Coll RG29 .... 95 F1
Lordsfield Rd RG25 .... 88 A4
Lordswood RG26 .... 27 F4
Lorraine Cty Fst Sch GU15, GU17 .... 36 A4
Lorraine Rd GU15 .... 36 B4
Louisburg Rd GU35 .... 164 B3
Louise Margaret Rd GU11 .... 76 C2
Loundyes Cl RG18 .... 2 C2
Love La Andover SP10 .... 106 A4
  Kingsclere RG20 .... 24 B1
  Newbury RG14 .... 1 C3
  Odiham RG29 .... 72 B1
Lovedon La SO23 .... 176 B4
Lovegroves RG24 .... 49 D2
Lovell Cl South Wonston SO21 .... 153 F2
  Thruxton SP11 .... 103 E4
Lovells Wlk SO24 .... 179 E3
Loveridge Cl Basingstoke RG21 .... 69 D1
  Knights Enham SP10 .... 83 D2
Lovers La GU10 .... 144 A4
Loves Wood RG7 .... 11 E3
Lovett Ho 1 GU9 .... 98 C1
Lovett Wlk SO24 .... 175 E2
Lovington La SO24 .... 178 B2
Low La GU9 .... 99 F3
Lowa Cl GU12 .... 77 E4
Lowa Rd SP9 .... 78 C3
Lowden Cl SO22 .... 197 E2
Lower Brook St Basingstoke RG21 .... 68 C3
  12 Winchester SO23 .... 198 A4
Lower Canes GU46 .... 33 F3
Lower Charles St GU16 .... 36 A3
Lower Chestnut Dr RG22 .... 68 C2
Lower Church La GU9 .... 98 C1
Lower Church Rd GU46 .... 34 B4
Lower Comm RG27 .... 15 E1
Lower Evingar Rd RG28 .... 86 B3
Lower Farm Ct RG19 .... 2 B1
Lower Farnham Rd GU10 .... 100 A4
Lower Hanger GU27 .... 189 D3
Lower Lamborough La SO24 .... 201 C3
Lower Moor RG46 .... 34 A3
Lower Neatham Mill La Alton GU34 .... 140 B3
  Alton, Neatham GU34 .... 140 C3
Lower Nelson St GU11 .... 76 C1
Lower Newport Rd GU12 .... 77 D1
Lower Paice La GU34 .... 159 E2
Lower Raymond Almshouses RG14 .... 1 B1
Lower Sandhurst Rd RG40 .... 16 C1
Lower South View GU9 .... 99 D2
Lower St GU27 .... 189 F3
Lower Stanmore La SO23 .... 197 F3
Lower Turk St GU34 .... 139 F2
Lower Way RG19 .... 2 C2
Lower Weybourne La GU9 .... 99 F3
Lower Wote St RG21 .... 69 D3
Lowicks Rd GU10 .... 144 C3
Lowlands Rd Basingstoke RG22 .... 68 A2
  Blackwater GU15 .... 35 D2
Lowry Cl GU15 .... 35 D3
Lowry Ct SP10 .... 82 C1
Loxwood Ave GU13 .... 74 C4
Loyalty La RG24 .... 70 A3
Lubeck Dr SP10 .... 82 C2
Lucas Cl GU46 .... 34 A3
Lucas Field GU27 .... 189 D3
Ludgershall Castle Prim Sch SP11 .... 57 D1
Ludgershall Rd SP9 .... 78 C4
Ludlow Cl Basingstoke RG21 .... 68 B3
  Camberley GU16 .... 56 C4
Ludlow Ct RG14 .... 2 B1

Ludlow Gdns RG21 .... 68 B3
Ludshott Gr GU35 .... 165 F3
Luke Rd GU9 .... 99 E4
Luke Rd E GU9 .... 99 E4
Lulworth Cl GU14 .... 55 F4
Lundy Cl GU14 .... 48 B1
Lune Cl 5 RG21 .... 69 E3
Lune Ct 18 SP10 .... 83 E1
Lupin Cl RG22 .... 91 D4
Lutyens Cl Basingstoke RG21 .... 69 F4
  Chineham RG24 .... 48 C1
Lyall Pl GU9 .... 98 C4
Lych Gate GU47 .... 34 B4
Lyde Cl RG23 .... 67 D1
Lydford Cl Camberley GU16 .... 56 C4
  Farnborough GU14 .... 55 F4
Lye Copse Ave GU14 .... 55 F4
Lyeway La East Tisted SO24 .... 182 B2
  Ropley SO24 .... 182 B2
Lyeway Rd Four Marks SO24 .... 182 A3
  Ropley SO24 .... 182 A3
Lyford Rd GU13 .... 69 D3
Lymington Ave GU46 .... 34 A3
Lymington Bottom GU34 .... 160 A1
Lymington Bottom Rd Four Marks GU34 .... 160 A2
  Medstead GU34 .... 160 A2
Lymington Cl Basingstoke RG22 .... 91 D4
  Four Marks GU34 .... 160 A1
Lymington Rise GU34 .... 160 A1
Lyn Ct 6 RG21 .... 69 E3
Lynch Cl SO22 .... 175 F1
Lynch Hill RG28 .... 86 B3
Lynch Hill Pk RG28 .... 86 B3
Lynch La GU11 .... 99 E1
Lynch The Overton RG25 .... 87 F4
  Whitchurch RG28 .... 86 B3
Lynchborough Rd GU30 .... 187 D3
Lynchford Rd Farnborough GU12 .... 77 D4
  Farnborough GU12 .... 77 E4
Lyndale Dr GU13 .... 54 B1
Lyndford Terr GU13 .... 74 C4
Lyndhurst Ave Aldershot GU11 .... 100 A3
  Blackwater GU17 .... 35 D3
Lyndhurst Dr RG22 .... 91 E3
Lyndhurst Sch GU17 .... 35 F3
Lyndsey Cl GU13 .... 54 C2
Lynford Ave SO22 .... 175 F1
Lynford Way SO22 .... 175 F1
Lynn Way GU14 .... 55 E4
Lynton Cl GU10 .... 121 F4
Lynton Ct RG14 .... 1 C2
Lynton Meadow SO20 .... 129 D2
Lynton Rd GU35 .... 164 B2
Lynwood Cl GU35 .... 165 D3
Lynwood Ct SO22 .... 175 F1
Lynwood Dr Andover SP10 .... 105 F4
  Mytchett GU14 .... 56 C2
Lynwood Gdns GU27 .... 51 D1
Lyon Way GU16 .... 36 A1
Lyon Way Ind Est GU15 .... 36 A1
Lyse Ct GU33 .... 207 F2
Lysons Ave GU12 .... 77 E4
Lysons Rd GU11 .... 76 C1
Lytham Cl GU35 .... 164 A1
Lytton Rd GU24 .... 69 E3

Mabbs La RG27 .... 52 B2
Mac Callum Rd Enham Alamein SP10 .... 83 D4
  Smannell SP10 .... 83 D4
Macadam Way SP10 .... 82 A1
Macdonald Rd GU9 .... 99 E2
MacDonald's Almshouses 10 GU9 .... 98 C1
Macklin Ho 16 SO22 .... 197 F4
Macrae Rd GU16 .... 34 A3
Maddocks Hill SO24 .... 181 D2
Madeira Cl RG24 .... 48 B1
Madeira Pl 5 RG14 .... 1 C1
Madeley Rd GU13 .... 75 D3
Madox Brown End GU47 .... 35 E3
Madrid Rd SP10 .... 83 E1
Magdalen Hill SO23 .... 198 A4
Magdalen Mews 41 SO23 .... 198 A4
Magellan Cl SP10 .... 83 F1
Magnolia Cl SP10 .... 105 F4
Magnolia Ho RG24 .... 48 A1
Magnolia Way GU13 .... 75 D4
Magnus Dr RG22 .... 91 D4
Magpie Cl Basingstoke RG23 .... 90 C4
  Bordon GU35 .... 164 C1
  Ewshot GU10 .... 98 A4
  Thatcham RG19 .... 2 C2
Mahler Cl RG22 .... 91 F4
Maida Rd GU11 .... 76 C2
Maidenthorn La RG22 .... 90 A1
Main Rd Littleton SO22 .... 175 D3
  Tadley RG26 .... 27 D3
Main St RG19 .... 6 C3
Maitland Rd GU14 .... 76 C4
Maitlands Cl GU11, GU12 .... 100 B3
Majendie Cl RG14 .... 1 A3
Majestic Rd RG22 .... 91 D3
Majorca Ave SP10 .... 83 E1
Makins Ct GU34 .... 179 E3
Maldive Rd RG24 .... 48 B1
Malham Gdns RG22 .... 91 D3
Mall The Andover SP10 .... 106 A4
  South Tidworth SP9 .... 78 B2

Mallard Cl Andover SP10 .... 83 D1
  Ash GU11 .... 77 D1
  Basingstoke RG22 .... 90 C4
  Haslemere GU27 .... 189 E3
  New Alresford SO24 .... 179 E3
Mallard Way 4 GU46 .... 33 F2
Mallards GU14 .... 139 F3
Mallow Cl GU35 .... 165 D3
Malmesbury Gdns SO22 .... 175 E1
Malmesbury Ho 2 SP9 .... 79 D3
Malmsbury Rd GU14 .... 164 B1
Malpass Rd RG21 .... 153 E1
Malshanger La RG23 .... 67 D2
Malt Ho 32 SO22 .... 197 F4
Malta Cl GU24 .... 48 A1
Maltbys GU34 .... 184 C4
Malters End GU26 .... 166 C2
Malthouse Bridge Cotts GU13 .... 74 B3
Malthouse Cl Fleet GU13 .... 74 C3
  Itchen Abbas SO21 .... 176 C2
Malthouse Cotts RG29 .... 72 B2
Malthouse Ct GU30 .... 188 A2
Malthouse La Bighton SO24 .... 158 B1
  Smannell SP10 .... 83 E4
  Tadley RG26 .... 27 D3
  Upper Chute SP11 .... 58 A4
Malthouse Meadows GU30 .... 188 A2
Malthouse Mews GU34 .... 140 B3
Maltings Cl GU34 .... 139 F2
Maltings The GU30 .... 188 A2
Malvern Cl RG22 .... 68 A2
Malvern Ct RG14 .... 1 B1
Malvern Rd Farnborough GU14 .... 55 D4
  Hawley GU47 .... 34 B1
  Hill Brow GU33 .... 208 A1
Mandarin Cl Farnham GU11 .... 99 D3
  Newbury RG14 .... 2 A1
Mandora RG11 .... 76 C2
Manfield Rd GU14 .... 77 F1
Manica Cl GU35 .... 164 B2
Manley Bridge Rd GU10 .... 121 E3
Manley James Cl RG29 .... 72 C2
Mann Cl RG22 .... 86 B2
Manningford Cl SO23 .... 176 A2
Manor Bridge Ct SP9 .... 78 C4
Manor Cl Abbotts Ann SP10 .... 105 D2
  Alton GU34 .... 140 A3
  Basingstoke RG22 .... 91 D3
  Haslemere GU27 .... 189 E3
  Shipton Bellinger SP9 .... 101 F4
  Tongham GU11 .... 100 B4
  Winchester SO23 .... 198 A4
Manor Copse SP10 .... 83 D3
Manor Cotts RG28 .... 87 D3
Manor Cres GU27 .... 189 E3
Manor Ct GU13 .... 75 D2
Manor Farm Bsns Ctr GU10 .... 100 B3
Manor Farm Cl GU12 .... 77 D1
Manor Farm Cotts SO21 .... 131 D1
Manor Farm La SO51 .... 193 F1
Manor Field Schs RG22 .... 91 F4
Manor Fields Liphook GU30 .... 188 A2
  Seale GU10 .... 100 C2
Manor Gdns GU10 .... 122 A3
Manor Ho The GU15 .... 36 A3
Manor House Farm SO24 .... 180 B2
Manor House Flats GU10 .... 100 B3
Manor La Old Basing RG24 .... 70 A3
  Thatcham RG18 .... 2 B3
Manor Lea GU27 .... 189 E3
Manor Park Cotts 8 Alton GU34 .... 139 F2
  Alton, Wilsom GU34 .... 140 A2
Manor Park Ctr Farnborough Coll of Tech GU11 .... 76 C1
Manor Park Dr Wokingham RG40 .... 16 B3
  Yateley GU46 .... 34 B3
Manor Pk Ind Est GU12 .... 77 D1
Manor Pl RG14 .... 1 A1
Manor Rd Aldershot GU9 .... 99 F4
  Alton GU34 .... 140 A3
  Andover SP10 .... 82 C1
  Ash GU10 .... 100 B4
  East Tytherley SP5 .... 191 F4
  Farnborough GU16 .... 56 A2
  Farnham GU9 .... 99 E2
  Sherborne St John RG26 .... 47 F2
  Tongham GU10 .... 100 B4
Manor Rise SP10 .... 105 F2
Manor Schs GU14 .... 55 E3
Manor View RG7 .... 8 B4
Manor Wlk GU14 .... 76 C1
Manorside Cl GU12 .... 100 B4
Manse La RG26 .... 27 D3
Mansell Dr RG14 .... 5 D3
Mansfield Rd RG23 .... 68 C1
Mansion House St GU14 .... 1 C2
Maple Cl Alton GU34 .... 139 F3
  Ash GU12 .... 77 E4
  Blackwater GU17 .... 35 E4
  Middle Wallop SO20 .... 126 A3
  New Alresford SO24 .... 179 E3
Maple Cres Basingstoke RG21 .... 69 D4
  Ludgershall SP11 .... 57 D1
  Newbury RG14 .... 1 C1
Maple Ct RG23 .... 68 A2
Maple Dr SO23 .... 176 A3
Maple Gdns GU17, GU46 .... 34 A3
Maple Gr RG26 .... 26 C4
Maple Leaf Cl GU14 .... 55 F2
Maple Leaf Ct GU35 .... 164 B2
Maple Ridge Special Sch RG21 .... 69 D4
Maple Terr 5 SP9 .... 79 D4

Maple Way GU35 .... 165 F3
Maple Wlk Aldershot GU10 .... 100 A4
  Andover SP11 .... 105 E3
Maplehurst Chase RG22 .... 91 D3
March Cl RG21 .... 83 D1
Marchant Rd SP11 .... 105 E3
Marchants Hill Activity Ctr GU26 .... 167 D4
Marconi Rd GU14 .... 1 C2
Mareth Cl GU11 .... 76 C1
Margaret Rd RG22 .... 68 B2
Margha Rd SP9 .... 78 C3
Marigold Cl RG22 .... 91 D4
Mariners Cl RG26 .... 27 D3
Mariners Dr GU16 .... 56 A3
Marino Way RG40 .... 15 F3
Mark La 17 RG21 .... 69 D2
Mark Way SO51 .... 191 E2
Mark Way Special Sch The SP10 .... 106 B4
Markall Cl SO24 .... 201 E3
Market La SO23 .... 198 A4
Market Pl Basingstoke RG21 .... 69 D2
  11 Newbury RG14 .... 1 C2
Market Sq 5 GU34 .... 139 F2
Market St Alton GU34 .... 139 F2
  Newbury RG14 .... 1 C1
  Winchester SO23 .... 198 A4
Markham Ct GU16 .... 36 A3
Markson Rd SO21 .... 153 E2
Marl's La RG24 .... 48 A3
Marlborough Cl GU13 .... 75 D3
Marlborough Cty Inf Sch GU12 .... 77 D4
Marlborough Gdns RG23 .... 67 D1
Marlborough Rise GU15 .... 36 B3
Marlborough St SP10 .... 106 A4
Marlborough Trad Mews RG24 .... 48 C1
Marlborough View GU14 .... 55 D3
Marley Combe Rd GU27 .... 189 E2
Marley Hanger GU27 .... 189 E2
Marley La GU27 .... 189 E2
Marlowe Cl RG24 .... 69 E4
Marlowes The RG14 .... 5 E4
Marnel Schs RG24 .... 48 B1
Marrowbrook Cl GU14 .... 55 F2
Marrowbrook La GU14 .... 55 F2
Mars Ho 12 RG22 .... 9 E1
Marsden Ct RG28 .... 87 E3
Marsh Cl GU35 .... 164 C2
Marsh La Bentley GU10 .... 120 B3
  Eversley GU46 .... 33 E4
  Newbury RG14 .... 1 C2
Marshall Cl GU14 .... 55 E4
Marshall Gdns RG21 .... 69 D4
Marshall Rd GU15 .... 35 E3
Marshall Sq SP11 .... 83 E1
Marshalls GU9 .... 121 F4
Marshalls Ct RG14 .... 1 A3
Marshcourt RG21 .... 69 F4
Marshfields SO21 .... 197 E1
Martin Cl Basingstoke RG24 .... 69 E3
  North Tidworth SP9 .... 79 D3
Martin Way Andover SP10 .... 83 D1
  Camberley GU16 .... 36 B1
Martingale Ct 8 GU11 .... 76 B1
Martins Cl Alton GU34 .... 140 A3
  Blackwater GU47 .... 35 D2
Martins Fields SO21 .... 197 E1
Martins La SO20 .... 129 E2
Martins Wood RG24 .... 48 C2
Mary La Newton Valence GU34 .... 183 D4
  North Waltham RG25 .... 89 F1
Mary Rose Ct RG22 .... 68 C2
Maryland RG40 .... 16 B4
Maskell Way GU14 .... 55 D2
Mason Ct RG20 .... 4 B1
Mason Pl GU17 .... 34 B4
Mason Rd GU14 .... 55 E3
Mason Way GU11, GU12 .... 99 F4
Mathew Terr GU11 .... 77 D1
Mathews Cl GU14 .... 77 E4
Mathias Wlk RG22 .... 91 E4
Matilda Dr RG22 .... 91 D4
Matilda Pl 3 SO23 .... 198 A4
Matthew Rd GU10, GU9 .... 99 E4
Matthews Rd GU15 .... 36 A4
Matthews Way RG23 .... 67 E3
Mattock Way RG24 .... 48 C2
Maultway Cl GU15 .... 36 C4
Maultway Cres GU16 .... 36 C4
Maultway N GU15 .... 36 C4
Maultway The GU15 .... 36 C4
Mavins Rd GU10 .... 122 A4
Maw Cl RG22 .... 91 F4
May Cl Headley GU35 .... 165 E2
  Old Basing RG24 .... 70 B3
  Sandhurst GU47 .... 35 D4
May Cres GU12 .... 77 E1
May Pl RG21 .... 69 D2
May St RG21 .... 68 C3
May Tree Cl SO22 .... 197 E2
May Tree Rd SP10 .... 82 B1
May's La RG7 .... 10 C2
Maybrook RG24 .... 48 C2
Maybury Cl GU16 .... 56 A4
Mayfair Dr RG14 .... 1 B1
Mayfair Ho 9 RG24 .... 69 D3
Mayfield GU10 .... 121 E2
Mayfield Ave Ind Pk SP11 .... 81 D1

Mayfield Cl Farnham GU11 ...... 99 F3
Shipton Bellinger SP9 ...... 101 E4
Mayfield Ct GU46 ...... 33 D4
Mayfield Cty Schs GU14 ...... 55 F3
Mayfield Rd Camberley GU47 ...... 35 F1
Farnborough GU14 ...... 55 E3
Mayfield Ridge RG22 ...... 91 E3
Mayflower Cl RG24 ...... 48 C1
Mayflower Dr GU46 ...... 33 F4
Mayflower Rd GU35 ...... 164 B1
Mayhill Cty Jun Sch RG29 ...... 72 C1
Mayors La RG14 ...... 1 C1
Maywood Dr GU15 ...... 36 C4
Mc Carthy Way RG40 ...... 16 B4
McCartney Wlk RG22 ...... 91 E4
McFauld Way RG28 ...... 86 B2
Mckay Cl GU11 ...... 77 D2
Mckernan Ct GU46 ...... 34 B4
McNaughton Cl GU14 ...... 55 D2
Mead Cl SP10 ...... 105 F4
Mead Hatchgate RG27 ...... 51 D1
Mead Hedges SP10 ...... 105 F3
Mead Hedges Footpath
SP10 ...... 105 F4
Mead La GU9 ...... 98 C1
Mead Rd Andover SP10 ...... 105 F4
Hindhead GU26 ...... 167 E2
Winchester SO23 ...... 197 F2
Mead The Farnborough GU14 ...... 55 F2
Liphook GU30 ...... 187 F3
Liss GU33 ...... 207 F2
Old Basing RG24 ...... 70 A3
Meade Rd SP11 ...... 57 D1
Meadham La RG26 ...... 44 C2
Meadow Bank GU9 ...... 98 C1
Meadow Cl Ash GU14 ...... 56 B1
Blackwater GU17 ...... 35 D2
Liphook GU30 ...... 188 A2
New Alresford SO24 ...... 179 E3
Meadow Ct
Farnborough GU14 ...... 55 E2
10 Fleet GU13 ...... 53 F1
Meadow Dr SP11 ...... 127 F4
Meadow End GU30 ...... 188 A3
Meadow La RG27 ...... 52 B3
Meadow Rd
Basingstoke RG21 ...... 69 D1
Farnborough GU14 ...... 55 E2
Meadow Rise GU25 ...... 89 F1
Meadow Special Sch
GU35 ...... 165 D2
Meadow Vale GU27 ...... 189 F3
Meadow View Bordon GU35 ...... 164 C2
Fleet GU13 ...... 74 C3
Micheldever SO21 ...... 133 D2
Ropley SO24 ...... 181 E3
Whitchurch RG28 ...... 86 A3
Meadow Way
Aldershot GU12 ...... 77 E2
Blackwater GU47 ...... 35 D3
Farnham GU10 ...... 121 E2
Liphook GU30 ...... 188 A3
Winchester SO22 ...... 197 E2
Meadow Wlk Fleet GU13 ...... 74 B4
1 Liss GU33 ...... 207 F2
Meadowbank RG20 ...... 3 F4
Meadowland Chineham RG24 ...... 48 C2
Kings Worthy SO23 ...... 176 A4
Meadowridge RG22 ...... 91 E3
Meadows The Ash GU12 ...... 77 F1
Churt GU10 ...... 144 B1
Sandhurst GU15 ...... 35 E3
Sherfield on Loddon RG7 ...... 29 E1
Meads The GU27 ...... 189 E3
Meadsview Ct **4** GU14 ...... 55 F2
Meadway Camberley GU15 ...... 36 B1
Haslemere RG27 ...... 189 E3
Mede Cl RG25 ...... 88 A4
Medina Cl **44** SP10 ...... 83 E1
Medina Gdns RG23 ...... 67 D1
Medlar Dr GU17 ...... 35 E2
Medonte Cl GU13 ...... 75 D4
Medstead CE Prim Sch
GU34 ...... 159 F3
Medstead & Four Marks Sta
GU34 ...... 160 A1
Medstead Rd GU34 ...... 139 D1
Medway Ave RG23 ...... 67 D1
Medway Cl RG18 ...... 2 C3
Medway Ct **46** Andover SP10 ...... 83 E1
13 Basingstoke RG21 ...... 69 E3
Medway Dr GU14 ...... 55 E4
Meerut Rd SP9 ...... 78 C3
Meitner Cl RG14 ...... 28 C2
Meldrum Cl RG14 ...... 5 D3
Melford Gdns RG22 ...... 68 A1
Meliot Rise SP10 ...... 83 D2
Melksham Ho **1** SP9 ...... 78 C3
Mellersh Cl GU13 ...... 74 C2
Melrose Ave GU14 ...... 55 D2
Melrose Cl GU35 ...... 164 B1
Melrose Wlk RG21 ...... 69 D4
Melville Ave GU15 ...... 36 B1
Membury Cl GU14 ...... 56 C4
Memorial Bglws RG25 ...... 87 D3
Memorial Rd RG29 ...... 72 A4
Mendip Cl RG21 ...... 68 A2
Mendip Rd GU14 ...... 55 E4
Menin Way GU11 ...... 99 D1
Meon Cl Farnborough GU14 ...... 55 D3
Tadley RG26 ...... 9 F1
Meon Rd RG21 ...... 67 D1
Meon Wlk RG21 ...... 69 E3
Mercer Cl RG21 ...... 68 B2
Merchants Pl **9** SO23 ...... 198 A4

Mercia Ave SP10 ...... 82 B2
Mercury Cl GU35 ...... 164 C2
Mercury Ho **7** RG7 ...... 9 E1
Merepond La GU34 ...... 204 A2
Meriden Ct **10** SO23 ...... 176 A1
Merivale GU13 ...... 74 B4
Merlin Ct GU15 ...... 36 A1
Merlin Rd GU34 ...... 160 A1
Merlin Way GU14 ...... 55 D2
Merlins Cl GU9 ...... 99 D1
Merriatt Cl RG21 ...... 69 D1
Merrieas Gdns RG22 ...... 91 D4
Merron Cl GU46 ...... 34 A3
Merrydown La RG24 ...... 49 D1
Merryfield RG24 ...... 48 C2
Merrywood Pk GU16 ...... 36 B2
Merryworth Cl GU12 ...... 77 E1
Mersey Ct **50** SP10 ...... 83 E1
Mersey Way RG18 ...... 2 C3
Merton Rd RG21 ...... 69 D3
Merton Schs RG24 ...... 69 D4
Meryon Rd SO24 ...... 179 E2
Mesh Rd SO51 ...... 193 D1
Methuen Rd GU33 ...... 186 B2
Meudon Ave GU14 ...... 55 F2
Mews La SO22 ...... 197 F4
Mews The Andover SP10 ...... 106 A3
Bramley RG26 ...... 29 D1
Farley Castle RG7 ...... 15 D4
Meyrick Dr RG14 ...... 5 D3
Michaelmas Cl GU47 ...... 34 A2
Michaelmas Dro SP11 ...... 81 D1
Micheldever Cl RG28 ...... 86 B2
Micheldever Prim Sch
SO21 ...... 133 D2
Micheldever Rd
Andover SP10 ...... 106 B4
Whitchurch RG28 ...... 86 C2
Micheldever Sta SO21 ...... 111 D1
Midas Ho **17** RG7 ...... 9 E1
Middle Ave GU10 ...... 122 A4
Middle Bourne La GU9 ...... 122 A4
Middle Brook St SO23 ...... 198 A4
Middle Church La GU9 ...... 98 C1
Middle Cl Camberley GU16 ...... 36 C3
Newbury RG14 ...... 5 D4
Middle Gordon Rd GU16 ...... 36 A3
Middle Head RG27 ...... 51 D1
Middle Hill GU12 ...... 76 C2
Middle Meadow GU33 ...... 208 A2
Middle Old Pk GU9 ...... 98 B2
Middle Wallop Airfield
SO20 ...... 126 A1
Middlefield GU10 ...... 121 F4
Middlefield Cl GU10 ...... 121 F4
Middlemead RG27 ...... 51 D1
Middlemoor Rd GU16 ...... 56 B4
Middleton Ct RG14 ...... 2 B3
Middleton Gdns
Basingstoke RG21 ...... 69 D4
Farnborough GU14 ...... 55 E3
Middleton Rd
Camberley GU15 ...... 36 B4
Middle Winterslow SP5 ...... 168 A3
Middleway The
Andover SP11 ...... 107 E3
Longparish SP11 ...... 107 E3
Midhurst Rd
Haslemere RG27 ...... 189 F3
Liphook GU30 ...... 188 A1
Midlane Cl RG21 ...... 69 D1
Mike Hawthorn Dr GU9 ...... 99 D2
Milden Cl GU16 ...... 56 C3
Milden Gdns GU16 ...... 56 C3
Mildmay Ct Odiham RG29 ...... 72 C2
42 Winchester SO23 ...... 198 A4
Mildmay St SO22 ...... 197 E3
Mildmay Terr RG27 ...... 52 B3
Miles Rd GU12 ...... 77 F2
Milkingpen La RG24 ...... 70 A3
Mill Chase Com Sch GU35 ...... 164 C2
Mill Chase Rd GU35 ...... 164 C2
Mill Cl Haslemere GU27 ...... 189 E3
Sherfield on Loddon RG27 ...... 29 F1
Mill Cnr GU13 ...... 54 B2
Mill Copse Rd GU27 ...... 189 F2
Mill Hill SO24 ...... 179 E3
Mill Hill Ave SP9 ...... 78 C4
Mill La Alton GU34 ...... 140 A2
Bishop's Sutton SO24 ...... 180 A3
Ecchinswell RG20 ...... 23 F2
Fair Oak Green RG26 ...... 29 E2
Frensham GU10 ...... 143 F4
Hawkley GU34 ...... 184 C1
Headley GU35 ...... 165 D3
Kings Worthy SO21 ...... 176 B3
Longparish SP11 ...... 108 B3
Middle Winterslow SP5 ...... 168 A4
North Warnborough RG29 ...... 72 A3
Rotherwick RG27 ...... 50 B3
Sandhurst GU17 ...... 34 A4
Sherfield on Loddon RG26 ...... 29 E2
Steep Marsh GU32 ...... 206 C1
Yateley GU46 ...... 34 A4
Mill Lane Ind Est GU34 ...... 140 A2
Mill Rd GU33 ...... 208 A3
Mill Reef Cl RG19 ...... 2 B2
Mill Rise SO51 ...... 192 B1
Mill Stream GU9 ...... 99 D3
Mill View RG29 ...... 71 F1
Milland Rd SO23 ...... 198 A3
Millard Ct RG21 ...... 68 C4
Millbridge Rd GU46 ...... 33 F4
Millbrook Cl GU33 ...... 208 A2
Milldown Ho RG25 ...... 88 A4
Millers La SO22 ...... 196 C2
Millers Rd RG26 ...... 26 C4

Millers Yd SO21 ...... 131 E2
Millgate Ct GU9 ...... 99 D2
Millgreen La RG19 ...... 7 E1
Millmere RG46 ...... 34 A4
Mills Ho GU12 ...... 77 D1
Millstream Cl SP10 ...... 105 F3
Millstream The GU27 ...... 189 E3
Millway Cl SP10 ...... 105 F4
Millway Rd SP10 ...... 105 F4
Milner Pl SO22 ...... 197 F3
Milnthorpe La SO22 ...... 197 F4
Milsons The SO20 ...... 149 F1
Milton Ave SP10 ...... 82 B1
Milton Cl RG21 ...... 69 E4
Milton Grange GU12 ...... 77 F3
Milverton Rd SO22 ...... 197 F4
Mimosa Cl GU35 ...... 165 D3
Mimosa Ct SP10 ...... 105 F3
Minchens La RG26 ...... 28 C2
Minden Cl RG24 ...... 48 C1
Minden Way SO22 ...... 197 E3
Minehurst Rd GU16 ...... 56 B2
Minerva Ho **9** RG26 ...... 9 E1
Ministry Rd RG14 ...... 6 C3
Minley Cl GU14 ...... 55 E2
Minley Gr GU13 ...... 54 A2
Minley Rd Farnborough GU13 ...... 54 C4
Fleet GU13 ...... 54 A2
Hawley GU13 ...... 54 C4
Minstead Cl Tadley RG26 ...... 26 C3
Winchester SO22 ...... 175 E2
Minstead Dr GU46 ...... 34 A3
Minster Ct Camberley GU15 ...... 36 A4
Camberley, York Town GU17 ...... 35 E2
Minster La **27** SO23 ...... 198 A4
Mint Rd GU33 ...... 208 A3
Minter Ct RG26 ...... 9 E1
Mistletoe Rd GU46 ...... 34 A2
Mitchell Ave RG27 ...... 52 B3
Mitchell Bldgs GU46 ...... 33 F3
Mitchell Cl SP10 ...... 82 B1
Mitchell Gdns RG22 ...... 91 E4
Mitford Rd SO24 ...... 179 E2
Moat Cl RG26 ...... 28 C2
Moffatts Cl GU46 ...... 34 C4
Mole Cl GU14 ...... 55 D3
Momford Rd SO22 ...... 197 D2
Monachus La RG27 ...... 52 B4
Monarch Cl RG22 ...... 91 D3
Mongers Piece RG24 ...... 49 D2
Monier Williams Rd SP11 ...... 108 A2
Moniton Trad Est RG22 ...... 68 A2
Monk Sherborne Ho RG26 ...... 47 D3
Monk Sherborne Rd RG26 ...... 46 C4
Monk's La GU14 ...... 5 E4
Monk's Wlk GU10 ...... 122 B4
Monks Cl Farnborough GU16 ...... 56 A2
North Tidworth SP9 ...... 78 C4
Monks Rd SO23 ...... 176 A1
Monks Rise GU13 ...... 53 E1
Monks' Well GU10 ...... 99 F1
Monkshanger GU9 ...... 99 E1
Monkswood Cl Newbury RG14 ...... 5 E4
Tadley RG26 ...... 26 C4
Monkton La GU10 ...... 99 E3
Monkton Ho RG9 ...... 99 E2
Monktons La RG7 ...... 12 A3
Monmouth Sq SO22 ...... 197 D3
Mons Cl RG14 ...... 77 E4
Montacute Cl GU16 ...... 56 A2
Montague Cl GU15 ...... 35 F3
Montague Pl RG21 ...... 69 D2
Montague Terr RG14 ...... 5 F4
Monteagle La GU46 ...... 33 F3
Montgomery Cl GU46 ...... 34 C4
Montgomery Ho **5** SP9 ...... 78 C4
Montgomery Rd
Farnborough GU14 ...... 55 E2
Newbury RG14 ...... 5 E4
Montrose Cl Bordon GU35 ...... 164 C1
Camberley GU15 ...... 36 B1
Fleet GU13 ...... 75 D4
Montserrat Pl RG24 ...... 48 A1
Montserrat Rd RG24 ...... 48 B1
Monument Chase GU35 ...... 164 B1
Monument Cl RG14 ...... 5 D4
Monxton Rd Amport SP11 ...... 103 E1
Andover SP10 ...... 105 D4
Grateley SP11 ...... 103 E1
Moody's Hill SP5 ...... 190 B1
Moons Hill Farnham GU10 ...... 122 A1
Frensham GU9 ...... 122 A1
Moor Cl Bordon GU35 ...... 164 A2
Wokingham RG40 ...... 16 B4
Moor Court La SO21 ...... 174 A2
Moor La RG14 ...... 1 B2
Moor Park La GU9 ...... 99 F2
Moor Park Way GU9 ...... 99 E1
Moor Rd Bordon GU33 ...... 186 B1
Camberley GU16 ...... 56 B4
Farnborough GU14 ...... 55 F4
Linchmere GU27 ...... 189 E1
Moor View RG24 ...... 70 A4
Moorcroft Cl SO21 ...... 131 E2
Moorcroft Gdns RG22 ...... 68 A2
Moore Cl Andover SP10 ...... 83 D1
Fleet GU13 ...... 75 D3
Moore Rd GU33 ...... 75 D3
Moorfield GU27 ...... 189 E3
Moorhams Ave RG22 ...... 91 D3
Moorings The
10 Basingstoke RG21 ...... 69 E3
Grayshott GU26 ...... 167 E2
Moorlands Cl Fleet GU13 ...... 75 D4
Hindhead GU26 ...... 167 E2
Moorlands Pl GU17 ...... 35 F2
Moorlands Rd GU15 ...... 35 F2
Moors Ct RG40 ...... 16 B4

Moors The GU10 ...... 100 B4
Moorside Cl GU15 ...... 35 F1
Moorside Rd SO23 ...... 176 B1
Moot Cl SP10 ...... 83 D2
Moray Ave GU15 ...... 35 D4
More House Sch GU10 ...... 122 A1
Moreland Ct GU34 ...... 140 A1
Morestead Rd
Chilcomb SO21 ...... 198 C2
Winchester SO21 ...... 198 A2
Winchester SO21 ...... 198 C2
Moreton Cl Churt GU10 ...... 144 B1
Fleet GU13 ...... 74 C2
Morgaston Rd RG24, RG26 ...... 47 F4
Morland Rd GU12 ...... 100 A3
Morley Cl GU46 ...... 33 F3
Morley Rd Basingstoke RG24 ...... 69 D1
Farnham GU10, GU9 ...... 99 D1
Mornington Ave RG40 ...... 16 B4
Mornington Cl
Andover SP10, SP11 ...... 106 A3
Baughurst RG26 ...... 9 E1
Mornington Dr SO22 ...... 175 E1
Mornington Rd GU35 ...... 164 A1
Morris Rd GU14 ...... 77 D4
Morris St RG27 ...... 71 F4
Morse Rd RG21 ...... 68 C2
Mortimer Cl
Hartley Wintney RG27 ...... 52 A2
Kings Worthy SO23 ...... 176 A3
Mortimer Gdns RG26 ...... 27 D4
Mortimer La
2 Basingstoke RG21 ...... 69 D3
West End Green RG7 ...... 29 D4
Mortimer Sta RG7 ...... 12 B3
Morton Cl GU14 ...... 56 B4
Morval Cl GU14 ...... 55 C2
Morval Rd GU46 ...... 34 B1
Moscrop Ct **8** RG21 ...... 69 D2
Moselle Cl GU14 ...... 55 D3
Moss Cl GU33 ...... 208 A2
Moss Rd SO23 ...... 198 A4
Mothes Ho RG26 ...... 27 D4
Mottisfont Abbey Gdns
SO51 ...... 192 C2
Mottisfont Abbey (NT)
SO51 ...... 192 C1
Moulsham Copse La GU46 ...... 33 F4
Moulsham La GU46 ...... 33 F4
Mount Carmel Rd SP11 ...... 124 C2
Mount Cl Highclere RG20 ...... 21 E3
Newbury RG14 ...... 1 C1
Winchester SO22 ...... 175 F2
Mount Hermon Rd SP11 ...... 124 C3
Mount Pleasant
Amport SP11 ...... 104 A3
Farnham GU9 ...... 98 C1
Hartley Wintney RG27 ...... 52 B3
Kings Worthy SO23 ...... 176 B3
Laverstoke RG28 ...... 87 D3
Tadley RG26 ...... 26 C4
Mount Pleasant Dr RG26 ...... 26 C4
Mount Pleasant Rd
Aldershot GU12 ...... 77 D1
Alton GU34 ...... 139 F1
Lindford GU35 ...... 164 C3
Mount The Fleet GU13 ...... 54 A1
Headley GU35 ...... 165 F3
Mount View Rd SO22 ...... 197 D2
Mountbatten Cl RG14 ...... 2 A3
Mountbatten Ct
14 Aldershot GU11 ...... 76 C1
Andover SP10 ...... 83 E1
Winchester SO22 ...... 175 F2
Mountbatten Pl SO23 ...... 176 B4
Mounter's La GU34 ...... 139 E1
Mountsom's La GU34 ...... 161 F2
Mourne Cl RG22 ...... 68 A2
Mowatt Rd GU26 ...... 167 D1
Mozart Cl RG22 ...... 91 F4
Mud La RG2 ...... 15 E1
Mulberries The GU9 ...... 99 E2
Mulberry Cl Ash GU11 ...... 77 F2
Sandhurst GU15 ...... 35 D4
Mulberry Ct GU34 ...... 160 B2
Mulberry Ho **3** SP10, SP11 ...... 106 A4
Mulberry Mead RG28 ...... 86 B3
Mulfords Hill RG26 ...... 26 C4
Mulgrave Rd GU15 ...... 36 B1
Mull Cl RG21 ...... 67 D1
Mullins Cl RG21 ...... 69 D4
Mulroy Dr GU15 ...... 36 C3
Munnings Cl RG21 ...... 69 E2
Munnings Ct SP10 ...... 82 C1
Munnings Dr GU14 ...... 35 E3
Murray Cl SP10 ...... 105 F3
Murray Rd GU14 ...... 55 E2
Murray's Rd GU11 ...... 77 D3
Murrell Green Bsns Pk
RG27 ...... 51 F2
Murrell Green Rd
Hartley Wintney RG27 ...... 51 F3
Hook RG27 ...... 51 F3
Murrell Rd GU12 ...... 77 F2
Murrells La GU47 ...... 35 F2
Mus of Army Flying SO20 ...... 126 A2
Muscott Cl SP10 ...... 101 E4
Museum of the Iron Age
SP10 ...... 106 A4
Musgrave Cl RG22 ...... 91 E4
Musgrove Gdns **17** GU34 ...... 139 F2
Musket Copse RG24 ...... 70 A3
Muss La SO22 ...... 172 A2
Myland Cl RG21 ...... 69 E4
Mylen Bsns Ctr SP10 ...... 105 F4
Mylen Rd SP10 ...... 82 C1
Myrtle Dr GU47 ...... 35 D3

Mytchett Cty Fst Sch GU14 ...... 56 B2
Mytchett Heath GU16 ...... 56 C2
Mytchett Lake Rd GU16 ...... 56 C1
Mytchett Place Rd GU16 ...... 56 C1
Mytchett Rd GU16 ...... 56 B2

Naafi Rdbt GU11 ...... 76 C1
Nadder Rd SP9 ...... 78 C3
Naini Tal Rd SP9 ...... 78 C3
Nairn Cl GU16 ...... 36 B1
Napier Cl Ash GU11 ...... 77 E4
North Tidworth SP9 ...... 79 D3
Napier La GU11 ...... 77 F2
Napier Wlk SP10 ...... 83 E1
Napoleon Ave GU14 ...... 55 F3
Napoleon Dr RG23 ...... 68 B4
Naseby Rise RG14 ...... 2 A3
Nash Cl Basingstoke RG21 ...... 69 E4
Farnborough GU14 ...... 55 E2
Nash Grove La RG40 ...... 16 B4
Nash Meadows RG25, RG29 ...... 95 D2
Nateley Rd RG27 ...... 71 F1
National Dairy Mus RG7 ...... 14 A1
Nations Hill SO23 ...... 176 B3
Naylors The RG7 ...... 14 A3
Neath Rd RG21 ...... 69 E3
Neelem Ct GU16 ...... 56 A1
Nelson Cl Aldershot GU12 ...... 77 D1
Farnham GU9 ...... 99 D4
Stockbridge SO20 ...... 149 F1
Nelson Rd Farnham GU9 ...... 99 D4
Winchester SO22 ...... 198 B3
Nelson St GU11 ...... 76 C1
Nelson Way GU14 ...... 55 E2
Nelson Wlk SP10 ...... 83 E1
Nene Ct **17** SP10 ...... 83 E1
Nepaul Rd SP9 ...... 78 C4
Neptune Rd GU35 ...... 164 C1
Nestor Cl SP10 ...... 82 C1
Nether Vell-Mead GU13 ...... 74 C2
Nethercliffe Sch SO22 ...... 175 F1
Netherfield Cl GU34 ...... 139 F2
Netherhouse Cl GU13 ...... 74 B3
Netherhouse Moor GU13 ...... 74 B3
Netley St GU14 ...... 77 D4
Nettlebeds La Bighton SO24 ...... 158 A1
Old Alresford SO24 ...... 158 A1
Neuvic Way RG28 ...... 86 B2
Nevada Cl GU14 ...... 55 D2
Neville Cl Andover SP10 ...... 106 A3
Basingstoke RG21 ...... 69 D1
Neville Duke Rd GU14 ...... 55 E4
New Barn Cl GU13 ...... 74 B4
New Barn Cotts SO21 ...... 152 C1
New Barn Farm SO24 ...... 181 D1
New Barn La Alton GU34 ...... 139 F1
Wherwell SP11 ...... 128 C4
New Bldgs SP11 ...... 58 B4
New Cotts Bighton SO24 ...... 158 B1
South Warnborough RG29 ...... 95 D2
Wonston SO21 ...... 131 E2
New Dawn Cl GU14 ...... 55 D2
New Farm Rd
East Stratton SO21 ...... 134 A2
New Alresford SO24 ...... 179 D2
New Greenham Pk RG14 ...... 6 C3
New House La SP11 ...... 81 E4
New La SO20 ...... 172 A2
New Market Sq **18** RG21 ...... 69 D3
New Mill La RG27 ...... 15 E1
New Mill Rd RG40 ...... 15 E2
New North Dr RG24 ...... 49 F4
New Odiham Rd Alton GU34 ...... 139 E3
Shalden GU34 ...... 139 E3
New Paddock Cl GU34 ...... 140 B3
New Rd Basingstoke RG21 ...... 69 D2
Blackwater GU35 ...... 35 E2
Bordon GU35 ...... 164 B1
Eversley GU46 ...... 33 E4
Fleet GU13 ...... 75 D3
Greenham RG19 ...... 6 A4
Hartley Wintney RG27 ...... 52 B3
Hook RG27 ...... 72 A4
Linchmere GU27 ...... 189 E1
Littleton SO22 ...... 175 D3
Micheldever SO21 ...... 111 D1
Newbury RG14 ...... 6 A4
North Warnborough RG29 ...... 72 B2
Over Wallop SO20 ...... 147 E4
Pamber End RG26 ...... 27 E2
Sandhurst GU17 ...... 34 C4
Stratfield Mortimer RG7 ...... 12 A4
Tadley RG26 ...... 26 C4
Tongham GU10 ...... 100 B3
New Rd Cotts GU34 ...... 184 C4
New St Andover SP10 ...... 83 D1
Basingstoke RG21 ...... 69 D2
Stockbridge SO20 ...... 149 F2
Stratfield Saye RG26 ...... 29 F4
New The GU12 ...... 77 F1
New Villas RG20 ...... 3 F2
Newall SP10, SP11 ...... 105 D4
Newark Rd GU47 ...... 34 B1
Newbold Rd RG14 ...... 1 A3
Newburgh St SO23 ...... 197 F4
Newbury Coll RG14 ...... 1 B1
Newbury District Hospl RG14 ...... 1 B1
Newbury L Ctr RG14 ...... 2 B2
Newbury Rd Andover SP10 ...... 83 D3
Enham Alamein SP10 ...... 83 D3
Kingsclere RG20 ...... 24 A2
Knights Enham SP10 ...... 83 D3
Tangley SP11, SP11 ...... 83 D3
Whitchurch RG28 ...... 86 B4
Newbury Sta RG14 ...... 1 C1
Newchurch Rd RG26 ...... 9 F1
Newcomb Cl SP10 ...... 106 A3

Newcome Pl GU11 .... 100 A4
Newcome Rd GU9 .... 99 E3
Newfield Ave GU14 .... 55 E3
Newfield Rd Ash GU12 .... 77 F3
   Liss GU33 .... 208 A3
Newlands Cl GU46 .... 34 A3
Newlands Dr GU14 .... 77 F2
Newlands Prim Sch GU47 .... 34 A3
Newlands Rd GU35 .... 35 F1
Newman La GU34 .... 140 A3
Newmans Ct GU10, GU9 .... 98 C4
Newnham La Newnham RG27 .... 70 C4
   Old Basing RG24 .... 70 C4
Newnham Pk RG29 .... 71 F4
Newnham Rd Hook RG27 .... 71 F4
   Newnham RG27 .... 71 F4
Newport Cl RG14 .... 1 C2
Newport Jun Sch GU12 .... 77 D1
Newport Rd Aldershot GU12 .... 77 D1
   Newbury RG14 .... 1 C2
Newton RG26 .... 9 F1
Newton La GU34 .... 183 F4
Newton Rd GU16 .... 56 A3
Newton Tony CE Prim Sch
   SP4 .... 123 D3
Newton Way GU10 .... 100 B4
Newtown RG26 .... 26 C4
Newtown Cl SP10 .... 105 F4
Newtown Rd Liphook GU30 .... 188 A2
   Newbury RG14 .... 5 F4
   Sandhurst GU17 .... 34 C4
Nicholson Pl SO24 .... 179 D3
Nickel Cl SO23 .... 198 A4
Nicola Ct GU12 .... 77 D1
Nicotiana Ct GU13 .... 74 C2
Nightingale Cl
   Farnborough GU14 .... 55 D3
   Winchester SO22 .... 197 E3
Nightingale Dr GU16 .... 56 C2
Nightingale Gdns Hook RG27 .... 51 D1
   Sandhurst GU46 .... 34 C4
   Sherborne St John RG22 .... 68 B4
Nightingale La RG7 .... 12 A3
Nightingale Rd GU35 .... 164 C1
Nightingale Rise RG25 .... 88 A4
Nightingales The RG14 .... 5 F4
Nightjar Cl GU9 .... 98 A4
Nine Acres GU32 .... 207 D1
Nine Mile Ride RG40 .... 16 B3
Nine Mile Ride Prim Sch
   RG40 .... 16 B3
Norden Cl RG21 .... 69 D3
Norman Cl GU35 .... 164 C2
Norman Court La SP11 .... 105 F2
Norman Ct GU9 .... 99 D1
Norman Gate Special Sch
   SP10 .... 83 E1
Norman Rd SO23 .... 197 F3
Normandy Mews **10** GU34 .... 139 F2
Normandy St GU34 .... 140 A2
Normans SO22 .... 197 F3
Normanton Rd RG21 .... 69 D4
Normay Rise RG14 .... 5 D3
Norn Hill RG21 .... 69 E4
Norn Hill Cl RG21 .... 69 E3
Norris Cl GU35 .... 164 A1
Norris Hill Rd GU13 .... 75 E4
Norris Ho RG25 .... 88 A4
North Acre SP11 .... 108 B3
North Ave GU9 .... 99 D4
   North Camp Sta GU12 .... 77 E4
North Cl Aldershot GU12 .... 77 E1
   Farnborough GU14 .... 55 F4
North Dr SO22 .... 175 D3
North End Farm Cotts
   SO24 .... 201 E4
North Farm Rd GU14 .... 55 E4
North Farnborough Inf Sch
   GU14 .... 56 A3
North Foreland Lodge RG24 ... 49 F3
North Fryerne GU46 .... 34 A4
North Gate Rd GU14 .... 56 A1
North Hampshire Hospl The
   RG22 .... 68 C4
North Hill Cl SO22 .... 175 F1
North Hill Ct SO22 .... 175 F1
North La Aldershot GU12 .... 77 D1
   West Tytherley SP5 .... 169 D1
North Mall **13** GU13 .... 53 F1
North Par RG25 .... 164 B3
North Rd Ash GU12 .... 77 E2
   Farnborough GU14 .... 77 D4
   Kings Worthy SO23 .... 176 A4
North Row RG26 .... 28 C2
North Side GU12 .... 100 B4
North St Bishop's Sutton SO24 ... 180 B3
   Kingsclere RG20 .... 24 B1
North View SO22 .... 197 F4
North View Gdns **14** RG14 ... 1 C2
North View Rd RG26 .... 27 D4
North Walls SO23 .... 198 A4
North Waltham Prim Sch
   RG25 .... 89 F1
North Warnborough St
   RG29 .... 72 A2
North Way SP11 .... 83 F1
Northanger Cl GU34 .... 139 F2
Northaw Sch SP5 .... 168 C1
Northbrook SO21 .... 132 C2
Northbrook Ave SO23 .... 198 A4
Northbrook Ct **11** SO23 .... 198 A4
Northbrook Rd GU9 .... 99 F4
Northcote Rd
   Ash GU12 .... 77 F4
   Farnborough GU14 .... 55 E3
Northcroft Ct RG29 .... 95 D2
Northcroft La RG14 .... 1 B2
Northcroft Terr RG14 .... 1 B2

Northern Ave Andover SP10 ... 83 D1
   Newbury RG14 .... 1 C3
Northfield Cl Aldershot GU12 ... 77 D1
   Fleet GU13 .... 75 E3
Northfield Rd Fleet GU13 .... 75 E3
   Sherfield on Loddon RG7 .... 29 E1
   Thatcham RG18 .... 2 C2
Northfields La GU34 .... 161 E4
Northgate La RG25 .... 92 A1
Northgate Way RG22 .... 91 D3
Northington Corner SO21 ... 134 A2
Northington Rd SO21 .... 177 F4
Northlands Dr SO23 .... 176 A1
Northmead GU14 .... 55 F2
Northside La SO24 .... 180 C3
Northumberland Rd GU35 ... 164 B1
Northway RG14 .... 1 C1
Northwood Dr RG14 .... 2 A1
Norton Cl RG14 .... 5 D3
Norton Cotts SO21 .... 131 E4
Norton Rd RG7 .... 14 A2
Norton Ride RG21 .... 69 F4
Norwich Ave GU16 .... 36 B2
Norwich Cl RG22 .... 91 D4
Norwich Rd RG22 .... 91 E4
Novello Cl RG22 .... 91 E4
Nuffield Rd RG40 .... 15 F4
Nuns Rd SO23 .... 176 A1
Nursery Cl Camberley GU16 ... 56 B4
   Chineham RG24 .... 49 D2
   Fleet GU13 .... 75 E4
   Hook RG27 .... 51 D1
Nursery Field GU33 .... 207 F2
Nursery Gdns SO22 .... 197 E4
Nursery Rd Alton GU34 .... 140 A2
   New Alresford SO24 .... 179 E3
Nursery Terr RG29 .... 72 B2
Nutbane La SP11 .... 81 F4
Nutbeam La RG7 .... 14 B3
Nutbourne GU9 .... 99 E4
Nutchers Dro SO20 .... 172 A2
Nutcombe La GU27 .... 189 E4
Nutfield Ct GU15 .... 36 A4
Nuthatch Cl GU9 .... 98 A4
Nutley Cl Bordon GU35 .... 164 B1
   Yateley GU47 .... 34 A3
Nutmeg Ct GU14 .... 55 D3
Nutshell La GU9 .... 99 D3
Nutter's La RG7 .... 14 C4

O'Connor Rd GU12 .... 77 E4
O'Gorman Rd GU14 .... 55 F1
Oak Bank SP10 .... 106 A3
Oak Cl Basingstoke RG21 .... 69 E3
   Baughurst RG26 .... 26 A4
   Middle Wallop SO20 .... 126 A4
   North Tidworth SP9 .... 79 D4
   Oakley RG23 .... 67 D1
   Overton RG25 .... 88 A4
Oak Cotts GU27 .... 189 E3
Oak Ct Farnborough GU14 .... 56 B1
   Farnham GU10 .... 98 C1
Oak Dr RG14 .... 1 B1
Oak Farm Cl GU15 .... 35 D3
Oak Farm Com Sch GU14 ... 55 E3
Oak Grove Cres SO17 .... 35 E3
Oak Hanger Cl GU34 .... 51 D1
Oak Hill SO24 .... 179 E3
Oak Ho **3** GU14 .... 55 F4
Oak Lodge GU35 .... 164 B1
Oak Rd GU14 .... 56 A2
Oak Tree Cl Aldershot GU10 ... 100 B4
   Ash GU16 .... 56 B1
   Chilbolton SO20 .... 129 D2
   Headley GU35 .... 165 E2
   Tadley RG26 .... 9 F1
Oak Tree Dr GU33 .... 208 A2
Oak Tree La GU27 .... 189 D3
Oak Tree View GU9 .... 99 E3
Oak Tree Way RG27 .... 51 D1
Oakdene GU34 .... 139 F3
Oaken Copse GU13 .... 75 D2
Oaken Copse Cres GU14 ... 55 F4
Oaken Gr RG14 .... 5 D4
Oakfield Rd Blackwater GU15 ... 35 E2
   Pamber Heath RG26 .... 10 B1
Oakfields GU17 .... 35 F3
Oakfields Cl RG20 .... 23 E2
Oakgreen Par GU34 .... 160 B2
Oakhanger Rd GU35 .... 164 A3
Oakhill Rd GU35 .... 165 F3
Oakhurst GU26 .... 167 D2
Oakland Ave GU14 .... 99 E4
Oakland Rd RG28 .... 86 B3
Oakland Terr RG27 .... 52 B3
Oaklands
   Hartley Wintney RG27 .... 52 B3
   South Wonston SO21 .... 153 E2
   Yateley GU47 .... 34 A3
Oaklands Way RG23 .... 68 B4
Oaklea GU12 .... 77 F3
Oaklea Dr RG27 .... 15 E1
Oaklea Gdns RG26 .... 29 E1
Oaklea Ho GU26 .... 167 D2
Oakley CE Jun Sch RG23 ... 67 C1
Oakley Dr GU13 .... 75 D4
Oakley Inf Sch RG23 .... 67 D1
Oakley La RG23 .... 67 C1
Oakley Pl **15** Fleet GU13 .... 53 F1
   Hartley Wintney RG27 .... 52 B3
Oakley Rd Bordon GU35 .... 164 B3
   Camberley GU15 .... 35 F2
   Hannington RG26 .... 44 C1
   Mottisfont SO51 .... 192 C2
   Newbury RG14 .... 2 A2
Oakmead RG26 .... 28 C2
Oakridge Ctr RG21 .... 69 E4
Oakridge Rd RG21 .... 69 D4
Oakridge Schs RG24 .... 69 D4

Oakridge Towers RG21 .... 69 E4
Oaks The
   Andover SP10 .... 105 F4
   Camberley GU17 .... 35 E2
   Farnborough GU14 .... 55 D2
   Tadley RG26 .... 26 C4
   Yateley GU46 .... 34 A3
Oaktree Rd GU35 .... 164 B1
Oaktrees Ash GU12 .... 77 E1
   Farnham GU9 .... 98 C3
Oakway Aldershot GU10 .... 100 B4
   Bentley GU10 .... 120 A3
Oakway Dr GU16 .... 36 B1
Oakwood Chineham RG24 ... 48 C2
   Fleet GU13 .... 75 D2
Oakwood Inf Sch RG27 .... 51 D1
Oast House Cres GU9 .... 99 D3
Oast House La GU9 .... 99 D3
Oast La GU9 .... 99 F4
Oasthouse Dr GU13 .... 54 B2
Oban Cl RG23 .... 67 D1
Obelisk Way GU15 .... 36 A3
Oberursel Way GU11 .... 76 B1
Observer Cl GU13 .... 74 C2
Ochil Cl RG22 .... 68 A2
Ockham Hall GU35 .... 142 A1
Octavia Hill SO22 .... 197 E3
Octavian Cl RG24 .... 91 D4
Oddfellows Rd RG14 .... 1 B1
Odette Gdns RG7 .... 10 A1
Odiham Cottage Hospl
   RG29 .... 72 C1
Odiham Rd
   Ewshot GU14 .... 98 B4
   Farnham GU12 .... 98 B4
   Heckfield RG7 .... 14 A1
   Odiham RG29 .... 73 D4
   Winchfield RG29 .... 73 D4
Odon Cl SP9 .... 79 E3
Officers Row RG7 .... 29 D1
Oglander Rd SO23 .... 176 A1
Olaf Cl SP10 .... 83 D2
Old Acre Rd GU34 .... 139 F1
Old Barn Cl RG25 .... 89 F1
Old Barn La GU10 .... 144 C1
Old Basing Inf Sch RG24 ... 70 A3
Old Basing Mall **22** RG21 ... 69 D3
Old Bath Rd RG14 .... 1 B2
Old Bisley Rd GU16 .... 36 C2
Old Brick Kiln Trad Est The
   RG26 .... 46 C4
Old Brickfield Rd GU9 .... 99 F4
Old Chapel La GU11 .... 77 D1
Old Church La GU10 .... 122 A4
Old Common Rd RG21 .... 69 E2
Old Compton La GU11 .... 99 E1
Old Cove Rd GU13 .... 54 A2
Old Ct RG20 .... 72 C1
Old Dean Rd GU16 .... 36 A4
Old Down Cl RG22 .... 68 A1
Old Down La GU32 .... 205 D1
Old Down Rd SP10 .... 82 C1
Old Farnham La Bentley GU9 ... 97 F1
   Farnham GU9 .... 122 A4
Old Forge Gdns SO24 .... 170 A4
Old Frensham Rd
   Farnham GU9 .... 122 B2
   Frensham GU9 .... 122 B2
Old Gdns SO22 .... 175 F1
Old Green La GU15 .... 36 A4
Old Guildford Rd GU14 .... 56 C3
Old Heath Way GU11 .... 99 D4
Old Hill The SP11 .... 128 C4
Old Hillside Rd GU27 .... 175 E1
Old Kempshott La RG23 ... 68 A2
Old Kennels Cl SO22 .... 197 D3
Old Kennels La SO22 .... 197 D2
Old Kiln GU35 .... 98 C1
Old Kiln Cl GU10 .... 144 B1
Old Kiln La GU10 .... 144 B1
Old La Aldershot GU9 .... 99 F4
   Ashford Hill RG7 .... 8 B1
   Frensham GU10 .... 143 F3
   Hamstead Marshall RG20 .... 3 E4
   Kintbury RG20 .... 3 E4
Old Litten La GU32 .... 206 B2
Old London Rd SO20 .... 150 A2
Old Micheldever Rd SP11 ... 107 D3
Old Newtown Rd RG14 .... 1 B1
Old Odiham Rd Alton GU34 ... 139 F3
   Shalden GU34 .... 139 F3
Old Orchard The GU9 .... 121 F4
Old Palace Farm SO20 .... 172 A1
Old Park Cl GU10 .... 98 C3
Old Park Farm GU35 .... 142 B1
Old Park La GU9, GU10 .... 98 C2
Old Park Rd SO24 .... 180 C1
Old Pasture Rd GU16 .... 36 B2
Old Pond Cl GU15 .... 36 A1
Old Portsmouth Rd GU15 ... 36 C3
Old Potbridge Rd RG27 .... 52 A1
Old Quarry The GU27 .... 189 E2
Old Reading Rd RG21 .... 69 E3
Old Rectory Dr GU12 .... 77 F1
Old Rectory Gdns
   Farnborough GU14 .... 56 A2
   Kings Worthy SO21 .... 176 B3
Old Salisbury Rd SP10 .... 105 D2
Old School Cl Ash GU12 .... 77 F2
   Fleet GU13 .... 54 A1
   Hartley Wintney RG27 .... 52 B3
Old School La GU46 .... 34 A3
Old School Rd Hook RG27 ... 71 F4
   Liss GU33 .... 207 F2
Old Station App SO23 .... 198 A4
Old Station Rd SO21 .... 177 F3
Old Station Way GU35 .... 164 A3

Old Stockbridge Rd
   Middle Wallop SO20 .... 125 D1
   Over Wallop SO20 .... 125 D1
Old Stoke Rd
   South Wonston SO21 .... 154 A4
   Wonston SO21 .... 154 A4
Old Vicarage La SO20 .... 172 A2
Old Vyne La RG26 .... 26 B1
Old Welmore GU46 .... 34 B3
Old Winton Rd SP10 .... 106 A3
Old Worting Rd RG22 .... 68 B2
Oldberg Gdns RG22 .... 91 F4
Oldbury Cl GU46 .... 56 B4
Oldcorne Hollow GU46 .... 33 F3
Olde Farm Dr GU46 .... 34 C3
Oldfield View RG27 .... 52 B3
Oldwood Chase GU14 .... 55 D2
Oliver Rise GU34 .... 139 F2
Oliver's Battery Cres SO22 ... 197 D2
Oliver's Battery Gdns SO22 ... 197 D2
Oliver's Battery Rd N SO22 ... 197 D2
Oliver's Battery Rd S SO22 ... 197 D2
Oliver's La RG26 .... 29 C2
Oliver's Wlk RG21 .... 69 F4
Olivers Cl SO22 .... 29 D1
Omega Pk GU34 .... 140 A2
Omni Bsns Ctr GU34 .... 140 A2
Onslow Cl RG24 .... 48 C1
Openfields GU35 .... 165 E3
Orange Gr SP11 .... 124 C3
Orange La SO20 .... 125 E1
Orbit Cl RG40 .... 16 B3
Orchard Cl Ash GU12 .... 77 F3
   Farnborough GU15 .... 35 E1
   Farnborough, Cove Green GU14 ... 55 F2
   Farnham GU9 .... 99 F3
   Linchmere GU27 .... 189 E3
   New Alresford SO24 .... 179 E2
   Newbury RG14 .... 2 A3
   South Wonston SO21 .... 153 E2
Orchard Cotts SP11 .... 58 A2
Orchard Ct GU10 .... 97 E3
Orchard End GU27 .... 121 E2
Orchard Gate GU46 .... 34 C4
Orchard Gdns GU12 .... 100 A4
Orchard Ho Alton GU34 .... 140 A2
   Tongham GU10 .... 100 B4
Orchard La GU34 .... 140 A2
Orchard Rd Andover SP10 .... 82 C1
   Basingstoke RG22 .... 68 B2
   Farnham GU11 .... 99 F3
   Mortimer RG7 .... 11 F3
   South Wonston SO21 .... 153 E2
Orchard Terr GU34 .... 140 A2
Orchard The Kingsclere RG20 ... 24 B1
   Overton RG25 .... 88 A4
   Tadley RG26 .... 27 D4
Orchard Way GU12 .... 100 A4
Orchard Wlk SO22 .... 175 E1
Orchardene RG14 .... 1 C2
Orchid Ct SP10 .... 105 E3
Ordnance Rd Aldershot GU12 ... 77 D2
   North Tidworth SP9 .... 78 C3
Ordnance Rdbt GU11 .... 76 C1
Oregon Wlk RG40 .... 16 B4
Oriel Hill GU16 .... 36 A2
Orient Dr SO22 .... 175 E2
Orkney Cl RG24 .... 48 B1
Orpheus Rd **4** RG26 .... 9 E1
Orts Rd RG14 .... 1 C1
Orwell Cl GU14 .... 55 E3
Osborn Rd GU9 .... 99 D2
Osborn Way RG21 .... 72 A4
Osborne Cl Alton GU34 .... 139 E2
   Camberley GU16 .... 56 B4
Osborne Ct GU12 .... 77 D4
Osborne Dr GU13 .... 75 D4
Osborne Rd Andover SP10 ... 106 A4
   Farnborough GU14 .... 77 D4
Osbourne Cl RG21 .... 69 D4
Osier Ho GU26 .... 26 C4
Osler Cl GU35 .... 28 C2
Osnaburgh Hill GU15 .... 35 F3
Osprey Cl RG22 .... 67 F1
Otterbourne Cres RG26 .... 26 C1
Our Lady of Providence
   Convent Sch GU34 .... 140 A3
Ouse Ct **49** SP10 .... 83 E1
Oval Rd SO51 .... 192 A1
Oval The Andover SP10 .... 83 E2
   Liss GU33 .... 207 F2
Overbridge Sq RG14 .... 2 B1
Overdale Pl GU35 .... 164 B1
Overdale Rise GU15 .... 36 B2
Overdale Wlk GU35 .... 164 B1
Overlord Cl GU35 .... 100 A3
Overton CE Prim Sch RG25 ... 65 D1
Overton Cl GU11 .... 100 A3
Overton Ho RG25 .... 88 A4
Overton Rd SO21 .... 111 E2
Overton Sta RG25 .... 65 D1
Owen Rd GU14 .... 1 C3
Owen's Rd GU22 .... 175 F1
Owlsmoor Rd GU15 .... 35 D4
Ox Dro SP11 .... 84 A1
Ox Drove Rise SP11 .... 84 A2
Oxenden Ct GU12 .... 100 B4
Oxenden Rd Ash GU11 .... 100 B4
   Tongham GU10 .... 100 B4
Oxford Rd Farnborough GU14 ... 56 A1
   Newbury RG14 .... 1 B3
   Wonston SO21 .... 131 E2
Oxford St RG14 .... 1 B2
Oyster Cl RG22 .... 91 D4

Packenham Rd RG22 .... 68 C2
Paddington Ho **13** RG21 .... 69 D3
Paddock Cl Camberley GU15 ... 36 C3
   South Wonston SO21 .... 153 F2
Paddock Ct RG27 .... 52 B3
Paddock Field SO20 .... 129 D3
Paddock Rd
   Basingstoke RG22 .... 68 B2
   Newbury RG14 .... 5 E4
Paddock The
   Farnham GU10 .... 121 E2
   Grayshott GU26 .... 166 C2
   Hartley Wintney RG27 .... 52 B4
   Haslemere GU27 .... 189 F4
   Headley GU35 .... 165 E3
   Kings Worthy SO23 .... 176 B3
   Kingsclere RG20 .... 24 B1
   Newbury RG14 .... 2 A1
Paddock Way Liphook GU30 ... 188 A3
   New Alresford SO24 .... 179 E2
Paddockfields RG24 .... 70 A4
Padwick Cl RG24 .... 69 D2
Padworth Rd RG7 .... 11 D4
Pages Yd RG28 .... 86 B2
Paget Cl Camberley GU16 ... 36 C4
   North Tidworth SP9 .... 78 B4
Paice La GU34 .... 159 F2
Paices Hill RG26 .... 9 F2
Painters Field SO23 .... 197 F2
Painters Pightle RG27 .... 50 C1
Palace Cl SO23 .... 171 F1
Palace Gate RG29 .... 72 B2
Pale La RG27 .... 53 D1
   Hartley Wintney GU13 .... 53 E2
   Winchfield RG27 .... 53 D1
Palestine Rd SP11 .... 124 C3
Palm Hall Cl SO23 .... 198 B4
Palmer Cl RG21 .... 69 E4
Palmer Dr SP10 .... 106 B4
Palmerston Cl GU14 .... 55 D2
Palmerston Ct **2** SO22 .... 197 F3
Pamber Heath Rd RG26 .... 10 B1
Pamber Rd RG7 .... 10 C1
Pan's Gdns GU15 .... 36 B2
Pankridge St GU9 .... 97 E4
Pannells GU10 .... 122 A3
Pantile Dr RG27 .... 51 E2
Pantings La RG20 .... 21 E3
Paper Mill La GU34 .... 140 A2
Papermakers RG25 .... 88 A4
Parade The Ash GU11 .... 77 F2
   Basingstoke RG21 .... 69 E3
   Tadley RG26 .... 9 F1
Parchment St SO23 .... 198 A4
Pardown RG22 .... 90 A4
Parfitts Cl GU9 .... 98 C1
Parish Cl Ash GU12 .... 77 F1
   Farnham GU10, GU9 .... 98 C3
Parish Rd GU14 .... 77 D4
Park Ave Camberley GU15 ... 36 A2
   Old Basing RG24 .... 70 A3
   Winchester SO23 .... 198 A4
Park Cl Binsted GU10 .... 120 C1
   Kingsley GU35 .... 142 B1
   Oakley RG23 .... 67 D1
   Winchester SO23 .... 176 A1
Park Close Rd GU34 .... 140 A3
Park Corner Rd RG27 .... 52 B4
Park Ct Farnham GU9 .... 99 D2
   1 Winchester SO23 .... 176 A1
Park Dro SO20 .... 125 F2
Park End RG14 .... 1 C2
Park Farm Ind Est GU15 ... 36 A1
Park Gdns RG21 .... 69 E2
Park Hill GU13 .... 74 C3
Park Ho **8** SO23 .... 198 A4
Park House Mews SP9 .... 101 F2
Park House Sch RG14 .... 5 E3
Park La Arborfield RG40 .... 15 F3
   Camberley GU15 .... 36 A3
   Hamstead Marshall RG20 .... 3 F4
   Kings Worthy SO21 .... 176 B3
   Lower Froyle GU34 .... 119 E3
   Newbury RG14 .... 1 C2
   Old Basing RG24 .... 70 A3
   Quarley SP11 .... 103 D2
   Ropley SO24 .... 181 D2
   Silchester RG7 .... 12 A1
Park Pl GU13 .... 74 C3
Park Prewett Hospl RG22 ... 68 B4
Park Prim Sch GU14 .... 100 A4
Park Rd Aldershot GU10 .... 100 A4
   Camberley GU15 .... 36 A2
   Farnborough GU14 .... 77 E4
   Farnham GU9 .... 99 D2
   Sandhurst GU17 .... 35 D4
   South Tidworth SP9 .... 78 C3
   Winchester SO22, SO23 .... 175 F1
Park Row GU9 .... 98 C2
Park St Bordon GU35 .... 164 B2
   Camberley GU15 .... 36 A3
   Newbury RG14 .... 1 C2
Park Terr RG14 .... 1 C2
Park View Beech Hill RG7 ... 13 D3
   Lockerley SO21 .... 191 F2
Park View Schs RG21 .... 68 B1
Park Way RG14 .... 1 C2
Parkfields GU46 .... 34 A3
Parkhill Cl GU47 .... 35 D2
Parkhill Rd GU47 .... 35 D2
Parkhouse Cnr SP9 .... 101 F2
Parkhouse Cross SP9 .... 101 E2
Parkhouse Rd SP9 .... 101 F4
Parkhurst Fields GU10 .... 144 B1
Parkland Gr GU9 .... 99 E4

Parkside GU9 ... 99 D3
Parkside Farm SO24 ... 181 D1
Parkside La SO24 ... 181 D1
Parkside Rd RG21 ... 69 E2
Parkstone Dr GU15 ... 36 A2
Parkstone Rd SO24 ... 181 E4
Parkview Cl SP10 ... 82 C1
Parkway GU15 ... 36 A2
Parkwood Cl RG24 ... 48 C2
Parliament Pl SO22 ... 197 E2
Parmiter Ho 45 SO23 ... 198 A4
Parnell Cl SP10 ... 82 B1
Parnholt Rd GU34 ... 161 F2
Parsonage Cl GU34 ... 161 F2
Parsonage Farm Inf Sch
  GU14 ... 55 D3
Parsonage Way GU15 ... 36 B1
Parsons Cl Arborfield RG40 ... 15 F4
  Fleet GU13 ... 74 C3
  Newbury RG14 ... 1 B1
Parsons Down Schs RG19 ... 2 C1
Parsons Field GU17 ... 34 C4
Parsons La GU26 ... 167 D3
Part La RG7 ... 14 B3
Partridge Ave GU46 ... 33 F3
Partridge Cl
  Barton Stacey SO21 ... 130 B4
  Camberley GU15 ... 36 B1
  Ewshot GU9 ... 98 A4
Partridge Down SO22 ... 197 D2
Partridge Gn GU34 ... 139 F3
Paschal Rd GU15 ... 36 B4
Passfield Ent Ctr GU30 ... 187 D4
Passfield Mill Bsns Pk
  GU30 ... 165 D1
Passfield Rd GU30 ... 165 E1
Pastures The Cheriton SO24 ... 201 E3
  Kings Worthy SO23 ... 154 A1
Paternoster Ho 31 SO23 ... 198 A4
Paternoster Row 30 SO23 ... 198 A4
Paterson Cl RG22 ... 91 E4
Paterson Rd GU34 ... 186 B1
Pathfinders The GU14 ... 55 D2
Patrick's Cl GU33 ... 208 A2
Patrick's Copse Rd GU33 ... 208 A2
Patten Ave GU47 ... 34 A4
Pattinson Cres SP11 ... 105 D4
Paul Cl GU9 ... 99 E4
Paul's Rd GU46 ... 33 D4
Paulet Pl Old Basing RG24 ... 70 A3
  Winchester SO22 ... 197 F3
Pavilion Rd GU11 ... 76 B1
Pavilions End The GU16 ... 36 A2
Paviors GU9 ... 99 D2
Pawley Cl GU10 ... 100 B4
Pax Hill GU34 ... 119 F2
Paxton RG22 ... 91 D4
Paynes Cl Broughton SO20 ... 170 A4
  Headley, Nr Greenham RG20 ... 24 B4
Paynes Hay Rd SO51 ... 194 B1
Paynes La SO20 ... 170 A4
Paynesdown Rd RG19 ... 2 C2
Peabody Rd GU12 ... 77 D4
Peach Gr SP11 ... 124 C3
Peach Tree Cl GU14 ... 55 F4
Peacock Pl 5 SO23 ... 198 A4
Peake Cl RG21 ... 69 F4
Peakfield GU10 ... 144 A4
Pear Tree Cl GU35 ... 164 C2
Pear Tree Ct GU16 ... 36 C4
Pear Tree La Farnham GU10 ... 121 E2
  Newbury RG14 ... 2 A3
Pear Tree Rd GU35 ... 164 C2
Pearl Ho SP11 ... 57 D1
Pearman Dr SP10 ... 106 B4
Peatmoor Cl GU13 ... 53 F1
Peddlars Gr GU46 ... 34 B3
Peel Ave GU16 ... 56 C4
Peel Ct Farnborough GU14 ... 77 D4
  Hartley Wintney RG27 ... 52 B3
Peel Gdns RG20 ... 24 B2
Pegasus Ave GU14 ... 77 E1
Pegasus Cl Linchmere GU27 ... 189 D3
  Thatcham RG19 ... 2 C2
Pegasus Ct
  Farnborough GU16 ... 56 B1
  4 Fleet GU13 ... 53 F1
  Whitchurch RG28 ... 86 B3
Pegasus Rd GU14 ... 55 E4
Pelham Cl Bordon GU35 ... 164 B1
  Old Basing RG24 ... 70 A3
Pelham Pl GU10 ... 121 F2
Pelican La RG14 ... 1 C2
Pelican Rd RG26 ... 10 B1
Pelton Rd RG22 ... 68 C3
Pembroke Bwy GU15 ... 36 A3
Pembroke Ct SP10 ... 106 A4
Pembroke Rd
  Basingstoke RG23 ... 68 A3
  Newbury RG14 ... 1 B2
Pembury Pl GU14 ... 77 D1
Pemerton Rd
  Basingstoke RG21 ... 69 E4
  Winchester SO22 ... 175 E2
Pen Cl SP10 ... 106 B4
Pendennis Cl RG23 ... 68 A3
Pendle Gn SO51 ... 191 F1
Penfold Croft GU11 ... 99 E2
Pengilly Rd GU9 ... 98 C1
Peninsula Rd GU12 ... 197 F4
Peninsula Sq 25 SO22 ... 197 F4
Penn Rd GU11 ... 1 A3
Penn's Yd GU9 ... 98 C1
Pennefather's Rd GU11 ... 76 B2
Pennine Cl RG21 ... 68 A2

Pennine Way
  Basingstoke RG23 ... 68 A2
  Farnborough GU14 ... 55 E4
Pennings Rd SP9 ... 78 C4
Penns Wood GU14 ... 56 A1
Penny La SO20 ... 150 A1
Penny's Hatch RG20 ... 24 C1
Penrhyn Cl GU12 ... 76 C1
Penrith Rd RG21 ... 69 D2
Penrose Cl RG14 ... 1 B3
Penrose Way GU34 ... 160 A1
Penryn Dr GU35 ... 166 A3
Pentangle The RG14 ... 1 C2
Pentland Cl RG23 ... 68 A2
Pentland Pl GU14 ... 55 E4
Penton La SP11 ... 81 F3
Penton Pl 8 SO23 ... 198 A3
Penwith Dr GU27 ... 189 E3
Penwood Hts RG20 ... 21 F4
Penwood Rd RG14 ... 5 D2
Perham Cres SP11 ... 57 D1
Perins Cl SO24 ... 179 D2
Perins Com Sch SO24 ... 179 E3
Periwinkle Cl GU35 ... 165 D3
Perowne St GU11 ... 76 B1
Perring Ave GU14 ... 55 E4
Perry Dr GU13 ... 53 E1
Perry Way GU35 ... 165 E2
Pershore Rd RG24 ... 48 A1
Perth Cl SP9 ... 79 E4
Peshawar Cl SP9 ... 78 B4
Peter Symonds' Coll SO22 ... 175 F1
Peters Cl SP9 ... 101 F4
Petersfield RG22 ... 90 A4
Petersfield Cl RG24 ... 49 D2
Petersfield Ho 6 SP9 ... 78 C3
Petersfield Rd
  Bordon GU35 ... 186 A3
  Cheriton SO24 ... 201 E2
  East Tisted SO24 ... 182 B1
  Greatham GU33 ... 186 A3
  Ropley SO24 ... 181 E2
  Winchester SO21, SO23 ... 198 B4
Petrel Croft RG23 ... 90 C4
Petty's Brook Rd RG24 ... 49 D2
Petunia Cl RG22 ... 91 D4
Petworth Cl
  Basingstoke RG22 ... 91 D3
  Camberley GU15 ... 56 B4
Petworth Ct GU15 ... 36 B2
Pevensey Way GU14 ... 56 C4
Peveral Way RG22 ... 68 B2
Peveral Wlk RG22 ... 68 B2
Pewsey Ho 4 SP9 ... 78 C3
Pheaben's Field RG26 ... 28 C2
Pheasant Cl
  Barton Stacey SO21 ... 130 C4
  Basingstoke RG22 ... 90 C4
  North Tidworth SP9 ... 79 D3
Pheasant Copse GU13 ... 53 F1
Pheasant La RG20 ... 6 B2
Pheby Rd RG22 ... 68 B1
Pheonix Cl RG24 ... 52 A2
Pheonix Terr RG27 ... 52 A2
Philips Ho GU26 ... 166 C2
Phillips Cl GU35 ... 165 E3
Phillips Cres GU35 ... 165 E3
Phoenix Ct
  16 Aldershot GU11 ... 76 C1
  Kingsclere RG20 ... 24 B1
Phoenix Park Terr RG24 ... 69 D3
Phoenix Wlk RG14 ... 5 D3
Pickave La GU34 ... 118 A3
Picket Twenty SP11 ... 106 C4
Picketts Hill GU35 ... 143 D1
Pickford St GU12 ... 76 C1
Picton Rd SP10 ... 106 A3
Pierrefondes Ave GU14 ... 55 F3
Pierrepont Sch GU9 ... 122 B1
Pigeon Cl RG26 ... 29 D1
Pigeons Farm Rd RG19 ... 6 B4
Pike St RG14 ... 1 C2
Pilcot Rd GU13 ... 74 B3
Pilgrims Cl GU10 ... 121 F4
Pilgrims Gate SO22 ... 175 F1
Pilgrims Sch The SO23 ... 198 B4
Pilgrims Way Andover SP10 ... 83 E1
  Headley GU35 ... 165 E3
Pilgrims Way
  Cty Prim Sch The GU10 ... 121 F4
Pimpernel Way RG14 ... 69 F4
Pinchington La RG14 ... 5 F4
Pindar Pl RG14 ... 2 B3
Pine Ave GU15 ... 36 A2
Pine Bank GU26 ... 167 E2
Pine Cl Middle Wallop SO20 ... 126 A2
  Sandhurst GU47 ... 35 E4
  South Wonston SO21 ... 153 F2
  Winchester SO21, SO22 ... 197 D2
Pine Cotts GU33 ... 208 A4
Pine Dr Blackwater GU17 ... 35 E2
  Mortimer RG7 ... 11 E3
  Wokingham RG40 ... 16 C4
Pine Gr GU10 ... 122 B3
Pine Grove GU13 ... 75 D3
Pine Mount Rd GU15 ... 36 A2
Pine Rd GU34 ... 160 B2
Pine Ridge RG14 ... 2 A3
Pine Ridge Dr GU10 ... 122 A3
Pine View GU35 ... 166 A3
Pine View Cl GU9 ... 99 F3
Pine Wlk Andover SP10 ... 105 E3
  Liss GU33 ... 208 A3
Pinehill Rd GU35 ... 164 B1
Pinehill Rise GU17 ... 35 D4
Pinehurst RG26 ... 26 C4
Pinehurst Ave GU14 ... 55 F1

Pinehurst Cotts GU14 ... 55 F1
Pines Rd Fleet GU13 ... 53 F1
  Liphook GU30 ... 187 E2
Pines The Andover SP10 ... 105 F4
  Camberley GU15 ... 36 B4
Pinetree Ho 6 SP9 ... 79 D4
Pineview GU14 ... 55 F2
Pinewood Cl Baughurst RG26 ... 9 D1
  Sandhurst GU47 ... 34 B4
Pinewood Cres GU13 ... 55 D3
Pinewood Cl 1 GU13 ... 54 A1
Pinewood Hill GU13 ... 54 A1
Pinewood Inf Sch GU14 ... 55 D4
Pinewood Pk GU14 ... 55 D4
Pinkerton Rd RG22 ... 68 B1
Pinks La RG26 ... 9 E1
Pinnell Cl RG22 ... 91 D3
Pipers Croft GU13 ... 75 D2
Pipers Patch 1 GU14 ... 55 F2
Pipit Cl RG19 ... 2 C2
Pipsons Cl GU46 ... 34 A3
Pirbright Rd GU16 ... 56 A2
Pitcairn Cl RG24 ... 48 B1
Pitfield La RG7 ... 12 A2
Pitfold Ave GU27 ... 189 D3
Pitfold Cl GU27 ... 189 E3
Pither Rd RG29 ... 95 E4
Pitman Cl RG22 ... 68 A1
Pitt Hall Cotts RG26 ... 45 F3
Pitt Rdbt SO22 ... 197 D3
Pitt Way GU14 ... 55 E3
Pittard Rd RG22 ... 68 C2
Pitter Cl SO22 ... 175 D3
Pitts La SO22 ... 106 A3
Place Ct GU11 ... 100 A4
Plantation Andover SP10 ... 105 F4
  Hill Brow GU33 ... 208 A1
  South Warnborough SP9 ... 78 C3
  Tadley RG7 ... 9 E1
Plantation Row GU15 ... 35 F3
Plantation The RG24 ... 49 E4
Plantation Way GU35 ... 186 A4
Plassey Rd SP9 ... 78 C4
Pleasant Hill RG26 ... 26 C4
Plough Gdns SO20 ... 170 A3
Plough La RG27 ... 31 F3
Plough Rd GU46 ... 34 B4
Plough Way SO22 ... 197 E2
Plover Cl
  Andover SP10 ... 83 D1
  Basingstoke RG22 ... 68 A1
Plover La RG27 ... 15 E1
Plovers Down SO22 ... 197 D2
Plovers Way GU34 ... 140 A3
Plumer Rd GU33 ... 186 B2
Plumpton Rd RG14 ... 2 A1
Plumpton Way GU34 ... 139 F1
Poachers Field RG29 ... 95 D2
Pococks La GU33 ... 206 C4
Poets Way SO22 ... 197 E4
Poland La RG29 ... 72 C3
Polden Cl GU14 ... 55 E4
Polecat Cnr RG24 ... 70 A1
Police Hos GU35 ... 164 B1
Polkerris Way GU13 ... 75 E2
Pollards The GU14 ... 120 A2
Pollen's Almhouses SP10 ... 106 A4
Polmear Cl GU13 ... 75 E2
Pond Cl Newbury RG14 ... 5 D4
  Overton RG25 ... 88 A3
Pond Croft GU46 ... 34 B3
Pond La Churt GU10 ... 144 A2
  Headley GU10 ... 144 A2
Pond Rd
  Bramley RG26 ... 29 D1
  Headley GU35 ... 165 F2
Pondtail Cl GU13 ... 75 E4
Pondtail Gdns GU13 ... 75 E4
Pondtail Rd GU13 ... 75 E4
Pool Rd
  Aldershot GU10 ... 100 A4
  Hartley Wintney RG27 ... 52 B2
Poors Farm Rd RG24 ... 70 C4
Popes Hill RG20 ... 24 B1
Popham La RG25 ... 112 C4
Poplar Cl
  Baughurst RG26 ... 26 A4
  Mytchett GU16 ... 56 C2
  Sherfield on Loddon RG26 ... 29 E1
Poplar Cotts GU16 ... 56 B3
Poplar Path SO20 ... 126 A2
Poplar Pl RG14 ... 1 C3
Poplar Wlk GU14 ... 99 D4
Poplars Cl GU34 ... 55 D3
Poppy Fields RG24 ... 70 A4
Poppyhills Rd GU15 ... 36 B4
Porchester Rd RG14 ... 1 C1
Porchester Sq 16 RG21 ... 69 D3
Port La SO21 ... 196 C1
Portacre Rise RG22 ... 68 C2
Portal Cl SP10 ... 105 D4
Portal Rd SO23 ... 198 A3
Portchester Cl SP10 ... 82 B2
Porter Cl RG29 ... 95 E4
Porter End RG14 ... 5 F4
Porter Rd RG21 ... 68 C1
Porters Cl
  Andover SP10 ... 82 B1
  Dummer RG22 ... 90 B1
Portesbery Hill Dr GU15 ... 36 A4
Portesbery Rd GU15 ... 36 B3
Portesbery Sch GU15 ... 36 A3
Portiswood Cl RG26 ... 27 D1
Portland Dr GU13 ... 75 D2
Portland Gr SP10 ... 106 A4
Portland Sq 5 GU33 ... 207 F2
Portsmouth Cres RG22 ... 68 B1
Portsmouth Ho 10 SP9 ... 78 C3

Portsmouth Rd
  Bramshott GU26 ... 167 D1
  Camberley GU15 ... 36 B2
  Grayshott GU26 ... 167 D1
  Haslemere GU26 ... 167 D1
  Liphook GU30 ... 187 F1
Portsmouth Way RG21 ... 68 B1
Portsmouth Wlk RG21 ... 68 B1
Portway Baughurst RG26 ... 9 E1
  Riseley RG7 ... 14 A1
Portway Cl SP10 ... 105 E4
Portway Cty Inf Sch SP10 ... 105 E4
Portway Ind Est SP10 ... 82 A1
Portway Jun Sch SP10 ... 105 E4
Portway Pl RG22 ... 68 A3
Post Office La RG22 ... 90 B1
Posting House Mews RG14 ... 1 B2
Pot La RG24 ... 70 C4
Potbridge Rd RG27 ... 72 C4
Potley Hill Prim Sch GU47 ... 34 C3
Potter's Cross SP9 ... 101 F2
Potter's Wlk 11 RG21 ... 69 D3
Potteries La RG24 ... 56 B2
Potteries The GU14 ... 55 D3
Potters Cres GU12 ... 77 F1
Potters Field GU33 ... 208 A2
Potters Gate GU9 ... 98 C1
Potters Gate CE Prim Sch
  GU9 ... 98 C1
Potters Ind Pk GU13 ... 75 E3
Potters La RG26 ... 29 F2
Pottery Ct GU9 ... 121 E3
Pottery La GU11 ... 121 E3
Poulters Cl RG25 ... 88 A4
Poultons Rd RG25 ... 88 A4
Pound Cl Bramley RG26 ... 28 C2
  Headley GU35 ... 165 E3
  Over Wallop SO20 ... 125 E1
  Upper Wield SO24 ... 137 D1
  Yateley GU17, GU46 ... 34 B3
Pound Gate GU34 ... 140 A3
Pound Hill SO24 ... 179 E3
Pound La Burghclere RG20 ... 22 B3
  Newbury RG14 ... 1 A2
  Thatcham RG19 ... 2 C2
Pound Meadow
  Sherfield on Loddon RG24 ... 49 F4
  Whitchurch RG28 ... 86 B3
Pound Rd 8 Aldershot GU12 ... 77 D1
  Kings Worthy SO23 ... 176 B3
  Over Wallop SO20 ... 125 E1
  Overton RG25 ... 88 A4
Pound St RG14 ... 1 B1
Poveys Mead RG20 ... 24 C1
Poyle Rd GU10 ... 100 C3
Poynings Cres RG24 ... 69 E1
Poynters Cl SP10 ... 82 C1
Poyntz Rd RG25 ... 88 A4
Pragnells Cotts SP5 ... 169 D1
Prentice Cl GU14 ... 55 F4
Prescelly Cl RG22 ... 68 A2
Preston Candover
  CE Prim Sch RG25 ... 136 A4
Preston Rd RG14 ... 2 A2
Pretoria Cl GU33 ... 186 B1
Pretoria Rd SP11 ... 57 D1
Preymead Ind Est GU9 ... 99 F4
Priestley Way RG14 ... 1 A1
Priestly Rd Basingstoke RG22 ... 68 C4
  Sherborne St John RG23 ... 68 C4
Primrose Ct SP11 ... 105 E3
Primrose Dr RG27 ... 52 B4
Primrose Gdns
  Basingstoke RG22 ... 91 D3
  Farnborough GU14 ... 55 E2
Primrose La GU33 ... 208 B2
Primrose Wlk 3 Fleet GU13 ... 53 F1
  Yateley GU46 ... 33 F3
Primula Rd GU33 ... 164 C2
Prince Albert Gdns 17
  SP10 ... 106 A4
Prince Charles Cres GU16 ... 56 A4
Prince Cl SP10 ... 83 E1
Prince Hold Rd RG19 ... 2 E2
Prince of Wales Wlk GU15 ... 36 A3
Prince's Ave GU11 ... 77 D3
Prince's Bldgs 10 SO23 ... 198 A4
Prince's Mead Sch SO22 ... 197 F3
Princes Cl GU35 ... 164 B1
Princes' Cres RG22 ... 68 C2
Princes Ct 15 SP9 ... 78 C4
Princes Mead GU14 ... 55 F2
Princes Pl SO22 ... 197 F3
Princes Way GU11 ... 76 C1
Princess Ct 7 SO23 ... 198 A4
Princess Dr GU34 ... 139 E2
Princess Marina Dr RG27 ... 15 E4
Princess Way GU15 ... 36 A3
Prinstead Cl 7 SO23 ... 198 A3
Prior Croft Cl GU15, GU16 ... 36 C2
Prior End GU15 ... 36 C3
Prior Heath Inf Sch GU15 ... 36 C3
Prior Place Cross Roads
  GU15 ... 36 C2
Prior Rd GU15 ... 36 C2
Prior's La GU17 ... 34 C3
Priors Barton SO23 ... 197 F3
Priors Cl Farnborough GU14 ... 55 F4
  Kingsclere RG20 ... 24 B1
Priors Dean Rd SO22 ... 175 E2
Priors Keep GU13 ... 75 D4
Priors Rd RG26 ... 9 F1
Priors Row RG26 ... 72 B2
Priors Way SO22 ... 197 D2
Priors Way The SO24 ... 182 A1
Priors Wood GU27 ... 189 E3

Priory Cl GU13 ... 74 B4
Priory Croft GU10 ... 122 A4
Priory Ct GU17 ... 35 E3
Priory Gdns RG24 ... 70 A4
Priory La Frensham GU10 ... 144 B4
  Hartley Wintney RG27 ... 52 B2
Priory Prim Sch The RG26 ... 27 D1
Priory Rd RG14 ... 1 C1
Priory St GU14 ... 56 A2
Privet La SP11 ... 80 C3
Privet Rd GU35 ... 165 D3
Privett Cl RG24 ... 70 A4
Privett Rd GU32 ... 205 F1
Prospect Ave GU14 ... 55 F3
Prospect Cott GU12 ... 77 F2
Prospect Hill GU35 ... 165 E4
Prospect Pl RG14 ... 1 C1
Prospect Rd Ash GU11 ... 77 F3
  Farnborough GU14 ... 55 F3
  Farnham GU10 ... 121 E2
  New Alresford SO24 ... 179 E2
Providence Pl 3 GU9 ... 99 D1
Pruetts La GU33 ... 207 F1
Puckridge Hill Rd GU11 ... 76 B3
Pudding La SO23 ... 176 A3
Puffers Way RG14 ... 1 B1
Pug's Hole SP5 ... 191 D3
Punshott La SO24 ... 203 F3
Purbrook Rd RG26 ... 26 C4
Purcell Cl GU9 ... 68 C1
Purley Way GU16 ... 56 B4
Purmerend Cl GU14 ... 55 D3
Puttenham Rd
  Chineham RG24 ... 49 D2
  Seale GU11 ... 100 C2
Puttock Cl GU27 ... 189 D3
Pyestock Cres GU14 ... 55 D2
Pyle Hill RG14 ... 1 C1
Pyotts Copse RG24 ... 49 D1
Pyotts Ct RG24 ... 49 D1
Pyotts Hill Chineham RG24 ... 49 D1
  Old Basing RG24 ... 70 A4

Quadrant The GU12 ... 77 F2
Quantock Cl RG22 ... 68 A2
Quarry La GU46 ... 34 B3
Quarry Rd SO23 ... 198 B4
Quarters Rd GU14 ... 56 A1
Quebec Gdns GU47 ... 35 D2
Queen Anne's Wlk 7 RG21 ... 69 D3
Queen Elizabeth Dr GU11 ... 76 B1
Queen Mary Ave
  Basingstoke RG22 ... 69 D3
  Camberley GU15 ... 35 F3
Queen Mary Cl GU13 ... 53 F2
Queen Mary's Coll RG21 ... 69 D2
Queen St GU12 ... 77 D1
Queen Victoria Cross Roads
  GU15 ... 35 F3
Queen Victoria Ct GU14 ... 55 F3
Queen's Ave Aldershot GU11 ... 76 C3
  Farnborough GU11 ... 76 C3
Queen's Cl GU11 ... 76 C4
Queen's Ct GU12 ... 77 D4
Queen's Par RG24 ... 69 D2
Queen's Rd Basingstoke RG22 ... 68 C3
  Newbury RG14 ... 1 C1
  Winchester SO22 ... 197 E4
Queen's Rdbt GU11 ... 76 C4
Queen's St RG22 ... 68 C3
Queens Ave SP10 ... 106 A4
Queens Cotts SP11 ... 61 F1
Queens Ct RG21 ... 1 C1
Queens Keep GU15 ... 36 A3
Queens La GU9 ... 98 C4
Queens Mead SO22 ... 197 E3
Queens Rd
  Aldershot GU11 ... 76 B1
  Alton GU34 ... 139 F1
  Bordon GU30 ... 187 D2
  Camberley GU17 ... 35 F2
  Farnborough GU12 ... 77 D4
  Farnham GU9 ... 99 D3
  Fleet GU13 ... 75 D4
  Kingsclere RG20 ... 24 C1
  North Warnborough RG29 ... 72 B2
  Whitchurch RG28 ... 86 B2
Queensberry Pl GU15 ... 35 D2
Queensfield RG25 ... 90 B1
Queensmead GU14 ... 55 F2
Queensway Andover SP10 ... 83 E1
  Camberley GU14 ... 56 C4
Queenwood Rd SO20 ... 170 A3
Queenwood Rise SO20 ... 170 A3
Quennells Hill GU10 ... 121 E3
Quilter Rd RG22 ... 68 B1
Quince Tree Way RG27 ... 51 D1
Quinneys GU16 ... 56 A1

R.E.M.E. Mus RG40 ... 15 F4
Race Course Rd RG14 ... 1 C1
Race Course Sta RG14 ... 2 A1
Racedown Cotts SP11 ... 102 C3
Raceview Bsns Ctr RG14 ... 1 C1
Rack Cl SP10 ... 106 A4
Rack Close Rd GU34 ... 139 F2
Rack & Manger Cotts
  SO21 ... 174 A3
Rackfield GU27 ... 189 D4
Rackstraw Rd GU47 ... 35 D4
Radcliffe Cl GU16 ... 56 C4
Radford Cl GU9 ... 99 E3
Radford Gdns RG21 ... 68 C3
Radical Rde RG40 ... 16 B4
Raeburn Cl SO24 ... 201 E3
Raeburn Way GU15 ... 35 D3
Raghill RG26 ... 10 A3

Raglan Cl Aldershot GU12 ...... 77 D1
Camberley GU16 ...... 56 C4
Raglan Ct RG22 ...... 91 E4
Ragmore La GU32 ...... 205 F3
Railway Cotts GU34 ...... 204 B3
Railway Rd Bordon GU33 ...... 186 B2
Newbury RG14 ...... 1 C1
Rainbow Cl GU12 ...... 70 B3
Rainham Cl RG25 ...... 90 C4
Rake Bsns Pk GU33 ...... 208 C2
Rake CE Prim Sch GU33 ...... 208 C3
Rake Rd GU33 ...... 208 A2
Rakemakers GU34 ...... 140 B4
Ramillis Cl GU12 ...... 77 E4
Ramparts The SP10 ...... 105 F3
Rampton Rd RG28 ...... 86 B2
Ramptons La RG26 ...... 10 C3
Ramptons Meadow RG26 ...... 27 D4
Ramridge Ho SP11 ...... 81 E2
Ramsay Rd SO23 ...... 176 B4
Ramsdell Cl RG26 ...... 26 C4
Ramsdell Rd Baughurst RG26 ...... 25 E1
Pamber End RG26 ...... 27 D1
Ramsey Cl GU15 ...... 36 C4
Ramsholt Cl RG25 ...... 89 F1
Rances Way SO22 ...... 197 F3
Randell Cl GU14 ...... 35 E1
Randolph Dr GU14 ...... 55 D2
Range Rd RG40 ...... 16 C4
Range Ride GU15 ...... 35 E4
Range View GU47 ...... 35 E4
Rank The Fyfield SP11 ...... 80 C1
Hurstbourne Tarrant SP11 ...... 60 C4
Penton Grafton SP11 ...... 81 E1
Rankine Cl GU9 ...... 99 F3
Rankine Rd RG21 ...... 69 E4
Rapallo Cl GU14 ...... 56 A2
Raphael Cl RG21 ...... 69 E2
Rapley Cl GU15 ...... 36 B4
Ratcliffe Rd GU14 ...... 55 E4
Rathbone Rd SP11 ...... 108 B1
Ravel Cl RG22 ...... 68 C1
Ravelin Cl GU10 ...... 97 E3
Raven Cl North Tidworth SP9 ...... 78 C3
15 Yateley GU46 ...... 33 F3
Raven Rd RG27 ...... 51 D1
Raven Sq GU34 ...... 139 F3
Ravens Wood Dr GU15 ...... 36 C3
Ravenscote Jun Sch GU15 ...... 36 C2
Ravenscroft RG27 ...... 51 D1
Rawdon Rise GU15 ...... 36 C3
Rawlings Rd RG29 ...... 72 A4
Rawlinson Rd GU17 ...... 35 F3
Rayleigh Rd RG21 ...... 69 D3
Read's Field GU34 ...... 160 A1
Reading Rd
Basingstoke RG24 ...... 48 B1
Blackwater GU17 ...... 34 B3
Chineham RG24 ...... 48 C1
Eversley GU17 ...... 34 B3
Farley Hill RG40 ...... 15 E2
Farnborough GU16 ...... 56 A1
Hook RG27 ...... 51 D3
Mattingley RG27 ...... 51 D3
Sherfield on Loddon RG24 ...... 49 E4
Yateley GU46 ...... 34 B3
Reading Rd N GU13 ...... 53 F1
Reading Rd S GU13 ...... 75 D3
Rebecca Cl GU13 ...... 74 C2
Recreation Rd
Andover SP10 ...... 106 A4
Farnham GU10 ...... 121 E2
Odiham RG29 ...... 72 B1
Rectory Cl Newbury RG14 ...... 1 B1
Sandhurst GU47 ...... 34 B4
Tadley RG26 ...... 27 D3
Rectory Cotts RG25 ...... 92 A4
Rectory Hill West Dean SP5 ...... 190 B2
West Tytherley SP5 ...... 169 A1
Rectory La Bentley GU10 ...... 120 A2
Bramshott GU30 ...... 188 A4
Broughton SO20 ...... 170 A4
Itchen Abbas SO21 ...... 178 A4
Kingsclere RG20 ...... 45 D4
Rectory Pl SP11 ...... 81 E1
Rectory Rd
Farnborough GU16 ...... 56 A2
Hook RG27 ...... 72 A4
Oakley RG23 ...... 66 C1
Padworth RG7 ...... 10 B4
Reculver Way SP10 ...... 82 B2
Red Hill Ashmansworth RG20 ...... 41 D4
Mattingley RG27 ...... 31 F1
Medstead GU34 ...... 160 A3
Red Lane Rd RG26 ...... 10 A3
Bradley RG25 ...... 115 E2
Headley GU35 ...... 165 F4
West Tytherley SP5 ...... 191 D4
Red Lion La
15 Basingstoke RG24 ...... 69 D2
Farnham GU9 ...... 98 C1
Overton RG25 ...... 88 A4
Red Oaks GU10 ...... 121 D2
Red Post La
Abbotts Ann SP11 ...... 104 C4
Monxton SP11 ...... 104 C4
Penton Grafton SP11 ...... 104 C4
Red Rice Rd SP10 ...... 105 E1
Redan Gdns 1 GU14 ...... 77 D1
Redan Hill Est GU14 ...... 77 D1
Redan Rd GU12 ...... 77 D1
Redbridge Dr SP10 ...... 105 F3
Redbridge La
Old Basing RG24 ...... 69 F3
Ropley SO24 ...... 182 A2
Redcrest Gdns GU15 ...... 36 B3
Rede Ct 4 GU14 ...... 56 A1

Redenham Dro SP11 ...... 81 D4
Redfield Ct RG14 ...... 2 A2
Redfields Cl GU13 ...... 74 C1
Redfields Pk GU13 ...... 74 C1
Redgrave Ct GU12 ...... 77 E1
Redhearne Fields GU10 ...... 144 B1
Redhouse Mews GU30 ...... 188 A1
Redlands La GU10 ...... 97 F4
Redlane Hill RG7 ...... 10 A3
Redon Way SP10 ...... 82 C1
Redvers Buller Rd GU12 ...... 77 D4
Redwoods Way GU13 ...... 75 D3
Reed Cl GU12 ...... 77 D3
Reed Wlk RG14 ...... 2 A2
Reeds La Liss GU33 ...... 208 B3
Rake GU33 ...... 208 B3
Reeds Rd The
Frensham GU10 ...... 122 B2
Tilford GU10 ...... 122 B2
Rees Rd GU12 ...... 77 D1
Reeves Rd GU12 ...... 77 D1
Regent Cl GU13 ...... 75 D4
Regent Ct Fleet GU13 ...... 74 C4
17 Winchester SO23 ...... 176 A1
Regent St GU13 ...... 75 D4
Regent Way GU16 ...... 36 C1
Regents Ct Andover SP10 ...... 83 F1
Newbury RG14 ...... 1 B2
Regents Pl GU15 ...... 35 D4
Regiment Cl GU14 ...... 55 D2
Regnum Dr RG14 ...... 1 C3
Reith Way SP10 ...... 82 A1
Rembrandt Cl RG21 ...... 69 E2
Remembrance Gdns RG24 ...... 48 C1
Remembrance Rd RG14 ...... 1 B1
Renoir Cl RG25 ...... 69 E2
Renown Way RG24 ...... 48 C2
Restormel Ct RG22 ...... 68 A3
Reubens Cres RG26 ...... 26 C4
Revelstoke Ave GU14 ...... 55 F3
Rewlands Dr RG29 ...... 175 E2
Rex Ct GU27 ...... 189 E3
Reynards Ct RG21 ...... 26 C4
Reynolds Cl RG24 ...... 69 F2
Reynolds Ct SP10 ...... 82 C1
Reynolds Gn GU47 ...... 35 D3
Reynolds Ho RG21 ...... 68 B1
Reyntiens View RG29 ...... 72 C1
Rhine Banks GU14 ...... 55 D3
Rhodes Sq SP10 ...... 83 E2
Rhododendron Rd GU14 ...... 56 C4
Ribble 5 SP10 ...... 83 E1
Ribble Pl GU14 ...... 55 E4
Ribble Way 14 RG21 ...... 69 E3
Richard Aldworth
Com Sch The RG22 ...... 68 B1
Richard Cl GU13 ...... 74 C4
Richard Moss Ho 6 SO23 ...... 198 A4
Richards Cl GU11 ...... 77 F3
Richborough Dr SP10 ...... 82 B2
Richmond Cl Bordon GU35 ...... 164 B1
Camberley GU15 ...... 36 B1
Farnborough GU14 ...... 55 D2
Fleet GU13 ...... 74 C3
Richmond Ho GU47 ...... 35 E4
Richmond Rd
Basingstoke RG21 ...... 69 D3
Sandhurst GU47 ...... 35 E4
Riddings La RG7 ...... 8 A1
Rideway Cl GU15 ...... 35 F2
Ridge Cl RG22 ...... 91 E3
Ridge La Hook RG27 ...... 50 C1
Newnham RG27 ...... 50 C1
Ridgemoor Cl RG26 ...... 167 E3
Ridges View SP10 ...... 83 E4
Ridgeway Par GU13 ...... 75 D3
Ridgeway The GU34 ...... 139 F1
Ridgeway Sch GU10 ...... 122 A4
Ridgway Hill Rd GU9 ...... 122 A4
Ridgway Rd GU9 ...... 122 A4
Ridings The Camberley GU15 ...... 36 C2
Liss GU33 ...... 208 A2
Ridley Cl GU13 ...... 74 C4
Ridleys Piece RG29 ...... 95 D2
Rifle Way GU14 ...... 55 D2
Riley La RG24 ...... 70 A4
Rimbault Cl GU11 ...... 77 D4
Rimes's La RG26 ...... 26 B3
Ringlet Way 6 SO23 ...... 198 B4
Ringshall Gdns RG26 ...... 28 C2
Ringway Ctr The RG23 ...... 68 C4
Ringway E RG21 ...... 69 E3
Ringway N RG21 ...... 69 D4
Ringway S RG21 ...... 69 E2
Ringway W RG22 ...... 68 C3
Ringwood Rd
Blackwater GU17 ...... 35 D3
Farnborough GU14 ...... 56 A4
Ripon Rd GU46 ...... 34 B1
Ripplesmore Cl GU17, GU46 ...... 34 C4
Rise The RG27 ...... 15 F1
River Cl GU34 ...... 160 A1
River Ho 59 SP10 ...... 83 E1
River La GU10 ...... 121 E4
River Park L Ctr SO23 ...... 176 A1
River Pk RG14 ...... 1 C2
River Rd GU46 ...... 33 F4
River Row Cotts GU10 ...... 121 E4
River View SP11 ...... 128 C2
River View Cotts GU34 ...... 140 A2
River Way GU10 ...... 83 E1
Riverdale GU14 ...... 121 E4
Riverhead GU24 ...... 180 B2
Rivermead Ho GU47 ...... 34 B4
Rivermead Rd GU47 ...... 35 F1

Rivermede GU35 ...... 164 C2
Rivers Cl GU14 ...... 56 B1
Riverside Bsns Pk GU9 ...... 99 D2
Riverside Cl
Farnborough GU14 ...... 55 E3
Liss GU33 ...... 207 F2
Old Basing RG24 ...... 70 A4
Overton RG25 ...... 88 A4
Riverside Ct GU9 ...... 99 D2
Riverside Gn SO20 ...... 172 A2
Riverside Rd GU14 ...... 55 E3
Riverside 44 SO23 ...... 198 A4
Riverside Ind Pk GU9 ...... 99 D2
Riverside Rd GU15 ...... 165 C1
Riverside Way GU15 ...... 35 F2
Riverway Ind Est GU34 ...... 140 A2
Robert May's Sch RG29 ...... 72 B2
Robert Mays Rd RG29 ...... 72 B1
Robert Sandilands
Cty Prim Sch RG14 ...... 1 B2
Robert Way GU16 ...... 56 B2
Roberts Cl SO23 ...... 154 A1
Roberts Rd Aldershot GU12 ...... 77 D1
Barton Stacey SO21 ...... 130 C4
Bordon GU35 ...... 186 B1
Camberley GU15 ...... 35 F3
Sandhurst GU17 ...... 35 F3
Robertsfield RG19 ...... 2 B2
Robertson Rd SO24 ...... 179 E2
Robertson Way GU12 ...... 77 E1
Robin Cl Ash GU11 ...... 77 F3
Basingstoke RG22 ...... 91 D4
Robin Hill Dr GU16 ...... 36 C2
Robin Hood Cl GU14 ...... 55 F4
Robin La Bishop's Green RG19 ...... 6 B2
Sandhurst GU47 ...... 34 C4
Robin Way SP11 ...... 83 D1
Robin's Bow GU15 ...... 35 F2
Robins Cl RG14 ...... 5 E4
Robins Grove Cr GU46 ...... 33 F3
Robinson Way GU35 ...... 164 C1
Rochester Cl RG22 ...... 91 D4
Rochester Gr GU13 ...... 75 D4
Rochford Rd RG21 ...... 69 D3
Rock Gdns GU11 ...... 76 B1
Rock La GU10 ...... 121 F3
Rockbourne Rd SO22 ...... 175 E2
Rockdale Dr GU26 ...... 167 D2
Rockdale Ho GU26 ...... 167 D2
Rockery The GU14 ...... 55 E2
Rockfield Way GU15 ...... 35 D4
Rockingham Rd RG14 ...... 1 B1
Rockmoor La SN8 ...... 18 B1
Rockpit Cotts GU33 ...... 208 A2
Rodfield La SO24 ...... 200 B3
Roding Ct 1 RG21 ...... 69 E3
Rodney Ct SP10 ...... 83 E1
Roe Downs Rd GU34 ...... 160 A3
Roebucks Cl RG14 ...... 5 E4
Roedeer Copse GU27 ...... 189 E3
Roentgen Rd RG24 ...... 69 F4
Roke La RG29 ...... 96 A4
Rokeby Cl RG14 ...... 5 F4
Rokes Pl GU46 ...... 33 F3
Roman Cl RG14 ...... 1 C1
Romans Bsns Pk GU9 ...... 99 D2
Romans Field RG7 ...... 10 C1
Romans Gate GU9 ...... 10 B1
Romans Ind Pk GU9 ...... 99 D2
Romans' Rd 1 SO23 ...... 198 A3
Romayne Cl GU14 ...... 55 F3
Romley Ct GU9 ...... 99 D1
Romsey Cl Aldershot GU10 ...... 100 A3
Basingstoke RG24 ...... 48 A1
Blackwater GU17 ...... 35 D3
Romsey Rd Broughton SO20 ...... 170 A3
King's Somborne SO20 ...... 171 F1
Nether Wallop SO20 ...... 147 F3
Wherwell SP11 ...... 128 B3
Winchester SO22, SO23 ...... 197 E3
Ronald Bowker Ct 1 SO21 ...... 197 F4
Rook La SO21 ...... 133 D2
Rookery Cotts SP5 ...... 190 B2
Rookery Ct RG40 ...... 15 F3
Rookery La SO20 ...... 170 B3
Rookery The RG28 ...... 86 B3
Rooks Down Rd SO22 ...... 197 E3
Rooksbury Rd SP10 ...... 105 F3
Rooksdown Ave RG22 ...... 68 B4
Rooksdown La RG26 ...... 47 E1
Rooksfield RG14 ...... 6 C1
Rookswood Cl RG27 ...... 51 D1
Rookwood Cl GU34 ...... 159 E1
Rookwood Sch SP11 ...... 105 F4
Room Cotts SO20 ...... 129 D3
Ropley CE Prim Sch SO24 ...... 181 E2
Ropley Cl RG26 ...... 26 C4
Ropley Rd GU34 ...... 183 D2
Rorkes Drift GU34 ...... 56 C2
Rosary Gdns GU47 ...... 34 A3
Rose Cl RG22 ...... 91 D4
Rose Cotts GU14 ...... 77 D1
Rose Gdns GU14 ...... 55 E2
Rose Hodson Pl RG23 ...... 68 B4
Rose Wlk GU14 ...... 53 F1
Rosebank Cl RG26 ...... 26 C4
Rosebay Gdns RG27 ...... 51 E1
Roseberry Cl RG22 ...... 91 D3
Rosebery Rd SO24 ...... 179 E2

Rosedale GU12 ...... 77 D1
Rosedene Gdns GU13 ...... 53 F1
Rosedene La GU35 ...... 35 A4
Roseship Way RG21 ...... 69 E4
Rosemary Ave GU12 ...... 77 F4
Rosemary Cl GU12 ...... 55 D2
Rosemary Gdns GU47 ...... 35 D3
Rosemary La
Blackwater GU17 ...... 35 D3
Farnham GU10 ...... 121 E2
Rosemary Terr RG14 ...... 1 B1
Rosetree Cotts GU34 ...... 140 A2
Rosewarne Ct 28 SO23 ...... 176 A1
Rosewood GU14 ...... 56 C2
Rosewood Ct 4 SP9 ...... 79 D4
Rosewood Rd GU35 ...... 165 D3
Ross Cl RG21 ...... 69 D1
Ross Terr RG14 ...... 1 B1
Rossini Cl RG22 ...... 91 F4
Rossmore Gdns GU11 ...... 76 B1
Rothay Ct 15 RG24 ...... 69 E3
Rother Cl GU47 ...... 35 D4
Rother Ho GU33 ...... 207 F2
Rother Rd GU14 ...... 55 E4
Rotherbank Farm La GU33 ...... 208 A3
Rotherwick Ct GU12 ...... 77 D4
Rotherwick La RG27 ...... 50 B4
Rotherwick Rd RG26 ...... 26 C4
Rotten Green Rd GU13 ...... 53 F3
Rotten Hill RG25 ...... 87 F3
Rotunda Est The 18 GU11 ...... 76 C1
Round End RG14 ...... 5 D3
Roundabouts The GU33 ...... 208 A3
Roundaway La SP11 ...... 58 C2
Roundhuts Rise 4 SO23 ...... 198 B4
Roundmead Rd GU24 ...... 69 D2
Roundway Ct SP10 ...... 105 F4
Rounton Rd GU13 ...... 75 D3
Row The SO21 ...... 177 F3
Rowan Chase GU10 ...... 121 F3
Rowan Cl Camberley GU16 ...... 36 A4
Fleet GU13 ...... 54 B1
South Wonston SO21 ...... 153 F2
Tadley RG26 ...... 27 D4
Rowan Ct 8 SP9 ...... 78 C4
Rowan Dale GU13 ...... 74 C3
Rowan Dr RG14 ...... 1 C3
Rowan Rd RG26 ...... 27 D4
Rowan Tree Cl GU33 ...... 208 A2
Rowans The Andover SP10 ...... 82 C1
Grayshott GU26 ...... 167 D1
Rowanside Cl GU33 ...... 166 A2
Rowanwood RG40 ...... 15 F3
Rowcroft Cl GU12 ...... 77 F3
Rowcroft Rd RG2 ...... 15 E4
Rowdell Cotts SO24 ...... 181 E3
Rowhill Ave GU11 ...... 99 E4
Rowhill Cres GU11 ...... 99 E4
Rowhills GU11 ...... 99 E4
Rowhills Cl GU11 ...... 99 E4
Rowland's Cl RG7 ...... 11 D3
Rowledge CE Prim Sch
GU10 ...... 121 E2
Rowlings Rd SO22 ...... 175 E2
Roxburghe Cl GU35 ...... 164 B1
Royal Cl RG21 ...... 91 D3
Royal Greenjackets Mus The
SO22 ...... 197 F4
Royal Hampshire
County Hospl SO22 ...... 197 E4
Royal Hampshire Regiment
Mus SO22 ...... 197 F4
Royal Military Academy Hospl
GU17 ...... 35 E4
Royal Naval Sch GU26 ...... 167 F1
Royal Par GU26 ...... 167 E2
Royale Cl GU10 ...... 100 A4
Royce Cl SP10 ...... 82 A1
Roycroft La RG40 ...... 16 B4
Roydon Cl GU12 ...... 197 F3
Rozeldene GU26 ...... 167 E2
Rozelle Cl GU34 ...... 175 D3
Rubens Cl RG21 ...... 69 E1
Rucstall Prim Sch RG21 ...... 69 E2
Rudd Hall Rise GU16 ...... 36 A2
Ruffield Cl SO22 ...... 175 E1
Rufford Cl GU13 ...... 75 D3
Runfold-St George GU9 ...... 99 F3
Runnymede Ct 1 GU14 ...... 55 F4
Runwick La GU10 ...... 98 A1
Rupert Rd RG14 ...... 5 E4
Rural Life Ctr GU9 ...... 122 B2
Rushden Way GU9 ...... 99 D4
Rushmoor Cl GU13 ...... 75 D4
Rushmoor Ct GU12 ...... 77 D4
Rushmoor Ind Sch GU16 ...... 56 A1
Rushmoor Rd GU11 ...... 76 A2
Ruskin Cl RG21 ...... 69 F2
Russel Rd RG21 ...... 69 D2
Russell Ct Blackwater GU17 ...... 35 D3
Hinchead GU26 ...... 167 E2
Russell Rd Newbury RG14 ...... 1 B1
Winchester SO23 ...... 176 A1
Russet Cl
New Alresford SO24 ...... 179 E2
Tongham GU11 ...... 100 A4
Russet Gdns GU15 ...... 36 A2
Russet Glade GU11 ...... 99 E4
Russett Rd GU34 ...... 140 A2
Russetts Dr GU13 ...... 75 D4
Rustic Glen GU13 ...... 74 C3
Ruth Cl GU14 ...... 55 D3
Rutherford Rd RG21 ...... 69 E4
Rutland Cl GU11 ...... 76 C2
Ryan Mount GU17 ...... 34 C4
Rydal
Bordon GU35 ...... 164 B3
Farnborough GU14 ...... 55 D2

Rydal Dr Fleet GU13 ...... 74 C3
Thatcham RG19 ...... 2 C2
Ryde Ct 7 GU11 ...... 77 D1
Ryde Gdns GU46 ...... 33 F3
Rye Cl Farnborough GU14 ...... 55 E4
Fleet GU13 ...... 54 B3
Rye Croft GU13 ...... 74 C2
Ryebeck Rd GU13 ...... 75 D3
Ryecroft Gdns GU47 ...... 35 E2
Ryeland Cl GU13 ...... 54 B3
Ryelaw Rd GU13 ...... 75 D3
Ryle Rd GU10 ...... 121 F4
Ryon Cl SP10 ...... 83 D2
Ryves Ave GU46 ...... 33 F3

Sabre Ct 3 GU11 ...... 76 B1
Saddleback Rd GU15 ...... 36 B4
Saddleback Way GU13 ...... 54 A2
Saddlers Cl SO21 ...... 131 E2
Saddlers Ct RG14 ...... 1 B2
Saddlers Scarp GU26 ...... 166 C2
Saddlewood GU15 ...... 36 A2
Saffron Cl Chineham RG24 ...... 49 D2
Newbury RG14 ...... 1 B2
Saffron Cl GU14 ...... 55 D2
Sages La GU34 ...... 204 B3
Sainfoin La RG25 ...... 90 A4
Sainsbury Cl SP10 ...... 105 F3
St Albans Rdbt GU12 ...... 77 D4
St Andrew's Ct 5 GU11 ...... 99 D1
St Andrew's Inf Sch GU10 ...... 98 C1
St Andrew's Rd RG22 ...... 68 B2
St Andrew's Way GU16 ...... 56 B4
St Andrews Bordon GU35 ...... 164 A1
North Tidworth SP9 ...... 78 C3
St Ann's Cl SP11 ...... 105 F4
St Anne's RC Prim Sch RG22 ...... 68 B2
St Annes Cl SO22 ...... 197 E2
St Aubins Cl GU34 ...... 160 A1
St Augustine's Cl GU12 ...... 77 D1
St Austins GU26 ...... 167 D2
St Barbara's Ct GU11 ...... 29 D1
St Bartholomews Sch RG14 ...... 1 B1
St Bede CE Prim Sch SO23 ...... 198 A4
St Bede's Ct 26 SO23 ...... 176 A1
St Bede's RC Prim Sch RG24 ...... 48 A1
St Benedict's Convent Sch
SP11 ...... 82 A2
St Benedicts Cl GU11 ...... 76 C1
St Bernadette RC Prim Sch
GU14 ...... 55 F3
St Catherine's Hill RG7 ...... 11 E3
St Catherine's Prep Sch GU15 ...... 36 A2
St Catherine's Rd SO23 ...... 198 A3
St Catherines Rd GU14 ...... 56 C4
St Catherines Way SO23 ...... 198 B3
St Christopher's Gn GU27 ...... 189 F3
St Christopher's Rd GU27 ...... 189 F3
St Christophers Cl
Basingstoke RG22 ...... 68 B2
Haslemere GU27 ...... 189 F3
St Christophers Pl GU14 ...... 55 E2
St Christophers Rd GU14 ...... 55 F2
St Clement St 23 SO23 ...... 198 A4
St Clements Ct GU14 ...... 55 F4
St Cross Ct 4 SO22 ...... 197 F3
St Cross Mede SO22 ...... 197 F2
St Cross Rd Camberley GU16 ...... 56 C4
Crondall GU10 ...... 97 E3
Farnham GU9 ...... 99 D2
Winchester SO22 ...... 197 F3
St David's Cl Farnborough GU14 ...... 55 E4
Farnham GU9 ...... 99 D4
St David's Rd Basingstoke RG22 ...... 68 C2
Newbury RG14 ...... 1 B1
St Davids Cl RG29 ...... 72 B1
St Donats Pl GU14 ...... 1 C1
St Edmunds Sch GU26 ...... 167 D2
St Faith Cl GU34 ...... 160 A1
St Faith's CE Prim Sch SO23 ...... 197 F3
St Faith's Rd SO22 ...... 197 F3
St Gabriel's Sch Sandleford Priory
RG14 ...... 1 C4
St George's Cl GU9 ...... 99 F3
St George's Rd Aldershot GU12 ...... 76 C1
Farnham GU9 ...... 99 D1
St George's Rd E GU11 ...... 76 C1
St George's St SO23 ...... 198 A4
St Georges Ave RG14 ...... 1 B1
St Georges Ind Est GU17 ...... 35 F2
St Georges Mews GU9 ...... 99 D2
St Georges Rd Farnham GU9 ...... 99 F3
North Tidworth SP9 ...... 78 C3
St Georges Yd GU9 ...... 99 D1
St Giles Cl SO23 ...... 198 A4
St Gregory's RC Fst Sch GU15 ...... 35 F3
St Helens Cres GU17 ...... 34 C4
St Hubert Rd SP10 ...... 105 F4
St James' Ave GU9 ...... 99 D2
St James Ct Farnham GU9 ...... 99 D2
Fleet GU13 ...... 74 C4
St James' La SO22 ...... 197 F4
St James Rd Fleet GU13 ...... 74 C4
Wokingham RG40 ...... 16 B4
St James' Terr Farnham GU9 ...... 99 D2
Winchester SO22 ...... 197 F4
St John the Baptist
RC Prim Sch SP10 ...... 105 E4
St John the Evangelist
CE Inf Sch RG14 ...... 1 B1
St John's CE Prim Sch RG21 ...... 69 D2
St John's Cotts RG27 ...... 71 F4
St John's Ct
Farnborough GU14 ...... 55 D3
10 Fleet GU13 ...... 54 A1

St John's Hospital (N) 🟦
SO23 .... **198** A4
St John's Hospital (S) 🟦
SO23 .... **198** A4
St John's Inf Sch RG7 .... **11** F3
St John's Piece RG22 .... **90** A4
St John's Rd Andover SP10 ... **106** A4
Farnborough GU14 .... **55** C3
Farnham GU10 .... **121** F4
Mortimer RG7 .... **11** F3
Newbury RG14 .... **1** C1
Oakley RG23 .... **67** E1
Sandhurst GU46 .... **34** C4
Winchester SO23 .... **198** A4
St John's St SO23 .... **198** A4
St John's Wlk 🟦 RG21 .... **69** D3
St Johns CE Inf Sch GU10 .. **144** B1
St Johns Cl RG27 .... **51** D1
St Johns Gr GU10 .... **121** F4
St Johns Rd RG27 .... **52** B3
St Joseph's Cres RG24 .... **48** C1
St Joseph's RC Prim Sch
RG14 .... **1** C2
St Joseph's Rd GU12 .... **76** C1
St Josephs Ct RG14 .... **1** C2
St Josephs RC GM Prim Sch
GU9 .... **99** F4
St Just Cl SP4 .... **123** D3
St Lawrence CE Prim Sch
GU34 .... **139** F2
St Lawrence Rd GU34 .... **139** F2
St Leger Ct RG14 .... **1** B2
St Leonard's Ave RG24 .... **49** D2
St Leonard's Rd SO23 .... **198** A3
St Lucia Pk GU35 .... **164** C3
St Margarets SP11 .... **81** F4
St Mark's CE Prim Sch
Basingstoke RG22 .... **91** E3
Farnborough GU12 .... **77** D4
St Marks Cl GU14 .... **56** A1
St Marks Pl GU9 .... **98** C4
St Martin Cl SO23 .... **198** A4
St Martin's CE Prim Sch
RG20 .... **20** C4
St Martins Ind Est SO23 ... **198** A4
St Mary Bourne
Cty Prim Sch SP11 .... **61** F1
St Mary Magdalen
Almshouses 🟦 SO23 .... **198** A4
St Mary St SO22 .... **197** E3
St Mary's Almshouses RG14 .... **1** B1
St Mary's Ave RG26 .... **29** D1
St Mary's CE Inf Sch GU10 ... **144** A4
St Mary's CE Jun Sch RG24 .. **70** A3
St Mary's Cl
Kings Worthy SO21 .... **176** B3
Old Basing RG24 .... **70** A3
St Mary's Coll SO23 .... **198** A3
St Mary's Ct
Basingstoke RG21 .... **69** E3
Bramley RG7 .... **29** D1
🟦 Newbury RG14 .... **1** C2
St Mary's Meadow SP11 ..... **105** D2
Newbury RG14 .... **1** C2
St Mary's Pl Farnham GU9 .... **99** D2
Newbury RG14 .... **1** C2
St Mary's Rd Ash GU12 .... **77** F3
Camberley GU15 .... **36** A3
Hartley Wintney RG27 .... **52** B3
Kingsclere RG20 .... **24** B1
Liss GU33 .... **207** F2
Mortimer RG7 .... **11** F3
Newbury RG14 .... **1** C2
St Marys CE Jun Sch RG7 .... **12** A3
St Marys Cl GU17 .... **35** D4
St Matthew's CE Prim Sch
GU33 .... **186** A4
St Matthews Rd SO22 .... **175** E1
St Michael's CE Inf Sch
GU9 .... **99** D1
St Michael's CE Jun Sch
GU46 .... **34** B4
St Michael's CE Prim Sch
GU10 .... **100** A4
St Michael's Cl RG25 .... **89** F1
St Michael's Gdns 🟦 SO22 ... **197** F4
St Michael's Hall GU9 .... **99** F4
St Michael's Pass SO23 ..... **198** A3
St Michael's Rd
Aldershot GU12 .... **76** C1
Basingstoke RG22 .... **68** B2
Farnborough GU14 .... **55** F3
Newbury RG14 .... **1** B1
Sandhurst GU47 .... **34** B4
Winchester SO22 .... **197** E3
St Michaels Ave SP9 .... **78** C3
St Michaels Cl Fleet GU13 .... **75** D4
South Tidworth SP9 .... **78** C3
St Michaels Rd GU15 .... **35** F3
St Michaels Sch RG20 .... **21** E3
St Neot's Rd RG14 .... **32** B4
St Neot's Sch RG27 .... **32** B4
St Nicholas CE Jun Sch RG14 .. **1** C1
St Nicholas Cl SP11 .... **57** D1
St Nicholas Ct RG22 .... **68** B2
St Nicholas Rd RG14 .... **1** B1
St Nicholas Rise SO23 ...... **176** A3
St Patrick's La Liss GU33 ... **208** B3
Rake GU33 .... **208** B3
St Patrick's RC Prim Sch
GU16 .... **56** A2
St Patrick's Rd RG22 .... **68** C2
St Patricks Ave SP9 .... **78** C3
St Paul's CE Inf Sch GU10 ... **100** C4
St Paul's Hill SO22 .... **197** F4
St Paul's Hospl SO22 .... **197** F4

St Paul's Rd RG22 .... **68** C2
St Pauls Pl 🟦 SO22 .... **197** F4
St Peter St SO23 .... **198** A4
St Peter's CE Jun Sch
Farnborough GU14 .... **56** A2
Yateley GU46 .... **34** B3
St Peter's CE Prim Sch
GU10 .... **121** F3
St Peter's Gdns
Farnham GU10 .... **121** E3
Yateley GU47 .... **34** A3
St Peter's Rd RG22 .... **68** B2
St Peter's Way GU16 .... **56** B4
St Peters Cl
Headley, Nr Greenham RG19 ... **7** D1
Tadley RG26 .... **26** C4
St Peters Mead GU12 .... **77** F1
St Peters Pk GU11 .... **99** E4
St Philips Ct 🟦 GU12 .... **54** A1
St Polycarp's RC Prim Sch
GU9 .... **99** D1
St Richards Rd RG14 .... **1** C3
St Stephen's Rd SO22 .... **175** D1
St Stephens Cl GU27 .... **189** E3
St Swithun St SO23 .... **198** A4
St Swithun's Sch SO23 ...... **198** B4
St Thomas' Cl RG14 .... **69** D4
St Thomas Cl SP10 .... **82** C2
St Thomas' Pas 🟦 SO22 .... **197** F4
St Thomas St 🟦 SO23 ...... **198** A4
Salamanca Pk GU11 .... **76** B1
Salcombe Rd RG14 .... **1** B1
Salcot Rd SO23 .... **176** A1
Salerno Cl GU11 .... **76** C1
Salerno Rd SP9 .... **79** E3
Sales Ct 🟦 GU11 .... **76** C1
Salesian Coll
Farnborough GU16 .... **56** A1
Farnborough GU12 .... **77** D4
Salesian View GU12 .... **77** E4
Salisbury Cl
Alton GU34 .... **140** A1
Odiham RG29 .... **72** B1
Salisbury Gdns RG22 .... **68** B2
Salisbury Gr GU16 .... **56** C2
Salisbury Ho 🟦 SP9 .... **78** C4
Salisbury La SO20 .... **147** E4
Salisbury Rd
Abbotts Ann SP10 .... **105** D2
Andover SP10 .... **105** F3
Ash GU12 .... **77** F1
Blackwater GU17 .... **35** D3
Broughton SO20 .... **169** F4
Farnborough GU14 .... **56** A2
New Alresford SO24 .... **179** E3
Over Wallop SP11 .... **124** C3
Shipton Bellinger SP9 ...... **101** F3
Upper Clatford SP11 .... **105** F3
Salisbury Terr GU16 .... **56** C2
Salmond Rd SP10, SP11 .... **105** D4
Salmons Rd RG29 .... **72** B1
Salters Acres SO22 .... **175** E2
Salters Heath Rd RG26 .... **47** D4
Salters La SO22 .... **175** D1
Saltram Rd GU16 .... **56** B1
Samarkand Cl GU15 .... **36** C2
Sampson Bsns Pk GU17 ...... **35** F2
Sampson's Almshouses 🟦
GU9 .... **98** C1
Samuel Cody Ho GU12 .... **77** F4
Samuel Cody Sch GU12 ...... **76** C4
San Carlos App GU14 .... **77** D1
Sand Hill GU14 .... **55** F4
Sand Hill Ct GU14 .... **55** F4
Sandbanks Dr RG22 .... **91** D4
Sandford Cl RG20 .... **24** C1
Sandford Ct GU11 .... **76** B1
Sandford Rd
Aldershot GU11 .... **76** B1
Farnham GU9 .... **98** C4
Tadley RG26 .... **26** C4
Sandheath Rd GU26 .... **167** D4
Sandhurst La GU47 .... **34** C3
Sandhurst Rd
Wokingham RG40 .... **16** C4
Yateley GU46 .... **34** B4
Sandhurst Royal Military Acad
GU17 .... **35** F4
Sandhurst Sch GU47 .... **35** D4
Sandhurst Sta GU47 .... **34** C4
Sandleford Hospl RG14 .... **5** F4
Sandleford Rise RG14 .... **5** F4
Sandown Cl
Alton GU34 .... **140** A1
Blackwater GU17 .... **35** D3
Sandown Cres GU9 .... **99** F4
Sandown Dr GU15 .... **36** A1
Sandown Way RG14 .... **2** A1
Sandpiper Way RG22 .... **90** C4
Sandpit Cotts GU13 .... **75** D1
Sandpit Hill GU34 .... **5** D2
Sandpit La RG7 .... **14** C3
Sandringham Cl
Alton GU34 .... **139** E2
Farnborough GU11 .... **76** C4
Sandringham Ct RG22 .... **68** B2
Sandringham Ho 🟦 SP10 ..... **83** D2
Sandringham Inf Sch
GU14 .... **56** B4
Sandringham Way GU16 .... **56** B4
Sandrock Hill Rd GU10 .... **121** F3
Sands Cl GU11 .... **100** A1
Sands Rd
Farnham GU10 .... **100** A1
Seale GU10 .... **100** A1
Sands The GU35 .... **164** A1
Sandy Cross GU10 .... **100** B2
Sandy Hill Rd GU9 .... **98** C4

Sandy La Bramshott GU27 ... **189** D4
Camberley GU15 .... **36** B3
Farnborough GU14 .... **55** D4
Fleet GU13 .... **75** D2
Frensham GU9 .... **122** A1
Frensham GU10 .... **144** C3
Hartley Wintney RG27 .... **52** B3
Haslemere GU27 .... **167** E1
Rake GU33 .... **208** C2
Tadley RG26 .... **27** D4
Sandys Cl RG23 .... **68** C2
Sandys Rd RG22 .... **68** C2
Sandys Road Rdbt RG22 ...... **68** C2
Sangro Rd SP9 .... **79** E3
Sankey La GU13 .... **54** B2
Santina Cl GU11 .... **99** D4
Saor Mews SP10 .... **105** F4
Sapley La RG25 .... **88** A4
Sarah Way GU14 .... **55** F2
Sarisbury Cl RG26 .... **26** C4
Sarson Cl SP11 .... **104** A3
Sarson La Amport SP11 ..... **104** A4
Thruxton SP11 .... **104** A4
Sarum Cl Over Wallop SO20 ... **147** E4
Shipton Bellinger SP9 ...... **101** E4
Winchester SO22 .... **197** E4
Sarum Hill RG21 .... **69** D2
Sarum Rd Tadley RG26 .... **9** F1
Winchester SO22 .... **197** D4
Sarum Road Hospl SO22 ... **197** E4
Saturn Ho 🟦 RG22 .... **9** E1
Saunton Gdns GU14 .... **55** F3
Savernake Rd 🟦 SP9 .... **78** C3
Savile Cres GU35 .... **164** B2
Saville Gdns GU15 .... **36** C2
Savoy Cl SP10 .... **106** A4
Savoy Gr GU17 .... **35** D2
Sawyer Cl SO22 .... **175** D1
Saxon Croft GU11 .... **99** D1
Saxon Cl 🟦 SP10 .... **83** D2
Saxon Leas SP5 .... **168** A3
Saxon Mews 🟦 GU34 .... **139** F2
Saxon Rd SO23 .... **176** A1
Saxon Way RG24 .... **69** F4
Saxon Wood Sch RG22 ...... **68** A4
Saxony Way GU46 .... **34** A2
Sayers Cl Camberley GU14 ... **56** B4
Newbury RG14 .... **5** F4
Scamblers Mead SP11 .... **81** F2
Scarlatti Rd RG22 .... **91** F4
Scarlet Oaks GU16 .... **36** B2
Scarlett's Rd GU11 .... **76** C2
School Cl SP11 .... **38** B3
School Fields GU35 .... **142** A1
School Hill Farnham GU9 .... **121** E3
Seale GU11 .... **100** C2
School La Bentley GU10 ...... **120** A3
Bishop's Sutton SO24 .... **180** A2
Broughton SO20 .... **170** A4
Ewshot GU9 .... **98** A4
Farnham GU10 .... **122** A3
Itchen Abbas SO21 .... **177** F4
Kings Worthy SO23 .... **176** A3
🟦 Liss GU33 .... **207** F2
Michelmersh SO51 .... **193** E1
Middle Wallop SO20 .... **147** F4
Riseley RG7 .... **14** B2
Ropley SO24 .... **181** E2
Silchester RG7 .... **10** C1
Yateley GU46 .... **33** F3
School Lane Cotts SO20 ... **147** F4
School Rd Bordon GU35 ..... **164** B2
Farnham GU10 .... **121** E2
Grayshott GU26 .... **166** C2
Linchmere GU27 .... **189** E3
Riseley RG7 .... **14** B2
Schubert Rd RG22 .... **91** F4
Scotland Cl GU12 .... **77** F3
Scotland Farm Rd GU12 .... **77** F3
Scotland Hill GU46 .... **34** C4
Scotland La GU27 .... **189** D3
Scotlands Cl GU27 .... **189** E3
Scotlands Dr GU27 .... **189** E3
Scotney Rd RG21 .... **69** D4
Scott Cl Andover SP10 .... **83** F1
King's Somborne SO20 ..... **172** A1
Scott's Ct GU14 .... **55** F4
Scrubbs La SO24 .... **180** A2
Scures Rd RG27 .... **50** C1
Seagull Cl RG23 .... **90** C4
Seal Rd 🟦 RG21 .... **69** D3
Searle Rd GU9 .... **122** A4
Searle's La Hook RG27 .... **51** D2
Hook RG27 .... **51** E1
Searles Cl SO24 .... **179** E3
Seaton Rd GU35 .... **35** F3
Sebastopol Rd GU11 .... **76** C1
Second St E RG14 .... **6** C3
Second St W RG19 .... **6** B2
Sedgefield Rd RG14 .... **6** A4
Sedgemoor GU14 .... **55** F4
Seebys Oak GU17 .... **35** E3
Sefton Ho 🟦 GU11 .... **76** C1
Sek Kong Cl SO20 .... **126** A2
Selborne Ave GU10 .... **100** A3
Selborne Cl Blackwater GU17 ... **35** D3
Hook RG27 .... **51** D1
Selborne Pl SO22 .... **197** E3
Selborne Rd Alton GU34 ..... **162** B3
East Worldham GU34 .... **162** B3
Selborne GU34 .... **162** B3
Selborne Way GU35 .... **164** A1
Selbourne Rd RG26 .... **26** C4
Selbourne CE Prim Sch
GU34 .... **184** B4
Selbourne Gdns GU10 .... **121** F4
Selby Wlk RG24 .... **48** A1
Seldon Cl SO22 .... **197** D2

Selwyn Dr GU46 .... **33** F3
Sepen Meade GU13 .... **74** C2
Seremban Cl SO20 .... **126** A3
Sermon Rd SO22 .... **175** D1
Seton Dr RG27 .... **71** F4
Sett The GU46 .... **33** F3
Seventh St RG14 .... **6** B3
Severals The RG26 .... **47** F2
Severn Cl Sandhurst GU15 .... **35** D4
Thatcham RG18 .... **2** C3
Severn Ct 🟦 SP10 .... **83** E1
Severn Gdns RG22, RG23 ..... **67** D1
Severn Rd GU14 .... **55** E3
Severn Way 🟦 RG21 .... **69** E3
Seville Cres SP10 .... **83** E1
Seymour Ct Fleet GU13 .... **54** A1
Odiham RG29 .... **72** C2
Seymour Dr GU15 .... **36** C4
Seymour P RG29 .... **72** C2
Seymour Rd
Basingstoke RG22 .... **68** B1
Headley GU35 .... **166** A2
Shackleton Sq SP10 .... **83** E1
Shady Nook GU9 .... **98** C3
Shaftesbury Ct
Bordon GU35 .... **164** B1
Farnborough GU11 .... **77** D4
Shaftesbury Mount GU47 ..... **35** D2
Shakespeare Ave SP10 .... **82** B1
Shakespeare Gdns GU14 ..... **55** D3
Shakespeare Rd RG21 .... **69** E4
Shalbourne Rise GU15 .... **36** A3
Shalden La GU12 .... **138** C4
Shalden Rd GU12 .... **100** A4
Shamrock Cl GU16 .... **56** A4
Shanklin Ct GU12 .... **77** D1
Shannon Ct 🟦 SP10 .... **83** E1
Shapley Heath RG27 .... **52** A1
Shapley Hill RG27 .... **52** B1
Shaw cum Donnington
Parochial Prim Sch RG14 .... **1** B3
Shaw Farm Rd RG14 .... **1** C3
Shaw Hill RG14 .... **1** C3
Shaw Ho SP11 .... **81** D3
Shaw House Comp Sch RG14 ... **1** C3
Shaw La RG26 .... **26** B4
Shaw Mill RG14 .... **1** C3
Shaw Pightle RG27 .... **50** C1
Shaw Rd RG14 .... **1** C2
Shawfield Cty Inf Sch GU12 ... **77** F2
Shawfield La GU12 .... **77** E1
Shawfield Rd GU12 .... **77** F1
Sheddon Pl SO21 .... **174** B1
Sheep Dro SO20 .... **147** E2
Sheep Fair SP10, SP11 .... **106** B4
Sheep Fair Cl SP10 .... **106** B4
Sheep Ho GU10 .... **122** A4
Sheephatch La GU9 .... **122** C3
Sheepwash La RG26 .... **26** A4
Sheepwash La RG26 .... **5** F1
Sheerlands Rd RG40 .... **15** E3
Sheffield Cl GU14 .... **55** E2
Shefford Lodge 🟦 RG14 .... **1** C1
Sheldon's La RG27 .... **51** D1
Sheldon's Rd RG27 .... **51** D1
Shell La GU34 .... **183** D1
Shelley Cl Basingstoke RG24 ... **69** E4
Fleet GU13 .... **75** D4
Itchen Abbas SO21 .... **177** F3
Winchester SO21, SO22 ..... **197** E4
Shelley Ct GU15 .... **36** A3
Shelleys La GU34 .... **140** C1
Shelly Rise GU14 .... **55** E3
Shenstone Cl RG40 .... **16** C4
Shepherds Cl SO22 .... **197** D2
Shepherds Ct GU9 .... **122** A4
Shepherds Down SO24 ...... **179** E2
Shepherds Rd SO23 .... **198** A4
Shepherds Rise SP11 .... **38** B3
Shepherds Row SP10 .... **106** B4
Shepherds Spring La SP10 ... **83** D1
Shepherds Spring Schs
SP10 .... **83** D2
Shepherds Way GU30 .... **188** A2
Shepherds Wlk GU14 .... **55** E4
Sheppard Almshouses
SP11 .... **104** A3
Sheppard Cl RG28 .... **86** B2
Sheppard Rd RG21 .... **69** D1
Sheppard Sq SP10 .... **83** E1
Sheraton Ave RG22 .... **91** D4
Sheraton Cl GU17 .... **35** E2
Sherborne Rd
Basingstoke RG24 .... **69** D4
Farnborough GU11 .... **77** D4
Sherborne St John RG26 ..... **47** F1
Sherborne St John
CE Prim Sch RG26 .... **47** F2
Sherbrooke Cl SO23 .... **176** B4
Sherfield Rd RG26 .... **29** D1
Sheridan Cl SO22 .... **197** E3
Sheridan Cres RG26 .... **9** E1
Sheridan Ct Camberley GU16 .. **56** A4
Newbury RG14 .... **2** A2
Sheridan Rd GU16 .... **56** A4
Sherlock Lea GU17, GU46 ..... **33** E4
Sherrard Mead RG14 .... **1** C3
Sherrington Way RG22 .... **68** C1
Sherwin Cres GU16 .... **56** A4
Sherwood Cl
Basingstoke RG22 .... **91** E3
Liss GU33 .... **208** A4
Sherwood Terr GU34 .... **140** A2
Shetland Rd RG24 .... **48** B1
Shetland Way GU13 .... **54** A2
Ship Alley GU14 .... **56** A4
Ship La GU16 .... **56** A3

Shipley Ct GU30 .... **188** A2
Shipton Bellinger
Cty Prim Sch SP9 .... **101** E4
Shipton Way RG22 .... **68** B1
Shire Ave GU13 .... **54** B2
Shire Ct 🟦 GU11 .... **76** B1
Shires Way GU46 .... **34** A4
Shoddesden La
Kimpton SP11 .... **80** B3
Ludgershall SP11 .... **57** D1
Shoe La GU11 .... **76** C3
Shooters Way RG24 .... **69** E3
Shop La RG14 .... **1** B3
Short Dale Rd GU11 .... **100** A3
Short La SP10 .... **82** A1
Short St Aldershot GU11 ...... **76** C1
Ludgershall SP11 .... **57** D1
Shortheath Crest GU10 ...... **121** F3
Shortheath Rd GU9 .... **121** F3
Shotter's La GU34 .... **183** F3
Shotterfield Terr GU33 .... **207** F2
Shottermill Cty Fst Sch
GU27 .... **189** E4
Shottermill Cty Jun Sch
GU27 .... **189** E4
Shottermill Rd GU27 .... **189** E3
Shrave The GU34 .... **160** C2
Shrewsbury Terr RG14 .... **1** B1
Shrivenham Cl GU47 .... **35** D4
Shrubbery The GU14 .... **55** D2
Shrubbs La GU9 .... **122** A4
Shyshack La Baughurst RG26 ... **9** E1
Tadley RG26 .... **9** E1
Sian Cl GU13 .... **75** D3
Sibelius Cl RG22 .... **91** F4
Sickle Rd GU27 .... **189** F3
Sickles Rd GU35 .... **142** A1
Sidbury Circular Rd SP9 ...... **78** B4
Sidbury Hill Ave SP9 .... **78** C4
Sidings The GU12 .... **77** D2
Sidlaw Cl RG22 .... **68** A2
Sidlaws Rd GU14 .... **55** D3
Sidmouth Rd SP10 .... **106** B4
Silchester CE Prim Sch RG7 ... **10** C1
Silchester Cl SP10 .... **82** C1
Silchester Rd Bramley RG26 ... **28** B2
Pamber End RG26 .... **27** F2
Pamber Heath RG26 .... **10** B1
Silchester RG26 .... **10** B1
Silk Mill La RG25 .... **87** F4
Silkweavers Rd SP10 .... **106** A4
Silver Birch Cl Fleet GU13 ... **74** C3
Liss GU33 .... **208** A2
Silver Birch Rd SP10 .... **82** C1
Silver Hill Sandhurst GU17 ... **35** E4
Winchester SO23 .... **198** A4
Silver La RG7 .... **10** C4
Silver Park Cl GU13 .... **75** D3
Silverdale GU13 .... **75** D3
Silverdale Rd RG26 .... **9** F1
Silverglades GU46 .... **34** A2
Silverwood Dr GU15 .... **36** C4
Silvester Cl RG21 .... **69** E4
Silvester Way GU13 .... **74** C3
Silwood Cl SO22 .... **175** E1
Simmondstone La GU10 ..... **144** A1
Simms Farm La RG7 .... **11** E2
Simms Wlk 🟦 RG21, RG24 .... **69** E3
Simonds Cl 🟦 SO23 .... **176** A1
Simons Cl RG24 .... **48** C1
Simons Rd RG24 .... **48** C1
Sine Cl GU14 .... **55** F4
Sinhurst Rd GU17 .... **35** F2
Sixth St RG14 .... **6** B3
Skates La RG26 .... **27** D3
Skew Rd Amport SP11 .... **103** D2
Quarley SP11 .... **103** D2
Skinners Green La RG14 .... **4** C4
Skippetts La E RG21 .... **69** E1
Skippetts La W RG21 .... **69** D1
Skippons Cl RG14 .... **5** D3
Skylings RG21 .... **2** A2
Slade Hill Gdns RG20 .... **4** B1
Sleeper's Hill Ho SO22 ...... **197** E3
Sleeper's Hill Rd SO22 ...... **197** E3
Sleepers Delle Gdns SO22 ... **197** E3
Sleepers Hill Gdns SO22 ..... **197** E3
Slessor Cl SP10 .... **105** D4
Slim Cl GU12 .... **77** E4
Slim Rd GU47 .... **35** F4
Smallfield Dr RG27 .... **51** E1
Smallridge GU14 .... **5** D2
Smannell & Enham
CE Prim Sch SP10 .... **83** E2
Smannell Rd
Knights Enham SP10 .... **83** E2
Smannell SP10 .... **83** E2
Smay Down La RG40 .... **17** D2
Smeaton Rd SP10 .... **82** A1
Smithfield La GU35 .... **143** F1
Smiths Mead RG25 .... **89** F1
Smithy Cl GU34 .... **140** B4
Smithy La GU35 .... **143** E1
Smugglers La SO24 .... **182** A1
Smugglers' Way GU12 .... **100** B1
Snailing La GU33 .... **207** E4
Snailslynch GU9 .... **99** D1
Snipe La Bishop's Green RG20 ... **6** B1
Linchmere GU27 .... **189** F1
Snoddington Rd SP11 .... **80** A1
Snode Hill GU34 .... **139** D2
Snowdon Rd GU14 .... **55** E4
Snowdrop Cl RG22 .... **91** D4
Snowdrop Wlk 🟦 GU13 .... **53** F1
Soame's La GU34 .... **181** F1
Sobers Sq SP10 .... **83** E1
Society of St Pius X
St Michael's Sch RG20 .... **22** B3

Soke Hill SO24 ... 159 F1
Soke Rd Aldermaston RG26 ... 10 B2
  Silchester RG26 ... 10 B2
Soke The SO24 ... 179 E3
Solarton Rd GU14 ... 55 F2
Solby's Rd RG21 ... 69 D3
Soldridge Rd GU34 ... 159 F2
Solent Dr GU14 ... 91 D4
Somborne Park Rd SO20 ... 172 B4
Somers Cl SO22 ... 197 E3
Somerset Ave GU35 ... 164 B2
Somerset Ct [11] GU14 ... 56 A1
Somerset Rd GU14 ... 56 A1
Somerville Cres GU47 ... 34 B3
Somerville Ct SP11 ... 83 E1
Somerville Rd SO23 ... 176 B4
Somme Rd SP9 ... 79 E4
Sonnige Cl GU47 ... 35 D4
Sonning Cl RG22 ... 90 C4
Soper Gr RG21 ... 69 D3
Sopwith Cl SO20 ... 172 B4
Sopwith Pk SP10 ... 82 A1
Sorrel Cl Farnborough GU14 ... 55 D3
  Newbury RG14 ... 2 A3
Sorrell's Cl RG24 ... 48 C2
Sotherington La GU34 ... 185 E3
South Atlantic Dr GU14 ... 77 D2
South Ave GU9 ... 99 D3
South Cl SO24 ... 179 D3
South Dr Littleton SO22 ... 175 D2
  Sherfield on Loddon RG24 ... 49 E4
  South Tidworth SP9 ... 78 C2
South End Rd SP10 ... 106 A3
South Farnborough Inf Sch GU11 ... 77 D4
South Farnborough Jun Sch GU14 ... 56 A1
South Farnham Sch GU9 ... 99 D1
South Gr GU13 ... 54 B2
South Ham Rd RG22 ... 68 C2
South Hill RG25 ... 94 B3
South Hurst GU35 ... 164 B1
South La GU11 ... 77 F1
South Mall [16] GU13 ... 53 F1
South Rd Broughton SO20 ... 170 B3
  Kingsclere RG20 ... 24 C1
  Liphook GU30 ... 188 A1
  New Alresford SO24 ... 179 D3
South Ridge RG29 ... 72 C1
South Side GU9 ... 100 B4
South St Andover SP10 ... 106 A4
  Ash GU11 ... 77 F2
  Farnborough GU14 ... 56 B1
  Farnham GU9 ... 99 D1
  Ropley SO24 ... 181 E2
South Town Rd GU34 ... 159 F3
South View SO22 ... 197 F4
South View Cl SO21 ... 131 E2
South View Cotts
  Bentley GU10 ... 120 A2
  Hook RG29 ... 72 A4
South View Gdns
  Andover SP10 ... 106 A4
  [16] Newbury RG14 ... 1 C2
South View Rd SO22 ... 197 D2
South View Schs RG21 ... 69 E4
South View Terr SP10 ... 85 D4
South Way SP11 ... 83 F1
South Wlk GU12 ... 77 D1
South Wonston Prim Sch SO21 ... 153 E2
Southampton Cl GU15 ... 35 D3
Southampton Ho [8] SP9 ... 78 C3
Southampton St GU11 ... 76 C4
Southbrook Cotts SO21 ... 133 D2
Southbrook Pl SO21 ... 133 D2
Southby Dr GU13 ... 54 A1
Southcote Dr GU15 ... 36 C3
Southdown Rd
  Tadley RG26 ... 26 C4
  Thatcham RG19 ... 2 B2
Southend Rd [1] RG21 ... 69 D3
Southern Haye RG27 ... 52 B3
Southern Rd
  Basingstoke RG21 ... 69 D2
  Bordon GU35 ... 164 B3
  Camberley GU15 ... 36 A3
Southern Way
  Farnborough GU14 ... 55 E2
  Farnham GU9 ... 99 D1
Southgate St SO23 ... 197 F4
Southgate Villas SO23 ... 197 F4
Southington La RG25 ... 87 F4
Southlands RG24 ... 48 C2
Southlands Cl GU12 ... 77 F1
Southlands Rd GU12 ... 77 F1
Southlea RG25 ... 92 A4
Southmead Rd GU9 ... 99 F4
Southrope Gn RG25 ... 116 B4
Southside Cotts SO20 ... 149 F2
Southside Rd SP11 ... 108 A3
Southview Cotts GU10 ... 122 A1
Southview Rd GU35 ... 165 F3
Southview Rise GU34 ... 139 F3
Southwark Cl GU46 ... 34 A3
Southway GU15 ... 35 F2
Southwell Park Rd GU15 ... 36 A3
Southwick Cl SO22 ... 175 E2
Southwood Cres The GU14 ... 55 D2
Southwood Inf Sch GU14 ... 55 D2
Southwood La GU14 ... 55 D2
Southwood Rd
  Farnborough GU14 ... 55 E2
  Hawley GU46 ... 34 B1
  Shalden GU34 ... 139 D4
Sovereign Ct [11] GU13 ... 53 F1
Sovereign Dr GU15 ... 36 C4
Sowcroft La GU34 ... 118 A3

Spain La Bentworth RG25 ... 115 F2
  Bradley RG25 ... 115 F2
  Lasham RG25 ... 115 F2
Sparkford Cl SO22 ... 197 F3
Sparkford Rd SO22 ... 197 F4
Sparrowhawk Cl GU10 ... 98 A4
Sparsholt CE Prim Sch SO21 ... 174 B2
Sparsholt Coll Hampshire SO21 ... 174 A2
Sparsholt Rd SO21 ... 196 B2
Sparvell Way GU15 ... 36 A3
Sparvells GU46 ... 33 E4
Spats La GU35 ... 165 E4
Speen Hill Cl RG14 ... 1 B2
Speen La RG14 ... 1 A2
Speen Lodge Ct RG14 ... 1 B2
Speen Pl RG14 ... 1 B2
Speenhamland Ct [3] RG14 ... 1 C2
Speenhamland Cty Prim Sch RG14 ... 1 B2
Spencer Cl Camberley GU14 ... 56 B3
  Fleet GU13 ... 75 E3
  Four Marks GU34 ... 160 A2
  Pamber Heath RG26 ... 10 B1
Spencer Ct GU35 ... 164 B1
Spencer Rd RG14 ... 5 D3
Spenser Cl GU34 ... 140 A3
Sperrin Cl RG22 ... 68 A2
Spey Ct [48] SP10 ... 83 E1
Spicer Ct [4] SO22 ... 197 F4
Spicers GU34 ... 140 A2
Spiers Cl RG26 ... 27 D4
Spiers La SO24 ... 135 F2
Spindle Ho [2] SP10 ... 106 A4
Spinney The Fleet GU13 ... 74 B4
  Grayshott GU26 ... 166 C2
  Hook RG27 ... 51 D1
  Wokingham RG40 ... 16 B4
  Yateley GU46 ... 34 A4
Spitalfields Rd GU34 ... 139 F2
Spitalhatch GU34 ... 140 A2
Spitfire End [7] SO23 ... 198 B4
Spitfire Link SO23 ... 198 A4
Spitfire Rdbt SO23 ... 198 B4
Spoil La GU12 ... 100 B4
Spokane Cl GU9 ... 99 E4
Sprat's Hatch La
  Dogmersfield RG27 ... 73 F4
  Winchfield RG27 ... 73 F4
Spray Leaze SP11 ... 57 D1
Sprents La RG25 ... 88 A4
Spring Cl RG26 ... 47 F2
Spring Gdns Camberley GU15 ... 36 C3
  Farnborough GU14 ... 55 F4
  New Alresford SO24 ... 179 E2
Spring Hill La SP11 ... 60 A1
Spring La Aldermaston RG7 ... 10 A4
  Burghclere RG20 ... 22 B3
  Mortimer RG7 ... 11 F3
  Swallowfield RG7 ... 13 F2
Spring La W GU9 ... 98 C3
Spring Mews SP10 ... 83 D1
Spring Way SO24 ... 179 E2
Spring Woods GU13 ... 74 C4
Springcross Ave GU17 ... 35 D2
Springdale RG40 ... 16 B4
Springfarm Rd GU27 ... 189 E3
Springfield [2] Liss GU33 ... 207 F2
  Oakley RG23 ... 67 E1
Springfield Ave RG27 ... 52 B4
Springfield Cl SP10 ... 106 B4
Springfield La GU13 ... 53 F1
Springfield Rd Ash GU12 ... 77 F3
  Camberley GU15 ... 36 C3
  Pamber Heath RG26 ... 10 B1
Springlakes Est GU12 ... 77 E2
Springmead Ct GU27 ... 189 D3
Springs The RG26 ... 29 D4
Springvale Ave SO23 ... 176 A3
Springvale Rd SO23 ... 176 A4
Springwell La RG27 ... 52 C4
Spruce Ave GU35 ... 164 A2
Spruce Cl Andover SP10 ... 105 E4
  South Wonston SO21 ... 153 F3
Spruce Way GU13 ... 54 B1
Spurs Cl [11] GU11 ... 76 B1
Spybush La SO24 ... 135 E1
Square Dr GU27 ... 189 F1
Square The Farnham GU9 ... 121 E2
  Grayshott GU26 ... 167 D2
  Liphook GU30 ... 187 F2
  Nether Wallop SO20 ... 148 A3
  Upper Froyle GU34 ... 119 D1
  Winchester SO23 ... 198 A4
  Wonston SO21 ... 131 E2
Squarefield Gdns RG27 ... 51 E1
Squirrel Cl GU17, GU46 ... 34 C4
Squirrel La GU14 ... 55 F3
Stable Cl RG27 ... 50 C1
Stable Ct RG14 ... 5 E4
Stable Rd GU35 ... 164 B3
Stable View GU46 ... 34 A4
Stables Rd SP9 ... 78 C2
Stables The RG26 ... 28 C1
Stacey's Ind Est RG26 ... 9 F1
Staddlestones Cotts SP11 ... 82 A2
Staff College Rd
  Camberley GU15 ... 35 F3
  Sandhurst GU15 ... 35 F3
Staff Rd
  Aldershot GU12 ... 77 D1
  Michelmersh SO51 ... 193 D1
Stag Hill RG22 ... 68 B1
Stainers La SO21 ... 153 E2
Stake La GU14 ... 55 F2
Stamford Ave GU15 ... 36 B1
Stanbury Cl SP11 ... 103 F4

Stanbury Rd Fyfield SP11 ... 80 B1
  Thruxton SP11 ... 80 B1
Stancomb Broad La GU34 ... 159 E1
Stancombe La GU34 ... 159 E2
Standford Hill GU35 ... 165 D1
Standford La GU35 ... 165 D2
Standing Hill SP5 ... 190 C4
Stanfield RG26 ... 26 C4
Stanford Rd GU22 ... 91 E4
Stanham Cl SO21 ... 153 E1
Stanhope Rd GU15 ... 35 E2
Stanley Dr GU14 ... 55 D2
Stanley Rd GU14 ... 1 C1
Stanmore Gdns RG7 ... 11 E3
Stanmore La SO22 ... 197 E3
Stanmore Prim Sch SO22 ... 197 F3
Stanton Dr GU13 ... 74 C4
Staple Gdns SO23 ... 197 F4
Stapleton Cl RG14 ... 5 D3
Stapley La SO24 ... 181 E1
Star Hill Churt GU10 ... 144 A1
  Hartley Wintney RG27 ... 32 C1
Star Hill Dr GU10 ... 144 A2
Star La GU17 ... 77 E1
Star Post Rd GU15 ... 36 B4
Starling Cl RG22 ... 90 C4
Starting Gates RG14 ... 2 A1
Statham Sq SP10 ... 83 E2
Station App Andover SP10 ... 105 F4
  Ash GU12 ... 77 F4
  Grateley SP11 ... 124 C4
  Haslemere GU27 ... 189 F3
  Medstead GU34 ... 160 A2
  New Alresford SO24 ... 179 E3
Station Cl SO21 ... 177 F3
Station Hill Farnham GU9 ... 99 D1
  Itchen Abbas SO21 ... 177 F3
  Overton RG25 ... 65 D1
  Ropley SO24 ... 180 C3
  Winchester SO23, SO23 ... 197 F4
Station Ind Est GU13 ... 54 A2
Station Mall [25] RG21 ... 69 D3
Station Rd Aldershot GU11 ... 76 C1
  Alton GU34 ... 140 A2
  Bentley GU10 ... 120 A2
  Binsted GU10 ... 120 A2
  Bordon GU35 ... 164 B3
  Camberley GU16 ... 56 A4
  Chilbolton SO20 ... 128 C2
  Cliddesden RG25 ... 92 A4
  Farnborough GU14 ... 55 F2
  Grateley SP11 ... 125 D4
  Hook RG29 ... 72 A4
  Liphook GU30 ... 188 A1
  Liss GU33 ... 207 F2
  New Alresford SO24 ... 179 E3
  Newbury RG14 ... 1 C1
  Newbury, Speen RG14 ... 1 A3
  Oakley RG23 ... 66 C1
  Over Wallop SO20 ... 125 E1
  Overton RG25 ... 65 D1
  South Tidworth SP9 ... 78 C3
  Stratfield Mortimer RG7 ... 12 B3
  Whitchurch RG28 ... 86 B3
  Woolton Hill RG20 ... 4 C1
Station Rd E GU12 ... 77 F4
Station Rd W GU12 ... 77 E4
Station Terr SO24 ... 181 D3
Station View GU14 ... 77 F4
Stavedown Rd SO21 ... 153 E2
Steele's Rd GU11 ... 76 C2
Steeple Dr GU34 ... 139 F2
Steepways GU26 ... 166 C3
Stenbury Dr RG25 ... 136 A4
Step Terr SP11 ... 197 F4
Stephen's Cl RG7 ... 11 E3
Stephen's Rd RG7 ... 11 E3
Stephendale Rd GU9 ... 99 D2
Stephens Firs RG7 ... 11 E3
Stephens Rd RG26 ... 27 D4
Stephenson Cl SP10 ... 82 B1
Stephenson Rd
  Arborfield RG40 ... 15 F4
  Basingstoke RG22 ... 68 C3
Sterling Pk SP10 ... 82 B1
Stevens Dro SO20 ... 171 E3
Stevens Gn SP11 ... 62 A1
Stevens Hill GU46 ... 34 B3
Stevenson Rd SP11 ... 108 B1
Steventon Rd RG25 ... 89 F1
Stewards Rise GU10 ... 121 E4
Stewart Rd RG24 ... 69 F4
Stile Gdns GU27 ... 189 E3
Stiles Dr SP10 ... 106 B4
Stillions Cl GU34 ... 140 A2
Stilwell Cl GU46 ... 34 B3
Stirling Cl Camberley GU15 ... 36 B1
  Farnborough GU14 ... 55 F2
Stirling Rd [1] ... 1 C1
Stoatley Hollow GU27 ... 189 F4
Stoatley Rise GU27 ... 189 F4
Stockbridge Ct RG24 ... 49 D2
Stockbridge Dr GU11 ... 100 A3
Stockbridge Prim Sch SO20 ... 149 F2
Stockbridge Rd
  Goodworth Clatford SP11 ... 127 D3
  King's Somborne SO20 ... 172 A2
  Upper Clatford SP11 ... 127 D3
  Wherwell SP11 ... 127 D3
  Winchester SO21, SO22, SO23 ... 175 E2
  Wonston SO21 ... 131 D1
Stockbridge Way GU46 ... 34 A2
Stocker Cl RG21 ... 69 D1
Stockers Ave SO22 ... 175 E1
Stockton Ave GU13 ... 53 F1
Stockton House Sch GU13 ... 53 F1
Stockton Pk GU13 ... 53 F1

Stockwood Rise GU16 ... 36 B3
Stockwood Way GU9 ... 99 E4
Stodham La SO23 ... 207 F1
Stoke Charity Rd SO21, SO23 ... 154 A1
Stoke Gate SP11 ... 61 E3
Stoke Hill SP11 ... 61 D2
Stoke Hills GU9 ... 99 D2
Stoke Ho RG26 ... 26 C4
Stoke La SP11 ... 61 D3
Stoke Rd Stoke SP11 ... 61 D1
  Winchester SO23 ... 176 A2
Stoken La
  Hartley Wintney RG27 ... 51 F4
  Mattingley RG27 ... 51 F4
Stone Cl Andover SP10 ... 105 F3
  Middle Winterslow SP5 ... 168 A3
Stone Copse RG14 ... 2 B4
Stone St GU10 ... 100 A4
Stonedene Cl GU35 ... 165 F2
Stonehill Pk GU35 ... 165 F2
Stonehill Rd GU35 ... 166 A2
Stonehills RG25 ... 89 D3
Stonehouse Rd GU30 ... 188 A2
Stonehouse Rise GU15 ... 36 B1
Stoneleigh Ct GU16 ... 36 B1
Stoner Hill Rd GU32 ... 206 A1
Stoney Bottom GU26 ... 167 D2
Stoney Cl GU46 ... 34 A2
Stoney La Cold Ash RG19 ... 2 B4
  Medstead GU34 ... 160 A2
  Newbury RG14 ... 2 B4
  Winchester SO22 ... 175 E1
Stoneycroft [18] GU11 ... 76 B1
Stoneyfields GU9 ... 99 E1
Stony La GU32 ... 205 F1
Stookes Way GU46 ... 33 F2
Stour Rd RG23 ... 67 D1
Stourhead Cl
  Andover SP10, SP11 ... 105 F4
  Farnborough GU14 ... 56 A2
Stovold's Way GU9 ... 99 E4
Stratfield Ave GU34 ... 26 C4
Stratfield Ct RG26 ... 27 D4
Stratfield Ho [61] GU11 ... 76 C1
Stratfield Rd RG21 ... 69 D4
Stratfield Saye Ho RG26 ... 30 B4
Stratfield Saye Rd
  Bramley RG26 ... 29 D3
  Fair Oak Green RG26 ... 29 D3
Stratford Ct
  Farnborough GU14 ... 56 A2
  Farnham GU9 ... 99 D1
  [9] Winchester SO23 ... 176 A1
Stratford Dr GU12 ... 77 E4
Strathfield Rd SP10 ... 106 A3
Strathmore Ct GU15 ... 36 A3
Stratton Cl SO21 ... 134 A2
Stratton La SO21 ... 134 A2
Stratton Rd Basingstoke RG21 ... 68 C1
  Winchester SO23 ... 198 B4
Stratton Wlk GU14 ... 55 F4
Strauss Rd RG22 ... 91 E4
Stravinsky Rd RG22 ... 91 F4
Strawberry Fields RG26 ... 28 C2
Strawberry Hill RG14 ... 1 B2
Stream Farm Cl RG26 ... 122 A4
Stream Valley Rd GU10 ... 122 A3
Streamside GU13 ... 75 D4
Street End RG27 ... 53 D2
Street The Aldermaston RG26 ... 9 F4
  Binsted GU10 ... 141 F4
  Bramley RG26 ... 28 B2
  Crookham Village GU13 ... 74 B3
  Farnham GU10 ... 121 E3
  Frensham GU10 ... 144 A4
  Frensham, Dockenfield GU35 ... 143 E3
  Long Sutton RG29 ... 95 E2
  North Warnborough RG29 ... 72 B2
  Old Basing RG24 ... 70 A4
  Rotherwick RG27 ... 50 C3
  Swallowfield RG7 ... 14 A3
  Tongham GU11 ... 100 B3
Streetway Rd SP11 ... 124 C4
Strokins Rd RG20 ... 24 B2
Stroller Cl RG19 ... 2 B2
Stroud Cl Chineham RG24 ... 48 C1
  Pamber Heath RG26 ... 10 B1
Stroud La GU13 ... 74 B3
Stroudley Rd RG24 ... 69 F4
Stuart Cl GU14 ... 55 F3
Stuart Cres RG22 ... 197 F3
Stuart Ct [2] SP10 ... 83 D2
Stuart Rd RG14 ... 5 D3
Stubbington Ave GU35 ... 164 B1
Stubbs Cl SP10 ... 82 C1
Stubbs Folly GU17 ... 35 D4
Stubbs Ind Site GU12 ... 77 E3
Stubbs Moor Rd GU14 ... 55 E3
Stubbs Rd RG21 ... 69 E1
Studland Ind Est RG20 ... 3 F2
Stukeley Rd GU13 ... 69 D2
Sturdee Cl GU16 ... 36 B1
Sturt Ave GU27 ... 189 F3
Sturt Rd Camberley GU16 ... 56 B3
  Farnham GU9 ... 98 C4
  Mytchett GU14 ... 56 B3
Stymies GU35 ... 164 A1
Suffolk Rd SP10 ... 105 F4
Sullivan Cl GU14 ... 55 F2
Sullivan Rd Basingstoke RG22 ... 68 C1
  Camberley GU15 ... 35 F3
Summer Down La RG23 ... 66 C2
Summerdown Cotts RG25 ... 66 C2
Summerfield La GU10 ... 121 F1
Summerfields RG24 ... 49 D2
Summerhouse Ct GU26 ... 167 D2
Summersfield GU33 ... 207 F2

Summit Ave GU14 ... 55 D2
Sumner Ct GU11 ... 99 D2
Sumner Rd GU9 ... 99 D2
Sun Brow GU27 ... 189 F3
Sun Hill Cres SO24 ... 179 E2
Sun Hill Cty Schs SO24 ... 179 E3
Sun La SO24 ... 179 E3
Sun Ray Est GU46 ... 34 B4
Sunbury Cl GU35 ... 164 C2
Sunflower Cl RG22 ... 91 D4
Sunley Cl RG14 ... 5 D3
Sunny Hill Rd GU11 ... 76 A1
Sunny Mead RG22 ... 90 A4
Sunny View Cl [5] GU12 ... 77 D1
Sunnybank SP11 ... 104 C3
Sunnybank Mews GU12 ... 77 F2
Sunnybank Rd GU14 ... 55 D3
Sunnydell La GU10 ... 121 F3
Sunnydown Rd SO22 ... 197 D2
Sunnyside Fleet GU13 ... 53 F1
  Kingsley GU35 ... 142 B1
  Newbury RG14 ... 1 B3
Sunnyside SP10 ... 82 C1
Sunnyside Cotts RG20 ... 24 B1
Sunnyside Rd GU35 ... 166 A2
Sunvale Ave GU27 ... 189 D3
Sunvale Cl GU27 ... 189 D3
Surrey Ave GU15 ... 35 F2
Surrey Inst of Art & Design The GU9 ... 98 C1
Sussex Gdns GU13 ... 54 B2
Sussex St SO23 ... 197 F4
Sutcliffe Sq SP10 ... 83 E2
Sutherland Cl GU35 ... 164 B1
Sutherland Ct SP10 ... 83 D1
Sutherlands RG14 ... 5 E4
Sutton Field GU35 ... 164 B1
Sutton Gdns SO23 ... 198 A4
Sutton Rd Basingstoke RG24 ... 69 D4
  Camberley GU16 ... 36 C4
  Newbury RG14 ... 1 A3
Suttonwood La SO24 ... 180 C4
Swains Cl RG26 ... 26 C4
Swains Rd RG26 ... 26 C4
Swale Rd GU14 ... 55 E3
Swaledale Gdns GU13 ... 54 A2
Swallow Cl Alton GU34 ... 140 A3
  Basingstoke RG22 ... 90 C4
  North Tidworth SP9 ... 78 C3
  Yateley GU46 ... 33 F3
Swallowfield Pk RG7 ... 14 B4
Swallowfield Rd RG7 ... 14 B4
Swallowfields SP10 ... 83 D1
Swan Ct [5] Andover SP10 ... 106 A4
  Newbury RG14 ... 1 B2
Swan Ho GU14 ... 34 C4
Swan La Sandhurst GU46 ... 34 C4
  Winchester SO23 ... 197 F4
Swan Mews RG29 ... 72 B2
Swan St RG20 ... 24 B1
Swan Way GU13 ... 74 B4
Swanmore Cl SO22 ... 175 E2
Swansdown Wlk RG19 ... 2 C2
Swanwick Wlk GU14 ... 26 C4
Swedish Hos RG26 ... 27 D4
Sweetzer's Piece RG7 ... 11 E3
Swelling Hill
  Four Marks SO24 ... 182 A3
  Ropley SO24 ... 182 A3
Swift Cl Andover SP10 ... 83 D1
  Winchester SO22 ... 197 E3
Swift Rd GU9 ... 99 D4
Swift's Cl GU10 ... 99 F1
Swindon Ho [9] SP9 ... 78 C4
Swing Swang La RG21 ... 69 F4
Swingate Rd GU10 ... 122 A4
Swiss Cl GU10 ... 121 F2
Switchback La
  Farnham GU10 ... 121 E2
  Farnham GU10 ... 121 F2
Sycamore Cl Camberley GU16 ... 36 B1
  North Tidworth SP9 ... 79 D3
  Sandhurst GU17 ... 34 C4
Sycamore Cr GU33 ... 74 C3
Sycamore Cres SO20 ... 126 A2
Sycamore Dr Ash GU12 ... 77 F4
  Camberley GU16 ... 36 B1
  Farnham GU9 ... 121 F3
  Kings Worthy SO23 ... 176 A4
Sycamore Ho RG24 ... 49 D2
Sycamore Rd GU14 ... 56 A1
Sycamore Rise RG14 ... 2 A3
Sycamore Way RG21 ... 68 B4
Sycamore Wlk SP10 ... 105 E3
Sycamores The
  Blackwater GU17 ... 34 C3
  Farnborough GU16 ... 56 A2
Sydings The RG14 ... 1 A3
Sydney Cl SP9 ... 79 E4
Sydney Rd GU35 ... 164 B2
Sydney Villas GU12 ... 77 F4
Syers Cl GU33 ... 207 F2
Syers Rd GU33 ... 207 F2
Sylvan Way GU13 ... 74 C3
Sylvaner Cl RG21 ... 69 D3
Sylvester Cl RG14 ... 1 B3
Sylvia Cl RG21 ... 69 D2
Symonds St SO23 ... 198 A4
Sympson Rd RG7 ... 10 A1
Syon Pl GU14 ... 56 A2

Tadley Common Rd RG7 ... 10 A1
Tadley Hill RG26 ... 27 D4
Tadley Prim Sch RG26 ... 27 D3
Tadpole La GU13 ... 75 D1

Taiping Rd SO20 .... 126 A3
Talavera Schs GU11 .... 76 C2
Talbot Cl Mytchett GU14 .... 56 C2
  Newbury RG14 .... 1 B3
Talbot Rd GU14 .... 121 F4
Talgarth Dr GU14 .... 56 A1
Tallis Gdns RG21 .... 68 C1
Tallywater Hill GU32 .... 205 E2
Tamar Dr RG23 .... 67 D1
Tamarisk Cl RG22 .... 91 E3
Tamworth Dr GU13 .... 54 A2
Tangier Ct 9 GU11 .... 76 B1
Tanglewood RG40 .... 16 C4
Tangway RG24 .... 48 C2
Tanhouse La GU34 .... 139 F2
Tank Rd GU47 .... 35 E3
Tanner Ct GU14 .... 1 C2
Tanner St 20 SO23 .... 198 A4
Tanners Way GU10 .... 67 D1
Taplin's Farm La RG27 .... 52 C2
Taplings Cl SO22 .... 175 E2
Taplings Rd SO22 .... 175 E2
Tarbat Ct GU15 .... 35 D4
Tarn Cl GU14 .... 55 E1
Tarn La RG14 .... 5 E4
Tarn Rd GU26 .... 167 E2
Tarragon Cl GU14 .... 55 D2
Tarrant Gdns RG27 .... 52 B2
Taskers Dr SP10 .... 105 E2
Tasmania Cl RG24 .... 48 B1
Tate Sq SP10 .... 83 E2
Taverner Cl RG24 .... 69 E4
Tavistock Gdns GU14 .... 55 F4
Tavistock Inf Sch GU13 .... 74 B4
Tavistock Rd GU13 .... 74 B4
Tawny Gr GU34 .... 160 A1
Tay Cl GU14 .... 55 E3
Taylors Cl GU35 .... 164 C3
Taylors Cnr SO23 .... 176 A3
Taylors La GU35 .... 164 C3
Teal Cres RG22 .... 90 C4
Tedder Cl GU14 .... 105 D4
Tees Cl GU14 .... 55 E3
Teg Down Meads SO22 .... 175 E1
Tegg Down Rd SO24 .... 180 C2
Tekels Ave GU15 .... 36 A2
Tekels Ct GU15 .... 36 B2
Tekels Way GU16 .... 36 B2
Teleconia Cl GU35 .... 166 A2
Telegraph La GU34 .... 160 B1
Telford Gate SP10 .... 82 A1
Telford Rd RG22 .... 68 C4
Templar Cl GU47 .... 34 C4
Temple Rd GU33 .... 208 A3
Temple Towers RG21 .... 69 D3
Temple's Cl GU12 .... 100 A1
Ten Acre Wlk GU10 .... 121 E2
Tenby Rd GU14 .... 56 C4
Tennyson Way RG23 .... 68 C1
Terra Cotta Ct GU9 .... 121 E3
Terrace The Camberley GU15 .... 35 F3
  Chawton GU34 .... 161 E4
Terrys Cotts RG29 .... 72 A2
Tesimond Dr GU46 .... 33 F3
Test Ct 57 SP10 .... 83 E1
Test Mews RG28 .... 86 B2
Test Rd RG28 .... 86 B2
Test Rise SO20 .... 129 D2
Test Valley Sch The SO20 .... 149 E1
Test Way RG21 .... 69 E3
Testbourne GM Com Sch
  RG28 .... 86 B2
Tewkesbury Cl RG24 .... 48 A1
Texas Dr SO22 .... 197 D2
Thackham's La RG7 .... 52 A3
Thames Cl GU14 .... 55 E3
Thames Ct
  56 Andover SP10 .... 83 E1
  7 Basingstoke RG21 .... 69 E3
Thames Rd RG18 .... 2 C3
Theal Cl GU15 .... 35 D4
Thibet Rd GU47 .... 35 D4
Third St RG14 .... 6 B3
Thirlmere Cl Bordon GU35 .... 164 B3
  Farnborough GU14 .... 55 E2
Thirlmere Cres GU13 .... 74 C3
Thistledown Cl SP10 .... 82 C1
Thomas La RG40 .... 16 B4
Thomas Merriman Ct 1 RG14 ... 1 C1
Thomas Rd SP11 .... 108 B1
Thorlands GU27 .... 189 F4
Thorn Cl GU10 .... 121 E2
Thorn Cres GU34 .... 160 A1
Thorn Ct GU34 .... 160 A1
Thorn Dr GU34 .... 160 B1
Thorn La GU34 .... 160 B1
Thorn Rd GU10 .... 121 F3
Thornburn Chase GU15 .... 35 E3
Thorneley Rd RG20 .... 24 B1
Thornfield RG19 .... 7 D2
Thornfield Gn GU47 .... 35 E2
Thornfield Rd
  Greenham RG19 .... 7 D3
  Headley, Nr Greenham RG19 ...... 7 E2
Thornhill Rd GU12 .... 77 D2
Thornhill Rdbt RG24 .... 49 D1
Thornhill Way RG24 .... 49 D2
Thornton Cl RG26 .... 29 D1
Thornton End GU34 .... 140 B3
Thornyhurst Rd GU16 .... 56 C2
Thorold Rd GU10 .... 99 D2
Thorpe Gdns GU34 .... 139 F2
Threadgill Way SP9 .... 101 E4
Threadneedle Ho 4 SP10 ...... 106 A4
Three Acre Rd RG14 .... 5 E4

Three Horse Shoes La
  GU34 .... 203 F1
Three Stiles Rd GU9 .... 98 B1
Three Ways GU35 .... 143 D3
Threshers Cnr GU13 .... 54 B2
Throakmead GU10 .... 120 A1
Throgmorton Rd GU46 .... 33 F3
Thrush Cl RG23 .... 67 F1
Thruxton Airfield Rd SP11 ...... 103 D4
Thuillier Rd SP11 .... 108 B1
Thumwood RG24 .... 48 C2
Thundery Hill GU10 .... 100 B2
Thurbans Rd GU10 .... 121 F4
Thurmond Cres SO22 .... 197 E3
Thurmond Rd SO22 .... 197 E3
Thurstons GU34 .... 141 F4
Thyme Cl RG24 .... 49 D3
Thyme Ct GU14 .... 55 D3
Tibb's Meadow SP11 .... 57 F4
Tiberius Cl RG22 .... 68 B4
Tiberius Rd SP10 .... 83 D2
Tiberus Cl RG21 .... 68 B4
Tichborne Cl GU47 .... 35 D3
Tichborne Down SO24 .... 179 E2
Tichborne Pl GU10 .... 100 A4
Tichbourne Cl GU15 .... 36 B2
Tickenor Dr RG40 .... 16 B4
Tidbury Cotts SP11 .... 109 D1
Tidworth Rd SP4 .... 101 D4
Tigwells Field RG29 .... 95 D2
Tilbury's Cl GU35 .... 164 B2
Tile Barn Cl GU14 .... 55 F3
Tile Barn Row RG20 .... 4 B1
Tilford Rd Beacon Hill GU26 ... 167 D3
  Farnham GU10 .... 122 B3
  Tilford GU9 .... 122 B3
Tilling Cotts GU34 .... 141 D1
Tilney Cl GU34 .... 139 F2
Timber Bank GU14 .... 56 C3
Timber Cl 6 GU9 .... 98 C1
Timbercroft Cl GU34 .... 160 A1
Timberlake Rd RG21 .... 69 D3
Timbermill Ct GU27 .... 189 E3
Timor Cl RG24 .... 48 B1
Tindal Cl GU47 .... 34 A3
Tinley Gdns RG29 .... 72 C2
Tintagel Cl Basingstoke RG22 ... 68 B3
  Knights Enham SP10 .... 83 D2
Tintagel Dr GU16 .... 36 B1
Tintagel Rd RG40 .... 16 C4
Tintern Cl RG23 .... 68 C4
Tippet Gdns RG22 .... 91 F4
Titan Ho 10 RG26 .... 9 E1
Titchfield Cl RG26 .... 27 D4
Tithelands La GU34 .... 202 C2
Tittymouse La SP11 .... 81 E1
Tiverton Rd GU13 .... 68 A3
Tiverton Way GU15 .... 36 B1
Toad La GU17 .... 35 E2
Tobago Cl RG24 .... 48 A1
Tobruk Cl SP10 .... 83 D4
Tobruk Rd SP9 .... 79 E3
Tockington Ct GU17 .... 34 A3
Todmore GU33 .... 185 F2
Toledo Grove SP10 .... 83 E1
Tollgate Cl RG23 .... 67 D2
Tollgate Rd SP10 .... 82 C1
Tollgate The 20 SO23 .... 176 A1
Tollway RG14 .... 49 D2
Tolpuddle Way GU47 .... 34 B3
Tomlins Ave GU16 .... 36 B1
Tomlins Cl RG26 .... 26 C4
  Tomlinscote Sch GU16 .... 36 C1
Tomlinscote Way GU16 .... 36 C1
Tomlison Dr RG40 .... 16 C4
Tongham Meadows GU10 ...... 100 B4
Tongham Rd
  Aldershot GU12 .... 100 A4
  Farnham GU10 .... 100 A3
  Farnham, Runfold GU12 .... 100 A2
Tope Cres SP11 .... 15 E4
Tope Rd RG2 .... 15 E4
Topiary The
  Farnborough GU14 .... 55 E2
  Old Basing RG24 .... 70 A4
Toplady Pl GU9 .... 99 D4
Tor Rd GU9 .... 98 B1
Torrington Cl GU35 .... 165 D3
Totland Cl GU14 .... 55 F3
Tottenham Cl RG26 .... 28 C2
Totters La RG27 .... 51 F1
Tournai Cl GU11 .... 77 E4
Tovey Ct SP10 .... 83 E1
Tovey Pl SO23 .... 176 B4
Tower Cl Charlton SP10 .... 82 B2
  Liphook GU30 .... 187 F2
Tower Ct 6 SO22 .... 197 F4
Tower Hill GU14 .... 55 F2
  Tower Hill Prim Sch GU14 ...... 55 E2
Tower Rd Hindhead GU26 ...... 167 E2
  Liphook GU30 .... 187 F2
  Winchester SO22 .... 197 F4
Tower St Alton GU34 .... 139 F1
  Winchester SO23 .... 197 F4
Town Centre West Junction
  RG23 .... 68 C3
Town Cl SO24 .... 181 A3
Town Hall Ct RG28 .... 86 B3
Town Mill RG25 .... 88 A4
Town Mill La RG28 .... 86 B3
Town Mills RG14 .... 1 B2
Town Sq GU16 .... 36 A3
Townsend Cl RG24 .... 48 B1
Townside GU15 .... 36 A3
Trafalgar Ct GU9 .... 99 D1
Trafalgar St
  Stockbridge SO20 .... 149 F2
  Winchester SO23 .... 197 F4

Trafalgar Way
  Camberley GU47 .... 35 E2
  Stockbridge SO23 .... 149 F1
Trafford Rd SO16 .... 56 A4
Trajan Wlk SP11 .... 83 D2
Travis La GU17 .... 35 D4
Treble Cl SO22 .... 197 D2
Trebor Ave GU9 .... 99 D1
Tredenham Cl GU14 .... 77 D4
Tree Tops Ave GU16 .... 36 C4
Treeside Dr GU9 .... 99 E4
Trefoil Cl RG27 .... 52 B4
Tregenna Ho GU30 .... 187 F3
Tregolls Dr GU16 .... 56 A2
Trellis Dr RG24 .... 70 A4
Trenchard Pk GU35 .... 164 B2
Trenchard Rd SP11 .... 105 D4
Trent Cl GU14 .... 55 E3
Trent Cres RG18 .... 2 C3
Trent Ct 54 SO10 .... 83 E1
Trent Way 8 RG21 .... 69 E3
Trenton Cl GU16 .... 36 C1
Tresham Cres GU46 .... 33 F3
Triangle The RG14 .... 5 F4
Trilakes Fishery & Ctry Pk
  GU46 .... 34 B4
Trimmer's Almshouses 8
  GU9 .... 98 C1
Trimmers Cl GU9 .... 99 D4
Trimmers Field GU9 .... 99 E1
Trimmers Wood GU26 .... 167 E3
Trinidad Cl RG24 .... 48 A1
Trinity Fields GU9 .... 98 C3
Trinity Hill Farnham GU9 ...... 98 C3
  Medstead GU34 .... 159 F4
Trinity Rd SO23 .... 137 F1
Trinity Rise SP11 .... 81 F2
Trooper Bottom GU32 .... 206 A2
Trout Rd GU27 .... 189 E3
Trout Wlk RG14 .... 1 C2
Trowbridge Ho 13 SP9 ...... 78 C4
Trowe's La Beech Hill RG7 ...... 13 D2
  Swallowfield RG7 .... 14 A3
Trueman Sq SP10 .... 83 E2
Trunk Rd GU14 .... 55 D3
Trussell Cl SO22 .... 175 E2
Trussell Cres SO22 .... 175 E2
Trust RG27 .... 50 C1
Tubb's La RG26 .... 47 D4
Tubbs La RG20 .... 21 E3
Tudor Cl GU26 .... 167 D1
Tudor Ct Ash GU11 .... 77 D1
  3 Knights Enham SP10 .... 83 D2
Tudor Dr GU46 .... 34 A2
Tudor Hall GU15 .... 36 B3
Tudor Rd RG14 .... 1 C1
Tudor Way Fleet GU13 .... 75 D2
  Kings Worthy SO23 .... 176 A4
Tulip Ct RG21 .... 91 D4
Tulls La GU35 .... 165 D1
Tunball SP11 .... 37 E4
Tunbridge Cres GU30 .... 187 F3
Tunbridge La
  Bramshott GU30 .... 187 F3
  Liphook GU30 .... 187 F3
Tunnel La RG2 .... 72 A2
Tunworth Ct RG26 .... 27 D4
Tunworth Mews RG26 .... 27 D4
Tunworth Rd RG25 .... 70 C1
Turbary Gdns RG26 .... 9 F1
Turf Hill Rd GU15 .... 36 B4
Turin Ct SP10 .... 83 D2
Turk St GU34 .... 139 F2
Turk's La RG7 .... 11 E2
Turner Cl RG21 .... 69 F2
Turner Ct SP10 .... 82 C1
Turner Pl GU17 .... 35 D3
Turner's Green La RG27 ...... 53 E3
Turnhill Ct SP10 .... 83 D4
Turnpike Ind Est RG14 .... 2 A1
Turnpike Rd Newbury RG14 ... 2 B2
  Thatcham RG18, RG19 .... 2 B2
Turnpike Sch The RG14 ...... 2 A2
Turnpike Way RG23 .... 67 D1
Turnstone End 3 GU46 ...... 33 F3
Tuscam Way GU15 .... 35 E2
Tweed Cl GU14 .... 55 E3
Tweedsmuir Cl
  Basingstoke RG23 .... 68 A2
  Farnborough GU14 .... 55 D2
Twelve Acre Cres GU14 ...... 55 E3
Tweseldown Inf Sch GU13 ...... 75 D2
Tweseldown Rd GU10 .... 75 D2
Twisell Thorne GU13 .... 74 C2
Two Gate La RG25 .... 88 A4
Two Gate Meadow RG25 ...... 88 A4
Two Rivers Way RG14 .... 2 B2
Twoways Ct GU35 .... 164 B1
Twyford Cl GU14 .... 55 E3
Twyford 15 SO23 .... 176 A1
Twyford La GU10 .... 121 F3
Tydehams RG14 .... 5 E4
Tyfield RG26 .... 47 F2
Tylney La RG27 .... 50 B1
Tylston Meadow GU30 .... 187 F3
Tyndalls Est GU26 .... 167 E2
Tyne Cl GU14 .... 55 E3
Tyne Ct 58 SP10 .... 83 E1
Tyne Way RG18 .... 2 C3
Tytherley Rd SP5 .... 168 B3

Ullswater Ave GU14 .... 55 E2
Ullswater Cl Bordon GU35 ...... 164 B3
  Farnham GU9 .... 98 C3
  Thatcham RG19 .... 2 C2
Ullswater Ct GU11 .... 77 E3
Ullswater Gr SO24 .... 179 E2
Underhill La GU9 .... 121 F4
Underwood Ave GU14 .... 77 D4

Underwood Rd GU27 .... 189 E4
Union La RG20 .... 24 B3
Union Rd GU11 .... 99 D1
Union Rise GU33 .... 186 B1
Union St Aldershot GU11 ...... 76 C1
  Andover SP10 .... 106 A4
  Farnborough GU14 .... 55 F2
  Winchester SO23 .... 198 A4
Union Terr GU11 .... 76 C1
Up St Dummer RG25 .... 113 E4
  North Waltham RG25 .... 89 F1
Upfallow RG24 .... 70 A4
Uphill Rd SO22 .... 175 E3
Upland La GU33 .... 207 D4
Upland Rd GU16 .... 36 A4
Uplands Cl GU46 .... 34 C4
  Uplands Cty Prim Sch GU46 ... 34 C4
Uplands La GU34 .... 160 A1
Uplands Rd Farnham GU9 ...... 99 E1
  Winchester SO22 .... 175 F2
Upnor Cl SP9 .... 79 E4
Upper Bourne La GU10 .... 121 F3
Upper Bourne Vale GU10 ...... 121 F3
Upper Brook St SO23 .... 198 A4
Upper Charles St GU15 .... 36 A3
Upper Chestnut Dr RG21 ...... 68 C2
Upper Chobham Rd GU15 ...... 36 C2
Upper Church La GU9 .... 98 C1
Upper College Ride GU15 ...... 36 B4
Upper Dro SP10 .... 82 B1
Upper Elms Rd GU11 .... 76 C1
Upper Farm Rd RG22 .... 90 A4
Upper Gordon Rd GU15 ...... 36 A3
Upper Grove Rd GU14 .... 139 F1
Upper Hale Rd GU9 .... 99 F1
Upper High St SO23 .... 197 F4
Upper Lanham La SO24 ...... 158 B4
Upper Mount SO23 .... 207 F2
Upper Neatham Mill La
  GU34 .... 140 B3
Upper Old Park La GU9 ...... 98 C4
Upper Park Rd GU15 .... 36 B3
Upper Raymond Almshouses
  RG14 .... 1 B1
Upper Sherborne Rd RG21 ... 69 D4
Upper Soldridge Rd GU34 ...... 159 F1
Upper South View GU9 ...... 99 D2
Upper St Michael's Rd GU9 ... 99 F4
Upper Union St GU11 .... 76 C1
Upper Union Terr GU11 ...... 76 C1
Upper Verran Rd GU15 ...... 36 A2
Upper Way GU10 .... 121 F4
Upper Weybourne La GU9 ...... 99 E4
Upron Field GU22 .... 91 D4
Upton Cl GU16 .... 56 A2
Upton Cres RG21 .... 69 D4
Upton Grey Cl SO22 .... 175 E2
Upton Grey Rd RG27 .... 71 F1
Urchfont Ho 1 SP9 .... 79 D3

Vale Cl Aldershot GU9 .... 122 A2
Vale Rd Ash GU12 .... 77 F3
  Camberley GU47 .... 35 F2
  Winchester SO23 .... 198 B3
Vale The RG22 .... 67 D1
Vale View Dr RG7 .... 13 D3
Vale Way SO23 .... 154 A1
Vale Wood Dr GU10 .... 122 A2
Vale Wood La GU26 .... 167 D2
Valencia Way SP10 .... 83 D1
Valentine Wood Ind Est
  RG26 .... 10 B2
Valley Ct The 4 SO22 .... 197 E3
Valley La GU10 .... 122 A4
Valley Mead SP11 .... 105 E2
Valley Rd Camberley GU16 ...... 56 C4
  Littleton SO22 .... 175 D3
  Newbury RG14 .... 5 E4
Valley Rise SP11 .... 105 F2
Valley Side GU30 .... 187 F3
Valley The SO22 .... 197 E3
Valley View GU46 .... 34 C4
Valley Way RG26 .... 10 B1
Valmeade Cl RG27 .... 51 D3
Valon Rd RG22 .... 15 E4
Valroy Cl GU15 .... 36 A3
Van Dyck Cl RG21 .... 69 F2
Vanburgh Gdns RG22 .... 91 D4
Vanners La RG20 .... 4 A3
Varna Rd GU35 .... 164 C2
Varney Cl GU14 .... 55 E3
Vaughans GU34 .... 140 A2
Vectis Cl GU34 .... 160 A1
Velmead Cl GU13 .... 75 D4
  Velmead Jun Sch GU13 ...... 75 D4
Velmead Rd GU13 .... 75 D4
Venice Ct SP10 .... 83 E2
Venison Terr SO20 .... 170 A4
Venning Rd RG2 .... 15 E4
Ventnor Terr GU12 .... 77 D1
Venture Rdbt RG21 .... 69 E1
Verdi Cl RG22 .... 91 E4
Verge Wlk GU11 .... 99 F4
Verity Sq SP10 .... 83 E2
Vermont Woods RG40 .... 16 B4
Verne The GU13 .... 75 D3
Verner Cl GU35 .... 165 E2
Vernham Dean Gillum's
  CE Prim Sch SP11 .... 38 B3
Vernham Rd SO22 .... 175 F1
Vernon Ct GU9 .... 98 C1
Veronica Cl RG22 .... 91 D4
Veronica Dr GU13 .... 74 B3
Vesey Cl GU14 .... 55 F3
Vespasian Rd SP10 .... 83 D2
Vetch Fields RG27 .... 51 E1
Viables La RG21 .... 69 D1

Viables Rdbt RG21 .... 68 C1
Vian Pl SO23 .... 176 B4
Vicarage Cl GU10 .... 122 A4
Vicarage Gdns Fleet GU13 ...... 74 C2
  Grayshott GU26 .... 167 D2
Vicarage Hill Alton GU34 ...... 139 F2
  Hartley Wintney RG27 .... 52 B3
Vicarage La Farnham GU9 ...... 98 C1
  Farnham GU10 .... 122 A4
  Farnham, Upper Hale GU9 ...... 99 D4
  Haslemere GU27 .... 189 E3
  Mattingley RG27 .... 31 D1
  Ropley SO24 .... 181 D2
  Yateley GU47 .... 34 A4
Vicarage Rd Alton GU34 ...... 139 F1
  Blackwater GU47 .... 35 E2
  Yateley GU46 .... 34 A4
Vickers Bsns Ctr RG22 .... 68 C4
Victoria Ave GU15 .... 35 F3
Victoria Cotts RG20 .... 20 C4
Victoria Ct Andover SP11 ...... 105 F4
  18 Fleet GU13 .... 53 F1
Victoria Dr GU15 .... 35 D2
Victoria Gdns 9 Fleet GU13 ... 53 F1
  Newbury RG14 .... 1 C2
Victoria Hill Rd GU13 .... 53 F1
Victoria Pl GU21 .... 68 A2
Victoria Rd Aldershot GU11 ...... 76 C1
  Alton GU34 .... 139 F2
  Farnborough GU14 .... 55 F2
  Farnham GU11 .... 99 D1
  Fleet GU13 .... 53 F1
  Mortimer RG7 .... 11 F3
  Winchester SO23 .... 175 F1
Victoria Rd E GU34 .... 140 A2
Victoria St RG21 .... 69 D2
Victory Rdbt RG21 .... 69 D3
Vidlers Farm RG26 .... 47 F2
Vienna Ct GU14 .... 55 F3
Vigo La GU47 .... 34 A3
Vigo Rd SP10 .... 83 E1
  Vigo Schs SP10 .... 83 E1
Viking Way SP10 .... 83 D2
Villa Pl RG7 .... 14 A3
Village St Bentworth GU34 ...... 138 A3
  Chilbolton SO20 .... 129 D3
Village The
  Finchampstead RG40 .... 16 B2
  Litchfield RG28 .... 63 E4
Village Way GU46 .... 34 A4
Villiers Way RG14 .... 5 D3
Villiers Wlk RG14 .... 5 D3
Vindomis Cl GU34 .... 140 B4
Vine Cl Farnborough GU11 ...... 76 C3
  Farnham GU10 .... 121 F2
Vine Ct RG14 .... 1 C1
Vine House Cl GU14 .... 56 C2
Vine La GU9 .... 121 F3
Vine St GU11 .... 76 C1
Vine Tree Cl RG26 .... 27 D4
Vine Way GU10 .... 121 F3
Vinns La RG25 .... 87 F4
Vinson Rd GU33 .... 208 A2
Violet Cl RG22 .... 91 D4
Violet La RG26 .... 26 A3
Virginia Gdns GU14 .... 56 A1
Viscounts Cl SP10 .... 83 F1
Vivaldi Cl RG22 .... 91 F4
Vivian Cl GU13 .... 75 D3
Vivian Rd RG22 .... 69 E4
Vo-tec Ctr GU11 .... 2 B1
Vockins Cl 2 SP9 .... 78 C4
Vulcan Cl GU46 .... 34 C4
Vulcan Ct GU17, GU46 .... 34 C4
Vulcan Ho 6 RG26 .... 9 E1
Vulcan Way GU46 .... 34 C4
Vyne Cl GU34 .... 139 F2
Vyne Meadow RG26 .... 47 F2
Vyne Rd Basingstoke RG21 ...... 69 D3
  Sherborne St John RG24 ...... 48 A3
Vyne Sec Sch The RG21 ...... 69 D4

Wade Rd RG24 .... 69 F4
Wadwick Bottom SP11 .... 62 A3
Waggoners Way GU26 .... 166 C2
Waggoners Wells Rd GU26 ...... 166 C1
Wagner Cl RG22 .... 91 F4
Wakeford Cl RG26 .... 10 B1
Wakeford Ct RG26 .... 10 B1
Wakefords Copse GU13 .... 75 D2
Wakefords Pk GU13 .... 75 D2
Wakes Cotts GU34 .... 184 C4
Walburton Ho RG27 .... 52 B3
Waldegrave Pl RG14 .... 1 C2
Waldorf Hts GU17 .... 35 D2
Wales St SO23 .... 198 A4
Walk The RG24 .... 49 F4
Walker's Ridge GU15 .... 36 B3
Wall La RG7 .... 11 D1
Walldown Rd GU35 .... 164 C1
Walled Meadow SP10 .... 106 A4
Wallins Copse RG24 .... 48 C1
Wallis Ct RG22 .... 68 B3
Wallis Dr RG14 .... 2 B3
Wallis Rd RG21, RG24 .... 69 D2
Wallop Dr RG22 .... 91 D3
Wallop Dro SO20 .... 147 E2
  Wallop Prim Sch SO20 ...... 147 F4
Wallop Rd Grateley SO20 ...... 125 D4
  Over Wallop SO20 .... 125 D2
Walmer Cl GU16 .... 56 C4
Walnut Cl Aldershot GU9 ...... 99 F4
  Alton GU34 .... 139 F3
  Yateley GU17, GU47 .... 34 A2
Walnut Tree Cl SO21 .... 153 E2
Walnut Tree Gr SP11 .... 80 C1
Walnut Tree Rd SP10 .... 105 F4
Walpole Gdns RG27 .... 52 B4

Walpole Rd SO22 ...... 197 E3
Walsh Meml CE Schs GU12 ...... 77 E1
Waltham Ct RG25 ...... 88 A1
Waltham La
  North Waltham RG25 ...... 88 B3
  Overton RG25 ...... 88 B3
Waltham Rd RG25 ...... 88 A4
Walton Cl GU13 ...... 74 C4
Walton Pl SO22 ...... 197 E3
Walton Way RG14 ...... 2 A2
Walworth Ent Ctr SP10 ...... 83 E1
Walworth Ind Est SP10 ...... 83 E1
Walworth Rd Andover SP10 ...... 83 E1
  Picket Piece SP11 ...... 84 B2
Wandle Cl GU12 ...... 77 F1
Wandsdyke Cl GU16 ...... 56 B4
Wantage Rd GU15 ...... 35 D4
Warblington Cl RG26 ...... 27 C4
Warbrook La RG27 ...... 32 C4
Ward Cl SP10 ...... 83 D1
Warehouse Rd RG14 ...... 6 B3
Wargrove Dr GU17 ...... 35 D4
Warminster Ho 11 SP9 ...... 78 C4
Warner Ct 11 SO23 ...... 176 A1
Warren Cl Bordon GU35 ...... 164 A1
  Fleet GU13 ...... 75 D4
  Hartley Wintney RG27 ...... 52 B3
  Sandhurst GU17 ...... 34 C4
  Wokingham RG40 ...... 16 B3
Warren Cnr GU10 ...... 98 A4
Warren Dr SP11 ...... 104 C2
Warren La Colemore GU32 ...... 206 A3
  Froxfield GU32 ...... 206 A3
  Wokingham RG40 ...... 16 B3
Warren Rd Bordon GU33 ...... 186 B1
  Liss GU33 ...... 208 A4
  Newbury RG14 ...... 5 D3
  Winchester SO23 ...... 198 B4
Warren Rise GU15 ...... 36 B2
Warren The Aldershot GU11 ...... 76 B1
  Farnham GU9 ...... 99 E4
  Tadley RG26 ...... 26 C4
Warren Way RG24 ...... 68 B2
Warrington Mews GU11 ...... 99 E4
Warton Rd RG21 ...... 69 E3
Warwick Aldershot GU10 ...... 100 A4
  Camberley GU15 ...... 36 C2
  Whitchurch RG28 ...... 86 B3
  13 Winchester SO23 ...... 176 A1
Warwick Ct 14 SO23 ...... 176 A1
Warwick Dr RG14 ...... 1 C1
Warwick Rd Ash GU12 ...... 77 F4
  Basingstoke RG22 ...... 68 B3
Wash Brook RG27 ...... 51 D1
Wash Water RG20 ...... 4 C2
Washbury Ho RG14 ...... 5 E4
Washford Cl GU35 ...... 164 C2
Washford La Bordon GU35 ...... 164 C2
  Lindford GU35 ...... 164 C2
Washington Gdns RG40 ...... 16 C4
Wasing La RG7 ...... 9 E4
Watch La RG28 ...... 64 A1
Watchetts Cty Mid Sch
  GU17 ...... 35 E1
Watchetts Dr GU15 ...... 36 A1
Watchetts Lake Cl GU16 ...... 36 A2
Watchetts Rd GU47 ...... 35 F2
Watchmoor Pk GU47 ...... 35 F2
Watchmoor Rd GU15 ...... 35 F2
Watchmoor Trad Est GU15 ...... 35 F2
Water Cl SO23 ...... 198 A4
Water End La RG24 ...... 71 D4
Water La Andover SP11 ...... 105 F2
  Bishop's Sutton SO24 ...... 180 A2
  Farnborough GU14 ...... 55 F4
  Farnham GU9 ...... 99 E2
  Greenham RG19 ...... 6 A4
  Upper Clatford SP10 ...... 105 F2
  Winchester SO23 ...... 198 A4
Water Rede GU14 ...... 74 C2
Water Ridges RG22 ...... 90 A4
Watercress Meadow SO24 ...... 179 D2
Waterfront Bsns Pk GU13 ...... 54 A2
Wateridge Rd RG24 ...... 69 E4
Waterloo Ave RG23 ...... 68 B4
Waterloo Cl GU15 ...... 36 C4
Waterloo Ct Andover SP10 ...... 106 A4
  Whitchurch RG28 ...... 86 B3
Waterloo Rd GU12 ...... 77 D1
Waterloo Terr SP11 ...... 105 E2
Waterman Cl GU35 ...... 164 C1
Watermills Cl SP11 ...... 105 F3
Waterside GU30 ...... 187 E4
Waterside Cl GU35 ...... 164 C2
Waterside Ct
  Alton GU34 ...... 140 A2
  Fleet GU13 ...... 54 A2
  Newbury RG14 ...... 2 A2
Waterside Mews GU13 ...... 54 A2
Watersmeet 36 SO23 ...... 198 A4
Watery La
  Andover SP10 ...... 83 D1
  Crookham Village GU13 ...... 74 C2
  Hamstead Marshall RG20 ...... 3 E3
  Kintbury RG20 ...... 3 E3
Watkins Cl RG40 ...... 16 B4
Watley La SO21 ...... 174 B2
Watling End RG22 ...... 91 D4
Watson Acre SP11 ...... 105 F4
Watson Way RG22 ...... 68 B3
Watt Cl SP10 ...... 82 B1
Watts Rd GU14 ...... 55 E3
Wavell Cl RG23 ...... 68 C1
Wavell Rd SP9 ...... 78 B4
Wavell Sch The GU11 ...... 76 C4
Wavell Way SO22 ...... 197 E3
Waverley Abbey GU10, GU9 ...... 122 C4

Waverley Ave
  Basingstoke RG21 ...... 69 D1
  Fleet GU13 ...... 54 A1
Waverley Cl Camberley GU15 ...... 36 B2
  Farnham GU11 ...... 99 D1
  Odiham RG29 ...... 72 C2
Waverley Dr Ash GU12 ...... 77 F3
  Camberley GU15 ...... 36 B3
  South Wonston SO21 ...... 153 F2
Waverley Gdns GU12 ...... 77 F3
Waverley La GU9 ...... 99 E1
Waverley Rd
  Farnborough GU14 ...... 56 A2
  Wokingham RG40 ...... 16 B4
Wayman Rd GU14 ...... 55 E4
Waynflete La GU9 ...... 98 B1
Waynflete Pl SO22 ...... 197 E3
Ways End GU15 ...... 36 B2
Waysend Ho GU15 ...... 36 B2
Wayside Cotts GU10 ...... 144 B2
Wayside Rd RG23 ...... 68 A3
Weale Ct GU12 ...... 69 D3
Weatherby Gdns RG27 ...... 52 B3
Weathermore La GU34 ...... 160 B1
Weaver's Wlk RG14 ...... 1 C2
Weavers Cl SP10 ...... 106 A4
Weavers Gdns GU10 ...... 121 E4
Webb Cl RG24 ...... 48 C2
Webbs Farm Cl RG28 ...... 86 B2
Webster Rd SO22 ...... 175 D1
Wedman's La RG27 ...... 50 C3
Wedman's Pl RG27 ...... 50 C3
Wedmore Cl SO22 ...... 197 D2
Weeke Manor Cl SO22 ...... 175 E1
Weeke Prim Sch SO22 ...... 175 E1
Weir Ave GU14 ...... 55 F2
Weir Cl GU14 ...... 55 F2
Weir Cotts GU34 ...... 42 C4
Weir Rd RG27 ...... 52 A2
Weirs The RG28 ...... 86 B2
Weirs The 4 SO23 ...... 198 A3
Welbeck Cl GU14 ...... 55 E2
Weldon Cl GU13 ...... 75 D3
Well Cl Camberley GU15 ...... 35 F2
  North Waltham RG25 ...... 89 F1
  Wooton St Lawrence RG23 ...... 67 F4
Well House La Bramshill RG7 ...... 14 C2
  Kings Worthy SO22 ...... 175 F3
Well La Long Sutton GU34 ...... 119 D4
  Lower Froyle GU34 ...... 119 D4
Well Meadow RG14 ...... 1 C3
Well Rd GU10 ...... 97 E3
Well St RG20 ...... 22 C3
Wella Rd RG23 ...... 68 C1
Wellburn Cl GU17, GU47 ...... 34 C4
Weller Dr Arborfield RG40 ...... 15 F3
  Camberley GU15 ...... 36 A2
Wellesley Cl GU12 ...... 77 E4
Wellesley Ct SP10 ...... 106 A3
Wellesley Gate 19 GU11 ...... 76 C1
Wellesley Gdn GU9 ...... 99 D4
Wellesley Rd Aldershot GU11 ...... 76 B1
  Andover SP10 ...... 106 A3
  Frensham GU10 ...... 144 C3
Wellhouse Rd GU34 ...... 138 C1
Wellington Ave
  Aldershot GU11 ...... 76 B1
  Bordon GU35 ...... 164 B1
  Fleet GU13 ...... 54 A1
Wellington Cl Newbury RG14 ...... 2 A3
  Sandhurst GU47 ...... 35 D4
Wellington Cotts RG20 ...... 3 F1
Wellington Cres RG26 ...... 9 D1
Wellington Ctr The 10 GU12 ...... 76 C1
Wellington Ctry Pk RG7 ...... 14 B1
Wellington Gdns 18 GU11 ...... 76 B1
Wellington La GU9 ...... 99 D4
Wellington Rd Andover SP10 ...... 82 C1
  North Tidworth SP9 ...... 79 D3
  Sandhurst GU47 ...... 35 D4
Wellington St GU11 ...... 76 C1
Wellington Terr
  Basingstoke RG22 ...... 68 B4
  Sandhurst GU15 ...... 35 D4
Wellmans Meadow RG20 ...... 24 B2
Wells Cotts GU10 ...... 121 F4
Wells's La RG28 ...... 86 A2
Wellspring Ho RG23 ...... 68 B1
Wellurn Ct SP10 ...... 106 A4
Welsh La RG7 ...... 13 F1
Welshman's Rd RG26 ...... 10 C3
Wendan Rd RG14 ...... 5 E4
Wensley Dr GU13 ...... 54 A2
Wentworth Cl Ash GU12 ...... 77 F4
  Farnham GU9 ...... 99 E3
  Yateley GU46 ...... 34 A3
Wentworth Cres GU12 ...... 77 F3
Wentworth Ct RG14 ...... 1 C1
Wentworth Gdns GU14 ...... 139 F2
Wentworth Grange SO22 ...... 197 F3
Wentworth Lodge RG14 ...... 1 B1
Wesley Rd SO23 ...... 176 B4
Wesley Wlk 17 RG21 ...... 69 D3
Wessex Ave RG29 ...... 72 B1
Wessex Cl RG21 ...... 69 D2
Wessex Cres RG21 ...... 72 B1
Wessex Dr Odiham RG29 ...... 72 B1
  Winchester SO22 ...... 175 D1
Wessex Gdns SP10 ...... 105 F4
Wessex Mews SO20 ...... 149 F2
Wessex Pl GU11 ...... 99 D1
West Ave GU9 ...... 99 D3
West Cl GU9 ...... 99 D4
West Cotts GU26 ...... 167 D3
West End Cl SO22 ...... 197 F4
West End Cl GU9 ...... 98 C1
West End Gr GU9 ...... 98 C1
West End Inf Sch GU11 ...... 76 B1

West End La GU34 ...... 159 D2
West End Terr SO22 ...... 197 F4
West Field Rd SO23 ...... 154 B1
West Fryerne GU47 ...... 34 A4
West Gn GU46 ...... 33 F4
West Green Ho RG27 ...... 51 F3
West Green Rd RG27 ...... 52 A3
West Ham Cl RG22 ...... 68 B2
West Ham Est RG23 ...... 68 C2
West Ham La
  Basingstoke RG22 ...... 68 B3
  Basingstoke, Worting RG22 ...... 68 A2
West Ham Pk RG22 ...... 68 B3
West Ham Rdbt RG22 ...... 68 B2
West Hayes SO22 ...... 197 E4
West Heath Rd GU14 ...... 55 E2
West Hill Dr SO22 ...... 197 F4
West Hill Pk SO22 ...... 197 E4
West Hill Rd N SO21 ...... 153 F3
West Hill Rd S SO21 ...... 153 F2
West Mills RG14 ...... 1 B2
West Mills Yd RG14 ...... 1 B2
West Pk SP11 ...... 81 D3
West Portway SP10 ...... 82 B1
West Rd Barton Stacey SO21 ...... 130 B4
  Camberley GU15 ...... 36 A3
  Farnborough GU14 ...... 55 F4
West Ring GU10 ...... 100 C4
West St Andover SP10 ...... 106 A4
  Burghclere RG20 ...... 22 B2
  Farnham GU9 ...... 98 C1
  New Alresford SO24 ...... 179 E3
  Newbury RG14 ...... 1 B2
  Odiham RG29 ...... 72 B1
  Tadley RG26 ...... 27 D4
West Tytherley CE Prim Sch
  SP5 ...... 191 D4
West View SO23 ...... 164 A1
West View Dr SO20 ...... 129 D2
West View Rd GU35 ...... 166 A2
West Way SP10 ...... 83 E1
Westbourne Rd GU47 ...... 35 E4
Westbourne Terr 2 RG14 ...... 1 C2
Westbrook Cl RG23 ...... 90 A4
Westbrook Ct RG22 ...... 68 A2
Westbrook Wlk 7 GU34 ...... 139 F2
Westbrooke Cl 15 SP10 ...... 106 A4
Westbrooke Rd GU34 ...... 139 F2
Westburn Fields GU34 ...... 119 E2
Westbury Ave GU13 ...... 75 E4
Westbury Cl GU13 ...... 75 E4
Westbury Gdns GU13 ...... 75 E4
Westbury Ho 5 SP9 ...... 78 C3
Westdeane Ct RG21 ...... 68 C2
Westerdale Dr GU16 ...... 36 C2
Western Ave Andover SP10 ...... 106 A4
  Newbury RG14 ...... 1 B2
Western CE Prim Sch
  SO22 ...... 197 E4
Western Cross RG29 ...... 72 B1
Western End RG14 ...... 1 B1
Western La RG29 ...... 72 B2
Western Rd Aldershot GU11 ...... 76 B1
  Andover SP10 ...... 106 A4
  Bordon GU35 ...... 164 B3
  Liss GU33 ...... 207 F2
  Winchester SO22 ...... 197 F4
Western Way RG22 ...... 68 B2
Westfield Cl RG26 ...... 27 D4
Westfield Cres RG18 ...... 2 C2
Westfield Ct 9 GU13 ...... 54 A1
Westfield Dro SO24 ...... 201 D1
Westfield Rd
  Basingstoke RG21 ...... 69 E2
  Camberley GU17, GU47 ...... 35 F1
  Littleton SO22 ...... 175 D3
  Thatcham RG18 ...... 2 C3
Westfield Way RG14 ...... 1 B1
Westfields Schs GU46 ...... 33 F3
Westgate Cl RG23 ...... 68 A3
Westgate Ct RG14 ...... 1 B1
Westgate Rd RG14 ...... 1 B1
Westgate Sec Sch SO22 ...... 175 F1
Westglade GU14 ...... 55 D2
Westland RG18 ...... 2 C2
Westlands Rd RG14 ...... 5 F4
Westley Cl SO22 ...... 175 E1
Westley Cotts SO21 ...... 174 A2
Westley La SO21 ...... 174 B2
Westlyn Rd RG26 ...... 10 B1
Westmarch Bsns Ctr SP10 ...... 83 D1
Westmead Farnborough GU14 ...... 55 F2
  2 Farnham GU9 ...... 98 C1
Westmead Dr RG14 ...... 5 E4
Westminster Cl
  Basingstoke RG22 ...... 91 D4
  Fleet GU13 ...... 54 A1
Westminster Gate SO22 ...... 197 D3
Westminster Ho 5 RG21 ...... 69 D3
Westmorland Dr GU15 ...... 36 C2
Weston Cl RG20 ...... 94 A3
Weston Colley SO21 ...... 132 B2
Weston Down Rd SO21 ...... 132 C3
Weston Ho RG14 ...... 29 E1
Weston La SP5 ...... 168 A3
Westover Farm SP11 ...... 128 A3
Westover Rd GU13 ...... 54 B1
Westray GU21 ...... 69 E4
Westside Cl RG21 ...... 68 B2
Westview Rd SO22 ...... 175 D1
Westwood RG14 ...... 2 A1
Westwood Rd RG14 ...... 6 A4
Westwood View SO24 ...... 201 D1
Wetherby Gdns
  Charlton SP10 ...... 82 C1
  10 Farnborough GU16 ...... 56 A1
Wetherby Ho GU15 ...... 36 A4
Wey Bank GU10 ...... 120 B2

Wey Cl Ash GU12 ...... 77 F1
  Camberley GU47 ...... 35 E4
Wey Hill GU27 ...... 189 E3
Wey Lodge Cl GU30 ...... 188 A2
Weybank Cl GU9 ...... 99 D2
Weybourne Cty Inf Sch GU9 ...... 99 E3
Weybourne Rd
  Aldershot GU9 ...... 99 E3
  Farnham GU9 ...... 99 E3
Weybridge Mead GU47 ...... 34 B4
Weybrook Ct RG26 ...... 47 E2
Weydon Hill Cl GU9 ...... 121 F4
Weydon Hill Rd GU9 ...... 121 F4
Weydon La GU9 ...... 121 F4
Weydon Mill La GU9 ...... 98 C1
Weydon Sch GU9 ...... 121 E4
Weydown Ct SO22 ...... 189 F4
Weydown Ind Est GU27 ...... 189 F4
Weydown Rd GU27 ...... 189 F4
Weyford Schs GU35 ...... 164 C2
Weyhill Cl RG26 ...... 26 C4
Weyhill Ct SP11 ...... 81 E1
Weyhill Rd Andover SP10 ...... 105 E4
  Penton Grafton SP11 ...... 81 F1
Weyland Cl GU30 ...... 188 A3
Weyside GU11 ...... 99 D1
Weysprings GU27 ...... 189 F3
Weysprings Cl 3 RG21 ...... 69 E3
Weywood Cl GU9 ...... 99 E4
Weywood La GU9 ...... 99 E4
Wharf Rd SO23 ...... 198 A3
Wharf Mill 2 SO23 ...... 198 A3
Wharf Rd Ash GU12 ...... 77 F2
  Camberley GU16 ...... 56 C3
  Newbury RG14 ...... 1 C2
Wharf St 1 SO23 ...... 198 A3
Wharf The Newbury RG14 ...... 1 C2
  Odiham RG29 ...... 72 C2
Wharf Way GU14 ...... 56 C3
Wharfenden Way GU14 ...... 56 B3
Wheatland SO22 ...... 197 E3
Wheatlands La RG14 ...... 4 C3
Wheatley La GU35 ...... 142 A3
Wheatleys Cl RG25 ...... 89 D2
Wheatsheaf La RG14 ...... 1 C2
Wheeler CE RG28 ...... 86 B2
Wheeler Hill RG27 ...... 51 E1
Wheelwrights La GU26 ...... 166 C2
Wherwell Cty Prim Sch
  SP11 ...... 128 A4
Whetstone Rd GU14 ...... 55 D2
Whin Holt GU13 ...... 75 D3
Whinchat Cl RG27 ...... 52 B4
Whins Cl GU47 ...... 35 F2
Whins Dr GU15 ...... 35 F2
Whistler Cl RG21 ...... 69 E2
Whistler Gr GU15 ...... 35 D3
Whistlers La RG26 ...... 10 C1
Whitchurch CE Prim Sch
  RG28 ...... 86 B2
Whitchurch Cl GU11 ...... 100 A3
Whitchurch Silk Mill RG28 ...... 86 B2
Whitchurch Sta RG28 ...... 86 B2
White Acres Rd GU16 ...... 56 B2
White Ave GU33 ...... 186 B1
White Cottage Cl GU9 ...... 99 D3
White Farm La SN8 ...... 18 A3
White Hart Ho GU15 ...... 35 E2
White Hart Ind Est GU15 ...... 35 E2
White Hart La
  Basingstoke RG21 ...... 69 E2
  Charter Alley RG26 ...... 46 C4
  White Hart Par GU47 ...... 35 E2
White Hill Burghclere RG20 ...... 22 A1
  Ecchinswell RG20 ...... 23 E2
  Kingsclere RG20 ...... 44 A3
  Long Sutton RG29 ...... 96 A1
White Horse Crossroads
  GU32 ...... 205 F3
White Horse La GU34 ...... 16 A3
White House Cl RG22 ...... 68 C1
White House Gdns GU46 ...... 34 A4
White House The SP9 ...... 78 C3
White House Wlk GU9 ...... 99 D4
White La Greywell RG25 ...... 71 E1
  Hannington RG26 ...... 66 B3
  Mapledurwell RG25 ...... 71 E1
White Lion Way GU46 ...... 34 A4
White Oak Way SP10 ...... 105 E2
White Post La GU9 ...... 121 F2
White Rd GU15 ...... 35 E3
White Rose La GU10 ...... 121 F4
White Swan Ct SO21 ...... 131 E2
Whitebeam Gdns GU14 ...... 55 D2
Whitebines GU9 ...... 99 D1
Whitedown GU34 ...... 139 F1
Whitedown Cotts 1 GU34 ...... 139 F2
Whitedown La GU34 ...... 139 E1
Whitedown Rd RG26 ...... 26 B4
Whitedown Special Sch
  GU34 ...... 139 F1
Whitehall Dr RG2 ...... 15 E4
Whitehall Rd SO20 ...... 172 C4
Whitehead Cl RG21 ...... 69 F4
Whitehill Cl GU16 ...... 36 A4
Whitehill La
  Bishop's Sutton SO24 ...... 179 F2
  New Alresford SO24 ...... 179 F2
Whitehill Pk GU35 ...... 186 C4
Whitehill Rd GU35 ...... 164 C1
Whites Cl RG27 ...... 50 C1
Whites Rd GU16 ...... 56 B1
Whiteshoot SO20 ...... 170 A3
Whiteshute La SO23 ...... 197 F3
Whitestones RG21 ...... 91 E3
Whitethorn Cl GU12 ...... 77 F1
Whitewater CE Prim Sch
  RG27 ...... 50 C3

Whitewater Rd RG29 ...... 72 B2
Whitewater Rise RG27 ...... 51 E1
Whiteways End GU10 ...... 100 A2
Whitewood RG24 ...... 48 C2
Whitlet Cl GU14 ...... 98 C1
Whitley Rd GU46 ...... 34 A2
Whitmoor Vale Rd
  Beacon Hill GU26 ...... 166 C3
  Grayshott GU26 ...... 166 C3
Whitmore Cl GU17 ...... 35 D4
Whitmore Gn GU9 ...... 99 E3
Whitmore Vale GU26 ...... 166 B3
Whitmore Vale Rd
  Grayshott GU26 ...... 166 C2
  Headley GU26 ...... 166 B4
Whitney Rd RG21 ...... 69 F4
Whittle Cl RG40 ...... 16 B4
Whittle Cres GU14 ...... 55 E4
Whittle Rd SP10 ...... 82 A1
Whittle Rdbt SP10 ...... 55 D1
Whynot La SP10 ...... 105 F4
Whyte Ave GU11 ...... 100 A4
Wick Hill La RG40 ...... 16 C3
Wicket Hill GU10 ...... 121 F3
Wickham Cl Alton GU34 ...... 139 E1
  Fleet GU13 ...... 74 C3
  Tadley RG26 ...... 26 C4
Wickham Pl GU13 ...... 74 C3
Wickham Rd Camberley GU15 ...... 36 B4
  Fleet GU13 ...... 74 C3
Wicklow Ct RG23 ...... 68 A2
Widgeons GU34 ...... 139 F3
Widmore Rd RG22 ...... 68 B1
Wield Grange SO24 ...... 136 C1
Wield Industries SO24 ...... 137 D2
Wield Rd SO24 ...... 159 E4
Wights Wlk RG22 ...... 91 D4
Wigmore Rd RG26 ...... 9 E1
Wilberforce Cl 2 SO22 ...... 197 E3
Wild Briar RG40 ...... 16 B4
Wild Herons RG27 ...... 51 E1
Wilderness Rd GU16 ...... 36 B1
Wilders Cl GU15 ...... 36 A2
Wildhern SP11 ...... 59 F1
Wildmoor La
  Church End RG24 ...... 49 E3
  Sherfield on Loddon RG24 ...... 49 F4
Wildwood Gdns RG26 ...... 9 D1
Wildwood Gdns GU46 ...... 34 A2
Will Hall Cl GU34 ...... 139 E2
Willems Ave GU11 ...... 76 B1
William Cobbett Cty Jun Sch
  GU9 ...... 99 E3
William Farthing Cl GU11 ...... 76 C1
William Hitchcock Ho 5
  GU14 ...... 55 F4
William Way GU34 ...... 140 A3
Williams Way GU13 ...... 54 B1
Willian Pl GU34 ...... 167 E3
Willington Cl GU15 ...... 35 F3
Willis La GU34 ...... 160 C1
Willis Mus The RG21 ...... 69 D2
Willis Waye SO23 ...... 176 B3
Willoughby Cl GU34 ...... 139 F2
Willoughby Way RG22 ...... 68 B3
Willow Cl Bordon GU35 ...... 164 C2
  Liphook GU30 ...... 188 A2
  Mytchett GU16 ...... 56 B2
  Newbury RG14 ...... 1 B1
Willow Cres GU14 ...... 55 F4
Willow Ct Ash GU12 ...... 77 F4
  Camberley GU15 ...... 36 A1
Willow Gdns GU30 ...... 188 A2
Willow Gr SP11 ...... 105 F4
Willow Ho RG24 ...... 49 D2
Willow La GU17 ...... 35 D2
Willow Mews 3 SP9 ...... 79 D4
Willow Pk GU12 ...... 77 E1
Willow Rd Bishop's Green RG20 ...... 6 B1
  Liss GU33 ...... 208 A4
  Tadley RG26 ...... 26 C4
Willow Way Aldershot GU12 ...... 100 B4
  Basingstoke RG22 ...... 68 B4
  Farnham GU9 ...... 99 D3
  Middle Wallop SO20 ...... 126 A2
  Sherfield on Loddon RG26 ...... 29 E1
Willowdale RG40 ...... 16 B4
Willowford GU46 ...... 34 A3
Willowmead Cl RG14 ...... 5 D3
Willows End GU46 ...... 34 C4
Willows The Andover SP10 ...... 105 F3
  Farnham GU12 ...... 100 A3
  North Warnborough RG29 ...... 72 B2
Wilmot Way
  Basingstoke RG22 ...... 68 B3
  Camberley RG26 ...... 36 B2
Wilmot Wlk RG14 ...... 5 D3
Wilsom Rd GU34 ...... 140 A2
Wilson Cl Alton GU34 ...... 140 A2
  Middle Wallop SO20 ...... 126 A2
Wilson Ho 14 SP9 ...... 78 C4
Wilson Rd Aldershot GU12 ...... 77 D1
  Farnborough GU14 ...... 55 E2
Wilson Valkenburg Ct RG14 ...... 1 B2
Wilsons Rd GU35 ...... 165 F3
Wilton Cl GU16 ...... 56 A2
Wilton Pl RG23 ...... 68 C2
Wilton Rd GU47 ...... 35 F2
Wilton Terr SP9 ...... 101 F4
Wimborne Ho GU14 ...... 56 A1
Wimbushes RG40 ...... 16 A3
Wincanton Cl GU34 ...... 140 A1
Winchcombe Cl GU13 ...... 75 D4
Winchcombe Cty Schs
  RG14 ...... 1 C2

Winchcombe Rd
2 Basingstoke RG24 .... **69** D2
Newbury RG14 .... **1** C1
Winchester Coll (New Hall)
SO23 .... **198** A3
Winchester College SO22 ...... **197** F3
Winchester Gdns SP10 .... **106** A3
Winchester Hill SO21 .... **131** E2
Winchester Ho 9 SP9 .... **78** C3
Winchester Rd Alton GU34 ... **161** E4
Andover SP10 .... **106** A2
Ash GU12 .... **77** F2
Basingstoke RG22 .... **91** D4
Chawton GU34 .... **161** E4
Four Marks GU34 .... **160** B2
Frensham GU10 .... **144** C4
Goodworth Clatford SP10 ...... **106** A2
King's Somborne SO20 .... **172** A2
Kingsclere RG22 .... **44** B4
Micheldever SO21 .... **133** D1
New Alresford SO24 .... **179** D3
Upper Clatford SP10, SP11 ... **106** A2
Wherwell SP11 .... **106** A2
Whitchurch RG28 .... **86** B2
Winchester Road Rdbt RG23 ... **68** C2
Winchester Sch of Art SO23 .. **198** A4
Winchester St
16 Andover SP11 .... **106** A4
12 Basingstoke RG24 .... **69** D2
Chilbolton SO20 .... **129** D3
Farnborough GU12 .... **77** D4
Overton RG25 .... **88** A4
Whitchurch RG28 .... **86** B2
Winchester Sta SO22 .... **197** F4
Winchester Way GU15 .... **35** D3
Winchfield Ct RG27 .... **53** D1
Winchfield Gdns RG26 .... **27** D4
Winchfield Hurst RG27 .... **52** C1
Winchfield Sta RG27 .... **52** B1
Windermere Ave RG22 .... **68** A1
Windermere Cl GU14 .... **55** E2
Windermere Ct GU12 .... **77** E2
Windermere Gdns SO24 ...... **179** E2
Windermere Rd GU35 .... **164** B3
Windermere Way Farnham GU9 **98** C3
Thatcham RG19 .... **2** C2
Winding Wood Dr GU16 .... **36** C2
Windmill Cnr RG7 .... **11** F3
Windmill Cl 4 Aldershot GU12 .. **77** D1
Mortimer RG26 .... **11** F3
Windmill Dr GU35 .... **165** F3
Windmill Fields
East Worldham GU34 .... **141** D1
Four Marks GU34 .... **160** B2
Windmill Hill GU34 .... **140** A1
Windmill La Alton GU34 .... **140** A1
Hurstbourne Tarrant SP11 .... **60** B4
Windmill Rd Aldershot GU14 ... **77** D1
Mortimer RG7 .... **11** F3
Windrush Cl 19 RG21 .... **69** E3
Windrush Hts GU46 .... **34** C4
Windsor Cl GU34 .... **139** E2
Windsor Cres GU9 .... **98** C3
Windsor Ct Camberley GU12 ... **36** A2
7 Fleet GU13 .... **54** A1
Windsor Gdns Ash GU12 .... **77** D1
Basingstoke RG22 .... **91** D3
Windsor Ho 18 SO23 .... **198** A4
Farnborough GU16 .... **56** A1
Lindford GU35 .... **164** C3
Medstead GU34 .... **160** A2
New Alresford SO24 .... **179** E2
Windsor Ride Sandhurst GU17 ... **35** F4
Wokingham RG40 .... **16** C4
Windsor Rise RG14 .... **6** A4
Windsor Way Aldershot GU11 ... **76** C1
Camberley GU14 .... **56** B4

Windsor Wlk GU35 .... **164** C3
Wingate Ct GU11 .... **76** B1
Wings Cl GU9 .... **98** C4
Wings Rd GU9 .... **98** C3
Winklebury Ctr RG21 .... **68** B3
Winklebury Schs RG22 .... **68** B3
Winklebury Way RG23 .... **68** B3
Winkworth La RG26 .... **10** A1
Winkworth Pl GU9 .... **99** D2
Winnall Ind Est 9 SO23 .... **198** A3
Winnall Cl SO23 .... **176** B1
Winnall Manor Rd SO23 .... **198** B4
Winnall Prim Sch SO23 .... **198** B4
Winnall Trad Est SO23 .... **198** B4
Winnall Valley Rd SO23 .... **198** B4
Winslade La RG25 .... **115** E4
Winslade Rd RG22 .... **175** E2
Winston Ave RG26 .... **27** D3
Winston Cl GU16 .... **56** B3
Winston Rise GU34 .... **160** A2
Winston Way RG19 .... **2** B2
Winterbourne Ho RG22 .... **68** B1
Winterbourne Wlk GU14 .... **56** B4
Winterdyne Mews SP10 .... **105** F4
Winterthur Way RG21 .... **69** D3
Winterton Dr RG14 .... **1** A3
Winton Chase SP10 .... **106** B4
Winton Cl SP9 .... **78** C2
Winton Cres GU46 .... **34** A3
Winton Hill SO20 .... **150** A2
Winton Rd 24 Aldershot GU11 ... **76** C1
Farnham GU9 .... **99** D2
Winton Sch SP10 .... **106** B4
Winton Sq RG21, RG25 .... **69** D2
Wiremead La Amport SP11 ..... **103** F4
Thruxton SP11 .... **103** F4
Wishanger La GU10 .... **143** F1
Wishmoor Cl GU15 .... **36** B4
Wishmoor Rd GU15 .... **36** B4
Wisley Gdns GU14 .... **55** D1
Wisley Rd SP10 .... **105** F4
Wistaria Cl SP10 .... **105** E4
Wistaria La GU46 .... **34** A3
Wisteria Dr GU35 .... **164** B1
Wisteria Mews GU34 .... **140** B3
Witan Cl GU17 .... **83** D2
Wither Rise RG23 .... **67** D1
Withers La GU10 .... **97** E3
Witherslack Cl GU35 .... **166** A2
Withes The GU10 .... **97** E3
Withies The SP11 .... **108** A3
Witt Rd SP5 .... **168** A3
Wittcomb Terr GU35 .... **164** B1
Wittmead Rd GU16 .... **56** B2
Witton Hill SO24 .... **179** E2
Wivelrod Rd GU32 .... **138** B1
Woburn Ave GU16 .... **56** A2
Woburn Cl GU16 .... **36** C1
Woburn Gdns RG22 .... **68** B2
Wolds The RG23 .... **68** A2
Wolf's La GU34 .... **161** F4
Wolfe Cl SO22 .... **197** E3
Wolfe Rd GU12 .... **77** D1
Wolfmere La GU33 .... **186** A1
Wolseley Rd GU11 .... **76** C1
Wolverdene Special Sch
SP10 .... **106** A4
Wolversdene Cl SP10 .... **106** B4
Wolversdene Gdns SP10 .... **106** B4
Wolversdene Rd SP10 .... **106** B4
Wolverton La RG26 .... **25** E1
Wolverton Rd Ashford Hill RG26 .. **25** F3
Baughurst RG26 .... **25** F3
Wolvesey Terr 3 SO23 .... **198** A3
Wonston Cl SO21 .... **131** E2
Wonston La SO51 .... **131** E1
Wood Cl RG21, RG22 .... **91** D3
Wood La Beech Hill RG7 .... **13** E3
Bramdean SO24 .... **202** C3
Farnborough GU14 .... **55** F2
Fleet GU13 .... **54** B1
Seale GU12 .... **100** C3

Wood Moor RG40 .... **16** B1
Wood Rd Beacon Hill GU26 ... **167** D3
Camberley GU15 .... **35** F1
Farnham GU9 .... **99** D4
Wood St GU12 .... **77** F3
Woodbarn The GU9 .... **99** D1
Woodbine Cl GU17 .... **35** D4
Woodbine La RG14 .... **5** E1
Woodbourne GU9 .... **99** E4
Woodbourne Cl Liss GU33 ..... **208** A2
Yateley GU47 .... **34** A3
Woodbridge Dr GU15 .... **36** A4
Woodbridge Rd GU46 .... **34** C3
Woodbury Rd RG22 .... **91** D3
Woodcock Cl SP9 .... **78** C3
Woodcot Gdns GU14 .... **55** D2
Woodcote Cotts SO24 .... **202** B2
Woodcote Gn GU13 .... **74** B4
Woodcote Rd SN8 .... **18** A4
Woodcott Ho RG26 .... **26** C4
Woodcott Terr GU10 .... **100** A4
Woodcut Rd GU10 .... **121** E3
Woodend Camberley GU15 ...... **36** C4
Farnborough GU10 .... **56** A2
Woodfield GU35 .... **142** A1
Woodfield Cotts GU32 .... **206** A2
Woodfield Dr SO22 .... **197** D3
Woodgarston Dr RG22 .... **91** D3
Woodgate GU13 .... **54** B2
Woodgreen Rd SO22 .... **175** E2
Woodhouse La RG7 .... **8** B1
Woodland Dr Bramley RG26 ... **29** D1
Farnham GU10 .... **121** F3
Woodland Rise GU13 .... **74** C3
Woodlands Andover SP10 ...... **106** B4
Chineham RG24 .... **49** D2
Farnham GU10 .... **100** A2
Fleet GU13 .... **53** F1
Highclere RG20 .... **21** F4
Overton RG25 .... **88** A4
Yateley GU46 .... **34** A2
Woodlands Ave GU9 .... **99** E4
Woodlands Bsns Village RG21 **69** E3
Woodlands Cl Ash GU12 .... **77** F3
Farnborough GU47 .... **35** E1
Woodlands Ct 18 SO23 .... **176** A1
Woodlands La
Haslemere GU27 .... **189** E4
Liss GU33 .... **208** A2
Woodlands Rd Baughurst RG26 ... **9** F1
Camberley GU15 .... **35** F3
Farnborough GU14 .... **55** F2
Woodlands The Bordon GU35 .. **186** B4
Kings Worthy SO23 .... **176** B3
Woodlands Way SP10 .... **106** B4
Woodlands Wlk GU47 .... **35** E1
Woodlane Cl SO24 .... **202** B3
Woodlea Cl SO22 .... **175** F1
Woodlea Prim Sch GU35 .... **164** B1
Woodleigh GU13 .... **75** D4
Woodleys RG20 .... **23** E2
Woodman Cl SO21 .... **174** B1
Woodman La SO21 .... **174** B1
Woodmanfield RG25 .... **94** B3
Woodmere Croft RG23 .... **90** C4
Woodpecker Cl
Basingstoke RG23 .... **90** C4
Bordon GU35 .... **164** B1
Ewshot GU9 .... **98** A4
Woodpecker Dr SO22 .... **175** E1
Woodpeckers 1 SP10 .... **106** A4
Woodroffe Dr RG22 .... **68** B1
Woodruff Cl GU35 .... **186** B4
Woods La RG25 .... **91** F4
Woodside Blackwater GU17 .... **35** D2
Farnborough GU14 .... **55** F4
Hawley GU15 .... **35** D2
Newbury RG14 .... **5** D4
Sandhurst GU17 .... **35** E4
Woodside Cl Bordon GU35 ..... **164** B2
Mortimer RG7 .... **11** F3
Wokingham RG40 .... **16** B4

Woodside Cres GU35 .... **164** B2
Woodside Gdns Chineham RG24 **49** D2
Fleet GU13 .... **54** B1
Woodside La GU34 .... **161** D2
Woodside Pk GU35 .... **164** B2
Woodside Rd Farnborough GU11 **76** B4
Farnham GU9 .... **99** E4
Woodstock Mead RG22 .... **91** D3
Woodstocks GU16 .... **56** A3
Woodville Cl Blackwater GU46 ... **34** C3
Chineham RG24 .... **48** C1
Woodville Rise RG24 .... **48** C1
Woodway GU17 .... **35** D3
Wool Gr SP10 .... **106** B4
Wooland Ct GU13 .... **74** C2
Wooldridge Cres RG29 .... **95** E4
Woolfield La GU34 .... **205** D2
Woolford Cl 1 SO22 .... **197** E3
Woolford Way RG22 .... **68** B3
Woollards Rd GU12 .... **77** F2
Woolley Sq SP10 .... **83** E2
Woolmead Cl GU9 .... **99** D2
Woolmead Rd GU9 .... **99** D2
Woolmead The GU9 .... **99** D2
Woolmead Wlk GU9 .... **99** D2
Woolmer Hill Rd GU27 .... **189** D4
Woolmer Hill Sch GU27 .... **189** D4
Woolmer La GU30 .... **188** A4
Woolmer Rd GU33 .... **186** A2
Woolmer Terr GU33 .... **186** A2
Woolmer Trad Est GU35 .... **164** B2
Woolmer View GU26 .... **167** D2
Woolton Hill CE Schs RG20 ..... **21** D4
Woolton Lodge Gdns RG20 ...... **4** B1
Wootey Schs GU34 .... **139** F3
Wooteys Way GU34 .... **139** F3
Worcester Ave RG25 .... **91** D4
Worcester Cl GU14 .... **55** F4
Wordsworth Ave GU46 .... **33** F2
Wordsworth Cl
Basingstoke RG21 .... **69** E4
Winchester SO22 .... **197** E4
Worldham Hill GU34 .... **141** D1
Worrell Sq SP10 .... **83** E2
Worsley Rd GU14 .... **56** B4
Worthy La SO23 .... **175** F1
Worthy Rd SO23 .... **176** A1
Worting Inf Sch RG22 .... **68** A2
Worting Jun Sch RG22 .... **68** A2
Worting Rd Basingstoke RG23 ... **68** A2
Basingstoke RG21, RG22, RG23 **68** C2
Worting Road Rdbt RG22 .... **68** B2
Wote St RG21 .... **69** D2
Wouldham SP9 .... **79** E4
Wrecclesham Hill GU10 .... **121** E3
Wrecclesham Rd GU10 .... **121** E4
Wrekin Cl RG21, RG22, RG23 ... **68** A2
Wren Cl Alton GU34 .... **140** A3
Winchester SO22 .... **197** E3
Yateley GU46 .... **33** F3
Wren Ct GU12 .... **77** F2
Wren Way GU14 .... **55** E4
Wrights Cl SO21 .... **153** E2
Wrights Way SO21 .... **153** E2
Wychwood Cl GU12 .... **77** E1
Wychwood Pl GU16 .... **36** C4
Wyck La Binsted GU34 .... **141** F3
Binsted, Wyck GU34 .... **141** D2
East Worldham GU34 .... **141** D2
Wye Ct 55 SP10 .... **83** E1
Wykeham Ct RG29 .... **95** E4
Wykeham Dr RG21, RG22, RG23 . **68** A2
Wykeham Ho GU12 .... **77** D4
Wykeham Ind Est The
SO23 .... **176** B2
Wykeham Pl SO22 .... **197** E3
Wykeham Rd GU9 .... **99** D2
Wykwood GU30 .... **188** A2
Wyld Green La GU33 .... **208** A3
Wylye Rd SP9 .... **78** C4
Wymering Ct GU14 .... **56** A2
Wyndham Cl GU17 .... **34** A4

Wyndham Rd Andover SP10 ... **105** F3
Newbury RG14 .... **2** A3
Wyndham St GU12 .... **77** D1
Wynfields GU16 .... **56** B2
Wynne Gdns GU13 .... **75** D3

Yarnhams Cl GU34 .... **160** A1
Yateley Common (Ctry Pk)
GU46 .... **34** B2
Yateley Inds GU17 .... **34** A4
Yateley Inf Sch GU46 .... **34** A3
Yateley Manor Prep Sch
GU46 .... **34** A3
Yateley Rd GU47 .... **34** B4
Yates Copse RG14 .... **2** B3
Yatesbury Cl GU10 .... **121** E4
Yellowhammers GU34 .... **139** F3
Yeomans GU46 .... **33** E4
Yeomans Cl Ash GU10 .... **100** B4
Farnborough GU14 .... **55** F3
Yeomans La Burghclere RG14 .... **5** F1
Liphook GU30 .... **187** F2
Yeomans Pl GU35 .... **165** E3
Yeomans Way GU15 .... **36** B3
Yeosfield RG7 .... **14** A2
Yeovil Cl GU14 .... **56** A1
Yeovil Rd GU14 .... **56** B1
Yetminster Rd GU16 .... **56** A1
Yew Cl RG20 .... **24** C1
Yew Gate GU46 .... **1** B3
Yew Tree Cl Bramley RG26 ..... **29** D1
Farnborough GU14 .... **55** D2
Goodworth Clatford SP11 ...... **106** A1
Oakley RG22 .... **90** A4
Yew Tree La
North Waltham RG25 .... **89** F1
West Tytherley SP5 .... **169** D2
Yew Tree Pl GU33 .... **208** A2
Yew Tree Wlk GU16 .... **36** B1
Yolland Cl GU9 .... **99** D4
York Cl Basingstoke RG22 ...... **91** D4
Bordon GU35 .... **164** B1
Newbury RG14 .... **1** C1
York Cres GU11 .... **76** B1
York Ct 4 SP10 .... **83** D2
York Ho 17 Aldershot GU11 ... **76** B1
Basingstoke RG23 .... **68** C3
32 Winchester SO23 .... **176** A1
York La RG27 .... **52** B3
York Mews GU34 .... **140** A2
York Pl GU15 .... **36** A4
York Rd Aldershot GU14 .... **76** B1
Ash GU12 .... **77** F2
Farnborough GU14 .... **56** A1
Farnham GU9 .... **99** D1
Newbury RG14 .... **1** C1
York Terrace La GU15 .... **35** F3
York Town Ind Est GU15 .... **35** F2
York Way GU17 .... **34** C4
Yorktown Rd GU15 .... **35** E4
Yorkwood GU33 .... **207** F2
Youlden Cl GU15 .... **36** C3
Youlden Dr GU15 .... **36** C3
Young Cres RG19 .... **6** A4
Young's Ind Est RG26 .... **9** E2
Youngs Dr GU12 .... **77** E1
Youngs Paddock SP5 .... **168** A3
Youngs Rd GU34 .... **139** F2

Zephyr Ho 13 RG26 .... **9** E1
Zinnia Cl RG22 .... **91** D4
Zion Rd SP11 .... **124** B3
Zodiac Ho 12 RG26 .... **9** E1
Zouch Ave SP9 .... **78** C4
Zouch Cl SP9 .... **78** C4
Zouch Farm Rd SP9 .... **78** C4
Zouch Mkt SP9 .... **78** C4
Zouch Prim Sch SP9 .... **78** B4

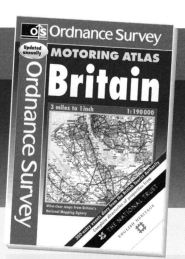

Ordnance Survey

Updated annually

MOTORING ATLAS
Britain

The best-selling *OS Motoring Atlas Britain* uses unrivalled and up-to-date mapping from the Ordnance Survey digital database. The exceptionally clear mapping is at a large scale of 3 miles to 1 inch (Orkney/Shetland Islands at 5 miles to 1 inch).

A special feature of the atlas is its wealth of tourist and leisure information. It contains comprehensive directories, including descriptions and location details, of the properties of the National Trust in England and Wales, the National Trust for Scotland, English Heritage and Historic Scotland. There is also a useful diary of British Tourist Authority Events listing more than 300 days out around Britain during the year.

Available from all good bookshops or direct from the publisher:
Tel: 01933 443863

The atlas includes:

- ◆ 112 pages of fully updated mapping
- ◆ 45 city and town plans
- ◆ 8 extra-detailed city approach maps
- ◆ route-planning maps
- ◆ restricted motorway junctions
- ◆ local radio information
- ◆ distances chart
- ◆ county boundaries map
- ◆ multi-language legend

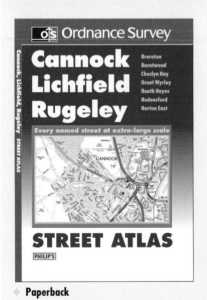

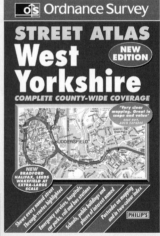